VICHY FRANCE

AND THE JEWS

VICHY FRANCE AND THE JEWS

MICHAEL R. MARRUS

AND

ROBERT O. PAXTON

Schocken Books · New York

First published by Schocken Books 1983
10 9 8 7 6 5 4 3 2 1   83 84 85 86
Originally published as *Vichy et les juifs* by Calmann-Lévy
Copyright © 1981 by Calmann-Lévy
Published by agreement with Basic Books, Inc.

Library of Congress Cataloging in Publication Data
Marrus, Michael Robert.
Vichy France and the Jews.
Translation of: Vichy et les juifs.
Reprint. Originally published: New York: Basic
Books, c1981.
Includes bibliographical references and index.
1. Jews—France—Persecutions. 2. Holocaust,
Jewish (1939-1945)—France. 3. World War, 1939-
1945—Deportations from France. 4. France—Politics and
government—1940-1945. 5. France—Ethnic relations.
I. Paxton, Robert O.   II. Title.
DS135.F83M3813 1983   940.53'15'0393240944   82–16869

Designed by Vincent Torre
Manufactured in the United States of America
ISBN 0–8052–0741–4

To the French men and women

who assisted persecuted Jews

during the Second World War

In a dreadful moment in history it was argued that one only carried out unjust laws in order to weaken their severity, that the power one agreed to exercise would have done even more damage if it had been placed in hands which were less pure. What a deceitful rationalization, which opened the door to unlimited criminality! Everyone eased his conscience, and each level of injustice found a willing executor. In such circumstances, it seems to me, innocence was murdered, with the pretext that it be strangled more gently.

BENJAMIN CONSTANT

Principes de politique,
applicables à tous les gouvernements
représentatifs et particulièrement
à la constitution actuelle
de la France (1815)

Contents

Introduction

URING the four years it ruled from Vichy, in the shadow of Nazism, the French government energetically persecuted Jews living in France. Persecution began in the summer of 1940 when the Vichy regime, born of defeat at the hands of the Nazis and of a policy of collaboration urged by many Frenchmen, introduced a series of antisemitic measures. After defining who was by law a Jew, and excluding Jews from various private and public spheres of life, Vichy imposed specifically discriminatory measures: confiscating property belonging to Jews, restricting their movements, and interning many Jews in special camps. Then, during the summer of 1942, the Germans, on their side, began to implement the "final solution" on the Jewish problem in France. Arrests, internments, and deportations to Auschwitz in Poland occurred with increasing frequency, often with the direct complicity of the French government and administration. Ultimately, close to seventy-six thousand Jews left France in cattle cars—"to the East," the Germans said; of these Jews only about 3 percent returned at the end of the war.

Vichy France bears an important part of the responsibility for this disaster, as the records of both French and German governments make clear. The deportations from France from 1942 to 1944 were made possible not only by direct French assistance but also by the course of earlier persecution; there were important links between the Nazis' "final solution" and the previous work of French governments—policies usually supported by French public opinion.

Our story begins at one of the clear dividing points of French history. In the 1930s, under the Third Republic, tolerant and cosmopolitan France had been a haven for thousands of refugees, many of them Jewish, who fled from Germany and eastern Europe, from fascist Italy, and from the battleground of the Spanish civil war. Then came France's stunning defeat by Nazi Germany in May and June 1940. Three fifths of the country were occupied by the German army; and a new French regime, camped temporarily in the southern hill resort town of Vichy, administered unoccupied France under the terms of an armistice negotiated with the victor. The Vichy regime, reacting against the Third Republic whose legitimacy had vanished in defeat, launched France on what many French people believed was a permanent new tack, the program called the National Revolution: authoritarian, traditionalist, pious, and neutral in the war between Hitler and the Allies.

Vichy was also publicly and conspicuously antisemitic. It has been customary to assume that what befell the Jews of France during the German occupation, beginning with discriminatory legislation in 1940 and culminating with the death of many thousands of French and foreign Jews between 1942 and 1944, was largely the work of Nazi zealots who imposed their views on a defeated country. That seemed the only possible explanation for so apparently abrupt a change of climate in June 1940.

No occupying power, however, can administer territory by force alone. The most brutal and determined conqueror needs local guides and informants. Successful occupations depend heavily upon accomplices drawn from disaffected, sympathetic, or ambitious elements within the conquered people. In fact, the study of a military occupation may tell one as much about the occupied as about the conquerors. The interplay between the two enhances divisions and antagonisms among the former and offers new opportunities for suppressed minorities among them to surface and come to power.

When we began several years ago to look closely at the measures taken against Jews in France during the German occupation, we found that the French had much more leeway than was commonly supposed, and that victor and vanquished had interacted much more intricately than we had expected. We found that, for the first year or so after June 1940, the German occupation authorities were not preoccupied by what happened to Jews in the unoccupied part of France. Short of manpower and concerned above all to focus their energies on the war against Britain and later Russia, the Germans preferred to leave to the Vichy authorities as much as possible of the expense and bother of administration. Without direct German prompting, a local and indigenous French antisemitism was at work in Vichy—a home-grown program that rivaled what the Germans were doing in the occupied north and even, in some respects, went beyond it. The Vichy regime wanted to solve in its own way what it saw as a "Jewish problem" in France. Beyond that, it wanted to reassert its administrative control over the Occupied Zone by attempting to substitute its own anti-Jewish program for the German antisemitic measures in the north.

Vichy's measures were not intended to kill. The regime initially sought the re-emigration of recently arrived Jews it deemed refractory to French culture, the submergence of longer-established Jews, and their ultimate assimilation into a newly homogeneous French nation. In the long run, the aim was to have few, if any, Jews remaining in France when, in 1942, the Germans launched a new policy of deporting Jews from western Europe to death camps in eastern Europe. Indigenous French restrictive measures against Jews had been in effect for two years; and Vichy's urge to expel them dovetailed neatly with the German project. Indeed, Vichy France became in August 1942 the only European country except Bulgaria to hand Jews over to the Nazis for deportation from areas not directly subject to German military occupation. Although this complicity aroused the first important protest to Vichy from elite groups, such as church leaders, internal opposition was never strong enough until late 1943 to prevent Vichy from contributing police support to the deportation operations. Right up to the Liberation in August 1944, Vichy sustained its own discriminatory measures against Jews.

Our book explores the indigenous French roots for the antisemitic measures adopted by Vichy after 1940, and explains just how these measures were applied, who in France supported them, and how they meshed with the separate and sometimes conflicting German policy. To clarify the situation, we had not only to review the intellectual traditions of antisemitism in France but to examine the measures taken against refugees by the Third Republic during the 1930s. Unexpectedly we found an important root of Vichy's anti-Jewish program in the increasingly severe restrictions imposed upon refugees by the Republic, and a hitherto unnoticed continuity between the anxiety and hostility aroused by refugees in the late 1930s and Vichy's xenophobia. Our subject belongs, in fact, to the larger history of the worldwide refugee crisis of the Depression years and to the narrowly defensive reaction to it by all Western countries.

More generally, our work belongs to the study of ethnic prejudice within predominantly liberal societies. France had been the first European nation to extend full civil rights to Jews, in the 1790s; Frenchmen were, however, also among the most influential pioneers of secular antisemitism in the later part of the nineteenth century. Both traditions existed in twentieth-century French society. During the Third Republic, the tolerant tradition prevailed, almost to the end, against the xenophobic one. Many outsiders, including Jews and a few cultivated Africans, managed to live comfortably among the French, as long as these outsiders were willing to renounce their own language and culture. Compared with eastern Europe and Russia, France was a liberal haven; and thousands of Jewish refugees arrived there after the 1880s. By 1940 about half of the 300,000 to 350,000 Jews in France were foreign-born. Although the xenophobic tradition clearly prevailed after 1940, there were still instances of generosity and idealism. As the novelist Serge Doubrovsky recently told us in recounting his childhood in wartime France, while the measures of 1940–42 against Jews were the work of French people, every Jew who survived in France during 1942 to 1944 owed his or her life to some French man or woman who helped, or at least kept a secret.

Wherever possible we relied upon the Vichy government's own accounts of what it did, and compared them with the surviving records of the German occupation authority and the German government. On the French side, we were permitted to see the voluminous files of the Commissariat-General for Jewish Affairs, the papers of Marshal Pétain's secretariat, the prefects' monthly reports to the minister of the interior between 1940 and 1944, and the postwar trial records of the successive commissioners-general for Jewish affairs (Xavier Vallat, Louis Darquier de Pellepoix, and Charles Mercier du Paty de Clam) as well as those of the commissariat's right-hand man in the final years, Joseph Antignac, and the drafter of the first Vichy Jewish statute, Justice Minister Raphaël Alibert.

On the German side, we used fragments of the papers of the supreme German military authority in France, the *Militärbefehlshaber in Frankreich* and of German police agencies in France, along with their special anti-Jewish office, the *Judenreferat,* which survive at the West German Federal Archives *(Bundesarchiv)* in Koblenz and at the Centre de Documentation Juive Contemporaine in Paris. Another source essential for understanding German policy was the daily dispatches to Berlin of Otto Abetz, German ambassador in Paris, and his staff, including Theodor Zeitschel, the former ship's doctor who became the German embassy's expert on Jewish affairs. These papers are preserved at the German Foreign Office Archives in Bonn and, in part, on microfilm at the U.S. National Archives (Microcopy T–120). We also examined microfilmed archives of the German military commands in France at the U.S. National Archives (Microcopy T–77 and T–78), and of the Franco-Italian Armistice Commission at Turin (Microcopy T–586).

In addition to its well-known collection of Resistance documents and interviews, the Comité d'Histoire de la Deuxième Guerre Mondiale in Paris has gathered a rich collection of documents on the Vichy government and its workings. Other papers that we were able to examine in Paris include the papers of Fernand de Brinon, the Vichy government's official representative in the Occupied Zone, the Archives Nationales, and some archives of the Paris Prefecture of Police dealing with the refugee question up to July 1940.

Reports of foreign observers in France were also useful. American diplomats filed dispatches from Vichy until their mission there was closed in November 1942; many of these have been published in the annual volumes of *Foreign Relations of the United States.* We have examined the unpublished State Department files in the U.S. National Archives in Washington. Although the British Foreign Office had no direct observers in France after the rupture of diplomatic relations in July 1940, the Public Record Office in London contains accounts from refugee workers and émigrés, as well as from British diplomats in neighboring countries who were well informed about events in France. We found significant information in the reports of foreign refugee relief workers from the Young Men's Christian Association (YMCA), the Quakers, Swiss relief agencies, the Organisation au Secours aux Enfants (OSE), and the Jewish refugee assistance organization HICEM which we consulted in London and New York.

Jews themselves observed events in France with mounting uneasiness, and we tapped these rich resources in the personal papers of survivors in London (the Wiener Library) and in New York (the Leo Baeck Institute, YIVO, the Jewish Theological Seminary Library). The life of Jews in Vichy France and their responses to Vichy's antisemitic measures were not, however, our central concern: that is a very different subject and would fill another large book. For this reason we did not extend our research in the papers and reminiscences of survivors to the collections of the Yad Vashem Archive in Jerusalem.

We devoted little effort to interviews. Many of the people who shaped Vichy policy toward the Jews are dead. Among the survivors, Darquier proved—in a controversial interview published by *L'Express* in October 1978—that he had learned nothing and forgotten nothing since 1942. Though one of the authors spent an afternoon with Xavier Vallat twenty years ago, their discussion centered upon the veterans' movements at Vichy rather than upon Jewish affairs. In any event, each participant's version has been so often retold and redefended since 1945 that it long ago lost all spontaneity.

In our researches we have been helped by many persons and institutions. The Connaught Fund of the University of Toronto and the American Council of Learned Societies provided travel and research assistance; and the Killam Program of the Canada Council supported Marrus for a year of research and writing. Paxton was supported for a year by the Rockefeller Foundation. We owe particular thanks to Pierre Cézard, director of the Contemporary Section of the Archives Nationales in Paris. Justice Minister Alain Peyrefitte, Interior Minister Christian Bonnet, and Minister of Culture Jean-Philippe Lecat permitted us to consult archives under their care. For his help, we most gratefully thank Jean-Claude Casanova, law professor and advisor to the French premier. We are also grateful to Professor Stanley Hoffman of Harvard University, to Georges Wellers and Ulrich Hessel of the Centre de Documentation Juive Contemporaine in Paris, and to Henri Michel and Claude Lévy of the Comité d'Histoire de la Deuxième Guerre Mondiale. We were assisted in our research by Vicki Caron, Paula Schwartz and Joseph Mandel.

Paxton was further aided by Dr. Maria Keipert of the Politisches Archiv of the Auswärtiges Amt in Bonn; Daniel P. Simon, director, and Werner Pix, archivist, of the Berlin Document Center; Dr. Ritter of the *Bundesarchiv* in Koblenz; Dr. Hans Umbreit of the *Militärgeschichtlischesforschungsamt* in Freiburg-in-Greisgau; Dr. Robert Wolff of the U.S. National Archives; and Dr. Hanno Kremer of the editorial department, R.I.A.S., Berlin.

Marrus received help from Dr. Elizabeth Eppler of the Institute of Jewish Affairs in London, from the keepers of archival and newspaper collections at the Royal Institute of International Affairs, the Wiener Library, and the Public Record Office—all in London—and from the Paris lawyer and scholar Serge Klarsfeld. For two years Marrus enjoyed the generous hospitality provided by the Warden and fellows of St. Antony's College, Oxford, and for far longer the unflagging moral support of Carol Randi Marrus.

Both authors benefited from conversations with colleagues and students too numerous to mention by name in New York, Toronto, Paris, Oxford, and elsewhere. Margaret Steinfels and Phoebe Hoss gave the English text their rigorous editorial attention. Finally, we offer special thanks to our friend Roger Errera, editor of the series in which the first edition of this work appeared in France, published by Editions Calmann-Lévy. From beginning to end, we counted on his wide reading and his expert and generous assistance.

CHAPTER
1

First Steps

DURING the summer and fall of 1940 the French government at Vichy began a legislative assault upon Jews living in France. The most conspicuous of these measures was the *Statut des juifs* ("Statute on the Jews") of 3 October 1940.[1] This law was virtually constitutional in scope. It assigned, on the basis of race, an inferior position in French civil law and society to a whole segment of French citizens and to noncitizens and foreigners living on French soil. The *Statut des juifs* began by defining who was Jewish in the eyes of the French state, and then excluded those Jews from top positions in the public service, from the officer corps and from the ranks of noncommissioned officers, and from professions that influence public opinion: teaching, the press, radio, film, and theater. Jews could hold menial public service positions provided they had served in the French armed forces between 1914 and 1918, or had distinguished themselves in the 1939–40 campaign. The law, finally, promised that a quota system would be devised to limit Jews in the liberal professions.

The *Statut des juifs* was not, however, the first Vichy legislation against Jews. On 27 August 1940, Vichy had repealed the *loi Marchandeau* ("Marchandeau Law").[2] That executive order of 21 April 1939—an amendment to the 1881 press law, sponsored by Justice Minister Paul Marchandeau—had outlawed any press attack "toward a group of persons who belong by origin to a particular race or religion when it is intended to arouse hatred among citizens or residents."[3] While the Marchandeau Law had been in effect, antisemitic newspaper articles had been effectively suppressed; after 27 August 1940, however, antisemitism was free to spread itself in French newspapers.*

---

*A contemporary press release accused the Marchandeau Law of establishing a "special legal status [*loi d'exception*] . . . which was no longer compatible with the new guidelines that are to preside over the creation of the new French state."[4]

Still earlier laws, without mentioning Jews explicitly, restricted the opportunities previously enjoyed by naturalized French citizens. The law of 22 July 1940[5]—rushed into effect only twelve days after Marshal Pétain's role as head of state and constitution maker had been established—set up a commission to review all the naturalizations accorded since 1927 and to strip of French nationality all those new citizens found undesirable. Eventually over fifteen thousand lost French citizenship in this fashion, including about six thousand Jews.[6] A law of 17 July 1940 restricted entry into the French public service to those born of a French father.[7] The law of 16 August 1940[8] set up a doctor's guild (the Ordre des Médecins) and limited access to the medical professions to those born of French fathers. The law of 10 September 1940[9] regulated admission to the bar in the same fashion. These last two measures were applied with particular rigor to Jews; and even though the word *Jew* does not appear in their texts, Jews were generally understood to be prominent among those whom the laws were designed to restrict.

Further legislation that followed the *Statut des juifs* was far more explicit. The law of 4 October 1940,[10] "concerning foreigners of the Jewish race," posed an even more immediate danger to many Jews than did the statute of the previous day. It authorized prefects (the local executive agents of the French state) to intern foreign Jews in "special camps" or to assign them to live under police surveillance in remote villages *(résidence forcée)*. Completing this first wave of anti-Jewish legislation, the law of 7 October 1940[11] swept away the Crémieux decree, that republican landmark of October 1870 that had granted French citizenship to Algerian Jews. Fully French for seventy-five years, these Jews not only were now subject to the incapacities and restrictions imposed upon other Jews on French soil but lost the civic rights of French citizens as well.

Where did they come from, these laws that seem so foreign to French political practice? Since the repeal in 1846 of provisions for different legal oaths for Christians and Jews, no French law had singled out for discrimination any religious or ethnic group in metropolitan France. Ethnic or religious distinctions had become so foreign to French civil law that for lack of evidence in the vital statistics it is even now virtually impossible to arrive at accurate population figures for Jews in Third Republican France (1875–1940) or to be certain about such matters as intermarriage between Jews and non-Jews in France.

Public opinion, even among the well-educated, has generally attributed these apparently radical measures to German orders. The novelist Maurice Druon, welcoming the art expert Maurice Rheims into the

Académie Française in February 1977, deplored "that tawdry period when the victors' laws were passed down, alas, by a captive state."[12] The memoirs of some Vichy leaders have fostered the impression of direct German pressure. Jérôme Carcopino, the great classicist, rector of the Academy of Paris in 1940 and soon to become minister of education, wrote that the *Statut des juifs* "dishonored only the Germans."[13]*

Any simple notion of German *Diktat* can be dismissed summarily. When Raphaël Alibert, minister of justice in 1940 and author of the *Statut des juifs*, came to trial in March 1947, the attorney-general found, to his astonishment, that the accused's dossier contained no evidence of contact with Germans, official or not, and was obliged to drop, from among the charges, the accusation of *intelligence avec l'ennemi*.[15] Years of scrutiny of the records left by German services in Paris and Berlin have turned up no trace of German orders to Vichy in 1940 —or, for that matter, to any other occupied or satellite regime of that year—to adopt antisemitic legislation.[16]

After all, the German officials who were hastily improvising their offices in Paris in summer 1940 had other irons in the fire. The principal German authority in occupied France, the *Militärbefehlshaber in Frankreich* (MBF), was concerned primarily with providing a secure base for continuing war against England. The Armistice Commission at Wiesbaden, where Vichy had its most regular contacts with German authorities well into fall 1940, was concerned primarily with French demobilization and the economy. The more politically aggressive German agencies—and we shall see that German agencies often differed sharply among themselves and competed for bureaucratic advantage— were not established until the summer's end. The German embassy in Paris was reopened only on 7 August, when Otto Abetz, who had hitherto been merely diplomatic advisor to the MBF, returned from a consultation in Berlin with autonomous authority as ambassador.[17] As for German police agencies, they gradually turned their attention from immediate military security to longer-term political matters. It was not until 12 August that Theodor Dannecker, the twenty-seven-year-old SS officer assigned to organize a special police branch for Jewish questions —the *Judenreferat*—in the Paris headquarters of the German High Security Office (*Reichssicherheitshauptamt*, RSHA), was finally assigned a secretary from Berlin.[18]

---

*Most participants' memoirs lack precision on this point, and Carcopino's, quoted here, especially so: "No matter how abominable it [the law] appeared, whether or not it was written into the agreements, it flowed inexorably from the armistice: like the armistice, it was the poisoned fruit whose bitterness the defeat forced us to taste for a time."[14]

Among highly placed German officials in France in 1940, Ambassador Otto Abetz was the one most eager to promote the racial "purification" of France. This young one-time art student, indolent, pleasure loving, and well connected with French rightist groups through marriage to the journalist Jean Luchaire's secretary and through years of work in Paris for the French-German Friendship Committee (Comité France-Allemagne)* never became the dominant force he expected to be in the shaping of German policy toward France. His appointment as ambassador represented the ascendancy of Foreign Minister Ribbentrop's amateurs and party enthusiasts over old-line professional diplomats, many of whom resented Abetz.

As early as 20 August, he wired an urgent *(sehr dringend)* proposal to Ribbentrop for a series of "immediate antisemitic measures that could serve equally well later as a basis for the exclusion [*Entfernung*] of Jews from Unoccupied France": refusal to readmit to the Occupied Zone Jews who had fled south; the obligation of a Jew in the Occupied Zone to register with his or her prefect; the marking of Jewish enterprises with a special placard; and the appointment of trustees *(Treuhänder)* over Jewish enterprises whose owners had fled. All these measures were to be carried out by the French administration in the Occupied Zone.

Abetz's enthusiastic proposals seem to have aroused little immediate interest in Berlin. The bankers and economists of the Four Year Plan† agreed on 31 August that the German occupation authorities should as a matter of course appoint trustees to any enterprise left idle by the departure of its owners, but thought that special measures singling out Jewish enterprises in this connection were "contrary to our aims." The RSHA had to be asked a second time for an opinion. Finally, on 20 September, Reinhard Heydrich, Gestapo chief Heinrich Himmler's deputy and chief of German police, replied that he had no objection to Abetz's proposed measures, nor to French services bearing "first responsibility" for their application, as long as German police watched them closely.[19]

Thus, the first German ordinance in the Occupied Zone concerned explicitly with Jews was not issued until 27 September 1940.[20] It followed Abetz's earlier proposals closely. After defining who was Jewish in the eyes of the German Occupation authorities, it forbade Jews who had fled the Occupied Zone to return there and required all Jews in the

---

*Abetz's work for the Comité France–Allemagne provoked the French government to expel him in July 1939.

†German agency for economic planning set up in 1936.

Occupied Zone to register with the *sous-préfecture* of their principal residence. Jewish community leaders were held responsible for providing the French authorities with all information they requested to enforce registration. Subsequent enforcement of this ordinance required that all Jews' identity papers in the Occupied Zone be stamped *Juif* or *Juive*.

When this first German ordinance appeared, Vichy had already repealed the Marchandeau Law and was busy reviewing naturalizations and purging the medical and legal professions. Without any possible doubt, Vichy had begun its own antisemitic career before the first German text appeared, and without direct German order.

Perhaps indirect pressures were at work, however. Hitler's antisemitic frenzy was a secret to no one, and some German authorities gave early indications of applying it to the French territory they controlled. No sooner had the German Propaganda Office taken over the main radio station in Paris than a stream of antisemitic propaganda issued forth. Even before the ordinance of 27 September, German border guards were refusing to let Jews back into the Occupied Zone.[21] In July over three thousand Alsatian Jews were brutally expelled from former French territory and dumped into Unoccupied France. On 7 September, General Benoît-Léon Fornel de La Laurencie, the French government's delegate in the Occupied Zone and Vichy's eyes and ears in Paris during the first months, reported to Vichy on Abetz's plans for an anti-Jewish ordinance.[22]

The most alarming aspect of General de La Laurencie's report concerned the German intention to appoint trustees (presumably Germans or German sympathizers) for abandoned Jewish property in the Occupied Zone. Indeed, a German ordinance of 20 May 1940[23] had empowered the MBF to appoint trustees to enterprises left vacant by the flight of their owners. Although this ordinance was aimed ostensibly at assuring economic continuity and did not explicitly refer to Jews, much of the property still vacant belonged to Jews unable to return to the Occupied Zone. The matter took a graver turn with the publication of the second German ordinance of 18 October 1940.[24] According to this new decree, all Jewish enterprises in the Occupied Zone were to be registered and placed under trusteeship—not merely those that had been abandoned by owners in flight. Some of the properties concerned were major enterprises (such as the Galéries Lafayette department store), vital components of national defense (Avions Bloch), or massive investment holdings (such as the Rothschild interests or Lazard Frères). It seemed possible that, under the cloak of the armistice, German interests might gain control of significant elements of the national economy. The fact that a special team, the *Einsatzstab* Rosenberg, was already at work seizing art works owned by Jews in France lent credibility to this supposition.

The French ministries of Finance and Industrial Production took immediate steps to counter the German seizure of property. Their measures were technical, devoid of overt antisemitic expression. The Ministry of Industrial Production set up the Service de Contrôle des Administrateurs Provisoires (SCAP), in Paris at 5 rue de Florence, whose business it was to insert French administration into the German projects concerning Jewish property in the Occupied Zone. SCAP chose French trustees, or *administrateurs provisoires,* instead of German ones, subjected their management to the scrutiny of the French administration, and tried to refuse the transfer of any property to foreign hands without the assent of the Ministry of Finance. It must be emphasized that SCAP functioned only in the Occupied Zone in these early days, and that it applied German law there. It was the MBF that gave legal appointment to the *administrateurs provisoires* nominated by SCAP. In return, Vichy was reassured in October 1940 by Dr. Blanke, of the MBF's civil administration staff, that Germany would not use the aryanization of Jewish property as a device for the intrusion of foreign interests into the French economy[25]—a promise observed often in its breach.

The German authorities had no objection to the Vichy strategy of providing the administrative muscle for tasks such as aryanization. As we have seen, this was Abetz's intention from the beginning. As long as they remained masters of policy direction, the Germans wished to be relieved so far as possible of the chores and expense of administration in the occupied areas. We shall attempt later to determine who won in this implicit bargain. Pursuing the French plan, on 27 October, 5 November, and 15 December 1940, General de La Laurencie instructed the prefect of police and the departmental prefects in the Occupied Zone to have all Jewish enterprises censused and put under SCAP trusteeship. He urged that the work be done completely and energetically. Zeal was the best means of keeping the Germans to their promise to limit the import of aryanization; the Jews' role in the French economy would be diminished, but France would not lose the properties that had once belonged to them.[26]

In late 1940 a distinguished civil servant, Pierre-Eugène Fournier, former governor of the Bank of France and director of the national railways, was placed in charge of SCAP and of what his successor, the senior military administrator de Faramond, was to describe in August 1941 as "this thankless and awkward task that has been imposed upon me." SCAP could be considered, in the words of the historian Joseph Billig, an attempt "to win the right of presence in an activity that made it [the French government] fear a German seizure of a part of the French patrimony." De Faramond described it as "the re-establishment of French sovereignty over aryanization."[27]

A similar pre-emptive strategy—heading the Germans off from doing something worse by doing it oneself—was often claimed after the war for the *Statut des juifs* and other Vichy anti-Jewish measures. At the 1947 trial of Xavier Vallat (the first commissioner-general for Jewish Affairs), André Lavagne, former chief of Marshal Petain's civilian staff, likened the *Statut des juifs* to the firefighter's tactic "of lighting small fires [*contrefeux*] to save the forest." Although he was ostensibly talking about the *Statut des juifs,* Lavagne seems to have had the SCAP in mind, for he explained that "there are some very full dossiers on the subject at the Ministry of Finance."[28] The *contrefeux* theory enjoyed a widespread vogue in the postwar trials and memoirs of Vichy participants. If Vichy had done nothing, wrote Paul Baudouin, foreign minister in fall 1940, "the Germans [were going] to take brutal measures in the Occupied Zone, perhaps even purely and simply extend their racial laws to the Occupied Zone."[29*]

Whatever one thinks of the pre-emptive strategy for the Occupied Zone—and, for our part, we are convinced that the Germans could have accomplished far less without French administrative help—it was legitimate to extend that strategy to the Unoccupied Zone only if it can be shown that the Germans planned to extend their racial laws and their seizures of property there. Responsible German officials had no such intention in 1940. Ambassador Abetz, it is true, alluded in August to a "later" exclusion of Jews from the Unoccupied Zone. But the immediate intention of German authorities was quite the reverse.

Through at least mid-1941 the German strategy was to encourage the emigration of Jews from Germany, from territory occupied by Germany, and from territory slated for German settlement. Indeed, it was not until the Wannsee Conference of 20 January 1942 that the Nazi regime began to give systematic form to a policy of deporting European Jews to the east and of exterminating them there, and not until June 1942 that this policy was extended to western European occupied areas and to Unoccupied France. The term *Endlösung* ("Final Solution")

---

*Baudouin claimed that the matter of the Jews was examined "for the first time" at the cabinet meeting of 10 September.

appears earlier than that, to be sure; and the murderous potential of Nazi antisemitism is evident in the working papers of German agencies. But up until mid-1941 even the most committed Nazi antisemites—and even among friends—discussed the ultimate fate of Jews in terms of exclusion, of sending them somewhere else in the world. Himmler's deputy Heydrich, in a 5 February 1941 memorandum, looked forward to the "later total solution to the Jewish problem" as a process of "sending them off to whatever country will be chosen later on." He explained to Martin Luther of the Foreign Office, on 14 February 1941, that "after the conclusion of peace, they [the interned Jews of German-dominated Europe] will be the first transport to leave Fortress Europe in the total evacuation of the continent that we plan."[30] Luther later explained to German diplomats abroad that it had been German policy until mid-1941 to hinder Jewish emigration from non-German areas in order to save every available shipping space for the accomplishment of Jewish emigration from Germany.[31] Ultimate measures, whose preparation Ambassador Abetz discussed with a rather reluctant *Militärbefehlshaber* in August 1940, included the "expulsion of all Jews from the Occupied Zone."[32] In its everyday application during 1940–41, German policy toward Jews—whatever its dreadful inner logic—was expressed in the expulsion of Jews from German and German-occupied territory.

That meant expulsion of Jews into Unoccupied France. German authorities, contemptuous of French racial tolerance and interested in drawing only the industrialized north and east of France into the eventual Greater Economic Sphere *(Grossraumwirtschaft)*,[33] did not yet think of Unoccupied France as an area to be made *Judenrein* ("purified of Jews"). Such would perhaps have been in their eyes more of an honor than the half-breed French deserved. Well into 1941, German authorities considered Unoccupied France a place to dump their unwanted Jews.

We have already alluded to the 3,000 Alsatian Jews sent into the Unoccupied Zone in July 1940. On 8 August, Polizeimajor Walter Krüger in Bordeaux, evidently acting on his own initiative, sent 1,400 German Jews across the Demarcation Line, assuring them that on the other side they would be free. The French authorities locked them up in the camp at Saint Cyprien (in the Pyrénées-Orientales department, on the Spanish border of southern France), where some among them, Jewish veterans of the German army in 1914–18, appealed to Berlin to save them from the "humiliating confinement" imposed on them by the French enemy.[34] At dawn on 22 October 1940, with advance notice ranging from a quarter-hour to two hours, gauleiters Josef Bürckel and

Josef Wagner rounded up 6,504 Jews in Baden and the Saarpfalz and, without notifying French authorities, dispatched them, each carrying only a hand parcel, in sealed trains for Lyon. The oldest Jew was one hundred and four (or ninety-seven according to German records), 2,000 were over sixty, and many were children. Behind this step was an embryonic project to send into France as many as 270,000 Jews from "the Altreich, the Ostmark, and the protectorates Böhmen and Mähren" (prewar Germany plus newly absorbed Austria, Bohemia, and Moravia).[35]

The unannounced arrival of these German Jews seemed at Vichy a gross breach of the armistice, all the graver since Hitler's willingness finally to accede to Pétain's requests for a meeting that very week had seemed to promise a more cooperative atmosphere. The French protests lodged with the Armistice Commission at Wiesbaden over this incident were surpassed in vehemence and number only by French protests over the expulsion of French citizens from Alsace-Lorraine.[36] As for the wretched occupants of the trains, they suffered as both French and Germans competed in inhumanity. After being shuttled back and forth in their sealed wagons while French and German authorities wrangled, these German Jews were finally deposited on 25 October in the French internment camp at Gurs, in the Pyrenees. When the cattle cars were unsealed at Pau, some of them contained dead bodies. At Gurs, more Jews died of cold, malnourishment, tuberculosis, and other diseases before the survivors were ultimately deported to the east in 1942 and 1943.

German records suggest that the intensity of Vichy protests stopped the next planned deportation of German Jews, from Hesse. Even so, local German officials continued, more discreetly, to dump Jewish refugees from Occupied France into the Unoccupied Zone. On 30 November 1940, German officials in Bordeaux sent a train with 247 Jewish refugees from Luxembourg to Pau, without French knowledge or authorization. The minister of the interior had them sent back to Othez; and General Paul Doyen, French delegate to the Armistice Commission at Wiesbaden, delivered a formal protest.[37] Vigilant French authorities detected a new case on 11 February when German police at Châlons-sur-Marne (in northern France, east of Paris) loaded 38 Jewish refugees from Luxembourg aboard a French train bound for the Unoccupied Zone, and dispersed them among the regular passengers so that French police would not notice.[38] As late as April 1941, German authorities in the Atlantic coastal area expelled 300 Jewish refugees from Luxembourg, some into Spain and others into Unoccupied France, though the subprefect of Bayonne could not obtain precise information.[39] These are the cases we know about. There were no doubt others, and Vichy officials seem to have been as eager to keep Jewish refugees out of the Unoccupied Zone as German officials were to keep them from returning to the Occupied Zone. "In fact," reported a 1941 compendium of new regulations concerning Jews in France, "the Demarcation Line is closed in both directions to Jews."[40]

Vichy policy toward Jews in the Unoccupied Zone thus ran at cross-purposes to German wishes in 1940. Put bluntly, the Germans wanted to dump Jews in the Unoccupied Zone; Vichy wanted to keep them out. Once German policy as it was in 1940 is clearly understood, it becomes apparent that Vichy policy was no simple copy of it. Vichy mounted a competitive or rival antisemitism rather than a tandem one.

Indeed, the Vichy *Statut des juifs* of 3 October went farther than the German ordinance of the previous week. Where the German ordinance defined Jewishness reticently by religious practice, the Vichy statute spoke bluntly of race. The Vichy statute was also more inclusive. The German ordinance defined as Jewish anyone with more than two Jewish grandparents—that is, with at least three grandparents who had observed Jewish religious practices. The Vichy statute included in its definition those with only two grandparents "of the Jewish race" in cases where the spouse was also Jewish. Thus some persons who escaped the Germans' anti-Jewish measures in the Occupied Zone fell under the Vichy statute in the Unoccupied Zone. While the German ordinance went beyond Vichy law in requiring that Jewish enterprises be marked, the Vichy law of 4 October, in authorizing the internment of foreign Jews, went beyond anything yet legislated in the Occupied Zone.

So far from heading off German measures, Vichy's antisemitic campaign may have actually precipitated the German ordinance of 27 September 1940. The German occupation authorities, whose antisemitic measures up to then had remained unsystematic bursts of propaganda and border controls, were well aware that Vichy was initiating anti-Jewish laws. They needed only their eyes and ears to tell them so. Moreover, as Vichy leaders tried desperately in late summer 1940 to find ways of access to the still unfamiliar (and only partly established) German centers of power, they talked eagerly of their anti-Jewish plans. Perhaps they expected to curry favor in this fashion; perhaps they hoped to soften the anticipated peace treaty.[41] In late July, Vice-Prime Minister Pierre Laval sent an emissary to the Armistice Commission at Wiesbaden to air proposals for broader economic and colonial cooperation; in the course of the visit, the Germans were told that Vichy planned anti-Masonic, antiparliamentary, and anti-Jewish measures.[42] On 28 August, Laval himself finally got to Paris where he tried with all his eloquence to persuade the German historian and propagandist Dr. Friedrich Grimm of the sincerity of France's new attitudes. Britain, he said, was now the enemy, particularly in Africa. As an earnest of France's new spirit, he called Dr. Grimm's attention to what France was already doing against the Masons, the old parliamentary system, and Jews.[43] In October 1940, Werner Best, chief of the civil administration arm of the MBF, even asserted that the Germans published their ordinance on 27 September lest a French statute on the Jews *precede* their own.

> It was established that the French government, for its part, intended to publish in the near future a sweeping law against the Jews. . . . The ordinance of the Chief of the Military Administration in France [that is, the German ordinance of 27 September 1940] was issued on the Führer's order, and it was consciously judged necessary to have it antedate the French law in order that the regulation of the Jewish question appeared to emanate from the German authorities.[44]

Vichy measures against Jews came from within, as part of the National Revolution. They were autonomous acts taken in pursuit of indigenous goals. The first goal was to block further immigration of refugees, especially Jewish refugees, into a country hardly able to feed and employ its own people. On 5 July 1940, Interior Minister Adrien Marquet sealed off French borders, "so that foreigners cannot trouble public order."[45] As we have noted, the German expulsion of more Jewish refugees into Unoccupied France roused Vichy to strenuous protests. Complaining that his government's notes on this subject had gone unanswered, General Doyen, French representative to the Armistice Commission at Wiesbaden, asserted in November that "the French government can no longer guarantee asylum to these foreigners." He asked the German government to accept their return and to pay for their sojourn in France.[46]

The second Vichy goal was to encourage the re-emigration of the refugees already there, insofar as wartime restrictions permitted. In July 1940, French authorities turned over to the Germans twenty-one Jews, nineteen of whom, it was claimed, had been arrested "because of actions in favor of Germany." The Germans forced the French to take them back, and argued that with respect to Jews "the voluntary principle obtains," and that no Jew could be forcibly sent by the French to the Occupied Zone.[47] Prefectoral authorities also tried to ship Jews north, but were often frustrated by their sneaking back across the Demarcation Line separating the northern Occupied Zone from the southern Unoccupied Zone.[48] In December 1940, Vichy was negotiating the emigration of up to 150,000 Spanish Republican refugees to Mexico—a project that the Germans feared might provide recruits for the British army.[49] French police agencies repeatedly declared their eagerness to facilitate re-emigration.[50] An anti-Allied Zionist movement called "Massada," with which Pétain's staff was in contact in 1943, submitted studies to the staff concerning Jewish resettlement in Palestine, and other groups—official and unofficial—studied Jewish resettlement in Madagascar and Indochina.

The third goal was the reduction of the foreign, the unassimilable, the "non-French" in public life, the economy, and French cultural life. An inward-turning, atavistic nativism permeated early Vichy actions. We have alluded already to the revisions of naturalizations, which *Le Temps* promised "will permit the rapid elimination of doubtful and even harmful elements that had slipped into the French community with the aid of certain administrative and political complicities that the present government intends to sweep away."[51] We have also referred to the laws closing public service and certain liberal professions to those not born of a French father (see p. 4). The *Statut des juifs* of 3 October, in closing top public offices to Jews and in promising a *numerus clausus* (a quota on Jews in the professions), was not out of step with these other measures. Jews had been singled out, "however valid some honorable exceptions may be,"—read a government press release on the *Statut des juifs* published in the *Journal officiel* and widely referred to in the press—because their influence "made itself felt in an intrusive and even disunifying manner." Jews had assumed "a preponderant role" in French public life in recent years, and the present national disaster obliged the government to "retrench the elements of French strength, whose characteristics a long heredity had fixed."[52]

In this inward-turning, inhospitable, even xenophobic climate of the summer of 1940, we can perceive the impact of defeat. We believe that the Vichy racial laws of 1940–41 are inconceivable without that seismic shock of June 1940. The world was turned upside down. German troops occupied three fifths of France. Physical destruction and death were far less massive than in 1914–18, though they were devastating enough in the battlefield areas in northern France, where, for example, half the houses in Beauvais had been destroyed and four fifths of Abbeville leveled. It was human dislocation, though, that was the main mark of this disaster. Four million French, Belgian, and other refugees, having fled before the German advance, were on the roads or camped in makeshift shelters. Beauvais had been evacuated twice; Orléans had suffered "successive pillagings"; only seven out of forty doctors remained in Le Mans.[53] A million and a half young Frenchmen were prisoners of war, on their way to prisoner-of-war camps in Germany. Their comrades-in-arms were being demobilized. They could hardly expect to return to normal pursuits, however, for the economy was beginning to be grossly distorted by the German occupation. With their 400,000,000 francs per day in occupation costs, the German armed forces were becoming the main clients of an emerging black market. What food, drink, and clothing their official purchasing agents did not buy, German soldiers bought on their own. The German army was also requisitioning draft animals, railroad wagons, shipping, and motor vehicles. Inordinate demand faced inadequate supply. The British blockade sealed off the usual sources of fuel, rubber, and tropical foodstuffs. There were no raw materials for industry, no fuel to drive machines, too few agricultural laborers. The four leanest, bitterest years in modern French experience were commencing.

It would be surprising if the exodus and the other hardships of summer 1940 had not brought out the worse in some people. The frictions of that dreadful time were further sharpened by the pervasive search for "the guilty parties"; and now and again that search stopped at the familiar, unpopular doors. Antisemitism surfaced in the acrimonious atmosphere of Bordeaux, where ministers and deputies gathered after 14 June. It surfaced among the crew of the steamship *Massilia* as Jean Zay and Georges Mandel boarded among the nearly thirty deputies who persisted on 21 June in trying to get to North Africa. "It is certain," reported Prefect Robert Billecard of the Seine-et-Oise on 5 August, "that antisemitism is growing among ordinary people."[54]*

But it cannot be said that Vichy launched its moves against Jews, Freemasons, and foreigners in response to insistent public pressure. Only about one third of the prefects referred at all to the *Statut des juifs* in their monthly reports during 1940. Nine prefects in the Unoccupied Zone reported public approval, but only three in the Occupied Zone, where Vichy actions tended to seem both more distant and less significant. All four prefects who referred to some degree of public disapproval (Calvados, Seine-et-Marne, Deux-Sèvres, Vosges) were in the

---

*A Popular Front prefect, Billecard was removed from office on 18 September 1940.

Occupied Zone, out of reach of Vichy propaganda, and where antise-mitism assumed a somewhat more clearly German coloration. Three prefects in the Unoccupied Zone and an equal number in the Occupied Zone reported that the Vichy racial laws aroused no public reaction. Fully two thirds of the prefects had nothing at all to say about the matter during 1940. If anti-Jewish and anti-Masonic activity began to deploy in Paris at the end of July, the prefect of police Roger Langeron believed it was the result of German intrigue, not of popular enthusi-asm.[55] Moreover, until 27 August, newspapers were relatively calm, for the Marchandeau Law against antisemitic campaigning remained firmly in place.[56]

Indifference seems to have been the predominant attitude. After all, ordinary people had other things on their minds as they attempted to piece their lives together again. The population is "crushed," re-ported the prefect of the Aube on 28 July; "people aren't talking about anything." The prefect of the Ain reported in October on the general "intellectual and moral anesthesia." In the Seine-et-Oise the population seemed "sceptical, soured, and disillusioned" and dominated by private cares.[57]

But this generalized indifference could easily become focused into indifference to the sufferings of others, especially if the others were perceived as in some way responsible for the disaster. Much depended, then, on the tone set by the new leadership of France, and, above all, by Marshal Philippe Pétain, who enjoyed in 1940 as nearly unlimited a personal mandate as any French leader since, say, Napoleon following the Peace of Amiens. Would the new leaders of the *Etat français* lend respectability and coherence to these scattered bursts of popular antise-mitism, or would they condemn or ignore them?

Marshal Pétain's speeches of 13 August and 11 October, and the series of articles in the *Revue des deux mondes* in the fall of 1940 in which he outlined the new order, did not refer to Jews at all. Indeed, the Chief of State never, to our knowledge, talked publicly about Jews. He preferred to sound as high a note as possible in speaking of a general policy of exclusion: "The review of naturalizations, the law concerning secret societies [that is, Freemasonry], the search for those responsible for our disaster, the repression of alcoholism—all bear witness to a firm will to apply, in all domains, a unified effort at healing and rebuild-ing."[58]

"Healing," "rebuilding": such terms were eminently positive and invited support. Who favored disease or chaos? The authors of official pamphlets describing the Marshal's program conscientiously avoided

words like "antisemitism" or even "Jew." One example—a large-format
booklet of seventy-nine pages intended for "the average Frenchman,
sometimes so shallow or thoughtless"—emphasized that restrictions
upon Jews (disguised as "defense of the race, the family, youth, professions") were not what they seemed. "It is not a matter, on the leaders'
part, of easy vengeance, but of an indispensable security." The exemptions *(dérogeances)* for those who had rendered exceptional services to
the state absolved the government of anything base. "They prove that
it has never entered into Marshal Petain's intentions to penalize for
their origins men who, in the realm of thought, have enhanced French
prestige."[59] The harsh fact of exclusion tended to be veiled behind
formulas of a cautious generality. But exclusion was clear enough. In an
essay in which Marshal Pétain tried to "open [French] eyes" to the
abuse "of the sweeping words and illusory hopes" of the old regime,
such as Liberty, Equality, and Fraternity, he warned that "true fraternity is possible only within natural groups such as the family, the ancient
town, the nation."[60]

In private, Marshal Pétain had no objection to the company of
those much less discreet in expressing contempt for Jews. His personal
physician and private secretary, the son of an old army friend, Dr.
Bernard Ménétrel, was to tell the German police official Herbert Hagen
in June 1943 that even though Pétain insisted on a humane solution, he,
Ménétrel, admired *(bewundere)* the resolution with which the Germans were carrying out a "final uprooting" *(endgültigen Entwur-
zelung)* of Jewry.[61] The Marshal's staff offices in the Hôtel du Parc were
the kind of place where it was necessary to preface with an apology the
occasional interventions that nearly every Vichy official made at one
time or another on behalf of individual Jews. "You have known for a
long time . . . how I feel about Jews," wrote the chief of the Marshal's
civilian staff André Lavagne in October 1941 to Guionin, an official in
the Ministry of Colonies, "so the very fact that I am intervening in favor
of a Jew constitutes a quite exceptional recommendation."[62]* The
American couple, Mr. and Mrs. Alfred D. Pardee, Pétain's good friends
at Cannes, warned him in March 1941 that "*la juiverie* is working its
ravages on the other side of the Atlantic too." Pardee wanted the
Marshal to know that he was going to bring financial pressure on his old
university, Yale, for having engaged as a professor the Popular Front
Air Minister Pierre Cot ("gravedigger" of the French Air Force): "Isn't
he Jewish?"[63] If we can believe the postwar testimony of Paul Bau-

---

*Lavagne did intervene in favor of a number of Jews, sometimes in sympathetic
terms.

douin, Pétain himself was "the most severe" of all the participants in the Council of Ministers which discussed legislation against Jews on 1 October: "He insisted that the judicial and educational systems should contain no Jew."[64] We do not know how the Marshal reacted to the pathetic letters that reached him from Jewish war veterans and other Jews for whom he was the last hope; he does not seem to have replied to any of them. He is probably best described as someone who took for granted a certain polite antisemitism in the social circles he had at last reached and whose company he so clearly relished. He found public name calling in poor taste, but he was perfectly willing to leave a free hand to those who felt strongly against Jews.

Vice-Prime Minister Pierre Laval—and it must be emphasized that his ascendancy in the government was only gradually growing up to the time of the meetings with Hitler at Montoire in October—was not one of those who did feel strongly about them. He had no history of overt antisemitism, nor had he taken any role in elaborating Vichy's first racial laws. Indeed, there were some whispers that the rather exotic-looking Auvergnat was Jewish himself. In the summer and fall of 1940, however, Laval adapted to the new climate. In early August he allowed himself a rather brutal comment to Robert Murphy, the American chargé d'affaires at Vichy. According to Murphy, Laval said that the Jews "were congregating in Vichy to an alarming extent. He believed they would foment trouble and give the place a bad name. He said he would get rid of them."[65]

A calculated antisemitism had a small but distinct place in Laval's grand strategy in the fall of 1940. During those first fluid months there was a kind of footrace to see which of the emerging Vichy leaders would establish the most rewarding contact with the elusive German authorities. Minister of the Interior Adrien Marquet had been the first to make contact, signing an agreement with German police officials for informal cooperation on 25 July 1940.[66] Another route was through the Armistice Commission at Wiesbaden, where successive French delegates tried to widen the agenda. After trying Wiesbaden, Laval settled on Paris and Ambassador Abetz, with whom he formed a close working relationship. Abetz saw in Laval a counter to the clericalist and reactionary elements at Vichy, a kind of popular tribune who could give the new European order a mass base in France. It had not hurt that Laval had been sending antisemitic signals to the Germans during July and August (see pages 229–30). When Hitler finally thawed, after Vichy's vigorous defense of Dakar against the British and the Gaullists, and acceded to a meeting with Pétain, Laval was well situated to make the most fruitful contact of all. At Montoire on

22–24 October, he became the only French leader who possessed an independent link to the Führer. A calculated antisemitism had helped him come out on top in this scramble for influence.

At the same time, Laval had to fend off the French far Right in Paris who never lost hope that, with German help, they could supplant Laval by showing that he was a mere parliamentary hack, incompatible with the new fascist spirit. Laval was playing a delicate game, not the last of his career. His fundamental attitude toward Jews in 1940 seems to have been indifference, laced with a keen appreciation that Jews were an obsession to others. As we shall see, he was capable of the most total callousness. In the view of a recent biographer, Laval "felt neither hatred nor pity for those being persecuted. He had adjusted to a tolerant France; now he adapted himself to intolerance because purges were in style."[67]

The basic indifference of Pétain and Laval left the field to the zealots. Vichy antisemitism seems to us neither the work of mass opinion nor of the men at the very top. It was pushed by powerful groups and fanatical individuals, given a free hand by the indifference of others ready to abandon the values of the hated *ancien régime*.

There was a substantial minority of convinced antisemites among the new governing team at Vichy in summer and fall 1940. When he visited Vichy at the end of July, Pastor Marc Boegner, the leader of French protestantism and favorably inclined at first to many aspects of the new regime, was struck by the "passionate antisemitism" of several ministers, which "gave itself free rein without any German pressure."[68] The neo-socialist Minister of the Interior Adrien Marquet, who hated the "reactionary" clericals such as Alibert and tried to persuade Abetz as early as August-September 1940 to get rid of them, found that anti-Jewish sneers set the tone at Vichy.[69] We know little about the position of General Weygand on the Jewish question while he was a dominant influence as defense minister at Vichy, up to 6 September; but thereafter he applied the racial laws zealously as Vichy's proconsul in North Africa.

Most ardent of all was Raphaël Alibert, a mercurial personality who had been long associated with the monarchist Action Française, and whose Justice Ministry prepared the *Statut des juifs*. Alibert's authority derived from his imperious temperament, from his rancor owing to his years of exclusion from public service and his failure in professional life, from his favored position in Pétain's inner circle, and from the ruthless consistency of his monarchical world view. With Alibert was fulfilled the long campaign waged by Action Française leader Charles Maurras against the *métèques*, or halfbreeds (by which he meant Jews, Freemasons, and Protestants), who, in his opinion, had weakened modern France.

Antisemitic spokesmen also occupied more modest public positions. We have mentioned some of those in the Pétain entourage. Presiding over French radio and cinema from Vichy was Jean-Louis Tixier-Vignancour, whom Maurice Martin du Gard described at Vichy in July 1940 as delighting "in Jew-baiting, and in looking for chances to cast more insults at Léon Blum, distant and forlorn."[70] Still other rightist stalwarts like Xavier Vallat, at this point secretary-general for veterans' affairs in the new government, applauded the racial legislation as the fruition of a "long national tradition."[71]

At the local level it was no longer taboo to avow antisemitism, and "Jew hunting" promised to offer possibilities for place or enrichment. The prefect of the Oise reported that "adventurers" and "gangsters of the press" were "trying to implicate in their anti-Jewish and anti-Masonic campaigns decent people who have always been adversaries of the Jews and Masons but against whom they bear old local grudges."[72] Prefects were alarmed by the number of letters of denunciation which arrived on their desks. The prefect of the Indre reported that the "tale-telling mania" brought him diverse denunciations "every day."[73] The position of *administrateurs provisoires* now being appointed by SCAP to oversee Jewish properties in the Occupied Zone was beginning to attract candidates, not always disinterested ones.

Vichy tried to reassure foreign opinion about these new developments. Before a group of American newsmen in October 1940, Foreign Minister Paul Baudouin declared that "we have decided to limit the action of a spiritual community that, whatever its qualities, has always remained outside the French intellectual community." No longer could the Jews, with their "considerable international influence," constitute "an empire within an empire." He wanted the American newsmen to know that Vichy had no intention to persecute. "Neither persons nor property will be touched, and, in the domains from which they will not be excluded, there will be no humiliating discrimination."[74] Foreign Jews were already in detention, however; and before nine months were out French officials would be seizing Jewish property in the Unoccupied Zone; before two years had passed, French police would be rounding up Jews for German deportation schedules. The momentum of antisemitism could hardly be contained within Paul Baudouin's benign expressions of good intentions, echoed by many at Vichy during 1940. Certainly not within Hitler's Europe.

But why should Vichy have launched itself in this direction at all?

Why, to an experienced official like Paul Baudouin, should being different have seemed so threatening, in October 1940? Why, with so much else to do, did the emerging National Revolution spend so much time and effort on the dangers posed by different "spiritual communities"? And why, among these, were Jews singled out with such insistent attention and manifest fear? Thus, in explaining a shift of attitudes that was far more widespread and profound than a mere foreign import, imposed at bayonet point, we give little credence to German pressures. It is the indigenous roots of those attitudes that we wish to explore in our next chapter.

CHAPTER

2

The Roots of Vichy Antisemitism

THE WINDS of antisemitism blew intermittently in modern French history, varying widely in intensity and the amount of damage they caused. Consider two events of quite different impact, recent enough to be remembered in 1940. The first began in Paris on 25 May 1926 when a mild-mannered Yiddish poet and watchmaker Scholem Schwartzbard made a dramatic appeal to public opinion on behalf of tens of thousands of Jews murdered in eastern European pogroms in 1919. At the corner of the rue Racine and the boulevard Saint-Michel, he shot and killed the Ukrainian nationalist and military leader Semyon Petliura. In a sensational trial a few months later Schwartzbard was acquitted, thanks to a moving address by his defense counsel Henry Torrès, the compassion of a French jury, and a relatively favorable climate for Jews. In August 1927, the French parliament passed a remarkably liberal law on naturalization which later eased the pain of exile for thousands of Jews.

The second event occurred twelve years later. On 7 November 1938, seventeen-year-old Herschel Grynszpan, a German-born Jew of Polish extraction, shot to death the German diplomat Ernst vom Rath in the German embassy on the rue de Lille in Paris. Grynszpan meant to draw public attention to the abrupt uprooting from Germany of his parents and fifteen thousand other Jews and their expulsion, without belongings, to Poland at the end of October. Grynszpan enjoyed little of the tolerant understanding that had favored Schwartzbard. Police seized not only the assassin but his uncle and aunt, who were sentenced to six months of imprisonment for harboring an illegal alien. Grynszpan's trial was eventually overtaken by the war; and in July 1940, after the Germans had imprisoned the state prosecutor of Bourges for allegedly allowing the young suspect to escape, French police turned Grynszpan over to the Nazis.

In Germany in 1938, Ernst vom Rath's murder tripped the wires of a murderous assault on Jews by the Nazi party. During the night of 10–11 November, 267 synagogues were burned, 91 Jews murdered, at least 7,500 shops and stores sacked across Germany, and nearly thirty thousand Jews imprisoned in concentration camps.[1]* The next morning, as German strollers crunched over the glass-strewn pavement, they referred ironically to "the night of crystal," *Kristallnacht.* French opinion was deeply troubled by the renewal of Franco-German tension just six weeks after the Munich crisis. French antisemitic spokesmen surged into the public arena, calling for stern measures against Jews, especially against Jewish immigrants, who, they alleged, were exposing France to grave risks. Many Frenchmen agreed. The year 1938 saw a crackdown on foreigners in France and a deteriorating situation for Jews.

The differing French reactions to these two cases show how volatile the social climate in regard to Jews had become in the late 1930s. Antisemitism burgeoned in France during the decade before Vichy. The government of Pétain did not invent the anti-Jewish program it so earnestly and eagerly put forward in 1940. Every element of this program was present in the years preceding the fall of the Third Republic.

But it is not enough merely to assert that anti-Jewish feeling grew in the 1930s in France. Closer examination reveals an antisemitic idiom somewhat different from that of the 1920s, to say nothing of the 1890s and the time of the Dreyfus affair. Antisemitism has been associated with remarkably different intellectual currents, from clericalism to socialism and nationalism; and it would be wrong to assume that it has been consistent either in behavior or in ideology. Anti-Jewish images permeated like a gaseous current beneath the cultural surface, periodically changing in composition, sometimes too weak to assert themselves, sometimes kept down by external pressures, then sometimes bursting forth, after having mingled explosively with some economic or social issue.

An explosion something like this seems to have happened in the decade before Vichy. A lively traditional antisemitism mingled first with the social crisis of the Depression and then with the nervous international situation of the late 1930s, when Nazism pushed Jews to center stage, casting them in the role of warmongers. So we must examine not only the traditional images of French antisemitism but also the contemporary issues with which they combined in the 1930s, and which gave them immediacy and shifted them from the journalism of

---

*Almost incredibly, Herschel Grynszpan survived a series of German prisons and was never brought to trial.

gutter or salon to the realm of ministerial staffs and senior civil servants
—to the very heart of the French state.

Traditional Images of the Jews

> We are a Kingdom of Christ. If the deicide nation comes near, the only
> reason can be to give a Judas kiss. . . . This Jewish people of ancient culture,
> experienced at every kind of bargain, skillful at arousing covetous feelings.
> . . . It is not possible to distinguish what was really the Jews' work from that
> of Calvinists like Jean-Jacques Rousseau and that of the Free-Masons, so
> closely did they already walk hand in hand, in common accord and under
> one banner, that of the Declaration of the Rights of Man and of the Citizen.
>   Le Marquis de la Tour du Pin (1898)[2]

French antisemitism had been part of a general Western tradition.
No Christian people had been exempt from it. Had not every church-
goer for a millennium heard the priest on Good Friday denounce "the
perfidious Jews" who "wanted to have the Lord Jesus Christ killed"?[3]*
Traditional society, grounded in orders and corporations, had considered the Jews as forever alien from a Christian tradition that they
rejected. In the past, Jews had adjusted to this climate by reinforcing
and cultivating their separateness. Christians sometimes tolerated Jews
in their midst as long as the latter fulfilled certain prescribed roles:
economically, they undertook tasks deemed necessary but reprehensi-
ble, such as usury; theologically, they served as reminders, by the
debased terms of their existence, of the true faith that they had chosen
to reject.

Secularization weakened the foundations of this arrangement, especially during the eighteenth-century Enlightenment; and Jewish
emancipation during the French Revolution made the Jews theoreti-
cally part of the European family. France led the way to full civil rights
with two important statutes in 1790 and 1791. Other countries in western
and central Europe followed suit, sometimes at the point of French
bayonets, more often drawn forward by middle-class tastes for a more
rational, more open society. But statutory interventions seldom transform with ease centuries-old patterns of thought and action. Old ways
died hard. Throughout Europe the nineteenth-century advance of Jew-

*From 1959 to 1963, Pope John XXIII removed from the liturgy this and other
passages offensive to Jews.[4]

ish emancipation went together with new, secular justifications for old habits of exclusion. Along with civic rights were to be found secular, modern reasons to deny them. Where once the Jews had been made pariahs because of their religion, they could now be singled out for a supposed Jewish *character*—itself ascribed variously to race, upbringing, or education. Inventive theorists from across the political or social landscape undertook to do what intellectuals have always done best: to provide sophisticated and clever reasons for people to believe what they already believed—in this case that the Jews were different and worthy of dislike.

Both social and political circumstances conditioned the attention that Europeans gave to such matters and the extent to which they remained hostile to the Jews. In Protestant Holland or in many states of Catholic Italy, for example, emancipation proceeded smoothly once legal barriers were crossed. Elsewhere, as in Protestant Germany, Jews ran into a wall of popular and official opposition. Outbreaks of popular hostility to Jews punctuated the nineteenth-century history of agrarian central Europe, where writers kept alive the ancient notions about Jewish perfidy, and both peasants and artisans nursed real or imaginary wounds inflicted by Jewish merchants. Spokesmen for conservatism or reaction made their contribution; but so, too, did an early generation of socialists, including Karl Marx. The revolutions of 1848 were the occasion for anti-Jewish riots in many German-speaking areas, including Alsace. From the early decades of the nineteenth century, antisemitism was tinged with radical protest against liberal, bourgeois society, symbolized by that society's emancipatory traditions of 1789.

New energy for the old hatred came in the last part of the nineteenth century, when liberal society everywhere in Europe endured a series of assaults. Common to them all was a profound disillusionment with the world wrought by parliaments, cities, industry, science, democracy, and civic equality. Such creations were seen as a package—unable to satisfy the cultural needs of an élite, incapable of realizing a just order, and inadequate to contemporary challenges like empire, war, or economic insecurity. At times, Left and Right joined: people unhappy with the failure of liberalism to offer enough justice and equality, found common cause with those whose attitude was that, in offering what it did, liberalism debased and cheapened worthwhile values. Syndicalists became nationalists, and conservatives appealed to the common man, rallying against a bankrupt liberal civilization.

Increasingly in the late nineteenth century, the cultural critics explained these failures by references to race, which added potency to their analysis. Modern society had failed, the argument went, because the biological fabric of its leadership had softened, either through miscegenation or through the infiltration of alien elements of lower racial standing. Racist ideas were popularized in the three decades before the First World War, working their way into language and ultimately providing the most durable of the theoretical bases of modern antisemitism. Racist thought, of course, had a much wider focus than the Jews; but it never avoided reference to them and never failed to rank them in the ugly classificatory schemes that absorbed racist energies. For antisemites, a biological basis for alleged deficiency was now available, to be added to the rationales offered by religion or social theory.

These trends were especially prominent in France. French had provided the language of revolution in the first part of the nineteenth century, and French thinkers now pioneered a rejection of that heritage, heaping contempt upon the liberal, rationalist doctrines their countrymen had helped establish in Europe. By the mid-1880s dozens of publicists were at work. Paris, according to a recent analysis, became "the spiritual capital of the European Right" during this period, and French politics the laboratory in which was forged an original synthesis of extreme nationalism and social radicalism.[5]

Antisemitism flourished as one of the principal expressions of this movement and one of the most appealing to a popular audience. Before this period, hostility to Jews in France had been principally the province of the Left—part of the anticapitalist or antibourgeois baggage of such eminent socialists as Proudhon, Fourier, and, most important, Fourier's disciple Alphonse Toussenel, the author of a two-volume work, *Les Juifs, rois de l'époque*, in 1845. Antisemitism remained congenial to much of French socialism, as was clear from the continuing polemics against the Rothschilds or against the supposed Jewish domination of international banking. But innovation and political vitality passed to a new anti-Jewish constituency, combining radical protest with nationalist and sometimes reactionary impulses. For this new current antisemitism came easily. It helped weld together new political coalitions by an eclectic doctrine appealing to both Left and Right. Its theme was the Jewish conquest of France.

The Jews who had benefited so much from the republic were now labeled its principal support and representatives. In the portrait created by the new agitators, Jews appeared as the central agents of republican culture: optimism, progress, centralization, industrialization, science, along with corruption, greed, materialism, and scandal. According to the socialist-turned-racial-theorist Georges Vacher de

Lapouge in 1899, Jews were becoming for Europe what the English were for India.

> The conquest of France . . . is taking place at this very moment before our eyes. To have made this conquest without fanfare, without a battle, without shedding a drop of blood, to have made it without any other weapons than the millions of French people and the laws of the country, that exploit is more remarkable than those of Alexander and of Caesar."[6]

An early milestone in this polemical path was the collapse of a Catholic banking house, the Union Générale, in 1882. The event is important because the antisemitic campaign launched during the economic stagnation of the 1880s had a heavily Catholic inspiration.[7] Popular Christianity was experiencing an unexpected revival in post-1870 France. Cut loose from more austere or intellectual sources of piety, the movement's extravagance often found its way to a furious hatred of Jews, the living foil to a newly awakened Christian consciousness. Though antisemites thereafter could and did flirt with the French Left, they could not easily forsake specifically Catholic tastes in formulating anti-Jewish views. Such was the case with Edouard Drumont, perhaps the pre-eminent nineteenth-century antisemite for his success in joining the old anticapitalist themes of the Left with the Right's new fears of French moral and material decadence. Drumont published his extraordinarily successful *La France juive* in 1886 and, with its huge royalties, founded a daily newspaper, *La Libre Parole*, in 1892. Sensationalist, provocative and popular, *La Libre Parole* helped launch a new journalistic style to go with its new message. No less scurrilous in its treatment of Jews was the widely distributed paper of the Assumptionist religious order, *La Croix*, which, with its affiliated publications, reached half a million readers during the time of the Dreyfus affair.[8] Together the two journals helped persuade a whole gamut of troubled social groups—declining artisans, agrarians, and aristocrats in an era of increasing commercialization; patriots transfixed by German and American growth—that their troubles were the fault of the Jews.

Along with this synthesis of appeals to the interests and fears of both Left and Right, changing styles of political behavior also aided antisemitism in the late nineteenth century. As manhood suffrage rooted itself in practice, politicians began looking for ways to recruit and manage a mass electorate. The political scientist Dan White has described how antisemitism was useful to new lower middle-class politicians wresting votes from entrenched Liberal notables in the German state of Hessen in 1889–90.[9] During the same years, on the fringe of the nationalist-authoritarian Boulangist movement (although General Boulanger himself had Jewish advisors and financiers), the first French candidates ran for the Chamber of Deputies on a largely antisemitic platform. Francis Laur, antisemite and scourge of the trusts, won a Paris deputy's seat in 1890. The Dreyfus affair provided an even better opportunity to test the new formulas in political combat. The bulk of the popular newspapers in France were anti-Dreyfusard, and of the fifty-nine deputies elected to the Chamber under the banner of the Ligue de la Patrie Française in 1902, most had espoused antisemitism openly in their campaigns.

No vehicle did more to carry forward the antisemitism of the Dreyfus era than Action Française. Founded in 1898 and sufficiently strong to mount a daily newspaper in 1908, the movement was led by Charles Maurras, an admirer of France's royalist past, at least as he imagined it. An inspiration to the Right for over forty years, Maurras was the most articulate of the antiparliamentary, antidemocratic, and antisemitic theorists for whom the Third Republic embodied everything they despised in political, social, and aesthetic life. His movement attracted some of the brightest minds of the Right, thus lending credence and respectability to antisemitism. The intense nationalism that clothed its hatred of Jews and foreigners similarly eased xenophobia into general acceptance. So solidly did the movement become entrenched in the French landscape that it remained the "principal source and the cutting edge of French antisemitism"[10] during a time of dearth for the extreme Right in the 1920s.

Yet, despite the exuberance of French *fin de siècle* antisemitism, one must not exaggerate. The Dreyfusards won, after all, in the end. Electoral nationalism collapsed after its apogee in 1902, and its energies fragmented. The historian Pierre Sorlin's exemplary study of *La Croix* from 1880 to 1899 (see note 8, page 377) suggests that even that venomous journal could step back from the brink, and seemed to be moderating at the end. The First World War and its spirit of *union sacrée*, above all, left people with little taste for reviling minorities in France. Even Maurice Barrès, the sharpest tongue of the far Right, had mellowed to the point of admitting that Jews were one of the "spiritual families" of France. Drumont's old newspaper *La Libre Parole*, whose circulation had reached three hundred thousand in 1889, died in 1924 for lack of readers. Other antisemitic sheets took on a shabby, dog-eared appearance that not even the publication and periodic republication of the

*Protocols of the Elders of Zion** could remedy. Pope Pius XI condemned Action Française in 1926, and antisemitism two years later.
Parish priests gave up their subscriptions to Maurras's journal. The
writer Georges Bernanos, always a solitary traveler among antisemites,
could observe defensively in the late 1920s that it was "good form" to
deny the existence of a Jewish problem. There was less antisemitism,
he reflected, than thirty or forty years before. He had the impression
of moving "against the current of his time."[12]

For our purposes, it is less important to trace the polemical chain
from one writer or one newspaper to the next than it is to note the way
in which all of them, cumulatively, and over a long period of time,
conditioned the responses of many French people who had never met
a Jew and would have been astonished to be labeled antisemitic. Reflecting on his own childhood in Lille, the historian Pierre Pierrard
recalled that Jews hardly entered his consciousness or that of his school
friends. But as pupils in the local parochial school, the Jews were with
them still:

> I can still feel the emotions triggered by the brusque shift of the
> prayer *Pro perfidis Judaeis* in the long, rather soothing series of
> "great prayers" of Good Friday: while the six preceding prayers
> and the eighth and final prayer ("for the pagans") were preceded
> by the *Oremus. Flectamus genua. Levate,* accompanied by a collec-
> tive kneeling, the prayer for the Jews was deprived of this rite,
> which naturally struck our young sensibilities. When I try to imag-
> ine what a "moral ghetto" is, then I refer to the discomfort that
> grasped me at that moment.[13]

Moreover, anti-Jewish sensibilities were exceedingly durable in
France, where divisions were profound and political memories long.
Over thirty years after the Dreyfus crisis, right-wing toughs broke up
the opening of a play about it in Paris in 1931. An inherited antipathy
to Jews could survive for generations. In October 1941, the commissioner-general for Jewish affairs, Xavier Vallat, discussed his recent measures against Jews with Cardinal Gerlier, archbishop of Lyon, who had
expressed some doubts about the rigor with which they were to be
applied. Even so, "no one recognizes more than I the evil the Jews have
done to France," said the cardinal. "It was the collapse of the Union
Générale that ruined my family."[14]

*A celebrated document purporting to demonstrate the existence of a Jewish con-
spiracy of world domination, probably forged by the tsarist secret police, and first published in France in 1924.[11]

Beneath the surface moderation of the 1920s, therefore, there remained a reservoir of antipathy to Jews in France, often stagnant and scarcely visible. The distribution of anti-Jewish feelings in French culture at the close of that decade might be likened to a series of concentric rings. An outer circle was composed of a relatively diffuse attitude of social exclusion, extremely widespread but not often given expression in speech or writing. These feelings expressed themselves in the choice of friendships, in the rules of access to social clubs, in the subtle pressures that governed the choice of a spouse. It is likely that social exclusivity directed against Jews was probably weaker in France in 1930 than in Britain and the United States, and perhaps even than in Germany where the assimilation of older families, despite certain flagrant exclusions such as from the officer corps, had been so thorough. The amount of intermarriage would make a useful comparison on this score, but it left no trace in the egalitarian and secular French vital statistics. Our subjective impression, at least, is that intermarriage was more extensive in France than in the United States between the world wars, certainly among the social élite.

A circle of higher intensity—narrower and more charged—lay within that one: it consisted of open feelings of antipathy based on cultural parochialism or professional rivalry, where dislike was colored by fear as well as by contempt. Such feelings were relatively relaxed during times of general confidence and prosperity such as the one ending in 1930, and were clearly weaker in France in the 1920s than in Germany, and perhaps even weaker in France than in Britain and the United States. The informal closure of many prestigious American university faculties to Jewish professors, for example, which was just beginning to be breached in the 1930s, was already unthinkable in France as it had become unthinkable in Weimar Germany.[15]

At the center was a hard core of overt hatred, the values of the committed antisemite. France had a history of particularly brilliant expositors of antisemitism, as did Germany, in contrast to Britain or the United States where antisemitic agitators were likely to be intellectually marginal. The verbal brilliance of the French and Germans gave their ideas a certain legitimacy that antisemites may have enjoyed less often outside France and Germany. At the popular level, however, overt hatred of Jews found no more direct expression in France than in comparable countries. At the time when Captain Dreyfus was being exonerated at long last by his third trial in 1906, the young Leo Frank was being lynched in Georgia and the rabble-rousing Tom Watson was finding antisemitism useful for a political career in the American Deep South. In 1911 there were antisemitic riots in several coal-mining villages in South Wales.[16] Violence against Jewish property had occurred in fifty-five localities of France in 1898;[17] but violence against Jewish people had probably become no more common in France since 1848 than in the Anglo-Saxon countries.

These rough and preliminary comparisons suggest that there was nothing in the widespread but partly submerged French antisemitism of 1930 that would make inevitable the French government's adoption of an anti-Jewish policy ten years later. Had not the young Jules Isaac —and many others like him—felt completely at ease in friendship with his schoolmates?[18] Indeed, many German Jews would have said the same thing before 1933. The crises of the 1930s were to strip away the veneer.

Second Wave: The Crises of the 1930s and the Revival of Antisemitism

> Almost everywhere reigns a latent antisemitism, more or less conscious, composed of suspicion, revulsion, and prejudices.
>   Joseph Bonsirven, S.J. (1936)[19]

When Georges Bernanos wrote in the late 1920s about the decline of French antisemitism, he stood, unknowingly, at the threshold of a new antisemitic era. "For France," says one student of this period, "the years 1930–32 were a time of cruel awakening which dispelled the dreams of peace and prosperity which she had nurtured since 1918."[20] In truth, during the troubled early and middle 1920s, those dreams had been clung to all the more passionately for their fragility. By the late 1920s, however, it seemed possible to believe that France had at last reaped the reward of her 1914–18 sacrifices: that finances were stable, that prosperity was increasing, and that France's international position was secure. The French economy grew even stronger during the United States financial collapse of 1929.

This serenity ended abruptly in the early 1930s. In 1931, France first felt the effects of economic disorder; by 1932, crisis seemed endemic. In that year production fell 27 percent; and well over a quarter of a million people were out of work, by official figures which were certainly underestimated. Political stability ended at the same time. Aristide Briand and Raymond Poincaré, two solid, familiar alternatives of the happier

1920s, disappeared from the political scene. Ministries began to succeed each other at an accelerated tempo. Affected later than other countries, affected less by some indices, France felt the Depression quite as deeply and much longer than most countries. Rather than a cataclysm, the French Depression was a long, slow rot. Even in 1938, industrial production remained 15 percent to 17 percent below that of 1928; and between 1935 and 1939 the number of assisted unemployed never dropped below 350,000, an unprecedentedly high figure, however low it may seem by our present standards.[21]

In a time of economic contraction, who could be more vulnerable than the masses of foreigners living in France? By 1931 there were close to 3,000,000 of them, 7 percent of the population of metropolitan France. Indeed, France had actively encouraged immigration in the 1920s. The bloodletting of 1914–18 had reduced the labor force by over 1,400,000 active young men. That hemorrhage affected a population that, since 1890, had hardly been replacing itself. During the 1920s, French government agencies recruited Polish miners and Italian agricultural workers, and many people welcomed the arrival of new workers and potential soldiers. With the onset of economic difficulties, some foreign workers returned home. Between 1931 and about 1936, more left France than entered it. The total number of aliens in France fell from 2,891,000 in 1931 to 2,453,000 in 1936.[22]

Dramatically, however, in the mid-1930s this decline was offset by a new factor which changed somewhat the composition of the immigrant population in France. This factor was the flood of refugees, victims of the politics of eastern and central Europe at that time.

The numbers of refugees are difficult to trace, partly because so many entered France illegally. There were relatively few in 1931, when French economic difficulties began; and until the collapse of the Spanish Republic in 1939, this influx did not begin to approach the volume of free immigration of the early 1920s. By the end of the decade, France had become "the leading country of immigration in the world," with a greater proportion of foreigners than any other. It had 515 immigrants for every 100,000 inhabitants, against 492 per 100,000 in the next largest country of immigration, the United States.[23] By the summer of 1938, according to one estimate, there were 180,000 refugees in France, not counting those who had re-emigrated or who had become naturalized citizens.[24] The country that had welcomed immigrants in the 1920s found them an extremely vexing presence a decade later. Refugees became a major public issue: they had arrived at the wrong time and in the wrong place—the usual fate of refugees.

We do not know exactly how many of the refugees were Jews, although it is certain that their numbers were highly exaggerated at the time. Although Jews began to leave Germany in large numbers when Hitler took power in 1933, many returned to the Reich during the calmer years of 1934–38. Jews were also leaving Poland during this period, fleeing conditions at least as hard as those in early Nazi Germany. Jewish agencies did their best to monitor the totals; and, if nothing else, their figures cast into relief the wild exaggerations. The first wave of 1933 reached between 17,000 and 20,000 German refugees. Then followed close to 6,000 people (fewer than half of them Jews) who left the Saar valley in 1935, when a plebiscite bound the region to the Reich. By the end of 1937, 7,000 German Jews lived in France. A new wave followed the absorption of Austria by the Reich in March 1938 and especially after the *Kristallnacht* of November. France may have received about 55,000 Jews of all nationalities in the decade after 1933—a figure subject to dispute.* Not all of the original entrants remained. Some took French citizenship and disappeared from the statistics, if not from public awareness; others went on to England, America, or Palestine, or even returned to the countries from which they had fled. To mention only one example which demonstrates the relative numerical insignificance of recently arrived Jews: there were over 720,000 Italians in France in 1936, among them thousands actively hostile to the Fascist regime.[26]

The refugees presented three kinds of threat to the French, whose confidence was already badly shaken. First, the threat to employment. More subtly, there was a threat to swamp French culture, already under assault, many Frenchmen feared, from the mass cultures of America and Russia—mass cultures created and spread, it was alleged, by Jews. Finally, and most urgently by 1938, the refugees threatened to involve a deeply anxious France in unwanted international complications. Spanish refugees might embroil France in trouble on the Pyrenees; Italian antifascists, the next most numerous category, could poison relations with Mussolini, whose neutrality in an eventual conflict was keenly desired by conservatives and the military; refugees from Germany and Austria might antagonize Hitler. Indeed, that is what Herschel Grynszpan did.

All the refugees bore the brunt of a newly aroused xenophobia in France. The Englishman Norman Bentwich, assistant to the League of

---

*Kurt R. Grossmann ranks France fourth among recipients of Jewish refugees during 1933–45 with 55,000 of them—after the United States (190,000), Palestine (120,000), and the United Kingdom (65,000).[25]

Nations High Commissioner for Refugees, was struck by the hostility toward aliens he encountered on a visit to Paris in February 1934.[27] At issue then was the French reception of thousands who had left the Sarre (Saar) basin anticipating its annexation by Germany. How much more intense were the feelings when the arrivals were not manifestly pro-French Sarrois but the unwanted and displaced from central and eastern Europe. Immigration into France, observed Georges Mauco in 1932, used to come from French-speaking neighboring countries—Belgium and Switzerland. Then came Mediterranean elements—from Spain, Italy, and Portugal. But the most recent period showed a "predominance of Slavic and exotic elements," much more truly foreign and much more exposed to the lash of anti-immigrant journalists.[28] "Canaan-on-the-Seine," wrote Georges Imann in *Candide*, describing Paris facing its first experience of German-Jewish refugees in 1933. The same newspaper worried about a proposed position for Albert Einstein in a French university.[29]

Competition for jobs became a particularly sensitive issue. Here was a novel antisemitic theme: Jews as predatory proletarians, job stealers, rather than Jews as usurious capitalists and exploiters of the poor. Right-wing publicists and candidates made ample use of the issue, and even Communists conceded its appeal. Each congress of the Communist trade union federation from 1925 to 1933 passed a resolution calling for equal treatment for immigrant workers and the repression of xenophobia within the French working class—a tacit admission of its existence.[30] Jews who tried to aid their co-religionists found the unemployment issue extremely awkward; as early as December 1933 the Jewish Welfare Committee of Paris (Comité de Bienfaisance Israélite de Paris) was taking steps to assure that "aid to refugees . . . must at no time tend to create, for the benefit of refugees, possibilities to engage in commerce or labor on French soil."[31] By late 1934, with over 400,000 unemployed in France, a French senator spoke of a "hatred, muffled but ready to explode [which] separated French workers from foreign workers."[32] In 1937 the French Communist party quietly changed its policy and opposed further immigration; it closed its separate foreign language sections.[33] The "liberal" press was even less discreet. *La République* and *l'Ere nouvelle* urged Jews to train their co-religionists to be miners.[34] In 1938, Jacques Saint-German referred in *La Liberté* to those who patronized or protected Jews as plotters "against our working class, against our artisans, against our shopkeepers."[35] And even when the word *Jew* was not spoken, it is difficult not to hear in some cases the antisemitic accent. The General Confederation of the Middle Classes, for example, whose members were required to be French citizens, launched an enquiry in October 1938 into "the daily increasing flood of foreigners who come to France to set up commercial, industrial, or craft enterprises . . . to practice there, in the most diverse ways, the activity of middlemen."[36] In an economic climate where the size of the pie was firmly believed to be fixed or shrinking, each new arrival necessarily seemed to entail a smaller slice for the others.

Among intellectuals, rivalry for places merged easily with another theme—the swamping of that tender plant, French culture, by the rank herbs of foreign mass culture. Wherever there was a violently frustrated talent, held back from some coveted position or acclaim, and able to link his private frustration with the ills of France, there was a potential antisemite. For Robert Brasillach, the critical *Wunderkind* of Parisian letters in the 1930s, nothing could be more obvious than the domination of the Jews: "The movie business practically closed its doors to aryans. The radio had a Yiddish accent. The most peaceable people began to look askance at the kinky hair, the curved noses, which were extraordinarily abundant. All that is not polemic; it is history."[37] The journalists Jean and Jérôme Tharaud revived in 1933 a theme that they had overlooked in *L'Ombre de la croix* of 1917: Jews caused revolutions, and threatened society by their corrosion of national culture. Jews were warned to watch their step, although in what manner was not made clear:

> If the thousands of Jews who emigrate here don't carry a lot of discretion in their baggage (but that is precisely the virtue that you most lack!), it is to be feared that just what you dread will be awakened, that old human passion you have unleashed so many times. . . . It depends on you alone to avoid that catastrophe.[38]

For the novelist Louis-Ferdinand Céline in 1937, reveling in cultural pessimism, there was no longer a point in warning the Jews; it was simply a matter of submitting with maximum ill grace: "Messrs. Kikes, half-niggers, you are our gods."[39]*

Few political leaders denounced the anti-immigrant mood more tellingly than the Socialist party leader Léon Blum. And few men in public life had Blum's capacity to draw a fusillade of prejudices, includ-

---

*Eugen Weber believes Céline's antisemitism, absent from earlier work, was precipitated by the rejection of his ballet project for the Exposition of 1937 by the minister of education, Jean Zay.[40] Technicalities never troubled proponents of the Jewish conspiracy idea; Zay had one Jewish parent but was a convert to Protestantism.

ing antisemitism, from virtually every political quarter. One Catholic deputy, for example, a man alleged to detest antisemitism, is reported to have confided to a friend, "When one hears Léon Blum, so destructive, one understands the pogroms, and one must resist the temptation to hate the Jews."[41] Such scruples, reported in 1935, were not commonly exercised when Blum won his dramatic victory and became the first Jewish prime minister of France in June 1936. Leading the charge, antisemitic newspapers made their angriest attack yet upon Jews in general and upon Blum's "Talmudic cabinet" in particular. When the deputy from the Ardèche, Xavier Vallat, lamented in the Chamber that his "old Gallo-Roman country will be governed by a Jew," he knew that his Maurrasian sympathies and nativist Catholicism were not a political liability. "Xavier Vallat was not entirely wrong to present his antisemitic spewings, at the Chamber podium, as the uncensored expression of an immense half-stifled murmur."[42]

Antisemitism was plainly an important focus for opposition to Blum's Popular Front government. Those years reshaped anti-Jewish sensibility into a political, economic, and social world view, giving it a combative edge, the *cri de coeur* of an opposition movement attempting to defend France against revolutionary change. In Spain another Popular Front provoked a military rising and civil war in July 1936. Illogically, but by the juxtaposition of events, French conservatives lumped together what to them had become related ills: bolshevism, Blum, the Jews. Indeed, the compounding of enemies became a linguistic exercise in which Jews figured importantly. Senseless neologisms peppered popular antisemitic prose: *judéo-bolshévique, judéo-allemand,* or *judéo-slav.* Strains of anti-Jewish opinion turned up now in unexpected places, united only by opposition to the Popular Front or its leader. The Right and the Catholics indulged, of course, but so also did neo-socialists, the pacifist Left (Simone Weil wrote to the deputy Gaston Bergery in the spring of 1938 that she preferred German hegemony to war, even though it would mean "certain laws of exclusion against Communists and Jews"[43]), and some grassroots Communist elements.

The war scares of 1938 sharpened the focus upon the image of the scheming Jewish warmonger. It was bad enough that Jews were taking Frenchmen's jobs, flooding into the country illegally, launching a "Jewish revolution" through Léon Blum; now, it was held, they wanted to involve France in their own war of revenge. "Today synagogues burn; tomorrow it will be our churches," reported one newspaper on 28 November 1938, in the wake of *Kristallnacht.* Whether such predictions were offered in solidarity or in a self-protecting recrimination, many French citizens concluded that it was the Jews who were causing the trouble. Long-established French Jews did their best to insist that their community wanted peace. General Jacob-Léon Weiller released a press statement on behalf of French-Jewish army officers, of whom he was the senior representative; French Jews did not want war with Germany.[44] Grand Rabbi Julien Weill assured his listeners that sorrow at the fate of German Jewry did not lead French Jews to oppose a Franco-German rapprochement. "No one sympathizes more than I with the pain of 600,000 German Israelites. But nothing appears to me more precious, either, and more necessary than maintaining peace on earth."[45]

Amidst the din of German propaganda, the shrill cries of the French Right, and the nearly universal sinking of hearts in France at the prospect of another experience like that of 1914–18, these efforts were not altogether successful. "Surely we are not going to war over 100,000 Polish Jews," declared Ludovic Zoretti of the pacifist Left review *Redressement.*[46*] From the other side of the barricades, *Action française* drove the point home: "behind Czecho-Slovakia . . . it is the Jews who are pulling the strings."[48] Following the *Anschluss* of Austria in March 1938, Darquier de Pellepoix's Anti-Jewish League (Rassemblement Antijuif) launched a tract that echoed the contemporary German propaganda line: "It is the Jews who want war because that is the only way to avoid defeat and to pursue their dream of world domination."[49] But it is not necessary to look as far as a street ruffian like Darquier, the recipient of secret German funds, to find a preoccupation with foreign Jews and their supposed desire for revenge against Germany. Emmanuel Berl, in his review *Les Pavés de Paris,* returned repeatedly to the theme in November 1938. The issue of peace or war for France simply must not be left to foreigners, insisted this most pro-Munich of French Jews.

During September 1938 there were demonstrations against Jews in Paris. Foreigners were attacked in the streets. Incidents also occurred in Dijon, Saint-Etienne, Nancy, and various other places in Alsace-Lorraine. During the Jewish High Holy Days of 1938, the Grand Rabbi of Paris warned his co-religionists not to gather in large numbers outside synagogues. Bernard Lecache, the militant president of the International League against Racism and Antisemitism (LICA) appealed to French Jews to avoid all political conversations.[50]

*According to David Weinberg, Paris Jews were not particularly against the Munich compromise with Hitler.[47]

It was at this sensitive juncture that the young Herschel Grynszpan shot a German diplomat. This time the slogan of *Action française* seemed to have concrete applicability: "no war for the Jews." At the very least, Jews were perceived as endangering delicate negotiations with Germany, as Foreign Minister Georges Bonnet awaited the visit of Ribbentrop. Even the semi-official *Le Temps* now found links between the dangers of war and an international Jewish problem. After *Kristallnacht, Le Temps* wondered how "what was at first only a purely internal German matter is tending, by the force of circumstances, to turn into an international matter which will not be easy to settle."[51] *Le Temps* favored some preliminary remedies: no more admission of foreigners into France ("Let's stop playing with fire") and a police crackdown on those already there:

> Public opinion does not want to hear any more about political refugees who are, by definition, either future public wards or future lawbreakers, competitors of the French worker or intellectual in the labor market, and whose contradictory ideologies can only create disorder, stimulate violence, and make blood flow by expressing themselves on our soil.[52]

Central to the whole 1930s anti-Jewish sensibility was an obsession with France's incapacities—what the novelist Pierre Drieu de la Rochelle called "the terrible French inadequacy"[53]—of which Jews were confusedly regarded as both symbol and cause. Added to the troubles we have already mentioned, a series of scandals rocked the Third Republic, culminating in the Stavisky affair of 1934 in which gangsters and parliamentarians seemed joined in a scheme to float fraudulent municipal bonds and then to cover over the matter. Commentators hardly noticed how the affair was pumped up by the press or by political interests, hungry to deride a political system. What they noticed was the involvement of foreigners, especially Jews, and the suspicion of some wider, more general plot against a society severely undermined from within. The connection was rapidly made: France's international weakness, its economic decline, its parliamentary disorder, its diminished sense of national purpose, its declining birthrate, its flagging bourgeois culture—all could be attributed to the Jews, so notoriously not French yet so vividly evident in so many spheres of French activity.

Since the public mood of the 1930s rested upon so radical a sense of insecurity, a conviction of decadence stronger even than that of the

1890s, its antisemitism was also different—more radical, more violent, more energetic. Its principal spokesmen were young writers who found their elders too soft. Though he had learned antisemitism at Charles Maurras's knee, Lucien Rebatet thought that the *Action française* should be called *Inaction française*, that Maurras

> had made his antisemitism inoperative by dangerous distinctions, the door open to the "well-born Jew," so many shadings that were suggested to him only by his horror of racism, the sole integral principle, sole definitive critique, but marked with a German sign.[54]

Céline, similarly, dismissed the cultural, assimilationist antisemitism of the Maurrasiens as outmoded. In a rare effort at programmatic lucidity, he advised:

> if you really want to get rid of the Jews, then, not thirty-six thousand remedies, thirty-six thousand grimaces: racism! That's the only thing Jews are afraid of: racism! And not a little bit, with the finger-tips, but all the way! Totally! Inexorably! Like complete Pasteur sterilization.[55]

When such writers as these set the outer limits, others could take middle positions with a show of moderation. When the prize went to the most clever denunciation, the sharpest barb, the best-turned insult, others could feel less constrained to adhere to strict logic. In the current antisemitic style, few seem to have worried overly about contradictions: Jews both a cause and a symptom of national decadence, Jews both bourgeois and revolutionary, Jews both rootless and a nation, Jews both mercantile and bellicose, long-established French Jews tarred with the same brush as recent German or Polish refugees, and so on.

Just who, after all, were the targets of the antisemites' wrath? Did a Jew cease to be dangerous after generations of assimilation to the ways of his country of residence? Hitler clearly thought that assimilated Jews were the most dangerous of all, as being the most hidden. By contrast, many French people who felt an aversion to Jews freshly arrived from some eastern European *shtetl* were conditioned by a long assimilationist tradition to accept those who spoke perfect French and who had fought in the French army. This was also, quite naturally, the position of long-established French Jews themselves, who were painfully torn

during the 1930s between charitable instincts, condescension, and uneasiness as they contemplated the horde of refugees. Emmanuel Berl
was the most outspoken on these matters. The new immigration of the
1930s, he said, was an "immigration of cast-offs," and a "veritable catastrophe" for France. After the Grynszpan deed, Berl proclaimed "the
impossibility for France to let her country and her capital be invaded
by the undesirables of every land."[56]* Berl, who insisted that he was
more French than Jewish and that those whom Hitler was expelling
were more German than Jewish, denied that there was a "Jewish problem." There was only an "immigrant problem." If France would revise
its too-generous immigration laws so as to refuse citizenship to all save
those who really intended to submerge themselves entirely in French
culture—that is, for Jews, those who renounced Zionism and *Yiddisch-
keit*—the problem would be resolved.

Perhaps Emmanuel Berl hoped that it would be so easily resolved,
but in the late 1930s the distinction he drew between the "undesirable"
foreign Jews and the long-established French Jews was already threatening to give way. Many hard-core French antisemites denied that it
existed at all, and insisted that Jews, by their very nature, could not be
assimilated. The writer Marcel Jouhandeau squirmed at the very
thought of Jewish intellectuals teaching the French classics in school to
young descendants of French warrior heros like du Guesclin and Jean
Bart: it was "monkeylike," a pure effort of mimesis. He vowed in 1939
to "point them out to the vengeance of my people," and not to rest "so
long as there remains one [Jew] in France who is not subjected to a
special statute."[57]

Jouhandeau's advocacy of a special statute for Jews was not exceptional in the late 1930s. A concrete program took more specific form in
the antisemitic writings of 1938–39. Robert Brasillach set the tone in his
editorial of 15 April 1938 in the right-wing newspaper *Je suis partout*
appealing to an antisemitism "of reason" as opposed to an antisemitism
"of instinct." He wanted nothing less than a *statut des juifs:*

> What we want to say is that a giant step will have been taken
> toward justice and national security when the Jewish people are
> considered a foreign people. . . . To consider Jews of foreign nation-
> ality as foreigners and oppose the most stringent obstacles to their
> naturalization—to consider all the Jews established in France as a
> minority with a special legal status that protects them at the same

---

*Berl was later to draft some of Pétain's speeches of the summer and fall 1940.

time that it protects us—never to forget services rendered. . . . These are the only way to assure the absolute independence of French soil.

A second special issue of *Je suis partout*, in February 1939—this one focused on Jews in France and put together by Lucien Rebatet—included the text of a "reasonable" *statut des juifs*. René Gontier advocated virtually the same strategy in *Vers un Racisme français* (Paris, 1939): a *numerus clausus* in the liberal professions and in commerce, the retraction of French citizenship from all naturalized Jews, and a "special statute for Jews" to ensure that they would not abuse their position as guests within French society. Jews should be made subjects rather than citizens and susceptible to a network of legislative control and regulation that removed from them the possibility of involvement in the future of French society.[58] In April 1938, Darquier de Pellepoix presented to the Paris Municipal Council a proposal that even more explicitly joined long-established French Jews with recent immigrants in exclusion from French public life. Darquier wanted all Jews—however many generations established in France—to be considered foreigners, disfranchised, and subjected to severe limitations in economic and cultural activity. "Hitler has known how to solve the problem by legal means," he reminded his listeners, following a long harangue about Jewish domination of French medicine, commerce, and the arts.[59]

In the spring of 1938, a respected journalist, Raymond Millet, published a widely read series on immigrants in *Le Temps*. Sincerely opposed to antisemitism—he called it, in Jacques Maritain's words, "impossible antisemitism"—he nevertheless described Jewish "invasion" of the Belleville neighborhood of Paris, and sounded a common antisemitic obsession with "the psychopaths [who] encumber our hospitals. They are mostly of Slavic or Israelite origin." Millet's final recommendation seems to hang in the air, as if to await the arrival of a more resolute political authority: "Measures must be taken against this disorder."[60]*

---

*To separate the "undesirables" from the welcome "immigrants," Millet proposed a *filtrage* ("filtering system") that would select those "whose blood type and psychology are the most like ours."[61]

The Reach of Antisemitism:
How Influential Was It?

> The xenophobic movement that is taking shape in the country can be contained within just limits only if no one misjudges its incontestable depth. A statute for foreigners is necessary—without delay—if we are to avoid graver and graver conflicts between French and foreigners.
>
> Emmanuel Berl (1938)[62]

It would be tempting to regard the upsurge of xenophobia and antisemitism in late 1930s France as the noisy but marginal enterprise of a handful of cranks and literary renegades and as distasteful to the great majority of the French people. In truth, there are no convincing measurements of public opinion in the matter. Public-opinion polling was taking its first infant steps in France in 1939; there were no 1940 elections to test public responses to issues concerning foreigners and Jews.

One explanation can be dismissed out of hand. French antisemitism was no mere import, a hothouse plant artificially nurtured by German secret funds. Darquier de Pellepoix did indeed receive German money, and the Office of National Propaganda of Henry Coston, the self-proclaimed successor to Edouard Drumont, was in contact with the Nazi party's propaganda center in Erfurt, the *Weltdienst.* Several other French organizations were on its payroll.[63] German propaganda agents were active in Paris and in Alsace, where French police identified Strasbourg as a distribution point for Paris-bound German antisemitic material.[64]

The Germans were singularly inept in their choice of pawns, however. Darquier must have been one of the few French antisemites of the 1930s unable to support himself; and, in any event, most of his backing came from the owner of a tire-recapping plant in Neuilly, Joseph Gallien. Moreover, most German agencies preferred not to stress antisemitism in their dealings with the French. The Comité France-Allemagne, one of the most important ideological links of the 1930s, did not make much of anti-Jewish feeling. There were so many willing French hands anyway that German funds and propaganda resources do not seem to have been necessary or significant. French writers were more than capable of launching an antisemitic campaign on their own.

In fact, antisemitism recruited some of the most formidable literary talents of 1930s France. One would have to search long and hard in the dingy annals of antisemitism to find prose more seductive and yet ultimately more inflammatory. Along with the older nonconformist Georges Bernanos, who opened the decade with his affectionate appreciation of Drumont—*La Grande Peur des bien pensants* (1931)—there arrived on the scene a whole new generation of young writers contemptuous of the soft complacency and woolly liberalism of their elders. Most of the major new talents angrily dismissed their elders' orthodoxies, in reaction to which, in the 1930s, the former tended to be closer to the energetic mass movements of the Right than to a Left that at that point was busily throwing in its lot with the bourgeois democracies. There was Robert Brasillach, a young graduate of the prestigious Paris Ecole Normale Supérieure and already at twenty-two editor of the literary page of *Action française,* who announced the arrival of his new postwar generation in 1931 with a celebrated essay in *Candide,* entitled "The End of the Postwar Period." There was Louis-Ferdinand Céline who, having dazzled even those whom he shocked with his powers of invective and spleen in the obsessive *Voyage au bout de la nuit* (1932), followed it with the violently antisemitic *Bagatelles pour un massacre* (1937). There was Drieu de La Rochelle, brooding over the decadence of Europe in the face of the Americans and the Russians, who wanted to culminate a brilliant career as novelist-essayist with *Gilles* (1939), the chronicle of a young Frenchman who had a strong resemblance to the author and "scorned and hated with all his man's heart the pious, petulant, and wheezing nationalism of this Radical party which left France childless, which let her be invaded and overrun by millions of foreigners, Jews, halfbreeds, Negroes, Indochinese."[65]

Yet the French Republic's censor deleted certain passages from *Gilles* in October 1939, and Drieu's integral text appeared only in July 1942. There were clearly powerful forces at work in the Third Republic to limit and repress the open expression of antisemitism, as the *Loi Marchandeau* showed. Significant voices in France denounced the campaign against the Jews. Despite the clamor of the extremist writers, it was not at all clear at the time that these could carry the day.

In mid-1938 the World Jewish Congress, recognizing the furor over Jews in France, prepared a report on French antisemitism with particular attention to Catholic opinion. The congress's conclusions were cautiously optimistic. It saw a rapprochement between Judaism and Catholicism, jointly persecuted by the Nazis.[66] And whatever one may think of the drift of certain Catholic attitudes at the time, most well-informed Catholic literature (Jacques Maritain, Robert d'Harcourt, for example) spoke firmly against racism and antisemitism. Pius XI condemned Nazi race hatred with his encyclical *Mit brennender Sorge* in 1937, and made similar interventions the following year. In their turn, Jean Cardinal Verdier in Paris and Monsignor Jules-Gérard Saliège, Archbishop of Toulouse, denounced racism as un-Christian; and Cardinal Maurin of Lyon, originally a supporter of *Action française,* came out strongly in the 1930s against its vilification of the Jews. His successor, Pierre Cardinal Gerlier, presided over a meeting against racism and antisemitism in 1938. And, in sharp contrast with its position during the Dreyfus years, *La Croix* told its readers that hatred of foreigners was a survival of paganism.[67]

On the far Left, the Communist party considered antisemitism a bourgeois diversion tactic; although many militants were unhappy about immigrants, and although some party policies worked against Jewish interests, the party's hands, officially, were clean. A high-ranking Communist trade-union official André Bothereau did his best to disentangle the working-class movement from xenophobia.[68]

Overt opposition to antisemitism could be found on the traditional Right as well. A rare nationalist who opposed the Munich compromise, like Henri de Kérillis, argued in *L'Epoque,* for example, that antisemitism contradicted "the entire French tradition" and threatened to isolate France from its natural ally, Great Britain.[69] In an interview with Emmanuel Berl in September 1938, Etienne Flandin, the future Vichy foreign minister ardently favorable to the Munich compromise, said that he refused any discrimination against Jews, although by April 1939 he wrote that France had been invaded by suspect foreigners who wanted to provoke revolution, and that the "obvious" lines of revival for France included race (France had been bastardized by foreigners), the family, and the willingness of individuals to take risks.[70]*

Colonel François de la Rocque, whose Parti Social Français (the successor to the banned right-wing paramilitary movement the Croix de Feu) certainly meant to be a new mass movement of the Right however short it fell of truly fascist violence and authoritarianism, refused pointedly to join the anti-Jewish bandwagon and thus occasioned divisions in the movement (Algerian and Alsatian members objected) and bitter attacks from more extremist groups.[72] The more overtly fascist party leader Jacques Doriot (subsidized by Mussolini rather than by Hitler at this point) remained relatively immune to

*By late 1940 Flandin had joined the chorus of those blaming Jews and Freemasons for French defeat.[71]

antisemitism until autumn 1938, though he took pains to make clear that
it was not for love of Jews. The Parti Populaire français (PPF)

> is a great national party which has more and better things to do
> than to struggle against the Jews. We have no intention of either
> defending or attacking the Jews. We do not oppose the French of
> the Israelite religion. But we reject those who call themselves Jews
> before feeling themselves French. We do not accept that a cate-
> gory of citizens puts its racial interests before the national inter-
> est.[73]

As late as May 1940 one can find, on a list of sponsors of a committee
to defend oppressed Jews, the name of the ex-socialist authoritarian
Marcel Déat.*

Cautious optimism was not based entirely upon Jewish self-delu-
sion in 1938, therefore, despite some handwriting on the wall. As with
graffiti, the wall carried several messages at once. Even the future
commissioner-general for Jewish affairs, Xavier Vallat, found it possible
to work with Jewish colleagues in the rightist Republican Federation
and in the interwar veterans' movements.[75] For all its susceptibility to
Jews at home, the French press found *Kristallnacht* abhorrent, with
the exception, of course, of a few diehards like *Je suis partout, Action
française* or *Gringoire.* As for Darquier de Pellepoix, his bimonthly *La
France enchaînée* was in periodic trouble with the police in the fall of
1938 and fell afoul of the Marchandeau Law in July 1939 for attacks upon
Jews.

The trouble was that French opponents of hard-core antisemitism
lacked the basis for a strong counterposition. It would be hard to find
any political or intellectual leader in France after the Popular Front
ready to argue the pragmatic case in favor of immigrants: that France
was the most thinly populated of industrial nations; that in a depression
immigrants were not so much rival job seekers as new consumers, a
stimulus to the market; that in any event France needed more workers,
not less, for increasing armaments production; that, faced with a more
populous Germany, France needed all the people it could get, however
exotic; and that any of Hitler's victims were likely to furnish highly
motivated workers and soldiers for French defense in any foreseeable
war. These arguments, which seem to us not unreasonable in view of
the economic stimulus afforded by immigrants to, say, West Germany

---

*Déat's signature is on an appeal to General Sikorski in London from the directors
of a "Committee for the Defense of the Rights of Oppressed Jewish Minorities."[74]

in the 1950s or to France after the loss of Algeria in 1962, were simply unthinkable in the 1930s. For one thing, this position assumed the inevitability of war with Hitler. For another, it was out of step with the prevailing economic assumption that the Depression was a crisis of overproduction rather than of underconsumption. And it assumed that assimilation was not necessary to make a people strong, a point admitted by neither Left nor Right in France. One would have to have been, simultaneously, an advocate of war, a Keynesian, and a cultural pluralist to make a frontal attack on xenophobia and antisemitism in France of the 1930s, and there were not many such in that static, fearful, inward-turning decade,

There remained only the moral argument in favor of immigrants. France had been traditionally hospitable, so it went, and should continue to be so. But that argument easily drifted into a feeling that France had already borne more than its share of the world's burdens since 1914, and that it was now the turn of others to be charitable. Refugees' difficulties getting into Switzerland or the United States during this period were hardly an encouragement.

Under these conditions, many sincere opponents of antisemitism unwittingly acquiesced in an integral part of the antisemites' world view: that exotic peoples weakened France, and that immigrants should be regarded exclusively as a burden. Thus even people committed to the moral case for helping refugees accepted the notion that there was "an immigrant problem," into which the notion of "the Jewish problem" nestled so comfortably.

Once it was accepted that Jews were a "problem," the way was open for other elements of the antisemitic world view to slip quietly into the consciousness of moderates. It is striking how widely fragments of the antisemitic position permeated moderate political vocabulary after the mid-1930s. Anti-Jewish expressions acquired new kinds of legitimacy. The old taboos against anti-Jewish language, widespread since the vindication of Dreyfus, were clearly softening. With the outer limits of acceptable discourse set by the Célines, the Brasillachs, and the Drieus, conventional people could, without shocking, become much more aggressive about foreigners and Jews. Even people setting out to denounce antisemitism had to begin with disclaimers: of course, undesirables must not be admitted; of course, there must be tougher regulation. No longer was the debate about whether such lines should be drawn; it was only about where to draw them.

The tendency to find foreigners—and especially Jews—at the root of France's problems permeated far beyond the hard core. Anti-Jewish language made steady headway into terrain that had been free of it before, at least publicly so. The end of the 1930s saw relative unknowns coming forward with modest proposals to curb foreigners, sometimes overtly anti-Jewish proposals. Often still couched in republican or liberal language, these projects threatened Jews at least as much as the blustering of hard-core antisemites. They pointed toward the middle-ground consensus upon which Vichy was going to be able to build. Vichy's measures would not shock, after the long habituation of the late 1930s.

In July 1938, for example, the Confederation of French Medical Associations called for strict enforcement of earlier quotas and even for the exclusion of foreigners from practising medicine "on any pretext whatsoever."[76] The Paris Chambers of Commerce studied the refugee question carefully in 1938 and at the beginning of the next year declared in favor of limiting foreigners "in professions where passage is easy from wage earner to craftsman to commerce." Strict controls were to be established for aliens proposing to set up a business in France.[77] Similarly, the National Confederation of Commercial and Industrial Groups of France and the Colonies asked the government to prepare a comprehensive "statute of foreigners" to regulate foreign businessmen in France.[78]

Once such eminently respectable commercial and professional groups had declared themselves, it became difficult for politicians to avoid concessions to xenophobia, especially if they represented threatened social groups. Thus, a number of his constituents in the department of the Moselle who lived near the Maginot Line petitioned Deputy Robert Schuman shortly after the Munich crisis "protesting against the attitude of certain recently arrived foreigners during the recent period of international tension." Schuman, in turn, undertook to propose a law immediately expelling foreigners from the area, examining all naturalizations pronounced since 1919, deporting all those fraudulently naturalized, banning any new naturalizations, and forbidding all naturalized aliens not mobilized in wartime from engaging in any commercial activity in the frontier departments.[79] Schuman's Meusien and Lorrain constituents were not alone; all kinds of special interests pressed their case against foreigners, who were deemed to be taking advantage now of a beleaguered society: Parisian taxpayers supporting aliens' children at school, French patriots suspicious of foreigners' evading military obligations, or small businessmen worried about a new vegetable stand in a local market.

With war in sight in 1938 and 1939, such concerns, petty or local though they may have been in specific instances, received national attention. International crises exposed painful, sensitive points in the national subconscious: old obsessions about French weakness, race, and the Jews re-emerged for anguished public recrimination. Pius XII lifted the interdict on *Action française* in 1939, freeing Catholics to read Maurras without fear of sin. By now, however, many of his diatribes had become commonplace.

Le Temps, for example, recalled worries about French demography:

> In a country with a low birthrate like ours, it is quite natural to try to overcome the disadvantages of chronic demographic deficiency by the arrival of new blood, provided that this arrival, prudently rationed and wisely administered, threatens neither national unity nor the integrity of the race.

But precisely the latter concerns had been made real of late by so many undesirables. It was high time, the journal argued, for a policy of "selective assimilation."[80] The same newspaper, which suddenly discovered another million foreigners in France (making up a highly exaggerated total of four million *allogènes,* or outsiders), declared that public opinion was seriously nervous *(inquiète)* over the issue. *Le Temps* welcomed the Statute of Foreigners—the Daladier government's series of decrees in April 1939—especially in light of the prospect of European hostilities. It seemed confirmed that foreigners posed a threat to French security. It seemed also confirmed that they endangered French unity, morals, and even physical health. "There is a danger," wrote Georges Mauco, an advisor on immigration and demography to the Third Republic, to Vichy, and to General de Gaulle, "that physically inferior or ethnically heterogeneous elements might bastardize the race and introduce into it germs of diseases that it had managed to diminish." And the threat was not merely physical. "No less pernicious is the moral delinquency of certain Levantine, Armenian, Greek, Jewish, and other *métèque* merchants or speculators. The intellectual influence of foreigners, although still difficult to discern, appears above all as contrary to the reason, finesse, prudence, and sense of measure that characterize the French."[81] Georges Mauco, we should stress, opposed racist fears and denounced doctrines based on a supposed racial purity; his occasional flights into a racist fog are a measure of the general acceptability of this language in the 1930s.

In this climate, it is not surprising that some of the concrete propos-

als of the antisemites crept here and there into moderate circles, sometimes in the guise of devices to prevent the development of anti-Jewish
feeling. J. Rossé, a deputy from Colmar, abjured antisemitism in the
Christian Democratic *L'Aube* of 14 October 1938, but favored a *numerus clausus* "to prevent the antisemitism already so strong in Alsace
from reaching proportions so powerful that it will impose excessive
measures against the Jews." Similarly, Stanislas Fumet, a liberal Catholic *opponent* of racism, noted "that nations have a right to defend
themselves against an excessive percentage of Jews in the ruling positions of a country," and that therefore there was legitimate grievance
"when a Léon Blum calls upon a disproportionate share of the Jewish
element to set up his ministry. It is this lack of discretion, this tactless-
ness typical of a certain Judaism. . . . It is possible that the quota system
[*numerus clausus*] is not an arrangement to reject out of hand."[82]

Elements of anti-Jewish sensibility penetrated deep into the parliamentary majority of Radical premier Edouard Daladier. Lucien
Lamoureux was a Radical Socialist deputy from the Allier department
and a frequent minister in the 1930s. An opponent of the Popular Front,
he was to be minister of finance under Prime Minister Paul Reynaud
in 1940. In the pages of the *Bourbonnais républicain* of 2 October 1938,
he reflected on the "terrible and legitimate settlements of scores" that
would have occurred had France been drawn into war over Czechoslovakia: "They would have extended . . . to the representatives of religious confessions who, for ideological reasons and in order to take a
racial revenge on Hitler, were reputed to be working in favor of war."*
A strong supporter of Foreign Minister Georges Bonnet, Neville Chamberlain, and the policy of rapprochement with Germany and Italy,
Lamoureux coupled this international aspiration with a call for internal
revival, very much à la mode at the time of Daladier: "re-establishment
of discipline and authority, increased production, restoration of financial health, economic stability."[83] Here, as in his conviction of Jewish
warmongering, Lamoureux prefigured the National Revolution of 1940
before its time.

Overt antisemitism reached into the ministry itself in the person
of Jean Giraudoux, the witty and widely celebrated dramatist whose
political reflections, *Pleins Pouvoirs,* were a major publishing event of
1939. Giraudoux's book exuded a technocratic antiparliamentarism increasingly acceptable to broad segments of opinion. Daladier could not
have found it distasteful, for within weeks of the book's appearance he

---

*Simone Weil made similar predictions of an antisemitic deluge in the event of war.[84]

named Giraudoux to a newly created Commissariat of Public Information. *Pleins Pouvoirs* stands as a kind of summation of republican antisemitism on the eve of Vichy. Giraudoux shared many of his countrymen's
anxieties about low population growth in France and the massive influx
of refugees. "Our land has become a land of invasion. The invasion is
carried out just as it was in the Roman Empire, not by armies but by
a continual infiltration of barbarians." Among these *barbares* he drew
special attention to "the bizarre and avid cohort of central and eastern
Europe . . . primitive or impenetrable races," and to the threat they
posed to French racial stock. Sorely needed since 1918 was some careful
attention to breeding:

> Since every immigrant in the present state of our country and
> Europe is a potential Frenchman, it is a question of defining the
> rules of a rational immigration [policy]. But it is also a question of
> turning back, by methodical selection and by ceaseless watchful-
> ness, every element that could corrupt a race which owes its value
> to twenty centuries' selection and refinement.

Candidates for citizenship had to be "healthy, vigorous, without any
mental or physical blemish," the sort that only a determined bureaucracy could competently assess. Giraudoux wanted a "Ministry of Race,"
whose task it would be to make the right choices. "What more beautiful
mission could there be than to shape lovingly one's own race."

In Giraudoux's view, France had been swamped by "hundreds of
thousands of Ashkenazis escaped from Polish or Rumanian ghettos,"
remarkably disposed to lawlessness and corruption—"constant threats
to the French artisan spirit of precision, trust, perfection." Naturalization had gone wild, and the result was Stavisky, unemployment, tax
evasion, and the insalubrious cluttering of Paris by Jews. Of course, the
republican Giraudoux favored traditions of asylum—"for many true
Europeans," at least—and, like all opponents of Action Française, he
rejected the slogan "France for the French." Exceptional Jews, like
Freud, Giraudoux would have accepted with open arms. "We agree
entirely with Hitler," concluded Daladier's commissioner for public
information, "to proclaim that a policy reaches its highest form only if
it is racial, for that was also the thought of Colbert or of Richelieu."[85]

The Administrative Response

> The main instrument of your Ministry of the Interior is expulsion or exclusion. I have noted the dossier where our vain appeals have piled up. I defy any man not entirely bereft of humanity to scan these pages without feeling real anguish.
>
> Victor Basch to P.-E. Flandin (1935)[86]

Historians succumb easily to the temptation to place intellectuals and journalists at the center of their universe—people of the word, who leave traces so readily accessible to research. To trace the roots of Vichy antisemitism merely by ascending a chain from writer to writer would, however, be seriously inadequate. For many of the most visibly antisemitic polemicists of the 1930s wound up after 1940 not at Vichy but in Paris, where they sniped at what they considered the irresolution of the new French regime in the matter of antisemitism. Some of the prewar antisemites, we might add, like Georges Bernanos or the industrialist Jacques Lemaigre-Dubreuil, wound up on the Allied side. Vichy began, pre-eminently, as a triumph of civil servants and experts. How did these prefects, inspectors of finance, councilors of state on special assignment to ministerial staffs—carefully trained professionals usually far removed from vulgar polemic—become deeply involved after 1940 in applying policies advocated by the antisemites? The quiet but thorough mobilization of the French public administration in the work of repression of "undesirable foreigners" during the final years of the Third Republic is an essential element of our story. There was no sharp break in 1940; there was, rather, a long habituation through the decade of the 1930s to the idea of the foreigner—and especially the Jew—as the enemy of the State.

Faced with intense popular concern with the foreign "invasion," the French administration had not remained idle. Beginning early in the 1930s, the French state machinery was mobilized to restrict the flow of immigrants, to bar the door to refugees, and to scrutinize and regiment those already arrived. To a far greater degree than during the earlier wave of antisemitism and xenophobia of the 1880s and 1890s,[87] the identification of needy foreigners with a threat to state security became, long before Vichy, a commonplace of administrative routine. It helped legitimize these practices that during Auden's "low dishonest decade" most other governments were reacting to refugees in much the same manner.

Unknown to the public, the French Ministry of the Interior had long been assembling lists of persons to be arrested in the event of mobilization for war—the now notorious Carnet B. By the mid-1930s, according to a historian who has examined them, the lists had changed in nature. In a departure from their original concentration on domestic subversives, nearly 60 percent of the names in the 1930s lists were aliens, thus betraying a conviction that foreigners were the chief threat to French internal security.[88]

Quite early in the decade, French governments devised a bold and original method for dealing with the foreign employment problem: a system of quotas. By a law of 10 August 1932,[89] Edouard Herriot's government armed itself with the authority to limit the proportion of foreigners in certain branches of professional activity. And although officials hesitated for a few years fully to use the powerful machinery, the cabinet of Pierre-Etienne Flandin, which took office in the autumn of 1934, authorized the forcible expulsion of foreigners whose papers were not in order. During the first four months of 1935, over three thousand were summarily ejected from France.[90] The Laval government which succeeded Flandin's continued this policy, extended quotas from workers to artisans, and prescribed imprisonment for aliens who refused orders to leave France. French officialdom soon decided that a Russian balalaika orchestra could employ only 15 percent of Russian musicians and a Russian church choir only 10 percent Russian voices.[91] Refugees now found it extremely difficult to earn a living in France, even when legally resident there. Many were forced into working illegally, producing the very conditions of lawbreaking the statutes were designed to repress.[92]

Regulations and restrictions abated during the Popular Front. Despite periodic calls from police officials to reinforce the surveillance of foreigners, especially in the Paris region, Minister of the Interior Roger Salengro pointedly reminded prefects and prefectures of police, in the summer of 1936, about French traditions of asylum and hospitality.[93] Froissard, the minister of labor, insisted reasonably enough that the right to asylum could not be separated from the right to work. Refugees and foreign workers had a brief respite.

A major escalation occurred in 1938. Not only did France face a series of war scares, but at home there was revived social conflict culminating in the general strike of November. Daladier's government and the "fighting bull of the Vaucluse" himself exuded energy for this sort of challenge. The result was a series of draconian police measures, beginning with the celebrated decrees of May 1938,[94] which were referred to by opponents as *super-scélérats* because their harshness toward aliens recalled the *scélérat* (perfidious) anti-anarchist laws of 1894. The chief intentions of these measures were to regulate entry of foreigners more strictly and to tighten scrutiny of those who had already entered. Prefects of frontier departments were now empowered to expel aliens on their own responsibility, and the decrees bristling with regulations offered abundant pretexts to do so.

Some refugees illegally in France simply could not be repatriated whence they had come, however. Some of them were stateless; some would not be accepted by Nazi or fascist authorities; some were subject to severe victimization if deported. The Daladier government recognized this state of affairs by a palliative measure. Those unfortunates who could not be sent back to a homeland that rejected them could be sent by the Ministry of the Interior to some "assigned residence" in some remote corner of the provinces, where they could be easily watched.

New and more complicated rules defined the precious "regular situation," without which the alien would become a hunted person. For those whose situation was in the slightest way *irrégulière,* for those whom the government called "clandestine persons," these were frightening times indeed. Interior Minister Albert Sarraut ordered radio broadcasts of the new law in several languages. Employers were pointedly warned of their obligation to hire only properly authorized aliens. A special filing system was set up to index those foreigners caught by the police; and within nine months, 8,405 had been sent to prison for violating some part of the maze of regulations.[95] Still other aliens found themselves floating between deportation, internment, and forced residence in what one of them called "a new, refined form of torture," the *régime de sursis* (parole regime). This was a formal denial of permission to stay in France, mitigated by short-term reprieves, at the expiration of which one could be jailed, interned or deported.[96]

The November 1938 war scare brought the administrative response to foreigners to a new climax. The decree of 12 November 1938 concerning the status and supervision of foreigners modified the generous naturalization law of 10 August 1927: French nationality could be stripped from those *already naturalized* in the event that they were judged "unworthy of the title of French citizen."[97] This new machinery for producing stateless persons was denounced by Joseph Barthélemy, professor at the Faculty of Law at the University of Paris, who defended Jews and Italian antifascist refugees that year.[98] Time, defeat, and the office of the Ministry of Justice under Vichy were to change Barthélemy's views.

As the official government statement put it, explaining its November decree:

> the supervision and surveillance [of foreigners] are now assured in the country under conditions never before realized, while at the same time a purge is being tirelessly carried out, which is inspired exclusively by the needs of the state and which serves the interest not only of public order but also of those foreigners of good faith who visit or inhabit our country.[99]

The word "purge" carries a distinct ring of Vichy, as do the words "undesirable foreigners" in Title IV of the decree of 12 November, and also the innocuous-sounding *centres* described in that statute—"centers that will be established by decree and organized by the Ministry of the Interior, and, if need be, by the minister of colonies." This was the basis for the establishment of concentration camps in France.

Jews may not have been mentioned in these statutes, but there are indications that Jews were on people's minds. However slight their numbers in all of France, economic fears became associated to some degree with Jews. Immigrant Jews concentrated heavily in Paris, where they paid a high price for being conspicuous. Some efforts at exclusion seem to have been tailor-made for them. The Laval law of 5 April 1935,[100] for example, to protect French artisans from aliens' competition, penalized foreign needle or garment workers—10,500 of whom were east European Jews in Paris. These now had to obtain an artisan's card, the issuance of which required approval of local craftsmen's associations *(chambres de métiers)*, sometimes notoriously hostile to Jews. The independent Left deputy Philippe Serre gave particular attention to the immigration issue after the summer of 1937 when he became undersecretary of state for immigration in the Ministry of Labor. Among several important projects that he proposed to the government of Camille Chautemps was one dealing with frequent antisemitic allegations that Jews clogged the cities of France, especially Paris. Serre's strategy specifically addressed Jews: the idea was to install them in the countryside and involve them in agricultural work.[101] This plan may have been well intentioned but, like all such schemes, easily lent itself to a coercive sequel. In March 1938, according to the historian Yehuda Bauer, Serre wanted to go even farther, to the point of forcibly repatriating Jews, the expenses to be paid by Jewish organizations in France.[102]

In the climate of the late 1930s, it was not difficult for a French civil

servant to become inured to dealing highhandedly with foreign refugees, among whom none were more conspicuous or more defenseless
or, evidently, more irritating than were Jews. The machinery was soon
in place to deprive thousands of them of the liberty they had sought in
France.

The Refugee Crisis, 1938-41

> Four million foreigners in France, including a million Jews, gave me the
> occupation blues long before you [the Germans].
>   Drieu La Rochelle (1941)[103]

Nineteen thirty-eight was the crucial year. Internal tensions and
alarms of war threw Jews into the spotlight. We have already seen the
escalation of public language, the proliferation of xenophobic projects,
and the strengthening of government action against foreigners that
year. Now we shall see how the French administration set in place the
machinery to deal with refugees which Vichy later used against Jews.

Four days after the *Anschluss* of Austria, in March 1938, the Gestapo captain Adolf Eichmann arrived in Vienna and unleashed a terror
campaign designed to force the Jews of Austria to emigrate. Three
thousand Jews a day besieged the American embassy in Vienna, and
comparable numbers tried to obtain visas for Latin America or Switzerland. Determined not to raise the United States's slender quotas, President Roosevelt called an international conference on refugees at the
French resort town of Evian-les-Bains in July. It has been calculated
that if each of the thirty-two rather reluctantly participating nations
had agreed to admit seventeen thousand German Jews, the stateless
persons of the summer of 1938 could have been absorbed. In the end
none of the nations made a substantial change in its immigration quotas;
and the Jews were left with expressions of sympathy and not much else.

In France, those who followed the debates at Evian learned at least
about the dimensions of the Jewish tragedy. "The Jewish drama is one
of the most painful in recent history," wrote an editorialist in *Le
Temps*.[104] But the ever-mounting flood of refugees, coupled with the
disinclination of other governments to admit large numbers, made
French authorities nervous. Evian spawned the Intergovernmental
Committee (IGC) to help German and Austrian refugees, and France

proved reluctant to cooperate. The committee's American director, George Rublee, reported in November that the French were suspicious, that they had not been in touch with the committee since its establishment, and had not made their financial contribution. French officials were "particularly emphatic" in forbidding to refugees transit rights across France when emigrating to other countries; they wanted them to go directly to their final destinations.[105] The French representative to the IGC, Henry Béranger, explained that "France has reached the saturation point which does not permit receiving any more refugees without tipping the social balance.... We have long since gone beyond the limit in our country."[106]

Béranger was a significant figure—president of the Foreign Affairs Committee of the Senate and vice-president of the IGC. In this matter, however, he was the voice of his Foreign Minister Georges Bonnet with whom he was in close touch on the question. From the fall of 1938, and especially after the near-war avoided at Munich, Bonnet seems to have felt that the situation's urgency dictated direct action: an amicable agreement with Germany on Jewish refugees. Among supporters of the accord reached in September, Munich gave rise to considerable optimism about the prospect of wider settlements with the Nazis. Bonnet believed there existed an atmosphere of détente in which differences with Germany over Jews, as over Czechoslovakia, could be solved "in a friendly manner."[107]

Herschel Grynszpan's act and the ensuing anti-Jewish frenzy in Germany did not help these prospects. But French efforts persisted. Not long after *Kristallnacht,* the British Prime Minister Neville Chamberlain came to Paris together with his Foreign Secretary Viscount Halifax to meet with Daladier and Bonnet. Bonnet told them that the French government was "much preoccupied with the question of Jewish immigration into France." Bonnet did not exaggerate the numbers; he said there were forty thousand Jewish refugees in France. But "France could not stand a Jewish immigration on a large scale," he told the British. "She was already saturated with foreigners, of whom there were about three million in the country."[108] Note that "saturation" had become governmental orthodoxy, long before it became a favorite phrase of Xavier Vallat in 1941.

In the face of similar views expressed by Chamberlain ("one of the chief difficulties [in accepting Jews]" he said, "was the serious danger of arousing antisemitic feeling in Great Britain"), and of the United States' manifest reluctance to grant more visas, only two courses of action seemed open. One was to find colonial settlement somewhere for

Jews, and the other was to seek agreement with Germany to allow Jews to emigrate "normally"—that is, to take their property with them, so as not to arrive penniless on some foreign doorstep. This, said Bonnet, "would greatly facilitate matters." The French decided to pursue both possibilities.

The visit of German Foreign Minister von Ribbentrop to Paris on 6 December gave Bonnet his occasion to pursue the matter. The key conversation occurred the following day, 7 December, at the Hôtel Crillon. In Ribbentrop's version, sent directly to Hitler on the ninth, Bonnet told the German that there was great interest in France "in a solution to the Jewish problem." The French, according to Ribbentrop, "did not want to receive any more Jews from Germany" and sought German help in keeping them out. Indeed, "France had to ship ten thousand Jews somewhere else. They were thinking of Madagascar for this."[109]*

After the war Bonnet claimed this account to be utterly false. According to his memoirs, the conversation was hasty and involved his relating "the wave of popular feeling and the human and material problems posed by Hitler's persecution of German Jews" to a curt and indifferent Ribbentrop. Bonnet insisted that he never spoke of sending Jews to Madagascar, "for the whole government and I myself were firmly opposed to it," and that France opened its frontiers "unreservedly" to the helpless Jews.[111]

We possess another contemporary account of the Bonnet-Ribbentrop encounter, however, for on 15 December, Bonnet told Edwin C. Wilson, the counselor of the American embassy in Paris, about it. In this version, Bonnet and Ribbentrop had talked for half an hour in the latter's room at the Hôtel Crillon without mentioning "popular feeling" or "human problems." A rather loquacious Ribbentrop claimed that there were good Jews and bad Jews; all Jews in Germany were bad, whereas France and Britain had good Jews. Bonnet had seized his opening and explained to Ribbentrop that "he had no wish to mix into Germany's internal affairs but that Germany was creating a problem for other countries by forcing them to accept people whom Ribbentrop himself referred to as bad Jews and that the settlement of this problem would be greatly facilitated by some cooperation from Germany." Bonnet had even formed a rather favorable picture of the German foreign

---

*It has been generally believed that the dinner for Ribbentrop and his party at the Quai d'Orsay on 6 December involved a snub of two cabinet members of Jewish descent, Georges Mandel and Jean Zay; but Anthony Adamthwaite has recently denied this interpretation.[110]

minister: he had the impression "that Ribbentrop personally regretted the way in which German authorities had treated the Jewish problem recently, and that Ribbentrop would be disposed to assist in so far as he could in efforts to handle this problem on a more reasonable basis."[112]* Everything points to a businesslike conversation between Ribbentrop and Bonnet in which there was no French protest on humane terms, and in which Bonnet optimistically envisioned Franco-German cooperation in diminishing the flood of refugees into France. In the first years of Vichy, French ministers pursued the identical aim.

On the subject of Madagascar, Bonnet's postwar version is entirely misleading. Since the issue was to arise again under Vichy, it deserves some brief discussion here.[114] A French colony since 1896, the island of about 228,000 square miles in the Indian Ocean off the east coast of Africa was inhabited in 1936 by 3,800,000 *indigènes* and 36,000 Europeans. For some reason the place had a special attraction for anyone eager to get rid of unwanted groups of people. Indeed, in 1946 the British Foreign Office was still interested enough in sending Jews there to sound out consular representatives about settlement possibilities.[115] Since 1931, German writers had periodically proposed that Madagascar be colonized by Jews. Himmler himself is supposed to have suggested the idea to Hitler in 1934. Three years later the Socialist deputy and minister of colonies Marius Moutet published an article in *Le Matin* favorable to the settlement of Jews in territories abroad, especially Madagascar. In Poland, where the government had its own anti-Jewish and colonial axes to grind, this proposition aroused great interest. The Polish ambassador to France had suggested sending Polish peasants there in 1926, but the idea had been abandoned after unfavorable reports of climatic and soil conditions. Now the suggestion was revived for Polish Jews.

With the consent of Léon Blum and his Foreign Minister Yvon Delbos, a new Polish mission went to study the possibilities in May 1937. Prospective Polish settlement was even envisaged in the Franco-Polish commercial treaty of that month. But there were serious obstacles (not least of which were violent objections coming from the colony itself), although elements of the Polish press remained enthusiastic. Apparently the French Colonial Office was still interested enough in June 1937 to press the idea upon representatives of the Jewish Joint Distribution Committee.[116] One year later the plan was still alive; and Georges Mandel, then minister of colonies, wrote about Madagascar to Georges

*In the British account, "M. Bonnet said [to Ribbentrop] that France could not go on admitting Jews indefinitely."[113]

Bonnet on 25 May 1938.[117] Mandel, a Jew who had borne harsh antisemitic attacks in his own political career, warned Bonnet that the Madagascar "affair," as he now called it, raised "ticklish political problems." Special territorial concessions for Jewish emigrants would involve the recognition of a "Jewish question":

> We would appear to be adopting the point of view of foreign governments that consider the Jews not as citizens but as outsiders properly subject to a special statute. We would thus risk encouraging the very persecutions and harsh measures that have helped provoke the exodus of Jewish populations.

Moreover, explained Mandel—no doubt having on his mind the agitation of the Sudeten Germans against their Czechoslovak rulers in the 1930s—it would be dangerous to implant groups of foreign Jews in French possessions: "For, supposing that in a more or less distant future Jewish colonists succeed in founding a large and prosperous community, could we not fear that the government of the state from which these colonists originated might not end up by claiming the colony populated by its former citizens?"*However odd they may sound now, such arguments appear to have been conclusive. Béranger repeated them in London six months later.

And yet the plan refused to die. In October 1938, the United States Undersecretary of State Sumner Welles expressed an interest in the Madagascar plan. The British government, uneasy about the pressures of Jewish emigration on Palestine, also made a sounding. Fortified by continued interest abroad, and after having been closely briefed by Bonnet, Béranger told U.S. Ambassador Joseph Kennedy in London on 2 December that "if all the other participating governments in the Evian Committee would make a specific contribution, France would consider the settlement in Madagascar and New Caledonia of ten thousand persons but not persons of German origin."[119]†

Were these the ten thousand Jews whom Ribbentrop reported the French wanted "to ship somewhere else"? It seems likely. Béranger knew what Bonnet was going to propose to Ribbentrop a few days later

---

*This view was shared by such others as George Rendel, head of the eastern department of the British Foreign Office, who believed in 1937 that the Jews in Palestine had strong German loyalties and that a Jewish state might eventually become a "spiritual colony" of Germany.[118]

†M. de Tessan, under secretary of state for foreign affairs, spent several months in summer 1939 in the United States further pursuing the matter; and U.S. Congressman Hamilton Fish was in Paris in August 1939 with the promise of support from private philanthropists.

—indeed, Béranger was even indiscreet enough to reveal this before-hand to the Americans and the British.[120] In any event, the larger point about this episode seems abundantly clear: the French government and its spokesman Georges Bonnet spoke the language of "saturation" and tried earnestly to conclude some agreement with the Germans to ease the Jewish-refugee burden on France. Another object was to get the British and Americans to do more, and to secure their understanding as the French did less, at least in metropolitan France.

Bonnet was later to make much of the Interfaith Committee on refugees set up in December 1938, with the cooperation of Cardinal Verdier, Pastor Marc Boegner, Grand Rabbi Israel Lévi, François Mauriac, Jacques Helbronner, Professor Robert Debré, and others. And it is true that the foreign minister, as well as Daladier, spoke publicly of the "heart-rending situation" of the refugees, promising that the new committee would devote itself to abandoned children, that the government would seek to establish some refugees in the French colonies, and that France would even continue to admit refugees "to the extent that the United States and Great Britain would make a comparable effort."[121] As with Jean Giraudoux, official declarations paid obeisance to traditions of asylum.

None of these declarations of good intention slowed the steady progression of harsher measures toward foreigners. The Ministry of the Interior announced in late October its program of "decongestion" for the Paris region: refugees could no longer go to Paris. Border surveillance was tightened, "to assure definitively," as a blunt communiqué put it, "an absolutely rigorous supervision over entry onto our soil."[122] We have already examined the tough law of 12 November 1938 that followed soon after. The minister of the interior, the eminent Radical Albert Sarraut, explained that these various measures permitted a "filtering of the frontiers, to dam up the flood of immigrants," and carefully balanced this firmness with rhetorical gestures toward historic French hospitality and openness.[123]

Eloquent declarations of French generosity contained important elements of truth: France, indeed, received proportionately more refugees than any other country—a point that Bonnet rightly stressed. The United States, too, was treating refugees with new rigor. The Aliens' Registration Act (Smith Act) of June 1939 imposed tighter admission requirements for aliens, all of whom would have to be finger-printed, and provided for deportation for "subversive activities" and other violations. But the defeat of Republican Spain in early 1939 strained French hospitality beyond the breaking point.

The flood of refugees from the Spanish Civil War far surpassed anything France had seen before. Many times more Spaniards came than Jews. In the ten days following the collapse of Republican resistance in Catalonia at the end of January 1939, more than four hundred thousand Spaniards and international volunteers crossed the French border in a state of panic, exhaustion, and hunger. Soldiers and civilians, people of all ages and backgrounds, burst the dikes in desperation.

French policy now crossed a new threshold: the resort to mass internment. The government was lashed on by the fire-eaters of the right, such as the deputy of the Basses-Pyrénées, Jean Ybarnégaray, who declared that "France can no longer bear this crushing burden on her own shoulders alone,"[124] and conditioned by widespread suspicion of criminal elements, revolutionaries, and anarchists among the Spanish and the international volunteers.[125] The French government did its best to persuade the Franco regime to accept the repatriation of as many as possible, and exiles feared they would be forcibly returned to Spain.[126] Finally, the government had little answer for thousands but the hasty expedient of concentration camps. These camps, constructed not far from the Spanish frontier in March 1939, were the sad end of the International Brigades, the cream of European and American idealism. In Gurs alone assembled the nationals of fifty-nine different states.[127]

From the internment of the Spanish republicans to the outbreak of war stretched six months of government uncertainty, improvisation, and unintended cruelty. The refugees cost the government dearly at a time when it could ill-afford such expenses. In March, Ybarnégaray estimated the costs, including material installations, at 200,000,000 francs a month.[128]* Humanitarians clashed with reactionaries over the issue. The League for the Rights of Man voiced demands for asylum, while deputies from the Right were obsessed with security. The state continued to add to its repressive machinery. On 12 April 1939, out of fear of an ill-defined fifth column, a law instituted rigorous government control over foreigners' cultural, artistic, and philanthropic associations. Then came another law—that of 6 May 1939—allowing the minister of the interior to seize foreign publications.† The authorities tried to impose fiscal and military obligations on the newcomers. It was a very poor time indeed to be a refugee. "Our liberalism, sometimes carried too far," said an authoritative voice in Le Temps, "must give way to our security."[129]

When war finally came in September 1939, many Spanish Loyalists

*About $6,000,000 a month in 1938 dollars.
†Both of these laws remain in force, over forty years later.

had returned. Their places in the camps were quickly filled by foreigners of all descriptions, swept up in a nationwide police action during the first days of national emergency. "Selection being impossible," as Interior Minister Sarraut admitted in the Chamber,[130]* the fifteen thousand foreign males, mostly German or Austrian nationals, locked up in *camps de concentration* (also Sarraut's term) included hundreds of distinguished anti-Nazi refugees. Leo Lania, for example, a well-known Austrian-Jewish writer and journalist, languished for over a week on the stone benches of the Colombes Stadium on the west side of Paris before being released.[131] Gradually those internees found to be politically innocuous or in categories such as those with children born in France were allowed to go home, so that by December only about eight thousand were left.

Internment seemed the simplest recourse in times of emergency to a harassed and distracted bureaucracy, however; and in May 1940, as the Germans swept into France, many foreign refugees were rounded up again. These were "administrative internments," without interrogation or the possibility of defense. This time both men and women were included. Leo Lania now found himself at the Roland Garros Stadium in Auteuil. Some refugees were held pending a routine "regularization" of their situation, like a Swiss traveling salesman arrested absurdly while on a sales mission to the French National Railroads. Others were bundled from camp to camp by confused officials. Few were given sufficient warning to assemble necessities or notify families.

The great exodus of June 1940, ahead of the German Army's advance, compounded the hardships of refugees. The administration was now buried in a human avalanche. In a panic born of military operations and whipped on by rumor, a terrorized population surged south under occasional strafing from German aircraft. Swelling their numbers were about a million Belgians and roughly two hundred thousand Luxemburgers, Dutch, Poles, and Jewish refugees from the Reich. Approximately eight million persons were uprooted and close to a million remained displaced a year later. These people jammed the roads, taxed relief facilities beyond the limit, and exasperated the officials charged with trying to control the situation. Repatriation of refugees to the north became a major French government preoccupation, and one that lasted for many months after the armistice.[132]

In this whirlwind, aliens received short shrift. Internment was the simplest recourse for beleaguered officials, but refugees could not un-

*The British government also interned, in September 1939, all German and Austrian nationals, regardless of political persuasion, as did the American and Canadian governments all Japanese in December 1941.

derstand why they were imprisoned or learn what their fate would be as the Germans approached. In the rich literature of foreign refugee experience in France during 1938–41—after all, a great many of the refugees were writers—a dominant theme is disillusion.

> The sufferings that we who were confined in French concentration camps underwent sprang not so much from personal privation as from bitter disappointment. France, for which most of us had conceived so deep a love; France, which had received us with such broad-minded hospitality; France, whose highest ideals seemed to be liberty and justice—this France suddenly revealed a totally different face to us, a grimace that inspired us with horror, for we had seen it once before, when we had fled before Hitler.[133]

Some of the German Jewish refugees were so exhausted and desperate after weeks of flight and internment that they turned to Nazi German officials for help against the French. One group of German Jewish refugee war veterans of 1914–18 found themselves in the makeshift camp at Saint-Cyprien in the fall of 1940, after having been uprooted in Belgium in May 1940, deposited in Bordeaux by the human tide, expelled by the Germans into the Unoccupied Zone in a typical scene of "underground emigration," and then locked up by the French. In November they appealed to the German Foreign Office for help against the "inhuman conditions" in which they found themselves, "too bad for black slaves"—treatment that was an insult to Germany. For "here we are Germans first, before anything else, and forevermore German." As veterans of the German army they felt entitled to German diplomatic protection. And to them, after the ministrations of French police and camp officials, Hitler's officials looked like a port in a storm.[134]

There is ample evidence of chilling cases of mistreatment, which prefigured the later fate of many Jews. Families were torn apart. After being sorted out at the great Paris indoor stadium, the Vélodrome d'Hiver, women were sent to the camp of Rieucros, formerly used for Spanish refugees, where facilities were utterly inadequate. Over five thousand *children* were interned, and were still in the camps in November 1940. Some men and women were shipped to camps in cattle cars, some with the doors sealed shut.[135] François Bondy described one such transport of one hundred refugees from Belgium to the camp at Le Vernet. It took a week. There was no food, and someone had painted *parachutistes* on the side of the car, which excited popular demonstrations of hatred. One of the internees went mad en route and was shot by the guards.[136]

The official targets in all this were enemy aliens, but Jews were caught in the nets like other foreigners, and their Jewishness seems to have compounded their vulnerability. Unofficially many irrationalities were at work, and in many instances it was each man's prejudice for itself. Usually stateless, often penniless, as often as not speaking a French that offended the ear, foreign Jews were prominent among the victims of harassments both calculated and unintentional. Already in December 1939 the Socialist deputy Marius Moutet had protested in the Chamber of Deputies about "immense majority of Israelites" among internees in France.[137] About forty thousand civilians remained interned in unoccupied France near the end of 1940; of these as many as 70 percent were Jews.[138]

Whatever the figures, there can be no doubt about the importance of this "administrative pogrom" of 1939–40 in preparing the explicitly anti-Jewish persecution that quickly followed. The apparatus of concentration camps, reputed to be no less degrading and brutal than those of prewar Nazi Germany by those who had experienced both, was now in place. Officials had become accustomed to herding about large numbers of miserable foreigners, among whom Jews figured prominently. The helplessness of many officials during the collapse, abetted by efforts to preserve an ambience of authority in the midst of defeat, encouraged callousness in dealing with aliens. One lady, pleading with French authorities for the release of her husband, a German lawyer interned in May 1940, had to remain standing before an officer, three feet from his desk.[139]

> A few years ago we had been called the martyrs of Fascist barbarism, pioneers in the fight for civilization, defenders of liberty, and what not; the press and statesmen of the West had made rather a fuss about us, probably to drown the voice of their own bad conscience. Now we had become the scum of the earth.[140]

The change of regime in July 1940 did not mark a radical departure, then, as far as refugee policy was concerned. It is true that anti-Jewish feelings became stronger amidst the anger and grief of a crushing national disaster. Far more important, the new regime legitimated freer expression of them, stripping away the republican law and custom that had helped inhibit anti-Jewish expressions. Did not the cabinet itself include outspoken antisemites? Had not the government repealed the Marchandeau Law?

Beyond that admittedly important change, however, Vichy policies toward refugees were not strikingly different from those of the late

Third Republic. They were rather a continuation and reinforcement of them, raised to a new power by the hunt for the guilty and by the effort to create an impression of vigor and authority. Refugees, after all, presented the same three threats to France after July 1940 as in the 1930s. The most preoccupying problems were the same, only magnified by defeat: unemployment, as the war effort stopped and as the German occupation began to bleed the French economy white; the fear of cultural swamping, as French prestige registered the shock of the 1940 collapse; and the fear of warmongers, stronger than ever now that Vichy set out resolutely to defend its neutrality against Gaullists, British, and Germans. No less than before, Jews seemed pre-eminent among aliens as threats to jobs, to the purity of French culture, and to a settlement with Hitler.

During the summer and fall of 1940, therefore, the administrative momentum already generated against foreign Jews ground on, meshing easily with the anti-Jewish laws of August and October. As before, for lack of something better, officials tended to fall back on internment. The provisions of the armistice provided some additional complications. According to its terms, the French army was limited to 125,000 officers and men in metropolitan France. Without German prompting, the Ministry of War had no trouble deciding to eliminate Jews from it entirely. We might add that the Ministry of War went even beyond the October *Statut des juifs* in eliminating even Jewish enlisted men, and boasted in its posters that recruits would not have to associate with Jews. That meant systematically demobilizing the foreign volunteers from the French army (about 30,000 of the 60,000 Jews who had volunteered for the French army in 1939–40 were foreign refugees, enthusiastically enrolled by Jewish organizations for the purpose), stripping them of the badly needed protection of military status, in crude disregard of Jewish support for the French war effort. Indeed, that warm support was now a liability, as a potential danger to French neutrality. These Jewish ex-soldiers were then interned or sent to labor camps. Some effort was made by the French officers with whom they had served to keep them regrouped in the Foreign Volunteers' Association (Amicale des Volontaires Étrangers) even within the camps, but most of these ex-soldiers were never released except to be deported to Auschwitz in August 1942.*

*Lieutenant-Colonel Puaud, honorary president of the Foreign Volunteers' Association, submitted to Marshal Pétain in July 1942 a plan for the "reorganization and moral and professional re-education" of foreigners in France, involving the segregation of "undesirable" Jews, the settlement in Madagascar or Indochina of carefully selected Jews who would be limited to agricultural pursuits, and the fulfillment of France's "moral

Officials directed the less unfortunate of these Jewish ex-volunteers to North Africa, where they joined Jewish servicemen already interned there. Eventually they were put to work, under conditions that can be described only as slave labor, building the first links of the now-revived ancient project of a Trans-Sahara Railway across uninhabited desert.[142]

These labor battalions—*groupements de travailleurs étrangers* (GTE)—were lineal descendants of 1930s schemes to avoid foreign competition for jobs, joined to the precedent of setting prisoners of war to work during the war of 1914–18. The Vichy regime would have greatly preferred the repatriation or the expulsion of these refugees. Since wartime conditions made either impossible, the regime could at least keep them under guard and isolated from the normal labor market. By a law of 27 September 1940 the government extended its authority to intern all immigrants "superfluous in the national economy."[143] The law applied only to males (aged eighteen to fifty-five); and so the separation of families followed. The Interior Ministry designated the foreigners for internment, and the Ministry of Industrial Production and Labor was in charge of work crews. Jews filled the GTE both in metropolitan France and in North Africa; and from the beginning, some were segregated in specifically Jewish units.[144] Mostly stateless, these Jews could more easily be treated as forced laborers than could the citizens of foreign countries, the governments of which might retaliate against French interests. Considerations of unemployment as well as ingrained fears for national security meant that proposals by international relief agencies to free Jews from concentration camps or from GTE went without answer.[145]

Another clause of the Armistice Agreement, article XIX, obliged the French to hand over to the Germans those German nationals on French soil whom the Reich would designate. To apply this French capitulation of the traditional right of asylum, a detachment of German officials and Gestapo agents, the Kundt Commission, combed French concentration camps in the unoccupied zone. Among those they seized were the former Weimar Socialist leader Rudolf Hilferding and the young Herschel Grynszpan, though the French declined to deliver the Rhenish separatist leader of the 1920s, Dr. Adam Dorten. The commission visited French camps freely, facilitated by the French administration. Its chairman, a young German diplomat, Dr. Kundt, observed that the internees constituted a serious economic and security burden for

---

mission" by returning Jews in France to agriculture, all while awaiting the postwar international solution to the "Jewish problem."[141]

the French, and that the French were eager to get rid of them. "The French government is thankful for every one we take off their hands."[146]

But the Vichy government was no more successful in winning German help in getting rid of its refugee burden than Georges Bonnet had been with Ribbentrop. Kundt pointedly declared his lack of interest in taking back Jews and ordinary emigrants from the Reich. In the end the Kundt Commission claimed only some 800 persons, almost none of them Jews, after examining some 32,000 internees in thirty-one Vichy camps and other centers—7,500 of these internees German, including about 5,000 Jews.[147] When Kundt's victims had been delivered, mostly by the end of September 1940, another somber precedent had been set. German agencies had gathered data on residents of the Unoccupied Zone and had deported some of them to Germany.

Far from aiding Vichy France with its bursting internment camps, the Germans, as we saw in chapter 1, continued at least until April 1941 to push more Jewish refugees into unoccupied France. They perfected the tactics that they had begun applying on a grand scale in eastern Europe after *Kristallnacht*, and that the French had been protesting on their own frontiers since 1938: to deliver Jews to the border, without belongings, and to force them to cross illegally—"underground emigration."[148]

We are now in a position to understand the fervor of Vichy's protests, also witnessed in chapter 1, against the Germans' continuing expulsion of Jews and residents of Alsace-Lorraine into the Unoccupied Zone. Not only was this "a direct blow at the right of French sovereignty." Not only were the new arrivals an unbearable added burden to a France that believed itself "obliged to take charge of these foreigners and intern them."[149] Not only were these expulsions an ominous signal with respect to the eastern provinces, insofar as they involved residents of Alsace-Lorraine. France, the French representative to the Armistice Commission at Wiesbaden asserted to the Germans, refused to become "a dumping ground [*déversoir*] for persons judged undesirable in Germany."[150] It had been the constant French cry since 1933, now made even sharper by a sense of French helplessness.

Vichy's anti-Jewish program was neither new nor limited to a small minority on the far Right. It fed upon a decade-long obsession with the alien menace. Even moderates had learned during the 1930s to think of foreign refugees—and Jews pre-eminently among them—as a threat to jobs, to the purity of French culture, to peace. Many civil servants had acquired years of unpleasant experience dealing with intractable and complaining foreigners. French policy toward foreigners had been incoherent: many had been admitted, but ever fewer had managed to obtain work permits or to lead normal lives. These wretched *clandestins* further fanned animosities. A vivid French tradition of antisemitism singled out the Jews among them, and anti-Jewish sensibility permeated even into moderate political attitudes.

When the regime changed in July 1940, the ground had been well prepared in advance. Even the idea of a *statut des juifs* had been floated, and a *numerus clausus* had made many liberal converts. The new regime offered opportunities hitherto denied. It made it acceptable to voice prejudices now sharpened by defeat. A few determined antisemites now rushed forward to settle old scores. Government leaders either shared their views, did not care, or kept silent out of warped motives of personal ambition or a sense of service to the state. Meanwhile, as we shall see, wide segments of opinion and a good part of the bureaucracy went along, covered by deeply ingrained habits of antipathy, by obsession with private griefs and woes, or by administrative routine.

CHAPTER
3

The Strategy of Xavier Vallat, 1941–42

A S FRANCE entered 1941 and a new year of German occupation, it was not clear where Vichy's anti-Jewish program of 1940 would lead. Its principal animator in the cabinet, Justice Minister Raphaël Alibert, had been forced out of the government under German pressure after he had taken a leading role in the ouster of Pierre Laval on 13 December 1940 (see page 83). By the time he left office, Alibert had begun to apply the *Statut des juifs* within his own ministerial department by removing Jewish magistrates and judicial officials, and he had begun to press other ministerial departments to do the same.[1] But although serious application had begun in some departments—notably in the Army—it was spotty elsewhere in the absence of a strong driving center.

Laval's would-be successor, Pierre-Etienne Flandin, outspoken enough in 1939 against the threat to the French "race," did not have time to establish a Jewish policy before the Germans indicated that they would not work with him. His successor, Admiral François Darlan, who finally brought Franco-German relations back to the point where they had been interrupted by Laval's removal, was far more interested in strategic and military affairs than in such domestic matters as refugees or the place of Jews in French society. Outside the government, public opinion at large had little time for Jews in its preoccupation with private woes: the absent prisoners of war, the fading hopes of early peace, the first pinches of the dreadful privations that the French would endure for the next four years. The new law's rather restricted application also diminished concern about them. A series of special exemptions allowed French Jews of notable prestige and accomplishment to remain in important posts. At the end of 1940, two Jewish officers were permitted to retain their commissions in the French Army, ten professors were allowed to keep their chairs, and a handful of other specialists remained in high government posts, mostly technical ones.* Things seemed to be settling into an uncomfortable but not mortally menacing normalcy: foreign and stateless Jews harassed and interned; French Jews forced from public service and teaching by an official discrimination softened by notable exceptions; the rest wounded and humiliated in their feelings, but—as the frequent Vichy phrase went—"neither in their property nor in their persons." There was no particular urgency among Jews at this point to leave the country; some French Jews even returned to Paris where they believed the French government would protect them.

Those appearances were deceptive. As is so often the case, persecution had a dynamic of its own. Vichy's anti-Jewish program was in motion again by mid-1941. New legislation narrowed Jewish access to the professions and intellectual posts, and previous restrictions were rigorously enforced. Far graver, the French government now became involved in stripping Jews of their property in the Unoccupied Zone. And a convinced antisemite, Xavier Vallat, now filled a new ministerial post as commissioner-general for Jewish affairs. He eagerly gave unity and impulse to a program that had been meandering.

Three forces were at work to push Vichy's policy beyond the first steps we examined in chapter 1 and to give it a new momentum. German pressures, hardly apparent in 1940, showed their first insistent signs in early 1941. Vichy's response to those pressures was the second factor. Amidst receding hopes for an early peace and for an end to the temporary expedients of 1940, the Vichy regime set out to recapture its administrative sovereignty in the Occupied Zone and to negotiate the substitution of French law for German ordinances there—a fateful bargain which we shall have to scrutinize in detail. And within both camps, the ambition and energy of committed antisemitic activists were given free rein by the general indifference of the rest of opinion.

*The officers were General Darius-Paul Bloch and Chief of Artillery Squadron Pierre-Salomon-Isaac Brisac.[2] Among the professors were Robert Debré, Louis Halphen, and Marc Bloch;[3] also the economist Jacques Rueff and Raymond Berr, mining engineer.[4] Subsequently six *lycée* professors, five more in universities, and a handful of scientists were added to this list.

The Beginnings of German Pressure

They [the *Militärbefehlshaber in Frankreich*] managed to steer the French government's own impulses and those of the French police in the same direction [as the Germans]. That way they not only saved effort. They also spared French self-respect and thereby brought even nationalist circles closer to the German positions. That reduced the odium of the use of force, since it was French force, or left it at French doors.

An MBF official (1942)[5]

For the Germans, anti-Jewish actions were nothing new. They were the continuation of a near-decade of escalating antisemitism at home, which had been given sweeping new scope by the opportunities for plunder and settlement opened up in the conquest of Poland. But in the specific context of France, matters changed subtly but importantly as 1941 progressed. The urgent concerns of security and support for German troops in preparation for the invasion of England lost some of their intensity as that plan was abandoned, and as France became a secondary theater with the invasion of the Soviet Union in June 1941. By then, the occupation of France had settled into an unexpectedly long duration. The expedients of 1940 were not going to be temporary. There was more time for considering long-term planning for Nazi Europe. German administrative offices had settled in and were ready for action. The time of first improvisations was over; the time for projects involving the future of Europe was at hand.

Typically, the Nazis never assigned an important task to one individual or one agency where two or more could be set to work, competing with each other in the preferred Nazi style of administration—dynamism unfettered by plan or chain of command, together with unquestioned control by a Führer who alone could arbitrate among conflicting jurisdictions and dominate the network of competing agencies. What this system lost sometimes in efficiency it more than made up in ideological subservience, as one branch competed with another for the Führer's favor. These methods certainly applied in Jewish matters, which in France were in the hands of no fewer than five branches of German government authority. In regard to Jewish affairs, Vichy officials were thrown off balance more than once by having to deal with several German agencies.[6]*

*For a chart of the Principal German Authorities Dealing with Jews from 1940 to 1944, see pages 374-75.

The ostensible high executive authority of the German occupation of France was the German army: the Military Command in France (*Militärbefehlshaber in Frankreich,* or MBF), headed in 1941 by General Otto von Stülpnagel. The MBF had twin chiefs of staff, military and civilian. The civilian administration staff (*Verwaltungsstab*) was presided over by Dr. Werner Best, who had first reached public notoriety in 1931 when, as legal counsel to the Nazi party in Hesse, he was implicated in a planned putsch in the event of an attempted Communist coup. An active proponent of ridding Europe of Jews, Best was later notorious as civil governor of Denmark. By 1958 he had become a lawyer for the Stinnes Company, one of West Germany's largest trading concerns. (Colonel Speidel, Best's opposite number as head of the military staff, served later as commander-in-chief of West German NATO forces.) Under Best, the economic section of the civil administration was led by Dr. Elmar Michel (after the war, executive of a large German corporation, Salamander Shoes). Dr. Michel was often involved in matters of aryanization, assisted by his chief specialist for Jewish economic affairs, Dr. Blanke. The sole authority at the beginning of the occupation, the MBF was forced to share its powers increasingly, and grudgingly, and without clear guidelines, with other German agencies.

First to acquire autonomy was the embassy, to which Otto Abetz returned in August 1940 with full authority as ambassador. The embassy was supposed, in theory, to advise the military and the police on the political implications of their acts in France. From the beginning, however, Abetz—no professional diplomat but a party activist, as we have seen—seized as much initiative as possible. Few subjects interested him more keenly than the Jewish question, for he regarded antisemitism as one of the levers to replace the reactionary grip of Church and Army in Vichy France by a popular, anticlerical, pro-European (that is, pro-German) mass movement. His consul-general, Rudolf Schleier, a German businessman in prewar Paris, also often became involved in Jewish matters. The embassy's specialist on the Jewish question after April 1941 was Carl-Theo Zeitschel, a former merchant marine doctor and long-time party member, who represented the embassy at the regular Tuesday meetings on Jewish affairs and was full of suggestions of his own, such as the mass sterilization of Jews.[7]

The most important rival to the military authority in Occupied France was the police. The Security Police was a subdivision of the RSHA (*Reichssicherheitshauptamt*), the gigantic Reich Security Division of Heinrich Himmler's SS (*Schutzstaffel*), under the direct command of Reinhard Heydrich in Berlin. The RSHA itself was an administrative labyrinth whose complexity need not detain us here. The miniature version set up in Paris and modeled on its Berlin headquarters was familiarly known as the "Gestapo" or the "SD" *(Sicherheitsdienst)*, terms that technically applied only to part of the apparatus but that effectively and interchangeably stood for it all. The head of the Security Police in France was SS-Obersturmführer Helmut Knochen, a talented intellectual thirty years old and known for his organizational ability and social grace. In the summer of 1940, Knochen and a small unit were introduced surreptitiously into France, so as not to upset the jealous military administration; and there was considerable friction both before and after the police won its administrative autonomy in May 1942. Thereafter the SD-Paris answered directly to Himmler's office in Berlin; but conflicts with the military did not cease, including disputes over Jewish matters. Knochen's apparatus included the twenty-six-year-old SS-Stürmbahnführer Herbert Martin Hagen, a specialist in Jewish affairs and a former colleague of Eichmann's in the RSHA head office in Berlin. Early in August 1940, Hagen established an RSHA office in Bordeaux which extended German police surveillance to the south Atlantic coast of France and to the Spanish border. In November, SS-Stürmbahnführer Kurt Lischka, another former Eichmann collaborator, joined the SD in France, becoming Knochen's assistant. The Gestapo's job was to keep an eye on all enemies of the Nazi regime, mainly Communists, antifascists, and Jews.

Within the RSHA Paris office was a special department for Jewish affairs. In the late summer of 1940, SS-Hauptstürmführer Theodor Dannecker was sent to Paris directly by Adolf Eichmann's bureau IVB4, the branch of the RSHA in Berlin devoted to Jewish matters. Only twenty-seven at the time, and a fanatical antisemite with three years' experience behind him in the anti-Jewish bureaucracy of the SS, Dannecker headed bureau IVB4 in the Paris RSHA office, or the *Judenreferat.* The SD *Judenreferat,* with its leader Dannecker, was to be the most active of the German agencies involved with long-range planning of Jewish policy in France and with efforts to prod Vichy into more active anti-Jewish measures.[8]

The *Einsatzstab* Rosenberg was a competing authority intensely interested in Jews. The fiefdom of Nazi theoretician Alfred Rosenberg, it had Hitler's personal authorization to plunder French archives (the original of the Treaty of Westphalia, marking French victory over the German states in 1648, was the object of a special search) and the art collections of Jews and other people judged hostile to the Reich. Deeply absorbed in the business of pillage, the *Einsatzstab* Rosenberg tended to leave high policy to others. Rosenberg's unit was represented in the Tuesday meetings in Paris and in other interagency sessions deciding the German policy toward Jews in France, but it seldom took an initiating role.

There was, finally, the Armistice Commission at Wiesbaden in which the details of applying the armistice were worked out by French and German officers, diplomats, and bankers. The most active center of Franco-German contact in 1940, the Armistice Commission tended to decline in significance as the embassy took over its role as the principal point of contact between the two governments by 1941. The Armistice Commission was the scene of frequent French protests against the German expulsion of further Jewish refugees into the Unoccupied Zone through the winter of 1940–41, but it did not become involved in many other aspects of the Jewish issue.

Over time, as the MBF shared its authority reluctantly with the embassy and the police, the agenda also changed. When the main issues had been French demobilization and the continued war against England, the Armistice Commission and the MBF were at the center of things. By 1941, other issues had come to the fore: the crowded refugee camps in both zones; the threat many Germans felt that the refugees posed to the German army's security; the burden these refugees imposed upon France; French economic revival and contribution to the Axis war effort; and the long-term construction of a New Europe, German-centered, and *judenfrei* ("free of Jews").

In early 1941, it was still general German policy to expel Jews from the occupied areas. There were clear differences of approach and tone, however, among the various German agencies. Although the MBF had initiated anti-Jewish activity in the Occupied Zone of France with the ordinances we have already examined, the soldiers tended to value stability and calm over ideological purity. They defined their long-range goal, menacingly enough, as to "banish Jewish influence forever in every area of public life including the economy"; and that goal was certainly not limited to the Occupied Zone. But military authorities worried about international law, feared antagonizing French public opinion and were eager to obtain the cooperation of the French government. As an MBF policy statement declared on 22 August 1940, the objective "will be realized only if the French People themselves decide to liberate themselves from Judaism."[9] Indeed, as German manpower in France was squeezed later by the demands of the eastern front, all

German officials recognized that French administrative support was indispensable.*

In private, Otto Abetz and the embassy made more aggressive proposals in 1940 than did the MBF, but at the same time the ambassador remained torn between his ambition to win favor with high Nazi ideologues and his more practical need to find responsive French elements without whose cooperation he could achieve nothing in France. Sometimes he attempted to impose a restraining hand and deferred to what he perceived as the reticences of French opinion. One such case was the plan to force all Jews to wear the yellow star on their clothing in the spring of 1942. In December 1940, therefore, Abetz threw his lot firmly with Laval against the more radical antisemite Alibert.

Dannecker and his *Judenreferat* had no such hesitations. His strategic context was the Führer's "mission to prepare the solution to the Jewish question in Europe." His bureau's task, he believed, was "to be able, when the proper time comes, to serve usefully as the external arm of the European commissioner for Jewish affairs [that is, Eichmann]."[11] There were times when the *Judenreferat* provoked the open hostility of the MBF. For example, when some of Dannecker's hired thugs— French rightist strong-arm men—burned several synagogues in Paris during the night of 2–3 October 1941, the MBF tried—without success —to have his boss Knochen recalled to Berlin. By and large, however, Dannecker found complaisant allies among the embassy and military officials (notably in obtaining trains later when the deportations began). Generally he was left free by the unconcern and indifference of most German diplomats and officers to the fate of the Jews.

The terrain was clear for the activists to press ahead in early 1941. An interagency meeting in Paris on 3 February 1941 marked a new firmness of purpose. The time had come to seek a "solution" for the Jewish problem, in the removal of Jews from all of Europe. By late February 1941, Dannecker had set up weekly meetings on Tuesdays of the representatives of all agencies interested in the Jewish question. In these meetings, he boasted, he had been able to bring the lukewarm soldiers and diplomats into line and put a stop to French maneuvers among different German offices.[12]

Dannecker came forward at once with a scheme to get the French to establish a *Zentraljudenamt* ("central Jewish office"). Such a French

---

*On 3 July 1943, Heinrich Müller (RSHA, Berlin) informed Karl Oberg and Helmut Knochen in Paris that only four SS men out of 250 requested could be sent. On 7 July, Heinz Röthke (Dannecker's replacement) observed that the planned arrests of Jews "must be accomplished almost exclusively by French police forces."[10]

agency would have much to recommend it to a convinced antisemite: the unifying and energizing of French anti-Jewish policy, and assistance to the Germans in their now clarifying "final solution." Dannecker realized that the Führer's plans might well exceed German capacities. To accomplish the tremendous task ahead, French help was essential.

Within weeks the other German agencies fell in behind Dannecker's plan. The MBF seems to have accepted because it was concerned about the large number of Jewish refugees in camps in the Occupied Zone, and about the French refusal so far to accept any more refugees in the Unoccupied Zone. Contact was made with Admiral Darlan, newly installed as head of the Vichy government, at the beginning of March 1941. Vichy agreed. In the early German version, the new office was to have operated only in the Occupied Zone. Vichy, with its nagging fear of permitting the division of France to harden, seems to have proposed to extend the scope of the new agency to both zones. This would make it possible, Vichy felt, to maintain both a unified policy for all of France and the outward show, at least, of French sovereignty.[13]

When Darlan accepted the German proposal for a "central Jewish office," it was not without reservations. As Vichy officials often did in delicate negotiations, Darlan took refuge behind objections he attributed to Pétain. At dinner in Paris on 5 March, Darlan told Abetz "that there was much vacillation in Marshal Pétain's attitude toward the Jewish question." The Marshal, he said, was worried about the impact upon native French Jews and about distinguished war veterans. Abetz advised Berlin to press on despite these Vichy reservations. Vichy, he predicted, would give the new central office "a valid legal foundation," and thereafter "its activity could . . . be stimulated through German influence in the occupied territory to such an extent that the unoccupied territory would be forced to join in the measures taken."[14]

In view of the unexpected degree of French cooperation, the Germans could afford to leave to Vichy the choice of a director of the new bureau. The German embassy had been at work sifting candidates suggested by certain unnamed "Frenchmen worthy of confidence." The list included Bernard Faÿ, Darquier de Pellepoix, Vacher de Lapouge, Ferdinand Céline, and others.[15] But now the Germans were eager to let the French proceed on their own. The latter took the bait. Having conceded the main point—to give a new impetus to the anti-Jewish program—Vichy now made two gestures of independence. First, the new office—now called in more appropriately French official language the Commissariat-General for Jewish Affairs (CGQJ)—was created by a French law of 29 March 1941, without prior submission to the German military administration.[16] Second, again without clearing it with the occupiers, Darlan named as head of the new commissariat a resolute antisemite, but one well known also as a nationalist and anti-German—Xavier Vallat. These gestures of independence gave the Germans no cause for alarm, for the main step had been taken. Vichy agencies would now become more closely enmeshed in the administration of anti-Jewish programs begun in the Occupied Zone by the Germans. The bargain gave more leverage to the Germans than to the French. If the French ceased to cooperate, the Germans' anti-Jewish program in the Occupied Zone would be performed less thoroughly, for lack of French manpower and administrative experience; but then the Vichy regime would lose its newly reacquired administrative sovereignty in the Occupied Zone.

To understand the ease with which Vichy slipped into the role cast for it by Dannecker and Abetz at the origins of the CGQJ, we must assess the Vichy leaders' preoccupations in early 1941 and the part played by each of them in the matter of the Jews.

Vichy Defines the Jewish Issue, 1941

> The way aryanization is carried out in the Occupied Zone is bound to have an influence on whether we can substitute French regulations for German regulations in the aryanization business.
> de Faramond, director of SCAP (1941)[17]

Early 1941 was a time of exceptional anxiety at Vichy. In the short term, there were the catastrophic effects of the dramatic coup of 13 December 1940 when Marshal Pétain had forced Pierre Laval out of the cabinet. While the motives of this step—whether related mainly to foreign or to domestic policy—have been widely debated, it does seem plain that Laval's opponents intended no basic new policy directions. The principal effect was to anger the Germans and to transform the tentative interest that, in fall 1940, they had had in a wider settlement with the French, into a suspicious reserve that Marshal Keitel himself described as a policy of the "cold shoulder."[18] Vichy's courting of Germany became if anything more eager now. It took months to resume contact. In February, Abetz offered signs of willingness to deal with the new government headed by Admiral François Darlan. The dinner in Paris on 5 March at which Abetz broached the "central Jewish office" to Darlan was, in fact, the first meeting of a Vichy government leader with a major German official since the rupture of 13 December. Both Darlan's colleagues and the Germans expected the admiral to repair the damage done two months before.

In a longer perspective, the Vichy government gradually came to the disagreeable realization that the hoped-for early peace settlement was not going to take place. The war and the occupation were going to be long after all. Armistice arrangements that might have been tolerable for a few months became intolerable when extended into the indefinite future. One of the intolerable situations was the gradual encroachment of German agencies in the everyday administration of the Occupied Zone. As the occupation became prolonged, it was essential, Darlan thought, to emerge from passive waiting. He wanted to reassert French sovereignty over the Occupied Zone and to restore unity of French administrative practice to both zones: in customs control, in police matters, in economic planning, and eventually—as we shall see —in the matter of dealing with Jews. This effort was a major feature of general Vichy policy in the spring of 1941.

The German authorities did not reject outright the expansion of French administrative control in the Occupied Zone. They clearly understood that they had insufficient manpower to govern directly, without the cooperation of French officialdom. Indeed, the economy of the armistice arrangement was one of its most appealing features to the Germans. On the other hand, German administrators remained suspicious of the French and loath to renounce direct control over matters that might be essential to the security or the supply of German armed forces. These subtle French and German counterpressures over how the Occupied Zone would be administered shaped the degree to which the new Commissariat for Jewish Affairs would regain French initiative in the Jewish question.

It is not easy to determine exactly how Darlan felt about Jews in France as he assumed the responsibility of government in the early spring of 1941. Like Laval, he had no history of overt antisemitism before 1940; but he differed from Laval in almost every other respect. Admiral Darlan had been the dominant force in the expansion of the French navy in the 1930s, and the commander-in-chief of French naval forces as admiral of the fleet since June 1939. He could claim to be the one French military chief not defeated by the Axis in 1939–40. A bluff, blunt technician, he surrounded himself with officers, engineers, and experts worlds removed from the parliamentary *bonhomie* of Laval. He had little time or inclination to devote to domestic issues. Too much depended on reopening the quest for a settlement with Germany and seeking a new colonial and maritime future for France in the German-dominated world that, until late 1942, he considered ineluctable. Like most of his fellow ministers, Darlan had absorbed the prejudices against foreign refugees so deeply ingrained in the 1930s. But he appears to have been perfectly content to turn the unpleasant matter of the Jews over to someone like Xavier Vallat.

Yet perhaps not without disquiet. Vichy's opening salvo had been directed at all Jews, French as well as foreign. German ordinances, even more damagingly, were stripping all Jews, French as well as foreign, of their property in the Occupied Zone. Darlan and other officials at Vichy felt prompted to shelter important and prestigious French Jews and their property from the Germans' lack of discrimination. Education Minister Jérôme Carcopino reported after the war what Darlan declared in a cabinet meeting: "The stateless Jews who have thronged to our country for the last fifteen years do not interest me. But the others, the good old French Jews, have a right to every protection we can give them. I have some, by the way, in my own family." A contemporary document strikes a similar note: his aim, Darlan wrote Moysset in January 1942, had been "not to bother the old French Jews."[19]

Because Marshal Pétain had nothing to say publicly about Jews, historians have had even greater difficulty assessing his role in this matter in 1941. Certainly Pétain's contacts with people in and out of government do not sustain the view—widely held at the time—that the Marshal somehow remained ignorant of the stronger anti-Jewish measures that he signed into law in summer and fall of 1941. It is conceivable that the old man was not shown the dozens of pathetic letters from Jewish veterans of Verdun and others who sought to penetrate the screen of the "king's friends," unable to believe that the Marshal himself could be aware of what French officials were doing to them and yet do nothing to stop them. In any case, he does not seem to have answered any of them personally.[20] When he replied to the stout protests of his speechwriter René Gillouin and Pastor Marc Boegner in the summer of 1941, it was only briefly and evasively.[21] And he certainly spoke repeatedly during 1941 with his "friend" Jacques Helbronner, the most important public figure among Jewish community leaders. As director of the military staff of War Minister Painlevé, Helbronner was said to have supported Pétain's appointment to lead the French armies in 1917. After a distinguished career in the Conseil d'Etat (Council of State), Helbronner had, in 1940, become president of the Consistoire Central (the top administrative body of French Jewry). During 1941, he strenuously protested every new anti-Jewish measure: Pétain's replies were polite but inconsequential.[22]* Furthermore, we cannot accept the view—often expressed after the Liberation—that the old man (he was eighty-five in 1941) was already senile. Senile he was in 1947 when the Haute Cour de Justice sent a delegation to interview him in prison on the Ile d'Yeu, off the Atlantic coast of France; but the earliest reference we have found to Petain's inability to cope with the duties of office is during the crisis of November 1942; and even during 1943 several German visitors' notes reveal the Marshal as alert and informed.[24] In 1941, Pétain *knew*.

The most persuasive assessment seems to us that of Pétain's some-time chief of civilian staff, Henri du Moulin de Labarthète: "the Marshal fastened upon individual cases."[25] Perhaps because of his age, perhaps because of his legendary aloofness, he showed concern only when individuals close to him were involved. He and his staff quietly came to the aid of a certain number of well-connected French Jews affected by French laws. When the Germans obliged Jews in the Occupied Zone to wear the yellow star in June 1942, Marshal Pétain asked exemptions for the wives of two prominent aristocrats, the Marquis Louis de Chasseloup-Laubat and Pierre Girod de Langlade.[26] Pétain's government, as we have seen, exempted important scientists and scholars and a few officers from the French laws; but he washed his hands of the great majority of Jews. We know of no intervention by the Marshal in favor of Jews in general before July 1943, when he asked Laval to remonstrate with the Germans about conditions at Drancy, a camp that they had recently taken over from French police.[27]† Pétain continued to have friendly contact with people, like Raphaël Alibert, who made no attempt to bridle their outspoken hatred of Jews, and with apparent enthusiasm forwarded to Justice Minister Barthélemy in June 1943 an antisemitic memoir prepared by Charles-Emile Roche. Roche championed a "Christian union of Europe" against two mortal enemies—"Nazi civilization," on the one hand, and the Anglo-Americans, on the other; the latter were seen as opening the way for "the Jewish invasion."[28]

Once known as a republican general, Pétain seems to have fit

---

*André Lavagne had written twice to Helbronner to this effect as late as November 1943. If the date of 24 November on the second of the two letters to Helbronner is correct, it did not reach him; he and his wife were deported, on 20 November 1943, to Auschwitz where they both perished.[23]

†We have no indication that Laval ever raised the subject with the Germans.

comfortably into the shrine that universal adulation prepared for him. Whether from age, prior conviction, or a sense of immense responsibility born of the near-total collapse of 1940, Pétain seems to have believed the paternalistic propaganda spread about him. But his paternalism had limits: it did not extend to Jews, at least to those outside his narrow circle of acquaintance. The "just measures taken against the Israelites" of which he approved in June 1942, when objecting to the yellow star imposed by the Germans in the Occupied Zone,[29] reflect a genuine preference for a society that imposed harsh restrictions on Jews. The details he could leave to someone else.

A number of Pétain's ministers also intervened on behalf of favored individuals. Pierre Laval obtained special permission in September 1942 from the new head of police forces in France, Brigadeführer Karl Oberg, for Mme. André Citroën to visit her children in the Occupied Zone, and intervened on behalf of a Paul Boron in the summer of 1943.[30] Pétain's chief of staff, du Moulin de Labarthète, tried to obtain the release of the senator and jurist Pierre Masse in March 1942, but it was rejected "sharply" and "with astonishment" by the Germans.[31] Ambassador Fernand de Brinon (Vichy's representative in Paris) bestirred himself with the Germans on behalf of Mme. Philippe de Rothschild—unsuccessfully, it turned out. More significant, the French government asked for the exemption of favored small groups: those Jewish veterans of the 1939–40 campaign who had earlier been released from German POW camps and were being rearrested in late 1942, and ten French Jewish families in Salonika who were being deported in the spring of 1943.[32]* But these particular interventions did nothing to deflect the general bent of Vichy policy. Justice Minister Barthélemy had Jewish friends, he confided publicly to a Toulouse audience in August 1941 as the new laws were going into effect; but one must not let personal regrets stand in the way of cruel necessity. Surgery, he said in an ominous metaphor, was necessary to cure the French patient.[33]

Xavier Vallat was to be the surgeon. He liked the metaphor himself, for it signified the use of a scalpel rather than a meataxe, and promised a return to national health. "We have tried to be surgeons and not butchers and certainly not torturers." Nevertheless a major operation was necessary—perhaps brain surgery. "France was stricken with a Jewish brain fever of which she almost died."[34]

The new commissioner general for Jewish affairs was born in 1891 in the Vaucluse, the tenth child of a poor schoolteacher. Deeply Catho-

---

*The German embassy was instructed to delay its response until the Salonika families were already on their way to Auschwitz.

lic, he inherited from his father the world view of the Action Française as well as a calling to public service. After teaching literature at the parochial school in Aix en Provence, he served valiantly in the First World War, during which he lost an eye and a leg.*

As deputy for the Ardèche (1919–24; 1928–40), Vallat became a familiar figure in conservative and Catholic political circles. During this period he did a tour of rightist leagues and parties, belonging at various times to the Action Française, to the right-wing Faisceau movement of Georges Valois, to Colonel de la Rocque's Croix de Feu, to Pierre Taittinger's Parti Républicain National et Social, and to the moderate rightist Fédération Républicaine. Closest to Vallat's heart were General Edouard de Curières de Castelnau's Fédération Nationale Catholique, a pressure group that lobbied for the election of Catholic legislators in order to reverse the republic's anticlerical position, and a series of veterans' organizations. In July 1940, Pétain appointed Vallat secretary for veterans' affairs, and supported his creation of a unified veterans' movement—the Légion Française des Combattants—whose supporters intended it to become the principal mass organization of the new regime.

For Xavier Vallat antisemitism had a vital contribution to make to France's national recovery. To the end, his ideas on Jews remained fixed. Before the Haute Cour de Justice that tried him after the Liberation, he explained his beliefs in language almost identical to a speech he had given in spring 1942 to the students of the Ecole Nationale des Cadres Civiques (a training school for young public service leaders). As he put it in his own apologia, "The Jew is not only an unassimilable foreigner, whose implantation tends to form a state within the state; he is also, by temperament, a foreigner who wants to dominate and who tends to create, with his kin, a super state within the state." At bottom was the ancient indictment against the people who had killed Christ: "the cursed race that deicide, collectively agreed to, has condemned never again to have a homeland but to wander across the world." Draining national resources, this "parasitical element" consistently weakened host societies everywhere. It had played an important role in undermining France in 1940. Jews could never really become French. With extensive quotations from Bernard Lazare's book (*Antisemitism: Its History and Its Causes*, 1894) on antisemitism, Vallat insisted

---

*According to Robert Debré, Vallat owed his life to the Jewish doctor Gaston Nora (who also testified in his favor in the 1946 trial). Nora and Robert Debré visited Vallat in 1941 to remonstrate with him over Jewish policy. Vallat received them politely but was deaf to their arguments. "Neither heart nor brain" was Debré's assessment of the man.[35]

upon the impossibility of cultural assimilation: Jews were fundamentally "foreign in thought and language in spite of excessive naturalizations." Action against them was simply a matter of self-defense.[36]

Like his friend Maurras, Vallat joined his antisemitism to a profoundly traditionalist world view. His was not what Maurras contemptuously called "gut antisemitism"—a visceral hatred undisciplined by reason, patriotism, or sense of public order. Using the habitual terminology of the Action Française, Vallat proclaimed himself a champion of "state antisemitism," the regulation of Jewish existence by state agencies for the benefit of all Frenchmen. "Neither hatred nor reprisals," Vallat told a press conference in April 1941, echoing a familiar promise from Vichy, "simply the strict defense of the national interest."[37] Again like Maurras, Vallat knew he had enemies on the Right. He spurned offers of help from German-financed publicists like Henry Coston and engaged in a running feud with the extremist Paris weekly *Au Pilori,* the two denouncing each other to the Germans. He insisted on distinguishing his anti-Jewish efforts from those of the German and French racialists and radical collaborationists who saw antisemitism as a means to overturn French society.[38]

Vallat had already brushed against German interests before becoming commissioner-general for Jewish affairs. As head of the veterans' Légion he had vigorously played the patriotic card, appointing departmental presidents in territories newly joined to the Reich and thereby incurring the wrath of Abetz, who secured his dismissal in October 1940. Vallat made no secret of his First World War veteran's nationalism, in which the traditional anti-Germanism was at least as vigorous as the pacifism of the trenches; it was one of the main emotional axes of his life. He was prepared to stand up to the enemy. But although this set him against German policy in 1940, he was more a rival than an opponent of the long-range German goals for the Jews as they were defined in 1941. In the short run, Vallat insisted, each nation should deal with its Jews on its own. This was what French independence meant for him. "There is unfortunately no 'standard solution,' and we must put in place a whole system that corresponds to French conditions."[39] Vallat did not want to be rushed by the Nazis, and he demanded allowances for complex French realities—North African Jews, old Alsatian and Marrano families, war veterans, and so forth. But ultimately each nation's individual efforts would be incomplete. After the war "it will certainly appear necessary . . . to unify this [national] legislation in order to find a European solution, if not an international solution, to the Jewish problem."[40] The *New York Her-*

ald Tribune of 14 June 1941 quoted him similarly: "a complete solution of the Jewish problem can only be found on an international or at least on a European basis, but this must be postponed until the conclusion of a peace."

How did Vallat see this postwar solution? Two of the most authentic contemporary guides to his long-range thinking are a speech to the students of the Ecole Nationale des Cadres Civiques in spring 1942, and a book written at the end of 1941 by a close collaborator, Gabriel Malglaive. Vallat contributed an enthusiastic preface to Malglaive's work, declaring it "quite close to what I believe myself to be the truth." Malglaive knew that each state's short-term "defensive measures" were only temporary adaptations to wartime circumstances. To settle the Jewish question finally, Malglaive proposed an international agreement defining Jewish nationality, locating Jews in their own state somewhere, and conceding those who chose to be left behind only the status of foreigner. In his 1942 speech to the students of the Ecole Nationale des Cadres Civiques, Vallat allowed that some twenty-five thousand old-established families (perhaps seventy-five thousand persons in all) would be "digestible," provided that access to the professions remained limited and means were found to block the "instinctive" desire to dominate. The rest would have to go. But go where? And under whose auspices? At whose expense? It is best to hear Vallat asking these questions and answering them on his own, vague as to territory, but explicit as to the victor's rights to dispose of the Jews:

> Send them where? Back home, that is to say throughout the whole vast world? By what means, so long as the war is going on? In reality, it will be the victor's business, if he intends to organize a durable peace, to find the means, worldwide if possible, European in any case, to settle the wandering Jew.[41]

It is sometimes suggested that Vallat eschewed the racist antisemitism so fundamental to nazism, preferring to rest his case upon more benign distinctions rooted in culture. Paris radicals felt this was so, and their castigations of the commissioner for his "weakness" in racial matters are probably at the origin of this perception of him. At his postwar trial, Vallat did nothing to dispel that moderate image. It is true that his occasional gestures on behalf of highly assimilated Jews reflected a willingness to tolerate small numbers of those whose cultural distinctiveness was virtually nil. "The Jew is acceptable in homeopathic doses," he told the students in his speech in early 1942, "which is to say, as long as he is sufficiently diluted that the incontestable qualities that he derives from his race are a stimulant and not a danger."[42]*

There is no doubt of Vallat's distaste for the cruder and more disorderly forms of *Blut und Boden* ("blood and soil") racism, a distaste he shared with most members of the Action Française, committed as they were to France's historic role of cultural missionary and to an orderly state. As a reactionary, Vallat preferred history to biology in his denunciation of the Jews. He made no effort to introduce, into the French *Statut des juifs,* Nuremburg-style laws regarding intermarriage; he admitted the existence of no races other than Jews; and he did not propose the definition of half-Jews such as racism seemed to require in Germany and as his successor Darquier was to propose later. As Joseph Billig reminds us, even the word *racisme* was not in favor in Vichy circles.[43] On the positive side, Vallat took pains to explain to German officials why some categories of French Jews, most particularly war veterans, deserved special consideration, albeit without disturbing his confidence in the general rule: "exemptions of Jewish war veterans constitute simple gratitude for a meritorious effort by a Jew, an essentially unassimilable element, toward integration into the national community that he defended on the battlefield." Moreover, such exemptions were necessary to dampen public protests.

> This exception is all the more necessary in France because, outside Paris and North Africa where the Jewish element had particularly proliferated, public opinion is little aroused against the Jewish danger, and because we must avoid over-radical measures which would look like unjust and needless persecutions.[44]

It will not do to confuse Vallat's prejudices, according to which the Jewish danger increased proportionately with exoticism, with those of Hitler and Himmler for whom the most assimilated Jews were the most dangerous, as being the best concealed. Vallat believed that sincere efforts at cultural assimilation were meritorious. Yet they were not enough. Léon Blum, French to his fingertips, represented to Vallat the quintessence of what he hated in Jewry.

So we cannot let Vallat off as a mere assimilationist, ready to clasp the sincere convert to the national bosom. The nub of the matter seems to be that Vallat believed assimilation came harder for Jews than for other peoples—if it was not altogether impossible. In the eclectic tradi-

*He used identical language in his 1946 trial.

tion of French antisemitism, racial, religious, cultural, and political elements were mingled in Vallat's image of the Jew—some mixture of cosmopolitan, mercantile, subversive, and rootlessly intellectual; and we should not expect any sophisticated effort on his part to untangle the strands. His working definition of the Jew was hammered out in his daily tasks as commissioner-general for Jewish affairs. He wanted the law enforced, and he wanted fewer Jews in France. If a dose of racism helped achieve this, he would accommodate to it. Repeatedly he came down on the side of race in his daily efforts to enforce the *Statut des juifs*. There is no better way to discern the contours of Vallat's reasoning than to follow him in this task.

One of the thorniest aspects of the search for a definition of who was Jewish was the role of religion. Vallat made religion more visible as a criterion of Jewishness in his new *Statut des juifs* of 2 June 1941. The second statute provided only one means of establishing non-Jewishness: "proof of adherence to one of the other confessions recognized by the state before the law of 9 December 1905 [separation of Church and State]." This clause exposed him to the criticism of the Paris radicals, and Vallat was eager to explain that the religious exclusion applied only to persons with only two Jewish grandparents. Where three grandparents or more were Jewish, as in Alibert's first statute, a Jew was a Jew, whatever the confessional status. As Vallat explained in an interview with a journalist of the French government press agency (AFIP) on 3 February 1942, "a baptized person or the son of a baptized person is Jewish" if three grandparents were Jewish. In these cases, he wrote in an internal memorandum at about the same time, it did not matter whether some of the grandparents had converted to Christianity. They remained "transmission agents of Jewish tradition. No matter if he [the grandparent] later converted to another religion, for he belongs to the Jewish race, and his son or grandson has received the Jewish imprint from him."[45] One might have expected Vallat, an ardent Catholic, to have followed the Church on this point, that the sacrament of baptism takes precedence over all else. It was not so. For Vallat, heredity was stronger than holy water. Only in cases where two grandparents or less were Jewish could baptism make a difference, and even there Vallat tightened up Alibert's statute by requiring proof of baptism prior to 25 June 1940, not merely prior to the date of the statute. Vallat's fear of expedient conversions was stronger than his Catholic orthodoxy.

Vallat's Catholicism was sufficiently strong, at least, to give short shrift to nonbelievers. In effect, the law accepted only baptism as proof of non-Jewishness. Pastor Marc Boegner raised the question in the summer of 1941 of certain "Jews by race" who, for several generations, "have established themselves in a state of nonbelief which French law seemed to authorize." *Raison d'état* was uppermost in Vallat's reply. If the strict definition of the law were not held firm, he wrote Boegner, there would be a rush of Jews claiming to be free thinkers.[46]*

Two months later Vallat opted again for a strict construction of racial determination. A group of about 250 Russians in France, the Karaites—whom, on the basis of complex religio-historical reasoning, the Germans did not consider Jewish—were firmly deemed Jews by Vallat because they were "impregnated with Jewish attitudes [*esprit*]." Again, Vallat's decision was firmly grounded in *antisémitisme d'état*. To let the Karaites slip off the racial hook, he explained, "would result in forcing us to examine the case of the Provençal and Alsatian Jews who claim they are descendants of Celts converted to the Mosaic Law before the arrival of the Catholic apostles in Gaul."[48] He and his subordinates reacted similarly to the appeal of two other tiny groups that claimed exemption from antisemitic laws—Georgian Jews living in Paris, closely linked to their emigré Christian countrymen, and the Jugutis, Jews from Central Asia. Here too the commissioner-general took a tougher line than the Nazis.[49] Vallat, it is clear, wanted the laws obeyed. To achieve this he was prepared, on occasion, to shape existing racial or historical definitions of the Jew to his administrative needs.

Indeed, race and religion were inextricably intermingled where Vallat's definition of the Jew was concerned. The Jews were more than a race, he told the students of the Ecole Nationale des Cadres Civiques in early 1942; around the "large racial kernel" was "a margin" of peoples "impregnated with Jewish attitudes"—such as eighty thousand observing Jews in Abyssinia. The important thing was that, for Vallat, the *esprit juif* could be inherited. Citing Bernard Lazare as his authority, he declared the Jew "a confessional type: as he is, it is the Law and the Talmud that have shaped him more powerfully than blood or climatic variation: they developed in him the imitative characteristics that heredity perpetuated."[50]

However feeble these neo-Lamarckian remarks are as anthropology, they show how the momentum of Vichy's accelerating discrimination policy forced Vallat ever deeper into a de facto racialism based on *raison d'état*. During the fall of 1941 he was drawn into the issuance of *certificats de non-appartenance à la race juive* (documents declaring that the bearer did not belong to the Jewish race). As soon as the French

*Barthélemy and Darlan also raised this point with Vallat.[47]

anti-Jewish legislation began to bite, people in ambiguous situations requested some means of proving that they were not Jews. Moreover, at the Demarcation Line, Darlan was informed on 1 July 1941, the Germans were requiring a certificate of *pur aryanisme* for travelers entering the Occupied Zone. During the summer a few certificates were issued, but these were called *certificats de non-appartenance à le religion juive*. Darlan called a meeting to set official policy on how the Vichy government would formally designate Jews and non-Jews. Vallat wanted the word *Juif* or *Juive* stamped on identity cards. Other officials apparently disagreed. In the end, Vichy fell into step, both with the exigencies of German racial policies and with the practical march of its own discriminatory laws: the CGQJ began issuing *certificats de non-appartenance à la race juive* in October 1941. Soon thereafter, Dannecker tried to attach a German racialist "expert" to Vallat's services to oversee the issuance of these certificates. To head him off, Vallat asked the Swiss racialist ethnologist Dr. George Montandon to join his staff.[51] Montandon seems to have remained rather isolated within Vallat's CGQJ, but with him the crudest forms of phrenology and cranial measurement had arrived within the commissariat.

During his entire tenure of office Vallat kept trying to tighten up the *Statut des juifs*. He brooded about its lax enforcement by indulgent law courts, "deeply rooted in a juridical culture still drawing upon the old individualism of the past," and about "tendentious" interpretations of the CGQJ's work which surrounded it with an "unfavorable climate."[52] He kept redrafting a new text which, by the time he had left office in March 1942, had been circulated to his colleagues, approved by Admiral Darlan, and analyzed by the Conseil d'Etat—a third *Statut des juifs* that was never promulgated and has since been forgotten. Since the Haute Cour de Justice failed to ask him about it in 1946, Vallat never mentioned this additional sign of zeal in his postwar memoirs. The draft "third statute" gives us a final look at the commissioner's image of the Jew and of his own mission as an antisemitic activist. In the draft *exposé de motifs* ("preamble"), Vallat claimed to have arrived at a new "guiding idea" for a specifically French antisemitism. Neither race nor religion had worked: race, he said, was a *tautologie;* religion led to false conversions. Vallat believed that a new jurisprudence could be built on national tradition. The simplest cases, where a majority of ancestors were "of the Jewish race," were already accounted for by the existing *Statut des juifs,* Vallat thought. Cases where only two grandparents were Jewish and—a new category—cases of "continuity of Jewish ancestry," where Jewish forebears went back uninterruptedly in a single line, had given no end of trouble, however. In these borderline cases, according to Vallat's reasoning, "the Jewish tradition and the national tradition are vying for influence in the family." Here everything depended on the choice of "moral atmosphere" made by each individual: for example, the choice to adhere to another religion; though, even then, if a convert was married to a Jewish spouse, the convert would still be considered Jewish because "the Jewish tradition could become preponderant in the household."

For the determination of these difficult cases, Vallat found that the traditional judicial presumption of innocence tended to "dejudaize" many authentic Jews. Yet he hardly dared thrust the entire burden of proof on the accused. His "third statute" proposed to divide the burden of proof: if the state could provide a "beginning of proof" of Jewishness, the "defendant" would then face the burden of proving the contrary.

The Jewish problem, Vallat concluded, is "a conflict between the French national tradition and an unassimilable Jewish tradition, and we will go on the assumption that anyone is Jewish who manifests, whether by decisive signs or by sufficiently strong presumptions, the presence or persistence of the Jewish tradition."

In his own way, Vallat wanted the total elimination of Jewish culture from the French scene: the foreigners by emigration, the French-born by exclusion, and the half-Jewish by assimilation. But he admitted the possibility of genuine assimilation only in cases with two Jewish grandparents or less. And even there assimilation meant an abandonment of Jewish culture so total that the very memory of it would vanish.

Vallat saw himself as a "serious antisemite." Thus, on the one hand, he did not want to compromise his program by accepting the wilder schemes of the Paris radicals or by acceding to German measures that would arouse French sympathy for Jews; and, on the other, he was determined to enforce to the hilt the French government's anti-Jewish programs. "In a revolutionary time," he wrote to Darlan's advisor Henri Moysset on 7 February 1942, after the admiral had expressed some concern about Vallat's zeal, "better too much than too little." Naturally, one must not give the Jews the occasion to "cry persecution. I protest ceaselessly to the occupation authorities about measures whose sole result is to arouse pity for 'the poor Jews.' But I call your attention to the need to keep a tight rein on the Jews of the Free Zone."[53]

Vallat: An Activist at Work

> The declarations have led to the creation of special file cards, which were
> centralized at National Police headquarters. Every French and foreign
> Jew living in France is thus known to the police. . . . Intelligent exploitation
> [of the 1941 census] by the central offices of the National Police, assisted by
> the prefectural and municipal administrations, has permitted us to achieve
> in one single step an operation that the German military authorities ac-
> complished only in two attempts. In a single move, the French administra-
> tion has enumerated both Jewish persons and Jewish property.
>   Henri Baudry and Joannès Ambre (1942)[54]*

Xavier Vallat settled with confidence into the offices found for the
new Commissariat-General for Jewish Affairs in the Hôtel d'Alger in
Vichy at the end of March 1941. He was going to show the Germans that
the French could design and execute an anti-Jewish program appropriate for France, and he was thereby going to get the Germans to withdraw their anti-Jewish ordinances in the Occupied Zone. In their place,
French services would administer a unified French anti-Jewish program throughout the country, in full sovereignty, and do a better job
of it than the clumsy occupying authorities.

Vallat's first meetings with top German officials in Paris on 3–4
April revealed a watchful reserve on both sides. The Germans, after all,
had learned of Vallat's appointment only from the press, and there
had been some friction when he had been in charge of the veterans'
Légion. Vallat, for his part, had behind him a lifetime of suspicion
of Germans.

When the new commissioner sat down with General von Stülpnagel in the Hotel Majestic in Paris on 4 April, the latter's top civilian
assistant Dr. Werner Best revealed that the Germans were now thinking in terms of "last solutions," the complete "dejudaizing" of Europe.
It would now be essential, he said, to expel all foreign Jews from the
Occupied Zone, and to intern there three to five thousand of the most
undesirable Jews of all nationalities. Could the French help? Vallat,
perhaps recalling his government's frantic protests against German
expulsions of refugees into the already crowded southern zone in the
previous autumn and winter, and sensitized by the 1930s to fear the
disruptive arrival of further refugees, hastily explained that expulsion

*Baudry was at the time professor at the National Police Academy; he became its
director in 1963. Ambre, a lawyer, was awarded the Médaille de la Resistance after the
war.

(Ausweisung) and internment *(Internienung)* were not his province at all. These were government and police matters, and the German authorities should refer to them.

Dr. Best's third demand *(Forderung)*, however—the systematic application to the Occupied Zone of French legislation that excluded Jews from French public life and the economy—fit Vallat's plans like a glove. Vallat said he wanted to be in constant touch with the Germans for those purposes. As Vallat explained his mandate, Marshal Pétain had given him three jobs: to broaden the statute of October 1940 to include the professions and business; to oversee the aryanization [*sic*] of the economy in order to prevent abuses that might provide leverage for pro-Jewish propaganda; and to examine the serious and difficult question of Jews in North Africa (a matter in which the Germans at no time expressed the slightest interest). In carrying out this mandate, Vallat explained, he would have to take into account the special susceptibilities of the French: their "sentimentality" and their penchant for fairness *(Gerechtigkeitsgefühl)*. Veterans, in particular, would have to be exempted. If not, persecution would only arouse sympathy for the Jews in France and would further the impression that the Germans were forcing antisemitism upon the country. If French feelings were kept in mind, however, and if the Germans were wise enough to avoid the unsavory opportunists *(unerfreuliche Konjunkturritter)* who were offering themselves as paid Jew fighters—here Vallat took the occasion to warn the Germans against his principal Parisian antagonists such as the journal *Au Pilori*—then "we could move in a thoroughly radical fashion against the Jews."[55]

Werner Best was disappointed, he told the embassy's anti-Jewish specialist Carl-Theo Zeitschel the next day. When he had read of Vallat's nomination as commissioner for Jewish affairs, Best had hoped "that all Jewish questions would be facilitated from that direction." But Vallat had refused "the disagreeable part" *(der unangenehme Teil)*— namely, "expulsions and internment."[56] The Germans thought they had explained to Vallat what they expected of him. He thought he had explained to them the limitations of Vichy policy. But neither side had revealed its ulterior aims. Dr. Best and the MBF were still primarily interested in dumping more Jews into the Unoccupied Zone. Vallat wanted to keep the Germans' hands off Jewish property in the Occupied Zone. For the moment, there appeared to be enough common ground to leave these ambiguities unexplored. As Otto Abetz reported back to Berlin, Marshal Pétain's feelings made it essential to proceed in France by stages, and the Germans would have to be satisfied with

Vallat who, after all, had led the antisemitic campaign against Léon Blum in 1936.[57]

Vallat's first job was to produce new Vichy legislation that would not only fit special French circumstances but also prove acceptable to the Germans to substitute for their ordinances in the Occupied Zone. His new legislative package contained three major elements. The first was a revised *Statut des juifs,* promulgated on 2 June 1941,[58] to replace Alibert's first *Statut des juifs* of 3 October 1940. Whereas the first statute had been hastily drafted, the new one was carefully prepared in cabinet meetings during May, with technical improvements added by Justice Minister Barthélemy. It was a properly French initiative without direct German intervention; no mere revision of the earlier statute, it was a new text based upon the experience of the first seven months of official antisemitism as well as upon "the study of measures taken abroad." It was designed to fill lacunae in the earlier law as well as to take into account more recent German measures concerning Jewish property in the Occupied Zone. For this law was designed "for the whole of France."[59]

As Vichy liked to think of the new statute, the increased "severity" of the interdictions was balanced by "more liberal provisions for exemption" than were in the 1940 statute. The elimination of Jews from public positions—"the principal aim of the first statute"—having been all but completed, it was necessary to add only a few categories of public posts closed to Jews. Then the new statute went on to settle "the role it is appropriate to attribute henceforth to their private activity in the national economy."[60] This clause opened the way to a massive purge of Jews from the liberal professions, commerce, the crafts, and industry. The first statute had promised to impose a *numerus clausus* in the liberal professions; this project was now implemented by a veritable assembly-line production of decrees of application between June and December 1941.* Jews were limited to 2 percent of one profession after

*For example:

	Decree Date	JO Date
lawyers	16 June 1941	17 July 1941
surgeons-dentists	5 June 1941	11 June 1941
doctors	11 August 1941	6 September 1941
university students	21 June 1941	24 June 1941
architects	24 September 1941	25 September 1941
midwives	16 December 1941	21 January 1942
pharmacists	26 December 1941	21 January 1942
actors	6 June 1942	11 June 1942

another—medicine, law, pharmacy, and so on; and Jews were limited as students to 3 percent in institutions of higher education. The new statute also reinforced those provisions of the 1940 statute that excluded Jews from activities having to do with the transfer of capital, publicity, or the media. Justice Minister Barthélemy undertook to defend this intensification of the anti-Jewish program:

> [The Jews] have refused for centuries to melt into the French community. . . . The French government has no intention of assimilating them by force. . . . It is not expelling them. It is not depriving them of the means of existence. It is merely forbidding them the functions of directing the French soul or French interests.[61]

In a widely heralded counterbalance, the second statute provided for somewhat more liberal exemptions—though Vallat never mentioned them without simultaneously promising to be "very strict" in granting them. The first statute, in addition to general permission for Jewish war veterans to occupy certain subordinate public posts, had provided for special individual exemptions only for exceptional "literary, scientific, or artistic" services. The new statute permitted special exemptions on the basis of family status as well: those established in France for at least five generations and whose families had served the nation notably and well. The immediate families of Jewish war dead were also now given the same exemptions as veterans. As before, however, these general exemptions for veterans and their families restored only the right to hold subordinate posts in public service and some occupations. As a cabinet minute explained, the idea was to grant a few favors "to those whose families count three generations of war veterans: 1870, 1914, 1939." And, in a curious observation, "the Jews of Sephardic origin, whose families came from Spain to France at the time of Henri II [*sic*] will be able to benefit from it." Similarly, a few crumbs thrown in the direction of the families of war dead "will let certain painful situations be rectified."[62]

In fact, a few Jews removed from their jobs under the first statute actually got them back under the second.* But one must read the text in detail to appreciate how mean-spirited were its provisions. The new statute reached the height of condescension with its half-hearted gesture in favor of Jewish prisoners of war. These unfortunates would face

---

*For example, a minor court official who was father of a prisoner of war.[63]

the full rigors of the law only after their return from the German camps; their immediate families would have a bit longer: the law would apply to them only two months after a prisoner's liberation. Vallat was as good as his promise to the press to be "very strict" in applying these liberalized exemptions. The abundant files of this driven man and of the Conseil d'État's review of each case show that they measured exemptions out with an eyedropper.[64]

The second element in Vallat's new legislative package was the detailed census of all Jews in the Unoccupied Zone[65]—a grave step which profoundly shocked Jewish opinion and was to have fatal consequences later when Jews were being rounded up and deported. This was a new departure in many ways. Religion or ethnicity had not been part of vital statistics in France for almost seventy years, although some incomplete data on Jews had been collected in the general census of 1941.[66] The Germans had required a census of Jews in the Occupied Zone with the ordinance of 27 September 1940, and French police had quickly and efficiently set up a complete card file of the Jews of Paris under the supervision of A.-L.-H. Tulard. For the Unoccupied Zone, however, this enumeration came as an unexpected menace.

Within a month (eventually extended to 31 July) all Jews had to make an elaborate declaration in person. Not only were they asked to enumerate children, parents, grandparents, religious affiliation, educational attainments, military service, and professional activity; but the census also enquired ominously about the most private details of economic activity: the enumeration of all property, income, debts, and so on.

The idea of censusing the number and the economic power of all Jews in France had appeared in antisemitic pamphlets as far back as the Marquis de la Tour du Pin in 1898,[67] and Vallat himself proposed such a census from the time he became commissioner. He intended it to be put to use at once in his increasingly aggressive policy against the Jews. Darlan's government threw its weight behind the census. Henri Chavin, secretary-general for police in the Ministry of the Interior, underscored its importance in a circular to prefects on 12 July: "I call your special attention to how important it is that this census, a measure of public order, be carried out carefully and supervised with all the means at your disposal."[68] Police, prefectural, and municipal administrations were all involved. No Jew was dispensed from the obligation to declare himself—not even those exempt from other laws.

The third part of Vallat's legislative program extended the "aryanization" of Jewish enterprises and property to the Unoccupied Zone.

The law of 22 July 1941[69] was the gravest step yet taken by Vichy with respect to Jews, and the first to arouse perceptible opposition within the government itself. For one thing, the aryanization law, like the statute and the census, applied indiscriminately to French and foreign Jews alike. For another, it violated the frequent Vichy promise to touch "neither persons nor property." It empowered the state to place all Jewish property in the hands of a non-Jewish trustee *(administrateur provisoire)*, who had the authority to liquidate it if it was deemed unnecessary to the French economy, or to sell it to a non-Jewish purchaser.* The census of 2 June already provided the government with detailed information on Jewish property; the law of 22 July empowered the state to confiscate it. Gravest of all, this law engaged the French administration even more deeply in the German-originated spoliation of Jewish property already underway in the Occupied Zone. In a fateful bargain, Vallat proposed to purchase Vichy's right to administer a unified anti-Jewish program throughout the country, including the Occupied Zone, by agreeing to "touch property" in the Unoccupied Zone.

A French role in aryanization was nothing new in the Occupied Zone. When the Germans had required that all Jewish enterprises in the Occupied Zone be marked with a special sign and placed in the hands of a trustee (ordinances of 27 September and 18 October 1940), they had wanted and needed the help of French administrative services. As Martin Luther, under secretary of state in the German Foreign Office, explained it to Abetz on 28 September, Vichy should carry out the measures against Jews in the occupied territories so that the French would "bear the responsibility in the event of failure."[70] Dr. Elmar Michel, head of the MBF's economic department, explained in a circular of 1 November that the Germans had neither the personnel nor the desire to rob the Jews in France exclusively for their own profit. The French were to participate fully in aryanization. So long as specific German interests were not at stake, the Jewish property should go to Frenchmen. The French administration should have a hand in choosing the *administrateurs provisoires*. "The aim, in principle, is to replace Jews by French in order to have the French population themselves take part this way in the elimination of the Jews, and to avoid the impression that the Germans only want to take the Jews' places."[71]

Vichy could not know that it was German policy to leave most Jewish property in France in French hands, except where exceptional

*The publication of this law was preceded by a thoroughly misleading communiqué which implied that only *prohibited* enterprises would be placed in trusteeship; in fact, every Jewish enterprise was subject to seizure.

German interests were at stake. The handful of flagrant exceptions were enough to raise major worries. The initial French reaction of keeping hands off aryanization* quickly gave way to an effort to establish a French administrative foothold in the process. The creation of a French agency to oversee aryanization in the Occupied Zone in October 1940—the Service de Contrôle des Administrateurs Provisoires, or SCAP—was a major step in that direction. By 1941, further developments tempted Vallat and Darlan into widening that foothold. Vallat had no doubt that, as he told the students of the Ecole Nationale des Cadres Civiques in early 1942, the Germans sought to "infiltrate in order to carry out germanization in the guise of aryanization."[73]

The fate of artistic property in the Occupied Zone was a chilling warning to Vichy of what could happen to Jewish property in general.† The pillage of Jewish art in France was the work of the *Einsatzstab Rosenberg* and associated henchmen, including Reichsmarshal Hermann Göring, "a born thief," as Jacques Delarue calls him; the *Militär-befehlshaber in Frankreich* had little to say in the matter. Indeed, the MBF later judged that German interests had lost more in moral reputation than they gained in property as Rosenberg's crews broke into private houses and museums, and obliged bank vaults to be opened, and carried away collections belonging to the Rothschilds, the Reinachs, the David-Weills, the Wildensteins, and other Jewish families.[74] A wide range of French interests joined in the ensuing protests: museum officials, the scholarly community, the Secours National (the state-run charity, which the French government intended to fund from the sale of property belonging to the émigrés of June 1940, such as the Rothschilds), the Direction Générale de l'Enregistrement des Domaines et du Timbre (the state property administration, whose director insisted on the right of *his* service to liquidate property and take charge of it), the CGQJ (which defended *its* priority in Jewish matters), and the secretary of state for the economy and finance (because the art was supposed to be sold for public benefit). Even Marshal Pétain wanted to dispose of some Jewish art. His eye was on the frescos by the Spanish painter José-Maria Sert, in the former Rothschild château of Laversine, which he wanted to donate to the government of Spain.[75]

Not that any of these protestors voiced serious objection to remov-

*In August 1940, French authorities in Paris told the MBF that their government was not prepared to take measures against Jews in the economy; it would take eleven months to prepare public opinion and to plot a comprehensive aryanization plan.[72]

†*France-soir* reported on 30 July 1950, at the opening of the trial of members of Rosenberg's group, that the Germans had taken an estimated 10,890 paintings, 583 sculptures, 2,437 peices of furniture, 583 tapestries, 5,825 porcelains, and so on.

ing the collections from Jewish hands; it was that "the Jewish collections make up a considerable part of the artistic patrimony of France," as Education Minister Jérôme Carcopino pointed out to Darlan in the spring of 1941.[76] The focus was no longer Jews, but a patriotic defense of French national treasure. What pushed Vichy to near-panic was its sense of powerlessness. Whereas the MBF needed French administrative muscle for the painstaking work of aryanizing business enterprises, a few dozen Nazis with a truck could carry off artwork—and did. When Rosenberg's office finally condescended after many months to reply to French protests, it gave the French a stinging lesson in antisemitic fundamentals: Jews had no rights; the war against *la Juiverie* in France had begun thanks only to the German victory; and the French should be grateful for it.[77] The pillage of Jewish art was an unpleasant reminder of how aryanization could become an entering wedge for German seizure of the commanding heights of French industry and finance.

A further disadvantage of limiting aryanization to the Occupied Zone, as Vichy saw it in the spring of 1941, was the flight of Jewish capital to the south. As Jewish businessmen tried to escape aryanization by smuggling economic resources across the Demarcation Line, Vichy became alarmed at what it saw as an "invasion." Not only did complications arise over Jewish enterprises with interests in both zones, with the MBF demanding ominously to extend to the south the rights of northern-zone *administrateurs provisoires;* the Unoccupied Zone, where there had been only about 5,000 Jews in 1940, now had a population that Vallat estimated in early 1942 at 150,000, "wanderers in every sense of the word . . . scouring the countryside," installing themselves and their friends, hoarding food, and disrupting the village economy.[78] Having pinched off one flood of refugees coming from Germany in the fall of 1940, Vichy now feared another coming from the Occupied Zone.

During May 1941, Vichy ministers planned together how to arm the *Etat français* against these various threats, preferably by replacing German aryanization ordinances with their own. De Faramond, head of the SCAP, Pierre Pucheu and Jean Bichelonne, minister and secretary-general—respectively—of industrial production, and Yves Bouthillier, minister of national economy and finance, took part as well as Vallat.[79] The result was Vichy's aryanization law of 22 July 1941 and a personal victory for Vallat. Both Bichelonne and Bouthillier had hoped to restrain his authority by attributing the main role to the economics ministries, but the SCAP was attached to the CGQJ on 19 June 1941. The minister of justice, Joseph Barthélemy, had last-minute scruples about aryanization, in which cavalier violation of property rights, he freely conceded, was "contrary to the general rules of French law." He went along in the end, however, persuaded that the interests of "general policy" outweighed his legal concerns.[80] Vallat pressed the scheme forward, negotiated precise language with MBF officials, and presented a draft to Darlan in early July.[81]* If we can rely on what Vallat himself told the Germans a few months later, he gave the French cabinet an explicit promise that the Germans would repeal their ordinances upon Vichy's passage of the law.[82] Finally, the cabinet fell in behind the proposal, as it had unanimously for the other new anti-Jewish legislation of June 1941.

The law provided a complex and shaky legal cover for the robbery of Jewish property. Its object was to eliminate "all Jewish influence from the national economy" (our italics). It empowered (though it did not oblige) the commissioner-general to appoint trustees, at his own discretion, to "every industrial, commercial, real estate, or artisanal enterprise; every building, share of real estate, or mortgage holding whatever;" "all movable property or title thereto" belonging to Jews. The trustees had the power not only to manage the Jewish property over which they had been given supervision, but to liquidate it if it was deemed to contribute nothing to the French economy, or to sell it to a non-Jewish purchaser if it did contribute to it. The proceeds from the liquidations or sales were to be placed in blocked accounts in the Treasury Department's Caisse des Dépôts et des Consignations, in the name of the former owners but without any mention of the future disposition of these accounts—building a transparent fiction that this was not outright theft. In fact, the accounts belonged to the despoiled Jews in name only. The commissioner-general disposed of their use, and the law obliged him to give the former owners a mere pittance "to assure some food to the Jew and his family." In keeping with the legalistic style of Vallat's *antisémitisme d'état,* it was not the law that despoiled; rather, the law authorized competent authority to despoil in effect, but according to properly designated bureaucratic agencies.

Jewish property was to be sold or liquidated, as Vallat later said, "under such honest conditions that no one will be able to cry scandal."[83] In that hope he was to be disappointed. Scandals emerged almost immediately, and many continued to echo beyond 1944. Not only was there corruption at every stage of the aryanization process; the program itself locked Vichy into endless quarrels. Aryanization may have

---

*Vallat made it sound as though the power would be used sparingly, and denied that any spoliation was intended.

not been slowed by them, but Vichy paid heavily in political capital. Increasingly the regime appeared to the outside world not only dishonest but incompetent. Even for those who accepted the principle of stripping Jews of their property, aryanization came to have a bad odor. The law grew ever more complicated in its provisions for the appointment of *administrateurs provisoires,* the use of funds generated by sales and liquidations, and its general operation. In a press conference near the end of his tenure, Vallat told reporters that aryanization involved 18 different laws, 18 *décrets d'application* (executive orders) for metropolitan France, 13 for Algeria, 5 for the colonies, plus special decrees for minor issues—altogether 67 texts with 397 articles.[84] And there was more to come. Moreover, the Germans did not retreat from the field. Their own ordinances remained in effect in the Occupied Zone, and they pestered the French unceasingly to do more in the Unoccupied Zone. They tried to override Vichy exemptions, to replace Vichy-appointed trustees, and supported a thinly disguised peculation in which more than one SS officer was involved. All of this was fertile ground for litigation and pressure from interest groups, as we shall see in chapter 4.

His legislative machinery in place, the new commissioner-general appeared bursting with energy to pursue his Jewish quarry. Vallat was everywhere, nipping at the heels of bureaucrats too slow to prosecute or too unimaginative in finding areas of Jewish influence to eliminate. The commissioner-general began a substantial program of spying, intercepting mail and telephone calls to monitor Jewish activity. He asked the police to expel Jews from the city of Vichy, where "their very presence at the seat of government was harmful."[85] His office probed the possibility that Jewish composers were being aired over Radio Marseille (Mendelssohn and even Reynaldo Hahn could be performed, but Darius Milhaud and Jacques Ibert should be limited "to the bare minimum"). "Insofar as light music is concerned," the director of programs was admonished, "I would be grateful if you would furnish me the list [of the artists] who fill your programs most regularly."[86]

Vallat's correspondence overflows with signs of his aggressive attention to detail. He took pains to see that 129 Jews who had been removed from other positions and were being allowed menial jobs with the postal services in Algeria, did not gain access to vital communications matters; he tried to sort out how insurance payments should be made to Jews whose property was under trusteeship; he called attention to Jewish shopkeepers who had somehow escaped the appointment of *administrateurs provisoires.*[87] Vallat continued his efforts to have Jews' identity cards stamped *Juif* against the opposition of René Bousquet, head of the French police, who observed that even the Germans had not gone so far.[88] And in keeping with his rigorous legalism and his struggles to make his definition of Jewishness airtight, Vallat made remarkable efforts to discover false baptismal certificates and to hunt down Jews posing as gentiles.[89]

Such zeal was not limited to metropolitan France. In August 1941, Vallat carried the antisemitic flag in person to French North Africa. Vichy legislation had already been extended to Algeria as it appeared; but, following Vallat's tour, an additional official, one Franceschi, was appointed to head a new aryanization service. By 17 November, Franceschi was asking to increase his staff from 60 to 230 agents, the cost to come out of the benefits realized from aryanization. In Morocco, a Royal Dahir of 5 August 1941 extended the law of 2 June 1941 to the kingdom just before Vallat's arrival, and the commissioner-general paid public tribute to the cooperative efforts of the Sultan.[90] A few months later, new decrees carried the Jewish census to the farthest reaches of the empire: Saint-Pierre and Miquelon, off the coast of Canada, French Guiana, and the French West Indies.[91] No stone was left unturned in the hunt for Jews to count, control, and deprive of their property.

Despite his preferred image as Vallat "the Incorruptible," the commissioner-general stooped often to vindictiveness. The names of prominent Jews were stricken from the Légion d'Honneur. Bernard Lecache, formerly president of the LICA (Ligue Internationale contre l'Antisémitisme), a major organization combatting antisemitism before the war, and a French citizen since 1905, was denaturalized along with other Jewish enemies of the new order.[92] Even non-Jews were victimized by the CGQJ. Ernest Mercier was an industrialist and technocrat with a record of militant antinazism and a Jewish wife. The Paris office of the CGQJ hounded him throughout 1941 and 1942, demanding proof of "pure aryan" ancestry."[93]

In the midst of this flurry of administrative activity, Vallat remained busy with legislative drafting in the fall and winter of 1941. There were three reasons for this. First, the commissioner-general had a horror of even a few Jews evading the full rigor of the law. No matter how he honed and sharpened the legal definition of the Jew, some Jews, armed with exceptional circumstances and an occasional complaisant judge, wriggled away. There was the problem of natural children of foreigners, whose grandparents' racial makeup could not be established. Some who practiced the Jewish religion, Vallat fretted, were not legally Jews. Somehow the statute had to be perfected to reach every Jew.

Second, Vallat had not completed the work of regulating the role of Jews in the economy—a task whose necessity, as he had written the Marshal in May, was becoming "even more imperious with the increase of their number in the Free Zone."[94] In particular, the status of Jewish artisans and small businessmen remained ambiguous, as well as that of Jews in agriculture. The third reason was perhaps the most pressing: the project to have the Germans withdraw their anti-Jewish ordinances in the Occupied Zone was meeting unexpected delay, as the German staffs in Paris found fault with Vichy's existing anti-Jewish legal arsenal.

It was simple enough to complete the economic restrictions upon Jews. On 17 November a further law added even more professions and occupations to the excluded list, bringing Vichy into line with the extensive exclusions imposed in the Occupied Zone by a new German ordinance of 26 April 1941. Now Jews could not be involved, except in menial or manual jobs, in banking, merchant shipping, financial brokerage, publicity, capital lending, commercial brokerage, real estate transactions, sales on commission, or wholesale trading in grains, horses, or livestock. Jews were banned from trade in antiques, forestry, gambling commissions, news services, the periodical press (except for strictly scientific journals or Jewish confessional publications), publishing, film making, theater, and radio.[95] Then Jews were forbidden to buy farms except land that they would cultivate themselves.[96] Throughout this period, moreover, Vallat was working on his draft "third *Statut des juifs*" which we have already considered. He also drafted a statute of artisans and merchants, which he submitted to the Germans in November. The basic principle was that Jews might be permitted to exercise a skilled craft if they worked alone or in a cooperative, but that they could not employ other people or own or direct a limited-liability corporation—"that vice of capitalism."[97]* The economic staff of the *Militärbefehlshaber* picked away at this text through the winter, withholding their approval, while Vallat quietly applied the text unofficially in the Unoccupied Zone.

As exclusion from jobs and professions and the aryanization of enterprises began increasingly to impoverish once-productive Jews, the problem of supplying them with basic social services became acute. Vallat had no intention of allowing his victims to become wards of the state. Article 22 of the aryanization law of 22 July 1941 already provided that the benefits realized by the sale or liquidation of Jewish properties would support a "common fund" for the support of the growing ranks of the Jewish new poor.

*Before 1940, Vallat had proposed a law in each session of the legislature for the abolition of the limited liability corporation.

Dannecker had somewhat more advanced notions of making the Jews pay for their own destitution. Since 1938, the RSHA had perfected devices for forcing Jews to abandon all their wealth upon emigration from Germany. As emigration routes were closed off, other devices were found to force wealthy Jews to subsidize the rest. A characteristic technique of German occupation policy in conquered eastern Europe was the *Judenrat*—a Jewish council implanted in the ghettos to assist the German occupation authorities. The *Judenräte* served to channel the remains of Jewish wealth into the maintenance of the population forced out of useful work, to spare the Germans the trouble of local administration, and eventually to help carry out the more sinister plans of the Germans—the elimination of the Jews altogether.

Dannecker wanted a *Judenrat* for France. He had his eye on the wealth of the Jewish relief agencies, and he wanted to merge and milk them, on the model of the *Reichsvereinigung der Juden in Deutschland* (National Union of Jews in Germany). The French situation differed radically from conditions either in Germany or in eastern Europe: there was no ghetto as in eastern Europe (although Dannecker kept urging such measures as separate educational systems to begin the segregation of Jews in France); and direct German control was limited to the Occupied Zone. Even there, as we have seen, the German authorities had neither the manpower nor the desire to run things without the assistance of French services. Here, as with other aspects of the Germans' anti-Jewish program, it was essential to secure French cooperation.

Vallat stalled Dannecker's pressures for a "forced grouping" of Jews in France until August 1941, when the latter forced his hand. While attempting to win Vichy's support for his own plan, Dannecker had already begun working directly with a few Jewish leaders who had remained in Paris: with a few Consistoire officials acting on their own; and then with a new umbrella organization of Jewish philanthropies, the Comité de Coordination des Oeuvres de Bienfaisance Israélites à Paris (Coordinating Committee for Jewish Charities in Paris) which he hoped would form the kernel of a full-scale French Jewish council. He also brought in two Jews from Vienna, Israelowicz and Bigerstein, to man a "section 14" of his office, the embryo of a self-administering and self-financing central Jewish council. As Vallat saw Dannecker's machinery taking shape, he feared losing control of such Paris-based funds as the assets of the Alliance Israélite Universel, which he estimated at 13,000,000 to 18,000,000 francs.[98] When Dannecker finally announced that by 25 September he would proceed to set up his own Jewish council for the Occupied Zone, Vallat agreed to present to the Vichy government a plan for such a council in *both* zones, answering to Vichy rather than to the Germans. The result was the Union Générale des Israélites de France (UGIF), created by the law of 29 November 1941.[99]

The UGIF swallowed up all the various philanthropies and social agencies created by Jews in France and put them under a new administrative structure subordinated to the commissioner-general for Jewish affairs. All Jews living in France had to pay dues to the UGIF, which was officially charged with "representing Jews to the public authorities, notably for matters of public assistance, mutual aid, and social readaptation." Although we find no trace of opposition within the French cabinet, French-Jewish leaders were appalled. Naturally they worried about the uses to which Jewish philanthropies' assets would be put. They found the definition of the UGIF's functions dangerously open-ended, since those functions were "notably" but not "exclusively" a matter of social services. What spoliations and physical restrictions might the new organization be forced to undertake? Some Jewish leaders also objected to the fact that "French Israelites are, by the application of principles altogether foreign to the spirit of our country, treated by the Marshal's government on exactly the same footing as foreigners and stateless persons." Even the title of the new agency lumped French and foreign Jews together—not *Israélites français* but *Israélites de France*. And "the French are quite unacceptably placed in a minority in comparison with foreigners, stateless persons, and the recently naturalized." Paying dues to the UGIF imposed a sacrifice on French Jews in favor of "foreigners merely passing through."[100] Instructed by the Consistoire to oppose the creation of the UGIF, the former's president Jacques Helbronner tried to enlist his fellow councilor of state André Lavagne, chief of Marshal Pétain's civil cabinet, in a scheme to have the UGIF text referred to the Conseil d'Etat for review. Lavagne promised Helbronner to help, but the former's tentative steps came to nothing. In any event, Vallat brushed the proposal aside.[101]

Once the UGIF was created, Vallat mixed cajolery and browbeating to enlist a sufficient number of Jewish leaders in its two councils—one for each zone. He promised that the philanthropic and social aid associations could retain their separate identity within the UGIF's administrative structure, that there would be no official tie to the Consistoire (Helbronner won at least that point), that the word "teaching" would not appear among the UGIF's enumerated functions (separate schooling was greatly feared by French Jews as a ghettoizing project), and that the UGIF Council for the Unoccupied Zone would be autonomous from that in the Occupied Zone. Admitting that the word "notably" in the list of UGIF's stated functions left a dangerous loophole, he gave his "word of honor" that, at least in the Unoccupied Zone, the UGIF would be charged exclusively with social aid. Vallat also asked the Germans to agree that the French would name the members of the UGIF Council and would administer it in both zones, and that UGIF leaders would not be considered hostages for the Jewish community in case of trouble.[102] Finally he had to threaten that if no French Jewish leaders would accept roles in UGIF, he would appoint outsiders to these positions of power over the whole range of Jewish philanthropies and social agencies. The pressure caused a bitter rift within the ranks of French Jewish leaders. Most of the officers of the Consistoire held back; René Mayer, Marc Jarblum, William Oualid, and David Olmer refused to serve. André Baur finally agreed to head the UGIF Council in the Occupied Zone, with the assistance of Marcel Stora and Georges Edinger; while Albert Lévy, seconded and later succeeded by Raymond-Raoul Lambert, headed the UGIF Council in the Unoccupied Zone.[103]

The UGIF had hardly begun to take shape when the Germans gave a stunning demonstration of how it could be used both to punish the Jews and to subvert French interests. Beginning in August 1941, several German soldiers and officers had been wounded or killed by the Resistance; among various German acts of reprisal was a fine of one billion francs levied on the entire French Jewish community (though there was no indication that the assassins were Jews) on 17 December 1941. This was a spectacular sum, much greater than all the value of aryanization up to that time; and it was not lost on Vichy that whereas the yield of aryanization went to the Caisse des Dépots et Consignations, this cash was destined for the Reich.

Using the tool that Vichy had just put into their hands, the Germans ordered the UGIF to raise the money immediately, and by any means it chose. The French were trapped. An MBF note made a neat observation of how Vallat as well as the Jews were being put to work for Germany:

> It would be opportune to have the Jews collaborate on deciding how to distribute the assessments [of the fine]. . . . The organism best suited for this task is the Union Général des Israëlites de France, which has just been created on German suggestion by French law. It is true that this union is of very recent creation and has hardly begun its activity. But that activity suits German interests, and receiving so important a task at the beginning would be a powerful support to the organism in question. At the same time,

the commissioner-general for Jewish Affairs would be brought in in an appropriate manner, for the union was created under his authority.[104]

Vichy attempted to salvage what it could. The Minister of Finance put pressure on French banks to lend the billion francs on short term to the UGIF. The UGIF paid the banks back by "borrowing" from several hundred of the largest "aryanized" accounts in the Caisse des Dépots et Consignations, subject to a later redistribution of the costs among the entire Jewish community (a redistribution that never seems to have taken place).* All concerned, except those Jews whose blocked assets had been used to pay the fine, managed to save something. Vichy helped tighten the screws by a law of 16 January 1942 which forbade Jews in the Occupied Zone to transfer their assets into Unoccupied France, where they might escape German seizure.[106] Vichy wanted to protect certain more nationally strategic Jewish resources from confiscation, and hoped the Germans would be satisfied with what they could get easily.[107] Time would show that this plan, too, would fail.

The way Vallat succumbed to German promptings over the UGIF suggests that his particular combination of nationalism, antisemitism, and personal pride crippled his judgment of Nazi intentions. As a nationalist, he could no more accept German leadership in the antisemitic field than he could concede the loss of Alsace-Lorraine. Like everyone at Vichy, he winced at increased German authority in the Occupied Zone; more than most Vichy leaders, he believed that only the French should direct the anti-Jewish program there—for, as a lifelong antisemite, he was proud of his achievement. He believed that the CGQJ and its leader had served French reconstruction well and had completed the foundations of an *antisémitisme d'état* appropriate for French conditions and traditions. The challenge posed by the youthful Dannecker touched him particularly keenly. Unaccustomed to admit outside direction in his life-long campaign against Jews, he found it hard to evaluate antisemites who were more dynamic and thoroughgoing than himself.

Like the French generals faced with blitzkrieg, Vallat had no feel for the demonic drive now impelling the German antisemites. He had finished constructing his edifice. The Germans were now entering a new phase. To the expulsion *(Auswanderung)* they had long envisaged, they now added segregation or ghettoizing *(Aussonderung)* at the end of 1941.[108] While Vallat was busy trying to arrive at an estimate of the

*The first 250,000,000 was taken from 18 large accounts; the next 50,000,000 from 218 large accounts.[105]

total number of exemptions anticipated for war veterans, Dannecker was urging upon him separate education, and the exclusion of Jews from any job requiring contact with the public. Soon, as the spaces of Russia opened before the Germans, they would send the first convoys from France to Auschwitz, in late March 1942. Following the political wisdom of Vichy, Vallat thought that the Germans would leave the French alone if only Vichy showed sufficient resolve. Legalistic to a fault, he thought that French laws would guarantee French interests. He seems to have been convinced that the UGIF, by virtue of being created by French legislation, would thereby enhance his own authority in the Occupied Zone, would reduce German control of Jewish affairs there, and would not compromise French interests north of the Demarcation Line. In the end, the UGIF was his own creation, not the Germans'. It was his last accomplishment as commissioner general.

The Emigration Deadlock

> M. Pinck head of the Sûreté Nationale] tells me, in effect, that their interest is the same as ours: to assure the departure of the internees as rapidly as possible and without administrative obstruction.
>
> Jewish emigration official (October 1940)[109]

Throughout Vallat's tenure as commissioner-general, Vichy's ultimate plans looked no further than the emigration of most foreign Jews. This, indeed, was the most palatable course for all concerned. Many foreign Jews wanted nothing else. The Germans, too, until the fall of 1941, encouraged Jewish emigration as a general principle—with one major qualification. They preferred to discourage the emigration of Jews from the occupied territories until evacuation from Germany was complete, lest a massive exodus elsewhere would absorb scarce transport and overseas entry visas needed by German Jews.[110] In any event the Germans left the French free to develop their own policy on Jewish emigration except for the armistice prohibition on the departure of men of military age. On more than one occasion the *Militärbefehlshaber* expressed its lack of interest in non-aryans south of the Demarcation Line. The French could do as they liked with these "undesirables," and their departure from Europe was obviously welcomed. Departure fit German policies toward Jews, long-range plans being officially postponed until after the cessation of hostilities. As Dr. Blanke, of the MBF economic staff put it in the spring of 1941, peace would see "the total European settlement of the Jewish question by their complete emigration."[111] Until then, it was reasonable to suppose, emigration on a smaller scale simply facilitated the Germans' grand design.

Even without German prompting, Vichy wished fervently for Jewish emigration. Admiral Darlan was once again discussing sending all the Jews of Europe to Madagascar, the German embassy reported in August 1941—"in itself no bad thing."[112] Various French officials cleared the way for the embarcation of Jews, either from Switzerland or from French colonies, or directly from ports in the south of France. The idea was to maximize the number of departures and to make sure that Jews from other countries (such as Hungary and Italy) passing through France not use up French quotas for emigration elsewhere.[113] Above all, France was not to take on any more Jews. As Vallat often explained, Jews coming to the Unoccupied Zone would only add to France's economic burden and contribute to unemployment. As for foreign Jews already there, he told a press conference upon taking office that they "will probably be sent back."[114] Vallat did not mention any precise destination, Madagascar or elsewhere; and expulsions in any significant number were simply not practicable under existing circumstances. Shipping spaces were rare, and few countries would take Jewish refugees. Like the Germans, Vallat was presumably putting the matter off until after the war.

Given the formidable obstacles and expenses involved in this aspect of its Jewish policy, Vichy did what the Germans did throughout occupied Europe: it turned to a Jewish organization. Ready at hand was the Jewish emigration society HICEM, a well-known agency founded in Paris in 1927 and composed of three organizations helping Jews—the American Hebrew Immigrant Aid and Sheltering Society, the English Jewish Colonization Association, and Emigdirect, a German-Jewish body assisting east European Jews in Germany.[115] HICEM did heroic work in the first years of the occupation, struggling tirelessly to bring together the French bureaucracy, the shipping companies, and the consular offices of many states to permit Jews to exit from France. Its efforts were doomed from the start. Everyone knew that, even with the best will in the world and with unlimited resources—the latter far from the case—only a fraction of the Jews who wanted to emigrate from France would be able to obtain the limited visas and shipboard space available.

Vichy brought HICEM into the emigration picture from the beginning and gave its efforts strong verbal support. During 1941 the Interior Ministry permitted HICEM to set up offices within the refugee internment camps and encouraged prefectures and local officials to assist in its work. Vallat supported HICEM and worked it into the UGIF as that organization's sixth division.[116]

For several months after the armistice, the tide of emigrants not of military age flowed freely, if haphazardly. American volunteer agencies helped hundreds of prominent refugees to escape to the United States, where special entry visas were quickly provided for scientists and artists. But severe difficulties appeared within less than a year, just when the demand to emigrate began to grow pressing. Shipping grew scarce in 1941 as the war spread into the Atlantic. HICEM was perpetually short of funds; and Vichy, while enthusiastically endorsing its efforts in principle, gave purely rhetorical help. The French offered no financial support. And while some officials were well disposed, the emigration bureaucracy established a labyrinth of absurd regulations and scarcely exerted itself as frantic HICEM officials tried to deal with the obstacles.

Worst of all, the doors were closing in virtually all Western countries by the fall of 1941. The Russell Act in the United States reduced the issuance of American visas in June. By the middle of the month U.S. consulates everywhere in occupied Europe had stopped functioning. Thereafter Washington had to pass individually upon each application for a United States entry visa, and immigration slowed to a snail's pace. While U.S. authorities relaxed their control slightly in October to permit the issuance of a few dozen visas daily, the American entry into the war at the end of the year raised new barriers in the way of immigration.[117] Other countries blocked access for Jewish refugees at the same time. Switzerland had been vigilant against their entry since 1938; the Swiss border was even more hermetically sealed, if possible, when growing numbers of desperate Jews sought a way out of France in 1942 and 1943.[118] The British government declined to accept any more Jewish refugees on the grounds that to do so would enflame antisemitism in England.[119] The British government also closed the gates of Palestine, where the Jewish immigration issue had already strained British-Arab relations in the 1930s. Even Spain and Portugal were refusing transit rights that had formerly been freely granted.[120]

HICEM did its best. Indeed, some of its less discerning workers viewed their activity as a patriotic duty to the French government as well as to the refugees.[121] When it was dissolved in March 1943, HICEM had assisted about twenty-four thousand Jews to emigrate legally since June 1940.[122] Vichy had done far too little to help. It had made no effort to move substantial numbers of Jewish refugees to North Africa when the deportations began. The rest of the world had turned its back. There was to be no solution by emigration of what European antisemites regarded as the Jewish problem. French and German organizers of their respective anti-Jewish programs would have to deal with the matter within Europe.

Vallat's Fall

I have the impression that M. X. Vallat is going a little too far and that he does not follow directions, which are not to bother the long-established Jews.

Darlan to Henri Moysset
(15 January 1942)[123]

Vallat ought to be called the Commissioner for the Protection of the Jews [*Judenschutzkommissar*].

Dr. Werner Best (March 1942)[124]

By the end of 1941, Vallat was rapidly losing credibility, both in Paris and in Vichy. His colleagues in government had been prepared to support the commissioner-general, especially if all went well. Antisemitism was tolerable if it worked smoothly; but none of Vallat's plans had succeeded.

The first malodorous whiffs of aryanization had strained his colleagues' loyalty. Then came the billion-franc fine and the patched-together confiscations that paid it, along with the first shocking mass arrest of Jews by the Germans: the thousand Jewish professional and business leaders rounded up in Paris on 14 December. Worst of all, Vallat had failed to achieve his main goal: the substitution of French law for German, and the withdrawal of the German anti-Jewish ordinances in the Occupied Zone.

Not that the *Militärbefehlshaber* was fundamentally opposed to withdrawing its ordinances. Dr. Best's early intention, as we already know, had been to draw the French into doing "the disagreeable parts." In January 1941, even before Vallat had arrived on the scene, Best had put his own staff to work to "find out to what extent the German legislation concerning the Jews may be abrogated, in the presence of parallel measures adopted in the meantime by the French." Best envisaged how French ambitions could be put to work: "We could let the abrogation of the German measures dangle before the French, in order to stimulate their initiative in settling the Jewish question."[125] Far from outwitting or outbargaining the Germans, Vallat had fallen into their trap.

In June 1941 he had formally requested the Germans to withdraw their economic ordinances concerning Jews now that the French had begun their own aryanization program. The MBF's reply on 25 July had held out some hope, provided the French would do more. Through the autumn of 1941, there followed an abundant correspondence between Vallat and Dr. Best's staff: the commissioner-general reminding the Germans of their promise and sending new texts for their review; and the MBF raising objections to one detail after another.[126] Finally, on 25 November, Dr. Best's office pulled the rug from under Vallat's feet. It was not the texts themselves, said the MBF, but how the French applied them that mattered. The French pace of aryanization had been far too slow. The withdrawal of the German ordinances now would create the false impression that the Germans were easing the pressure on Jews. The Germans had not wanted to take on these functions, the MBF claimed, but the French had not been vigorous enough since 1940, and the Germans were obliged to take their own measures against Jews to guarantee the security of their troops. Now German policy had become one of total elimination. Jews could not be allowed to return. German ordinances could not be repealed unless French laws were brought fully into line with them.[127]

The price of German repeal and of a unified anti-Jewish policy under French direction now began to seem much higher than before. Among the French who began to have doubts, Admiral Darlan was the most eminent. On 8 January 1942 he wrote to the commissioner-general strongly objecting to a new proposal closing additional commercial professions to Jews. Darlan thought the measure excessive and certain to increase Jewish unemployment.[128] Aryanization was also causing trouble. Darlan told his political advisor Henri Moysset that Vallat had been given instructions "not to bother the long-established French Jews." The vice-president of the Council had learned of a particularly flagrant outrage: "Fontaine's brother, a pure aryan, who bought a Jewish business at Béziers a little over a year ago, has had a trustee slapped on him because the business is considered Jewish." Some Jews with visas were also being prevented from leaving France. Darlan did not think these were trivial matters. "The Jews are winding up as martyrs." On 15 January he ordered Moysset to conduct an investigation of "the way Jewish matters are being handled."[129]

Other French officials joined in undermining Vallat. Justice Minister Barthélemy and Prefect of Police Admiral Bard sniped at new legislative proposals from Vallat's office.[130] On 20 February, Ambassador de Brinon, the French government's spokesman in Paris but one who tended to say what his German listeners wanted to hear, told Dr. Best that Pétain himself was unhappy with Vallat, that the Marshal recognized that anti-Jewish activity had to be accelerated, and that the government was ready to recall the commissioner-general.[131]

Vallat was caught between an increasingly hesitant government and an increasingly aggressive German occupation. His report to Henri Moysset, on 7 February, reflects both of these pressures and shows a commissioner-general anxious above all to defend his original anti-Jewish strategy. Vallat would not be pressed further in negotiations with the Nazis:

> I have no intention of going any farther in concessions to the German point of view, for if the harmonization we finally achieve turns out to be a mere alignment on the German position, I could not personally assume political and moral responsibility for that.

But neither would he retreat from the principles enunciated in the spring of 1941 to Admiral Darlan. He insisted that France must continue to keep "a tight rein" on the Jews in the Unoccupied Zone.[132] It could not have escaped Vallat's attention that he was being attacked from that quarter for being too harsh, just as the Germans accused him of being too lax. He liked to think of himself as occupying an antisemitic middle ground.

In the German camp there was no doubt that Vallat's usefulness was at an end. From the first meeting, MBF officials had suspected him of being lukewarm. A half-year later Dr. Elmar Michel, head of the MBF economic branch, had decided that the problem was not inactivity on the part of Vallat but his fundamental hostility to Germany. By December 1941 the Gestapo was treating him with open contempt; they raided his Paris office and took away important papers, and placed under surveillance some of his close associates in the Occupied Zone.[133]

Disillusioned by his failure to achieve German repeal, Vallat became short-tempered. His competence had been called into question as well as his commitment to antisemitism. Defensively he boasted of Vichy's anti-Jewish achievements, such as 800,000 francs of Jewish property already aryanized at Lyon. If the Germans were not going to permit the unification of the two zones' anti-Jewish programs as they had promised, he told Dr. Blanke on 3 December, he would limit his activity to the Unoccupied Zone until a more normal climate had returned. At least in the latter zone, Vallat said, "my antisemitism is not called into question."[134] In January he lashed out at the December arrests of a thousand Jewish professional leaders in Paris, a "grave psychological error" which undermined Vichy's efforts to prepare a "climate propitious to antisemitism." If the Germans had arrested foreign Jews, he said, no one would have complained. Instead, they had singled out the "most honorable" French Jews, including war heroes before whom all should show respect. Warming to his diatribe, Vallat went on to ridicule the tougher German proposals then under discussion in the *Judenreferat*, such as the requirement that Jews wear a yellow star of David, as "a clumsy piece of childishness which was bound to embarrass the French government in its effort to eliminate the Jewish influence in this country. They match Lieutenant Dannecker's series of hasty initiatives whose most certain result was to arouse an atmosphere of pitying sympathy for the Jews." At this point, according to Vallat's notes, the SS representatives walked out of the meeting.[135]

Open rupture came in a stormy personal confrontation with Dannecker on 17 February. Vallat accused the Germans—in terms that Dannecker described as "unheard-of insolence"—of "childish methods." The French, Vallat claimed defensively, were going farther in aryanization than the Germans. "I have been an antisemite far longer than you," he told the SS officer. "What's more, I am old enough to be your father!" Upon hearing this "effrontery," Dannecker broke off the meeting.[136] German officials had already been dropping hints to other French ministers visiting Paris that Vichy should start looking for a replacement for Vallat. After this last outburst, Best told de Brinon, who hastened as usual to agree, that the Germans wanted a new commissioner-general. It was also Best who said, in late March, that Vallat ought to be called the "Commissioner for the Protection of the Jews."[137] On 19 March, Darlan wrote to Vallat letting him go. Vallat was even excluded from the Occupied Zone at the end of March, and his chief of staff, Lionel Cabany, arrested, in a dispute over the failure of the French to supply, through UGIF, the shoes and blankets that the Germans demanded for the first trainload of Jews being sent to Auschwitz from France.

By the spring of 1942 the Germans were embarking on vast new anti-Jewish projects in France. The time of mass deportations had arrived. Vallat's separate and rival French antisemitism, previously an irritation, now seemed an obstacle. To achieve their new aims, the Germans now needed a French anti-Jewish leader with fewer scruples and less independence. Already, on 11 November, Dr. Blanke, the official on the economic staff of the MBF charged directly with aryanization, reflected on the future. The greatest danger seemed to him "precisely the Jews who enjoy a certain consideration." Existing laws and those in preparation were sufficient for a nearly total aryanization; what was needed was "an energetic commissioner-general for Jewish affairs who will get ready to give the question its final solution."[138]

Vallat was not the man for the "final solution," in whatever sense the Germans intended. As Nazi objectives clarified at the end of 1941 and the beginning of 1942, the Germans wanted a new kind of anti-Jewish politics and a new style of antisemitism. Nevertheless, they appreciated what Vallat had done and recognized how indispensable his work had been. Dannecker himself paid generous tribute to Vallat in a note sent to Berlin only five days after their exchange of insults. "Even though the Jewish commissioner is personally very difficult on a number of grounds, it must nevertheless be said that through the preparations of [his] Jewish commissariat anti-Jewish legislation was activated and driven forward."[139]

CHAPTER
4

The System at Work, 1940–42

But it is the law. It must be obeyed.

Jules Jeanneney (1941)[1]

ORE THAN one historian has gone astray by taking legal texts too literally. Were the laws we have been examining really enforced? Was the whole machinery of anti-Jewish repression a mere façade, intended to appease the Germans? If a handful of zealots tried after all to enforce these laws, were they quietly ignored by the traditional French administration? Was the Commissariat-General for Jewish Affairs placed in quarantine by the other ministries and by the prestigious state agencies, or was there an effective working relationship among them?

Generalizations will not do to answer these knotty questions. We shall have to look with as much precision as the evidence now permits at various levels of French government—the central administration, the judiciary, local government. We shall have to keep geographical variations in mind, ranging from the differences between the Occupied and the Unoccupied zones to the special climate of French Algeria. We must also be aware of time. Even the best-informed officials knew less in 1940–41 about the ultimate effects of anti-Jewish policies than the most casual observer knows today; and while we see Vichy's anti-Jewish measures, inevitably, through the prism of the Holocaust, people at that time saw what they called "the Jewish problem" through the prism of the decade through which they had just lived: the Depression, the flood of refugees, an unwanted war, a humiliating defeat. We shall concentrate here on the period of Vichy's own initiatives, before the summer of 1942 when the Germans began their massive deportations that changed everything.

It might be well to open with a concrete case: the passage and implementation of the law of 21 June 1941, which imposed a quota on Jews in secondary and higher education.[2] The first *Statut des juifs* of October 1940 had excluded Jews from the teaching as well as other professions. The question arose, Should Jews be allowed to enroll in teacher-training courses? It came to a head in early 1941 when the Faculty of Letters and the Faculty of Sciences of the University of Paris appealed to the Ministry of Education to permit Jews to enter the final teacher-qualifying examination *(agrégation)*. Ministry officials addressed the issue in narrowly legalistic terms. The Directorate of Secondary Education argued that since Jews could not be teachers, they should not be allowed to take the *agrégation,* whose main purpose was to license people to teach. The minister, Jérôme Carcopino, agreed. Successful Jewish candidates for the *agrégation* would not be able to teach unless granted a special exemption; and "the principle of such an exemption raises a political problem that goes beyond my competence, and that is the government's business to settle."[3] General Weygand, the highest Vichy official in North Africa, was independently following the same line of reasoning. In a letter to Pétain (his position was too high for direct contact with Vallat) he wondered whether, since Jews were excluded from the liberal professions, there should not also be restrictions on the access of Jews to universities in North Africa.[4]

There were more insistent pressures—all from outside the Commissariat-General for Jewish Affairs—for a quota on Jews in the universities. One source of pressure was the National Union of Students, which —at its annual meeting in Grenoble on 18 April 1941—passed a resolution proposed by the Algiers delegation to limit to "2.5 percent at the very most" the number of Jewish students permitted to enroll in each discipline in French faculties. The union further urged that the same limit be imposed upon Jewish students already enrolled in universities who presented themselves for examinations at the end of the 1941 spring term. The student association urged this measure upon the government "with the utmost urgency," for, the students maintained, the steadily rising number of Jews in the universities threatened to make illusory the government's efforts to limit Jews in the professions. The union sent along statistics of Jewish increases in certain faculties, especially in Algiers. The other principal source of pressure was the medical profession, which had just organized its members into France's first nationwide doctors' association (Ordre des Médecins). Doctors had been more sensitive to foreign competition than had any other profession during the 1930s, and, in the absence of a professional association, they were alarmed by their inability to defend themselves.

Our documentation permits no firm conclusion about whether the CGQJ or the Ministry of Public Instruction took the first initiative to set up the interagency drafting committee that prepared the new law in May. There is no doubt, however, that the ministry hurried the matter along. On 29 May the secretary-general for public instruction, Ter-racher, drew the CGQJ's attention to the need to "set certain anxieties at ease" about the number of Jews in the university. The minister himself, Jérôme Carcopino, wrote Vallat on 24 May to express his agree-ment with the principle of a quota, though he thought that 3 percent was low enough. He further urged that "the quota be applied as soon as possible, at least in the medical faculties." Veterans and the children of war dead should not be counted in the quota. As for its application, Carcopino was not sure whether the 3 percent should apply to each faculty or to the university system as a whole. He leaned toward the former solution, "considering the very special situation of the Algiers campus."

After passage of the new law on 21 June, four interministerial con-ferences took place between August and November 1941 to determine how the quota should be applied in detail. Representatives of every ministry involved in universities or professional schooling took part, along with representatives of the CGQJ: Agriculture, National Educa-tion, Industrial Production, Communications, Colonies, and the three military services. According to the minutes of those meetings, no objec-tions of principle were raised to restricting the number of Jewish stu-dents. The intention was to apply the law "equitably"—that is, without personal favoritism—and to settle vexed questions of priorities. For example, should the selection of Jews to fill the quota be based upon intellect or upon some political criterion, such as being a veteran or the child of a soldier killed in action? Carcopino himself intervened to support selection by intellect and to object to the narrow view that any fractional place left over in the calculation of 3 percent of the student body could not be filled. That rigorous interpretation, Carcopino pointed out, would exclude Jews integrally from any program with fewer than thirty-four students, and there were many such programs. This intervention no doubt marked Carcopino as a liberal in this matter, though he evidently preferred not to mention these meetings at all in writing his memoirs.

We may draw a preliminary conclusion, then, that the drafting and implementation of Vichy's anti-Jewish statutes involved representa-tives of many ministries. They appear to have dealt with anti-Jewish measures with the same scrupulous attention to detail that the public administration devoted to rationing, to paying German occupation costs, or to any other measure considered disagreeable perhaps, but a wartime necessity. Throughout the French administration the general rule, when confronted with anti-Jewish measures, seems to have been business as usual.

That conclusion is strengthened by many other examples. Xavier Vallat consulted other ministries often while drafting legislation. He circulated his stillborn third *Statut des juifs* to the entire cabinet in several drafts in late 1941 and early 1942, and most of the replies survive. Justice Minister Joseph Barthélemy objected to some minor details but approved the measure in general. The most substantial objection came from Admiral Paul Auphan, chief of staff of naval forces, who complained on 15 March 1942 that yet another definition of who was Jewish would give the public an impression of improvisation and would subject his services to useless paperwork. The naval services, the admiral grumbled, had already filled eighty thousand file cards in applying the first two *statuts des juifs*. Admiral Auphan, however, gave his "entire agreement" to the draft's basic "dispositions of principle." The other ministries approved without comment.[5]

Not only were other state services consulted by the CGQJ; they took the initiative from time to time. The Army, the Navy, and the Air Force went beyond the letter of the *Statut des juifs*. Whereas the statute excluded Jews from the officer corps, the military excluded them from the enlisted ranks as well. The CGQJ even expressed some doubts about the legality of extending the law in so important a fashion by a mere ministerial ruling. In justification, Vice-Admiral Bourragué, chief of staff of national defense (Admiral Darlan was the minister), replied on 5 November 1941 that "in the professional army that we are working toward, it is indispensable that every soldier be qualified to become a noncommissioned officer." The admiral thus remained on strictly legalistic terrain and permitted himself none of the remarks about Jews as security risks that appear in less official correspondence, such as the warnings periodically sent to Vichy by General Marie-Jules-Victor-Léon François, head of the veterans' Légion in North Africa, about the Jewish danger there.* The admiral went on to assure Vallat that the services were entirely within their rights in forbidding Jews to volunteer for enlistment. In any event, he said, it was unthinkable to reopen a matter that had been decided by the common accord of the three

---

*For example, General François and General Martin, head of the veterans' Légion in Algeria, warned in January 1942 that Jews were still permitted to bid for military supply contracts, which might enable them to obtain defense secrets.[6]

services.[7] The decision to exclude Jews from the Vichy regime's obligatory youth service corps (Chantiers de la Jeunesse) after the first two classes had already accepted them, was taken at the request of the corps's commissioner-general, General Paul de la Porte du Theil, because of the situation in Algeria where Jews were "harmful" and "a source of disunity." Jews would not profit much from the experience of the youth camps anyway, according to the general, because they were "little accessible to the work of moral education."[8]* The CGQJ was clearly not the sole source of antisemitic measures taken by Vichy.

That being the case, it is not surprising to find that Vichy's anti-Jewish laws were seriously enforced. To return to the concrete case with which we began, Jewish students' careers were indeed interrupted or detoured by the *numerus clausus*. It would be difficult to establish exactly how many were affected without a laborious calculation within each faculty, for the law established a jury of five in each faculty (including the dean, one professor who was a war veteran, and one professor who was the father of a large family) to select the Jewish students to be admitted under the quotas. No doubt there was much variation from faculty to faculty. Moreover, some students probably quietly shifted their course of study to less crowded fields, an indirect impact of the law which it would be impossible to measure. We suspect that the ablest Jewish students usually found support within the universities to continue their studies in some fashion, at least outside Paris (where faculties were closely scrutinized) and Algiers (where there was genuine animosity to Jews among the students).

No such guesswork is necessary concerning the application of the *Statut des juifs* to civil servants. After an initial period when each ministry was left to its own devices, enforcement became strict and thorough. By early 1942, Vallat could report that 1,947 civil servants had been removed from their jobs in metropolitan France;[10] detailed reports from the ministries show that these figures were not inflated.[11] By October 1941, 2,169 out of 2,671 Jewish civil servants had already been dismissed in Algeria.[12] The CGQJ took some interest in the re-employment of Jewish civil servants in lesser jobs, but in a time of unemployment the ministries indicated that they had no suitable posts available.[13] Enforcement doubtless varied considerably at the level of local government, where much depended upon the temper of local officials and the zeal of local antisemites. Some local officials took pride in the

---

*The MBF recommended on 4 February 1942 that Jews be excluded from the youth corps, but General de la Porte du Theil went out of his way to give his own reasons for the exclusion.[9]

rigor with which they enforced the law. Others quietly covered Jewish employees. The prefect of the Landes was embarrassed in late summer 1942 when his services were found to contain three Jewish employees, one of them a purchasing agent for supplies destined for the occupation forces![14] It is quite possible that this kind of quiet circumvention of the law was more common in the Occupied Zone, where anti-Jewish policy seemed at least partly German, than in the Vichy zone where the law acquired all the legitimacy of the Marshal and his regime.

There is no indication, then, that the antisemitic laws were widely ignored within the French administration, or that the CGQJ was isolated from other agencies. Far from being an excrescence on the margin of the French administration, the Commissariat-General for Jewish Affairs—at least under Vallat—functioned as an integral part of it.

The CGQJ and Other State Agencies: Rivalries and Border Disputes

Any new government agency is likely to engender some friction with established agencies as it makes a place for itself. The CGQJ was in many respects an exaggerated instance of that rule.

From its beginnings, the CGQJ had an uncertain status within the French administration. It was expected to be a temporary structure, intended to solve a problem in French society and then to disband. Unlike Germany, where the Jewish question was a central obsession of the Nazi regime, Vichy's anti-Jewish measures were merely one of the many tasks of the National Revolution. It was never given top priority, and the regime did not feel comfortable accentuating it before the French public. The commissariat thus never attained the status and solidity to which its successive directors felt it was entitled. The CGQJ was first attached directly to the office of the head of government, Admiral Darlan, and Vallat had the rank of under secretary of state. In May 1941 the responsibilities of the commissioner-general were considerably enlarged to include an ill-defined but ominous task "to set in motion eventually with regard to the Jews . . . all police measures dictated by the national interest."[15] Perhaps as a result of these new police functions, the CGQJ moved to the Ministry of the Interior a few months later. But within less than a year its organizational home changed again. In May 1942, Pierre Laval, suspicious of the conduct of anti-Jewish policy and less than enthusiastic about Vallat's replacement, Darquier de Pellepoix, joined the CGQJ once again to the office of the prime minister.[16] The government also considered placing the CGQJ within the Justice Ministry.

Wandering among ministerial offices, the CGQJ also suffered in recruiting and retaining personnel. Since the commissariat was expected to be temporary, it was not thought appropriate to grant its employees the normal status of civil servants. They were either detached from other agencies on temporary assignment, hired as temporary employees, or *chargés de mission* (specialists) engaged by contract. There were constant complaints about crushing workloads, low pay, poor working conditions, and the absence of material benefits equivalent to those of the civil service. The CGQJ drew all sorts of people— true believers like Xavier Vallat, but also a wide circle of profiteers and adventurers. Commissariat officers, in turn, bemoaned the poor quality of workers, their insufficient numbers, and the high turnover. Regional Director de la Chassaigne, in Marseille, complained to Vallat on 16 December 1941 that he could not find candidates willing to take jobs in his office. The problem was not one of moral scruples: "Almost all turned my offers down, judging that the salary proposed would not permit them to live decently at Marseille; they prefer to become *administrateurs provisoires* [of Jewish property] which, in some cases, permits them to earn 10,000 francs a month."[17]

The work of aryanization, which came to absorb two thirds of the commissariat's activity, put an exceptional strain on both the honesty and the competence of personnel. De Faramond, director of economic aryanization for the Occupied Zone, warned Vallat in August 1941 that in a few days "my agency won't be able to do its job" for lack of suitable personnel. Each of his sections had to oversee the *administrateurs provisoires* of 2,500 to 3,000 sequestered Jewish enterprises. This was exacting work—"work that required a very keen critical intelligence from three points of view: economic, juridical, and aryan." De Faramond drew Vallat's attention to ways in which inadequate personnel could "compromise very seriously the re-establishment of French sovereignty in the business of aryanization . . . at the moment when all your efforts and all ours are bent to obtaining the substitution of French legislation for the German regulations."[18] This observation, aside from reminding us how the struggle for "sovereignty" accelerated the spoliation of the Jews, shows that the CGQJ suffered from morale problems perhaps greater than, but not much different from, those of civil servants in general—insufficient appreciation, too little pay, unsatisfying status.

Improvements in personnel came slowly, if at all. There were over four hundred CGQJ employees at the outset, in mid-1941, before aryanization had begun in the Unoccupied Zone. At the end of that year the total strength had reached 766. More people were requested, particularly to staff the Sections d'Enquête et Contrôle (SEC), a police arm of the CGQJ created in October 1942. In the spring of 1944 there were a total of 1,044 CGQJ agents.[19] During its three and one-half years of life, the CGQJ budget grew sixfold,[20] so it could hardly complain that the government refused support. (The CGQJ budget was 50,169,000 francs in 1944, of which 36,500,000 was for salaries; inflation, however, reduced the effect of the budget's growth.) Yet the commissariat never obtained the quantity of personnel it felt it needed, nor workers of sufficient quality to deal easily with the highly trained permanent civil servants of the established agencies.

Xavier Vallat may not have fully appreciated this problem, for he was inexperienced in administration and seems to have been largely uninterested in such questions. But administrative rot set in quickly within his commissariat. Procedures were not followed; recruitment was irregular; discipline and work routines were lax; and morale was poor. On the outside at least, observers blamed the commissioner-general. To help put the house in order, Vallat called in his old wartime comrade Colonel Pierre-Paul-Marie Chomel de Jarnieu, who found "grotesque confusions and misunderstandings, which totally obstruct the work of aryanization."[21] When Darquier de Pellepoix took over in 1942, one of the first tasks he undertook was a substantial reorganization of the CGQJ; but rapid turnover, laxity, and corruption were, if anything, worse by 1944 than before. CGQJ agents never enjoyed a high reputation in the general public; and by 1944, when opinion had shifted decisively against them, they "had to buck the whole current of French opinion."[22] Even at that late date, with the end in sight, complaints about morale seem more shaped by frustrated bureaucratic expectations than by feelings of extreme political isolation:

> Temporary agents of a temporary agency, the employees of the commissariat are not attached to their duties by any thought of the future; no career perspectives or desire for the esteem of leaders as ephemeral as themselves arouse their zeal and provoke emulation among them. Is it surprising, then, that aside from a few who devote themselves entirely to their task out of pure professional

conscientiousness, most see in their work only a temporary meal ticket, and that a few weak characters have not managed to resist questionable propositions?[23]

In a curious way, the very offensiveness of the CGQJ's job may have integrated it into the administration more than it isolated it. The commissariat did not usurp any agency's traditional functions, and the other services seem to have been glad to have someone to whom to refer the uncomfortable tasks of official antisemitism and the swelling volume of business that it unleashed: the tide of letters of denunciation, the headaches of trying to census a fugitive population, the laborious and tangled problems of aryanization, and all the rest. On the other hand, matters like aryanization tended to spill over and affect the workings of other ministries, which could hardly ignore what the CGQJ was doing to the economy. Most of the conflicts that arose between the commissariat and other agencies, therefore, were boundary disputes rather than outright challenges to the CGQJ's legitimacy or refusals to work with it.

Boundary disputes were all the more likely because anti-Jewish policy had been left to the individual ministries for the first seven months, from October 1940 to April 1941. In the opinion of Joseph Billig,

> The leaders of the French state would have preferred that the various cabinet ministries take charge of the racist program, as was the case in the Third Reich itself. They would have preferred a decentralized program, in order not to expose it in full and at each moment to Nazi scrutiny, and that this program develop at a pace appropriate to the Vichy government and according to its own views.[24]

Vallat considered it his duty to put an end to this variety, to coordinate the purge of Jews from public life, and to keep track of how various branches of government enforced the law. The administrations sometimes regarded this as abusive meddling. Justice Minister Joseph Barthélemy, who had attempted to preserve the competences of the various cabinet branches, insisted that the CGQJ's role was one of coordination, not interference.[25] Sometimes the CGQJ was treated with lofty condescension and its circulars went unanswered.[26] The refusal to cooperate could even be direct. In reply to a query about Jewish economic activity, the tax division of the Ministry of Finance opposed the obligation of professional secrecy. These officials defended what they felt was properly their own authority. Resistance collapsed, however, when Vichy gradually strengthened the hand of the CGQJ and threw its weight increasingly behind the persecution. Thus a law of 17 November 1941 gave the commissariat the right to look into certain property matters, and the Ministry of Finance had to go along.[27] In the course of 1941, it became the rule that agencies that had traditionally managed to resist meddling from other government branches—such as the postal service, which for a short time would not let the *administrateurs provisoires* receive the mail of their wards—gradually to give way.[28]

This situation hardly made antisemitic laws popular among civil servants who had to enforce them. The sheer paperwork could be annoying. In the Occupied Zone, for example, when the Germans decided in July 1942 that Jews' telephones should be removed, the postal service faced the impossible task of identifying all Jewish subscribers. Even Vallat opposed this project, arguing that the service would lose revenues, and that the French administration would lose its capacity to listen to Jews' conversations.[29] More generally, civil servants resented the way in which persecution could upset their work routines and abuse their sense of professional responsibility. The Committee for Review of Military Decorations, to take another case, was accustomed to grind out decisions, in a leisurely fashion and without overt outside influence, for the War Ministry on the award of military decorations. In 1942, however, a military decoration of sufficiently high grade could mean the difference for a Jew of retaining or losing his livelihood; eventually it would mean the difference between life and death. In January 1942, Xavier Vallat learned that a number of cases in his office could not be finally settled because the Jews in question were awaiting confirmation of military decorations—an obstacle that clearly annoyed him. Vallat asked the Committee for Review of Military Decorations to hasten its decisions and, for good measure, told it how to run its business: "Given the special impact of approving [a military decoration] when the recipient is a Jew, I call your attention to the grave consequences of approving them too easily or too liberally." The response was polite but bristling. These matters took time; they were proceeding through proper channels. "To accomplish its difficult task, the Committee for Review has the absolute moral duty to bring a total impartiality to its judgments. . . . Jews have neither benefited from any indulgence whatsoever nor been treated with exceptional severity."[30] The War Ministry was normally among the harshest in its application of the antisemitic laws, but in this case one small office of the French bureaucracy proved too much for the zealous commissioner-general.

One of the most important boundary disputes set the CGQJ at odds with the ministries of Finance and Industrial Production over aryanization. The two economics ministries had established the principal role in aryanization in the Occupied Zone from its beginnings in October 1940. When aryanization was extended to the Unoccupied Zone in July 1941, and the Vichy government attempted to gain control over the process in the entire country, it was not clear who would have authority over these expanded functions, so vital for the future of the French economy. The Ministry of Industrial Production was determined to retain the right to countersign the appointments of all *administrateurs provisoires* to Jewish enterprises (the Ministry of Finance in the case of banks and insurance companies).[31] On the other hand, Vallat won primary control over the whole aryanization project, and the SCAP (Service de Contrôle des Administrateurs Provisoires) was transferred to the new commissariat in July 1941. Dr. Blanke and the other German officials directly concerned with aryanization were not consulted on this shift in SCAP's place in the administrative hierarchy, and they protested that the "uniform direction of the French economy" would be "compromised." Vallat reassured them that he would do nothing without the approval of the ministry concerned, and that the SCAP would function in the Occupied Zone exactly as before.[32] It was no longer clear who had the ultimate responsibility of choosing the *administrateurs provisoires*, at least in the Occupied Zone, or of deciding whether a Jewish enterprise should be liquidated or kept in operation under an "aryan" purchaser. Each month an interministerial conference brought together representatives of the ministries of Finance and of Industrial Production, along with representatives of the CGQJ, in the offices of Jacques Barnaud, French delegate in Paris for Franco-German economic relations, in an effort—not always successful—to iron out a common policy on the more important Jewish enterprises before dealing with the Germans.

When German interests became involved, the trump card was still held by the Ministry of Finance which had to approve any transfer of property from French to foreign hands. At times this confusion of authorities was a useful device to obstruct the plans of German investors to buy important French Jewish enterprises. Dr. Elmar Michel, the chief economic official in the MBF, came to feel that the ministries of Finance and Industrial Production were hampering Vallat's work, and supported Vallat in his desultory efforts to gain independence of them.[33] In fact, it is not easy to discern any real difference of policy between Vallat and the chief economic ministries. Later on, when

Darquier was commissioner-general for Jewish affairs, the CGQJ sometimes authorized the sale of Jewish properties to German interests
without consulting the Ministry of Finance; and the latter complained
bitterly on these occasions. (For example, the Krupp purchase of the
Austin farm machinery plant and the Wetzel purchase of Helena
Rubinstein cosmetics in 1943, after years of discussion.)[34] At no time,
however, did either economics ministry appear to raise fundamental
objections to the notion that Jewish property should be sequestered and
placed in the hands of "aryans" as a matter of policy.

Out in the departmental capitals, friction between prefects and the
newly installed services of the CGQJ had little to do with the prefects'
personal feelings about Jews or about the government's anti-Jewish
measures. It was a function of the prefect's efforts to gain fuller control
over all the branches of government agencies within his department.
The prefects wanted to stop the tendency of some local officials to
bypass the prefect and contact their home offices in Paris (or Vichy)
directly. In the Alpes-Maritimes, for example, Marcel Ribière was one
of the most vigilant prefects in the Unoccupied Zone about interning
foreign or suspicious Jews, about attributing anti-governmental propaganda and black market activities to them, and about urging massive
nationwide internment of all "suspect" Jews (French as well as foreign)
in "concentration centers." Yet the same Marcel Ribière was incensed
when the CGQJ, as well as two other new agencies (the secretariats for
Unemployment and for Family Affairs), named departmental delegates
without consulting him. Prefects, he complained in his monthly report
of 4 August 1941 to the minister of the interior, did not yet have sufficient means to govern. They needed unquestioned primacy over all
government officials in their departments. In the CGQJ instance, Ribière knew derogatory information about the delegate, and asked his
removal.[35] This type of border conflict involved the most vigorous and
ideologically loyal of prefects, each of whom was offended not by what
the CGQJ was doing but by its failure to subordinate all its local activities to him.

A more complex variant of prefectoral conflict with the CGQJ
involved excess of zeal against well-established Jews with local roots.
Prefect René Le Gentil at Tarbes (Hautes-Pyrénées department) was
angered by the "clumsiness" of CGQJ agents who failed to distinguish
between foreign "scheming Jews," who belonged in *camps de concentration* (and Le Gentil sent some there), and "long-established Jews"
whom the agents pursued "indiscriminately." He denounced the aryanization of the Rosengart foundry in Tarbes, fearing that it would lead

to massive unemployment, and protested the aryanization of a leather works "following one of those clumsy blunders" that seemed to him characteristic of the CGQJ, and especially of its supplementary police, the Police for Jewish Affairs (PQJ).[36]

The creation of a special anti-Jewish police force raised a particularly delicate point of administrative order and competency. Vallat's state antisemitism was intended to be a lawful exercise, the very opposite of mob rule or popular pogrom. It rested upon a legislative program, devised by jurists and enacted by duly constituted authority. The Vichy state had little in common with the Nazi state's proliferation of parallel organizations—the single party, the party courts, and, above all, the special police and army units of the SS that stood outside the law and answered only to the Führer. Although, during his one visit to Paris, on 6 May 1942, Reinhard Heydrich, Himmler's second in command and head of the ˙Reich Security Office *(Reichssicherheitshauptamt)*, urged the French to create a special police and security force "outside the administration,"[37] Vichy remained a regime governed by law, and the traditional administration remained, by and large, master of its household. The special anti-Jewish police force was a rare and tentative move in the direction of a parallel administration entrusted with "dirty work" (the Sections Spéciales, the special anti-Communist courts of August 1941 were the other main example)—a move that was quickly and effectively limited and isolated by the regular forces of order.

It was the minister of the interior, Pierre Pucheu, who set up the Police for Jewish Affairs (PQJ), in the autumn of 1941, under the control of his own ministry. Repression was intensifying. The regime was experimenting with exceptional courts and executive justice following the first assassinations of German officers in France and the ensuing crisis over two German actions: the taking of hostages and the Germans' first massive internment of Jews in Paris.[38] The occupation authorities preferred to leave this repression to the French, and the regular French police were overwhelmed by the sudden rush of anti-Communist and anti-Jewish activity in the Occupied Zone.

One possibility was expansion of the CGQJ to fulfill these tasks, but Vallat had told Werner Best in April 1941 that internment and expulsion were police work, and not part of his functions as commissioner-general at all. In any case, Vallat did not inspire confidence as an administrator. Dannecker had already taken steps of his own that no doubt helped nudge the French in the direction of a special police unit devoted to Jews. On 27 May 1941 he had detached six French police inspectors from the Paris Prefecture to work directly with the SS as an "action squad," and soon thereafter set up a force of twelve French police inspectors in a special office in the rue de Teheran to deal with Jewish matters.[39] Later, when Vichy had absorbed this office into its own Police for Jewish Affairs, Vallat claimed paternity for the whole scheme. The youthful Dannecker normally ignored such claims contemptuously; but in this case, when relations with Vallat were deteriorating, he was humorless enough to force Vallat to sign a letter on 17 November 1941 acknowledging that the idea for a PQJ had been Dannecker's own.[40]

The PQJ fit the pattern of Vichy's grand strategy for dealing with the Germans: by internalizing parts of the German project, stamping them "made in Vichy" and extending them to the Unoccupied Zone, they seem to have hoped that they could both extend French authority and diminish the German grip over the Occupied Zone. Schweblin, the French director-general of the new PQJ, repeated the familiar formula in one of his first reports to Vichy:

> In our opinion it would be very adroit to accede to Lieutenant Dannecker's wish, carefully and with certain reservations. That would procure for us, without doubt, certain facilities in our dealings with his services in order to obtain our increasingly exclusive control over measures intended to resolve the Jewish problem in France, a problem that we still judge ought to be considered in strictly national terms and resolved by entirely national measures.[41]

The PQJ operated in both zones, although it clearly functioned more freely in the Occupied Zone. Its authority was supposed to be limited to gathering information on infractions of the *Statut des juifs*, in cooperation with the regular Police Nationale and under the guidance of the CGQJ.[42] In practice, however, the PQJ did not confine itself to intelligence operations. In direct contact with the Gestapo, its agents ignored the statutory limits imposed by Vichy, and arrested Jews and turned them over to the regular   police. Usurping ever more regular police functions, the PQJ was reinforced by inspectors detached from the Prefecture of Police. Dannecker admired its work. He considered it an "elite troop" which his own services had helped to educate.[43]

While the SS were pleased, the regular French police were not. They resented the establishment of a police unit operating outside normal controls and normal recruitment procedures and constantly ingratiating itself with the Germans. As a concession to the Police Nationale, the PQJ was put under regular police authority in January 1942;

but this move by no means ended independent action or the resulting friction. Relations were never cordial. Indeed, in Lyon, Marseille, and Toulouse, the PQJ had great difficulty finding lodging with the regular police and had to seek shelter with the CGQJ. In Lyon, the PQJ was still looking for office space in March 1942.[44] Regional prefects sometimes ignored the PQJ's recommendations for pressing charges or for administrative punishments. In Bordeaux, where SS Sturmbannführer Hagen made a direct request of the PQJ for the arrest of three Jews, the local intendant of police refused to go along, and the Jews escaped, probably fleeing to the Unoccupied Zone;[45] on the other hand, there was often cooperation, for the PQJ relieved the regular police of many unpleasant tasks.[46]

The regular French police thus remained the principal enforcers of Vichy's anti-Jewish legislation. This did not mean that the anti-Jewish measures were enforced slackly. In the Occupied Zone, the MBF staff found in early 1942, despite all their suspicions, that French police tasks were "generally carried out loyally."[47] In the Unoccupied Zone, the regular French police showed little hesitancy in enforcing Vichy policy. In the spring of 1941, even before the CGQJ had been created, the Marshal's staff became concerned by the number of Jews gathering on the Côte d'Azur. Someone in Pétain's office—the Italian Armistice Commission thought it was the Marshal's economic advisor Lucien Romier and his personal physician and confidant Bernard Ménétrel— was preparing to observe the regime's first May Day with a number of striking gestures to illustrate the new social order. Along with statements by such prominent pro-regime union leaders as Labor Minister René Belin and Georges Dumoulin about the replacement of class conflict by corporatism, the staff proposed to amnesty several labor leaders and to make what they assumed would be popular arrests: notorious black marketeers, some conspicuous Gaullists such as General Cochet, and four hundred Jews in Marseille, Nice, and Cannes.[48] On 25 April, as scheduled, Henri Chavin, secretary-general for the police in the Ministry of the Interior, rounded up seventeen foreign Jews accused of black market activities: "This is just an hors d'oeuvre, of course." Marshal Pétain's chief of civilian staff, Henri du Moulin de Labarthète, replied to Chavin on 3 May that "I am particularly grateful for your firm execution of the purge [*l'épuration*] authorized by the Marshal in the present circumstances." The identification of foreign Jews with black marketeering seems to have been immediate and unthinking. The subsequent police operation in the Alpes-Maritimes, the Var, and the Bouches du Rhône sent 61 foreign Jews into internment and 632 into assigned residence in another area by 5 July; there was no further mention of black market or of non-Jewish suspects. Du Moulin acknowledged these "impressive figures" which "correspond to the government's "expressed wishes"; and someone on the Marshal's staff penciled in the margin an admiring remark about "Chavin's terrific dragnet operations" (*fameux coups de filet de M. Chavin*).[49]

Vichy's *antisémitisme d'état* rested upon the regular judiciary no less than upon the regular police. The various exceptional jurisdictions created during the hostage crisis of fall 1941—Sections Spéciales, Tribunal d'Etat—dealt with relatively few cases, mostly Communists. The regular French courts saw to it that the anti-Jewish laws were obeyed; and the courts' role was essential, for Vallat and the other proponents of *antisémitisme d'état* intended their campaign against the Jews to fit into the larger legislative effort of the National Revolution. Toward the end of 1941, a legal manual entitled *Les Institutions de la France nouvelle* observed that the National Revolution involved about fifteen hundred new laws—not to mention the decrees, ministerial rulings, and circulars that controlled their application.[50] Several hundred of these texts concerned Jews. The lawyer and author Wladimir Rabi has observed recently that French antisemitism "has always been essentially juridical," in its ambition to repeal the emancipation of 1791.[51] But an orderly *antisémitisme d'état* meant nothing unless violators of the new anti-Jewish statutes could be convicted before regularly constituted courts of law. The French magistracy enforced these statutes, for the most part, with professional thoroughness and without any conspicuous opposition. That they did so was a reflection not necessarily of active hostility to Jews but of a desire to restore the normal functioning of the state, of professional acceptance normal to a system of positive law in which any duly promulgated statute undergoes no further test of constitutionality, and of genuine enthusiasm for the new regime.

The French judiciary gave its blessing to Marshal Pétain and the National Revolution, including the *Statut des juifs* which formed an integral part of that revolution. Prestigious jurists gave striking public endorsements of the new regime. At the summit was Joseph Barthélemy, a widely respected professor of constitutional law at the University of Paris, who became Darlan's justice minister and remained a leading figure in Laval's government after April 1942. Georges Ripert —member of the Institute and dean of the Paris Law Faculty and a man who had stirringly opposed racial and religious prejudice in 1938— applied the antisemitic laws as minister of education in 1940. Roger

Bonnard, rector of the Bordeaux Law Faculty, told his students at the opening of school in 1940:

> We are invited to turn back to the acceptance of authority. So we must detach ourselves from that old ideology that has perpetuated itself as a dogma since Rousseau: the democratic prejudice that holds that, in every domain, individuals govern themselves, so that, obeying only themselves, they remain as free as before.[52]

Bonnard was co-editor of the *Revue de droit public*, an erudite journal founded in 1894 and intended for an audience of specialists. In the first number to appear after an interruption caused by the *débâcle*, Bonnard put his periodical at the service of the head of state: "with our 'chief,' Marshal Petain, France has a guide of incomparable and almost super-human wisdom and mastery of thought, who will keep us from erring and will lead us on the path of truth."[53]

The most respected legal journals and scholars commented upon Vichy's anti-Jewish laws with a tone of scientific detachment. Roger Bonnard, who had written a "scientific" study of Nazi law in 1936, urged his colleagues in 1941 to embark upon the task of legal analysis in the interests of "our new Weltanschauung."[54] Distinguished authorities from the universities, the courts, and the bar contributed regularly to the *Semaine juridique* and the *Gazette du Palais*, keeping their colleagues abreast of new laws against Jews and court decisions based upon them. Typical of many of these commentaries was the work of E.-H. Perreau, honorary professor at the Toulouse Law Faculty, who in fact was critical of certain aspects of the anti-Jewish legislation. He insisted, however, upon his neutrality. In a long article discussing the new *Statut des juifs* of 1941, he took these laws "as juridical facts," important to study in a "purely objective manner": "We want *to facilitate their application* by clearing away misunderstandings, and to contribute, in our modest sphere, to the understanding of the new texts" (our italics).[55] Roger Bonnard's co-editor at the *Revue de droit public* was Gaston Jèze, a man of the Left reputedly hostile to Vichy. Nevertheless he continued in the "neutrality" followed by others. In 1944 he thought it opportune to publish his own note entitled "The Legal Definition of the Jew in Terms of Legal Incapacities," with a dry and careful summary in a section devoted to notes on jurisprudence.[56] Once more at the Paris Law Faculty, Georges Ripert contributed a preface to a book on Nazi laws published in 1943, and emphasized how important it was to study such matters objectively: "The scientist has the right to take no interest in the practical consequences of his studies."[57]

Books or articles on the maze of antisemitic laws became a flourishing academic industry under Vichy. The very first textbook on constitutional law published under the new regime, the work of a professor at the Dijon Law Faculty, repeated almost word for word the injunctions of Xavier Vallat:

> We must first eliminate the foreign or doubtful elements that have slipped into our national community, or put them in a position where they can do no harm. . . . Given his ethnic character, his reactions, the Jew is not assimilable. So the regime considers that he must be kept apart from the French community.[58]

The same year an even more comprehensive study appeared, devoted entirely to the anti-Jewish statutes and graced with a preface by Rear-Admiral Ven, commandant of the National Police Academy.[59]* The University of Paris granted at least one doctorate for an analysis "of pure legal technicality" of the *Statut des juifs*, written by a civil servant attached to the Prefecture of Police and approved by three French jurists of high academic standing.[60]

In the courtroom, judges generally adopted a viewpoint of "strict construction," holding to the letter of the law and insisting upon due process, even when they clashed with a battery of emergency laws and with the less scrupulous intentions of the prosecution. The administration, led by the CGQJ, wanted the courts to enforce the anti-Jewish statutes much more harshly. Although Xavier Vallat assured a skeptical Dannecker that the French courts were not as lenient as the latter believed, Vallat complained privately to Darlan that the judges were letting obvious Jews go in cases where the state had insufficient evidence—in cases with unknown fathers, for example, or with foreign ancestry that precluded documentation.[61] That is why, in the draft third *Statut des juifs*, Vallat wanted to reverse the burden of proof and place it on the accused.

An accurate assessment of how firmly the French courts enforced the anti-Jewish statutes would require taking into account wide local variation. In the Occupied Zone, the obligation to enforce German ordinances as well as French law imposed special circumstances. In the Territory of Belfort, the president of the Commercial Tribunal was "declared incompetent [by the Germans] to try such cases" after a

---

*The admiral referred to the *Statut des juifs* as "a characteristic monument of the legislative system now under construction in the new France."

dispute over liquidation of Jewish property in early 1941;[62] but, by and large, most French courts complied, going farther than their counterparts in Belgium where the highest appeals court (Cour de Cassation) protested solemnly against the measures of the occupation.[63] In the Unoccupied Zone, we have the impression that the courts tended to check the CGQJ's zeal. They did not challenge the legality or the principle of the *Statut des juifs* but rendered judgment, as has been said, "in a spirit of just measure, with respect for principles."[64] Sometimes this policy told in the Jews' favor, and sometimes it did not. In all, over six hundred Jews were condemned in French courts for violating the anti-Jewish statutes during the eighteen months between June 1941 and the end of 1942. A further forty-six were condemned during 1943 by French courts, at the height of the deportations; and eleven more, on the very eve of the Liberation, in 1944.[65]

At the pinnacle of the French legal and administrative system, the Conseil d'Etat had an important and varied role to play in these matters. Not only did it decide on the procedures of removing Jews from the civil service; its approval was required on each exemption allowed by the statutes; it reviewed prospective laws, regulated the nominations to posts of *administrateurs provisoires*, and rendered some independent decisions on its own. So significant was the new jurisprudence growing up around the new anti-Jewish laws that, in 1941, the Conseil d'Etat established a special Commission du Statut des Juifs, presided over by its vice-president Alfred Porché. It has recently been suggested that the Conseil d'Etat tried to attenuate the consequences of Vichy's antisemitic measures.[66] The Conseil's reputation at the time was rather different, however. Pétain's chief of civilian staff, Henri DuMoulin de Labarthète, reported after the war that the Marshal's efforts to obtain exemptions for his Jewish friends were partly frustrated: "we were irritated by the slowness, sometimes even the stinginess, with which the Conseil d'Etat, charged with ruling on demands for exemption, went about this work of reparation."[67] Jérôme Carcopino's memoirs leave a similar impression.[68] Official communications of the Conseil d'Etat, reread today, can even present a distinctly antisemitic cast. In December 1941, in an opinion issued over the signature of Vice-President Porché, the Conseil d'Etat advised the government against Vallat's proposal to direct some Jews toward agricultural pursuits:

> In the eyes of the Conseil, it would be risky to spread around the countryside, under the guise of a "return to the soil," an almost exclusively urban and commercial population that has always shown itself radically inadept at farm work, from the most distant

past to today, even in Palestine despite the Zionists' efforts, and in eastern France where it has been established in certain villages for centuries.

It is to be feared that we will only wind up by spreading usury and the so-called "black market," no matter what precautions we take and however we arm ourselves. What is more, . . . we run the risk of favoring the spread in the countryside of the extremist doctrines dear to too many Jews from eastern Europe.[69]

Although anti-Jewish dispositions clearly existed within the Conseil d'Etat, these seem to have taken second place to the assertion of legal prerogatives and the desire to render judgment in what was seen to be a professional manner. The Conseil issued a mass of decisions that established legal interpretation for lower courts to follow. Sometimes the results gratified the antisemites. On 21 March 1941, for example, the Conseil declared that Jewish *greffiers de tribunaux,* a category of court clerks not explicitly mentioned in the *Statut des juifs,* should also lose their jobs.[70] In the administrative purge, the Conseil placed the burden of proof upon the accused to prove he or she was *not* Jewish, and thus legalized the removal from office of an appellant unable to offer evidence on his or her own behalf.[71] In other cases, the Conseil d'Etat was more lenient, to the exasperation of the CGQJ. In cases before the lower courts, the Conseil d'Etat, they thrust the burden of proof upon the state prosecutor, a cause of considerable headache to the anti-Jewish bureaucracy in 1943.[72] A significant decision that same year quashed a prefectural ruling in the Haute-Savoie ordering *all* travelers to note their religion on hotel registers. And in 1944, long after North Africa had passed out of Vichy's control, the Conseil d'Etat annulled the decision of the governor-general of Algeria to impose a *numerus clausus* in primary and secondary schools.[73]

It may seem astonishing that such litigation extended beyond the summer of 1942, as Jews were being rounded up, torn loose from their homes and families, and deported to Auschwitz. Yet this was the case. Throughout the war, a tiny handful of Jews and non-Jews continued to apply to the courts for relief from what they claimed were abuses of the anti-Jewish laws. And the courts kept on with their job, amidst all the horrors of deportation, even through the summer of 1944, reflecting the magistrates' determination to assert control over statutory persecution.

To understand how the French judiciary became so extensively involved in this area, we must look more closely at the kinds of issue in dispute. One series of cases involved the legal identification of Jews, a matter that never ceased to give the authorities trouble. No matter how refined were Vichy's definitions, they were never completely effective in settling identities. Important rulings in 1941 set some of the terms for deciding cases where there were only two grandparents and the law left room for interpretation.[74] But problems kept arising. How was the religion of grandparents to be established? What about people from areas annexed by Germany who could not procure an exonerating document, such as an ancestral baptismal certificate? The CGQJ pressed the courts to accept presumption of Jewishness, so that Jews whose grandparents were not born in France—against whom the commissariat had a special animus—would not escape. One lawyer even suggested in a respected legal journal that French courts should refer to German jurisprudence "objectively and broadmindedly."[75] This suggestion was not, to our knowledge, taken seriously by any French jurisdiction. The courts continued to insist upon traditional French judicial procedures, including placing the burden of proof upon the administration and the CGQJ, in criminal cases.

The great bulk of cases involved property matters—the unforeseen residue of persecution which Vichy did not dare dispose of otherwise than through the courts. The division of France into two zones caused one set of problems. In one case a Jewish lady applied to the Tribunal of the Seine, through her attorney, for release from a Paris rental agreement contracted before the Germans arrived. Having fled south during the exodus, she was prevented as a Jew by German ordinances from returning to her apartment in the Occupied Zone. The court decided against her, ruling that her obligation under the lease remained intact, even though she was not in a position to enjoy use of it.[76] Then there were questions of allegedly concealed Jewish ownership or of direction of enterprises seeking to escape aryanization. What determined whether an enterprise was "Jewish"? Other disputes involved the possessions of mixed couples. The courts were sympathetic to the appeals of non-Jewish spouses against the damages caused by aryanization, and permitted the separation of marital property in such cases.[77] Despite the regime's celebration of the family, Justice Minister Joseph Barthélemy did his best to hasten divorce proceedings where the existence of mixed couples threatened to frustrate some of the intentions of aryanization. In a circular to state prosecutors in September 1942, he reminded them of "the importance of settling these cases promptly."[78] Aryanization also caused problems for third parties. What about partnerships between Jews and non-Jews? What about the rights of creditors in the event that a Jewish enterprise was dissolved? The fact that creditors of aryanized enterprises were granted rights roughly analogous to those in bankruptcy cases did not prevent thorny issues from arising.[79]

With tribunals allowed full latitude to decide these matters, and with property rights figuring heavily in the cases brought to court, it is hardly surprising that French judicial authorities generally resisted administrative interference. According to Billig, "the courts were among the public authorities least shaped by the Vichy government's racist pressures."[80] Yet there is no doubt that the judicial system facilitated legal persecution, permitting it to go forward relatively smoothly, without the sort of administrative bullying that could only have discredited *antisémitisme d'état.*

Broadly speaking, the antisemites got what they wanted. Moreover, after 1942, Jews were in physical danger, and judicial decisions about them made less difference. By that time, moreover, one can even discern a contrary trend in judicial action, favoring the administration and building up a tough jurisprudence in support of aryanization. There may well have been a lack of conviction in 1940 when the courts first began to enforce the anti-Jewish statutes; but like the rest of the French administration, the courts seem to have become habituated to their new routine.[81]

Business as Usual

The reason for the exclusion of Jews from public positions is the same as the reason for the exclusion of naturalized citizens: defense of the interest of the public services. Since the new regime recognizes that public positions have a certain political quality alongside their technical quality, it logically requires of every civil servant not only technical capacity but a certain political suitability [*aptitude*]. They judge that Jews, like naturalized citizens, do not generally have that suitability; hence, their exclusion from public positions.

Maurice Duverger (1941)[82]

French civil servants could have no doubt that anti-Jewish policy was now part of the legal order. It is hard today not to be surprised at the routine fashion with which this new legal order was explained and applied. The rising young jurist Maurice Duverger, supporter of corporatism and, in his student days, a member of Doriot's Parti Populaire Français, was neutral, cool, and matter-of-fact as, in a 1941 article, he summarized Vichy policy toward Jews in public life. He repeated the frequent Vichy disclaimers: "The laws of 3 October 1940 and 2 June 1941 have the character not of reprisal measures but of measures of public interest." But his article was unambiguous. The new political regime in France was authoritarian, and, as such, could not live with a liberal administration. Consequently, "the first administrative reforms have tended to restore the state's authority over civil servants." At the same time, "this new regime is also deeply *national*: it is mounting a very clear reaction against the cosmopolitanism inspired by the philosophy of the eighteenth century. This national character explains notably the measures taken to exclude Jews and naturalized citizens from public functions."[83]

If Duverger had any critical views of Vichy's anti-Jewish legislation, he transmitted no signal of it to his 1941 reading public. In general, the French public administration followed the same neutral pattern of business as usual. It is the business of bureaucracies to enforce the law with an outward appearance of uniformity, and the public services of the Vichy state may well have felt even more need to reinforce state authority than in normal times. Never had the authority of the state seemed more precious than when defeat and foreign occupation had shaken it. It was not heroic to flee, argued René Bousquet, former prefect of the Marne in 1940 and later head of the Vichy police, on trial in 1949; the essential step for French revival was to restore the "armature" of the public administration.[84] The duty of each public servant to keep the wheels turning seems to have extended easily to cover the new anti-Jewish measures. We know of no public official who resigned in protest against them in 1940–41. At that time it was Vichy's own program—quotas, a purge of the professions and the administration, a reduction of the Jewish role in the economy—that was at issue; and things no doubt seemed different when Vichy's project was supplanted by the far more drastic new German project of mass deportation in summer 1942. Many civil servants who recalled a secret opposition to Vichy's antisemitism after the war may have been thinking of the later period. It is exceedingly difficult to find contemporary evidence for such claims during the first two years of the Vichy regime. In general, to all who recorded their impressions at the time, the French public administration accepted the new laws as legitimate and went about its business of enforcing them much as it would enforce any law. There was no massive repugnance toward the Vichy anti-Jewish program of 1940–41 to match the widespread evasion of the obligatory labor service in 1943 or, for that matter, the widespread criticism of the deportation proceedings of late 1942.

Having said this, one must add at once that beneath the surface impression of conformity there was a good bit of diversity in the zeal or thoroughness of that enforcement. In contrast to the Nazi war machine, the French administration was not infused with a clear anti-Jewish intention. Vichy's long-range antisemitic goals remained limited, moderated by discrimination among different kinds of Jews, and blurred by the government's care to offer exemptions and exceptions. Since Jews remained only one focus of enmity for Vichy, and were probably never the principal one, civil servants were sometimes able to go their own way, within the important limit that they not deny publicly the legitimacy of what the regime was doing.

Foreigners involved in helping Jews reported a wide variability in their everyday dealings with French official services. In December 1940, before the CGQJ had injected more sense of purpose, a Dr. M. Kahany reported to British officers in Geneva that the intent of the first *Statut des juifs* was ignored here and there, or its provisions were enforced selectively.[85] Vallat recalled in 1945 that the first statute had been applied unevenly—to civil servants but not to many others.[86] Donald Lowrie, who was active in relief work for the World Alliance of the YMCA, dealt mostly with the Ministry of the Interior. "Like other ministries in Vichy," he wrote, "this one exhibited a curious mixture of subservience to German orders and more or less secret sympathy with the Allied cause. Success in Vichy depended on the man you had to deal with, and whether or not he was willing to bear the responsibility for any decision the Nazis might not like."[87] Lowrie had witnessed a provisional revolutionary government in Moscow in the spring of 1917; and he felt in 1940, at Vichy, the same porousness of an administrative system as yet unsure of its direction and its priorities.

Even after the CGQJ had imparted more coordination and more impetus to anti-Jewish policy, there was room for individual variation at the local level. It would require a multitude of local studies to trace the exact contours of these variations, and some of them were no doubt kept prudently quiet; but there is considerable evidence even in the central archives that we have been able to see. The prefects' role was crucial for the life of Jews in France. The law of 4 October 1940, as we have seen, gave prefects an enormous discretionary power in the internment of Jews, in their assignment to forced residence, or in their enrollment in work camps. Regional prefects had some authority over the six regional directorates of the CGQJ in Limoges, Clermont-Ferrand, Lyon, Marseille, Toulouse, and Montpellier. It was the prefects' responsibility to carry out the census of Jews; they could handle some difficult questions of definition, sifting Jews from non-Jews. They issued travel passes, enabling some Jews to move about, and they could take initiatives in police investigations to uncover Jews in hiding. They had an essential role in emigration during the period when Vichy was favoring the departure of Jews. The help that HICEM received from François-Martin, prefect of the Tarn-et-Garonne,[88] for example, may merely have reflected official policy; but some prefects were helpful on their own, and some Jews who survived the war in Montauban have kind memories of him. One refugee reported that the prefecture of the Creuse assisted Jews to escape to the Italian Occupation Zone in 1943 by providing the necessary documents,[89] but this example takes us ahead into the period of deportations. The regional director of the CGQJ in Clermont-Ferrand complained frequently that the prefecture of Puy-de-Dôme ignored requests for internment of Jews.[90] On the other hand, the prefecture of the Ardèche was held up as a model for others because of its stringent police measures.[91] Pujès, prefect of the Seine-Inférieure, reported proudly to the Ministry of the Interior in October 1942 that he had not only interned a Jew and his "aryan accomplice" active in the black market but had also arrested "another Jew who came arrogantly into my office without wearing his star."[92]

A major prefectoral concern, beyond maintaining the authority of their office, was to avoid the accumulation in their department of any exceptional concentrations of errant refugees. Monique Luirard gives this account of Jews being chased from one department to another:

> [A Jew] sometimes wound up in the Loire Department after having been expelled by prefectoral order from other departments, for periodically local authorities expelled surplus individuals from the colonies that formed by chance. Thus the prefect of Périgueux several times sent north of the Loire the Jews for whose upkeep the sub-prefect of Roanne did not want to be responsible. In January 1941 the regional prefect of Lyon decided that his city had been invaded by Jews from everywhere and that the food supply of the people of Lyon was threatened by this more or less parasitic population. So he decided to disperse 3,100 of them among the departments under his jurisdiction. The Loire received about a hundred of them that way.[93]

These games of refugee tennis, a continuation of the practices of the 1930s raised to new urgency by wartime scarcities, point up how the treatment a Jew received in one particular prefecture often depended upon timing, his financial circumstances, and sheer luck. The sufferings of the uprooted—whether refugees or French Jews expelled from jobs or businesses—were made all the greater by such uncertainties.

At one more remove from the center, the mayors and police departments in the thirty-eight thousand communes of France also had an important role in the enforcement of the anti-Jewish laws. This was the period when the traditional village mayor, often a farmer who devoted a few hours a week to his official charge, became obsolete: the avalanche of government instructions concerning rationing, food deliveries, labor service, and all the other wartime obligations forced even small communes to engage some full-time help. The anti-Jewish measures added their burden to local government. Local authorities were supposed to know at all times where Jews were living. A ministerial circular of 18 April 1942 required elaborate reporting procedures for Jews entering and leaving communes; a law of 9 November 1942 forbade foreign Jews to leave the commune where they lived without special documents issued by the police.[94] Since 30 May 1941, all Jews had been required to report any change of address, even when moving within a commune. In addition local governments were supposed to keep an eye on aryanization and the elimination of Jews from certain professions. They could propose heavy sanctions for any violation of the antisemitic laws, although it belonged to the prefectures to impose the penalties. Jews became somewhat easier to trace when the law of 11 December 1942 required the word *Juif* to appear on all identity cards and individual ration cards, but this requirement, in turn, imposed a new round of chores. In 1943 the CGQJ produced a small booklet on the anti-Jewish laws, designed to assist local authorities in what had become a nearly overwhelming task of regimentation, information, and exclusion.[95]

At this local level, too, there was inevitably a variety of ways to apply the law. Here and there Jews received support, even in the period before the roundups of 1942 changed opinion. Raoul Laporterie, mayor of the small town of Bascons (Landes department) helped several hundred Jews escape to the Unoccupied Zone in 1940–41.[96] Other mayors took advantage of their access to baptismal records to help conceal or protect Jews. In the summer of 1942, to the chagrin of the CGQJ, some mayors even presumed to issue *certificats de non-appartenance à la race juive"* (see pages 93–94), for which both Vallat and Darquier claimed exclusive competence. The most celebrated case was the Protestant village of Chambon-sur-Lignon,[97] though its sheltering of Jewish refugees belongs more properly to the period of deportations; it was far from being the only case at that later date. By contrast, other localities were consistently inhospitable. After February 1943, when French workers were being conscripted for work in Germany, some communes found a new use for antisemitism. In the Corrèze, foreign Jews were seized illegally by authorities on the lookout for workers. Jews were obviously vulnerable targets, and they may have relieved some communes with quotas to fill.[98]

One of the few institutions capable of taking an independent course was the French parliament, even in its dormant state since voting all power to Marshal Pétain in July 1940. Here the strategy of two opponents of Vichy was to force Marshal Pétain to take personal responsibility for the purge. Toward the end of 1940, Jules Jeanneney and Edouard Herriot—presidents of the Senate and the Chamber of Deputies, respectively—had declined to cooperate in the task the government wished to impose on them. Treating the parliamentarians like civil servants and Jeanneney and Herriot like so many administrative subordinates, the government had expected them to name and identify the Jews among the senators and deputies. In a letter of 23 January 1941, Marshal Pétain himself asked these leaders to find the names of all Jewish parliamentarians and report them promptly. The deadlock was finally settled in a personal meeting at the Hôtel du Parc on 27 January. Pétain, solemn and courteous before the redoubtable political veterans, had no choice but to take upon himself the identification of Jewish parliamentarians. Jeanneney and Herriot had not questioned the law's validity (although Jeanneney disputed its justice), but they considered it a major victory to have forced Pétain to take the onus of applying it. Three days later Jeanneney wrote to all senators in both zones: "If you are affected by the *Statut des juifs*, please be so kind as to declare that fact to the Chief of State." Ultimately, six Jewish senators and twelve deputies were relieved of their electoral mandates.[99]

This example shows not only how limited were the modes of resistance which the two distinguished veterans of the Third Republic considered available in their genuine opposition to the proscription of Jews, but also how vulnerable public officials were, whether elected or appointed, no matter how high the rank. "I disapprove of the Jewish statute," Jeanenney recalled having told Pétain, "for all the ways in which it is contrary to justice, to respect for the human person, and to French tradition, as well as because the Germans imposed it on you. But it is the law. It must be obeyed."[100]*

In Jeanneney's last phrase lies the heart of the matter. At least up

---

*He continued: "It is not the law I am resisting, but an order that you do not have the right to give me."[101]

to the major change in 1942 with the beginnings of massive deportations
to the East, the anti-Jewish program was French law, and the weight
of administrative traditions and sanctions lay on the side of conformity.
Several factors gave conformity the upper hand. A law of 17 July 1940[102]
enabled the government to remove from office all officials deemed
unsuitable for the new regime; and subsequent provisions empowered
the minister of the interior to replace elected communal governments
with appointed officials. Although the government moved cautiously in
removing mayors, and many more resigned for overwork and doubt
than were dismissed, the regime clearly had the means to punish any
official who disobeyed it. Moreover, there was considerable peer pressure not to show disunity at a time of national peril. During the first two
years, there was no knowledge of the more drastic project brewing in
Hitler's inner circle, and of the ways in which the more modest Vichy
project could facilitate it. Sheer bureaucratic inertia also played a role.
The state had spoken, the law was the law; and traditional bureaucratic
routine was on the side of enforcement.

Inertia was also on the side of maintaining government functions
in activity, even if they might endanger Jews. It was unthinkable in
1940–41 to close down a government agency. In the Paris Prefecture of
Police, for example, the Bureau of Foreigners had been active since
1937, keeping tabs on suspicious foreigners and refugees. When they
reached Paris, the Germans seized its files, the police having failed to
keep them out of Nazi hands. It was obvious that the Germans meant
to use the data to hunt down their own enemies. Rather than disband
the office, which in any event had been utterly swamped by the press
of refugees since 1939, Prefect of Police Roger Langeron, an anti-Nazi,
attempted to put it back on its feet—a move that could only serve the
cause of the occupation. At the beginning of 1941, Langeron even ordered a census of foreigners in the department of the Seine![103]*

Senior officials also persuaded themselves not to resign, confident
perhaps that they could defend things more effectively by subtle devia-
tions than by outright opposition. As Education Minister Jérôme Carcopino reasoned:

> If all the public officials who, in the name of educational freedom
> or of their legal conceptions, had quit, who would have softened or
> deflected the blows in their stead? I stayed at my place and said
> nothing. If I had risen up against the law in proud and vain words,

---

*Similarly, the Ministry of Foreign Affairs had a Stateless Persons Office which occa-
sionally looked into the "Jewish quality" of some individuals.[104]

I would have revealed my intentions to the occupying authorities and paralyzed my action. I thought it was more useful to buckle down to the task.[105]

By his own account, Carcopino kept finding reasons to obey the letter of the law and administer it with dispatch. As rector of the Academy of Paris in 1940, he assembled dossiers on Jewish teachers and sent them speedily to Vichy—"all the more quickly, I thought, could the various safeguard clauses of the law enter into play," such as pensions, early retirement, and the like. He avoided any public gesture of protest and tried to dissuade a close colleague, Gustave Monod, from doing so, by arguing that such efforts would be sterile and could vitiate his opportunity to render kindness to someone in trouble. Carcopino took great care to limit to two occasions a petition on behalf of Jews who had rendered "exceptional services" (article 8 of the *Statut des juifs* of 1940) lest he wear out his credit with the Conseil d'Etat, the final judge in such matters.[106] Carcopino was no hard-core antisemite, and he may even have helped a few Jews; but he rationed his influence with such parsimony, and submitted so easily to what he later called "cruel necessity," that the result was faithful service to the regime and its laws. This pattern was followed by armies of civil servants, many of whom comforted themselves with the same reflection and accomplished equally little for Jews in great trouble.

Some went along with persecution in a misguided effort to protect their own agency. Thus, Paul Jourdain, vice-president of the Senate in 1942, opposed even legal reintegration of a deposed Jewish employee, in order to spare the senate the risk of being placed "in an unfavorable position in the eyes of the government and public opinion."[107] There were courageous gestures on behalf of individuals, as in the case of Professor Robert Debré who was strongly supported by his medical colleagues in Paris in 1940. But support came easier for distinguished doctors or those with long records of public service than for humble civil servants. Following a close reading of the law, Jules Jeanneney felt powerless to assist a typist at the Senate Secretariat, despite an opinion (erroneous, as it turned out) from the head of the Status of Persons branch of the CGQJ, Jacques Ditte, that he had the authority to do so.[108]* In time, of course, all interventions became extremely risky, no

*Intervention on behalf of persons in trouble with the *Statut des juifs* sometimes seemed to have more to do with political opinions in the 1930s than with "the fact of being Jewish." Cf. the letter from an official of the Ministry of the Interior to the CGQJ, 9 January 1942, assuring the CGQJ that one Fels, who claimed to be Catholic but lacked the papers to prove it, could be helped because he "was never pro-Popular Front."[109]

matter who was involved; and the extreme prudence of Carcopino and others had gone to waste. They had accomplished little at a time when even mild obstruction might have been productive, and set a pattern of compliance which later proved essential to the Nazi war effort. The German occupation authorities reported repeatedly to Berlin that they had insufficient personnel to apply their policies toward Jews without the help of the French administration.[110] The compliance of that administration, in the end, made things much worse for the Jews.

And so an ever-widening circle of public and private agencies were drawn into working with Vichy's antisemitic policy. Military units were requested to provide extensive information on former Jewish soldiers, whose service records might be relevant to the application of the *Statut des juifs*.[111] The Ministry of the Interior tried to get the hotelkeepers' association to refuse Jews as hotel guests.[112] Curious new private enterprises sprang up to help serve official antisemitism. French doctors were called upon to certify that a man had not been circumcised.[113] The Vichy anti-Jewish program, given legitimacy by what was most learned and devoted in the French public service, spread out through French life like ripples from a stone thrown into a pond.

Aryanization

Given the delicacy of the Jewish Question in France, it is important to keep personal considerations or commercial rivalries from becoming involved with the measures taken concerning the Israelites. We would have good reason to fear such [conflicts of interest] if the elimination of Israelites from the professions that they encumber were carried out on the initiative of former colleagues or rivals.

Xavier Vallat (spring 1942)[114]

Greed has been unleashed.

Xavier Vallat (spring 1942)[115]

None of Vichy's anti-Jewish enterprises reached more widely into public life than the project to "eliminate all Jewish influence from the national economy."[116] The law of 22 July 1941 was no empty gesture. Without ever quite matching the hyperbole of its opening lines, the CGQJ acted vigorously to place Jewish property in the Unoccupied Zone under trustees, or *administrateurs provisoires,* as soon as the law allowed. Vallat wanted to prove to the Germans that he could organize as effective an economic purge as they could; he was determined to block the extension of the competence of the Occupied Zone's *adminis-trateurs provisoires* into the economy of the southern zone; and he was genuinely worried by the flow of Jewish wealth and economic power to the south. Of a total of 7,400 *administrateurs provisoires* named to Jewish enterprises for all of France throughout the war, 1,343 (18 percent) were in the Unoccupied Zone.[117]* Since Jewish property had been heavily concentrated before the war in what was to be the Occupied Zone, and particularly in the Paris basin, 18 percent may not be far from the actual distribution of property. At any rate this figure gives us no reason to conclude that aryanization was half-hearted in the area under Vichy's sole authority.

The *administrateurs provisoires* were supposed not only to take full charge of the Jewish enterprises over which they had been placed, but to transfer them to "aryan" owners. If the enterprises added nothing to the French economy, they were to be liquidated, and the assets auctioned off. If they were important to the economy, they were to be sold to new owners who would continue to operate them. By 1 May 1944, 42,227 Jewish enterprises had been placed in trusteeship. Of these, 9,680 had been sold to "aryans" (including 1,708 apartment buildings, 4,869 commercial enterprises, and 1,930 artisan establishments), and 7,340 had been "liquidated"—that is, put out of business by the trustee.[119] During the year 1943 alone, over 200,000,000 francs realized by these sales and liquidations were deposited in the blocked accounts numbered 501 and 511 which the Caisse des Dépôts et des Consignations kept very carefully for the CGQJ.[120]† The share of the Unoccupied Zone in this spoliation was 1,954 properties aryanized (554 by sale, 421 by liquidation, and 979 by unspecified procedures); and, on 29 February 1944, another 2,991 dossiers were still being studied in the Unoccupied Zone. There is no trace of leniency in the CGQJ's files: only 73 of these Jewish enterprises were exempted from the law as being too small to notice, and only 53 "because of military service."[122] Again, the fact that the properties involved were far less numerous than in the Occupied Zone reflected the actual distribution of Jewish property. This was not as large a forced sale of property as that imposed on church lands in the 1790s, nor as extensive an inventory as that imposed on church property

---

*As of 1 May 1944, 825 out of 5,522, or 15 percent, were in the formerly Unoccupied Zone.[118]

†The dossier "Caisse des Dépôts et des Consignations" contains monthly statements for accounts 501 and 511 for the year 1943. About 20,000 Jewish accounts were held there, totaling approximately 3 billion francs in total deposits.[121]

in 1905; but there is nothing else to compare with it in recent French history.

A transfer of property on this scale inevitably sent shock waves throughout the economy. Every line of business faced potential changes in the concentration of firms and in competitive positions. Every profession involved in business transactions found itself drawn willy-nilly into decisions involving Jewish property, for which there was no traditional jurisprudence. Bankers, insurance agents, and notaries labored over complex problems for Jewish and non-Jewish clients—the payment of money owed to Jews and owed by them, complicated frequently by the Demarcation Line, non-Jewish spouses, companies of mixed ownership and direction, Jews trapped in one zone with property in another, and the disappearance of Jews who were in hiding or internment or were victims of deportation. The simple payment of a month's rent could spin an impenetrable tangle of blocked accounts, contractual arrangements between spouses or partners, and squabbles over the limits of a trustee's powers. Bankers, insurance agents, and notaries turned to their national associations; and these, in turn, asked the CGQJ for clarification and guidance.

Roger Lehideux, president of the national bankers association, corresponded frequently with Vallat in an effort to resolve such difficulties. Lehideux found that settling on procedures for the banks' transactions with Jewish clients took time, effort, and tact, not only because mail had to pass German controls at the Demarcation Line, but because all communications between the CGQJ and banks had to have the concurrence of the Ministry of Finance, and transfers of currency within the Occupied Zone had to have the authorization of the German occupation authority's foreign exchange control service.[123] Insurance payments were complicated by the German requirement in the Occupied Zone that they be paid exclusively into blocked accounts. This German rule applied to payments due to Jews now in the Unoccupied Zone on insurance policies initially opened in the Occupied Zone; and as a result, when Vallat left office at the end of March 1942, the CGQJ was in the process of giving these arrangements "juridical weight from the standpoint of French jurisprudence by means of a French law establishing analogous arrangements."[124] The association of French exporters of Indochina, in Marseille, asked about commissions owed to Jewish brokers and were instructed that the commissions should be paid only to the *administrateur provisoire* of the brokerage house.[125] The net of aryanization kept widening, and more and more ordinary business and professional people were drawn into it by the feelings that life must go on, that they must try to obey a novel and confusing law, and that these new arrangements were probably permanent.

Aryanization called into play at least five competing interests. The first was Vallat himself, who had a zealot's conviction that he was serving France. He gained not a franc out of the whole operation. He took steps to have an independent auditor—a Commissaire aux Comptes— assigned to each aryanized business, and attempted to establish the practice of receiving multiple sealed bids for each sale of Jewish property. Running the vast aryanization bureaucracy proved to be more than the administratively inexperienced commissioner-general could manage, however. Nonetheless, he drove the machine forward, hoping eventually to win the confidence of the German occupation authorities and to secure the withdrawal of all German control over Jewish property matters. We know from the estimates that Vallat gave the *Militär-befehlshaber* staff that he envisaged a purely French program that would leave a remnant of exempt French Jews (mostly war veterans) numbering perhaps two thousand heads of families as managers of firms and three thousand heads of families in the artisan trades,[126] but leaving none in decisive sectors like banking or in the limited liability corporations that he hated.

Next came a complex of German interests. Individual German entrepreneurs hoped to acquire important French holdings, though the MBF tried with varying success to restrain them. The main MBF interest was continued French economic production for the German war effort, with a minimum of disturbance. The main MBF aryanization official, however, Dr. Blanke, wanted to retain full control over the aryanization process in the Occupied Zone. Moreover, he kept trying to extend German influence south of the Demarcation Line. Vallat managed only with some difficulty to retain separate *administrateurs provisoires* for those parts of Jewish property situated in the Unoccupied Zone.[127]

A third set of pressures came from Vallat's ministerial colleagues and some of the prestigious public agencies. Insofar as aryanization had already been launched in the Occupied Zone by the Germans in the fall of 1940, the economics ministries wanted to retain the role they had established there in this process from the beginning. They shared that role with Vallat only grudgingly. Bichelonne felt that Vallat threatened to compromise French economic interests in the Occupied Zone by ruining some healthy firms; he even carried his complaints to German authorities.[128] René Bousquet, head of the French police, quarreled with Vallat's office over certain transfers of landed property involving

Jews, a dispute that extended from December 1941 until the summer of 1942, when more pressing issues took over.[129] Darlan warned Vallat about "the risk of fraud and scandalous exploitation whose political consequences could not be extinguished even by eventually singling you out for responsibility."[130] Later Darlan was outraged when the confiscation of property turned, as it was inevitably supposed to turn, to well-established assimilated French Jews. Ministers tended to blame the CGQJ for a program that they themselves had endorsed. By 1943, Pierre Laval had serious plans to remove aryanization entirely from the CGQJ and lodge it in the state's Property Management Office (Administration des Domaines) or in the Ministry of Industrial Production. By then, however, Vichy's leverage in these matters had been lost, and the necessary German endorsement of the scheme never came.[131]

The fourth group of interests was the *administrateurs provisoires* themselves. Vallat admitted in public that aryanization had produced an "unleashing of greed." That was putting it mildly. When an *administrateur provisoire* was appointed to the publishing house of Calmann-Lévy, for example, the Paris police soon discovered that the individual concerned, Gaston Capy, had served two terms of imprisonment as a convicted burglar and pimp.[132] At times several trustees claimed legal authority over the same enterprise, setting German authority against French to prove their legitimacy. Some trustees accumulated impressive strings of Jewish enterprises to manage. No doubt the most blue-blooded was Ambroise Désiré Guy Augustin de Montovert de la Tour, "scion of an ancient and authentically French family, Catholic and aryan, from the beginning," as he declared in a letter protesting his innocence. He claimed also to be a reserve officer and both a correspondent for and member of the administration of the *Osservatore Romano*. He had no less than seventy-six letters of authorization to administer Jewish enterprises.[133]

It would perhaps be best to base our assessment of the *administrateurs provisoires* upon the views of French senior civil servants in a position to know, and resist the temptation of mere rumors, however diverting. On 8 May 1942, the man who was directly responsible for their work, Bralley, director of the Service de Contrôle des Administrateurs Provisoires (SCAP), took a pessimistic view of their selection:

> In effect, some have been named by the Prefecture of Police, others by the German authorities, still others by the SCAP, under time pressures that prevented sufficient selection. Only since several months ago have police files been asked for, and some immediate

replacements will have to be made. It is nonetheless true that [*administrateurs provisoires*] who do not present the necessary guarantees are very numerous: the timid ones who do not dare do anything without asking for instructions; the clumsy ones who take unfortunate steps; the negligent ones who carry out their duties only irregularly; the unconscientious ones who let things slide; the unscrupulous ones who enter into collusion with the Jews or with the purchasers."[134]

Near the end, in May 1944, Louis-Gabriel Formery, inspector of finances and a man of scrupulous integrity, was asked to scrutinize the CGQJ. He was shocked by "the innumerable and incredible abuses carried on, and still carried on, by a good many *administrateurs provisoires* of Jewish property." Some, he found, were honest; but the majority were not: "a very large proportion are defrauders [*concussionaires*]." It is soon apparent to a reader of Formery's reports that, as a conscientious civil servant, he wanted to make aryanization work better, not to obstruct it. He was full of suggestions for turning it over to the traditional financial agencies that would do an honest job. Moreover, among his *concussionnaires* are clearly included those who, with a mixture of heroism and guile that can never be unraveled, had entered into secret compacts with Jewish proprietors to camouflage a false aryanization.[135] During the same spring of 1944, a report by the civil servant Paul Houël indicated that 271 *administrateurs provisoires* had been revoked since December 1942 for having "betrayed" the commissariat.[136] This figure, too, includes those who tried to cover and conceal Jewish property as well as those who defrauded the Jews and the state. There will be no way to get to the bottom of this murky business, and it is perhaps best left at that.

The fifth and last competing interest in aryanization was the *comités d'organisation* (CO), the semi-public corporatist associations that grouped each trade, profession, and branch of industry in order to regulate the economy. It has been shown that these associations were run, for the most part, by the same interests—and often by the same individuals—who had run the various business and professional associations before the war.[137] The leaders of the *comités d'organisation*, not unnaturally, took an intense interest in any development that could alter fundamentally the degree of concentration in their line of work and thus redistribute shares of the market. Which among their competitors would acquire the shops or factories stripped from Jewish owners? Should the former Jewish enterprises be put out of business and liquidated rather than sold? Should a *comité d'organisation* seize the occasion to rationalize its branch of the economy or to reduce the total number of enterprises active in that branch? The *comités d'organisation*, and the business and professional leaders for whom they spoke, wanted to have a major role in deciding the answers to such questions.

Some *comités d'organisation* played active roles in aryanization, though their roles were never as autonomous as they wished, nor clearly defined in a legal text. From the beginning, the Ministry of Industrial Production consulted these associations about whom to name as *administrateurs provisoires*. In some instances, they tried to place their own members in these posts. The *comités* objected when an *administrateur provisoire* "unknown in our business" was named, but the CGQJ preferred "not to have competitors as *administrateurs provisoires.*"[138] Once, seizing the occasion offered by a request for advice from the SCAP, the National Furniture Group circularized its local branches asking for the names of Jewish enterprises in the Unoccupied Zone, but was soon called to order by the CGQJ.[139] Beyond the mere choice of *administrateurs provisoires,* the *comités d'organisation* wanted to have their say in the decisions subsequently taken about whether to close down an erstwhile Jewish enterprise or sell it to a new "aryan" owner. They lobbied actively with the commissariat and with the Ministry of Industrial Production to have things done their way.

In these instances anti-Jewish measures became a vehicle for the expression of broader economic concerns. With a decade of depression behind them and no alleviation in sight under the occupation, many French businessmen were preoccupied by what they diagnosed as a long-term overcapacity and overcrowding in their fields of activity. In the opinion of many, there had long been too many enterprises producing and selling in the French economy. In the immediate short term, moreover, "the shortage of goods to sell imposes . . . severe restrictive measures to contract our sales network: stocks must be concentrated, enterprises no longer needed must be eliminated." The retail merchants' *comité d'organisation* drew the conclusion that the necessary cleansing of the market could most conveniently be applied to Jewish enterprises. "So it seems to us logical to apply these measures [of elimination] very strictly to enterprises whose suppression could be easily obtained by applying laws already on the books. . . . Every Israelite enterprise that does not fill a demonstrated need for consumers should be liquidated." After conceding that certain "houses of long-established reputation or occupying an important role in foreign trade" should be preserved, and that liquidation of an enterprise should be avoided in cases where creditors would suffer heavy losses, the CO for Commerce concluded that "in our opinion liquidation of Jewish enterprises should be the rule, sale the exception."[140]

Aryanization opened the way for settlement of many old economic scores. A group of independent electric-light-bulb makers wanted to make sure that Jewish light-bulb works were sold to French independents and not to the prewar consortium, which they accused of being a mere French front for Dutch, British, and American electric light interests.[141] Small furniture makers sought revenge against the giant retail furniture chains, especially Levitan and the Galéries Barbès, for the "pushy methods" practiced by this "trade carried on by outsiders [to furniture making]" and "directed by Israelites." They urged Vallat in January 1942 to place the branches of Jewish furniture sellers in the Unoccupied Zone under *administration provisoire*, "as already done with the branches of the Galéries Barbès."[142]* Independent clothing retailers complained that large Lyonnais textile manufacturers were seizing the opportunity to acquire direct retail outlets from Jews and thus to integrate their operations vertically. The small retailers perceived this as "a veritable offensive by the trusts. . . . Was the decree forcing the Jews to sell their shops passed to favor the manufacturers at the expense of the retailers?"[144] Although we cannot get to the bottom of all these allegations, it seems evident that aryanization promoted the concentration of business in France.

The *comités d'organisation* were not all equally active in aryanization, for obvious reasons. COs in heavy industry had less occasion to be, although the CO of the automobile industry seems to have set up a *bureau de questions juives*.[145] The COs in crafts and trades with a large Jewish participation before the war had the most at stake and the greatest opportunity to reshape their competitive positions. The CO of the fur business, which had been 80 percent Jewish before the war, wanted the Jewish enterprises liquidated rather than sold to "outsiders." There ensued quarrels over the redistribution of the closed furriers' stocks. Since the leaders of the CO were also prominent in the branch of the Ministry of Industrial Production that allocated raw materials, other furriers complained that the privileged ones were getting the best of the irreplaceable North American and Russian furs. It was "immoral," they said, to sell off their stocks to one bidder when all dealers faced shortages.[146] The leather industry's CO set up a new corporation—SIFIC (Industrial and Financial Corporation for the

---

*Bichelonne agreed to the dissolution of the Galéries Barbès in February 1942, an uncharacteristic move by this technocrat and partisan of concentration.[143]

Leather Industry), financed jointly by the CO and the Banque de Paris et des Pays-Bas—to absorb Jewish shoe manufacturers and makers of leather goods. The aim was to rationalize an industry that had been, in their view, overly fragmented before the war.[147] The CO des Industries et Métiers d'Art (the CO for luxury hand-made goods) advised the remaining diamond merchants to form a cooperative to take charge of the stocks of the 70–80 percent of their trade that was Jewish and to sell them under supervision of the CO.[148]

It seems evident that the economic and professional purge carried further when there was an organized corporate interest to pursue the matter. *Comités d'organisation* in trades and businesses that had suffered severely during the 1930s from the inroads of chains or from intense competition, or where Jewish entrepreneurs had played a conspicuous role, gave a strong impetus to aryanization. So did professional organizations. The new doctors' association, the Ordre des Médecins— providing at long last an organized voice for the profession that had been most resentful of refugee interlopers in the 1930s,—took charge of deciding which Jewish doctors might receive exemptions and which should not. The bar performed the same function for lawyers. The Paris bar, for example, proposed twelve làwyers for exemption from the *Statut des juifs*, although a subsequent dispute between Vallat and Barthélemy prevented any action from being taken on special exemptions for lawyers[149] (as distinct from those already exempted because of veterans' status or being related to war dead). The bars seem to have been somewhat more lenient in this matter than the Ordre des Médecins, but both groups worked within the system and thus helped to legitimize the very principle of the purge.

Economic interest sometimes cut the other way. The hotel keepers of the Côte d'Azur wanted the business of the wealthy Jews whom the prefect wanted to intern, and so did the casino operators.[150] The leather-goods manufacturers wanted skilled Jewish cutters and shapers, though they did not want Jewish competitors.[151] The Limoges regional office of the clock industry's CO wanted to have some Jewish watchmakers released from the camps, as their skills were needed. Darquier refused, for he thought that French artisans should get the work "for the advantage of the community." The CO official then felt obliged to assure Darquier that "I am an old antisemite," but that it took a long time to train a watchmaker, and that demand was twenty to one for every French watchmaker available. Such was the climate of the times.[152]

Emigration

> The French population would prefer to see these foreigners leave our soil for good.
>
> Prefect of the Tarn-et-Garonne (May 1941)[153]

Compared with aryanization, Jewish emigration was a matter of comparative secrecy—a secrecy of uninterest, for the most part. The Jews involved were almost entirely foreign. No organized French interests gave an impulsion to policy. Matters were left to a few sections of the French bureaucracy that worked in relative autonomy. Incoherence of policy, an air of routine, and no little hostility and contempt for foreign Jews ingrained since the refugee crisis of the 1930s produced a tragic tangle of obstruction.

One might have anticipated a significant effort on Vichy's part to help a maximum number of Jews emigrate. Having ensured that so many of them could not earn a living, and having complained so bitterly that they were parasites, there seemed little alternative. Darlan, Vallat, and high police figures declared that Jewish emigration was their goal.[154] In practice, however, the fact that Vichy left essential steps in the emigration process up to many ill-coordinated agencies, each of which practiced business as usual, proved a real hindrance.

As in other areas, Vichy built upon the precedents of the previous regime. After the outbreak of war in 1939 it became even more difficult for refugees to leave France. Republican officials worried about young men escaping military service, and they had become habituated during the 1930s to regarding foreigners as potential subversives.[155] The police had to be satisfied with a formidable array of documents, as did the Army and special services dealing with foreigners. Given severe shortages of shipping and additional French restrictions (emigrants could leave only through French ports, in French or British ships), not to mention the difficulty of obtaining an entry visa from the United States or another potential country of settlement, few foreign Jews were able to escape.[156]

Things became even worse immediately after the armistice. At the beginning, all requests for exit visas went directly to Vichy, where the administration was not yet fully organized, and then on to the Armistice Commission at Wiesbaden for German approval. According to the American relief worker Varian Fry, once an application set out on this route, it was never heard of again.[157] When Vichy finally obtained full authority over this field, it set up a bureaucratic maze that frustrated its own stated policy. It was difficult enough for most emigrants to get the rare and cherished entry visa to another country, to raise the money for an overseas voyage (about $500 US at the time), and somehow to find a berth on the few ocean-going vessels taking passengers in wartime. In late 1941 there were reckoned to be only about a score of ships available for such traffic anywhere. Vichy's formalities presented an obstacle at least as formidable as the others.[158]

Relief workers helping Jews in the Unoccupied Zone, coordinated by a body known as the Nîmes Committee, outlined, in October 1941, the procedure for Jews wishing to emigrate.[159] Since emigrants usually embarked in Lisbon, they had to obtain, in addition to an entry visa for the country of destination, a Portuguese transit visa, a Spanish transit visa, and a French exit visa. In order to secure the latter, the would-be emigrant applied to the prefecture in the department where he lived. Sometimes the prefecture demanded a certificate of good behavior, which sent the applicant to the commissariat of police. The dollars necessary for tickets had also to be sought through the Bank of France. Further arrangements had to be made for the voyage across Spain and Portugal.

For Jews interned in concentration camps or work battalions, these formalities could not be concluded unless one were released (which was extremely difficult) or transferred to the transit camp at Les Milles. For those outside camps, passes were required for the travel needed to obtain all the papers. Here was another problem: all of these documents, including the passes, were issued for short periods of time. When a document expired before all were in order, it had to be renewed, or the whole chase had be resumed from the start.

Some Jews escaped via the French colonies. To take this route, they had to request a colonial safe-conduct from a special office in the Ministry of Colonies, transit visas from the colony concerned, and then line these up with all the other papers.

Finally, when all was in order, would-be emigrants had to apply to the Prefecture of the Bouches-du-Rhône, designated by the Ministry of the Interior as responsible for allocating places on ships. Of course, there were ways out of France other than through Spain and Portugal or the colonies. One direct route of exit went through Shanghai. By way of example, the Nîmes Committee summarized the French documents necessary to emigrate via Shanghai:

1. permit to disembark at Shanghai
2. traveling papers or national passport
3. French exit visa
4. travel pass of the Ministry of Colonies
5. transit visa for Indochina
6. registration of the dossier at the prefecture of the Department of the Bouches-du-Rhône, or at the military service department of the Ministry of Colonies
7. letter from the prefecture or the Ministry of Colonies authorizing the steamship company to deliver a space on the emigrant's boat.

Officials could hold up the quest for documents at any point along the line. Since so many foreign Jews were either stateless or came from countries considered belligerents, the local prefectures could not issue exit visas without consulting the Ministry of the Interior at Vichy. Since the Ministry of Colonies was situated in Clermont-Ferrand, the transit of dossiers back and forth slowed things down further. One could get to the last stage of the process only to find that places on a ship had been allocated to another ministry. And so it went.

Here was an arrangement tailor-made for bureaucratic obstruction and for the fullest indulgence of antisemitic impulses or tyrannical dispositions. Some highly placed Vichy officials tried to help Jews depart. André-Jean Faure, the prefect placed in change of inspecting the concentration camps, attended meetings of the Nîmes Committee. More than once the Nîmes Committee acknowledged official support. Some prefects and camp commanders cooperated usefully. The government authorized HICEM to act as a semi-official emigration agency, and the Ministry of Finance eventually facilitated currency exchanges. The Nîmes Committee could even offer

> praise for the comprehension, the humane sentiment, and the benevolence of the authorities who are *now* facilitating our task by permitting us to act more surely and more rapidly. This last possibility is particularly precious, for the success or failure of a departure often depends under current conditions on the speed with which a decision can be made.[160] [Italics added]

Are these phrases to be read as proof of bureaucratic good will, or rather as the Nîmes Committee's efforts to fan a few sparks of sympathy into a full blaze? In any event, the system proved too heavy to be moved. New instructions designed to ease contacts among government agencies never caught up with the old. Certain camps would not release Jews until they had visas, while in order to obtain visas they had to appear in person at a consulate. Prefectures differed with commissariats of police and with each other over the issuing of some documents. The Prefecture of the Bouches-du-Rhône, a key element in the process, jealously fought against receiving too many Jews in Marseille who, with incomplete dossiers, had been drawn there by a vague hope of embarcation. As long as emigration remained legal, HICEM representatives kept urging the government to find ways to speed up the process.

By late 1942, when German pressures put an end to legal departures, the cost of Vichy's obstruction was painfully evident. Far fewer Jews left France than could obtain entry visas elsewhere. According to HICEM, three thousand persons could have emigrated during the first half of 1942 instead of two thousand. And without the work of HICEM, there would have been barely a few hundred departures.[161] No one at Vichy with sufficient authority took the matter in hand. No one cut through the red tape. Except for a few, Jews were not permitted to exit through Casablanca after transit through Algeria and Morocco, although this route would have made it unnecessary to get to Lisbon (ships sailing from Lisbon stopped in Casablanca).[162] Individual cases of good will were overwhelmed by bureaucratic inertia.

There seems to have been no special reason for this failure of Vichy to bring procedures into line with its stated policy on encouraging emigration. The weight of bureaucratic structure, the atmosphere of business as usual, and an unwillingness on the highest level to expend energy on Jews' behalf took their toll. The inclination after 1940 was for each agency to reinforce its own authority and the authority of the state. Wartime measures added many layers of control. The loud and clear message from Vichy, as indeed from the last days of the Third Republic, was to consider foreigners, and especially Jews, as suspect. No one gave Jewish emigration a high enough priority to bother about contradictions between policy and application or to assess the cost in human terms. The Jews who wanted to leave France would have to manage as best they could.

The Camps

Now foreigners have to leave the coastal departments. They [my fiancée's family] obeyed this order. But no department is obliged to receive them. They have now been on the road for two weeks. Everywhere the same answer: impossible to receive foreigners. But they can't just evaporate. And I am afraid that at the end of these wanderings the camp awaits them.

Simon Hertz (4 January 1942)*

The camp! An immense sewer, where twenty thousand persons live pell-mell, aristocrats, intellectuals, scientists, dubious characters . . . My friend, Dr. Christensen, terribly diminished physically and morally . . . I came away sickened and ashamed at the same time.

A. Plédel (27 February 1941)†

. . . I refused to visit the camps, for I didn't want my presence there to be interpreted by the internees as a sign of acquiescence to measures that were solely the fault of the invader.

Xavier Vallat (1957)[165]

Camps de concentration—this was the term often used by French officials, beginning with Interior Minister Albert Sarraut in 1939—contributed one of the darkest chapters in Vichy policy toward the Jews,[166] and were responsible for several thousand deaths in France—mostly of Jews, but also of gypsies and other political prisoners such as veterans of the international brigades in Spain. This part of the anti-Jewish system involved few ordinary French citizens and, indeed, only a narrow sector of the French administration. But it was one in which a combination of scarcity and callousness produced horrors and suffering to a degree that shocked French and foreign opinion when the truth began to leak out at the end of 1940.

At the end of September 1940, immediately after the débâcle, there were no less than thirty-one camps in the southern zone. This is the total that was reported to the Kundt Commission, which was authorized by article 19 of the Franco-German armistice to visit French camps and extract prisoners whom the Germans wanted. This total includes a few small, temporary camps, some with only a handful of prisoners.[167] The major centers were Rivesaltes (Pyrénées-Orientales), with almost six thousand internees at the end of 1941; the disciplinary camp of Le Vernet (Ariège); the women's camp of Rieucros (Lozère); the very large

*Simon Hertz to Dr. Bernard Ménétrel, 4 January 1942, asking for help in obtaining exit visas for the parents of his fiancée.[163]
†Paris pharmacist A. Plédel to M. Allix, 27 February 1941, reporting on a visit to a German doctor friend imprisoned in Gurs.[164]

camp at Argelès (Pyrénées-Orientales), with a population of fifteen thousand near the end of 1940—mainly Spanish refugees; Les Milles, near Aix-en-Provence, a transit center for those expecting to emigrate; Gurs (Basses-Pyrénées) which received the thousands of Jewish deportees from Germany; the camp of sick and old people of Noé (Haute-Garonne); and the nearby center of Récébédou, just south of Toulouse. And there were others.[168] Internees were also to be found in ten hospitals and sixteen prisons in Unoccupied France.

For the northern zone, one is less certain. Joseph Weill, a physician doing his best to alleviate conditions of internment in what he called *l'Anti-France,* reported some fifteen camps soon after the armistice in the Occupied Zone.[169] A number of these were soon closed, as the Germans preferred to group the Jews together. During 1941, Jews interned north of the Demarcation Line ended up in one of three camps: Beaune-la-Rolande (Loiret), built during the winter of 1939–40 to receive Canadian troops, but converted into a German camp to hold French prisoners and then, after March 1941, into a center for interned Parisian Jews; Pithiviers (Loiret), established by German authority in 1940 to intern French prisoners of war, and used after May 1941 to house French and foreign Jews; and finally Drancy, established in August 1941 in a dingy suburb northeast of Paris to receive Jews rounded up that month in the capital. All three of these camps were under French administration. Lastly, we must not forget North Africa, where in 1941 between 14,000 and 15,000 Jews also found themselves interned. These included men, women, and children of all ages at Boghari, Colomb-Béchar, and Djelfa in Algeria; in Morocco, in Azemmour, Bou-Arfa, Oued-Zem, and in boats at anchor off Casablanca.[170]

The quantities of internees, especially Jewish internees, are difficult to determine, and various estimates were made at the time. One must remember the extreme confusion of 1940, with literally millions of refugees on the road during the summer. It took months to sort things out, and it was a long time before authorities had time to bother about interned Jews. Joseph Weill cites a figure of 50,000 Jews in camps in both zones in September 1940 and estimates that, at the beginning of November, Jews made up 70 percent of internees in unoccupied France. A report reaching the Marshal's staff in February 1941 indicated that 68,500 foreigners of all nationalities were interned in the Occupied Zone. Dannecker referred at about the same time to 40,000 Jews interned in the Unoccupied Zone.[171] Most commentators forgot the 14,000 to 15,000 Jews interned in North Africa.

From the end of 1940 to the end of 1941, the numbers declined.

Several thousand perished, as we shall see; thousands were released. The most fortunate received overseas visas and emigrated. Investigators from the Jewish emigration agency HICEM in November 1941 found 17,500 internees in the principal camps of the southern zone— a figure that is close to the 16,400 reported by the American Friends Service Committee (Quakers) for March 1942. Of the 17,500 HICEM discovered, 11,150 were Jews—approximately 63 percent. The numbers continued to fall until the summer of 1942 when German deportations transformed the situation dramatically. Just before the deportations began, the camps had reached their lowest ebb since 1939. The deputy high commissioner for refugees of the League of Nations reported 9,000 or 10,000 internees in the southern zone at the end of July 1942 (down from 30,000 a year before), and 7,500 in North Africa.[172]

As we have seen, Vichy inherited the camps and thousands of inmates from the Republic, but soon contributed internees on its own. We have also seen the extraordinary internment powers given to prefects by the law of 4 October 1940, according to which "foreigners of the Jewish race" could be placed in a camp on the prefect's personal decision. With the law of 2 June 1941, "administrative internment" became the principal club with which to beat *all* Jews, not merely foreigners. Any Jew whom the prefect considered in violation of the *Statut des juifs,* or whom he wished to punish for any other reason, could be sent to a concentration camp. Juridically, as a contemporary manual noted, the distinction between native and foreign-born Jews collapsed. Although in practice foreigners remained much more vulnerable than French citizens, Vichy's statutes put all Jews outside the law. Two authorities in the field, Henri Baudry and Joannès Ambre, explained this clearly:

> Internment is not a simple administrative punishment for the obligations imposed on Jews by the law of 2 June 1941. It is a security measure which the prefect can use *against any* Jew for any reason *whatever. . . .* The prefectoral authority, which is not encumbered by strict rules of penal procedure, thanks to the right of internment, can remedy the shortcomings of judicial repression. [Italics in original][173]

Moreover, as the same authors pointed out, one could be interned on the mere *suspicion* of being a Jew, whether or not one had declared oneself at the Jewish census, and whether or not the Police Nationale headquarters had one registered as such. Although the courts in some cases put the burden of proof on the state prosecutor to establish an individual's Jewishness for the purpose of the law of 2 June 1941, internment was not subject to this limitation.[174]

Like the last governments of the Third Republic, Vichy considered poor refugees even more "undesirable" in a time of severe unemployment and economic stress. At the end of 1940 and the beginning of 1941, internees who could show proof of an income of twelve hundred francs per month were set free.[175] By contrast, there was a tendency to intern automatically any foreigner who had formerly received relief allowances from the French government.[176] One practical reason for this practice was the desire to economize on the expenses of poor relief. Even a relief agency sponsored by the Quakers observed that it was easier to succor large numbers of people in a camp than to do it outside.[177] Vichy's intentions, however, were not mere benevolence.

The motives for internment sometimes exceeded all rational purposes of assistance, internal security, or remedies for unemployment. Foreign relief workers felt that roundups went on capriciously. Varian Fry believed that, especially in big cities where French police treated foreign refugees "with a mixture of muddle and brutality," arrests and consequent internment could result from mere chance. The prefect of the Seine-Inferieure who interned a Jew for "arrogance" might perhaps have wanted his report to be seen by the Germans; but the prefect of the Alpes-Maritimes commented directly, and with satisfaction, to Vichy in November 1940 that his internments of foreign Jews in Gurs should make their co-religionists more "prudent."[178] Admiral Darlan singled out Jews in a July 1941 circular to the prefects: "In agreement with the commissioner-general for Jewish affairs, I have decided that no foreigner of the Israelite race shall henceforth be liberated from shelters or internment camps if he was not resident in France before 10 May, 1940." Darlan did not want to stand in the way of their emigrating (everything should be done, he stressed, to "bring about their departure from France"), but these last arrivals must not be integrated into the French collectivity.[179] These attitudes among officials help explain why the internment of foreign Jews in the Vichy zone ran *ahead* of what was done in the Occupied Zone. Consul-General Schleier reported to Berlin in March 1941:

> The French government has also taken in hand the placing of alien Jews in concentration camps in the Unoccupied Zone; the French Jews are to follow later. So far about 45,000 Jews have been in-

terned in this manner, all of whom, however, belong to the poorer classes. Parallel measures are to be taken in the Occupied Zone as soon as the necessary camps have been prepared.[180]

Foreign Jews in any circumstances perpetually risked internment, without necessarily breaking a law, especially in the cities where normally lay their only prospect of assistance. One German-Jewish scientist who had escaped to Paris after Hitler's ascent to power, and who fled on foot to the Unoccupied Zone in the summer of 1940, was arrested thirty-three times until he finally emigrated in February 1943. He managed to escape because his son was in the Foreign Legion.[181] Other Jews were not so lucky.

Prefectures had other weapons in their arsenals besides internment. Jews and other "undesirables" could be sent to "assigned residence". This looser form of police restriction was intended for those who had sufficient resources of their own to feed and shelter themselves. In these cases, the suspect was sent to live under police surveillance in a remote place—usually a rural area with adequate hotel and police facilities. In these cases, too, people could be victimized for the slightest of reasons: because "their general attitude can be criticized," or for "reasons of pressing local circumstances, even though there is nothing to criticize in their behavior."[182] Like internment, "assigned residence" or "forced residence" (*résidence forcée*) (see page 4), as it was also called, was an act of police power rather than a judicial procedure, and thus carried few safeguards. Begun in the Third Republic by 1938 legislation, this technique was put to active use at Vichy.

By the summer of 1941, however, the government became aware of a reaction against Jews in the rural localities to which they had been assigned to residence. Arriving in localities often suspicious enough of outsiders in the best of times, the Jews drew special ire in a time of economic crisis and national stress. As newcomers, they seemed to be competing with the local inhabitants for increasingly scarce resources; they often had money (if not, they would have been interned)—usually proceeds from the sale or liquidation of their enterprises; and rumors circulated about them, not least because they were obviously the object of official surveillance for unknown reasons. By early summer 1941, eleven prefects of the Unoccupied Zone—more than had commented on Jewish affairs during 1940—were beginning to show alarm at the local strains created by Jews assigned to rural villages or arriving in their departments on their own. The prefect of the Haute Savoie was particularly concerned, as the summer season approached, about the expected arrival of large numbers of Jews for the summer, competing for hotel space, driving up food prices, and arousing a "lively discontent" in the Savoyard population.[183] André Dupont, the CGQJ representative in Limoges, warned that Jews in his region were stimulating Gaullist propaganda, inflating prices on the black market, and arousing resentment among the peasantry. "It appears to us that the question of Jewish refugees is a question of government which must be treated as a whole [dans son ensemble]."[184] This tentative groping toward a solution d'ensemble has an ominious tone against the background of the gathering holocaust.

The logic of these protests pointed toward increased internment. André Dupont's specific proposal was that "foreign and suspected Jews" be put into concentration camps.[185] Legal grounds for doing so would not be hard to find. The CGQJ was receiving reports indicating that Jews were now involved in massive illegality, if only by incomplete declarations in the census of 1941 or by failure to declare themselves at all. In the Occupied Zone, the Germans were applying pressure for internment. In May 1941, after an order from Dr. Werner Best, the Paris police sent almost four thousand Jews to Pithiviers and Beaune-la-Rolande.[186] Vichy was already taking its own initiatives in the Unoccupied Zone. This was the period of Chavin's "terrific dragnet operations," on the Côte d'Azur, from April to July 1941. The dispatch of several hundred Jews into résidence assignée and several dozen into the camps did not solve the problem, however, as Prefect Marcel Ribière of the Alpes-Maritimes saw it. Foreigners and Jews (he seemed to include French Jews) were still gathering on the Côte d'Azur, he complained in November: "The problem of their internment and especially of the Jews' internment should be taken up on the national level." Ribière proposed the creation of a camp d'internement in his department.[187] In November 1941, Interior Minister Pucheu was already turning his attention to the inadequacies of local measures of résidence assignée, and to the increasing numbers of indésirables in certain departments. On 26 January 1942 he became categorical: internment was to be the general rule for all stateless persons and foreigners who had lost the protection of their country of origin.[188]

One more prefectoral weapon against "undesirables" was the foreign labor battalions (groupements de travailleurs étrangers, GTE), which had originated in the struggle against unemployment. They were organized in Vichy under the authority of Commandant Doussau, inspector-general of foreign labor battalions, a subsection of the General Commissariat for Unemployment Relief; and the law authorized the assignment to GTE of able-bodied male foreigners between fifteen and sixty years old who were "superfluous in the national economy."[189] In 1940, authorities began to separate Jews into special units—the "Palestinian companies." A veteran of these has recalled the special dark gray uniforms with blue and white insignia on the left arm.[190] A CGQJ note dated some time in 1941 estimates that twenty thousand out of sixty thousand members of the GTE were Jews; most of the rest were Spanish refugees.[191] With time, assignment to GTE seemed to take on a punitive or disciplinary tone. In January 1943, a circular of the Interior Ministry authorized the assignment to work camps of all foreign Jewish males arrived in France since 1936.[192] Labor camps existed in both zones; and in the north, thousands of foreign Jews, originally taken from Unoccupied France, were forcibly employed by the Germans in building the "Atlantic Wall" fortifications against an Allied landing.[193] The numbers of Jews in GTE almost certainly continued to rise, for, unlike the situation in concentration camps, it was difficult to secure release in order to emigrate.[194] During the summer and fall of 1942, the GTE helped fill the deportation trains to Auschwitz.

It was in the camps that the greatest sufferings were endured. The responsibility for the camps lay entirely with Vichy. It would be possible to assemble a damning indictment of their insufficiencies and inhumane administration from the recollections of survivors, both French and foreign. We have chosen, instead, to draw upon the documentation concerning the camps prepared for Marshal Pétain himself, although we have reason to doubt that he ever saw it.

The situation in the camps became known to the foreign press, beginning with an article on Le Vernet (the "French Dachau") in the *New Republic* on 11 November 1940. The *New York Times* and the British papers the *Daily Telegraph* and the *Sunday Times* took up the theme, spurred on by various foreign relief organizations such as the American Friends Service Committee.[195] The Vichy government grew concerned when damaging articles appeared in the *New York Times* and in the *Journal de Genève* ("The Shame of the Internment Camps in France"). In April 1941, Vichy named the Prefect André Jean-Faure to the new post of inspector general of camps and internment centers, attached to the national police office within the Ministry of the Interior; and Jean-Faure departed on an inspection tour of the camps.

Jean-Faure was in no way ill disposed to the regime. The National Revolution seemed to arouse his enthusiasm. As prefect of the Ardèche in late 1940, he reported that the population of his department sincerely regretted its past errors and was accessible to reform since it had a peasant spirit, uncorrupted by cities. He found his charges enthusiastic for the new *Statut des juifs.*[196] The camps shocked him deeply, however; and his vivid reports stirred Pétain's cabinet. "The internees' living conditions put the honor of France on the line," wrote André Lavagne, chief of Marshal Pétain's civilian staff. "Everything must be done, for humane reasons as well as to avoid the commentaries of foreign journalists."[197]

We shall begin with the camp at Gurs, one of the largest, since it was used for the internment of Jews, and since, in Jean-Faure's words, it was the "object of severe criticism in the foreign press" and "for foreign anti-French propaganda, a source of severe criticism that is dangerous *because justified*" (our italics).*

Gurs had been built in 1939 in the Basses-Pyrénées to house refugees of the Spanish Civil War, especially former soldiers of the International Brigades. German Jewish refugees—including the political philosopher Hannah Arendt—were interned there in September 1939. "Of very vast extent," the camp consisted of large numbers of "shacks in deplorable condition." After his second visit to Gurs, in July 1942, Jean-Faure reflected that "there is no way to prevent shaky old wooden barracks, blackened by the weather, from presenting a poor appearance even if the interior provides a nearly acceptable living space." The interiors, however, could hardly have been livable. At the peak moment, eighteen thousand men, women, and children were packed into a camp built for fifteen thousand men. It was only by the summer of 1942 that what Jean-Faure called "a deplorable promiscuity" had been diminished by building a separate shelter for children, and that leaking roofs had been repaired. Even after he had recommended "urgent" improvements in November 1941, by July 1942 "the camp definitely does not offer even the minimum that one has the right to expect of an internment center."

The internees at Gurs could never be adequately fed. In November 1940, when the German Jews rounded up by Gauleiter Bürckel were deposited in Gurs, the German Red Cross was alarmed about deaths by starvation.[199] And with good reason. During the first winter stocks of dried beans and the like had remained in the open, where they "rapidly deteriorated." By July 1942, they were at least stocked under a roof, but there was simply not enough food available on local markets. Residents of the locality, hungry themselves, opposed the sale of food to the camp. Although 11 francs 50 per internee had been allotted each month, only

*The following pages are based, except where otherwise indicated, on reports sent by André Jean-Faure to Marshal Pétain's office.[198]

10 francs 62 were actually spent: and "a large part" of this sum was taken up by transport costs.

Only foreign charity made up for what André Jean-Faure called "the present dietary insufficiencies." The Secours Suisse, the Quakers, the YMCA, and a French-Jewish charity for children, the Organisation de Secours aux Enfants (OSE), brought the prisoners' diet up to a point where life could be sustained, as the French administration seemed unable to do. In his report Jean-Faure generously acknowledged the help of these organizations, though he observed that aid was distributed unevenly. "Block L" with 125 men and 55 women, he reported, was now "overfed" because the internees received 60 grams of salted sardines in the morning and 45 grams of meat and 15 grams of fats per day. Some inmates had even put on three to five kilos (suggesting the amount of weight they must have lost before). In an appendix to Jean-Faure's July 1942 report, Dr. Jean Roche, professor at the Faculty of Medicine and Pharmacy at Marseille, reported that inmates were receiving 1,600 calories per day per person, and that the Secours National was supplying an extra 350 calories a day to five hundred "needy cases," (suggesting that internees were expected to supplement their rations out of their own funds). Under this regime, according to Dr. Roche, a quarter of the camp's population had undergone "a significant weight loss, exceeding 25 percent."

Jean-Faure sent his reports dutifully to the Chief of State. On the July 1942 report on Gurs, however, some member of the Marshal's staff penciled the instructions "not to be acknowledged." It was perhaps wiser not to seem to know.

Conditions were no less scandalous at Rivesaltes (Pyrénées-Orientales), another large camp used for Jews in the Unoccupied Zone. This camp dated back to the First World War, when it had been constructed as a transit center for colonial troops. In other words, a camp built thirty years earlier for brief stays by young men from Senegal and Morocco was now used to house Central Europeans, mostly women and children, for an indefinite period. Rivesaltes was a vast encampment of wooden barracks spread over 3 kilometers of open, stony plain not far from the Mediterranean. It was subject, said Jean-Faure, to "glacial winds in winter, torrid heat in summer." The *tramontane* whirled dust through the camp for about one hundred days per year, in gusts up to 120 kilometers per hour. The main health problem was lack of water, which made it difficult to provide "basic conditions of cleanliness." At his first visit, Jean-Faure (whose standards for camps were austere at best) called it "almost a reprisal camp."

Sanitary conditions were so primitive that even the sick had to go
150 meters from the infirmary to an outdoor water closet. There was no
heat in the infirmary in winter. The camp had no refectories. The food
—what there was of it—arrived stone cold after being carried long
distances. In August 1942, Jean-Faure could report an improvement: the
internees could now eat from dishes. But even then, "short rations,
insufficient heat, sometimes a shortage of straw for mattresses have a
negative effect on many internees." The prisoners were not even getting the food allocation provided. The sole furnisher of food was "a
well-known local shady businessman"; and the veterans' Légion became involved in a local scandal over the sidetracking of parcels destined for the camp.[200] Children were separated from their mothers,
who could visit them only briefly after a circuitous trip via Narbonne.
Jean-Faure observed that the interned mothers regarded this as a
"harassment."

Rivesaltes seems to have hit its low point during the winter of
1941–42. Of the seventeen to eighteen tons of fuel needed each week,
the camp received three and one half. Conditions of existence became
"extremely harsh." Not only was heat insufficient; the internees did not
have "any suitable clothing at all. . . . And so some managed to make
some out of blankets. Of course that was deplorable, but, in justice and
reason, could one blame them? The women have no more undercloth-
ing. There are no shoes." And so, "mortality was high." According to
Jean-Faure's figures, the death rate rose at Rivesaltes in January 1942 to
twelve per thousand (an annual rate of 144/1000), and then to fifteen per
thousand in February (an annual rate of 180/1000). It is clear that many
hundreds of internees died in Rivesaltes during that winter for lack of
the most elementary provisions of food and shelter.

The third of the large camps used extensively for Jews was Le
Vernet, near Pamiers (Ariège). This camp had been built during the
1914–18 war for military prisoners of war and had been used in 1937–38
for refugees from the International Brigades in Spain, who were lodged
mostly in tents. When the camp was turned over the Ministry of the
Interior in December 1941, it provided "highly precarious living conditions." Le Vernet was a disciplinary camp: common-law prisoners were
in unit A; veterans of the International Brigades, in unit B; and Jews,
in unit C, "the most inadequate of all." Jean-Faure reported that "the
Israelites enclosed in unit C are piled up in wooden shacks in a deplorable state, dark, unclean, where the most elementary conditions
of hygiene cannot be observed"; and, in October 1942, that the
public works service had finally rebuilt unit C—but by then there

were no longer any Jews there. All had been taken "to the East."

Although there is not sufficient space to follow Jean-Faure in his rounds of all the camps, we cannot forego mentioning one special camp that played a role in the odyssey of any Jewish refugees during 1940–42 —Les Milles. This was an abandoned brickworks just outside Aix-en-Provence and was meant to be a temporary way station for Jews whose papers were at last in order for emigration. Many Jews waited there for weeks or months under appalling conditions, however, as they became entangled in one bureaucratic snarl or another. In November 1941, there were 1,365 persons jammed into this camp. When André Jean-Faure revisited the camp in October 1942, its former director had just been removed for fraud. Food and heat had been seriously lacking; the inmates had been receiving 150 to 200 grams of dried vegetables per day, while they needed 600. "Overcrowding had brought about the spread of lice and fleas. . . . This state of affairs was completely unacceptable."

Cruelty, neglect, and incompetence in the administration of the camps followed one regime to the next. In the enforced idleness behind barbed wires, as the Republic melted into Vichy, inmates reflected on their recent past. It was commonplace that in most respects the French camps were as bad as the Nazis, at least up to the beginnings of extermination in 1942. Arthur Koestler, having been sent to Le Vernet before France fell, pondered the subject carefully:

> In Liberal-Centigrade, Vernet was the zero-point of infamy; measured in Dachau-Fahrenheit is was still 32 degrees above zero. In Vernet beating up was a daily occurrence; in Dachau it was prolonged until death ensued. In Vernet people were killed for lack of medical attention; in Dachau they were killed on purpose. In Vernet half the prisoners had to sleep without blankets in 20 degrees of frost; in Dachau they were put in irons and exposed to the frost. . . . [As] regards food, accommodations and hygiene, Vernet was even below the level of Nazi concentration camps. We had some thirty men in Section C who had previously been in various German camps, including the worst-reputed Dachau, Oranienburg, and Wolfsbuettel, and they had an expert knowledge of these questions. I myself could confirm that the food of Franco's prison had been far more substantial and nourishing.[201]

The inmates were not the only ones to complain of the systematic hostility of the guards. The Paris pharmacist A. Plédel visited a German doctor friend, a Dr. Christensen, at Gurs in February 1941 and wrote a friend a shocked letter that reached Pétain's cabinet:

> The visitor who comes to see a husband, a wife, a dear friend (that was my case) has the distinct sensation of entering a penitentiary cell where reigns not the slightest humane sentiment. At the entry he must give a thousand reasons for his visit, hand over his ration cards (?) [sic]. . . . In a word, endure all the harassments that are usual in a prison establishment; then, next, sign two cards, one to fetch the person visited, the other for the guard of the visiting room who will watch over your presence.[202]

The French lawyer Serge Klarsfeld has estimated that there were a total of 3,000 deaths in internment camps in France, mostly in the period 1940–42; thereafter, deportation emptied these centers, and the inmates died elsewhere. In Gurs, during the first few months after the arrival of the Jewish deportees from western Germany, over 1,000 people died—of starvation, dysentery, and typhoid—out of a total camp population of 13,500.[203] In the camp cemetery at Gurs 1,187 persons are buried: 20 of these are Spanish; all the rest are Jews.[204]

CHAPTER
5

Public Opinion, 1940–42

When it comes to Jews, I was struck by the weakness of reactions aroused in the Free Zone by the first measures that affected them. This lack of reaction seems to me to derive from a kind of confusion, perhaps voluntarily entertained, between French-born Israelites . . . and foreign or recently naturalized Israelites.

The problem probably would not have arisen in France in the wake of the armistice, so far as the Jews are concerned, if the gates of immigration had been less liberally open since 1933.

Henri du Moulin de Labarthète (1946)[1]

EVEN AFTER THE WAR, Xavier Vallat claimed, with some reason, that Vichy's antisemitism had reflected popular wishes.[2] In the records kept by the French administration during 1940–44 there are unmistakable signs of popular antipathy for Jews, particularly for foreign Jewish refugees, but not infrequently spilling over onto French-born Jews as well. Letters to the Marshal, petitions from mayors of districts who wanted to get rid of their unwelcome visitors, vigilante actions that broke shopwindows and scrawled slogans on Jewish homes and businesses, the writings and speeches of prominent figures—all testify to a widespread hostility toward Jews that was both sincere and home-grown, for it not infrequently accompanied hostility to both the Germans and the British.

To make some accurate measurement of these feelings is, however, a delicate historical undertaking. How widespread was popular antisemitism after 1940? In what social and geographical settings was it most pronounced? What range of nuance may we be subsuming under one pat label? The complexities of public opinion are too fine grained for most historical techniques, even in the best of circumstances. For the Vichy regime, we face the additional obstacles of a diminished and controlled press, personal reserve during a time of uncertainty and suspicion, and profound change from one period to another. The perspectives of late 1943, when the people of metropolitan France awaited an Allied landing in an anguish of mingled hope and dread, bear only a tenuous relation to the perspectives of early 1941.

We shall concentrate in this chapter on Vichy's early, activist years, 1940–42. And we shall focus upon public responses to antisemitic projects that were clearly Vichy's own program: the removal of Jews from the public services and from teaching, the quotas imposed upon the professions and higher education, the forced sale or liquidation of certain Jewish businesses and real estate holdings.

Vichy's anti-Jewish program was not so blatantly foreign to the French political tradition that it could be rejected out of hand. It conformed to one strand of that tradition that led from Gobineau and the anticapitalists around Fourier and Proudhon to Maurras and to the more racialist twentieth-century French antisemites. On the other hand, it clearly violated the deepest commitments of another strand, that of tolerance and fraternity. These commitments strand had been deeply shaken by the failures of the 1930s and the defeat of 1940. Moreover, upon closer inspection, the French tradition of fraternity and universal mission contains an impulse to assimilate others to French culture, and an uneasiness about cultural pluralism that can turn intolerant in adversity. Retracing the intellectual roots of the French Right and Left would not, by itself, give us a clear map of popular antisemitism in France after 1940.

Things would be simpler if we had the results of opinion polls, such as the one taken in 1954 in which Parisians and inhabitants of the banlieu were asked, "Do you think that the Israelites are Frenchmen like any others?" While only 12 percent of the respondents identified as belonging to the Left answered No, 46 percent of those identified as belonging to the Right answered No, and some of them embroidered their replies with additional comments: Jews "are readily domineering. . . . They keep together and think only of exploiting others."[3] This poll was conducted by professional pollsters from the Institut Français d'Opinion Publique (IFOP), and the sample was distributed among socioprofessional categories but contained only 208 persons limited to Paris and the suburbs, results were not broken down by age or sex, and the criteria for assignment to Right or Left are unclear.[4]

No valid public opinion polls were conducted in the France of Vichy, however. Although IFOP had been founded in 1939, such public probings of popular feelings were considered impossible under conditions of war and occupation.

The CGQJ did conduct an opinion poll in the Unoccupied Zone in early 1943, but it violated nearly every canon of scientific poll taking. The investigators were not professionals but officials of the CGQJ; and the CGQJ itself recognized that, out of fear or suspicion, many respondents concealed their true opinions, and that the results from Limoges and Montpellier (86 percent and 90 percent antisemitic) were "too perfect." Perhaps the most important results of the poll were the fact that 31 percent of the respondents openly opposed "the measures taken against Jews in the Free Zone," and another 17 percent expressed indifference—nearly half of a clearly skewed sample under conditions of manifest pressure.[5] Otherwise this poll offers no real help.

Vichy officials themselves, however, kept close tabs on public opinion. Prefects submitted monthly reports, plus additional reports on special occasions. The office of the minister of war prepared for Marshal Pétain weekly and monthly evaluations of public opinion based on extensive sampling of letters, telegrams, and telephone calls. During the month of December 1943—the figures are scarcely believable—this service read 2,448,554 letters, intercepted 20,811 telephone calls, and inspected 1,771,330 telegrams.[6] We have the impression that they made a conscientious effort to record opinions accurately, for the reports can hardly have always been pleasing at Vichy. These materials, plus the letters from ordinary French men and women that poured into the Marshal's office, tell us after all a great deal about what French people were, at least, willing to commit to paper or the telephone.

The Climax of Popular Antisemitism

> The Jews excite a violent antipathy in the Free Zone. Their insolent attitude, the luxury that they indulge in shamelessly, the black market that they help support, make them hated.
> Postal Surveillance Service (August 1942)[7]

The most striking revelation of a study of Marshal Pétain's own intelligence sources is a powerful surge of popular antisemitism in the Unoccupied Zone during 1941–42. As we have already seen, public opinion as reflected in the prefects' reports had seemed largely indifferent to Vichy's antisemitic campaign at the beginning. Only fourteen prefects out of forty-two in the Unoccupied Zone reported any public reaction to the first *Statut des juifs*—nine of them favorable to the *Statut*, four unfavorable, and one mixed. Only twelve reported some public reaction to the second *Statut des juifs* and the further measures of June–July 1941—six favorable and six mixed. Then, with a nearly unanimous voice, during the fourteen months between the second statute and the first massive roundups for deportation in the southern zone in August–September 1942, thirty of the forty-two prefects commented on the influx of additional Jewish refugees from the Occupied Zone and on the sharp hostility these newcomers provoked. Twenty-two prefects wrote at great length on the matter, in tones of unmistakable urgency.*

Of course, all refugees drew attention as outsiders, even if they were native Frenchmen adrift in the Unoccupied Zone, far from their homes in the north; but Jews were insistently singled out for particular suspicion and hostility. The greatest animosity by far was directed at foreign Jews or the recently naturalized. French Jews who fled to the south also shared some of the animosity. At least one prefect (Marion, l'Aveyron, 3 September 1942) expressed the personal hope that the deportation measures would also be extended to French Jews. Sometimes there was physical violence. Incidents of window smashing and slogan painting were reported in Lyon, Nice, and other major urban centers. A more subtle form of violence was the robbery of some Jewish refugees at the Demarcation Line by unscrupulous frontier guides *(passeurs)*. Prefects always reported such depredations with distaste and declared that the public welcomed the action they took against youth groups from the collaborationist Parti Populaire Français and other people responsible for overt anti-Jewish violence. *Antisémitisme d'état* and the public feelings supporting it insisted upon legal means.

The themes of public animosity were remarkably uniform throughout the Unoccupied Zone. Blame for the black market was by far the most insistent of them. It was repeated both in the old haunts of antisemitism, such as the columns of *Action française*,[9] and also in villages and hamlets where Jews had never been heard of before the war. Food was becoming an obsession. "A single preoccupation: the stomach" (Pyrénées-Orientales, 30 October 1942). Stripped of its rich produce by the German occupation forces, France was becoming one of the worst

---

*Unless otherwise indicated, the following pages are based on prefects' monthly reports.[8] The prefects' contacts may have been one-sided, and prefects may have wished to demonstrate how thoroughly they had their populations in hand; but they also risked their careers if they failed to prepare the government for bad news. On balance, the regime preferred honest reporting to flattery. Thus, one finds frank opinions in the prefects' reports about public distrust of Laval or preferences for the BBC, which can hardly have pleased the minister of the interior. We take the prefects' reports seriously as a source, when used with appropriate caution.

fed of the occupied territories.[10] To make matters worse, food was inequitably distributed by a flawed rationing system. Scarcity pitted townspeople against farmers, shoppers against merchants, and practically everyone, it would seem, against new arrivals. No new arrivals seemed more conspicuous than the Jews. The black market was probably the one issue on which the Vichy regime could have built a successful popular appeal against them. According to Pierre Limagne's journal for 10 May 1942, "Darquier de Pellepoix defines his antisemitic program. Unfortunately, he is likely enough to be applauded in speaking of the place of Jews in the black market—the only [market] that remains accessible to those natural businessmen."[11] Jews were considered "synonymous" with the black market in unoccupied parts of the Jura (1 September 1942). Nine tenths of black market cases in the Alpes-Maritimes.could be traced to Jews, reported the prefect (4 October 1941), making popular prejudice his own. He thought that Gaullism and anti-governmental remarks were also attributable mostly to Jews. The regional prefect of Limoges liked so much the phrase "grabbing up everything that could be eaten" to describe what Jews were doing in the Limousin countryside that he used it twice (departmental report, 4 March 1942; regional report, 5 June 1942). Jews, reported the prefect of the Dordogne, had "corrupted" the local populations, "previously so honest," and peasants and merchants were now ensnared in temptations.

It is worth pondering this simplistic projection upon Jews of behavior widely indulged in by a broad cross-section of the French population in the Unoccupied Zone. The government knew that German purchases—both official ones and the clandestine forays of German soldiers and officers—were a principal cause of black market operations. Laval went so far as to tell the assembled public prosecutors in 1943 that Germans "were at the bottom of all black market deals."[12] Efforts to get the Germans to limit their purchases and to stop blocking judicial action against some of their illicit suppliers had become a major item of Franco-German negotiations. It was a point that the regime could not, or would not, explain to the public. As for the public, it was certainly aware that persons of all kinds were involved in illicit deals over food. It was French sellers who, in many cases, demanded the exaggerated prices that Jews sometimes had to pay. In the fragmentary arrest reports we have seen, Jews figure no more prominently than anyone else among black marketeers. Even if a careful study eventually demonstrates that they were arrested for black market operations beyond their proportion in the population, it was the Vichy state that had uprooted them from normal occupations and scrutinized them with particular suspicion.

The next most frequent charge against Jews was "the easy life that they are leading" (Rhône, 5 July 1942). They were "lazy" (Ariège, Creuse, Dordogne, Haute Garonne, Savoie, Tarn, Haute Vienne). This reproach took on a new edge of bitter jealousy in 1943 when young Frenchmen, but not Jews, were drafted for work in German factories. The program of labor conscription for Germany, known as the Service du Travail Obligatoire, then came to seem the real deportation, and the journey of young Frenchmen to the Ruhr or the Saar distracted attention from the journeys to Auschwitz of Jewish men, women, and children.

In spas and resort areas, Jews were taxed with "ostentatious and excessive expenditures" (Hautes-Pyrénées, 2 March 1942), with the "impudence" of their "luxury" (Alpes-Maritimes, July–August 1942), and with the "shameless way they behave in public." "In Aix-les-Bains, in particular, they are riding high, live in the best hotels, spend lavishly, and lead a lazy, luxurious life, making a fortune at the gambling tables" (Savoie, 1 July 1942).

The other resentments that fed the groundswell of popular antisemitism in the Unoccupied Zone in 1941–42 were more diffuse. It was mostly officialdom that fretted that Jews were responsible for "insidious and demoralizing activity," for propaganda hostile to the regime, for arousing political feelings against Pétain, for their political attitudes in general (Alpes-Maritimes, Indre, Jura). The real popular resentment was subpolitical and had to do with food and with allegations of conspicuous consumption—often wholly imaginary—at a time of penury.

It seems grotesque today that signs of distress among Jews were misread, according to an ancient symbolism, as signs of privilege. If many Jews were "lazy," it was because one government or another had excluded them from useful work. If they had cash, it was often because their business or property had been forcibly sold off, as often as not at a fraction of the real value. If they spent the cash, it was often because they found themselves sent to rural villages where they were outsiders, isolated from the network of friends and family from whom ordinary people could obtain an occasional illicit ham without raising an eyebrow, because they desperately needed the services of *passeurs*, suppliers of false documents, and furnishers of packages to camp inmates, and because *not* to demonstrate financial independence was to court internment in a concentration camp or in a *groupement de travailleurs étrangers*. No doubt there were some Jews who spent money in a kind of dizzy despair. The vast majority were neither rich nor ostentatious, but the traditional symbolism had it otherwise, and no responsible voice could, or would, explain these verities. In the absence of any moderating explanations, the Jews became a kind of lightning rod for generalized urban-rural tensions, merchant-consumer tensions, fears about future scarcities and price increases, envy at certain not clearly specified "others" who were rumored to have it easy, and even guilt about practices widespread within the general public.

As in the 1930s, hostility to Jews was nurtured by a broader xenophobia. But this time, within the crabbed perspectives of wartime suspicion and scarcity, foreigners included people from the other side of the hill. A defensive localism now treated any visitors as outsiders. "In a country formerly open to tourists and particularly interested in the development of the hotel industry, there is a violent reaction against the Jewish or aryan summer visitors unanimously seen as parasites, in the small mountain resorts" (Basses-Alpes, 5 August 1942). The prefect of the Haute Loire reported that his department had been "literally plundered by the tourists" (29 August 1942). It is not surprising, in a climate of real material want and diminishing social solidarity, that popular resentment against foreign Jews sometimes splashed over onto the French-born Jews who found themselves fleeing to the Unoccupied Zone. In the opinion of the regional prefect of Limoges, French-born Jews, in their turn, "cut themselves off" from foreign Jews whom they blamed for antigovernmental propaganda and the black market[13]—and perhaps also for endangering their place in French society.

These reactions are probably best seen as aggravations of familiar antipathies, resentments that we have already encountered in our consideration of the refugee problem of the late 1930s. The issues were still those of the 1930s, now raised to a new power by the tensions of defeat, occupation, and deprivation: unemployment, the fear that French culture was menaced by dilution, and the fear of being dragged back into the war. Once again there was a flood of refugees, concentrated this time in the narrower confines of the Unoccupied Zone. This time the refugees included the uprooted from the Occupied Zone, city populations on the prowl for food or safe havens for their families, as well as the Spaniards, Italian antifascists, and Jews from Central Europe of the 1930s. Even more exposed, in the summer of 1942, were the Jewish fugitives who had recently fled the Occupied Zone as German policy took a much more severe turn. One of the first mass arrests of Jews— the thousand important Jewish professional and intellectual personalities rounded up in Paris in December 1941—and the massive roundup of July 1942 (see pages 250–52) set off a "veritable exodus" across the Demarcation Line.[14]

The tide of Jewish refugees that had begun in 1933 now reached its high-water mark in the Unoccupied Zone of France, and so did fear and resentment of these "undesirables." The months culminating in autumn 1942 form the only period of the occupation when the "Jewish problem" figures in almost every monthly prefectoral report from Unoccupied France. Illegal crossings of the Demarcation Line were a growing preoccupation. Near the line, there was no longer "the slightest place to live," and the "presence of this well-heeled foreign population stands in the way of effective food distribution" (Indre, 31 July 1942). The regional prefect of Limoges called for urgent measures to "clear out" his region, to avoid a rise in prices and a "heating up of tempers" (13 August 1942). The prefect of the Dordogne said something must be done and proposed a new census and special passes to limit the mobility of Jews (4 August 1942). "A quick solution is needed" (Indre, 31 July 1942).

Quite independently of the prefects' worries, and unknown to them, a solution had been hatched in Hitler's inner circle; and at the very moment when the Final Solution was about to be applied to western Europe, exasperated officials in the Vichy Zone, egged on by a deprived and resentful populace, were looking for some remedy too. "There is growing concern to find a solution that will permit the reduction of the number of Jews living in France" (Cher, unoccupied section, 3 December 1941).

The Distribution of Popular Antisemitism

The prefects' reports form too blunt an instrument to draw a precise social or geographical map of the popular antisemitism that reached its peak in the Unoccupied Zone in the summer of 1942. Much depended on the predilections of each prefect, and his reports usually treated public opinion as a bloc. We have the impression that the most inhospitable areas for Jews were the villages and towns of rural areas, where highly visible conflicts of interest over food supply coincided with the least habituation to outsiders. Other centers of irritation were located in the vicinity of resort areas and along the Côte d'Azur. Some parts of rural France, particularly in the southwest, felt so strongly

about the "abuses" that they attributed to their Jewish visitors, that
when the deportations began in August-September 1942 the inhabitants
"have not hidden their satisfaction at this departure" (Ariège, 31 January 1943). In addition to the prefect of the Ariège, those of the Aude,
Creuse, Loiret, Lozère, Saône-et-Loire, Gers, and Indre departments
reported in late 1942 or early 1943 that relief outweighed disapproval
at the first deportations from the Unoccupied Zone. Around Limoges,
the prefect reported that the presence of Jews still aroused opposition
as late as February 1944.

Most of these reports pointed to towns as the setting most hostile
to Jews. Antagonisms were particularly acrid in villages to which Jews
had either fled or been banished for assigned residence, where they had
to use the proceeds of hurried sales of property and businesses to support themselves and their families and to keep out of internment
camps. Sometimes their numbers were exaggerated by local authorities, eager to attract outside assistance and block further arrivals. Sometimes non-Jewish refugees, of whom there were many, were indiscriminately labeled Jews to convey their general unpopularity.[15] Outsiders
sometimes recklessly amplified local opposition to Jews. Charles Maurras took the trouble to pass along some gossip to Xavier Vallat about
Jews flooding into the village of Bourbon l'Archambault (Allier) in 1941.
Investigating the matter, Vallat found that Bourbon l'Archambault,
with 2,784 inhabitants, had received 362 refugees, of whom 31 were
Jews; only 5 of the latter were foreigners.[16]

Popular antisemitism seemed less intense down the Rhône valley,
in the Pyrenees, and in Protestant areas. Prefects devoted little attention to it, or expressed it in relatively mild terms, in the Drôme, Gard,
Isère, Vaucluse, and Var departments. In major cities, where foreigners
were less novel, indifference seemed more common than outright hostility, although the prefect of the Rhône believed that the Lyonnais had
welcomed Vichy's anti-Jewish measures and even found them "too
mild" (5 November 1941, 5 February 1942). Prefects reported little evidence of strong antisemitic feelings in Saint-Etienne and Clermont-
Ferrand; while the Toulousains "worried little" about the Jews until
they were shocked by the roundups of August-September 1942 (5 October 1942).

Weaker popular antisemitism hardly fits a prewar map of the
French Left in the south and southwest—on the contrary. Districts in
the Allier, near Vichy, seemed particularly sensitive to the presence of
those Jews left after successive expulsions from the vicinity of the temporary capital. Municipal councils in Lapalisse (Allier), in the Lyonnais,

and on the Côte d'Azur all raised the alarm during the fall of 1941 about a Jewish "invasion" which was putting pressure on food supplies and lodging and was likely to aggravate conditions in the coming winter.[17] Feelings seem to have run particularly high in the Limousin, partly because it was close to the Demarcation Line where large numbers of Jews accumulated in regions little exposed to strangers in the past, partly perhaps because of the endeavors of Joseph Antignac, a particularly zealous regional representative of the CGQJ there from 1941 to 1943 (after which he was promoted to Darquier's staff and, at the very end, to effective control of the CGQJ).[18]

Resort areas were a particular case. Even if one admits that some wealthy Jews seemed to have lived extravagantly there, one has to ask why they were so much more bitterly resented than were the French or Germans who did the same. The prefect of the Hautes-Alpes was preoccupied in the late winter of 1941 by the brilliant crowd that frequented Mégève, skiing by day and indulging in "the most dissolute orgies" by night. He expelled a certain number of foreigners and closed some establishments, but reported that he could hardly ban people like the Princess de Polignac and the German officers who were prominent among the revelers (Hautes-Alpes, 18 March 1941). What the prefect identified as "aristocratic or Israelite circles" became foreshortened in some imaginations to "Israelite circles." The following winter a group of community leaders complained to Vallat about the presence of Jews in Mégève, "which formerly prided itself on its select clientele." Villars de Lans, in the Isère, claimed to be known for "its basic reputation as a family center." Jews there were bad for the tourist trade.[19]

We have almost no guideposts to the social distribution of antisemitic feelings. The remark of the prefect of the Loire that while intellectuals were opposed to antisemitism, the mass of the population "remains very hostile toward Israelite merchants" (4 January 1942) is plausible but far too crude a generalization to carry us far; and one must recall the prominent role played by antisemitic intellectuals in preparing the climate for Vichy's measures.

Even opponents of Vichy's persecution were affected by the general climate of opinion concerning foreign Jews and the number of them who had managed to acquire French citizenship in recent years. André Siegfried, who refused to serve on Vichy's Conseil National, could also write at the end of 1941 about immigrants' tenacious way of clinging to their particular ethos, "which threatens surreptitiously to make of the people something other than it believes itself and wants itself to be." Against this tendency, "a policy of defense, at least of prudence, is therefore entirely justified and even imperative."[20] One of the earliest and most forthright critics of Vichy's antisemitism was the Protestant leader Pastor Marc Boegner, who denounced the anti-Jewish laws forcefully in the spring and summer of 1941. In at least three of his letters, however—to Darlan, to René Gillouin, and to the Grand Rabbi of France—Boegner stressed that his sympathies extended only to "*French* Israelites." "I underline French," he told Gillouin, "for . . . I have indicated clearly our belief that the immigration of great numbers of non-French Jews and massive and unjustified naturalizations do pose a problem for the state."[21] This statement was not included in Pastor Boegner's postwar account of his interventions, but it was noted at the time. The Jewish Telegraphic Agency picked up his letter to the Grand Rabbi on June 22. Nor was this opinion shocking in 1941. Many French Jews felt the same way, and expressed such feelings freely in their official correspondence.[22]

This general sentiment that Jewish immigrants were a "problem" connected in some way with French decline, and that upon them any French government must know how to impose some limitations, permeated even into some parts of the Gaullist and Resistance movements. Some of the people gathering around Charles de Gaulle in London, in the very first days of the French Resistance, concluded that antisemitism was a political reality one had to take into account in 1940. Such was the view of the jurist Pierre Tissier, a financial advisor to Free France who published a book about Vichy in London in 1942. While Tissier found it unjust to deprive citizens of their citizenship, he thought it "legitimate . . . to reserve public office and certain management posts to those who have been completely assimilated, legitimate that certain French regarded as insufficiently assimilated should be deprived of certain rights, in other words, should enjoy only a restricted citizenship."[23] At his trial Xavier Vallat quoted some of Tissier's work to show how widespread his own ideas were. Georges Boris described in his memoirs how he hesitated to rally to de Gaulle too soon, lest the hostility to Jews be turned against the fledgling movement. When he did join officially, on 1 July 1940, he felt reluctant to put himself too much *en avant* for fear that his own involvement might be a liability.[24] On almost exactly the same date, René Cassin decided that as a Jew he should not embarrass de Gaulle by too close an association at the very beginning. De Gaulle agreed, although he himself in no way shared antisemitic views.[25] These were not the sentiments of *Juifs honteux* ("self-hating Jews"), anxious to mask their own identity; these were the judgments of political realists, sensitive to the groundswell of anti-Jewish feeling that followed the débâcle.

Anti-Jewish feeling never became significant within Gaullism or the Resistance movement, as it did within the Polish Resistance, for example. Nor was it completely absent either, as is indicated by a remarkable document published in mid-1942, at about the same time as the first convoys of Jews began to depart for Auschwitz. Dated June 1942, the first number of the *Cahiers O.C.M.*, the clandestine organ of a conservative resistance group, the Organisation Civile et Militaire, was a special issue devoted to "the national minorities." In fact, it was a small antisemitic book, apparently written by Maxime Blocq-Mascart, an economist of Jewish background and a leader of the OCM. This study insisted that the Jewish problem would have to be solved after the war: "The fact is that Frenchmen insist that certain situations not be allowed to recur, that certain ascendancies no longer be felt, and that [remedy must come] by preventative measures, rather than by sanctions."[26] Such "preventative measures" included "a statute for non-Christian and foreign minorities in France," a thinly veiled Jewish statute that would end Jewish immigration, encourage Jews to assimilate, and limit their access to professions. The project called for the establishment of a population commissariat and suggested, incredibly, that it draw its inspiration from a well-known racist writer, Dr. René Martial.[27]*

A copy of the *Cahiers* found its way to the desk of Simone Weil in London, where she was putting her talents at the service of the French Resistance. Weil, also of Jewish background but deeply involved shortly before the war in studying Christianity with friends such as René Gillouin, commented favorably on the basic thrust of the proposed *statut des minorités*. "The central idea is valid," she wrote, including the notion that "the Jewish minority . . . has as a bond a certain mentality, corresponding to the absence of Christian heredity." On the other hand, she thought it unwise to give official recognition to the Jewish minority, "for that would crystallize it. . . . The existence of such a minority does not constitute a good in itself; the objective must be to prompt its disappearance." For that, she thought the best instruments were "the encouragement of mixed marriages and a Christian education for future Jewish generations, . . . the inculcation . . . of an authentic spirituality."[29]

In its very first number, in December 1941, the clandestine Resist-

---

*Dr. Martial taught a course on *l'anthrobiologie des races* at the Paris Faculty of Medicine in 1938–39 and, under Vichy, was a member of the executive committee of Darquier de Pellepoix's Institut d'Anthropo-Sociologie.[28]

ance journal *Franc-tireur* denounced "the Hitlerian fable of a so-called Jewish conspiracy," whose only purpose was to confuse and divide Hitler's enemies. *Franc-tireur's* affirmation that "the Jew who works, produces, and conforms to the laws of the land has the same full rights as the non-Jew"[30] seems slightly reticent, however, when one remembers what the "laws of the land" were in December 1941. Is there an echo here, however faint, of the widespread complaints of that period against the "lazy" and their "abuses"? Veterans of the *Franc-tireur* movement have assured us that they never summoned Jews to obey anything but the laws of the Third Republic, and that the article was composed under conditions of haste and danger that made careful drafting impossible.

Similarly, when the underground Resistance paper *Combat* courageously raised its "strenuous protest" against Vichy's betrayal of "the national conscience and our most sacred traditions" in an October 1942 article entitled "The Jews, our Brothers," the editors could not resist displaying what two historians have considered "a touch of xenophobia." *Combat* called for a special law fixing the rights and obligations of foreigners, restriction upon immigration, and "naturalization that rewards their assimilation instead of initiating it."[31]

These texts suggest that even the most resolute Resistance movements could seem not fully aware of the penalties and indignities being forced upon Jews at that time by French law. It reminds us how difficult it is to reconstruct the precise tone of popular attitudes before the turning point of the summer of 1942—before the first shocking roundups, separations, and deportations of Jewish families in the Unoccupied Zone in August 1942 transformed Jews in French sensibility from problem to victim.

A Special Case: Algeria

Support for Vichy's antisemitic initiatives came from many quarters, but from nowhere more strongly than Algeria. That region's emotional tide had been running against the Jews for several generations. According to the census of 1931, French North Africa contained almost 294,000 Jews out of a total population of well over 13,000,000; 66,248 Jews lived in Tunisia, 117,603 in Morocco, and 110,127 in Algeria. Although a handful of Algerian Jews were wealthy, the great majority gained a precarious living in trades and handicrafts, made worse by a high rate of population growth.[32] They were deeply affected by the Depression. A study published in 1936 indicated that for every 10 Jews employed there were 53 dependents. Their material prospects were bleak: "an indescribable poverty afflicts the majority of our co-religionists in North Africa," wrote Maurice Eisenbeth, Grand Rabbi of Algeria at the time of the Popular Front.[33]

The Algerian Jews were also French. Only 2 percent or 3 percent lacked citizenship papers in 1931; most had been citizens since the Crémieux Law of 1870 by which France's Government of National Defense, set up after the collapse of the Second Empire, naturalized *en bloc* Jews born in Algeria. Thereafter, the small Jewish minority found itself plunged into the vortex of Algerian politics. Strongly republican, and identified with the government to which they owed their emancipation, Jews were the natural enemies of the European community's leaders. The latter represented a large part of the wealth of North Africa and tended to join forces with the local civil administration to oppose central control from Paris. To this group, the Crémieux decree symbolized political manipulation by republican elements in metropolitan France. Many Europeans resented Jewish emancipation because they considered these Jewish "natives" fit to be ruled but not to participate in colonial society. They feared that Jewish emancipation was one step toward their great nightmare: extension of the franchise to the Moslems who formed the vast majority of Algerian inhabitants.

Antisemitism became a powerful current among the European population in Algeria. Its expression there in local politics even antedated its development in metropolitan France. Algeria offered a natural constituency for such anti-Jewish careerists as the Marquis de Morès, Edouard Drumont, and Fernand Grégoire. The most famous of the local agitators was Max Régis, the young mayor of Algiers and president of the Anti-Jewish League. Régis terrorized local Jews and reveled in rhetorical excess. "If necessary, we will water our liberty tree with Jewish blood," he wrote in *Le Réveil algérien* in 1898.[34] More racist perhaps than on the Continent, certainly more violent in tone, Algerian antisemitism spread throughout Algerian cities. It acquired an important revolutionary dimension in the 1890s, when antisemitism became a common denominator of the Algerian extreme Left. These years saw the anti-Jewish movement take on a radical, populist hue in contrast to what were seen as the more sedate "clerical antisemites" of metropolitan France. Dislike of Jews was particularly powerful among European immigrants to Algeria, whether from metropolitan France, Italy, Spain, or neighboring colonies in North Africa. (Max Régis himself was of Italian origin; he had changed his name from Massimiliano Milano.) Yet, as several specialists in this field have noted, the remarkable spread of antisemitism generally stopped short at the borders of the European population; for the most part, Moslems tended to remain aloof from the campaign against the Jews.[35]

Algerian antisemitism flourished in the 1930s. Metropolitan extremist movements like Action Française and Doriot's Parti Populaire Français found their most fanatical and important following in Algeria. The Algerian wing of Colonel de la Rocque's Parti Social Français (successor to the dissolved Croix de Feu after 1936) affected a sharp antisemitism that was relatively absent in the parent movement. Anti-Jewish riots in Constantine in 1934 left more than a score of Jewish dead. Tension reached its sharpest point during the Popular Front. Léon Blum, together with a former governor-general, Maurice Viollette, made a modest proposal to extend French citizenship to about twenty-seven thousand Moslems without obliging them to abandon as heretofore their special legal status as Moslems. This proposal mobilized enraged Algerian opinion not only against the government but against the Jews who were somehow seen to be behind the move. This was the French-Algerian equivalent of the financial collapse of the Union Générale. In the fall of 1938, Jacques Doriot appeared at an Algerian conference of the PPF and called for the abrogation of the Crémieux decree. This proposal became common currency in Algerian politics, as public opinion increasingly lumped the Jews with the Moslems as a supposed challenge to existing institutions. Wide circles of North African opinion now equated a defense of French domination with opposition to the Jews.[36]

Paris and republican discipline restrained some antisemitic elements before 1940. The advent of Vichy, however, removed all limits upon the expression of anti-Jewish feelings. When Marcel Peyrouton, a former governor-general of Algeria sympathetic to the European settlers became minister of the interior at Vichy in September 1940, he saw to it that the Crémieux decree was abrogated, and forged new legal machinery to refuse any extension of French citizenship to either Jews or Moslems.[37] Algerian Jews found themselves in the position of their German co-religionists after the Nuremberg laws: having previously been citizens, they were reduced to subjects.

Anti-Jewish feelings so permeated the Algerian administration and colonial society that Morinaud, a veteran of the Algerian antisemitic movement, could write credibly of "the joy that gripped the French when they learned that the Pétain government was at last repealing the odious [Crémieux] decree."[38] It was Vichy that felt pressured by Algiers in Jewish matters, rather than vice versa. General Maxime Weygand, the delegate-general of the government in North Africa (September 1940–November 1941), and the successive governors-general—Admiral Jean Abrial and, at the end of 1941, Yves Châtel—all supported the anti-Jewish mood and the battery of antisemitic laws that followed. We have already noted the various proposals to Vichy from generals François and Martin of the veterans' Légion, and the role of Algerian promptings in the imposition of student quotas and in the closure of the Chantiers de la Jeunesse (the obligatory youth camps) to Jews. Darlan cited the intensity of Algerian feelings when he urged in the summer of 1941 that the Jews remaining there in civil service posts be removed.[39]

With the support of Abrial and Weygand, the *numerus clausus* was applied not only to Jewish university students but—beyond the provisions of the Vichy statutes—to primary and secondary school pupils. Although this measure was not the equivalent of the hermetic segregation of children attempted by the Nazis after 1938, the expulsion of 18,500 Jewish children from public primary schools (6,500 remained) was a far more substantial step toward segregation than anything envisaged in metropolitan France (separate schooling was a particularly strong fear among the French Jewish leaders who were negotiating with Vallat over UGIF in late fall 1941). Even Monsignor Leynaud, the archbishop of Algiers who believed Marshal Pétain was sent by Providence, transmitted his private dissent to Governor-General Châtel.[40] Châtel was particularly zealous. A few days before the Allied landings in North Africa, he ordered the fabrication of yellow star of David armbands for Algerian Jews, though not even Darquier de Pellepoix had succeeded in marking the Jews of the Unoccupied Zone of metropolitan France.[41]

Moslems continued to abstain from the anti-Jewish campaign. Although North African anti-Jewish measures have sometimes been explained as a French concession to Moslem pressures, the Western-educated Moslem élite, leaning toward the Resistance, seems to have even supported the Jews. As the lawyer A. Boumendjel wrote to the Jewish deputy Jean Pierre-Bloch, the Moslems "could not reasonably align with those who were attempting to impose a racial policy, when they themselves were continually abused in the name of 'racism'."[42] On 29 November 1942, a group of Moslem leaders including the lawyer Boumendjel and the Cheik-el-Okbi, one of the spiritual leaders of the Algerian Moslem community, wrote to Dr. Loufrani, a proponent of Jewish-Moslem understanding:

By putting down the Jew, one only brings him even closer together with the Moslem. It was thought that at the abrogation of the Crémieux decree, the Moslems would rejoice; but the latter can easily see the dubious worth of a citizenship that the granting authority can take away after seventy years' enjoyment.

If the antagonism between Jews and Moslems had existed, it would not have failed to show itself during the events of recent years. And yet nothing has been spared to set the Moslem and Israelite communities against each other.[43]

During the April 1943 session of the Oran Conseil Général, the regional governing body, all the Moslem members signed a declaration affirming their "sincere friendly understanding with Frenchmen of the Israelite religion" and their support for efforts to abrogate the repeal of the Crémieux decree.[44]

So deeply rooted was hostility toward the Jews in European circles that the anti-Jewish laws were not repealed when the Allies landed in North Africa in November 1942. The new French regime in Algiers, under Admiral Darlan and General Henri Giraud, defended French sovereignty against the Allied presence and continued to fly the colors of the National Revolution, despite being disavowed by the now totally occupied metropolitan France. In a remarkably obtuse gesture, the new rulers in Algiers named Pétain's former interior minister Marcel Peyrouton to be governor-general of Algeria. Peyrouton maintained Vichy laws against the Jews, with the sanction of the British and the Americans.

To a group of hand-picked Jewish leaders assembled in Algiers at the beginning of 1943, the new governor-general justified in an extraordinary statement the maintenance of the racial legislation. He recapitulated the arguments of the colonial administration: the Jews "have been declared responsible for the defeat," which had prompted "an explosion of antisemitism in all social strata in the country." The racial laws were "one of the essential conditions of the armistice," to which France was still presumably bound. Abrogation of these laws would provoke the Moslem population, itself denied full citizenship. Since Algeria was "still France," it could not go its own way and repeal them. And, in a final outburst, "the Jews go to see the American and the English authorities too often. Christians, Moslems, and Jews who do that are bastards [*sont des salauds*]."[45]

Peyrouton and General Henri Giraud seem to have been genuinely surprised when British and American protests crystallized over Jewish policy. Peyrouton was evasive in answering journalists' questions on the subject, and urged gradualism. He reminded his listeners that Giraud was a man of forty-three years of experience in North Africa.[46] The new governor-general claimed the right to pursue French "internal policy" without interference. But were not the racial laws themselves the product of German interference in French affairs, asked one Jewish official, referring to the *numerus clausus* in education? Peyrouton's answer was hard. "Don't kid yourselves; this measure was taken by the French government at the request of French students." The Jews, he added, ought to be aware of how many enemies they had: "You know very well all the harm that has been done to France and to all of you by that man whom you know . . . [that is, Léon Blum]. He is the cause of this current of antisemitism which swept France after the defeat; before, I did not even know what antisemitism was; no one ever spoke of Jews at home."[47]

The open expression of antisemitic sentiments remained acceptable in French North Africa after November 1942. Very few knew clearly, of course, what the recent beginning of the deportations to the East meant, and in North Africa, where there had been no roundups for deportation like those that shocked and altered opinion in metropolitan France, Vichy's policy could be detached in people's minds from its murderous sequel. General Auguste Noguès, another veteran colonial administrator who had served as French commander-in-chief in North Africa in 1940 and who as governor-general of Morocco had made at least one anti-Jewish proposal to Vichy,[48] did not even bother to change his tune when assuming the guise of a postwar statesman. At Casablanca, in January 1943, he told President Roosevelt and other high-ranking American officials "that it would be a sad thing for the French to win the war merely to open the way for the Jews to control the professions and the business world of North Africa." Nor did he need to mute his hostility. In the climate of French North Africa, even F.D.R. felt free to deliver some gratuitous anti-Jewish shots. According to the American account of the meeting, the U.S. President proposed that "the number of Jews engaged in the practice of the professions (law, medicine, etc.) should be definitely limited to the percentage that the Jewish population in North Africa bears to the whole of the North African population." The President continued that

> his plan would further eliminate the specific and understandable complaints which the Germans bore toward the Jews in Germany, namely, that while they represented a small part of the population,

over fifty per cent of the lawyers, doctors, school teachers, college professors, etc. in Germany were Jews.

Roosevelt repeated these views to Giraud the same day.[49]

It took months to end the discrimination begun under Vichy, and almost a year to restore the Crémieux decree and full Jewish political rights. Intense efforts were necessary on the part of the Algerian Jewish community, Jewish organizations the world over, and friendly individuals such as the jurist Henry Torrès. The delay was excruciating for many Jews and offered a sobering commentary on the strength of anti-Jewish feeling in French North Africa and on the lukewarm Allied interest in the problem.*

The Churches and the Jews

We have no right to criticize the Leader himself or his orders. The subordinate obeys without question or enquiry. . . . In the name of our religious conscience we will be the most united and the most disciplined of citizens.
Monsignor Cholet (1 September 1941)[51]

In the face of the "Jewish problem" almost all Catholic France was as if anesthetized.
Pierre Pierrard (1970)[52]

The changes of summer 1940 seemed to offer Catholic France the prospects of deliverance. After decades of growing secularism, declining official support for the Church and its values, and images of violent hostility to religion evoked by the Popular Front and the civil war in Spain, Marshal Pétain promised order, hierarchy, discipline, and respect for religious and traditional values. It was not specific programs that did most to draw Catholics to the new regime, for material concessions to the Church were less sweeping than many churchmen might have wished. Some state aid to parochial education, the return to the church of properties still unsold since the separation of Church and State, reduced legal restrictions on religious orders—all were welcome gestures; but the return of religion to the classroom lasted only until

---

*The prefects of several departments (Aude, Eure-et-Loire, Lozère, with mixed opinions in the Cher) reported strong disapproval of the repeal of the anti-Jewish legislation in North Africa. The French police commander Bousquet told SS officer Hagen that the United States would make a grave error if it changed Vichy's policy there.[50]

1941; and tentative steps in the direction of a restoration of official Church-State relations revealed great caution on the part of both.

The main attraction was a change of tone, a new world view, in which the new regime took on the imprint of a moral order and made public expressions of deference to the Church. No Vichy public ceremony was complete without some form of religious observance. When, in a tremulous voice, Pétain offered France "the gift of my own person" and spoke of the penitence and suffering that must come before redemption, the Christian symbolism of his gestures was lost on no one. The eminent Cardinal Gerlier of Lyon believed that Pétain's reconstruction of France would make it "more Christian." As he noted, "The Marshal said one day: 'Our fatherland must recover the beauty of its roots.' What is then the most authentic and the most beautiful of all its roots if not Christianity, which gave it birth?"[53]

In return, with virtual unanimity, religious leaders poured out their adulation for the old Marshal, who in earlier life had given little sign of piety and some grounds for condemnation as a roué married late and by civil ceremony to a divorcée. Cardinal Suhard, the new archbishop of Paris, called Pétain "the Frenchman without reproach." Monsignor Piguet, bishop of Clermont-Ferrand, was another who thought that the Marshal had been given to France by Providence.[54] The small clerical Left was, if anything, happier with the end of the godless and laissez-faire Republic than were the traditionalists, so that by the end of 1940 Frenchmen seemed joined in an intense new Christian commitment, encouraged by churchmen of the most varied persuasions and political beliefs.

The Jews were easily forgotten in this atmosphere of *reconquista*. Few churchmen had anything at all to say about them. Religious euphoria was at its height as the first *Statut des juifs* was being promulgated. Pierre Pierrard refers to "the almost total silence of the Catholic hierarchy in the face of anti-Jewish legislation." After the war, Xavier Vallat reminded everyone that Catholics had not opposed the anti-Jewish legislation, and in a handful of important cases had given their approbation. Dissent came, he admitted, but only in 1942 with the deportations.[55] Vallat may have exaggerated the extent of active support for antisemitism among the hierarchy, but he could have cited many individual cases as evidence. An article on Algeria in the Jesuit journal *Construire,* for example, referred to the anti-Jewish laws as "measures of moral purification as useful for Algeria as for France."[56] The bishop of Marseille wrote optimistically about the *Statut des juifs:* "Already we see the face of a more beautiful France, healed of her sores which were often the work of . . . foreigners."[57] In his Easter sermon of 1941, the elderly bishop of Grenoble congratulated Pétain on his repression of Freemasons, as well as of "that other, equally harmful power, the *métèques*, of which the Jews are a particularly outstanding specimen."[58] Such samples of Church opinion may not be representative, but they remain the views most commonly heard in 1940 and 1941. Silence was doubtless more common; but in the flush of enthusiasm for the "man sent by Providence," silence could fairly be taken as approval.

The Jewish census and the beginnings of aryanization brought the first murmurs of disagreement, in the summer of 1941. By then the intensity of Jewish suffering was apparent to anyone who would look. But we should not confuse these stirrings with the full-blown opposition, still of a minority, that was born a year later. Dissenters in the summer of 1941 tended to accept the *principle* of the anti-Jewish laws; they worried about their application. In June four professors of the Catholic University of Lyon attempted to launch a declaration against the persecution but apparently failed to obtain the necessary official support[59]—although some historians have wrongly assumed that this protest was actually made.[60] In general, the voices of opposition were neither loud nor clear. Consider, for example, the views of J. M. Etienne Dupy, in a letter to all heads of religious houses of his order in the region of Toulouse to guide them in their own responses: "While accepting the legitimacy of the measures taken, we have the charitable duty to help out with the individual suffering that results." Charity, however, had its limits. "The common good of the nation comes before that of the Jews alone, and a baptized Jew, son of the Church, before him who is not, and spiritual goods before temporal goods." What was the answer? Prudence, he replied. Take care not to be seduced by stories of individual miseries or by promises of conversion, he warned his subordinates. "The Jews, according to an often well-deserved reputation, require us to exercise extreme prudence." Catholics should guard against "a hate-filled antisemitism" while carrying out their obligations of Christian charity.[61]

Cardinal Gerlier, archbishop of Lyon, perhaps best epitomizes the hesitations of much of the hierarchy, torn between charitable impulses and the pull of Pétainist loyalties and anti-Jewish stereotypes. Like many of his peers, Gerlier was ripe for *redressement* in 1940. He was outspoken in his veneration for Pétain and the National Revolution, seeing in them a hope for a French resurrection, the kind of moral revival so longed for in the late 1930s. Gerlier was not a theologian; nor was he a political enthusiast for the Action Française. He was a practical, courtly man of affairs, a brilliant lawyer who had been a classmate of Jacques Helbronner at law school and who was on good terms with Jewish officials. He was a life-long follower of Action Catholique, a movement that advocated constructive social action rather than political engagement. But he had a weakness for traditionalist, authoritarian regimes with a veneer of Catholicism. While he abhorred Nazi ideology, he showed great sympathy for Franco in Spain. He thought Pétain was following the same path. Despite his enthusiasm for the head of state, however, Gerlier believed in "loyalty without subservience"— a conditional loyalty to legitimate authority. He was prepared to criticize.[62]

On a number of occasions in 1940–41, Cardinal Gerlier intervened on behalf of Jewish internees and, after the prompting of Abbé Glasberg, he protested against the terrible conditions at Gurs.[63] By the summer of 1941, after his visit to Pétain, Gerlier began to stand out more conspicuously. In September he met with the regional director of the CGQJ, and the following month, in order to convey his misgivings, he received Xavier Vallat himself. Even at this point Gerlier had no objections to the principle of the *Statut des juifs*. According to Vallat's account, the cardinal called the commissioner-general "an excellent Christian," and said, "Your law is not unjust, . . . but it lacks justice and charity in its enforcement."[64] The worldly priest particularly understood the economic case against the Jews. "He did not agree to the racial viewpoint," reported the CGQJ regional director, "but on the other hand was extremely understanding from the economic and financial viewpoint. The Jewish problem exists, he told me; it is indeed inescapable, and I approve [of the anti-Jewish measures] within the framework of justice and freedom."[65]

Did Cardinal Gerlier reflect a general disposition within the Church? Indirect evidence indicating precisely this situation comes from no less a source than the Holy See itself. During the summer of 1941, Pétain seems to have been troubled by critical opinions. He wrote on 7 August 1941 to his ambassador in the Vatican, Léon Bérard, asking for the papal view of Vichy's anti-Jewish measures. Bérard replied quickly, saying that he had heard nothing at the Vatican that might suggest disagreement. He promised to find out more. On 2 September, Bérard submitted a full report—a lengthy document of several closely typed pages, which could only have comforted the Marshal.[66] Bérard's first point was that France's anti-Jewish program had hardly concerned the Vatican. "At no time did the papal authority seem occupied or preoccupied with this part of French policy." The Church was fundamentally opposed to racist theories, being long committed to "the unity of mankind." Within the human species, however, the Jews were not merely a religious community but a group with "ethnic . . . particularities." There was consequently every reason to "limit their activity in society and . . . restrict their influence." Important theological and legislative precedent on this point went back to Saint Thomas Aquinas. Therefore, reported Bérard, "it is legitimate to deny them access to public office; also legitimate to admit them only in a fixed proportion to the universities *(numerus clausus)* and the liberal professions."

Bérard noted that, by focusing on race, French law was in formal contradiction to the teaching of the Church: the latter "has never ceased to teach dignity and respect for the individual." Moreover, a racial interpretation was in conflict with the sanctity of the sacrament of baptism. The Holy See could not accept that a person who had duly converted to Catholicism, and had been baptized, was still a Jew because he had three Jewish grandparents. Church law was explicit: "a Jew who has been properly baptized ceases to be Jewish and merges with the 'flock of Christ.' " This was "the sole point on which the law of 2 June 1941 [the second *Statut des juifs*] is in opposition to a principle espoused by the Roman church." Even so, Vichy got off lightly. "It does not follow from this doctrinal divergence that the *Etat français* is threatened . . . with censure or disapproval." When it came to the exclusion of Jews from the civil service or to the *numerus clausus* in certain professions and schools, "there is nothing in these measures that can give rise to criticism, from the viewpoint of the Holy See."

In conclusion, Bérard reassured Pétain that the papacy would not make trouble over the issue. "As an authorized source at the Vatican told me, they don't intend to get into a fight over the *Statut des juifs.*" Papal spokesmen had insisted upon two things, however. First, Vichy should not add to its anti-Jewish law any provision touching marriage. This was a point on which the Holy See felt that Mussolini had broken the Concordat of 1929,* by imposing restrictions on marriage between Jews and non-Jews. According to the Church, marriage was a sacrament, and the State had no business regulating it by racial laws. Second, Vichy should take care that its laws be applied with due consideration "for justice and charity"—the precise words Gerlier had used in his meeting with Vallat. In particular, the Vatican felt concern about the liquidation of businesses in which Jews had an interest.

---

*In the Lateran Pact of 1929, Mussolini made concessions to the Holy See, agreeing to papal sovereignty over Vatican City and conceding Catholic authority in certain areas of life, in exchange for which the Church came to terms politically with the fascist state.

Pétain put this message to use at once. A few days after receiving it, he was at dinner with a number of diplomats, including Monsignor Valerio Valeri, papal nuncio in France. In the presence of the ambassadors of Brazil and Spain, the Marshal referred to Bérard's letter, telling them that the papacy had no serious objections to the anti-Jewish legislation. The nuncio, an opponent of the *Statut des juifs*, was embarrassed. When Valeri suggested that the Marshal must have misunderstood the intentions of the Holy See, Pétain replied good-humoredly that it was the nuncio who was out of line. Pétain offered to show Valeri the text of the letter. Valeri took him up on the offer. Writing to the papal secretary of state, Cardinal Maglione, Valeri protested that the antisemitic laws contained "grave indiscretions [*inconvenienti*]" from the religious viewpoint. He wondered openly who had given Bérard his information. Maglione thought the matter worth pursuing and looked into it. Bérard's sources, it turned out, were highly placed within the secretariat of state and included monsignors Tardini and Montini (the future Pope Paul VI). At the end of October, Maglione replied to Valeri, affirming the substance of Bérard's report but dissenting from what he thought were Pétain's "exaggerated deductions" from it. The feeling at the Vatican was that the *Statut des juifs* was "an unfortunate law [*malaugurate legge*]" which should be limited in interpretation and application. There is no record, however, of Pétain's having been told any of Maglione's conclusions.[67]

Whatever this curious exchange signified, Vichy assumed Vatican support and acted on that assumption. Vallat had sent Bérard's report around to high officials as a circular. He brandished it in his conversation with Gerlier on 9 October; but at the time, the latter claimed not to have seen it.[68] Shortly afterward, Vallat told the Vichy press to deny rumors of Vatican reservations about the government's anti-Jewish measures. "We are in a position to issue the most firm denial of these allegations; according to information taken from the most authoritative sources, it is clear that nothing in the laws passed to protect France from Jewish influence is in opposition to Church doctrine."[69]

For about a year, indeed, everyone seems to have assumed that the Church's support for the existing legislation was solid, despite occasional dissent by individual clerics.[70] One regional director of the CGQJ with a flair for analogy told an inquiring prefect that no one had any business protesting because the Church itself had counseled obedience. "If Pontius Pilate had ordered a census of Jews, Jesus Christ himself would have complied; his most humble representative on earth should therefore submit to the requirements of the law, especially when these requirements are not at all vexatious, and also because humility is a Christian virtue."[71]

German officials involved in the Jewish question were relieved to note that France seemed unlikely to pose any obstacle to a general European settlement of the fate of the Jews. Under Secretary of State Martin Luther, in charge of Jewish matters in the German Foreign Office, reported to his superiors in December 1941: "Lately criticism comes only from Hungary, Italy, and Spain. We must expect resistance from these states to a common European solution. This is the result of Catholic ideas and Jewish influence in these countries."[72] That France posed no problem for him at the time was not entirely typical of Catholic Europe.

Later, when part of the French Catholic hierarchy denounced the massive deportations of Jews which began in the summer of 1942, some antisemites were taken by surprise. One local CGQJ official in Toulouse, horrified at Cardinal Saliège's pastoral letter decrying the deportations, called for "an energetic interdiction [*sic*] with the nuncio's office to punish the impropriety of such an action."[73] The nuncio was hardly in a position to act so independently, of course; but if he had been, he might well have criticized official papal policy rather than the aberrant archbishop.

The Opposition

The bakery workers' union asks me to call to your attention the situation of several of its members of Polish Jewish origin, who are presently interned in the camp of Pithiviers.

Secretary of State for Labor to CGQJ (24 June 1941)[74]

God is in your hearts? The true God, by whom I mean the God of Abraham, Isaac, and Jacob, who spoke through the prophets, who sent us his Son, Jesus Christ.

Monsignor Saliège (23 November 1941)[75]

The first clear voice of opposition from among non-Jews to Vichy's antisemitism came from French Protestantism. Soon after the débâcle, when future policies were still unclear, some French Protestants felt apprehensive that the National Revolution might prove hostile to them. Indeed, in French nationalist journalism, Protestants had often been lumped with Jews and the rest of "anti-France." The regime seemed about to manifest a "new clericalism" which made Protestants uneasy.[76] However ill founded these apprehensions, they persisted. Pastor Marc Boegner, president of the National Protestant Federation, still heard menacing rumors "virtually everywhere" in the summer of 1941: "After the Jews and the Freemasons, the Protestants."[77] Periodically, too, French Protestants with foreign-sounding names were harassed by CGQJ agents because they could not produce baptismal certificates.[78]

At the end of 1940, the council of the Protestant Federation decided that Pastor Boegner, its leader and a member of Vichy's Conseil National, should raise discreet objections. In March 1941, following the creation of the CGQJ, these were put in writing in the form of two letters, one to Darlan and the other to the Grand Rabbi of France. The latter was made public, appearing in *Au Pilori* in Paris, and widely distributed in the Unoccupied Zone.[79] Although Boegner couched his protest in polite terms and also alluded to the "hasty and unjustified naturalizations," his statement was a dignified and open challenge to the injustices of the *Statut des juifs*.

Like many people at the time, Boegner assumed incorrectly that Vichy had acted under German pressure: "We know after all that in the present circumstances there must be powerful pressure upon the French government in order for it to decide to promulgate an anti-Jewish law."[80] If this supposition led Boegner to hope for greater Vichy independence in the future, these hopes were quickly dashed in the months that followed. In May, Darlan told Boegner that the former's sole concern was protecting the Jews who had been in France for several generations—"French Israelites," as they were generally known, to distinguish them from "the Jews." "As for the others," Boegner reported Darlan to have said, "he only asked that they leave."[81] Protestant interventions became more numerous after the June 1941 second *Statut des juifs* and the beginnings of aryanization in the Unoccupied Zone. Boegner wrote to Pétain at the end of August and apparently mobilized Cardinal Gerlier to make the representation on behalf of Catholic opinion which we have already encountered.

The most dramatic appeal came from René Gillouin, a Protestant and an authentic traditionalist who was a close friend of Pétain and had helped draft some of his major speeches. Gillouin passed Boegner's message to the Marshal and added an anguished appeal of his own. Gillouin's letter was particularly compelling, coming from a man who had once shared anti-Jewish views:

I have always thought that there was a Jewish problem for France as for all nations, and I professed a state antisemitism at a time when it took some courage and involved some risk to do so; but I am ashamed of my country for the anti-Jewish policy that it has borrowed from Germany and even aggravated, and I do not know any Frenchman worthy of the name who does not in his heart condemn it as being neither Christian, nor humane, nor French.

Comparing this twentieth-century persecution to the seventeenth-century repeal of the Edict of Nantes, Gillouin added that the latter was a "picnic beside your Jewish laws, Monsieur le Maréchal." Gillouin was hard, one of the few of Pétain's correspondents who did not address him with fawning obsequiousness. Racism was a Christian heresy, he insisted. Its adoption meant for France "a denial of its *spiritual faith* and its *moral personality*" (italics in original). The anti-Jewish measures were "infamous laws" that dishonored the country. Gillouin also sent Pétain a lengthy study of the *Statut des juifs* which tore to ribbons its legal foundation as well as its claim to be mere national self-defense. According to Gillouin, Vichy's aryanization provisions were even more severe than the German ones. There were, in Gillouin's letters, no mitigating remarks about "strong German pressure."[82]*

Pétain may well have been moved by these appeals, but he was either unable or unwilling to do anything about them. In the summer of 1941 he attempted to play the opposition off against the strong Church support he still retained. According to Boegner, the Marshal later called Xavier Vallat on the carpet and asked for "moderation in the enforcement of the law." If true, this coincided with a similar gesture by Darlan which we noted in chapter 3. But by the time Pétain received Boegner again at the beginning of 1942, the elderly head of state may have wearily given up. "He saw clearly that great injustices had been committed. But it is equally true that he had a sorrowful sense of impotence in preventing injustices or in speedily rectifying them. 'Certain things can only be resolved after a peace settlement,' he told me."[84] The end of the war would clear up all the difficulties. Much the same, one will remember, was the view of Xavier Vallat.

Until the massive roundups of summer 1942, open denunciation of Vichy's antisemitism did not extend far beyond these few instances that we have cited. Pastor A.-N. Bertrand, leader of the Protestants in the Occupied Zone, claimed after the war that on several occasions Catho-

---

*Gillouin fled to Switzerland in 1943.[83]

lic authorities had been unwilling to act together with Protestants to intervene on behalf of the victims of racial laws. "I always received from those prelates a courteous and warm response, but also a clear refusal to oppose in any way the actions of those in charge."[85] One exception to this rule was Archbishop Saliège, once a member of Sillon, an organization of idealistic Catholic social activists which fell from the favor of the Vatican before the First World War. Saliège condemned doctrines of racial superiority from the first days of the regime, with notable popular impact in the Unoccupied Zone.[86] Paul Claudel, strongly Pétainist in 1940, wrote a stirring letter of sympathy to the Grand Rabbi of France at the end of 1941.[87] Some Catholic priests considered it outrageous to use baptismal records for the purposes of certifying "aryan background," and did not hesitate to say so.[88] Within the Church, such resistance stemmed largely from the lower orders of the clergy and the laity rather than from the hierarchy. This was certainly the case with *Témoignage chrétien,* the first Catholic Resistance publication. Its first brochure, entitled *France, prends garde de perdre ton âme* and published clandestinely in November 1941, directly addressed the issue of antisemitism. Three more brochures appeared before the deportations began in summer 1942, and each raised fundamental issues and left untouched no important aspect of Vichy's racism. Everything was there: concentration camps, the implications of Nazism, and the hypocrisies of Vallat, universally known for his role as a Catholic political leader.[89]

Little groups and individuals began to take action, often clandestine action, against Vichy's racial program and thus provided some precedent for the more important work that began in late 1942. In unoccupied France, overt sympathy toward Jews involved marginal risks at the very beginning of the regime, but a year later such action could mean the loss of one's job, arrest, or far worse. In the Occupied Zone, Admiral Bard, the Paris prefect of police, posted a decree in December 1941 forbidding Jews in the department of the Seine from spending the night outside their homes, and forbidding anyone from taking them in, "under pain of the gravest penalties."[90] By the summer of 1942 assisting Jews in any way was extremely dangerous in either zone.

Protestants and left-wing Catholics, disenchanted with Vichy's link with traditionalist elements within the Church, were frequently the first to aid Jews in trouble.[91] Help came from particular urban centers despite the real hazards: from Lyon, where there were good contacts with Switzerland and possibilities of escape in that direction; from Toulouse which, with its large concentration of Spanish exiles, was an important assembly point for refugees arriving across the Demarcation Line from the Occupied Zone or awaiting *passeurs* to take them across the border to Spain. Despite the reticence of their elders, idealistic leaders of Catholic youth groups, such as Germaine Ribière, eagerly aided the Jews.[92] Particularly outstanding was Abbé Alexandre Glasberg, a priest of Jewish origins, whose relief work after 1940 drew him inexorably into underground activity. Glasberg joined another cleric, Father Pierre Chaillet, in the Amitié Chrétienne, also centered in Lyon, an association of priests and laity which was organized, in the first months of 1942, under the patronage of Cardinal Gerlier and Pastor Boegner.

Small Protestant groups, often deriving similarly from prewar youth movements, were at least as important. Vital relief work, and later clandestine assistance to Jews, were organized by the Protestant Comité d'Inter-Mouvement auprès des Evacués (CIMADE), led by Madeleine Barot and Pastor J. Delpech. In heavily Protestant areas, such as isolated communes of the Haute Loire, the Hautes Alpes, or the Tarn, Jews found shelter and assistance, some of it illegal, for leaving the country. Chambon-sur-Lignon (Haute Loire) is probably the most celebrated of these Protestant communes. Frequently cut off by snowdrifts in winter, this almost homogeneously Protestant enclave helped thousands of refugees who passed through it. Jews received the solid support of the local population as well as of the Cévenol Normal School, headed by the nonviolent pastors André Pascal Trocmé and Edouard Theis.[93]

The traditional Left was not conspicuous in the early protests against Vichy antisemitism—those formulated before the mass deportations of summer 1942 changed things; nor was it well equiped for the direct practical aid that drew some religious groups into the Jewish question. The Socialist party had not yet reemerged from its stunned silence. The Communist party was implacably hostile to Marshal Pétain, the Vichy regime, and all their works; but the racial laws were never at any time during 1940–44 a major theme in its clandestine publications.[94]

Nor were the racial laws a major Gaullist theme. The general himself seems never to have mentioned Vichy's antisemitic program over Radio London. Personally De Gaulle seems to have been altogether exempt from antisemitism, remarkably so for someone of his social and professional background. But his attack upon Vichy took more general form.

The government of France no longer exists. In effect, the organism situated in Vichy and which claims to be such is unconstitutional and subject to the invader. In its present state of servitude, this organism can only be and is only an instrument used by the enemies of France against the honor and interests of the country.[95]

The overall tenor of his position was clear enough, when he denounced the National Revolution as the "abolition of the last French liberties," and when he promised to help "remake the world on the sacred foundations of human liberty."[96] But it was left to Maurice Schumann, the regular spokesman for the Free French on the BBC, to deal with more mundane details; and he duly denounced the first *Statut des juifs* as "imposed" by the Germans and as "contrary to all our national traditions and condemned by the Church."[97]* Good propaganda, but poor history. In focusing the attack upon alleged German pressure, the Gaullist line helped subtly to exonerate the domestic forces at work.

The world of higher education provided another setting for some organized, practical help for Jews. In the Occupied Zone, Education Minister Jérôme Carcopino strained the law to assist certain individual Jews. Henri Bergson, of course, received support. South of the Demarcation Line individual rectors could afford to be more forthright. Some went rather far and refused to report Jews on the teaching staff or to give information on students. At Clermont Ferrand, to which had fled the faculties of Strasbourg, and at Lyon, Montpellier, and Toulouse, there were noted refusals to cooperate in persecution.[98]

Personal kindness was extended here and there to individual Jews, of course; but for most of the victims of Vichy's racial policy, the first years were lonely and bewildering. Marc Haguenau, head of the Jewish Boy Scouts, took some comfort in the belief that "the *Statut des juifs* is translated from German"; this was his "sole consolation."[99] Those who shared Haguenau's view, however, that only German pressures were at work were mistaken. The French administration, especially the imposing legal system, provided daily evidence that the *Statut des juifs* was indeed composed in French.

---

*If Schumann delivered further attacks on Vichy racial laws during 1941, they were not published in his *La Voix du couvre-feu.*

An Indifferent Majority

> They [the French] show no understanding of the racial problem; they consider that a black or a yellow man has the same rights as they do.
> Dr. R. Csaki, director of the Deutsches Auslands-Institut
> (spring 1941)[100]

> It is almost impossible to cultivate among the French an anti-Jewish sentiment that rests on an ideological foundation, while the offer of economic advantages much more easily excites sympathy for the anti-Jewish struggle.
> SS-Standartenführer Helmut Knochen (January 1941)[101]*

In the first years of Vichy's own antisemitic program, most French people seem to have given little thought to Jews. Other matters—the future of France, an absent husband or son, the next meal—occupied the attention of many. Some of those who took note of Jews did so trivially or idiosyncratically and had no comprehension of the gathering tragedy, like the bad-tempered spinster who complained to the CGQJ in Lyon about Jewish neighbors in the apartment below. For her, the main issue was noise, and also *"an incessant and inexplicable coming and going of their co-religionists,* both *day* and *night"* (italics in original).[102]

French and German antisemitic leaders despaired of raising such petty annoyances into true racial consciousness. When, as an excuse for not expanding some aspect of the anti-Jewish program, Xavier Vallat drew the Germans' attention to a "still unenlightened French opinion," he was referring to real limitations.[103] The prefects' reports suggest a clear distinction between legal disabilities (approved by many French people and accepted by most) and the vigilante actions of slogan painters and shopwindow smashers, on the *Kristallnacht* model (disapproved by most). The German proposal to place a distinguishing mark —the yellow star of David—upon individual Jews was instantly perceived by Vichy as transgressing deep-seated French feelings of personal dignity. The Vichy regime's opposition to extending this measure to the Unoccupied Zone was the sharpest dispute involving Jewish affairs since the German expedition of trainloads of refugees into that zone in October 1940; and it was the first German proposal on Jewish matters that Vichy rejected outright. Darlan warned the Germans in January 1942 that the order to wear the star of David might "profoundly shock French opinion" and "risked the provocation of a movement in

*Knochen advocated the internment of one hundred thousand Parisian Jews, which would, he said, allow more French to rise into the bourgeoisie.

favor of the Israelites, considered as martyrs."[104] He might have concluded that it would compromise perhaps irrevocably Vichy's claims to
legitimacy.

The German taint placed particular limits on Vichy's antisemitic
projects. Despite Vichy's best efforts to declare antisemitism authentically French, the public often assumed it to derive from German inspiration. As one old-line antisemite could tell the future prime minister
Pierre Mendès-France: "If we have an account to settle with the Jews,
we'll take care of that after the war, when we will be free; today
antisemitism is a German strategy, and we won't fall into that trap."[105]
The ugly side of aryanization was another source of disenchantment.
Even though German propaganda asserted that the property transfers
would be permanent, potential buyers could not help wondering—
particularly by 1942—where these transactions would leave them if
Germany lost the war. The regime's efforts to summon up the precedent of the sale of Church property during the French Revolution was
an unfortunate analogy and may have led readers to unhappy associations.* Already in 1940 a British observer concluded that "the whole
[Jewish] problem is perhaps more a propaganda line than a deeply
rooted feeling in the public."[107] Commenting on the apathetic response
to the second *Statut des juifs* of summer 1941, the American ambassador
to France, Admiral William Leahy, believed that the French government planned even more measures but was treading slowly for fear
of adverse public reaction and too close an identification with
Germany.[108]

Perhaps because he had little faith in French public opinion, or
perhaps because he had neither the talent nor the resources for
manipulating opinion, Xavier Vallat put very little effort into antisemitic propaganda. This reticence fit Vichy's general understanding of
the CGQJ role: its mission was not to prepare some global "final solution" and drastically reorder French society, but rather to adjust the
social, economic, and intellectual role of Jews and then hold the line
until the conclusion of the war in Europe would permit a general
resettlement of Jews overseas. The Germans wanted more and hoped
that Vallat would help prepare the French public for increasingly drastic measures. They wanted the new CGQJ to assume much of the
burden of antisemitic public relations. Vallat delayed on this matter and
let other agencies do the work. In the Unoccupied Zone, the veterans'
Légion undertook some of the tasks of an anti-Jewish publicity director.

---

*"To buy a Jewish household is an excellent investment which carries no risk," said
Le Matin on 23 July 1942. A German officer assured the Troyes Chamber of Commerce,
on 26 February 1941, that the property sales would be guaranteed in the peace treaty.[106]

Its director, François Valentin, declared "stateless Judaism" to be one of the causes of France's woes, and some of the Légion's cantonal and communal correspondents kept the Jewish issue alive. The Légion circulated a bibliography containing many antisemitic works to provide background explanation for the National Revolution.[109] Vichy radio also lent a hand, inspired in part by the heavily anti-Jewish programming of its Paris competitor.

In May 1941, pressing forward in the Occupied Zone, Dannecker tried to outflank Vallat by creating a Nazi-sponsored propaganda outlet, the Institute for the Study of Jewish Questions (IEQJ).[110] Entirely French but with an ample budget from the Germans, the IEQJ remained under tight Gestapo control and in close contact with Rosenberg's anti-Jewish institute in Frankfurt. At its head was Captain Paul Sézille, a former comrade in arms of Darquier de Pellepoix and one of the most grotesque characters thrown up by the collaborationist milieu in Paris. A heavy drinker of marginal literacy, he quarreled with virtually everyone on the French side except a small band of followers. He became a specialist in denunciations and even suggested that Laval was Jewish.

For over a year German agencies in Paris struggled to hold the IEQJ together despite Sézille's corruption, mismanagement, and pugnacity. In an attempt to widen its activity, the journalists' branch of IEQJ launched the *Cahier jaune,* an antisemitic periodical that attracted such marginal members of the collaborationist literati as Henry Coston, Jean-Hérold Paquis, Pierre-Antoine Cousteau, and Henri Labroue, who later occupied a chair of contemporary Jewish history at the Sorbonne created by Darquier de Pellepoix. The IEQJ never managed to do more than satisfy a handful of careerists who gloried in anti-Jewish rhetoric. It tended to drift away from the drudgery of serious propaganda toward the more lucrative spheres of aryanization. Before long, the Germans began to despair of the entire enterprise. By the beginning of 1942 there were even signs of popular disgust with some of the IEQJ's efforts.[111] Eventually—Sézille having become an embarrassment to all concerned—Dannecker had him removed as decently as possible in the summer of 1942. By then, Darquier was ready to take over anti-Jewish propaganda, and the IEQJ re-emerged in the spring of 1943 as the Institute for the Study of Jewish and Ethno-Racial Questions under Dr. George Montandon.

The most conspicuous accomplishment of the IEQJ was the exposition "The Jews and France" which opened at the Palais Berlitz in September 1941. In reality, Sézille's institute was merely the nominal sponsor; the initiative for the exposition had come from Zeitschel in the

German embassy, and the funds (the total German budget was 1,285,-786.30 francs) and the impresarios came from the embassy and the security services (SD).[112] Commissioner-General Vallat was formally associated with the enterprise, much against his will, and conspicuously snubbed the formal opening. Later, when the exposition went on tour, it was limited to cities of the Occupied Zone.

The exposition presented to the French public an obscene cornucopia of anti-Jewish artifacts, posters, and graphic displays. The German plan was to stimulate French propaganda efforts and to prepare the French for a radicalization of anti-Jewish measures. As it turned out, the exposition merely confirmed Nazi apprehensions about public opinion and its management in France. Despite a huge publicity effort, the organizers were disappointed with the results.[113] The displays were not always taken seriously; Sézille found himself the object of a flood of criticisms from non-Jews who felt unjustly accused; and rumors flew concerning his gross financial mismanagement. He reported to Dannecker in January 1942 that all was not well: "A pro-semite tendency seems apparent, and people take pity on a certain category of Jews."[114]

Nudged forward by Dannecker's propaganda extravaganzas in the Occupied Zone, Vallat made some tentative efforts at Vichy. Nothing he had tried so far had been very successful. The screening of the German antisemitic film "The Jew Süss" (with a French soundtrack) in cinemas south of the Demarcation Line, with strong official patronage, had led to some of the first open displays of resistance a few months previously. Both the Catholic weekly Le Temps nouveau and Emanuel Mounier's Esprit denounced the film; and the latter even publicly approved the students who interrupted one performance with cries of "No Nazi films!"[115] At the end of 1941, Vallat made plans for a Department of Information and Propaganda for Jewish Questions, which he intended as a more respectable version of the IEQJ. The strategy seems to have been mainly defensive: to explain Vichy's anti-Jewish policy rather than to build up demand for harsher measures. As director, Vallat wanted Gabriel Malglaive, who envisioned a monthly review with contributions from George Montandon, Lucien Rebatet, Jean and Jérôme Tharaud, Bernard Faÿ, and others—a somewhat more presentable group than the team around Sézille.[116] Preferring literary efforts, Vallat showed less interest in spectacular expositions, radio, or cinema. This prudent scheme was backed by Paul Marion, Vichy's propaganda chief; but events soon swallowed up Vallat as well as his feeble propaganda efforts. Within weeks, with Darquier de Pellepoix, Vichy devised a vast new racial campaign. Its meager results, given previous efforts, were predictable.

Although Vichy France offered stony soil for the cruder forms of Jew baiting and window smashing promoted by a Dannecker or a Sézille, it did not offer fertile ground for sympathy toward or understanding of Jews in trouble. The irritations against foreigners and refugees which had been swelling in France since the 1930s, helped divert awareness of the scale of Jewish suffering in 1940–42 and of the way in which, historically, systematic antisemitism had tended to degenerate into bloody reckoning. Many French people had troubles enough of their own to occupy them. It was a time when suspicion and blame came more easily to the fore than did comprehension of strangers or social solidarity.

Vichy's own anti-Jewish program appeared to have strict limits. It was circumscribed by law and legitimated by reassuring statements from eminent jurists like Barthélemy, not to speak of the Marshal himself. Could anyone believe that the old man would be unable or unwilling to protect the Jewish veterans? Many observers, no doubt, would have agreed with Vercors's fictional character, in *L'Imprimerie de Verdun,* who is incredulous at Pétain's support for anti-Jewish legislation: "You know that in the end I couldn't give a shit about the Jews myself, but guys like you . . . Verdun and all that . . . the Old Man would let down his troops? You must be crazy."[117]

Deportations had not yet begun. A certain number of distinguished Jews were exempt from the Vichy discriminations, and certain classes of Jewish veterans enjoyed lesser penalties. It took more than a year for the process of aryanization to begin in the Unoccupied Zone. The regime seemed remarkably flexible on such matters as the Israelite Boy Scouts of France (EIF), especially after the EIF called for a "return to the land" in 1940. Although the EIF was dissolved at the end of November 1941, the decree did not appear in the *Journal officiel* until mid-March 1942; and two months later, Jewish scouts were marching alongside their French counterparts for the festival of Joan of Arc. The EIF were still in existence in January 1943, when Darquier de Pellepoix finally ordered them to disband.[118] In contrast to increasing German efforts to segregate Jews—by means of curfews, restricted hours for shopping, forbidden zones, and the like—in the Occupied Zone and elsewhere in Occupied Europe, Jews were never cut off from the surrounding society in Vichy France, either by ghettos or by a watertight wall of legislation.* Even in the Occupied Zone, Vichy laws still applied, and Jews continued to appear in public throughout the war. There were

---

*Uwe Dietrich Adam argues that as Jews were progressively cut off from the rest of German society, especially with the measures of 1941–42, they virtually disappeared from public consciousness.[119]

no Vichy restrictions on intermarriage or adoption. Jews communicated openly with each other and, indeed, were even encouraged to do so to maximize Vichy's capacity for spying on them. Bulletins from the Jewish Telegraph Agency, a worldwide Jewish news service, were distributed freely through the mails until the end of March 1942.[120]

Appearing limited in these many ways, the Vichy anti-Jewish program remained just under the emotional horizon for most of the French population, substantial enough to wreak real damage but restrained enough to leave most people unmoved until well into 1942. Even when the worst happened and the police took someone away, rumor and predilection encouraged the assumption that such a Jew had done something wrong. Everyone knew that these measures struck mostly at foreigners and stateless persons, and that many such persons were breaking the law. The Republic, too, after all, had been rounding up foreigners since 1939. And there were many liberations from internment. People were still returning from the French camps—they would not after the spring of 1942.

For a rational person, it takes an effort of historical imagination to suspend, for a moment, the dreadful knowledge revealed to the world by the Allied liberation of the death camps in May 1945. We have tried in this chapter to excavate an even earlier layer of consciousness: the time before the first mass arrests of whole Jewish populations, including women and children, in Paris in July 1942 and their extension to the Unoccupied Zone in August. After that turning point, for many individual French people (if not for their government) it was sufficient to witness the French police loading Jews into cattle cars, and the terrible attendant conditions, to see Jews principally as victims. Before this point, most French people saw them principally as a problem. The eyes of the French were still firmly fixed on the worries of the decade 1930–40. They saw the surfeit of refugees and the supposed damage done by them to France; the French joined the search for someone to blame for French decline and for their own sufferings; in Vichy they saw a regime that offered a restoration of national pride and hope. Other details did not matter. Vichy's anti-Jewish program still met with the indifference of most French people, with the approval of a growing number, the doubts of some, and the open opposition of very few. Even as the machinery was being put in place for the Final Solution, a growing number of French officials and individuals were looking for "a solution that will permit a reduction in the number of Jews living in France."[121]

CHAPTER
6

The Turning Point: Summer 1942

I have the honor to report that two trains carrying Israelites from the Paris region and heading for Germany passed through the Bar le Duc railway station on 22 June.

These convoys were made up of men under forty years of age whose hair had been very closely cropped. Two cars were filled with girls, the eldest of whom could have been twenty-five years.

No incidents to report.

The Prefect of the Meuse (24 June 1942)[1]

CONVOYS FOREIGN JEWS DEPORTED TOWARD OCCUPIED ZONE INCLUDE IN ACCORD FORMAL INSTRUCTIONS YOUNG CHILDREN GIRLS SICK WOMEN AND DYING STOP BEG YOU TO SPARE UNFORTUNATES GUILTY ONLY OF CRIME BEING BORN NONARYANS STOP ESPECIALLY URGE THAT FRENCH WAR VOLUNTEERS NOT HAVE TO BURN THEIR MILITARY DOCUMENTS TO ESCAPE HARASSMENT DURING DEPORTATION STOP EMBARCATION INVOLVED HEARTRENDING SCENES UNWORTHY OF FRENCH TRADITIONS AND SUSCEPTIBLE OF BLACKENING FRENCH REPUTATION IN ALL NEUTRAL AND CHRISTIAN COUNTRIES

Albert Lévy, president of the
UGIF, to Marshal Pétain (4 September 1942)[2]

Monsieur le Maréchal,

A French woman of eighteen respectfully makes a personal appeal to you.

They took away our mama. French policemen arrested her last 29 September at home, because she is Belgian and because she is Jewish. We learned that she was sent on 30 September to Drancy, and that she left from there, on the same day, for an unknown destination. . . .

I am well aware that my case is not one that would be considered exceptional . . . but she is nevertheless a praiseworthy person [who] has never—I swear it—done anything to merit the slightest reproach. . . .

Letter to Marshal Pétain (6 October 1942)[3]

New Men, New Measures

In a remarkable coincidence, all the important officials in France most directly responsible for the fate of the Jews changed during the spring and summer of 1942. In May 1942, Xavier Vallat was replaced as commissioner-general for Jewish affairs by Darquier de Pellepoix. The German supreme commander in France, the *Militärbefehlshaber in Frankreich,* General Otto von Stülpnagel had expressed grave reservations about the hostage policy and the reprisals of late 1941; he resigned his post in February 1942 and was replaced by his cousin, General Karl Heinrich von Stülpnagel.

More ominously, German police operations in France were removed from the MBF's control and placed under a new official who answered only to SS chief Heinrich Himmler: the Höherer SS- und Polizeiführer (HSSPF) Carl Albrecht Oberg. The position of HSSPF in the German power hierarchy symbolized the centralizing and ideological resolve of the SS and its leader Himmler. The first appointments of HSSPF in Germany in 1937 and in newly absorbed Austria in 1938 had displayed Himmler's success at gathering all police operations under Nazi party control without interference from other branches of the German state. Later the arrival of such officials in occupied Europe had marked the importance the Nazis assigned to the Final Solution, which began in late 1941 in Russia, East Prussia, and Poland.

As if to underscore France's integration into the new European vision of Hitler's élite, the new HSSPF, SS-Brigadeführer and Police Major-General Oberg came to Paris fresh from the east. He had been the top Nazi police official in Radom, about one hundred kilometers south of Warsaw. Oberg visited the French capital on 7 May 1942, with Heydrich, and took up his new post on 1 June. In consequence, Werner Best, Oberg's equivalent in rank as an SS-Brigadeführer and head of the civil administration staff of the MBF, found himself reduced in importance. Best soon left to take up a higher position as German plenipotentiary *(Bevollmächtige)* in Denmark.[4] Theodor Dannecker, head of the *Judenamt* (Jewish office) within the German police hierarchy in France, went on to more important work in July as Eichmann's representative in Bulgaria, then Italy, and still later Hungary. His successor, the likeminded SS-Obersturmführer Heinz Röthke, carried on actively until the end of the war. After these major changes in German police organization, the SS had a free hand in France.

On the French side, the new head of the French national police network was a young prefect, René Bousquet, only thirty-three and former prefect of the Marne, who had begun a brilliant prefectoral career under the Third Republic as a protégé of Albert Sarraut. In early May 1942, Bousquet took over as secretary-general of the Police Nationale in the Ministry of the Interior, bringing with him his former assistant from the Marne, Jean Leguay, to serve as police representative in the Occupied Zone.

The most significant change of personnel on the French side was the return of Pierre Laval to the cabinet on 26 April 1942. Laval received the key portfolios of Interior, Information, and Foreign Affairs as well as the vice-presidency of the Council. Although Pétain remained nominally president of the Council, as well as Chief of State, Laval was effectively head of the government.

Laval's arrival in power coincided with a sharp increase in German demands upon France. Having failed to defeat the Soviet Union by blitzkrieg, the Nazi regime was obliged during 1942 to put the German people for the first time under the constraints of total war; but the Nazi leaders preferred to shift onto the shoulders of the occupied peoples as much as possible of the burden of manpower and goods. In his first months in office, Laval received three high-ranking German visitors who announced these new demands. In May 1942, Gauleiter Fritz Sauckel, the plenipotentiary for foreign labor in the Reich, visited Paris and asked for 250,000 French workers for German industry—the first of a stream of demands that the French never fully met, but that saddled the Laval government with its most unpopular burden. Before it was over, more than 730,000 French workers were to go to work in German factories: at first voluntarily under the *relève* or exchange system by which Laval tried to buy the liberation of a French prisoner of war for every three skilled workers he could send to Germany, and later, after February 1943, by obligatory service. By late 1943, the French formed the largest male foreign-worker group in Germany. This was the real "deportation" for most of the French people, and it was an unremitting preoccupation for Laval.* Some observers thought his government would collapse under the strain.[6] The second visitor, Reinhard Heydrich, Himmler's second in command, came to Paris in early May 1942 to introduce General Oberg to French and German

---

*One Resistance broadcaster, only recently arrived in London from occupied France, delivered an empassioned denunciation of these deportations of French laborers in the summer of 1943, calling for resistance to them, without ever mentioning the "other" deportations, destined not for factories in the Reich but for the death camp of Auschwitz.[5]

authorities. Heydrich urged the French to create "a new police" composed of "militants" and led by ideologically commited chiefs from outside the regular police forces, as in the Nazi state.[7] The third German visitor was Adolf Eichmann, head of the *Judenamt* of the central German security office (RSHA). Eichmann arrived in Paris on 30 June 1942, bearing a brutal directive from Himmler: all the Jews of France were to be deported, apparently without distinction or regard for French citizenship. The Final Solution had begun.

The Final Solution

It is not possible to determine an exact date on which Hitler resolved to exterminate the Jews of Europe on European soil. The earlier policy of provoking the emigration of Jews from Germany and German-occupied Europe easily lapsed into periodic massacres, as on *Kristallnacht* and in the wake of the invasion of Poland in September 1939. Killing came easily to the Nazis, and a murderous intention may well have slumbered in their antisemitic ideology from the beginning. In any event, the spread of war after September 1939 made it ever more difficult to carry out a policy of mere emigration on any but a minor scale. Thereafter the Nazis faced the choice of postponing the matter until the end of a steadily lengthening war, or of doing something drastic at once. Locked up with the Jews in Fortress Europe, the Nazis' emotional pressure continued to rise.

The German attack on the Soviet Union on 22 June 1941 opened a new phase. On the one hand, the Reich's anticipated new frontiers promised to contain millions more unwanted and unexpellable Jews. On the other hand, the space opening up to the east offered vistas for the most grandiose schemes. Above all, the Nazis faced their new subjects in Russia without moral constraint. In the Hitlerian world view, Russia always represented a dark and demonic force—an implacable rival, the home alike of bolshevism and Judaism, confused in one insane vision. Faced with a foe like this, Hitler declared, everything was permitted. War with Russia was not to be an ordinary conflict. Describing it as a clash of *Kultur* with inferior peoples, the Führer gave the Germans license to destroy and lay waste. Orders were prepared in the spring of 1941 for the outright liquidation of those considered the enemies of Nazism—mainly Jews and Communist party cadres. *Einsatzgruppen,* special squads following the advance of the Wehrmacht, carried out systematic killings. At first they machine-gunned their victims. In the fall, the *Einsatzgruppen* experimented with gas, filling specially constructed motorized vans with carbon monoxide. Within four months, some 600,000 Jews perished by these hurried and sometimes chaotic means. As experience accumulated, the Nazis began to replace their improvisation with more coordinated and centralized techniques. At the very end of 1941, permanent facilities for mass executions by gas were established at Kulmhof (Chelmno), north of Lodz, in reconquered East Prussia, and at Birkenau, part of the vast Auschwitz complex in Upper Silesia, former Polish territory incorporated into the Reich. In the months that followed, Belzec, Sobibor, Majdanek, and Treblinka joined the list. Once in place, the death factories needed to be supplied with people to kill. Coordination was now essential, and Europe would have to disgorge its Jews.

As early as 31 July 1941, Hermann Göring wrote to Heydrich to "carry out all necessary preparations with regard to the organizational and financial matters for bringing about a complete solution of the Jewish question in the German sphere of influence in Europe."[8] It was, however, the conference of Nazi leaders in Berlin on 20 January 1942, at 56–58 Am Grossen Wannsee, that systematized the new Nazi policy of outright extermination and set the wheels into motion.

The Wannsee meeting was convoked by Reinhard Heydrich, head of the Reich Central Security Organization (RSHA) and Himmler's deputy in the SS. Representatives from the Reich's Four-Year Plan, the Interior Ministry, the Foreign Office, the Justice Ministry, various occupation authorities, the Nazi party, and, of course, the SS were present. Adolf Eichmann, head of the Jewish section within the RSHA, took the minutes, of which only thirty copies were made. The surviving copies of these minutes, even with their silences and ellipses, give us the most complete and chilling account up to that time of Nazi intentions with respect to the Jews of Europe.

Heydrich reviewed previous anti-Jewish efforts which had centered upon the emigration of Jews from Reich territory, "the only possible provisional solution." Problems had arisen, however—financial difficulties, lack of transport, visa restrictions, and so forth. Recently Himmler, the Reichsführer SS, had forbidden further emigration because of dangerous wartime conditions and "in view of the possibilities in the east." Following Hitler's authorization [*Genehmigung*], Jews were now to be evacuated to eastern territories as a further possible solution [*Lösungsmöglichkeit*]. The minutes are not precise about what would happen next, but Heydrich spoke of huge labor columns whose hardships would accomplish the "natural decline" of the majority, and of some undefined special treatment for the tenacious hard core of Jewry which survived this process of "natural selection." He indicated that practical experience was being gathered at that moment—an evident allusion to the *Einsatzgruppen*—which would be of major significance in the "final solution of the Jewish question."

Reich and occupation authorities, Heydrich continued, were to begin work on this "final solution." It would affect eleven million Jews, including even England. Europe was to be combed from west to east. Martin Luther, an under secretary of state at the Foreign Office and its specialist on the diplomatic aspects of the Jewish question, noted that the "thoroughgoing treatment of this problem [*tiefgehende Behandlung dieses Problems*]" would encounter difficulties in some countries, notably Denmark and Norway; but neither he nor Heydrich expected difficulties with France. The number of Jews in that country was reckoned to be 165,000 for the Occupied Zone, and an absurdly high 700,000 for the Unoccupied Zone. In both zones, a proper census of the Jews "for the purposes of their evacuation" could be conducted without much trouble. No timetable was set, but the tenor of the meeting indicated that the period of drift and improvisation was over. Two participants urged that preparations be made at once for Poland and other eastern territories to receive the deportees.[9]

From the very beginning, anti-Jewish activists among German occupation officials in France hoped eventually to include the Unoccupied Zone in their projects. When Abetz first asked Berlin's approval in August 1940 for immediate anti-Jewish measures in the Occupied Zone, he noted that these would later serve as a basis for the removal [*Entfernung*] of Jews from the Unoccupied Zone also.[10] A few months later, when Zeitschel, the German embassy's Jewish expert, was planning what eventually became the CGQJ, he set it in the context of the Führer's postwar vision of "a great deportation of the Jews," involving some ill-defined "colonial activity . . . in a territory that remains to be determined."[11] As Werner Best explained to the MBF in April 1941, in preparation for Xavier Vallat's first visit, "the Germans want progressively to rid all the European countries of Judaism and have undertaken to free Europe of the Jews completely." Although this goal could not be realized until after the war, Best wanted Vallat at once to begin "preliminary measures"—massive arrests and internments.[12]* Abetz

---

*Best wanted three to five thousand Jews of all nationalities interned in the Occupied Zone, including French Jews "who are particularly dangerous or undesirable for political, criminal or social reasons."

knew very well that Vallat had his own ideas, notably a tendency to favor native Jewish war veterans. There would be a "subsequent stage," however; and Abetz expected that eventually privileged Jews, too, would be "forced to emigrate definitively."[13]

Intermittently, from the moment they had set foot in Paris, the Germans had been rounding up Jews. Insofar as these spasmodic arrests reflected any settled policy, they seemed to respond to military security concerns. All Jews along the English Channel coast, for example, had been deported to the Yonne and Aube departments in north-central France in March 1941.[14] A few weeks later, the German military authorities decided to reduce the number of foreign Jews in Paris. Dr. Werner Best, head of the MBF's civil administration staff, told Jean-Marie Ingrand, the French Ministry of the Interior representative in Paris, that the French should expel or intern an unspecified number of foreign Jews living in the Occupied Zone. Since expulsion could only mean sending these Jews into Vichy's territory—clearly unacceptable to its government which wanted no more Jews—the orders for internment were given to the Prefecture of Police. On 14 May 1941, over 3,700 foreign Jews, all males, received individual summonses to the Paris commissariat of police. Jewish men who presented themselves (and most did) were arrested and sent to the camps at Pithiviers and Beaune-la-Rolande.[15]

The German invasion of the Soviet Union opened a new phase in France also. While the French police carried out preventive arrests of Communists throughout the country, the German authorities imposed sweeping new restrictions on Jews in the Occupied Zone. On 13 August, they ordered the seizure of radio sets belonging to Jews. Although the Vichy government considered this step a violation of the property rights guaranteed by the Hague Conventions of international law concerning military occupation, Commissaire François, head of the special Jewish section of the Prefecture of Police, had to carry out the order.[16] Then Jews' bicycles were taken away. On 15 August, the populous eleventh *arrondissement* of Paris was sealed off by French police, allowing German police and some inspectors of the Prefecture of Police to make arrests. On 20 August, the *arrondissement* was sealed again, and arrests were concentrated this time on Jewish lawyers. Altogether, about four thousand Jews were interned and taken to Drancy.[17] The Germans brushed aside a Vichy protest against this seizure of "some very prominent personalities,"[18] including French citizens. After all, as the German embassy official Rudolf Schleier pointed out to his superiors in Berlin, it was a French statute (the law of 4 October 1940) that created a legal basis for putting both French and foreign Jews into concentration camps.[19]

Tensions escalated sharply in August 1941 as Communist resistance groups began a new policy of direct attacks upon members of the German occupation forces. On the day after the arrests of the Jewish lawyers, two men shot and killed the German naval cadet Moser in the Barbès-Rochechouart Métro station, on 21 August. The outraged German authorities immediately announced a policy of taking French hostages and, in the event of future assassinations, of shooting them. The Germans also demanded that Vichy condemn six Communists to death in reprisal for the cadet's murder. Vichy, hoping for leniency in the long term and believing that it was protecting its police power from German usurpation, went even farther than the German authorities asked. The Interior Ministry's Ingrand and Fernand de Brinon, the French government's official spokesman in Paris, assured Captain Beumelburg, the German liaison officer, not only that six persons had been chosen for execution, but also—something that the Germans had not asked—that "the sentence handed down by the special tribunal be executed in an exemplary fashion by decapitation by guillotine in a public square in Paris."[20]

Interior Minister Pierre Pucheu tried energetically to supplant the Germans' executions of hostages with a home-grown repression that would work even more effectively—at least it would be French. He had already seized the opportunity offered by the German war against the Soviet Union to carry out mass arrests of the French far Left and other enemies of the National Revolution. Within days of the first assassination, he set up a series of exceptional tribunals to apply summary justice to people suspected of troubling public order; and before two months had passed, he organized three special new police units—the Police for Jewish Affairs, the Anti-Communist Police, and the Police for Secret Societies. The new authoritarian measures of August 1941 altered the character of the Vichy regime, but they did not suffice either to stop the Resistance's resort to direct action, or to persuade the German authorities to leave public order exclusively to the French. Between 21 August and 20 October, when the Feldkommandant of Nantes was shot, five Germans were assassinated in Occupied France.

Soon the Germans were shooting hostages on their own, without even bothering with Vichy's "exemplary" executions. The MBF issued a decree later known as the *code des hôtages:* for every German killed, they would shoot between fifty and one hundred hostages. In October, close to one hundred were shot, at Chateaubriant and Bordeaux. The barbarous spirit of the war in Russia had reached French soil. Eventually, between 500 and 550 Frenchmen were shot as hostages, creating "an unbridgeable gap of hatred between the population and the occupying authority."[21]

The entire hostage episode provided a dress rehearsal for the massive roundups, internments, and deportations that were soon to follow. Although the hostage code did not mention Jews, and although the MBF focussed at first on Communists and anarchists, the proportion of Jews among the hostages was high from the beginning.[22] In their haste to show the Germans how vigorously they both condemned violence against the Germans and were pursuing the real guilty parties, the Vichy authorities slipped easily into familiar charges of Jewish responsibility. The government declared that it responded to the German execution of hostages "with emotion," and left no doubt that it condemned Nazi brutality and the affront to its sovereignty, but promised to strike out on its own at "those responsible."[23]

For Vichy, "those responsible" always included Jews. Ambassador de Brinon, wired Göring, after the execution of one group of hostages, that he joined "the entire French people" in deploring "the actions of criminals incited daily by radio broadcasts of Jewish *émigrés* in the pay of the British government and the bolshevik plutocrats."[24] *Le Matin* phrased it more soberly, but the message was the same: "Jews, Communists, and foreign agitators constitute a national danger."[25] In a press communiqué issued on 10 December, Darlan announced that the *Etat français* was going to subject all foreign Jews who had come to France since 1 January 1936—even if they had acquired French citizenship— either to service in labor battalions or to internment in special centers. "Exhaustive research," he said, had established that those responsible for the crimes "were at once foreigners (parachutists, bomb throwers, hoodlums of the Spanish Reds), Jews, Communists."[26] On 2 January 1942, Interior Minister Pucheu followed up with a circular to all regional prefects, specifying just how these foreign Jews were to be censused and assigned to camps or forced residence.[27] As Darlan noted, in his own communiqué of 10 December, the Vichy government's new measures of repression were designed "to reach not only the immediate authors of these outrages, but also those directly or indirectly responsible for this rash of murder."[28] In that loose sense, it hardly required "exhaustive research" to declare foreigners, Jews, and Communists guilty.

Not satisfied by Vichy's measures against the assassins or their supposed supporters, the German authorities in the Occupied Zone turned their violence more directly against Jews in December 1941. On 12 December, they arrested 743 Jewish professional men and intellectuals in Paris, all French citizens and many of them decorated war veterans; and, after rounding out an even 1,000 with foreign Jews picked up at random in Paris, they interned these hostages in a prison compound at Compiègne. A notice published in the press of the Occupied Zone on 14 December announced a fine of a billion francs imposed upon the Jews of the Occupied Zone, and the deportation to the East for forced labor of "a large number of criminal Judeo-bolshevik elements." It was the first public mention of the deportations to come. Finally, the notice announced the execution of 100 more hostages in reprisal for recent attacks on German soldiers. The next day 95 hostages—including the Communist writer Gabriel Péri and including 53 Jews—were shot at Mont-Valérien.

In the fever of the hostage crisis, the Vichy government seems to have given a low priority to trying to save even the French citizens among the Jews caught in these roundups. When de Brinon asked, from Paris in October, what to do, Darlan suggested intervening on behalf of war veterans[29]—a tactic that, in effect, wrote off all the French Jews who were not war veterans. And in the usual progression, Vichy ended up by compromising even further. At first, Xavier Vallat reported that the German authorities were willing to hear appeals on behalf of Jewish war veterans. Then Dr. Werner Best permitted de Brinon to present requests about certain limited categories of war veteran ("victims of wounds or those with especially noteworthy military qualifications"). Finally, after 13 December, the MBF would hear no applications from the Vichy government about any arrested Jews.[30] In the end, a few dozen of the prominent Jews arrested on 12 December were released by the Germans, but according to criteria of the latter's choosing, such as illness. The Vichy government made no comprehensive remonstrances defending these Jews as French citizens, either on the basis of the armistice terms, or on that of the Hague Conventions concerning the rights of an occupying power.

Deportation had been announced on 14 December. As early as January 1942, only a shortage of trains prevented the RSHA from shipping to the east a first batch of the internees held at Compiègne.[31] General Otto von Stülpnagel, the *Militärbefehlshaber in Frankreich,* who seems to have been revolted by the reprisal executions imposed on him by Berlin, and eventually resigned his office, urged deportations as a more effective reprisal measure than the shooting of hostages. Before leaving Paris in February 1942, he proposed that instead of executions the Germans should deport to the east "great masses of Communists and Jews"—a tactic that he thought would be less provocative yet more intimidating. In April, von Stülpnagel's successor, his cousin Karl Heinrich von Stülpnagel, issued a circular citing Hitler's latest order: for every subsequent outrage, not only would hostages be executed but five hundred Jews and Communists would be handed over to Himmler for deportation to the east. Reserves for this purpose were to be kept interned at Compiègne.[32]

The first deportation trainload of Jews left France, then, supposedly in reprisal for attacks upon German servicemen in France. The RSHA *Judenamt* having finally succeeded, after three months' effort, in obtaining a train, 1,112 Jews left Drancy for Auschwitz on 27 March 1942 in third-class carriages—the only deportees to escape the ordeal of freight cars before the inevitable massacre in Poland. These first deportees included those swept up in the Paris arrests of August 1941 (mostly foreign Jews) and December 1941 (mostly French Jews, chosen for their prominence), plus some others arrested subsequently. Only 19 of them returned after the war.[33]

The two successive *Militärbefehlshabers* had preferred to see the first deportation as a police action, related in some loose legal way to acts of terrorism in France.[34] Already the RSHA was thinking more radically in terms of a total purge of the race. They were held back only by the shortage of railway cars. After the first train left on 27 March, there was a lull in the deportations while logistical preparations were being made. Eichmann had told Helmut Knochen, head of the *Sicherheitsdienst* in France, that five thousand Jews could follow the first transport to the east, and that 95 percent of these should be able-bodied men.[35] When rolling stock became available in June, these Jews were dispatched; and more followed. As we saw at the beginning of this chapter, the prefect of the Meuse reported vividly to de Brinon as the third transport (including many women) went through Bar-le-Duc on its way to Germany. Vichy remained silent.

Meanwhile, a number of German offices were planning something much more ambitious. Heydrich, meeting the new French police chief Bousquet in Paris in early May, alluded to additional deportations.[36] Then Dannecker saw the Wehrmacht's railway director General Kohl on 13 May and achieved a major opening of the transportation bottleneck. The general, it turned out, was sympathetic to the deportation project and promised enough trains to send between 10,000 and 20,000 Jews from France in the months ahead.[37] Just over a week later, Ambassador Abetz told Knochen that the embassy would have no objections on political grounds to the deportation of Jews from France as long as foreign Jews were taken first—only now the figure of deportees under discussion had swollen to 40,000.[38]* On 11 June a decisive meeting took place in Berlin, a sort of Wannsee Conference in miniature, with far more precise details. Dannecker, together with the other *Judenreferenten* in Brussels and The Hague, assembled in Eichmann's office at the RSHA. According to Dannecker's account, Himmler had ordered more Jews from southeastern Europe (Rumania) and occupied western Europe to be sent to Auschwitz "for labor service." The Netherlands were to yield 15,000 Jews; Belgium, 10,000; and France, "including the Unoccupied Zone," 100,000. Arrangements were to be made with the French government to strip all French deportees of their citizenship. Finally, the French were to bear the costs. Transportation amounted to 700 Deutsche marks per Jew, plus "equipment and food for the Jews for a period of fifteen days from the day of their deportation."[40] (Vichy was shortchanged by this allowance: most deportees did not live more than four or five days after they left France.)

Back in Paris, Dannecker set a figure of half the French total—50,000 Jews—to ask Vichy to deliver from the Unoccupied Zone. A senior embassy official, Rudolph Rahn, made an appointment with Laval for 27 June to present this demand officially to the French government.[41] Eichmann was due in Paris three days after that to get the project moving. Laval would have to decide how to respond.

Laval and the Final Solution

> Laval . . . stated flatly that these foreign Jews had always been a problem in France and that the French government was glad that a change in German attitude towards them gave France an opportunity to get rid of them.
>
> U.S. diplomat Tyler Thompson (August 1942)[42]

The RSHA found it difficult to pursue its anti-Jewish activities in the Occupied Zone without the help of the French administration and public services. Of all the operations we have mentioned so far, only the arrest of the thousand Jewish leaders on 12 December 1941 was carried out largely by German police forces. To mount a much larger operation

*On 10 March 1942, the German Foreign Office (Martin Luther) had asked Abetz's opinion on the first deportations.[39]

and, above all, to extend it to the Unoccupied Zone, the cooperation of French services was indispensable—a point about which the German authorities were always explicit. To achieve their ends, the Nazis now had to win the cooperation of the new government leader Pierre Laval.

Unlike most of the servants of the National Revolution, Laval was closely identified with the Third Republic and its political system. He had no links to the Croix de Feu or with Doriot's Parti Populaire Français as had Pucheu and Propaganda Minister Paul Marion. He had not been shaped by the military bureaucracy as had General Weygand or Admiral Darlan, by the civil service as had Baudouin or by the colonial administration as had Peyrouton or General Noguès. Nor did he have sentimental attachments to a traditionalist vision of a rural France set in an orderly hierarchy, as had Education Minister Jacques Chevalier or the head of the youth corps, General de la Porte du Theil. In any of these milieus hostility to Jews was common, if not always evident. Laval, by contrast, liked to present himself as a man involved with down-to-earth practical matters, as were his fellow Auvergnats.

During a long political career launched in 1914 and carried on as a deputy and senator, as minister repeatedly after 1926, and twice as prime minister (fall 1931, fall 1935), Laval was one of those who gravitated from a youthful socialism to a more rewarding centrist position. He won a seat in 1924 as an adherent of the Cartel des Gauches (a leftist political bloc which included the Socialists), obtained his first ministerial post a year later in the second government of Paul Painlevé, and then served repeatedly under Aristide Briand, the "Pilgrim of Peace." By the early 1930s, Laval was an indispensable centrist *ministrable* ("ministerial material"). His associations were all firmly republican. True, he was a strenuous opponent of Léon Blum, whose Popular Front victory in May 1936 removed Laval to the political sidelines and filled him with a deep and abiding resentment. Moreover, Laval's principal opponents in his home base of Aubervilliers, a Paris working-class suburb, were the Communists, which gave his local campaigning a somewhat more overt ideological tone than his national position. Nationally, he was known as a pragmatic figure committed to conciliation abroad and a balanced budget at home even at the cost of social services during the Depression. Above all, he was linked to a political style of bargaining and coalition building which probably underestimated the real consistencies in the man's convictions.

Laval may possibly have dropped an anti-Jewish phrase or two before the war, and he may even have picked up a germ of the prejudice that infected his society. This was hardly uncommon. But at no time did he resort to the mudslinging of a Xavier Vallat or to the easy assumption of Jews as scapegoats common in the late 1930s. Indeed, some antisemites indulged their own fantasies to the point of branding Laval himself a Jew—a form of abuse that could hardly have endeared him to their campaign.[43] It seems reasonable to agree with one biographer that Laval "was never an antisemite," at least never out of conviction—which is not to say that he was incapable of massive lapses of humanity when it came to Jews.[44]* They were simply not among his priorities.

Other concerns pressed heavily upon him when he took over the government in the spring of 1942. We have already mentioned the sharply escalating German demands for support in the war effort against the Soviet Union, the most preoccupying of which was German labor boss Sauckel's ever-mounting quotas for French workers to go and work in German factories. Laval also had to contend with a world strategic situation in which Vichy's carefully defended neutrality was growing more and more precarious as the Western allies threatened to invade continental Europe. Confronted with these daunting challenges, Laval hardly felt secure in his grip on power. The prefects' reports brought him steady reminders of his unpopularity in public opinion. The memory of his sudden ouster in December 1940 reminded him how quickly Pétain's somewhat grudging tolerance could evaporate. Laval retained the warm support of Otto Abetz in the German embassy, but just as the embassy had managed to pressure Vichy with a threat to impose Laval during his period of waiting in Paris, now the embassy could pressure him with the threat of Doriot. There remained Darlan in the wings, still commander in chief of the armed forces and, perhaps more ominously, still the officially designated successor to the Chief of State. At the moment when Laval returned to power, the sensational escape of General Henri Giraud from the German prison fortress of Königstein showed him how much his relationship to the German occupation authorities was subject to the actions of a host of other Frenchmen, most of them cool at best to his efforts. To retain his grip, Laval would have to deliver: workers, food, supplies, and public order to the Germans; and, to the French population, some striking proof of his capacity to win some improvement in their daily lives—the return of prisoners of war, or more to eat.

As he approached the difficult encounter with the Germans, Laval was buoyed by a remarkable self-confidence. He had always placed

*Philippe Erlanger claims that, as head of the government in 1935, Laval asked him for a copy of the *Protocols of the Elders of Zion* and seemed to attach importance to it.[45]

great faith in his ability to manage a difficult situation by a frank man-to-man bargain. In 1931, as prime minister, he had gone to Washington to try to solve in person the decade-old war debts imbroglio. In the fall of 1940, not yet foreign minister, he had sought out Ambassador Abetz and then a personal meeting with the Führer himself. The meager results of these summit negotiations did not discourage him; indeed, the bleak prospects of spring 1942 seemed to confirm his sense of indispensability. In public, Laval was prepared to go through the motions of friendship which in his mind constituted part of the currency of a Franco-German deal. "I hope for the victory of Germany," he told the French in a poorly received radio broadcast on 22 June 1942, "because without her communism would take over everywhere in Europe." In private, he lost no opportunity to attempt to engage German officials in a bargaining session. It was Laval who bought off Sauckel for a while by devising the *relève*, the bargain whereby for every three skilled French workers who volunteered to go to work in German factories one French prisoner of war would be released. It was Laval who started as early as May 1942 reminding Germans that the French population would be inclined to favor an Allied invasion unless the occupation authorities made concessions to French living standards and national pride.[46] It was Laval who asked Hitler for concessions that would impress the French people, "to hit them between the eyes" *(die ins Auge fallen)*. In February 1943, Laval told Knochen that the Americans had promised France all the Italian colonies and the Rhine frontier (a total invention on Laval's part), while the Germans had promised nothing.[47] He never lost the conviction that Hitler wanted, or would eventually need, France as a partner in the antibolshevik campaign. In order to launch the real substantive bargaining for his long-range purposes, Laval kept giving in on issues at a shorter range.

What Laval wanted most, like his predecessors, was a final peace treaty with the Germans that would replace—with some more comfortable permanent arrangement—the awkward and galling restrictions of the Armistice Agreement, which had been intended to be temporary but had dragged along for two years. Short of such a treaty, he hoped for some German assurances about future frontiers and overseas possessions, a return of the million and one half French prisoners of war still held in German prison camps, an improvement in food and fuel supply, the suppression of the crippling Demarcation Line sealing the Occupied off from the Unoccupied Zone, and the restoration of French administrative autonomy in the Occupied Zone. He gained only the last two goals, since—as we shall see—they were to German advantage. In his quest for the others, he gave the Germans most of what they wanted.

Knochen came away from his 12 February 1943 meeting with Laval convinced that the French premier would "swallow" a complete *Endlösung*—the wholesale removal of all Jews from France, French citizens included—if he thought that he could thereby win political concessions for the rest of the French people.[48] Knochen knew Laval well, and we see no reason to doubt that assessment of the latter's priorities.

Indeed, the Germans did not have to bargain hard to get Laval to agree to the deportation of foreign Jews, at least. Vichy wanted to get rid of its foreign Jews. The French government had been trying to persuade the Germans for years to take their refugees back. Long preoccupied by the burden of its refugee population, Vichy was beginning to hear the rising voice of popular resentment at the ever-swelling tide of foreign Jews in the Unoccupied Zone which we discussed in the previous chapter. When Dannecker had toured the Unoccupied Zone in February 1942, Roland von Krug von Nidda, the German consul-general in Vichy, told him that the French would likely hand over between one thousand and five thousand Jews a month and would even supply the necessary railroad cars, provided that the cars would be returned to France.[49] Where could Krug have gotten such an idea, unless it was making the rounds in Vichy? Later, when the deportations of foreign Jews from the Unoccupied Zone began, some observers were quick to claim that the Germans were simply taking back the Jews they had so inconsiderately dumped in France in October 1940.* The Vichy regime never raised any real objection to shipping *foreign* Jews back to Germany.

In fact, Vichy sounded rather afraid at one point that the deportations might *not* extend to the foreign Jews in the Unoccupied Zone. The subject arose when Heydrich visited Paris in early May 1942. The first deportation train had left six weeks earlier, carrying Jews arrested exclusively in the Occupied Zone. Would it be possible, asked French police chief René Bousquet, to include in future deportation trains some of the foreign Jews who had been interned in the Unoccupied Zone for the last year and a half?[51] Heydrich seemed evasive, saying that it depended on the availability of trains. At this point, Vichy was the eager party.

On the eve of his appointment with Rudolph Rahn in Paris at the end of June 1942, Laval clearly realized that something much more sweeping than a few refugees was at stake. He could not avoid taking

---

*As Pastor Boegner wrote to Pétain, "It will be claimed, I am sure, that France is merely giving back those Jews to Germany whom the latter sent us the autumn of 1940."[50]

the matter up with his cabinet colleagues. The cabinet assembled weekly during June in Vichy, but the question of French labor for German factories dominated the discussions. Finally, on 26 June, on the eve of his meeting with Rahn, Laval raised "a most sensitive matter: the Jewish question." He pointed out that the question had been resolved in Germany "in an extremely severe fashion," unacceptable in France where the Jewish problem "has never been so acute." Vichy was under German pressure "to strengthen the measures of constraint against the Jews," he said, in the face of which the French had to act "with the utmost prudence." No specific guidelines were set, and Laval clearly intended to keep this awkward matter in his own hands. He assured his ministerial colleagues that he would do nothing without reporting beforehand to Pétain. Finally, he reiterated the long-standing Vichy policy of favoring native Jews over immigrants. He had decided on another Jewish census, he said, "in order to distinguish French Jews from the foreigners."[52]

Back from hearing directly from Rahn (and possibly even from Eichmann, though there is no direct evidence that the two actually met) what the Germans now proposed to do with the Jews of France, Laval raised the matter once more in the cabinet, this time obliquely, on 3 July. He did not mention the plan for massive deportations. He repeated his proposal for a new census which would distinguish French Jews from foreigners. Pétain intervened to support Laval's efforts: "The Marshal considers that this distinction . . . is just and will be understood by public opinion."[53]

During these days the Germans formed an impression of uneasy hesitancy on the French side. At a meeting in Oberg's office on 2 July, Bousquet suddenly declared that the French police could *not* undertake the massive roundup: "The French were not opposed to the arrests, but . . . the fact that they were to be undertaken by the French police was embarrassing for Paris."[54] Laval himself had asked to see Oberg about the matter, and Leguay had refused to submit a plan of operations. Exasperated, Dannecker referred to "a wait-and-see, often refractory attitude of the French government representatives and officials on the subject of the solution of the Jewish question."[55]

Laval finally set the course on 4 July. That day the head of the French police relayed the Vichy government's decision to the Gestapo in Paris. Dannecker's notes suggest that Vichy issued a virtual blank check, signed by the Chief of State and the head of government: "Bousquet declared that, at the recent cabinet meeting, Marshal Pétain, the head of state, together with Pierre Laval, agreed to the deportation, *as a first step* [*pour commencer*], of all stateless Jews from the Occupied and Unoccupied zones" (our italics).[56]

Pour commencer. Was this really the impression that Laval wanted to convey? Or was Dannecker coloring Bousquet's statement with his own preferences? What seems most likely is that Laval hoped that giving up, first, stateless and, then, foreign Jews might satisfy the Germans. But he could hardly have been under real illusion on that point, for the German authorities repeatedly insisted that *all* Jews were targeted for deportation. Eichmann had clearly said so. Just over a month later, Röthke and Dannecker reminded Leguay of where things stood:

The delegate-general of police [Leguay] was told that we have no cause to doubt the fulfillment of promises made by Laval in the presence of Bousquet, during the meeting with the BdS [Knochen, who was *Befehlshaber der Sicherheitsdienstes*]. It was made very clear to Laval on that occassion that this was a definitive action, the last phase of which would also include Jews of French nationality."[57]

The *Sicherheitsdienst* was willing to humor Laval up to a point. Discussing the situation with his colleagues in Brussels, Dannecker indicated that, in agreement with Vichy, deportations were being temporarily limited to stateless and foreign Jews, apart from some French Jews deported in reprisal actions. In the future, however, the French would be asked to undertake massive denaturalizations of French Jews so they could be reported, too.[58] Laval may have thought that in postponing things he had won a real concession; but he had never won any suggestion of agreement by the German authorities to what is generally considered to have been the cardinal point of his response to the final solution: to buy off French Jews with stateless and foreign ones.

The Effort to Segregate: The Jewish Star

Throughout Europe, the Nazis aimed to segregate the Jews from the rest of society, in preparation for the Final Solution. The restrictions on intermarriage and other provisions of the Nuremberg decrees of 1935 were one step in this direction, and the withdrawal of Jewish children from German schools after *Kristallnacht* was another. Periodically the Nazis had also discussed a scheme to label the person of each Jew in some way in order to facilitate the isolation of the Jews from the rest of the population; but the scheme had been rejected for practical reasons.[59]

The war gave the Germans their chance to realize it; and in eastern Europe, the site of so many ghastly Nazi experiments, occupation authorities first imposed a distinguishing sign on Jews. In 1939, the Gouvernement General, the civil administration of occupied Poland, ordered all Jews to wear a blue star of David. In those parts of Poland annexed to the Reich, a Jew had to wear two Jewish stars sewn on the left breast and the back of an outer garment. Eventually, in September 1941, the star was extended to the whole territory of the Reich. Though it was costly to implement in terms of both world opinion and the sensibility of Germany's allies, and cumbersome to administer, especially in view of divergent views within the German administration, its partisans thought it worth considerable effort to humiliate the Jews and mark out one further step toward their elimination from Europe.

As early as December 1941, in a menacing list of anti-Jewish measures he wanted for the Occupied Zone, General Otto von Stülpnagel suggested to Vichy that French Jews wear a star. Darlan replied on 21 January 1942, disagreeing with the proposals for two reasons. First, he argued that the anti-Jewish regulations already decreed were "adequate to attain the desired goal, that is to say . . . to expel [Jews] from public employment and command posts of the country's industrial and commercial activity." Second, he warned, the measure might "profoundly shock French public opinion which would see these measures as mere harassment without any real utility either for the future of the country or for the security of the occupation troops." Indeed, the proposal "threatened to provoke a swing in favor of the Israelites, who could be considered martyrs."[60] If Darlan's arguments impressed anyone within the MBF staff, they were insufficient to restrain the antisemitic activists. Dannecker vigorously pressed the introduction of the star upon his colleagues in Belgium in early 1942, and meetings under Eichmann's auspices in Berlin and Knochen's in Paris during March settled the details. Jews in Holland, Belgium, and Occupied France would be required to wear the star.[61] As Knochen explained to Eichmann's office on 20 March, the star would be "one more step on the road to the final solution of the Jewish problem in all the occupied territories in the West." He hoped that by putting it forcefully he could persuade the authorities in Berlin to override the reluctance of top German military figures in Belgium—Brigadier General Eggert Reeder and General von Falkenhausen.[62]

Various complications delayed the project and the original date for imposing the star—15 March 1942—had to be changed several times. Diplomatic officials had to iron out wrinkles created by the presence in France of Jewish nationals of belligerent states, such as Great Britain and the United States, neutral states, or allies of the Axis, such as Rumania, Italy, or Bulgaria. Would these also have to wear the star? Eventually, the Germans agreed to exempt these Jews (amounting to almost ten thousand persons) for fear of adverse political repercussions. Further, the MBF was sensitive to Darlan's prediction of a negative French reaction. Dr. Werner Best realized that the cooperation of the French administration, and particularly the police, would be needed. He hoped the delay would enable the new French commissioner for Jewish affairs, Darquier de Pellepoix, to assume the risks and burdens of the new measure and impose a French star decree for *both* zones. Dannecker, who agreed with Best's assessment of Darquier's willingness to impose a star on all the Jews of France, doubted that the latter would be able to carry the Vichy government with him. In the margin of Best's remarks about Darquier, Dannecker penciled "too optimistic."[63]

Dannecker, it turned out, was right. Vichy refused to impose the star, and not even the advent of Pierre Laval shook the government's resolve to stay out of the matter. In the event, the Germans went ahead on their own in the Occupied Zone only. As of 7 June 1942, all Jews over the age of six had to wear, on the left side of an outer garment, a star of David the size of the palm of a hand, upon which was written in black letters the word *Juif* or *Juive*. At the local commissariat of police, each Jew was to obtain three stars, to be charged against him on his textile ration card. The French police estimated that over one hundred thousand Jews were subject to the decree, and after a few weeks eighty-three thousand had received stars.[64] Clearly, many Jews were refusing to obey the ordinance. This was not the first indication that the enforcement of the decree was running into difficulty.

It is worth pondering why the Vichy government was so much more recalcitrant about the star than about the deportation of foreign Jews. It was not that the star branded Jews, but that it discriminated against the wrong kind of Jew. Above all, it removed authority over such discrimination entirely from French hands. Nothing could have been more calculated to embarrass the Vichy government than to stigmatize native French Jews and to exempt certain groups of foreigners. An outraged citizen wrote to the CGQJ at once to point this out.[65] *Le*

Matin made the same observation, which the Germans did their best to silence.[66] Abetz, more sensitive to French public opinion than were other German officials, wrote Knochen that although the French population "is generally speaking in absolute agreement with the introduction of a distinctive sign for the Jews . . . [it] takes a very dim view of seeing foreign Jews exempt, in part, from German measures, foreign Jews who are perceived as outsiders much more than are long-established French Jews."[67]

On 12 June, Pétain ordered de Brinon to explain to the German authorities that "natural and necessary distinctions" had to be made among Jews. He wanted the French government, in the person of the new commissioner-general Darquier de Pellepoix, to make the distinctions:

> I am convinced that the German high command understands perfectly well that certain exceptions are indispensable. . . . And that seems to me necessary in order that the just measures taken against the Israelites [*pour que de justes mesures prises contre les Israélites*] be understood and accepted by the French.[68]

German refusal of this request reduced Pétain and other Vichy grandees to the role of humble suppliants, each with his own list of Jews for whom he sought exemptions. As if to rub salt into the wound and underscore the fact that the French were strangers in part of their own country, all official requests had to go to the Germans through Ambassador de Brinon in Paris. Pétain wanted exemptions for three society ladies: the Comtesse d'Aramon, the Marquise de Chasseloup-Laubat, and her sister Madame Pierre Girot de Langlade.[69] Cardinal Suhard, archbishop of Paris, appealed to de Brinon on behalf of Catholic converts or descendants of converts whom he feared might have to wear the star.[70] Most embarrassing of all, Madame Fernand de Brinon herself, *née* Frank, was the object of a special appeal.*

To these and several other petitions the Germans turned a cold eye. They authorized a handful of temporary exemptions (Pétain's three friends, Madame de Brinon, and the widow of Henri Bergson among others), but in general they refused to entertain such requests. The head of the Paris fire department learned that twenty-eight Jewish

---

*The exemption for Madame de Brinon was limited, according to a note of Hagen's of 13 July 1942, "to her residence in the de Brinon property in the Basses-Pyrénées Department near Biarritz. Ambassador de Brinon will hear from Ambassador Abetz in person that it would be desirable for his wife to live continuously on their estate . . . if she does not live in the Occupied Zone."[71]

firemen would have to wear the star on their uniform. Even Pétain's personal requests would not be approved unless countersigned by Laval.[72] Ambassador Georges Scapini, the blind war veterans' advocate who had often conducted high-level negotiations for Vichy, telephoned General Reinecke in Paris, approving the marking of Jews in general but asking that decorated war veterans be exempted. Wearing a French decoration side by side with a Jewish star, Scapini argued, "was unseemly [*war nicht schön*]" and made the decree unpopular among French people. General Reinecke's response was blunt: "The Jews should be forbidden to wear decorations, as is the case in our country, and then the question would be settled."[73]

The Germans intended the star to isolate the Jews of the Occupied Zone in preparation for their deportation from France. Once marked, it would be possible to segregate them in the rounds of everyday life. In July, the MBF rushed forward with the rest of its segregation measures. Jews were prohibited from frequenting public swimming pools, restaurants, cafés, theaters, cinemas, concerts, music halls, markets and fairs, museums, libraries, public exhibitions, historical monuments, sporting events, campgrounds, and public parks. Jews could not use public telephones and were obliged to ride in the last car in the Métro. Jews' shopping was strictly limited to certain afternoon hours—a particular hardship since in times of scarcity the stores had little to sell after early morning.[74]

Previous to the star decree, persecution of the Jews was hidden from most of the French public. Now it was visible—on the most fashionable streets of Paris where, on the Sunday following the ordinance, Jewish veterans strolled, wearing their star along with their military decorations; in the Métro, where it was reported that gentiles had given up their seats for Jews; and even in churches, where some practicing Catholics and one priest, classified Jewish by race, appeared with the Jewish sign.[75] Newspapers in the capital stoutly defended the new measures, at least in public; *Le Matin* warned that Jews occasionally removed their stars or did not sew them on properly.[76] But few pedestrians could ignore the mounting public nausea. Unlike the special notices affixed to Jewish stores in the Occupied Zone in 1940—apparently many shops lost customers—the star was perceived as an offense against individual dignity. Although several prefects in the Occupied Zone mentioned the star—there were few Jews left in many rural areas of the north—four of them (Morbihan, Seine-et-Oise, Vienne, Vosges) reported that the sign aroused more pity than repugnance, especially when it was worn by veterans or "long-established French Jews."[77] No prefect reported any favorable opinion.

Dr. Friedrich, official representative in France of the German Propaganda Ministry, conceded on Paris radio that the public response was hostile. "There are some who consider antisemitism as a kind of barbarism, and would like more regard shown to Jews than is now the case. . . . I have never heard so much talk about 'good' and 'bad' Jews since the introduction of the yellow star."[78] At least two Nazi reports referred to public indignation at the sight of children forced to wear the star. By October, General Oberg, the SS chief in France, was complaining openly about the failure of propaganda efforts to make the star acceptable.[79] By then, however, the French people had been exposed to a great deal worse.

The star provoked the first extensive, open resistance to the anti-Jewish persecution in France. One theme was ridicule, a kind of black humor inspired by the bizarre extravagance of the Nazi obsession with race. In Paris, Bordeaux, and Nancy, German police and counterespionage agents discovered Jewish sympathizers wearing yellow flowers, yellow handkerchiefs, or bits of papers with ironic inscriptions like "Auvergnat," "Goy," or "Danny," the name of a Jewish boyfriend.[80] Such protests were immediately picked up by foreign news services. London reported that Paris university students wore badges with an inscription *Juif* purporting to stand for "Jeunesse Universitaire Intellectuelle Française." In Geneva it was said that the star was mockingly called *pour le sémite*, an allusion to the Prussian decoration *pour le mérite*. From Zurich came a story of protesters ironically reminding Vichy of de Brinon's Jewish wife.[81]

Dannecker ordered the *Feldgendarmerie* (the German military police) to intern the demonstrators. Many, of course, were not caught. But twenty non-Jews arrested in such manifestations remained at Drancy at the end of the summer, finally to be released in September.[82] Moreover, the public incidents that troubled the police were only the tip of an iceberg. Other French people recorded their revulsion in some other fashion. The Council of the Protestant Federation of France wrote to Pétain expressing the "painful impression" created by the star, despite the Protestants' recognition of the need for a "solution to the Jewish problem."[83] The political scientist Maurice Duverger later recalled that it was the star that first conveyed the gravity of the persecutions and the true implications of fascism to people previously unaware of antisemitism except in a theoretical way.[84] Jean Galtier-Boissière headed the discussion of the star in his wartime journal with the phrase "in the depths of the Middle Ages."[85]

Some Germans remained confident. Dannecker boldly scrawled "to Drancy" in the margin of one of Zeitschel's more pessimistic assessments of French response. Other Germans, on the other hand, had their worst fears confirmed. The SS heard rumors on 17 June that Otto Abetz, who had been persuaded a few weeks before to support the star, once again opposed it.[86] Segregation, moreover, imposed extremely unpleasant new duties upon the French police. They now had to ensure that Jewish children did not leave the city to attend summer camps, that Jewish housewives did not shop at forbidden hours, that all stars were properly attached. Encounters between French police and Jews were bound to increase, as Jews hid their stars behind briefcases, or tried illegally to buy cigarettes, or dared to attach a star with pins so that it could easily be removed. Anyone with a "Jewish appearance" but without a star was a potential violator of the ordinance, and people who denounced the innocent made the situation nearly impossible for those police who tried conscientiously to enforce the law.

Thus, while the Germans needed the French police more than ever after the imposition of the star, they began discerning a certain "vacillation" as early as the beginning of June. The MBF staff noted at that time that police units "knowingly favored Jews' breaking the regulations."[87] This was certainly an overstatement, for throughout this period the French police handed out stars and cooperated with their German counterparts in the enforcement of the ordinance.* Nevertheless, the Germans were obliged thereafter to weigh the amount of French police support they were likely to get when imposing future measures. No doubt some calculation of this sort persuaded the Germans not to extend the star to the southern zone even after they occupied all of France in November 1942. Although Darquier de Pellepoix kept advocating it publicly, the Vichy government never imposed the star on its own, and the Germans did not insist. Instead, the Vichy government took an action that in some ways was even more threatening. On 11 December 1942, it ordered all Jews' vital personal documents stamped *Juif* or *Juive*—the identity card, the work permit, and the ration card.[89] Vichy did mark its Jews, but—instead of the cloth of the outer garment, which everyone could see—it preferred paper, concealed from all eyes but the civil servant's.

---

*The French police in Poitiers handed out 1,257 stars in summer 1942.[88]

Preparing the Deportation

> Bousquet then asked Heydrich whether the Jews who had been interned
> for a year and a half in the Unoccupied Zone could be included in the
> deportation transport. The question was left open, depending on railway
> traffic conditions.
>
> René Bousquet (May 1942), as quoted
> by Consul-General Schleier (September 1942)[90]

The summer of 1942 marked a passage in the history of Vichy's
anti-Jewish program from its legislative stage—exclusion from the public function, the *numerus clausus* in professions and higher education,
and aryanization of the economy—to a stage dominated by police actions—roundups, internment, and deportation. Hereafter the Jews'
great peril was the policeman's knock at the door, the midday roundup,
or arrest at the frontier. From the summer of 1942 on, the burden of
antisemitic policy weighed increasingly on the French police. It was
inevitable that it should be so, for as the Nazis' intentions grew more
violent, their own resources grew more and more scarce. There were
simply not enough Germans to do the job.

In mid-1942 the German occupation authorities maintained only
three battalions of police in France—between 2,500 and 3,000 men.[91]
Relatively isolated in French society and often hated by the population,
German police functioned with difficulty even in optimum conditions.
Few of them spoke French, and fewer still were familiar with the urban
and rural landscape where many Jews sought to hide. From the beginning, German police commanders relied heavily upon French police
for the day-to-day enforcement of the anti-Jewish ordinances in the
Occupied Zone. The arrest of the 1,000 leading Jewish personalities in
Paris in December 1941 was one of the rare operations carried out
mostly by German personnel. In the second half of 1942, reliance turned
into outright dependence as Nazi Jewish policy radicalized. Rounding
up Jews, watching border posts, guarding deportation trains—these
tasks, as well as being distasteful, were a severe drain on German manpower. Then when the Germans found themselves after November
1942 in occupation of the entire country (except for a small Italian zone),
their police resources were spread even thinner. Moreover, all this
occurred while the great military encounters in North Africa and the
Soviet Union put massive new demands on German forces. The following year, when General Oberg asked for 250 more German police to
carry out a major new deportation effort in July 1943, he was told that

he would have to content himself with four.[92] All the more critical, then, was the role of the French police.

In contrast to the Germans, the French had a powerful police apparatus. It had survived the débâcle of 1940 largely intact; and while the Germans were torn between their reluctance to entrust much transport and modern weaponry to the French police and their desire for a large indigenous force to assume the primary task of keeping internal order,* Vichy managed to build its strength considerably. The entire complement, at close to 100,000 men, was about the same size as the army permitted the French under the Armistice Agreement. It consisted of *gendarmerie,* municipal police, *gardes mobiles* (motorized police), and 30,000 police for Paris alone with its proudly separate Prefecture of Police, whose responsibilities extended well beyond the city of 3,000,000. The police followed the Vichy tendency toward administrative centralization. In April 1941, the regime nationalized the municipal police of every city of more than 10,000 inhabitants and set up a new layer of "super prefects" who were intended to solidify central control over the two crucial areas of food supply and police. Each regional prefect was flanked by an intendant of police and, after June 1942, had at his disposal a rapid striking force, a regiment of *gardes mobiles,* which he could despatch anywhere within his area of a half-dozen departments. Step by step, also, Vichy won new specialized police forces, such as the *gardes des communications* set up in December 1941 —but always at the price of involving the French police ever more directly in the protection of German war-making interests. After June 1942, when the *gendarmerie* was shifted back from the Ministry of War to the Ministry of the Interior, the whole apparatus was held firmly in the grip of Pierre Laval himself, through his close associate René Bousquet, secretary-general for police in the Ministry of the Interior.

Although the *Militärbefehlshaber in Frankreich* exercised a general supervision over all French police forces, Dannecker assigned a liaison officer from his *Judenreferat* to the Paris Prefecture of Police as soon as he arrived. In a long report of July 1941, he indicated that he had found an "undependable attitude" at the beginning among several high police officials, but that since spring 1941 things had gone smoothly.[94] The prefecture's own Jewish section had been in existence since October 1940. Directed by Commissaire François, this unit dealt regularly with various occupation authorities, administered concentration camps

---

*Werner Best wrote on 19 November 1941 that it was German policy to secure internal order in the first instance" through "indigenous police forces."[93]

in the Paris region (notably Drancy), and rounded up Jews in Paris.

The pride of this section was a remarkable card-file system which listed almost 150,000 Jews registered in the department of the Seine, alphabetically, by street, profession, and nationality. Administered by André Tulard, a career police official, this system was a model of organizational efficiency. It was continually updated. Cards of different colors distinguished French Jews from the rest.[95] The crucial first step in its creation seems to have been the census of Jews in the Occupied Zone which was prescribed by the German ordinance of 27 September 1940, and which General de La Laurencie, French government representative in the Occupied Zone, had ordered the French police to carry out.[96] Dannecker claimed that the card-file system was created after his urging; but, whatever its origins, it developed beyond the letter of German ordinances by bureaucratic momentum and by a long-standing police disposition to scrutinize and control foreigners. The Germans had full access to the file. They put it to its first systematic use in their arrest of the thousand leading Jewish personalities on 12 December 1941, and referred to it constantly after the deportations began in 1942.

Using tools such as this, the Paris municipal police kept track of Jews and enforced the laws against them—and, as far as one can tell without access to police archives, did so rigorously and efficiently, at least up to the summer of 1942. On a daily basis the police arrested and questioned individual Jews who appeared to be breaking some of the myriad regulations. On occasion, the police carried out mass sweep-ups of Jews: the roundup of 14 May 1941 netted about 3,400 mostly Polish Jews in Paris, and that of 20 August about the same number of mostly French Jews, all of whom were locked up in the special camps run by the Prefecture of Police. In December 1941, the Prefect of Police subjected all Jews under his jurisdiction to a periodic check of home address and activities.[97] In February 1942, the Germans added an 8 P.M. to 6 A.M. curfew to the battery of interdictions against Jews enforced by the Paris police.[98] The police administered the imposition of the Jewish star in June. Only when the weight of these measures became too great with the massive roundups of the summer of 1942 did the Paris police seriously worry the German authorities. And even then, in a letter to Bousquet on 29 July, Oberg acknowledged the "honorable conduct" of the French police; and Abetz told Berlin in October that the French police had provided "exemplary assistance" in the struggle against "terrorists."[99]

As they began to plan the more systematic deportation of Jews from France to the east, then, German officials could assume that the

French police would continue to cooperate. The efforts of Pierre Laval to strengthen Vichy's administrative autonomy in the Occupied Zone made that assumption a certainty. Like his predecessors, Laval was eager to roll back the German administrative encroachment in the Occupied Zone and to make Vichy the administrative master of its own house, of all of France.

The arrival of General Oberg as the new Höhere SS- and Polizei-führer (HSSPF), on 1 June 1942, provided the opportunity for a deal. In an exchange of letters concluding with Oberg's letter of 29 July and his briefing to the French regional prefects on 8 August, the Germans recognized the "free hand" of the French police "in certain areas . . . which did not immediately affect German interests." In particular, the Germans promised to furnish information about cases that concerned the French, to give orders to French police only through channels, to permit the French to establish reserve units of *gardes mobiles* in the Occupied Zone, and—most important—to relieve the French of the ugly task of designating hostages. The Germans also agreed to exclude from future execution as hostages persons whom the French police had handed over. Those accused of crimes that did not affect the Germans would remain in French hands. In exchange, the French police resolved to act vigorously against "communists, terrorists and saboteurs" and to assure "the repression of all the enemies of the Reich, carrying on this struggle itself, on its own responsibility."[100]

Though the Oberg-Bousquet accords were still under negotiation when the great roundups of July began, they reflected accurately the spirit in which the Vichy government responded to the dilemma posed by Eichmann's project. However disagreeable, police cooperation was deemed better than letting the Germans encroach on French administrative territory. Vichy even renewed the Oberg-Bousquet agreements in April 1943,[101] in the new circumstances produced by the German occupation of the south of France, even though the old accords had neither given the French police real "autonomy" nor improved public order in France. The Germans continued to execute hostages and even, in flagrant violation of the accords, took from French hands people whom the French police had arrested. The French government, complained Bousquet, was still under attack "notably by terrorists, communists, Jews, Gaullists, and foreign agents." Reaffirming police cooperation in April 1943 in the name of Laval, Bousquet spoke warmly, however, of the collaborative effort that had given the French police a "new push." He closed an address to Oberg with the same fearsome promise as in the previous summer:

What I wish to see is that the French police, whose task has never been so hard, technically and morally, can in the full expression of its independence, which is the most striking sign of the sovereignty of its government, pursue with a fierce energy the struggle against all the enemies of French internal security, against all the foreign agents who want anarchy and disorder to prevail in our land, against all those who, taking orders from abroad, want to serve a cause that is not that of France.[102]

The Jews, long since designated one of Vichy's "adversaries," were to pay heavily for this chimera of sovereignty and independence. Without these accords, the Germans would never have been able to take such a heavy toll of the Jews in France.

Bousquet also wanted to rein in the free-wheeling and unprofessional Police for Jewish Affairs, whose relationship to the regular police had always been awkward. Since Darquier de Pellepoix fancied having his own police arm, and since he enjoyed great credit with the Germans, liquidation of the PQJ was not a simple operation. Bousquet and Laval had to negotiate with Darquier over this issue, rather than give orders. Moreover, as the hour approached for the planned roundup of Jews in Paris, Bousquet and Laval wanted things to go smoothly. They decided to postpone a direct confrontation with Darquier over the PQJ. They gave him positive assurances about a reorganization of the PQJ, and although the unit was officially abolished on 5 July, it continued to function. Indeed, its inspectors played an important part in the roundups and deportations later that month. The dramatic events of July seem to have tipped the scales in favor of the obstreperous commissioner-general. Although Laval had clearly tried to prevent the renaissance of an anti-Jewish police outside regular police authority, he gave Darquier what he wanted a few weeks after the Vel d'Hiver roundup. In mid-August Vichy created the Sections d'Enquête et Contrôle (literally, investigation and inspection teams), a new anti-Jewish police with no more power of arrest than the old PQJ but with no less capacity for harassment. The SEC carried on to the end of the war.[103]

With questions of police responsibility more or less settled, the availability of trains became an all-important element in planning the deportations. Dannecker's first deportation projects had been frustrated for months by the scarcity of rolling stock, much of it devoted to the expanding needs of the campaign in Russia. When Dannecker finally obtained an allocation of trains from the Wehrmacht's director of railway transportation, General Kohl, on 13 May, their efficient use became an obsession with Dannecker and the other organizers of deportation. Deportation was a complex logistical process on a Europewide scale: timing and coordination were crucial. Railway schedules came to dominate the entire program. If a carefully arranged train had to depart less than full, the whole enterprise might be compromised. In mid-June, Dannecker noted that Berlin had just dispatched to the Occupied Zone some 37,000 freight cars, 800 passenger cars, and 1,000 locomotives, but many of these were needed for the 350,000 French workers required for Sauckel's labor program and for regular traffic between France and Germany. When cars were finally available for deportation purposes, under no circumstances could the timetable be broken or the pace allowed to slacken.

When a deportation train missed its schedule once, on 15 July 1942, Eichmann was furious. He telephoned the *Judenreferat* in Paris to deliver a blast that must have withered Heinz Röthke, the new man in charge. Röthke's own account tells the story:

> The SS-Obersturmführer [Eichmann] pointed out that it was a matter of prestige: difficult negotiations had been successfully conducted with the Reich Transport Ministry for these convoys, and now Paris was canceling a train. Such a thing had never happened to him before. The whole affair was "disgraceful."[104]

At this point Eichmann made his ultimate threat: "he wondered whether he shouldn't drop France entirely as a country to be evacuated." France could be denied the privilege of being included in the Final Solution. Thrown on the defensive, Röthke begged him not to do so, and promised that all future deportations would leave on time.[105] And they did.

Railway schedules, too, required close coordination between the two zones and depended upon the cooperation of the Vichy government—a cooperation Dannecker knew how to obtain. "A change of railway schedule is impossible," he noted on a list of points to be raised with Laval. If Vichy did not supply enough Jews from its own territory, "we should be obliged to arrest on our own, without distinction, the required Jews in the Occupied Zone"—a threat to deport French citizens as well as immigrant Jews.[106] By mid-August, schedules had been worked out for all of September. Röthke communicated these to Leguay, the French police representative in the Occupied Zone, so that Vichy could have ready the necessary number of Jews. According to Röthke, Leguay understood the logic of the timetable and made the necessary proposals—Jews to be rounded up at the right time, to be held in reserve, and other exigencies to be met.[107]

Before the trains could leave in a regular cadence, reserves of Jews had to be accumulated. We have seen how the spasmodic roundups of Jews in the Occupied Zone became more systematic under German pressure in the fall of 1941. In the Unoccupied Zone, too, the French concentration camp population, which had been falling through the year 1941, began rising again as the prefects began carrying out Darlan's order of 10 December 1941 to subject all foreign Jews who had come to France since 1936 to either internment or impressment into labor battalions.[108] When the Germans' trains had to be filled, the reserves of Jews would be ready to go.

The Jews' ability to emigrate from France would also have an effect on the Germans' capacity to fill their trains. With some active support from the French administration, Jews continued to leave the Unoccupied Zone despite the continued scarcity of shipping, the difficulties in obtaining visas, and the tangles produced by local bureaucracies.[109]* During the first six months of 1942, approximately 2,000 Jews emigrated legally from the Unoccupied Zone, compared with just over 3,000 during all of 1941.[110]† When Darquier de Pellepoix took over the CGQJ in May 1942, his office insisted on prior consultation on each individual case, imposing the delay of another tier of bureaucracy on Jewish emigration. Pierre Laval reminded the commissioner-general that it was government policy "to facilitate in every possible way the emigration of foreigners and Frenchmen superfluous to the national economy." Three months after Laval's complaint, however, the CGQJ was still intervening in emigration cases on its own.[111]

Meanwhile, in a clear early sign of a new direction in Nazi policy toward Jews, the German authorities had reversed their previous encouragement of emigration. As late as May 1941, when Göring ordered Jewish emigration from Bohemia and Moravia speeded up, the Nazi leaders may even have wanted to accelerate Jewish departures. At that time, it was official German policy to discourage Jewish emigration from western occupied territories in order to leave all available shipping space to emigration from the Old Reich, though policies differed rather confusingly from one jurisdiction to the next.[112] Soon after the German invasion of the Soviet Union, however, the Final Solution took com-

---

*A HICEM report on emigration for the first half of 1942 emphasizes new American restrictions since the United States had imposed additional limitations on the admission of Jews from Axis states when it entered the war in December 1941.

†These figures include only those who emigrated with the help of HICEM.

mand. On 23 October 1941 the Gestapo chief Heinrich Müller passed along an order from Himmler: apart from a few exceptions judged to be in the German interest, no more Jews were to emigrate from Germany or occupied Europe.[113] It seems to have taken some time for this injunction to have worked its way through the German bureaucracy. After additional notices, the MBF instructed 290 persons and services in occupied France on 4 February 1942: without the prior approval of Himmler, no more Jews could emigrate from the Occupied Zone.[114]

As it became important to produce foreign Jews from the Unoccupied Zone in August and September 1942 to meet its deportation quotas, the Vichy administration began to change its mind, too, about Jewish emigration. HICEM began encountering more obstacles to Jewish departures for North Africa and less cooperation from some prefects and camp officials. On 20 July, the Ministry of the Interior suspended exit visas previously issued to all foreign Jews except Belgians, Dutch, and Luxemburgers.[115] On 5 August, Henri Cado, member of the Conseil d'Etat and deputy secretary-general of the Police Nationale, sent an important telegram to regional prefects: apart from a few exceptions, all foreign Jews who had come to France after 1 January 1936 were to be sent to the Occupied Zone. Any exit visas they possessed would be canceled.[116] The *volte-face* appeared complete, and the UGIF pleaded in vain for help from Laval, getting as far as the head of government's chief of staff, Jacques Guérard.[117] At the end of September, when pressed by newsmen to explain the new policy, Laval declared that "it would be a violation of the armistice to allow Jews to go abroad for fear that they should take up arms against the Germans."[118] The number of Jews who managed to emigrate from the Unoccupied Zone declined sharply to only about 600 in the second half of 1942, although a few still managed to slip through without being counted in those figures.[119] Finally, on 8 November, Vichy ended the issuing of exit visas to Jews. Jewish emigration to any destination came to a standstill. Three days later, as French agencies were still being informed of Vichy's new decision, German troops swept across the Demarcation Line and extended their occupation to the Mediterranean Sea. The emigration door was closed.[120]

As soon as Eichmann returned to Berlin from his Paris visit on 1 July 1942, the German officials charged with the Final Solution began applying his instructions. They started planning a huge roundup of Jews in Paris for the middle of July, for which they expected to have the cooperation of the French police.

After the hesitations we have already noted, the Vichy government had ended by agreeing on 4 July to "the deportation, as a first step, of all stateless Jews in the Occupied and Unoccupied zones." While action was to take place all over France, the top French and German officials soon concentrated upon a spectacular coup in Paris. Dannecker lost no time setting up a "technical commission," composed of representatives of the CGQJ, the French police, and the *Sicherheitspolizei,* to plan the details of the roundup. Bousquet, who had raised objections on 2 July to the use of French police, now went along. He insisted only that "the direction of this commission be exclusively in the hands of the Commissariat for Jewish Affairs." According to Dannecker, Darquier de Pellepoix "was practically floored" at having this unexpected responsibility thrust upon him.[121]

When the commission went to work on 7 July, Darquier was only nominally in charge, for Dannecker outlined the plan and extracted the necessary commitments from the officials present. In the report of this meeting from his own hand, the other participants seem unusually silent. In a matter of two days, the Germans wanted 28,000 Jews arrested in the Paris region; of these, 22,000 would be deported. (Those who were sick, "unfit to travel," or too old were to be held aside). Full use was to be made of Tulard's card file at the Prefecture of Police. Jews of both sexes between the ages of sixteen and fifty were to be taken. Those under sixteen were to be left behind with the UGIF, which would transfer them to childrens' homes. The Municipal Police would carry out the arrests, and then assemble the prisoners at the Vélodrome d'Hiver, before taking them on to camps at Drancy and Compiègne and to two in the Loiret, Pithiviers and Beaune-la-Rolande. From there, the Jews would be deported to the east. French *gendarmerie* would guard the weekly deportation trains but would in turn be "watched over by a German police detachment made up of a lieutenant and eight soldiers." The operation, christened *Vent printanier* ("spring wind"), was to begin in a week.[122] After a last-minute postponement to avoid an embarrassing coincidence with Bastille Day on 14 July, everything appeared to be in order.

The Vel d'Hiv Roundup

The Vélodrome d'Hiver was a large Parisian indoor sports arena in the fifteenth *arrondissement,* not far from what is now known as the Pont de Bir Hakeim. In addition to sporting events, the Vel d'Hiv had seen its share of political rallies, including xenophobic and antisemitic demonstrations. When Charles Maurras was released from prison in July 1937 (the directness of his attacks upon premier Léon Blum having won him a sentence for incitement to murder), the Vel d'Hiv was the site of a large demonstration attended by Xavier Vallat, Darquier de Pellepoix, Léon Daudet, Philippe Henriot, and other notable antisemites. With the outbreak of war in 1939, internees of German nationality—mostly Jewish refugees—were assembled there before being sent to concentration camps in the Paris region. In May 1940 the stadium was used for interned foreign women, who in some cases huddled on wooden benches for days and nights in the cold, under conditions reportedly even worse than those of the interned foreign men at the Roland Garros Stadium.[123] There could have been few illusions, then, about the Vélodrome d'Hiver's suitability as an internment center when it was chosen as the principal concentration point of Jewish family groups seized in *Vent printanier* on 16–17 July 1942. But there was a precedent; and for the administration, that was sufficient reason to proceed.

The objective was twenty-eight thousand Jews in the greater Paris region—what the Germans called *"der Gross-Paris."* Hennequin, the municipal police chief, drew up the orders of the day, as French police were to do the job. They were to concentrate on stateless and foreign Jews, excepting sensitive categories such as British or American Jews. Everyone on the lists carefully prepared at the prefecture was to be seized, regardless of state of health. Children living with arrested persons were to be taken, too, unless a member of the family remained behind; they could not be left with neighbors. All Jews subject to arrest were to assemble specified clothing plus food for at least two days. Gas and electricity were to be turned off; animals were to be left with the concierge. Arresting officers were to fill out a card giving the relevant information concerning each arrest, including the name of the person in whose care apartment keys had been left.[124]

On the morning of 16 July, 9,000 French police went into action. The force was composed of gendarmes, *gardes mobiles,* bailiffs, detectives, patrolmen, and even students from the police school. Three or four hundred young followers of Doriot also turned out to help, wearing blue shirts, cross-straps, and armbands bearing the initials "PPF."[125] The police and their auxiliaries divided into almost nine hundred arresting teams of three or four men each, which fanned out across the city, concentrating particularly on certain *arrondissements:* the third, fourth, tenth, eleventh, twelfth, eighteenth, and twentieth. The Germans scarcely appeared on the scene at all. The Jews were often reassured by the French uniform, the instructions in French, and the "correct" deportment of the arresting officer. For two days the manhunt continued.

Although both German and French authorities had hoped for a quiet, orderly roundup, things went awry from the start. Word leaked out a few days before from sympathetic police. A clandestine Jewish newspaper advised Jews to flee or hide. Some well-intentioned policemen made a preliminary visit and announced that they would return for the arrest in an hour or two. Many of the victims did not profit by the warnings, however, remaining stunned or unbelieving to the end. Others despaired. According to one source, there were over one hundred suicides during the roundup and the days that immediately followed.[126]

Most of the victims had no idea of what awaited them. What they found was administrative chaos, combined with utter neglect. Drancy received some 6,000 internees, single men and women or families without children. The Vel d'Hiv, which could hold 15,000 spectators, was to receive the rest of the 28,000. Clearly, if the arrests had reached even near the intended total, there would not have been room at the stadium. As it was, when 7,000 people, including over 4,000 children, were packed into it, there was hardly enough space to lie down. Worse still, hardly any physical preparations had been made. There was neither food nor water nor sanitary arrangements. The Germans permitted only two doctors at a time to attend the internees. At first the victims experienced thirst, hunger, the heat of the day, the cold of the night. Then diarrhea and dysentery. A terrible odor infected the place. Then came a sense of abandonment as hours stretched into days. The confinement lasted for five days.

Pierre Laval was in Paris during this time, meeting with Darquier and others.[127] Though he was certainly briefed on the events of 16 and 17 July, there is no record of his having taken any active part. The following day he returned to Vichy and reported to the cabinet. According to the minutes, Laval put the events into the wider context of Franco-German relations: he "briefed the cabinet on measures decided upon by the German security services in the Occupied Zone, and on the agreement worked out between General Oberg and Monsieur Bousquet, secretary-general for the National Police."[128] Thereafter, Laval kept the matter to himself. The meetings of the Council of Ministers never, even indirectly, referred to the Jews again.

From the German standpoint, *Vent printanier* yielded mixed results. Only 12,884 Jews had been taken—9,800 on the first day and just over 3,000 on the second—less than half of the original objective. Many thousands had escaped. Some French police had proven unreliable. The Paris population had shown sympathy toward the victims, especially the children. Even so, Dannecker returned from a tour of the Unoccupied Zone on 19 July in a relatively optimistic frame of mind. Frenchmen had cooperated sufficiently to fill the deportation trains then beginning to roll. As Röthke put it, "the program can be achieved if the French government makes a commitment to it with the necessary dynamism."[129]

Drancy

The next stop for the Jews taken to the Vel d'Hiv was one of the camps in the Loiret—Pithiviers or Beaune-la-Rolande—or Drancy, where an enormous, half-finished apartment complex in a suburb northeast of Paris served as an antechamber to Auschwitz. For the events described in this book, Drancy assumes special importance as the destination of transports of Jews from the Unoccupied Zone, and as the most important assembly center for deportations to Poland. All but twelve of the seventy-nine deportation trains carrying Jews to the east left from Drancy, as did over 67,000 of the close to 75,000 Jews deported from French soil.[130] Regular departures began in the summer of 1942 and continued until 31 July 1944. About 70,000 Jews passed through its gates—and, except for a very few, this was the last they saw of France.

The camp was established in August 1941, when the *Judenreferat* ordered the buildings used as a detention center for an expected 6,000 Jews rounded up in Paris. From a detainee's perspective, however, Drancy was a thoroughly French institution. French gendarmes provided the guard until the Liberation. Commissaire François's department at the Prefecture of Police looked after internal administration until July 1943, when the *Sicherheitspolizei* took over. On the eve of deportations, CGQJ personnel arrived to take charge of searches, loading, and unloading. Three French police officials—Savart, Laurent, and Guilbert—succeeded each other as camp commandants until replaced by the German Alois Brunner in July 1943. Dannecker's office prepared administrative guidelines; and these, when translated into French and signed by Prefect of Police Admiral François Bard and General Guilbert, commandant of *gendarmerie* for the Paris region, became the order of 26 August 1941 regulating camp life.[131]

From the beginning, no French authority wished to take proper responsibility for Drancy. Admiral Bard wanted the prefect of the Seine to supply food, bedding, and other necessities. Prefect Charles Magny of the Seine protested that he had no funds for this purpose, and wanted the prefect of police to take charge.[132] Between them, they did the very minimum; and conditions at Drancy rapidly became a major scandal. When four thousand Jews arrested in the August roundup arrived, there were only twelve hundred wooden bunk-bed frames. Forty or fifty internees lived in one room. Weeks later there had been no improvement. The prefect of the Seine learned in September that a shipment of toilet paper and straw for mattresses would be available in a month. Food depended upon local markets, which produced a steady diet of cabbage soup. When mortality levels began to rise in November and a serious outbreak of dysentery made the inmates look like skeletons, the French administration called in a German sanitary team to investigate. According to a French intelligence report in December, the German officer who saw the camp "raised hell." The *Judenreferat* decided to free some of the prisoners, more than a thousand of the most seriously ill. The French report concluded on a somber note:

> Those who have not with their own eyes seen some of those released from Drancy can only have a faint idea of the wretched state of internees in this camp which is unique in history. It is said that the notorious camp of Dachau is nothing in comparison with Drancy.[133]*

When the Germans took over administration of the camp at Drancy in July 1943, material conditions actually improved, according to Georges Wellers, an inmate at the time: "Rations became more abundant and more varied; the camp benefited from new equipment,

---

*Dr. Joseph Weill estimated that there had been 950 deaths in the first ten months.[134]

was kept cleaner, major improvements were undertaken, its appearance transformed and was in better trim." The new regime was controlled by SS-Hauptsturmführer Brunner, who arrived with a team of only four permanent assistants. As in other Nazi camps in occupied Europe, inmates did some of the work of camp administration, and indigenous police mounted guard. Brutality, cynicism, and blackmail now replaced the privations of near-starvation and disease. Meanwhile, deportations continued, though at the reduced rate of about one convoy per month.[135]

The fact that the camp administration was French until July 1943 facilitated deportation by blurring the process of turning Jews over to the Germans, as Jacques Delarue has pointed out. For Jews arriving at Drancy from intermediate camps, "at first sight, it seemed to involve a simple passage from one camp to another and the handing over to the Germans for deportation was to some degree obscured because it happened inside the camp of Drancy, at the last moment before embarcation."[136] One should add that the French administration assumed the appalling task of deciding who would fill the German quotas for each convoy. Camp authorities and the .Prefecture of Police made up the rules as they went along. The convoy of 22 June 1942, for example, had only 756 Jews ready to go when Dannecker insisted on a full complement of 930. Feeling that he had no choice, Laurent, the camp commandant, dipped into a pool of "the least noteworthy war veterans" to make up the difference.[137]

After the Vel d'Hiv roundup of July 1942 added women, children, and old people to the camp population, life at Drancy became even more pathetic, and the selection process more callous. Even with the destination unknown, the voyage itself meant an ordeal that many might not survive. Who would fill the trains? In September the police drew up an elaborate table of priorities, indicating by the initial R those "to retain in camp," and by the initial D those "to deport." Assignment to categories followed no clear principles. Generally, those most integrated into French society were favored. French citizens had the best chance of being saved, along with pregnant women, French children whose parents were free, unaccompanied blind people, and non-Jews, legitimate spouses of non-Jews, war widows, and wives of prisoners of war. On the other hand, the weakest and those most difficult to care for in the camp were most vulnerable: foreigners, of course, but also nursing mothers, mothers with a child under two years, widows or widowers of non-Jews, children under sixteen one of whose parents were free and the other deported, certified French children between sixteen and twenty-one whose parents were deported or deportable, the infirm who were otherwise deportable, accompanied blind people, those over seventy.[138]

Terrified at the prospect of being unable to fill deportation trains, the police in charge improvised. A handwritten note dated 12 September 1942 considered the case of parents whose children were hospitalized:

> Under our current obligation to come up with one thousand deportees on Monday, we must include in these departures, at least in reserve, the parents of sick [children] and advise them that they could be deported, with their child remaining in the infirmary.[139]

Near the end, the thinnest veils of decency were torn away. More than 300 children were deported from Drancy in its last regular convoy on 31 July 1944, including at least one baby born in the camp. Some 14,400 Jews left Drancy that year for Auschwitz. When the camp was finally liberated on 18 August, it held only 1,500 Jews.[140]

Roundups in the Unoccupied Zone

> Departure of Israelites (Ministerial Circular No. 12392 of 14 August 1942 and additions).
>
> From lists drawn up by the prefecture or sent to my departments, 95 Israelites are affected by government instructions.
>
> In the night of 26 August *gendarmerie* units, with police cooperation, apprehended 65 individuals. These were asked to bring about fifty kilos of baggage and several buses took them to the camp of Ruffieux at the end of the morning of 26 August [sic] following predetermined routes.
>
> A substantial meal was served around noon.
>
> In the afternoon three doctors examined those Jews who requested it, and unanimously agreed that all were physically fit. A board of inquiry headed by the secretary-general examined the administrative circumstances of all individuals who came before it; two among these were deemed exempt from the departure in conformity with instructions.
>
> Around 6 P.M., 63 Jews left by bus for the camp of Vénissieux. Six had been apprehended on the day of the 26th and were directed to that camp. Twenty Jews have not yet been found, but as they are hiding in the woods surrounded by *gendarmerie*, it is likely that they will be apprehended little by little. Prefects in relevant departments have been advised about six others who moved.

The entire operation went forward without a hitch, according to plan, and all departments displayed both tact and resolution. Nothing regrettable happened.

The prefect of the Savoie Department (September 1942)[141]

In Béziers these measures have even caused profound indignation, for despite the early hours of the morning the population witnessed heartrending scenes.

The prefect of the Hérault Department (3 September 1942)[142]

The Vichy government had agreed, on 4 July 1942, to the deportation of foreign Jews from both zones. Indeed, Police Chief Bousquet had volunteered the inclusion of foreign Jews from the Unoccupied Zone. To facilitate planning, Dannecker decided to conduct a personal inspection of the important camps in the south. On hearing of Dannecker's proposed tour, Bousquet objected to this "violation of national sovereignty in the Unoccupied Zone,"—a protest that lacked force since Dannecker had already made a similar visit the previous February.[143] Dannecker dismissed the French objection and set out on 11 July accompanied by his aide Ernst Heinrichsohn and the Frenchman Schweblin, head of the Police for Jewish Affairs. In the course of a week, they visited several cities, plus the camps of Fort-Barraux, Les Milles, Rivesaltes, and Gurs.

The young SS officer was plainly disappointed by the number of Jewish internees that he found. Dannecker had been favorably impressed by the Vichy law of 4 October 1940, which authorized the regime to intern foreign Jews. In 1941 he had believed that these internees would make possible a "lightning strike" in the southern zone once the signal was given. When he set out for the south in July 1942, he had reason to expect to find over 40,000 foreign Jews interned.[144] But the French internment camp populations were lower than they had been in 1940. When Dannecker reached Gurs, where he anticipated at least 20,000 Jews, the camp in fact contained 2,599 internees, not all of whom were *déportables.*[145]

Dannecker was much more pleased by the way French officials received him. Generally speaking, he felt that "middle-ranking French officials and departments are interested in an early solution of the Jewish question and are only waiting for the necessary orders to come down." The police intendant in Grenoble confided that local Jews should be interned; if they were not, he said that too much police time would be needed to keep watch on them and investigate their crimes. His colleague in Nice longed to get rid of about 8,000 Jews whom he had on his hands. In Périgueux the local police chief spontaneously announced "that a rapid solution of the Jewish question by means of deportation was eminently desirable in his region," although he wanted to exempt a few "decent Jews."[146]

The authorities were ready, therefore; but the Jews were not. On 27 July, Röthke told Leguay, the French police representative in the Occupied Zone, that 3,000 to 4,000 Jews must be sent to Drancy within a week; and when Leguay proposed a more leisurely timetable, the SS officer cracked the whip.

> I told Leguay that handing these Jews over to us can only be considered as a small down payment [*ne pouvait être considérée que comme un premier petit accompte*]. According to exact information which we have, more than 5,000 Jews liable to being deported because they have no. nationality are presently concentrated in French camps in the Occupied Zone.

Röthke insisted on immediate new measures of internment: "The French government must now do everything necessary to gather together the greatest numbers of deportables." He reminded Leguay that, in the long run, French Jews would also be deported, and that Laval had in effect given his consent.[147] In early August, Dannecker insisted upon a supplementary shipment of 11,000 Jews from the Unoccupied Zone in a few weeks. Laval himself promised Knochen that not 11,000 but 14,500 extra Jews would be turned over, and Bousquet assured Knochen that the first 3,000 from Unoccupied France would be in German hands before 10 August.[148]

In order to meet the Germans' demands—now set at 32,000 Jews to be deported by the end of the summer—the Ministry of the Interior sent secret instructions to all regional prefects on 5 August. The circular, signed by Henri Cado, Bousquet's deputy in the police secretariat, directed the regional prefects to prepare to send to the Occupied Zone foreign Jews who had entered France since 1 January 1936. These included all Germans, Austrians, Poles, Czechs, Estonians, Letts, former inhabitants of Danzig and the Saar region, Soviet citizens, and Russian refugees, with exceptions permitted for unaccompanied children under eighteen, war veterans, and pregnant women. Other ministerial directives followed, culminating in one by Bousquet himself on 22 August ordering the regional prefects to take personal charge of the forthcoming operation, to "crush all resistance you encounter," to deal firmly with "indiscretions" or passivity, in order to "free your area totally of foreign Jews as provided for in my circular of 5 August."[149]

Some of these foreign Jews were taken from camps at Noé and Récédébou, near Toulouse, early in August and shipped north as early as 11 August. The main operation, however, took place in the nights of 26–28 August. Bousquet had decided "that it is preferable to arrest all the Jews in a single roundup rather than to go ahead with several isolated roundups that will enable the Jews to hide or to flee toward neighboring neutral countries," Leguay explained to Heinrichson.[150] Whereas the *Feldgendarmerie* occasionally did the work in the Occupied Zone—as in Rouen, Châlons, Dijon, Nantes, Saint-Malo, and La Baule—south of the Demarcation Line, of course, the operation was exclusively French. Police, *gendarmerie, gardes mobiles,* firemen, and French soldiers went into action in every department of the Unoccupied Zone according to carefully prearranged plans before dawn on 26 August.

The major roundup of 26–28 August in the Unoccupied Zone was made far easier by the actions that had already been taken in late 1941 against foreign Jews who had entered France since 1 January 1936. To find the proper doors to knock on, police used the censuses that Darlan had ordered on 10 December. Many of these Jews, in fact, were already in camps or labor battalions or had been assigned to residence under police surveillance by Pucheu's order of January (see page 170).[151]* After the first day, the police looked for those who had prudently stayed away from home. They searched for concealed children in convents and religious boarding schools. They watched forests where fugitives tried to subsist without food or shelter. For many Jews, the game was up at month's end when they had to renew their ration cards.

Once arrested, the Jews were taken to assembly points and thence to concentration camps in the Unoccupied Zone before going on to Drancy. Despite the authorities' best efforts to camouflage the deportations and to take them as quickly as possible out of the public eye, these processes of final loading and departure produced what even the most laconic of prefects' reports called "heartrending scenes."[152] The means of transport was, as the prefect of the Haute Garonne reported, "freight cars." Witnesses in train stations were shocked by the *wagons de marchandises,* where already stinking straw was the only sanitary facility; women were fainting in the heat.[153] The American relief official Donald Lowrie was appalled at these convoys: "Men and women pushed like cattle into boxcars, thirty to a car, whose only furniture was a bit of

*Most of the prefects' monthly intelligence reports from the Unoccupied Zone contain some reference to this operation.

straw on the floor, one iron pail for all toilet purposes, and a police guard. . . . The YMCA put a box of books into each car."[154]

It was the separation of families that produced the most searing impressions. Interned parents with children under eighteen were usually given the choice of leaving their offspring behind or being deported with them. In most cases, according to Donald Lowrie, the parents decided to meet their fate alone. "Eyewitnesses," he wrote in August 1942, "will never forget the moment when these truckloads of children left the camps with parents trying in one last gaze to fix an image to last an eternity."[155]

The deportees were shipped to Drancy. Then the transport continued to the east, sometimes immediately, sometimes after a day or two. From the first deportation train in March 1942, these transports were guarded by French police. The few German police could not be spared for this sort of work. Indeed, the manpower required to guard convoys was one reason that the Germans preferred freight cars. Whereas it took two hundred men to mount a proper guard for a passenger train, a freight train required far fewer. French police accompanied the deportees to the German frontier at Novéant, where the Germans took over.[156] It took three days to reach Auschwitz. There, Jews apt for hard physical labor were sometimes put to work in the I. G. Farben plants attached to the Auschwitz camp, under conditions that few survived. Most Jews were killed at once.

Although the prefects' reports indicate that French police and other officials followed orders virtually universally, there were many signs that they were not comfortable doing so. As in Paris, some officials let the word out, and many Jews were warned. At least three prefects knew of warnings over Radio London (Aude, Bouches-du-Rhône, Hérault), and rumors of what had already happened in the Occupied Zone had certainly alerted Jews in the south. The most valiant gesture from an official was the refusal of General Robert de Saint-Vincent, commander of the Military Region of Lyon, to use his troops to help deport Jews from that city. Within forty-eight hours Vichy relieved him of his post.[157] The Protestant prefect François-Martin at Montauban warned the government in advance of the adverse effect on opinion at home and abroad and, in his department, won a reputation as a sympathizer with opponents of deportation. His advice to the government, however, was to blame the Germans; he thought the French people would be grateful that their government had not "compromised the very basis of national existence by a pointless resistance."[158] In Bordeaux, police rebuffed certain demands of the local *Sicherheitspolizei.* Pierre Li-

magne observed in September that "the gendarmes are more ashamed
of their profession than when they drove out the religious congrega-
tions [a reference to the enforcement of measures against the Catholic
Church in 1905]; sometimes heroic resignations from the police have
occurred."[159] But disciplinary problems did not seriously hamper these
operations. Not until August 1943 were German officials having to take
account in their planning for a general unreliability of the French
police in serious cases.[160]

The results of the August 1942 roundups in the Unoccupied Zone
disappointed the Germans, however. In the Ardèche, the police
managed to send along 137 out of the 201 on their list. In the Haute
Savoie, they got 42 out of 91; but Prefect Edouard Dauliac, in an excess
of zeal, took the occasion to annul the residence permit of all Jews,
French or foreign, who had come into the department's mountain
resorts for the summer and had put a strain on the resources and
tempers of the inhabitants.[161] When the whole operation had been
completed, Bousquet reported that 11,184 Jews had been seized, though
the total was later revised to a modest 7,100.[162]

The Germans responded to these meager results by trying to widen
the category of "deportable"—logically enough since from the beginning they had meant to deport all Jews sooner or later. Bousquet now
agreed to include Belgian and Dutch Jews, which he had refused to do
up to that point.[163] From his work with the Nîmes Committee, Donald
Lowrie perceived that the various conditions for exemption from
deportation—age, family status, military record, and so forth—were
being altered "almost daily" in September so as to catch more Jews in
the police net.[164] The French administration was doing its best to fill the
quotas without having to resort to denaturalization of French citizens;
although, in conversations with Knochen on 3 August and with Oberg
on 2 September, Laval conceded the denaturalization of those who had
become citizens since 1933.[165]

By the beginning of September, just over 27,000 Jews had been
deported from both zones of France; and the German authorities hoped
to add another 25,000 before the end of October when the transports
might have to be suspended for the winter.[166] During September, the
Nazis' quota was precisely met—thirteen convoys. Suddenly, however,
the transports were stopped—possibly because numbers of "deportables" were insufficient, but more likely because of an unexpected interruption of railway timetables.[167] No trains left during October. There
were four in November, and then nothing again until the massive
roundups and deportations of February 1943 from both zones. The first

phase of deportation had therefore ended. No massive denaturalizations had been necessary to fill the trains. At the close of 1942, the Germans could count about 42,500 Jews sent from France to Auschwitz —a total they were never to match again in the two years of of war that remained.

How much did Laval and Pétain know of all this? Laval followed these events closely. We have seen that he was in Paris on the first day of the Vel d'Hiv roundup and had a report on it within a week from the CGQJ. He received a letter from the vice-president of the UGIF thanking him personally for exempting native French Jews during the July roundups and for securing the immediate release of some mistakenly arrested. As the massive roundups in the Unoccupied Zone approached, he met Knochen on 3 August.[168] A group of American Quakers from the Nîmes Committee led by Lindsley Noble saw Laval three days later and found him openly eager to get on with the deportations. According to the minutes of the Nîmes Committee, Laval "gave our delegates to understand that the deportations were inevitable and were undertaken on his own initiative." The Quakers talked to the U.S. representative in Vichy, who cabled their version to Washington the next evening:

> Laval made no mention of any German pressure but stated flatly that these foreign Jews had always been a problem in France and that the French government was glad that a change in German attitude towards them gave France an opportunity to get rid of them. Laval inquired why the United States did not take these Jews and concluded with a rather bitter discussion of the Jewish problem. . . . Laval gave the impression that the general policy of ridding France of foreign Jews had been definitely decided upon.[169]

In August and September, the American chargé d'affaires in Vichy, H. Pinkney Tuck, had a series of conversations with Laval on the deportations which led him to the same conclusion as the Quakers: "It was evident from Laval's attitude," he told Washington, "that he had neither interest nor sympathy in the fate of any Jews, who, he callously remarked, were already too numerous in France."[170]

Some of Laval's attitude may have been bravado designed to conceal the reality of French subjugation. To the Germans he also displayed irritability at the constant pressures upon him to meet the quotas. At a dinner party given by de Brinon in Paris on 2 September,

Laval talked to Oberg about his problems with the deportations. While confirming all previous agreements, including giving up Jews naturalized since 1933, Laval said he could not turn over Jews "as in a discount store" [*wie in einem Einheitspreisgeschäft*].[171] The Germans thought he was beginning to drag his feet.

Pétain was far less directly involved in these events and, when first approached, gave petitioners the impression that he only dimly understood the enormity of the roundups and the deportations. Relentlessly, however, the information was pressed upon him. Tracy Strong, of the American relief organization Young Men's Christian Association (YMCA), saw Pétain on 4 August and told him how the news coming out of Vichy was adversely affecting American public opinion. Together with Père Arnou, representing Cardinal Gerlier, Donald Lowrie tried to break through the screen of officials surrounding the Marshal and gave full accounts of atrocities to General Campet, his military aide, to Jean Jardel, his secretary-general, and to Dr. Bernard Ménétrel, his personal physician and confidant. Lowrie concluded that Pétain "knew" but could do nothing.[172] By this time an important wave of Church protest had broken over Vichy; and Pétain was drawn into numerous confrontations: with the papal nuncio, with other Catholic leaders, and with French Protestants. It is most likely that he was briefed by his chief of staff André Lavagne on details of the Vel d'Hiv roundup in Paris, submitted by officials of the Secours National.[173] Pétain knew enough about what was going on to intervene on rare occasions on behalf of some personal acquaintance or war veteran.[174] Whatever his personal knowledge and conclusions, there were—as late as the end of September, when the Vatican itself had warned him about the deportations—people close to him who continued to see something positive in these terrible events. A report (unsigned) was prepared for him on the roundups in the Unoccupied Zone; and, while admitting the brutality of the summer's deportations, it concluded "that this measure will considerably help to clear the air in the Unoccupied Zone. From all quarters, for a long time, we have been receiving complaints about the illicit activities of these foreign Jews: antigovernment activity, clandestine trade, black market, etc."[175]

The Massacre of the Innocents

In the biological perspectives of Hitlerian racism, Jewish children posed as grave a threat to the New Order as did their parents. Whether in Poland or in France, the plan was simply to murder them. But when it came to France, the Germans believed they had to exercise some care to obtain at least a degree of French cooperation. Vichy's official *antisémitisme d'état*, qualified by the weight given to cultural assimilation and national service, admitted the possibility of exceptions. Would these exceptions include children? Would the Vichy regime attempt to withhold children altogether from the categories of "deportables"?

Far from attempting to save the children of the foreign Jews whom they delivered to the Germans, French authorities offered them, too, for deportation. Vichy suggested that children be sent along with the adults even before the Nazis were ready to accept them. During 1942, according to Serge Klarsfeld's estimate, 1,032 children under six years of age were sent to Auschwitz from France, along with 2,557 between six and twelve, and 2,464 between thirteen and seventeen. Over 6,000 children in that year alone.[176] How did this happen, and why?

The Nazis did not want to be bothered with children in the first deportation convoys. Dannecker explicitly excluded them from his plans, as he noted in a memorandum on 15 June 1942: "The essential thing is that the Jews (of both sexes) be between sixteen and forty years of age. Ten percent of the convoys can include Jews unfit for work."[177] Laval raised the subject as soon as he became aware of the scope of German planning, just after Eichmann's visit on 1 July. Dannecker reported to Berlin on 6 July: "President Laval proposed that, in the deportation of Jewish families from the Unoccupied Zone, children under sixteen can also be taken. The question of the Jewish children remaining behind in the Occupied Zone does not interest him."[178] Would Berlin agree? Dannecker pressed repeatedly for a reply. Several weeks later, no response having arrived, Röthke noted that the French police had "on different occasions expressed the desire to see the children also deported to the Reich with their parents."[179] Finally, on 20 July, Eichmann telephoned his answer. Jewish children and old people could be deported as well as those capable of work.[180]

Laval's proposal, one should note, was made before the children had become a practical problem for the French authorities. But if he was anticipating difficulties, he was certainly correct. From the very first, the children were a problem. Whether they were rounded up in the *rafles*, or whether they were left behind, they suffered acutely in ways that were very hard to conceal.

In the massive July roundups in the Occupied Zone, children were taken along with their families. The four thousand children interned at the Vel d'Hiv in Paris, and those rounded up in the following weeks with their families, made the *Vent printanier* operation even more unspeakable. By contrast, many families in the Unoccupied Zone took the option of leaving their children behind. Even so, families with children arrived from the Unoccupied Zone in the trains bound for Drancy. Since in both cases, the parents were soon taken to the east, thousands of children were left interned.

In the squalid and disorganized conditions of camp life, where nothing had been prepared for them, the arrival of these newly orphaned children brought many of the inmates to the limits of despair. Georges Wellers has described some of the results at Drancy:

> The children were in bare rooms in groups of one hundred. Buckets for toilet purposes were placed on the landings, because many of them could not walk down the long and inconvenient stairways to the toilets. The little ones, unable to go alone, would wait agonizingly for help from female volunteers or another child. This was the time of the cabbage soup at Drancy. This soup wasn't bad, but it was hardly suited for children's digestion. Very quickly all the children suffered from acute diarrhea. They soiled their clothing, they soiled the mattresses on which they spent night and day. With no soap, dirty underclothing was rinsed in cold water, and the child, almost naked, waited for his underclothes to dry. A few hours later, a new accident, and the whole process had to be repeated.
>
> The very young often didn't know their names, and then one asked their friends who sometimes gave some information. Family and first names then being established, these were inscribed on little wooden dogtags. . . .
>
> Every night one heard the perpetual crying of desperate children from the other side of the camp, and from time to time the distraught calling out and the wailing of children who had lost all control.[181]

Germain Bleckman, a pediatrician hopelessly overworked at Drancy, counted 5,500 children who passed through the camp from 21 July to 9 September, many arriving in sealed cattle cars. Some 20 percent of them had to be hospitalized within the camp—between 900 and 1,000 according to a rough estimate.[182]

During July the deportation trains included many adolescents. During August younger children were also taken. Children often constituted the bulk of the transport in late August. They traveled in sealed freight cars, each carrying between forty and sixty children and a handful of adults. The Germans were little involved in the deportation of the children, and there are even signs that they disapproved of it. In August, Donald Lowrie reported that the Germans had "begun to shove across the Demarcation Line the Jewish children left alone in the Occupied Zone" after their parents' arrest. Sixteen hundred had already appeared, and more were expected. The French were not happy with having these new charges forced upon them, and this conflict of interest is reminiscent of the Franco-German disputes over the refugees in 1940.[183]

It was the French police who took the initiative in allocating children to specific convoys leaving France for the east. Jean Leguay, French police representative in the Occupied Zone, explained the whole system in a letter to Darquier de Pellepoix at the beginning of August. The Germans set the schedules, and the French police, in agreement with the SS, decided how the transports would be composed. The transports from Drancy set for 19, 21, 24, and 26 August would be "composed of the children of families who had been interned in Pithiviers and Beaune-la-Rolande."[184]

Notes prepared for briefing Marshal Pétain on the July roundup in Paris were not only accurate on what was happening to the children; they also made it clear that in the higher reaches of the administration the children were seen not as victims but as a problem:

> When the Jews will be taken to Drancy [i.e., from camps in the Loiret department] a sorting will occur to send the parents in groups of 50 in sealed freight cars to the east after having been separated from their children. The question of the children will therefore be posed very soon. These children, in groups of 4,000, cannot in short order be taken in hand by public charity.[185]

Some observers have contended that Laval tried to help obtain diplomatic visas so that 5,000 Jewish children could escape.[186] There was an effort to rescue Jewish children, but Laval's role in it was far from glorious. What happened can be pieced together from the records of a number of relief organizations—the American Friends Service Committee (Quakers), the YMCA—and those of the U.S. State Department and the German Foreign Office. The affair is worth examining in some detail.

Thanks to the efforts of both the Quakers and the Jewish Joint Distribution Committee, a few hundred Jewish children had been able to get out before ordinary emigration channels were blocked in the summer of 1942.[187] While the UGIF implored Bousquet in August 1942 to let out fifty more Jewish children who had already been granted entry visas by the United States, a much more ambitious plan grew out of conversations between Laval and U.S. chargé d'affaires H. Pinkney Tuck. When Tuck remonstrated with Laval on 26 August about the deportations and raised the question of children, Laval asked him sarcastically why the United States didn't take them all. Stung, but lacking official instructions, Tuck was caught short. He then urged the State Department to make a concrete offer to Laval. Well informed about the deportations by Donald Lowrie, Tuck estimated that between five thousand and eight thousand Jewish children would soon be in welfare homes. In view of the character of the Nazi deportations, he added, "many of these children may already be considered orphans." On 28 September, Secretary of State Cordell Hull offered one thousand entry visas with a possible further five thousand for Jewish children, "subject to approval by the French authorities of permission to depart from France."[188]

Laval was still determined, as late as 9 September, that the children should remain with their parents who were being deported. "Not a single one is to remain in France," he told Pastor Marc Boegner in a harsh interview that day.[189] And while Laval expressed interest in Tuck's proposals, he reported on them in detail to the German diplomat Roland Krug von Nidda. The Germans warned Laval repeatedly in the course of the following month not to let the departure of Jewish children for the United States become an occasion for anti-German or anti-French propaganda. On 12 October, in response to German pressures, Laval told Krug that he would insist that Tuck's project *not* include children separated from parents who were departing for the east. On 24 October he agreed not to let any children go without a United States promise to hold no public ceremonies upon the children's arrival or otherwise to call attention to the matter.[190]

Consequently, the Americans found that negotiations advanced only sluggishly. When Bousquet finally met with Tuck on 16 October, a day after the U.S. State Department had made public its offer to accept some five thousand children, the former hedged his government's position with numerous qualifications. He emphasized one of Laval's primary concerns, that this emigration not occasion "publicity unfavorable to the French or German governments." Bousquet eventually agreed to grant five hundred exit visas; he would consider more only when these children reached the United States. Then Bousquet "insisted that we [the rescuers] should limit the convoy to bona fide orphans, i.e. children whose parents were actually deceased or had not been heard from for several years." The head of the Nîmes Committee protested that five hundred Jewish orphans in Bousquet's strict sense probably did not exist. But Bousquet was adamant: "no information existed as to the fate of deported Jews, and therefore he could not assume that their children left behind were orphans."[191] Laval's promise to Krug had been kept.

When the Quakers went to Marseille, however, to handle the details of the five hundred emigrants they believed had been authorized, they found that the local French authorities there claimed to have no instructions. On 20 October, Tuck advised the Quakers that Laval had been upset by American publicity over the project and was reconsidering. When he saw Tuck again on 23 October, Laval agreed to 150 visas and restored the figure of 500 only on the American's insistence. As the Quakers began trying to assemble qualified children, the intendant of police in Marseille, du Prozic, required that only "bona fide" orphans be considered. Then he imposed ever more extravagant demands: he wanted information as to the status of parents of each child, for example, and insisted that all requests for exit visas be reviewed by the UGIF. The Quakers worked feverishly to fulfill these requirements. By 5 November everything seemed in order.[192] Still, there were no exit visas. On 9 November a final appeal went to Laval; but by this time the Allied landings in North Africa had begun, and the French leader was in no mood to do business with the United States. Diplomatic relations with this nation were broken; and on 11 November, the Germans moved into the southern zone. According to one account, 350 children managed to emigrate clandestinely to the United States after that[193]—but the Vichy government had not helped to save any of them.

What can explain Vichy's posture with respect to these children? Or Laval's personal delaying of the exit visas, and his harsh comments to Tuck, Pastor Boegner, and the Quakers? Or the police's eagerness for the deportation of the children, even before the Germans wanted to include them? One possibility is that the inclusion of children helped Vichy meet the deportation quotas. As the pressure to find "deportables" mounted, the regime may have wanted to use thousands of foreigners' children to stave off the deportation of native French Jews.[194] Joseph Billig, on the other hand, attributes Vichy's posture to "the terrifying spirit of inertia at the top of all sorts of responsible agencies; the authorities on the French side evading rescue possibilities because these would disturb administrative routine. Laval supported this tendency."[195]

It was undeniable that the children posed an administrative problem. When Leguay tried to find out, after Eichmann's visit, how many homes were available for the children of deportees, the answer was discouraging: there were 300 places available, with the possibility of 700 more if Vichy would restore requisitioned Jewish communal properties, and 550 in addition if the Germans would do the same. But over 4,000 children were camped in the Vel d'Hiv on the morning after the *grande rafle* of 16 July in Paris. Darquier, who had earlier favored putting the children in homes, now spoke for deportation. So did the police.[196] Even more children would be on their hands after the deportations were extended to the Unoccupied Zone. To many officials concerned, deporting the children together with their parents probably seemed the easiest solution.

The separation of children from parents had become, in fact, an acute political embarrassment for the Vichy regime. It was an aspect of the roundups which prefects' reports often mentioned as upsetting to public opinion.[197] It was a central theme of the most important voices raised against the deportations—particularly from French high clergy. International concern focused on this point. The Canadian government indicated concern, and the dictator of the Dominican Republic, Rafael Trujillo, offered to take 3,500 refugee children. Madame Laval was approached by the wife of the French ambassador to Spain, to whom an American relief agency had appealed.[198] Even the German diplomatic representative at Vichy, Krug von Nidda, found that the French police had been clumsy *(ungeschickt)* in separating families at home, in full view of the neighbors.[199]

Vichy was especially sensitive to any charge of disregard for the sanctity of the family. Merely mentioning the idea brought on a menacing investigation by agents of the anti-Jewish police squad, the SEC.[200] When Tuck and Boegner appealed to him, Laval denied strenuously that children were being separated from families. Indeed, the regime seems to have changed its policy in response to these criticisms. A report to Pétain on the deportations from the Unoccupied Zone regretted that some dismemberment of families had taken place, but observed that "in response to the outcry produced everywhere by this barbarous measure, President Laval requested and fixed things so that the children will not be separated. Thus in the arrests in the Unoccupied Zone the children have followed their parents."[201] When families were being taken from the camps at Noé and Récébédou in mid-August, Vichy issued an official denial that families were being separated.[202]

Incredibly, Laval seems to have believed that deporting children to Auschwitz would improve his image. Paris Radio declared in mid-September:

> M. Laval at a press conference last Friday announced that the Vichy government was prepared to make a concession [*sic*] with regard to the deportation of Jewish children. Henceforth they will be deported together with their parents instead of being separated. He added, however, "No one and nothing can deter us from carrying out the policy of purging France of undesirable elements, without nationality.[203]

If Laval was so eager to rid France of foreign Jews, why, then, was he so reluctant to cooperate with the plan to send five thousand children to the United States? It is impossible to know his inmost thoughts, but there is every indication that he thought the matter not worth arousing tension with the Germans. During September and October 1942, his main interests certainly lay elsewhere. On 4 September he had been obliged to decree obligatory labor service for all young Frenchmen—a tacit confession that the voluntary *relève* had not worked, and a step widely recognized as a move toward forced labor for Germany. This measure was likely to affect directly far more French people, and public response to it was far more negative than the response to the deportations of foreign Jews.* Laval found himself caught between an increasingly exigent German demand for labor service and an increasingly recalcitrant French population. Why, then, add to his difficulties with what seems, for him, to have been a minor issue? In the end, Laval did what promised least to burden the French administration and his relations with Germany.

---

*This measure created a *véritable sensation* in the Haute Garonne.[204] The prefect of the Vaucluse said, on 5 October 1942, that it had a "deeper" effect than the Jewish deportations.[205]

The Turn in Public Opinion

The scenes of terror and despair that took place across France as Jews were rounded up for deportation in July–August 1942 also marked a turning point in French public opinion.

Before, anti-Jewish policies followed the law and could be tolerated, or even approved, as one of the many planks in Marshal Pétain's program of national revival. Now they were police actions, with their share of violence and cruelty.

Before, only men had been taken away, almost always foreigners and usually of military age. Now women and children were loaded into cattle cars along with the men, and some of them were French citizens.

Before, many of the internees were later released. Now nothing was heard of the deportees again, save for a few curt and enigmatic postcards which only added to the anxieties raised by the official phrase "destination unknown."

Before, there appeared to be a distinction between the Occupied Zone and the Vichy Zone, and systematic abuse—such as the star—could be attributed to the Germans. The occasional cases of window smashing and graffiti scrawling in the Vichy Zone were clearly the work of disapproved minorities. Now, however, the roundups occurred throughout France and French police were conspicuously in charge of them.

Before, many French people could persuade themselves that Jews were suffering no more than anyone else in a dark time. Now, for anyone who witnessed the loading or the departure of a deportation train, there could be no mistaking the extraordinary nature of what was happening.

For the first time since the founding of Marshal Pétain's regime, significant numbers of moderate or conventional French people who had accepted the regime as a matter of course, or supported it enthusiastically, were deeply offended by something it had done. For the first time, voices of open opposition arose from establishment figures in positions of power. Those raised within the Catholic hierarchy had by far the most impact, in view of the Church's previous solid support for Vichy and all its works. To be sure, some of the most zealous secular collaborators had found the Church's antisemitism tepid; to be sure, some individual Catholics had worked against the regime's anti-Jewish measures, such as the group around the underground journal *Témoignage chrétien*. No doubt the hierarchy felt somewhat less close to Pierre

Laval, whose image was one of opportunistic republicanism, than to his predecessors. But for the first two years of the Vichy regime, no public utterance by any member of the Catholic hierarchy had troubled the apparently solid front between Church and State.

The last crying infant and despairing mother had hardly been moved on from the Vel d'Hiv to Drancy in July when the annual assembly of French cardinals and archbishops took place, in Paris. The assembled prelates did not make any public pronouncement, but they could hardly ignore the *Vent printanier* operation which had just taken place, nor the commanding French role in it. Cardinal Suhard carried to Pétain the assembly's unpublished protest. Like statements from the Holy See itself, the appeal limited itself to "the exigencies of justice and the rights of charity." Not all prelates felt this was strong enough, and the papal nuncio judged it "a platonic protest." Nevertheless, there was a new tone of urgency, on the side of both justice (now described as "the imprescriptable rights of individuals") and charity ("pity for the immense suffering, especially that of mothers and children.")[206]

Other churchmen followed at their own pace, some hesitantly, some with alacrity, and some not at all. Cardinal Gerlier of Lyon, known as a staunch Pétainist, was approached by Grand Rabbi Jacob Kaplan on 17 August, and by Pastor Boegner the following day. The letter Gerlier wrote to Pétain supporting the appeal previously made by Cardinal Suhard reflected, in the words of François Delpech, "an astonishing moderation."[207] Alerted to the departure scenes taking place in mid-August within his diocese, at the camps of Noé and Récébédou, Monsignor Jules-Gérard Saliège, the elderly and partly paralyzed archbishop of Toulouse—a man of great character and public popularity who had stood apart from Vichy to some degree from the beginning—drafted a pastoral letter to be read in all the parishes of his diocese the following Sunday, 23 August. It was the clearest voice yet heard in France on the persecution of Jews:

> That children, that women, fathers and mothers be treated like cattle, that members of a family be separated from one another and dispatched to an unknown destination, it has been reserved for our own time to see such a sad spectacle. Why does the right of sanctuary no longer exist in our churches? Why are we defeated? . . . The Jews are real men and women. Foreigners are real men and women. They cannot be abused without limit. . . . They are part of the human species. They are our brothers like so many others.[208]

It was the public roundups in the Unoccupied Zone on 26–28 August that swept away many hesitations. French police were seizing Jews on Marshal Pétain's doorstep and delivering them to the Germans; the complicity of the Vichy regime could no longer be veiled. The pastoral letter of Monsignor Pierre-Marie Théas, bishop of Montauban, read in his diocese on Sunday, 30 August, was no less resounding:

> I give voice to the outraged protest of Christian conscience, and I proclaim that all men, Aryans or non-Aryans, are brothers, because created by the same God; that all men, whatever their race or religion, have the right to be respected by individuals and by states.[209]

Prominent clerics found themselves drawn into the direct actions undertaken on behalf of Jews by certain of their subordinates. In the diocese of Lyon, Père Pierre Chaillet and his ecumenical group *l'Amitié chrétienne* dispersed Jewish children among a number of religious houses and refused to give them up to the police, even when Père Chaillet—known to be close to Cardinal Gerlier—was placed under house arrest in the Privas mental hospital in the Ardèche for three months. The cardinal himself refused to give the addresses of these children's shelters to Alexandre Angéli, the regional prefect of Lyon.

But when Cardinal Gerlier himself issued a public protest on Sunday, 6 September, he felt compelled to couch it in terms of loyalty to the regime and recognition "that there is a problem for the French authorities to resolve." Loyalism was the keynote of more than one protest. Monsignor Delay, bishop of Marseille, denounced indiscriminate arrests of men, women, and children to "send them possibly to their deaths"; but he hastened to add:

> We do not ignore the fact that the Jewish question poses difficult national and international problems. We are well aware that our country has the right to take all appropriate steps to defend itself against those who, especially in recent years, have done her so much harm and to punish those who abuse the hospitality that has so liberally been extended to them. But the rights of the state have limits.[210]

It is tempting now to depreciate such statements today because of the traces of ancient anti-Jewish prejudice they contain. Moreover, as Père Chaillet noted, these protests were "unfortunately more than matched by much reticence."[211] Fewer than half the prelates of the Unoccupied Zone made public statements from the pulpit; and not one in the Occupied Zone, where of course the possible penalties were much higher and the flow of information much less free. One curious silence was that of Cardinal Liénart of Lille, who had stood out before the war for his denunciations of racism and antisemitism; but his diocese was now administered by the German occupation authority in Brussels.[212] There were even a few signs of clerical approbation. *La Semaine religieuse* of the diocese of Evreux (in the Occupied Zone) agreed to publish a *Propagandastaffel* note justifying anti-Jewish measures by citing the example of Pope Paul IV (champion of the Inquisition in the mid-sixteenth century), after the archbishop of Rouen's diocesan bulletin had been interdicted for refusing to publish the note.[213] Of those who protested publicly only monsignors Saliège and Théas felt no need to allude to the "Jewish problem" or to express loyalty to the regime. And even they intimated that Germans, not French, were to blame.

Even with these limitations, the clerics' courageous statements resounded through the country and abroad precisely because they sounded a new note that all could hear. "God is using you, Monsieur le Maréchal," Monsignor Delay had proclaimed in a prestigious national journal the year before; now he sent a stinging letter to *Gringoire* (Marseille edition) when it applauded the deportation of the Jews. Such actions, the bishop said, were "contrary . . . to the true spirit of the National Revolution."[214] Cardinal Gerlier, with the episcopal title of *Primat des Gaules,* could now become known—quite incorrectly—as *le Primat des Gaullistes.* * It was because these blunt calls to conscience came from among the most ardent supporters of the new regime that they carried so far.

The Catholic clergy, of course, had no monopoly on public protests against the deportations. The Protestants added another public message to their long series—an eloquent statement by Pastor Boegner read in almost all Protestant pulpits on 22 September; but Protestants were already known to be troublesome and marginal. After relative silence on this subject, underground political groups now stressed the horrors and injustice of deportation. More significant, voices were raised within Pétainist inner circles. Pierre Regnier, head of a committee of war invalids, appealed to de Brinon for "protective measures" for Jewish war invalids and their families. Raymond Lachal, director-general of the War Veterans' League, told Laval publicly that the Jewish

---

*Abetz had already called him the *Primat de de Gaulle* in November 1941, but Abetz was congenitally anticlerical and poorly informed.[215]

problem "is on many people's consciences."[216] War veterans were known to return decorations in disgust, and protest letters rained steadily upon government offices.[217] "A militant supporter of the National Revolution, who does not consider that incompatible with a certain spirit of tolerance," intervened on behalf of an interned Jewish uncle, with the support of Marcel Déat—"while at the same time approving the measures designed to limit the Israelites' intrusion into many areas."[218]

It was, however, the clerical protests that had the most impact. The July protest of the cardinals and archbishops had been private, but it was hardly secret, having been sent to parishes throughout France. By December it had been published in the *Contemporary Jewish Record* in New York, together with statements of several other religious dignitaries. Despite a prefectoral interdiction, Monsignor Saliège's letter "spread like wildfire throughout the southwest," and was read in a majority of the churches of the diocese of Toulouse (not just half, as Laval assured Abetz), carried from hand to hand, and sold clandestinely in Catholic bookstores. It was published in *Témoignage chrétien, Franc-Tireur, Combat,* and other Resistance journals as well as broadcast over the BBC.[219] And however moderate were the opinions of Cardinal Gerlier, they were thought compelling enough to be carried by teams of cyclists from parish to parish along the Rhône and the Loire, often at considerable risk to the messengers.[220]

One measure of the importance of these clerical appeals is the authorities' efforts to stop them and to reduce their effects. Prefect François-Martin persuaded Monsignor Théas not to read his pastoral letter at an open-air mass for the Légion, in his presence, at Montauban on 30 August, though it was read at other services. Prefect Cheneau de Leyritz forbade the distribution of Monsignor Saliège's letter—to no effect.[221]

Vichy successfully imposed a blackout on all press reports of the arrests in the Unoccupied Zone, but it was quite another matter to force newspapers to justify what had been done. Laval gave strict instructions to the regional government spokesman to crush "a sinister propaganda, the only object of which was to compromise the work of the Marshal." The press was urged to remember "the true teaching of Saint Thomas and the popes"—an echo of Léon Bérard's memorandum of 1941 (see pages 200–202).[222] The Information Ministry also tried to get editors to take up an article from *Le Grand Echo du Midi* (Toulouse) designed to counter misguided "excitement" about the Jews with "the general and traditional teaching of the Catholic Church about the Jewish problem." No one was forbidden to feel concern for his neighbor; but, the article warned, "no one is permitted to launch a movement that could seriously compromise the work of the Marshal." Some journals complied, but others did not—notably *La Croix* (now published in Limoges). Almost immediately the Vichy censorship backed down.[223] The civil authorities were not successful in this effort to tell the Church what Catholic racial doctrines really were.

Rumors that the papal nuncio, Monsignor Valerio Valeri, had conveyed strong disapproval to Marshal Pétain were particularly threatening to Vichy, eager as that regime was for the appearance of papal support. The nuncio seems to have spoken to Laval on his own initiative —at least that is what Laval wanted the Germans to think—and the Pope himself remained resolutely silent.[224]* Laval was sufficiently worried to overcome his discomfort at dealing with clerics and visit Cardinal Suhard in Paris. Capitalizing upon papal reticence, Laval warned Church officials repeatedly that these protests damaged France's international position. He urged them to stay out of politics, and pointedly reminded Suhard that the Pope had not personally spoken out on the affair. At the end of August, Laval summoned Valeri's assistant to condemn Saliège's pastoral letter and to ask the nuncio to tell the Pope and Papal Secretary of State Maglione that France was not pleased with papal intervention in French internal affairs.[226]

These steps show that Laval understood clearly what was at stake for him—whether French and world opinion would still consider the Vichy government master of its own house after these events. The regional prefect of Lyon, Angéli, knew what was at stake when Père Chaillet refused to give up the addresses of the Jewish children he had hidden in various orphanages and boarding schools, "blocking in this way . . . the will of the government." The situation "required a show of authority." Laval hastened to tell Abetz about Chaillet's arrest and about how tough he, Laval, was with the French clergy.[227] Laval was less successful persuading his own people that Vichy was still sovereign. A sense of national humiliation is almost as strong a current in the prefects' reports as is a sense of pity for the victims. Vichy had not been able to limit the deportations to the Occupied Zone. These deeds were considered, according to several prefects, a sign of "subjection," a "national disgrace," and certain to diminish "the esteem that our country enjoys abroad."[228]

There was no denying the profound impact of these events on

*Monsignor Bruno de Solages, rector of the Institut Catholique at Toulouse, was already trying to explain papal silence to "an enormous crowd" at Montauban in June 1942 —before the deportations—by arguing that communism and racism were equally Catholicism's enemies, and that Catholic doctrine had always supported equality of rights, Jewish and aryan, white and black.[225]

opinion in the Unoccupied Zone. Every prefectoral report there had something to say about Jews during the summer of 1942, in sharp contrast to the relative lack of interest earlier and later. Twenty-four prefects in the southern zone stated without qualification that public opinion in its overwhelming majority was moved and shocked by the deportations there. Not that all the prefects agreed with their citizens; they used the word "sentimental" with striking unanimity to describe the latter's reactions, and marveled that such a sudden transformation could overcome people who only days earlier had been complaining about too many Jews, and that people could have so little sense of *raison d'Etat.* "The Frenchman remains ungovernable," lamented Prefect Didkowski of the Isère, contemplating this startling turnabout: "Everyone complains of the Jew"; but after the arrests these same people— even German and Italian liaison officers!—were at his door to intervene in favor of "a good Jew."[229]

By contrast, only two prefects in the Unoccupied Zone reported their departments generally happy to see the Jews go: the Gers, and the Indre, where early feelings of sympathy had vanished when masses of Jewish refugees arrived across the Demarcation Line. Another five departments (Ariège, Aude, Isère, Lozère, Saône-et-Loire) were reported to have mixed reactions. It was resort towns and towns in rural areas where well-to-do foreign Jews had been sent in forced residence that seemed to bear the most enduring ill-will. The deportations offended opinion in urban centers where numbers of people actually witnessed the loading of trains and the separations of families.

Critics who disapproved violently of handing Jews over to the Germans did not necessarily oppose Vichy's own more limited measures. The prefect of the Alpes-Maritimes thought that many of his people who were shocked to see Jews delivered to the Occupied Zone would have accepted with "relief" their internment in the Unoccupied Zone. The prefects of the Lozère and the Bouches-du-Rhône reported that their people hoped that the regime would continue to pursue its goals of "a purge" by social and economic measures applied with the necessary "discrimination," which "would eliminate [the Jews] from the jobs where they are not wanted."[230] Vichy's own anti-Jewish program did not lose its constituency overnight in August 1942.

The agitation was rather short-lived, also. Most prefects reported, to their surprise, that a matter of "great moment" in August had receded into "the background" by October (Pyrénées-Orientales). The new law of 4 September instituting obligatory labor service for young men took a great deal of wind out of the sails of the deportation excitement. Many prefects thought it had an even more profoundly unset-tling effect on public opinion (Vaucluse, Haute-Garonne). French work-ers taken to Germany would soon occupy center stage, in the awareness of most French people, as the *real* deportation.

Church leaders, too, drew back from the possibility of a rupture with the regime. Sensitive to the widespread reproduction of his pasto-ral letter in Resistance organs, Monsignor Saliège objected forcefully to "the indecent use that certain people have made of his letter," and went on to renew "his complete loyalty to the Marshal and to the powers that be."[231] Cardinal Suhard made a similar declaration, and Gerlier followed suit in a letter to the mayor of Lyon affirming his "loyalty in conformity with traditional Church doctrine."[232] Pétain's office carefully monitored the prelates' declarations of support as they flowed in—on 19 September from a gathering of bishops of the south-east, headed by the archbishop of Aix, and on 2 October from the archbishops of Paris, Rheims, and Besançon and the bishops of Châlons, Verdun, Mans, Chartres, Soissons, Beauvais, Nancy, Saint-Dié, Langres, Troyes, and Vannes. By the end of the month, the Marshal received a report contending that the crisis was over, and the Church "ap-peased."[233] As if to seal publicly some kind of rapprochement, cardinals Suhard and Gerlier, the two princes of the church in the two zones, met Laval and Pétain in Vichy on 29 October and appeared together with them at a military review.[234]

More than sociability was involved in that meeting. At lunch the same day, the government reaffirmed its intention to grant state subsi-dies for the first time to the Institut Catholique and other Catholic institutions of higher education. Pastor Boegner's National Protestant Federation was to get some state funds for its theology faculties, too, as was its smaller rival, Pastor Lamorte's Reformed Evangelical Church, which had supported the Vichy regime vigorously, had abstained from any mention of the Jewish issue, and, in a lawsuit, had challenged the federation's control of Church property.[235] Other concessions were offered the Church during this period, such as tax advantages and mea-sures favorable to diocesan associations. There is no record of any direct link between them and the Jewish question, but the recent confronta-tions can hardly have been far from anyone's mind. Almost two months before, Bousquet had told Hagen about a plan to use state subsidies for Catholic schools as a stick to beat down Church protests.[236] Relying instead upon a carrot, Laval wrote to Ambassador Léon Bérard at the Vatican that the concessions were "so many expressions of good will on the part of the *Etat français* and, in that sense, I hope that they will encounter reciprocal good will in certain religious circles." He could hardly have been more plain. Valeri accepted the measures gratefully, declaring them to be "clear testimony to the underlying objective of Monsieur le Maréchal Petain to build the new France on the only worthwhile foundation, that is, on spiritual values."[237]

As negotiations proceeded, the Jews slipped out of sight in relations between Vichy and the Church. In January 1943, Cardinal Suhard went to Rome to discuss important matters affecting France and the Vatican. Léon Bérard's report on 18 January of the results provide a tantalizing glimpse of Pope Pius XII's feelings about Vichy France:

> I have learned from an associate close to the sovereign pontiff that the latter was favorably impressed by his conversations with the archbishop of Paris. He saw things very much eye to eye with the latter. He very warmly praised the work of the Marshal and took a keen interest in government actions that are a sign of the fortunate renewal of religious life in France.[238]

Nothing at all was said about the Jews.

When the deportations resumed in February 1943, and once again French police took charge of massive roundups in the hitherto unoccupied zone as well as in the north, the French Catholic hierarchy did not renew its protests. Cardinal Suhard wrote to Pétain asking him to issue discreet orders to moderate the conditions under which some arrests were taking place. "At issue is the way in which actions against the Jews are carried out." He drew special attention to the arrests of Jewish mothers or fathers in "aryan families." Except on the question of how the deportations were managed, however, his resignation was complete:

> Everyone knows that the French government cannot be held entirely responsible for the steps taken. By one of those dramatic turns of fate in the present time, it happens that it is the French who must execute the orders. If the orders cannot be avoided, we would at least like to see that they not be executed with excessive severity and inhumanity.[239]

The main issue now straining relations between Vichy and the Church was obligatory labor for Nazi Germany, and the question of whether priests might accompany them. Cardinal Suhard was proud of the Church's restraint: "Our bishops refuse to take responsibility for certain protests that now circulate in Catholic circles," he told Monsignor Chappoulie, the hierarchy's representative at Vichy, in May 1943.[240] But there was no mention of the Jews.

The furor over the deportations had died down. But Marshal Pétain's claim to have spared his people something had been gravely damaged. The prefects made plain that "the best supporters of the National Revolution were among the most disaffected.[241] The first significant break had occurred between Vichy and major parts of the establishment. Vichy had lost part of its claim to legitimacy.

CHAPTER
7

The Darquier Period, 1942–44

I T WOULD BE HARD to find a more complete contrast to the first
commissioner-general for Jewish affairs, Xavier Vallat, than his
successor, Louis Darquier de Pellepoix. To be sure, both men were
capable of the coarsest expressions of antisemitism. Jews, Vallat said
in an address to students of public administration in the spring of 1942,
were "worms who are attracted by gangrenous wounds."[1] Darquier's
epithets took a more scatalogical turn. His description in print of Bernard Lecache, head of the Ligue Internationale contre l'Antisémitisme
as—among other things—"that excrement of the ghetto," "that circumcised little pig,"[2] won their author a fine and a prison sentence under
the Marchandeau Law in 1939. Darquier also liked to express his hatred
of Jews with his fists. He was arrested in 1936, 1937, and 1939 for picking
fights with Jews in public places.

Vallat had been a member of the conservative establishment—a
one-time teacher of literature, a deputy with a lifetime of experience
in Catholic and war veterans' movements and with friendships within
the highest military and clerical circles. Darquier was an unsuccessful
businessman and a marginal journalist whose top electoral position
before the war was the Paris Municipal Council. Vallat was a personage
of rank and distinction at Vichy, where he maintained his center of
operations. He was a welcome guest at Pétain's lunch table even after
leaving office. The Germans consented to issue him a special pass to visit
the Occupied Zone only on a case-by-case basis.[3]* Darquier always
remained an outsider at Vichy. He spent most of his time in Paris and
moved his offices there completely in November 1943. Vallat had been
hard-working and diligent, a man who took pride in his attention to
detail even though the commissariat escaped his efforts to control cor-

*Vallat was provided with a post in the Ministry of Foreign Affairs after leaving the
CGQJ.

ruption and administrative confusion. Darquier was indolent and pleas-ure-loving. He spent little time in his office, leaving the commissariat's daily operations to associates of dubious character. Vallat was a national-ist who hated Germans as much as he hated Jews, and whose antisemit-ism was tempered by a desire to shelter some Jewish war veterans. Darquier had been receiving secret funds from the Germans since 1937 or 1938, and no conception of *raison d'état* seems ever to have entered into his calculations. Indeed, while Vallat had been named to his post without German foreknowledge, Darquier was the candidate of the German embassy and *Sicherheitsdienst.*

Louis Darquier—he assumed the aristocratic-sounding compound surname of Darquier de Pellepoix only later—was born in Cahors in 1897, the son of a doctor. After making a good military record in the First World War (a record that he marred slightly by leaving his unit before being officially demobilized in fall 1919), the young war veteran, like so many in the 1920s, had trouble finding his place in the world. He worked for a publicity agency in Strasbourg and then for a Franco-British grain wholesaling firm in Antwerp and Rotterdam; in 1927 he even tried his hand on a ranch in Australia. It was the nationalist demonstrations of 6 February 1934 in Paris that gave Darquier a career. Making use of the wound he received while confronting the police alongside his Action Française comrades on the Place de la Concorde, Darquier founded the Association of the wounded of 6 February and made himself its president. Within less than a year, in May 1935, he had been elected to the Paris Municipal Council from the Ternes district. He had found his métier as a right-wing agitator.

For Darquier, however, everything came down to one issue: the Jews. Resigning from the Croix de Feu in 1935 because he found its leader, Colonel de la Rocque, a "tin-pot dictator," Darquier managed to quarrel even with the Action Française by siding with Urbain Gohier when the latter called Daudet and Maurras Jews in 1939.[4] Darquier certainly shared none of Maurras's principled anti-Germanism. He was asking the German embassy in Paris discreetly for money in early 1937, but Ambassador von Welczek was cautious. The German funds that Darquier eventually received came rather from such unofficial sources as the Geneva-based International Antisémite, a Nazi-front organiza-tion linked to Julius Streicher, and from Colonel Fleischauer, an agent of the *Weltdienst,* an anti-Jewish press agency supported by the Nazi party in Erfurt.[5]

These funds helped Darquier launch an antisemitic weekly, *La France enchaînée,* which seems to have soaked up cash as rapidly as the

Germans would provide it. He also founded a series of propaganda organizations: the National Club against Métèques, then the Anti-Jewish Union. He told the German embassy in 1937 that he had three thousand members, mostly lawyers and other prominent people—no doubt a gross exaggeration. He had notoriety, however, without doubt. He made a sensation on 7 April 1938 with a long speech before the Paris Municipal Council; in it, he asserted that all the professions and arts in France had been invaded by Jews, that Jews had begun and then stalemated the First World War, that Blum had ruined the country, that France was being forced to receive the 80,000 to 100,000 Jews that Poland was exporting "under threat of asphyxiation"—in short, "the definitive *youpinisation* ["kike-ification"] of France. Hitler, Darquier pointed out, "knew how to solve the problem legally"; if France did not pass some similar "sound laws" in its turn, violence would erupt. The response to this speech was stormy to the verge of open fighting, though Darquier was not completely alone. A certain Dr. Torchausse followed by transmitting to the council the wish of the Academy of Medicine that, to avoid "an assault upon the very fiber of our race," all naturalizations be made conditional upon a medical examination.[6] Darquier added to the notoriety he won that day by the conviction for defamation and slander already mentioned, and by a reputation for high-living, recklessness, and venality.

On the outbreak of war in 1939, Darquier's mobilization as a lieutenant in the artillery suspended his legal problems (his conviction was officially set aside in fall 1940) and gave him the chance once more to show bravery under fire. He was cited for covering his battery in retreat, and was taken prisoner. He continued his anti-Jewish propaganda in the German camp Oflag 2D, from which he was soon released.

Back in Paris, Darquier moved during 1940–42 in the shady world of antisemitic propaganda that he knew best, and which now seemed to offer a bright future. He founded the Association for the Defence of the Race and worked with the German-sponsored Institute for the Study of Jewish Questions. Together with Bernard Faÿ, Léon de Poncins, Claude Vacher de Lapouge, and others, Darquier was considered by the *Judenreferat* as a possible director of the "central Jewish office" (see chapter 3) which the Germans were urging upon Vichy in the spring of 1941. Instead Darlan seized the initiative by giving the post to Xavier Vallat. After Vallat had lost the Germans' confidence in early 1942, they settled upon Darquier as their candidate to succeed him, following a momentary consideration of Doriot. According to René Gillouin, Darlan offered the post to René Dommange, a right-wing

Parisian deputy on close personal terms with Pétain and a disciple of some of the more nostalgic aspects of the National Revolution; but Dommange refused.[7] Vallat, by his own account, warned the government about Darquier, as did others. When Laval took office, however, he seems to have decided to placate the Germans on what he considered a minor post. Unlike some of the Parisian zealots, moreover, Darquier had been a soldier and one of the earliest Pétainists—a sign perhaps that he could be controlled. Otherwise preoccupied, Laval gave in on Darquier. To cover himself, he named to the watchdog post of deputy commissioner Georges Monier, a member of the highest French administrative law court, the Conseil d'Etat.[8]* On 6 May 1942, Darquier's hour came: Pétain named him, at the age of thirty-five, commissioner-general for Jewish affairs.[9]

Darquier's CGQJ and Its Place in the Regime

> Moreover, he [Laval] often points out that Darquier de Pellepoix is an "excellent chap," to be sure, but useless for any serious administrative work. (The repeated ironic allusions to the actual incompetence of Darquier de Pellepoix suggest that President Laval wants him removed. This was especially evident when he remarked in today's conversation that Darquier de Pellepoix attended formal conferences without raising any objections, but that after meetings he constantly wrote letters of accusation against different ministers.)
>
> SS-Sturmbannführer Hagen, reporting on his meeting with Laval
> (3 September 1942)[10]

Darquier's appointment was hardly calculated to revive the flagging fortunes of *antisémitisme d'état,* which had been intended as a lawful discrimination and purge, carried out in an orderly manner to reinforce the authority of the state and the homogeneity of the culture. Darquier, however, fell naturally into a role that was more theatrical and ideological than administrative. He devoted his energies more to propaganda designed to excite public opinion about the purity and grandeur of the race than to drafting legal texts. Under Darquier, the persecution of the Jews lost whatever claims it had had to moderation and legalism. The Vichy promise "neither against persons nor against property" (see chapter 3)—never truly kept—was now flouted daily in

---

*Monier quit the post after several weeks.

the most brutal fashion. *Antisémitisme d'état* had been meant to be but one plank in a larger Vichy platform of order and national security. With Darquier it was an obsession, an end in itself that demanded ever more government resolve and commitment. The Jewish problem, said Darquier in 1943, "is the preliminary question for any internal and external policy, and for any French renewal."[11] *Antisémitisme d'état*, above all, had been meant to increase French independence and control. Vallat had even believed that he could obtain the repeal of German racial ordinances in the Occupied Zone by doing the same job better. Under Darquier, the last pretenses of French independence were swept away. The French program had been swallowed up in the far vaster German design of extermination. And while French police made the arrests and guarded the trains, and while the French administration coordinated the whole inhuman operation, few French people doubted that the Germans were in charge.

The commissariat's standing was also affected by the war situation. However fully Vichy's antisemitism reflected indigenous attitudes, its fortunes were ultimately linked to the success of German arms, much as was the credibility of the Vichy government itself. Antisemitism had stood nearly unchallenged in 1940 when the New Order seemed to have supplanted forever the cosmopolitan liberalism of the Third Republic. But as the war dragged on into 1943, as the dream of a compromise peace began to recede, as the burdens of occupation increased, and as the Reich suffered reverses in Russia and North Africa, Vichy policies in general were more exposed to second thoughts.

Under these circumstances, it is not surprising that the commissariat's old troubles with the recruitment of competent and honest personnel were compounded. Darquier set the worst possible example at the top. Bored by the tasks of everyday administration, he could not or would not surround himself with competent professional staff. The shift from Vallat to Darquier was typical of Vichy's general slide toward younger and more marginal leaders after 1942, though that process began earlier in anti-Jewish affairs than elsewhere. Darquier's subordinates reinforced that trend all the more strongly since the commissariat lost whatever legitimacy it had enjoyed more rapidly than the more traditional or technical public services.

One by one those CGQJ officials who had previously held major responsibilities in one or another of the most prestigious government agencies gave way to newcomers, often from the worlds of journalism, right-wing political movements, or para-police organizations. At the crucial Service de Contrôle des Administrateurs Provisoires (see chapters 1 and 3), a sequence of top civil servants came to an end with the resignation of Louis Bralley, controller-general of the Army. He was replaced by Lucien Boué, an old crony of Darquier's who had moved over from the Prefecture of the Seine a few years earlier and had worked his way up in the CGQJ. Boué was suspected by the Germans themselves of corruption.[12] As assistant head of SCAP, René Dagron, an industrial engineer, gave way to Pierre Gérard, a twenty-eight-year-old editor who had been a friend of Darquier's since 1934 and a journalist on *Le Jour.*[13] One Regelsperger, an investigator borrowed from the Bank of France to run aryanization affairs in the Occupied Zone, was let go, as were other officials drawn from the Bank of France and the Ministry of Finance. So was Jean Giroud, an officer of the Conseil d'État, formerly the top advisor to the CGQJ as head of its legal claims department. There is no certainty that the replacements of these men were less skilled or scrupulous (though many of them were), but it is plain that the replacements had fewer ties with the senior civil service. People of little experience or training could now move up quickly in the CGQJ. One Auguste Mudry, who had only a primary education, rose, as a friend of Gérard, from a post paying 2,000 francs per month to one paying 10,000 francs per month.

The new men in charge set the tone. Colonel Chomel de Jarnieu, who had tried to bring some order into Vallat's operations, departed with Vallat. The Germans refused to let him into the Occupied Zone after the mixup about supplies for the first deportation train of March 1942.[14] Darquier replaced him as private secretary with the free-wheeling Pierre Gallien. Gallien, owner of a tire-recapping plant in Neuilly, had become involved with Darquier's affairs as early as 1937. He lent Darquier money and served as co-editor and chief distributor of the latter's antisemitic weekly *La France enchaînée.* The two had been arrested together for beating up distributors of Bernard Lecache's *Le Droit de vivre* in 1939. After only five months at the CGQJ, in November 1942, they were at fisticuffs with each other in Darquier's office. It is not clear just what caused the breach, but Darquier paid off his debts to Gallien and fired him. To the Germans he explained that Gallien had been involved in corruption.[15] There is plenty of independent evidence for that charge; but, in view of Darquier's usual tolerance in such matters, something else must have been involved.

After Gallien, Darquier named Joseph Antignac his private secretary in November 1942. Antignac was as fervent an antisemite as Gallien but differed in almost every other respect. Where Gallien had been a brawler and agitator, Antignac was a former cavalry officer raised to the level of parody. He was one of the rare First World War reserve cavalry officers who managed to obtain a regular commission by passing through the prestigious Saumur Cavalry School after the war. Captain Antignac was forced out in 1926, however, by a peacetime contraction of the officer corps and condemned to a series of brief and uncongenial business jobs. He really found himself in the CGQJ after brilliant military service again in 1940. As regional director of the Police for Jewish Affairs in Limoges he formed a reputation for punctilio and harshness. Darquier brought him to Vichy in August 1942 to head the whole police operation as the Sections d'Enquête et Contrôle replaced the PQJ. After November 1942 as private secretary, and as chief of staff after January 1943, Antignac in fact ran the CGQJ. He did so with single-minded firmness to the very end. After May 1944, as secretary-general under the ephemeral Charles du Paty de Clam, he was commissioner in all but name.[16]

The CGQJ had always had the reputation of closer involvement with the Germans than had other Vichy agencies. Indeed, some of its branches, such as the SCAP and the Police for Jewish Affairs offices in the Occupied Zone, worked with their German counterparts on a day-by-day basis from the beginning. Vallat had taken some pains to give the rest of the CGQJ an outward impression of distance from occupation authorities. Under Darquier, the CGQJ forged links with the Germans at the very top. Gallien had been reporting to the Gestapo for years as agent Ju1. As Darquier's private secretary, he regularly passed documents to them. They valued his services, and Knochen himself tried to intervene when Gallien was fired. Antignac routinely forwarded interministerial correspondence to the *Judenreferent* Röthke for his inspection in 1943.[17] Darquier, never one to bury himself at Vichy far from the excitement of Parisian nightlife, spent far more time in the capital had than his predecessor. He referred constantly to the *Judenreferat* and took pains to display his rigor to the Germans. He reminded them of details and recommended harsh solutions. Referring to them the question of whether French parents could adopt Jewish children, for example, he made it clear that he expected a negative answer in terms of both German law and racial theory. He told Röthke that he wanted to see the Germans represented in the Vichy government, and reported compromising details in the lives of high-ranking Vichy personalities.[18]

The Germans repaid Darquier's obsequious attention with contempt. They did not permit him the slightest discretion in the enforcement of German anti-Jewish ordinances; and on the rare occasions when he asked for an exemption, they generally refused.[19] The CGQJ had to petition the occupation authorities for the most menial favors— opening a blocked bank account here, prying loose a few Jewish paintings there, or an automobile for one of Darquier's propaganda institutes.[20] The crowning ignominy came in early 1944 when the Gestapo required CGQJ employees to furnish meticulous documentation—birth registration plus baptismal certificates of all four grandparents—to prove that they *themselves* were not Jewish.[21]* Two months later Röthke tightened up still further and required the CGQJ to furnish weekly reports of all Jews turned over to the French police by the SEC. Darquier did not earn their respect, and in the end it was the Germans themselves who got rid of him.

None of this improved Darquier's relations with his constitutional colleagues and superiors in the Vichy government. Darquier never made the transition from his earlier role of propagandist and critic to that of member of a government. Far from becoming a spokesman for duly decided policy, he was unable to break his habit of criticizing Vichy from Paris. Vichy's anti-Jewish policy, he charged, forgetting that he bore constitutional responsibility for it now, was "in total confusion." Jews were still ensconced in high positions in the French administration. "Everywhere," the Jews could still rely on "a Judaized clique who will strive by every means to check and to sabotage the [anti-] Jewish laws."[23]

It was in the style of a propagandist and not as a member of a government that Darquier offered up his new program. If he discussed his proposals in advance with the head of government or colleagues, these courtesies have left no trace. Instead, his first act on being named commissioner-general was to issue an extravagant programmatic statement on 6 May as he emerged from a meeting at the German Propaganda Service in Paris. As other ideas occurred to him, he called more of the press conferences that he so obviously relished. Invariably critical of Vichy law on these occasions, he proposed to close the loopholes for long-established Jewish families and for war veterans which, he asserted, permitted them to infiltrate the administration. He thought that the different anti-Jewish programs in the two zones should be standardized, and he made it clear that standardization meant alignment on the German model. He urged the extension of the yellow star to the formerly Unoccupied Zone, denaturalization of all Jews who had become French citizens since 1927, and a law restricting the rights of "half-Jews"

---

*Technically, Darquier need not have felt humiliated: all SS officers had to file similar documents before marriage.[22]

who escaped the current laws. He regretted the weakness of the Police for Jewish Affairs and its successor, the Sections d'Enquête et Contrôle. On 12 May he proclaimed "his intention of settling the Jewish question once and for all." He later applauded deportations which he hoped would amount to "total expulsion." On 23 May he repeated his proposals of the sixth and urged an aggressive treatment of the Jewish question in school curricula. By early 1943, he had announced no less than twelve proposed statutes that amounted to a complete overhaul along racialist lines of the Vichy anti-Jewish program. "It's a matter of will. We have to make up our minds."[24]

Darquier's concern about "half-Jews" who had hitherto been left in peace (Vallat's statute had exempted those with two Jewish grandparents who were not married to a Jew) deserves closer attention. The bizarre obsession with half-Jews, whom the Nazis called *Mischlinge*, had hitherto been a German peculiarity. On this subject Darquier appeared to outstrip even the Nazis: "The half Jews are much more numerous than is often thought, especially among the common people. They are often more dangerous than pure Jews, precisely because of their hybrid character."[25] As we have seen, it is hard to disentangle the strands of racial and cultural antisemitism in Vallat; but he showed a clear disposition to reward such signs of deep rooting in French culture as several generations of public service and war heroism. With Darquier, as with German racialists, the more assimilated a Jew became, the more dangerous he seemed, because hidden. No concerns of *raison d'état* or religion modified his otherwise uncomplicated racialism.

None of Darquier's proposed statutes was adopted by the Vichy government. We do not know whether they were even debated there. Indeed, no new basic anti-Jewish legislation emerged from Vichy after the law of 11 December 1942 requiring that all Jews' personal documents be stamped *Juif* or *Juive*—something that Vallat had advocated in his time. Darquier had no legislative impact upon the government with which he was ostensibly associated. The legislative period of Vichy's anti-Jewish program was over, and Darquier could not revive it.

At the very top, Darquier's own place in the Vichy hierarchy was certainly very much lower than Vallat's had been. Marshal Pétain avoided him and—according to postwar recollections—referred to him publicly as "Monsieur le tortionnaire" ("Mr. Torturer").[26] Darquier met Laval regularly, once or twice a month during his tenure of office at CGQJ, but there was no cordiality between them. Laval openly disparaged Darquier when talking to German officials, scarcely concealing his irony and contempt.[27] The CGQJ's efficacy as a government agency is not to be measured in personal good will, however, or in invitations to lunch at the Hôtel du Parc. We need to return to the question of whether the CGQJ received the cooperation of other government agencies or whether it was put in administrative quarantine.

Relations between the CGQJ and other government agencies had never been smooth. Under the quarrelsome and hot-headed Darquier, they deteriorated even further. Faced with a magistracy perfectly willing to enforce the law but in its own way, Darquier took the legal offensive, filing briefs with the courts to argue the commissariat's hard line on current cases.[28] He denounced to the Germans the Ministry of Industrial Production's reluctance to supply scarce shoes and blankets for deportation convoys.[29] He quarreled with Bousquet over emigration.[30] He even fought with the anti-Jewish specialists at the Prefecture of Police and opposed the latter's occasional entry into sealed apartments to procure necessary personal effects for Jewish children whose parents had been deported.[31] In the notorious Schloss affair, he allowed a collection of Jewish paintings discovered in a bank vault in the formerly Unoccupied Zone to be taken to Paris for evaluation, over the objections of French fiscal, police, and cultural officials, and without adequate guarantees that these paintings would remain in French hands.[32] Vichy seems to have sent secret notes to prefects advising them to resist Darquier's projects; and, according to some postwar testimony, Laval winked at or even encouraged prefectoral undermining of anti-Jewish measures.[33] The government forbade press publicity for some of Darquier's more outrageous proposals and refused some of his administrative and police demands.[34]

Nothing, however, prevented Darquier's agents from simply going their own way when the CGQJ lost one of these interbureau confrontations. The CGQJ was known to ignore judicial decisions that went against it—for example, its refusal to accept the jurisdiction of the Court of Appeals of Amiens in June 1943 in determining Jewishness under the *Statut des juifs.*[35] The SEC commonly exceeded its supposedly limited police powers. In the long-standing tug of war between the CGQJ and the economics ministries over control of aryanization, Darquier's agency sometimes "forgot" to clear with the Ministry of Finance before allowing a foreign (that is, German) purchaser to acquire former Jewish property.* Many of the conflicts between the CGQJ and other agencies turn out, on closer inspection, to involve border disputes rather than conflicts of principle, perhaps out of prudence. As late as January 1944,

---

*For example, that of Austin and Helena Rubinstein.[36]

a prefect could complain bitterly that the CGQJ had given direct instructions to a local branch without passing through the proper chain of command.[37] In the spring of 1944, when Inspector-General of Finance Formery prepared a report on the functioning of the CGQJ, he addressed himself to correcting its abuses and making it function correctly rather than objecting to its fundamental purposes.[38]

Thus, nothing in the frictions between his agency and the rest of the French administration prevented Darquier from continuing to run the anti-Jewish machinery set up by his predecessors, or even from accelerating the rate of persecution. If the Vichy government had tried in any serious way to clip his wings, those restraints do not show up in the CGQJ's budget appropriations. In keeping with his extravagant personal style, Darquier tried to obtain 4,000,000 francs *per month* for his propaganda projects when he assumed office, along with comparable sums for other programs.[39] Though he was not successful to that degree, Darquier managed nonetheless to command a significant budgetary increase each year—a mark of bureaucratic momentum as well as of powerful support from Paris. A law of December 1942 fixed the next annual CGQJ budget at well over 47,000,000 francs (up from nearly 30,000,000 in the preceding year), of which over 28,000,000 was for salaries. For 1944, the CGQJ was allowed to devour over 50,000,000 francs, and certain credits were still open after the Liberation. As the jurist J. Lubetzki observed upon reporting these figures, "it is difficult to stop a functioning administrative machine."[40]

It is worth asking how Darquier managed to hold on to his office for nearly two years, when the better-connected and more capable Vallat lasted only one. The support of the German embassy and the *Sicherheitsdienst* in Paris counted for a great deal, although Darquier's German backers had few illusions about his capacities. From the Vichy side, Darquier was perhaps useful as a lightning rod, to draw public criticism away from the most sordid aspects of Vichy policy. Above all, this was simply not an area in which Laval wished to spend his diminishing bargaining power; and for more than a year he chose not to pick a quarrel with the Germans over Darquier.

Darquier's CGQJ in Action

Firmly supported by the German embassy and the *Judenreferat*, and evidently considered too costly to challenge by the French government, Darquier had a freer hand than Vallat in some respects. Blocked in legislative channels, he had the funds and the personnel to expand the anti-Jewish administrative machinery. Not that administrative detail interested him very much; he left such things to his subordinates who made up for his indolence.

Deportation was largely the work of the police. The actual arrests, concentration, and delivery of the victims were planned and carried out by officials of the Ministry of the Interior answerable to Laval and headed by Secretary-General for Police René Bousquet and his assistant Leguay—yet one more reminder that anti-Jewish policy at Vichy was a government function and not merely the private preserve of the CGQJ. Darquier was present at the planning sessions for the first great roundup in Paris in July 1942, however, and even received nominal authority over the operation. His private secretary Gallien was responsible for the preparations—or lack of them—that made conditions so intolerable in the Vélodrome d'Hiver. The CGQJ entered the picture in its efforts to browbeat the Ministry of Industrial Production into releasing a few shoes and blankets for the convoys, and CGQJ personnel assisted on loading days at Drancy. But it was not the PQJ who conducted the arrests and guarded the trains, but regular police; and the deportations were not the CGQJ's principal activity.

Much of the CGQJ's energies were drawn into aryanization. The majority of the agency's personnel were employed here. CGQJ offices throughout France became, in effect, property brokers. Each regional prefecture contained a commissariat officer who managed the transfer of property taken from Jews. In the northern zone, Darquier's agents assumed the functions that the prefectures had performed under the first German aryanization ordinances in 1940. Pressing his agency's old claims against the economics ministries, Darquier also managed to supplant the minister of industrial production, with the support of the German authorities, in the nomination of *administrateurs provisoires*. The CGQJ's Direction of Economic Affairs and SCAP had always been primarily responsible for overseeing these trustees' performance and were limited only by outside auditors *(commissaires aux comptes)*. Despite repeated proposals from within the administration to turn aryanization over to a better-supervised and professionally correct agency such as the Administration des Domaines, the CGQJ kept its grip on the aryanization process until the end of the war. Responsible French officials looked on helplessly as both the scale and the mismanagement of these property exchanges grew larger.[41]

Disregarding the law, the CGQJ extended aryanization to those properties still left to Jews who had been deported. Legally, this capital was supposed to go to the UGIF or to trustees named by the courts.[42] For almost two years the commissariat simply took what it wanted. In 1944 a CGQJ report spoke of "a complete breakdown of morality with too many *administrateurs provisoires*," as bribery and special favors riddled the aryanization bureaucracy. A French government official estimated in January 1943 that Jewish apartments were selling for 30 percent below market value. No one faulted Darquier's agency for going too slowly. By the end of 1943 the most important part of the task had been completed, according to reports from both zones. It is doubtful that much property remained in Jewish hands in France in the summer of 1944.[43]

The temptations to fraud were almost irresistible when the CGQJ was awash with confiscated businesses, dwellings, and personal effects. Again, the tone was set at the top. Gallien was known inside the agency itself for bestowing Jewish properties on his friends and rewarding other people with apartments and commissions.[44] In addition to corruption, there was incompetence. The French administration took it for granted that Jewish enterprises were being ruined by their CGQJ trustees, and the French economy correspondingly was damaged. The Ministry of Justice wrote to Antignac, by then secretary-general of the CGQJ, in July 1944 that "trusteeship most often leads to the decline or ruin of a business." Antignac was indignant at this reproach to his agency. Had not the Ministry of Industrial Production and the *comités d'organisation* themselves urged the liquidation rather than the sale of Jewish properties, in order to reduce competition?[45] Darquier's CGQJ was hardly of a stature to deal with these competing interests and temptations efficiently, let alone honestly.

As early as 1943, the lure of quick gains in aryanization began to be counterbalanced by anxieties about the future. Purchasers and trustees of Jewish property sensed that the ship might one day sink, despite German assurances that the legitimacy of their transactions would be guaranteed in the eventual peace treaty.[46] One solution was to unload the new acquisitions as speedily as possible, and new purchasers found vexing the restrictions on resale of the properties before three years. As for *administrateurs provisoires*, they began to give thought to insuring themselves against civil suits brought by former Jewish owners. To advance these various interests, purchasers and *administrateurs provisoires* considered forming societies for mutual defense. De Faramond, head of the SCAP in 1941, had opposed the formation of an association of *administrateurs provisoires* since he saw them as temporary agents of a public service. But by 1943, anxiety was greater, and administrative control less scrupulous. Darquier attempted to reassure the holders of aryanized property (he reminded readers that nationalized Church property in the 1790s was retained by purchasers even after the defeat of the French Revolution.)[47] but had increasing difficulty doing so. In September 1943, the purchasers founded the French Association of Owners of Aryanized Property to defend their interests; and it was followed in January 1944 by the French Association des Administrateurs Provisoires.[48]

The Sections d'Enquête et Contrôle, the para-police organization of the CGQJ, successor to the Police for Jewish Affairs of 1941, were also given a free rein under Darquier. The long rivalry between the regular police and these often embarrassing auxiliaries had ended in a compromise in August 1942 when Laval, stopping short of total abolition of the PQJ, permitted its replacement by the SEC under what were supposed to be strict limitations. There remained the problem of obtaining the cooperation of the regular police. The secretary-general of police, René Bousquet, was eager to explain the limits of the SEC's authority to the prefects. In a circular to the prefects on 11 September 1942, he advised them that the SEC was excluded from all judicial acts (arrests, searches, et cetera) and charged them to reserve for themselves any decisions about what further should be done about suspects identified by the SEC. With this charge, however, Bousquet granted the SEC a form of official recognition. Joseph Antignac, head of the SEC, believed that "the doors of the police departments will be open once again." In early 1943 further assistance came when terms of collaboration were worked out between the SEC and the Gendarmerie Nationale.[49]

The SEC became a nationally coordinated center for anti-Jewish espionage. At its top, the ex-cavalry captain Joseph Antignac was able to satisfy his taste for struggle and command denied him between the wars. From his Paris offices, Antignac directed several dozen SEC officials who fanned out like so many representatives on a mission to squeeze the revolutionary juices of the provinces in the service of an increasingly unpopular crusade. The SEC agents, nominally subject to regional CGQJ offices, enjoyed a wide independence.[50] They made liberal use of informers and expected the *administrateurs provisoires* to act as auxiliaries and pass along useful intelligence. They worked closely with the *Sicherheitsdienst*. They inspected aryanization proceedings, spied on individuals, searched out culpable leniencies in the other administrative services, denounced Jews in hiding, and investigated people who had helped them. During the month of January 1943 alone and in the former Unoccupied Zone alone, SEC agents carried out 527 inquiries which led to twenty-five administrative internments, fourteen expulsions from cities, nine assignments to forced residence, and forty-eight other indictments.[51]

SEC agents probed the slightest infraction of the anti-Jewish laws with a pedantry hitherto found only in the SS. In Rennes, representatives had the formidable task of exploring every bookstore to make sure none stocked books by Jewish authors. Rooting out Jewish books was an uphill task, for, particularly in rural areas, old texts such as Jules Isaac's forbidden *Cours d'histoire* was still in use in 1943 even though Hachette had removed it from sale in 1941.[52] In Paris, at the request of the Gestapo, the SEC submitted a long report on gymnastic classes at two *lycées* where Jewish and non-Jewish students still mixed together. Much of the SEC's work involved burrowing in church archives to find baptismal documents to detect forgery. Not infrequently, as a result, the SEC accused clerics of falsifying records. Sometimes it even complained that the police destroyed records or lacked stomach to arrest the individuals whom it had uncovered.[53]

Despite the efforts of Laval and Bousquet to contain it, the SEC continually overflowed the boundaries set in August 1942. In the northern zone, it made outright arrests from the beginning. When Joseph Darnand took over the police in both zones in January 1944, the way was clear for the agency to assume the long-coveted powers that had previously been withheld. In July 1944 these were extended to the southern zone in a final paroxysm of anti-Jewish vigilantism.[54]

Darquier's own predilection was propaganda. This was the world familiar to this former employee of a publicity agency, and he enjoyed the attention that mass media could provide. In a curious reversal, he seems to have been more drawn to the form than to the substance of anti-Jewish persecution, which he gladly left to others. While Vallat had relatively little energy for propaganda and had let antisemitism be aligned with the larger interests of the National Revolution, Darquier announced a vast publicity campaign which was "indispensable" for his anti-Jewish effort. He demanded over two million francs for this undertaking for the remainder of 1942 alone, and within a few weeks the government complied.[55]

The Propaganda Directorate attached to Darquier's office, and assigned to Alex Delpeyrou, coordinated a pyramid of institutes, each one designed to reach a specific clientele. The Anthropo-Sociology Institute under Claude Vacher de Lapouge, son of the racist author, catered to "scholarly and specialist circles." The Institute for the Study of Jewish and Ethno-Racial Questions, headed by George Montandon, constituted a sort of anti-Jewish academy. Most broadly geared to the masses was the French Union for the Defense of the Race. The first two institutes were outfitted with the symbols of scholarly and literary respectability: "serious" journals and other publications, lecture series, and guest speakers.

In a parallel bid for scholarly respectability, Darquier took the initiative in establishing a Sorbonne chair in the history of Judaism to which Minister of Education Abel Bonnard appointed Henri Labroue in November 1942. Labroue, a history professor who had written on the French Revolution in the Dordogne, veered into antisemitism between the wars with a pamphlet entitled "Voltaire juif." He served as a right-wing deputy from Bordeaux and after the defeat founded the Institute for the Study of Jewish Questions on his own in Bordeaux. When the sixty-two-year-old Labroue held forth in the Amphithéâtre Michelet, a German observer reported that he had only three to five regular students.[56] The room was sprinkled with hecklers, and the CGQJ sent photographers to the lectures to help identify them. A second Sorbonne chair was simultaneously announced, dealing with "racial studies" and probably intended for George Montandon; but this was never filled.[57] Montandon, as we shall see, found more lucrative employment conducting clinical racial examinations.

Darquier himself directed the French Union for the Defense of the Race, whose popular appeal suited his own tastes and ambitions. He intended this organization to be the center of his propaganda effort. He set up regional offices in Marseille, Lyon, and Toulouse and drew up an impressive battle plan at the close of 1942 that left no weapon unused in the propaganda war. Darquier called for antisemitic books, brochures, posters, and cinema. He wanted anti-Jewish agents sent everywhere in social life, even into sporting clubs. He proposed to commission "detective stories, romances, or sword-fighting novels in which Jews play pernicious parts."[58]

Radio programs became the particular specialty of the new commissioner-general, in a sharp departure from Vallat's more traditional deputy's orientation toward personal contacts. Beginning in the autumn of 1942, regular anti-Jewish "chats" were broadcast from Vichy at peak listening hours, usually four times a week. According to a German source, René Bousquet cleared the way for Darquier to broadcast his talks.[59] Assisted by other specialists such as Léon de Poncins and the Abbé Jacques, Darquier delivered dozens of these talks himself, often in crude and violent terms.

Not that Darquier neglected the press. The commissariat showered thousands of francs on various newspapers to carry CGQJ notices. Beyond the Parisian collaborationist newspapers where antisemitism was secure, the CGQJ could count on the support of a number of regional dailies, among them the *Nouvelliste de Lyon*, the *Grand Echo du Midi*, the *Mémorial de Saint-Etienne*, the *Courrier du Centre*, the *Petit Dauphinois*, and the *Eclaireur de Nice*.

The one persistent theme in all Darquier's propaganda was race. Since Gobineau, there had been French racial theoreticians[60] who—unlike their generally well-received counterparts in Germany—remained on the margins of social and scientific discourse. In France universalism still held sway, bolstered by Catholicism on the right and republican idealism on the left. While social prejudices were common in popular attitudes, it was usual to make individual exceptions rather than to ground one's prejudices in biology. The champions of race seemed much too rigid, foreign indeed to French national traditions. Vallat, whose thinking was colored by racialist attitudes as we have seen, had deliberately shunned Nazi-style arguments based on biology; and in this he was probably closer to the popular mood in France.

Darquier's public pronouncements, by contrast, took on the full panoply of National Socialist racialism. Deportations, he declared on the radio in December 1942, were a matter of "public hygiene":

Settling the Jewish problem is not an end in itself, it is only the preparation, a preliminary cleaning-up thanks to which there can arise in the foreseeable future (and the catastrophic circumstances we are going through, far from being an obstacle, will help) an *aristocracy of young men*, freed of this Jewish scum, who will be capable of bringing France back to her true ideals. (Emphasis in original)

Under his predecessors, Frenchmen had remained profoundly ignorant of the Jewish problem, he said. Now, thanks to the French Union for the Defense of the Race and the other institutes he had founded, they would be able to combat "the sinister Jewish propaganda." France had reached a low point. She had lost her army, her navy, her empire. "There is only one resource left to us: the strength of our own race."[61] Out of this perspective, Darquier drew the inspiration for a "complete plan of de-Judaizing": a redefinition of the Jew, a ban on intermarriage and other steps toward isolation of Jews, and, eventually, "total expulsion."[62]

Around Darquier gathered a group of French racialist thinkers whose sectarian aggressiveness had been nurtured by long years as outsiders. At last, their word was taken as law. The seventy-year-old René Martial lectured at the Paris Faculty of Medicine, as well as gracing Darquier's Anthropo-Sociology Institute. Claude Vacher de Lapouge, that institute's president, lent the name of his father who had spent a lifetime in master-race speculation. At the Institute for the Study of Jewish and Ethno-Racial Questions, a series of courses was offered for the uninitiated by lecturers with newly won credentials: Eugenics and Demography, by Gérard Mauger; Social Genealogy by Armand Bernardini; Judeocracy, by Charles Laville; and Ethno-Racial Philosophy by Pierre Villemain.

No one thrived in the new climate more exuberantly, however, than George Montandon. A Swiss physician who became French in 1936, Montandon published widely on his anthropological research conducted in Ethiopia, the Soviet Union, Japan, and the United States. Indeed, Montandon claimed to be a pioneer in the field of identifying Jews by physical characteristics. He even disparaged the celebrated German theorist Hans F. K. Gunther. Unlike the simple-minded who saw only *one* Jewish race, Montandon argued in *L'Ethnie française* (1935) that there were *two*—"the Alpine-Armenian race (that is to say, the Armenoid sub–race)" and "the Mediterranean race (that is to say, the Araboid sub-race)." Among the physiognomies chosen to illustrate his points was that of Léon Blum. As the Jewish question rose in the public's attention, Montandon churned out a number of works to satisfy new curiosities: books on how to recognize Jews, on their moral character, and a translation of a handbook on eugenics by the Nazi Othmar von Verschuer.[63]

Montandon had gained a toehold in the CGQJ when Vallat was pressured by the Germans to add a racial theorist to his staff. Under Darquier, Montandon was elevated to the position of the foremost Vichy expert on the Jewish race. Already since 1933 professor at the private Ecole d'Anthropologie, he now became head of the Institute for the Study of Jewish and Ethno-Racial Questions, and professor of its leading course "Ethno-Raciology." Darquier's CGQJ offered Montandon the dazzling prospect of rising from the purely theoretical plane to applied ethno-racism—physical examinations to discover Jews. The professor, who had trained in medicine at Zurich, jumped at the chance. Although the government would not cooperate to the extent of forcing people to undergo racial examinations, the services of Montandon became essential for doubtful cases wishing to prove they were not Jewish. Some people went to see the professor on their own initiative; others were "invited" by the CGQJ or the Prefecture of Police. Sometimes Montandon intervened at the eleventh hour at Drancy, where his decision was literally a matter of life or death. And, of course, money changed hands. Quite apart from the thousands of francs in bribes Montandon often required for a favorable answer, there were regular fees for his services. The UGIF paid these, and was bullied into doing so even when Montandon decided the examinee was not a Jew.[64]

Surviving texts of Montandon's diagnoses are framed in an elaborate pseudo-scientific terminology. First, he outlined the "ethnic antecedents." Then, for men, he displayed his full clinical wizardry with an exhaustive assessment of their circumcisions. (At issue was whether the operation, usually performed many decades before, had been "ritual" or "surgical.") Then came an exploration of the "biological race," a hodgepodge of crude measurements ("average nose," "feet slightly arched," "lower lip slightly more prominent than the upper"), other learned judgments ("nostril very arched," "partition between nostrils very low," "face rather elongated"), and miscellaneous incriminatory or exculpatory data ("general facial expression; not specifically Judaic" or "more or less Judaic"; "gestures: slightly Judaic"). From all of this, Montandon offered his highly paid conclusion: sometimes Jewish; sometimes non-Jewish; and sometimes he was just not sure.[65] In July 1944, Montandon was shot and killed by the Resistance.

Two final details will serve to indicate the atmosphere that reigned in the CGQJ offices under Darquier. Henceforth no Jews were to enter these offices, not even officials of the UGIF who worked for it. Soon after settling into the commissariat, Darquier warned all its employees against using the term "Israelite"—"the principal Jewish means of defense, which involves claiming that the Jewish problem is only a religious problem." Henceforth, he ordered, correspondence must never refer to a Jew as *"monsieur,"* but only as "the Jew so-and-so."[66]

Total Occupation and the Resumption of Deportations

> The entire operation in the southern French territory was much more dependent on the French police than in the formerly occupied territory. The German strike force there could only exercise a weak supervision over the operation.
>
> Heinz Röthke (July 1943)[67]

"Attila" was the code name under which the German army planned to seize the previously Unoccupied Zone of France in case of an Allied landing. When an Anglo-American force landed on 8 November 1942, however, it was limited to the French North African colonies of Morocco and Algeria; and for several days Laval struggled to persuade the Germans that the French could defend their own neutrality.[68] Ignoring Laval's offers of continued collaboration in exchange for better conditions for France, Hitler ordered his armies to sweep south to the Mediterranean coast on 11 November. Italian forces moved up to the Rhône River at the same time. Neither of the invading forces met any resistance, and within hours the French government faced a *fait accompli:* all of France was now under occupation.

Not yet willing to assume all the burdens of administration, the Führer declared that the armistice was still in effect and that the Vichy government was still sovereign. He conceded a few crumbs of form to save appearances as long as the French stayed in line. The Armistice Commission remained in existence, as it was a useful means to transmit orders to the French. Neither the German embassy nor the *Militärbefehlshaber in Frankreich* had its authority extended to the newly occupied zone, which was taken into the somewhat less confining grasp of the supreme German commander in the west, General von Rundstedt *(Oberbefehlshaber West)*. The German detachment stationed near Vichy to guard Marshal Pétain was kept at a discreet distance. In outward appearances, the French government still governed.

In practical terms, things changed radically. Vichy's principal bargaining counters slipped out of its hands. The fleet at Toulon was scuttled by its commanders as the Germans tried to seize it on 28 November. Simultaneously the Armistice Army* was dissolved. By then, most French overseas territories had fallen into the Allied camp. From the standpoint of the Jewish question, the most important change was the enhanced powers of the German police. Previously the *Sicherheitsdienst* had been limited to a representative at Vichy and to occasional

*The military force allowed to Vichy in 1940.

brief inspection tours of the southern zone. Now the authority of the Higher SS and Police Leader extended throughout the south, except for the Italian zone. General Oberg immediately entered into direct relations with the French government. At the local level, Knochen's SS *Einsatzkommandos* established themselves in regional prefectures, as in the old Occupied Zone. While the government in Vichy remained outwardly intact, its policy of independence lay in ruins.

The Germans liked to think of "Attila" as a lightning move. After the first advance parties of the Wehrmacht, however, most German occupation units moved laboriously into the southern zone. There was also a serious problem of numbers. Even before occupying the southern zone, the Germans had been stretched thin, with no more than three thousand *Ordnungspolizei* for all territories from the Belgian frontier to the Mediterranean. Now virtually the same number of men had tens of thousands of additional kilometers to control. Essential reinforcements were slow in coming. In February 1943, several thousand police, some with heavy weapons, were reported to be on the way, but their numbers were still insufficient.[69] Police detachments were established in Lyon, Marseille, Montpellier, Toulouse, and Vichy; but it took some time for their tentacles to extend and their presence to be felt elsewhere. The Gestapo showed up in Saint Etienne only in February 1943, for example; and, for this city of about two hundred thousand, the most important in the department of the Loire, there were only four men and a commander.[70]

This penury of manpower constantly troubled the German occupation in France. The relative scarcity of German personnel in the southern zone helps explain the German authorities' insistence that the French remain "sovereign." To maintain public order, things could hardly be different. In addition, these thin-stretched German police faced more difficult tasks every day. Quite apart from the roundups and deportations of Jews, the organized and armed *maquis* began to form after the imposition of obligatory labor in Germany for young men of military age. The struggle against "terrorists," Knochen had reported on the very day of the "Attila" operation, had required energetic action. Over two hundred hostages had already been shot, he told the military authorities, thanks to the help of the French police; but it would be advisable, in future, not to shoot hostages too hastily, presumably so as not to dilute the force of this counterterror.[71]

Had Vichy wanted to protect the Jews and political prisoners while the Germans were setting their insufficient forces into place, there was plenty of time to do so. During the blitzkrieg of May 1940, when a complete German occupation of France was widely expected, police and camp officials released Jews and other prisoners in some cases to enable them to evade the Nazis.[72]* In November 1942 they had the opportunity again, and even more reason to do so, knowing more about what lay in store. The British embassy in Madrid reported a few such cases—prefects who ordered Jewish registration records destroyed, and others who freed Jews from camps or prisons. Some refugees who made their way to the Spanish frontier reported aid by the French police.[73] But these were exceptions. For the most part, French police cooperated with their German colleagues. French guards continued to watch the barbed wire at Gurs and the other camps. No significant numbers of escapes were reported, no massive disappearance of documents, no breach of the civil peace.

To the contrary, the French police busied themselves extending repressive measures against Jews. Hagen saw Bousquet a few days after "Attila" and emphasized the special urgency of settling the Jewish question once and for all now that the American forces had landed in North Africa. Within a few weeks, as Jews were scattering in terror of the newly arrived German forces, Bousquet ordered the prefects of the southern zone to apply rigorously the law of 9 November which forbade foreign Jews to move freely from place to place or to leave their commune of residence without police authorization. Bousquet told prefects to grant such permissions only sparingly, particularly in those cases where foreigners "were no longer under the protection of their countries of origin."[74] These, of course, were the remaining stateless Jews who, by the previous summer's arrangements between Vichy and the Germans, had first priority for deportation. This was also the moment when prefectures were hard at work applying the stamp *Juif* or *Juive* to the ID cards and ration cards that were an essential lifeline, in accordance with the law of 11 December 1942. Without these cards, one went hungry; with them, one risked arrest. Generally, especially in big cities, the stamp was red and very prominent; here and there some police more sympathetically made a light impression in black with smaller letters. But there were no exemptions, not even for those who received special consideration under the *Statut des juifs*. Prefects' monthly reports make it clear that the work was carried out in earnest during the early months of 1943.[75]

On 10 December 1942, Hitler ordered the arrest and deportation of all Jews and other enemies of the Reich from France—Communists, Gaullists, and the like.[76] Now that the Allies were just across the Medi-

---

*The state prosecutor for the appeals court of Bourges was arrested in 1940 for having released Herschel Grynszpan.

terranean, he was nervous about their potential supporters in the event of an invasion of metropolitan France. This same order decreed the removal of Daladier, Gamelin, Reynaud, and Blum to a fortress in Germany. The French were not informed about the sweeping order concerning the Jews, for—as Knochen explained in a long report to Müller, head of the RSHA Section IV, in Berlin, on 12 February 1943—it was still preferable to deal with the Jewish question in France in stages. Pétain opposed using French police to arrest French Jews, Knochen believed, and it was impossible to do anything without the help of the French police. Laval might agree, Knochen thought, but he would always wriggle out of his agreement at the last minute by blaming Pétain or the Italians. Laval might also let the French Jews go in exchange for some major political concession, Knochen speculated; but for the time being (and no one with real authority in Germany ever seriously proposed making France a partner rather than a defeated enemy), there was nothing to do but proceed step by step.[77]

The French soon enough felt the effects of Hitler's 10 December order, however. In order to concentrate the Jews prior to their deportation, the SS proposed three steps to Bousquet in December: the evacuation of all Jews from coastal or border departments; the internment of foreign Jews, except for British, Americans, or neutrals, pending deportation to the east; and the grouping of French and exempted foreign Jews in three or four interior departments where they would be assigned to residence and forbidden to leave their commune. Bousquet complained about various practical problems created by these measures—the Italian refusal to allow anti-Jewish measures to be applied in their occupation zone, the effort of Spain and Rumania to protect their nationals[78]—but, in general, the Vichy government complied. Several ordinances in early 1943 forbade Jews to reside in fourteen departments: those on the Spanish and Italian frontiers, plus the Allier and the Puy-de-Dôme. A 16 March decree further tightened the vise on foreign Jews: they had to report to the police wherever they moved, even within a single commune. The Ministry of the Interior assumed the right to expel foreigners from any department or to fix their residence in any locality.[79]

In accordance with these new measures, foreign Jews were moved away from the coast and frontier departments and concentrated in the interior. The expulsions took place under very harsh conditions, as only three days' notice was given. The prefect of the Creuse provided a particularly vivid report of the arrival of three such convoys in his department during January; they came from the Ariège and the Pyrenees border departments and totaled nearly seven hundred persons.

Upon their arrival in the Creuse, the newly uprooted Jews were given a hot drink, supplied by the UGIF and the Red Cross, and a leaflet, supplied by the prefect. The leaflet was a kind of compendium of the abuses commonly attributed to Jewish refugees; and in it, the prefect welcomed his new charges and urged them to obey the laws, to shop only in markets and not directly at the farm, to have their ID and ration cards stamped, to send their children to school, and not to leave the commune where they were assigned to residence. While the inhabitants of the Ariège "did not conceal their satisfaction at this departure," the Jews' arrival in the Creuse "prompted strenuous complaints" and reawakened all the old fears of rising prices, black market, and scarcity.[80]

Things were now in readiness for a resumption of the deportations from Drancy. The *Judenreferat* had trains available again, after several months of waiting; and Knochen ordered on 26 January the dispatch of all deportable Jews to Drancy so that they would be ready for the first trains in mid-February.[81] Eichmann visited Paris again in February to hasten the process. The expulsion and concentration measures just described made new groups of Jews in the previously Unoccupied Zone available for deportation. All Jews' ID and ration cards in the southern zone were now being stamped. This procedure facilitated a new census. While the enumeration of Jews in the Unoccupied Zone completed in March 1942 had indicated a total of almost 110,000 Jews, 140,000 ration cards had been stamped by February 1943 in the southern zone, excluding the areas under Italian occupation.[82] The assassination of two German officers in Paris on 13 February added the further order to deport 2,000 more Jews in reprisal.[83]

To fill these new convoys, another round of mass arrests of foreign Jews was carried out by French police in the southern zone in February 1943. This roundup was second only to that of August 1942 in size and extent. When Knochen discussed the operation with Bousquet, the French police chief argued that his men could become uncooperative if the French Jews whom they had arrested for violations of the star decree or other statutes, were ordered to be deported; the French police, Bousquet said, had arrested 1,300 foreign Jews with the stipulation that these be deported instead of French Jews. But as Knochen told his superiors privately, he would of course deport both.[84*] Bousquet was ready, however, to help deport foreign Jews. On 18 February the order went out from the Ministry of the Interior to regional prefects to assemble foreign Jews and send them to Gurs, the first step in the

*Both the French and the foreign Jews left for Auschwitz the next day, their train guarded by French gendarmes.[85]

journey to Drancy and the east. Like the August action, the February roundup was exclusively the work of the French police. In the Limoges region alone, 509 Jews were sent to Gurs during 24–27 February.[86] Unlike the August action, however, this one did not arouse a public outcry or provoke protests by prominent churchmen. Only interior rural departments where Jews had been concentrated were involved, and the populations there seem to have always been particularly sensitive to unwanted aliens and their abuses. In February 1943, moreover, they were distracted by their own miseries and the "real deportation" of the French factory workers to Germany.[87]

The *Judenreferat* was dissatisfied with these results. Taking stock on 6 March 1943, Röthke calculated that 49,000 Jews had been sent from France to the east. But 270,000 remained, 200,000 of whom were in the newly occupied zone. Along with the stateless, Jews of seventeen different nationalities had been deported, plus 3,000 French Jews, carefully designated as "criminals." Now Röthke envisaged a vast program of deportation. He looked forward to the departure of convoys totaling 8,000 to 10,000 Jews per week, beginning in April. Transport would not pose a problem, but there were other serious difficulties. The attitude of the Italians in their occupation zone was "particularly revolting." The French, whose police support was indispensable, would have to be pressured to make more Jews available for deportation, even by stripping the recently naturalized of their citizenship.[88]

The main difference now, of course, was that the German police could for the first time carry out direct arrests in the southern zone. During January 1943 alone they seized 150 Jews in Lyon.[89] The Vichy practice of stamping ID and ration cards of Jews was a great help to these direct German arrests. The limited number of German police, however, remained a serious handicap. The German police authorities experimented with various ways to use their small force to maximum advantage. When the German police, newly arrived in Marseille, found the crowded old port city a haven for both opposition and crime, their reaction was strongly colored by a sense of being few in a hostile country. Writing to Oberg on the subject of Marseille on 18 January, Himmler said there was simply not enough German manpower to mount guard indefinitely over such a city. Better to destroy its slum areas by a "radical and complete solution" which would then liberate personnel for other tasks.[90] Thus, the very thinness of German police forces in France encouraged drastic action. On 22–27 January 1943, 10,000 French police and several thousand German police were concentrated in Marseille to move 22,000 inhabitants to other areas and to raze the Old Port.[91]

A similar sense of beleaguerment and urgency presided over the Germans' direct arrests of Jews in the newly occupied zone. They grouped their scarce forces into flying squads, the better to concentrate radical action on particularly fruitful points. We may take as an example the descent of the Gestapo on the Midi in April–May 1943. Massive arrests began on 19 April in Nîmes, Avignon, Carpentras, and Aix. Whole families were rounded up and taken to St. Pierre prison in Marseille and from there to Drancy, at the rate of forty a week. After the arrest of the subprefect of Arles, they stepped up the pace. On 28–30 April they boarded trains and picked up all passengers whose papers were stamped *Juif* or *Juive*. On 1 May, a Resistance attack on a Marseille house of prostitution wounded two SS men. Thereupon on 4 May German police arrested every Jew on trains to and from Nice. The French authorities tried to intervene by demonstrating that they were finding the real guilty parties; but when they declined to hand over the names of all persons whom they had questioned, the Germans threatened to arrest the leaders of UGIF unless they were given a list of Jewish leaders. Still acting on the assumption that any Resistance attack called for action against Jews, the Gestapo invaded the UGIF offices in Marseille on 6 May and took away sixty Jews in two buses, including a number of elderly people, 80 percent of them French. One woman jumped from the window in a futile escape attempt. On 7 May, the SS resumed making arrests in trains. On 8 May they interrupted a synagogue service in Marseille to ask for any foreigners present.[92]

Similar brutalities were visited upon Clermont-Ferrand after a German medical corps captain was assassinated in the night of 26–27 April. The German authorities asked the French for three lists—all suspects who had been questioned, all foreign Jews in Clermont, and all French Jews there. After checking with Bousquet, the regional intendant of police delivered the first two lists but refused the third.[93]

The image of France as an asylum, resistant to the shocks of the last two years, was now finally shattered. Thousands of Jews attempted to flee France, and many of the rest tried to go into hiding. It has been estimated that some 22,000 refugees of all backgrounds, many of them Jews, illegally crossed the Spanish frontier immediately after "Attila." By the end of 1942, this figure had swollen to 30,000.[94] Both Spain and Switzerland discouraged refugees and often turned people back. In October 1942, the Swiss tightened their controls, refusing entry to anyone not provided with a normal visa issued by the Swiss consulate.[95] Along both frontiers began a desperate traffic. Local guides took these people across, and to the hazards of police and border guards were added the hazards of fraud and robbery by some unscrupulous opportunists. Up to 50,000 francs were demanded for passage into Spain, and 8,000 for Switzerland; prefects reported that Jews were sometimes robbed in these journeys and sometimes shaken down by people posing as police.[96] Many of those who did not or could not attempt a flight abroad tried to go underground. Still others drifted into illegality without even choosing to, unable to comply with the changing and enveloping network of regulations.

Some hunted Jews found refuge in homes or religious institutions. More than one third of the Jews of Roanne, for example, were hidden in the private homes of non-Jews.[97] Often only part of a family went underground, the husband or employed children usually being obliged to declare themselves.[98] Young children had the best chance of survival in hiding. The very young were sometimes sent to foster mothers in rural areas, though this mode of care was subject to abuses and to harrowing child custody disputes, as social workers discovered.[99] Many children were placed in Catholic institutions. There they were obliged to assume new names (the real names being preserved in secret by Jewish social agencies where possible), and new names sometimes led subtly to new identities. In the worst cases, there was overt proselytism.[100] Even in the best cases, it was not possible for a child not to respond to loving foster parents and to suffer a corresponding ambiguity of identity when the truth was revealed. The experience of Saul Friedländer reveals all the ambiguity of the best-intentioned efforts to shelter Jewish children. The revelations of his parents' identity and fate on the eve of his entry into the Catholic priesthood plunged him into a cycle of name changes and self-exploration that he has movingly described in *When Memory Comes* (1979).

All these developments put severe strains upon the French police. On the one hand, prefects complained that German arrests of French Jews were "one of the gravest violations of national sovereignty," which placed the prefects in the position of being unable to protect French citizens.[101] This did not, however, prevent the French police from participating in the arrests of foreign Jews. Quite the contrary: prefects' reports refer to the arrests of foreign Jews (and even of some French Jews) by French police at least to January 1944. Moreover, as an increasing number of French Jews found themselves—willingly or not—in a position of illegality, the police could consider their arrest a simple matter of common law and not of deportation. Not only were Jews violating the regulations at the frontiers; they were refusing to report for the census that continued in many departments, or they were taking part in a lively false papers industry. HICEM, whose official task had ended with the last legal emigration, closed its office in Marseille and began organizing clandestine escapes from Brive-la Gaillarde (Corrèze) where it had good relations with the local subprefect Chaussade.[102] At the beginning of April 1943, the Germans assumed direct control of the Pyrenees border themselves, establishing a special frontier zone in which French police authority was suspended.[103] In some ways this step removed an awkward burden from the shoulders of the French police, who would otherwise have been obliged to assure the deportation of Jews trying to flee abroad. We do not know how many Jews were seized trying to cross the border illegally during 1943, but the number who tried may be gauged by the fact that 12,000 succeeded in reaching Spain and another 10,000, Switzerland during that year, in addition to a handful who crossed the Mediterranean by small boat.[104] But the loss of sovereignty over the borders was a painful amputation to those committed to maintaining the myth of Vichy independence to the bitter end. In April 1943, Bousquet renewed the police accords with Oberg, reaffirming the willingness of the French police to continue the struggle against "terrorists, Communists, Jews, Gaullists, and foreign agents."[105] More than ever, and with good reason, the Jews had become assimilated into Vichy's list of outlaws.

Vichy, the Abbé Catry, and the Massada Zionists

> The tremendous advantage of Kadmi Cohen's scheme . . . [it] could lift the very black cloud that hangs over [France] because of an excessively violent antisemitic policy. In effect it is France, together with Germany, which is persecuting the Jews the most.
>
> André Lavagne (February 1943)[106]

Around the turning of 1942–43, René de Chambrun, Laval's son-in-law, introduced a rather unorthodox Catholic priest to André Lavagne, Marshal Pétain's private secretary. The Abbé Joseph Catry had left the Jesuit order under a cloud after publishing a violently antisemitic pamphlet on the Jews and the Church, and was forbidden to say mass. He had been working with Vallat's associate Gabriel Malglaive and with Paul Creyssel, propaganda chief for the southern zone and soon to be national propaganda director, and he was trying to support a marginal publishing venture for his brochures at Vichy, the Editions de la Porte Latine.

Catry brought a letter from a Jewish lawyer in Paris, Kadmi Cohen. Born in Poland and raised in Palestine by parents who had been early associates of Theodor Herzl, Kadmi Cohen had volunteered for the French army in August 1914 and had been accorded citizenship under the law of 5 August 1914 concerning foreign volunteers. After the war, Cohen married a Frenchwoman of Catholic background, obtained a law degree, and entered the legal profession in Paris. At the same time, he maintained close relations with the World Zionist Organization, to which he was an advisor in the late 1930s. He wrote prolifically on the ancient and modern history of the Jewish people and earned a doctorate in oriental studies; one of his works received an award from the Académie Française. Cohen was among the Jewish leaders arrested in Paris and taken to Compiègne on 10 December 1941; he was subsequently released for reasons we are unable to discover.

While imprisoned at Compiègne, Cohen had founded a movement he called Massada. Massada was the *cri de coeur* of a handful of anti-assimilationist intellectuals who, out of the depths of prison, wanted to prove to the authorities that it was in Vichy's interest to help the Jews found their own state. Like Zionists generally, Cohen believed that settlement in a national state would promote the moral and intellectual elevation of Jews who had been spiritually deformed by life in the Diaspora. Unlike a majority of Zionists, Cohen proclaimed himself a follower of Vladimir (Zeev) Jabotinsky, leader of the Zionist Revisionist party and an opponent of the resolutely pro-Allied leadership around Chaim Weizmann. Cohen was bitterly hostile to what he regarded as the slack materialism of assimilated Jews in the Anglo-Saxon countries, as was already becoming apparent in his *Nomades: essai sur l'âme juif* (1929, preface by Anatole de Monzie) and, even more strikingly, in *L'Abomination américaine* (Flammarion, 1930). The catastrophes of 1940–41 only strengthened his determination to help European Jewry break away from its assimilationist leaders.

There was something in both Catry and Cohen to attract the attention of the increasingly distraught circle around Marshal Pétain. Catry's promise of an authentically Christian antisemitism aroused interest among men still scarred by the clerical protests against the deportations of August–September 1942. Catry was also hostile to Darquier, in whom he saw "an unvarnished criminal complicity with Germany."[107] Here, perhaps, was an alternative to *monsieur le tortionnaire*.

In his rambling and prolix style, the former Jesuit spun a bizarre "antijudaisme chrétien," a doctrine and a policy that he stressed was consistent with papal teaching. Vichy's Jewish policy, Catry warned, had been "negative and destructive." It was time, he said, to reward Jews who kept a national sentiment rather than those who lost it. An exodus should replace assimilation as the ancient goal of French policy. "For the first time in 150 years the current would flow in the opposite direction." Here is where the Massada movement came in. Kadmi Cohen's movement claimed to offer the possibility of getting Jews out of France no less effectively than the Germans were doing—but humanely, voluntarily, and by international agreement instead of under duress, in cattle cars, in a fashion gravely damaging to French prestige abroad. Cohen seemed to have arrived at some *modus vivendi* with the Germans, who had, after all, released him from Compiègne. Perhaps he could work something out with them.

Catry called his program "Christian anti-Judaism." Cohen called his project a means to "restore the dignity of Judaism and to effect its concentration in a Jewish state."[108] In their desperation, these two outsiders clung to what was complementary in their mutual antagonism; and some of Pétain's advisors saw possibilities in this curious conjunction of ideas.

The interpretation of the world situation offered by Catry and Cohen, also, struck a responsive chord at Vichy. When Catry wrote that German victory was no longer clear, and that a compromise peace was likely (and he had the pugnacity to say so outright to German officials during 1943), he touched upon a desperate hope for a French mediatory role, for a revival of French room for maneuver in the mutual exhaustion of the belligerents, a hope to which some officials at Vichy clung to the very end. Why not grasp the initiative in the Palestine question and use it as the British had used the Balfour Declaration in the First World War? The clumsiness of Darquier was only helping the Jews of the Anglo-Saxon countries, by backlash. A friendly Jewish state in the Near East would be an antidote to Communist expansion in the area; and as for the Arabs (he mentioned them rarely), they would be mollified by economic development.[109]

Speaking in a somewhat different tone to the Germans, Catry suggested that the Jewish question could be turned against Britain and the United States. A friendly Jewish state in Palestine would weaken the British Empire and would provide a defense against the "major threat, American imperialism." Kadmi Cohen pushed these arguments even farther in a letter to Dr. Klassen, of the German embassy in January 1943. Switching to a "positive, constructive antisemitism" would encourage European Jews to make the necessary break with assimilation. A Jewish state in Palestine, Transjordan, and the Sinai would block both Britain and Russia and protect the oil and eastern trade routes for the continent of Europe. This policy would divide the Jews in the Anglo-Saxon countries. The "plutocrats" would remain there, of course; but the "hostage Jews," the mass in those countries who had never had any influence on the plutocrats, would rally to the new state and abandon the spineless assimilationism that both Cohen and the antisemites despised.[110]

Kadmi Cohen warned Marshal Pétain directly in June 1943 where the present anti-Jewish moves might lead France in the event of the compromise peace for which Vichy longed. The current French policy toward Jews could only arouse a desire for vengeance when the war was over. He reminded the Marshal that this policy was not necessary. Neither other defeated countries (Belgium, Holland, Yugoslavia, or Greece) nor Germany's allies (Finland, Italy, or Hungary) had adopted an active official antisemitism. To make matters worse, Cohen said, France was temporizing by working with the Consistoire. This sign of weakness would only embolden Jews to take an active part if things came to a civil war in France. He warned Pétain that the only solution was to "turn Jewish dynamism in the direction of Jewish national-ism."[111]

Cohen wanted, in return for his cooperation with the Vichy government, a cessation of deportations, an official position as special assistant to the French government for Jewish national affairs, and a system of ID cards whereby his followers would not be subject to arrest. Catry wanted state support for his Editions de la Porte Latine and for the institute and journal that he hoped to found.

André Lavagne warmed to the possibilities offered by the Massada movement. He met Kadmi Cohen and confirmed his interest with a letter to him on 18 January, a document probably intended to assist the latter in drumming up support. Lavagne was happy to have exchanged ideas with the Jewish lawyer, and declared that "from many perspectives it would be a good thing if these projects could be carried out." He promised to study the matter more thoroughly, and expressed the hope "that you will not meet any obstacles in your preliminary discussions and activity."[112] There is no evidence that the Vichy government took any further steps toward giving official accreditation to Kadmi Cohen or to any of his followers; but the Germans were made to believe that Catry was a close advisor to Pétain, and that Cohen had received an official letter of recognition.[113]

The Massada scheme had its opponents at Vichy, of course. The

Consistoire repaid Cohen's hostility with interest; and its president, Jacques Helbronner, refused to meet Cohen in the spring of 1943. Cohen wrote him an insulting letter offering another meeting in terms that Helbronner could hardly accept. As for Catry, the Catholic hierarchy had little use for him. Cardinal Gerlier (who had been Helbronner's classmate) was cool, and Cardinal Suhard in Paris named someone else when the Germans urged him to appoint Catry editor of an important and long-established anti-Masonic review.[114] Darquier was disturbed by this rival to his authority and warned the Germans against him.

German acceptance, of course, was crucial to any such project's success. With the naïve optimism of the single-minded, Catry thought that a remark in one of Goebbels's speeches in March 1943 signaled a change of German policy toward support for a Jewish state and a general exodus to it.[115] On the scene in Paris, however, only one German, from Rosenberg's Paris office, was a consistent supporter of Catry. No German official at all saw any possible benefit in the Massada movement —neither policemen, nor soldiers, nor diplomats. Foreign Office representatives in Berlin thought the scheme would "work against our radical solution."[116]

As late as February 1944, the Germans in Paris continued to toy with the idea of using Catry by himself for anti-Jewish propaganda in Catholic circles, but they were not sure he would have much impact. The Gestapo watched him closely. Matters came to a head when Kadmi Cohen was once more interned. When the Abbé insisted upon Cohen's release in order to coordinate their common scheme, the Germans acted.[117] They broke relations with Catry. As for Cohen, they placed him aboard the deportation train for Auschwitz that left Drancy on 27 March 1944.[118] He never returned.

Vichy's interest in the Massada movement seems utterly harebrained today. To understand its appeal in the circle around Marshal Pétain, one must strip away all that has happened since and reconstruct the hopes and fears of 1943. Beginning with the conviction of German victory and the expectation of an early peace, Vichy had been forced to fall back on lesser evils in its search for a world strategy to fit an unexpected long war of attrition. Vichy leaders grasped desperately at straws—such as the plan to turn the French merchant fleet over to the Pope in exchange for uninterrupted commerce through this new Vatican armada[119]—that might protect France from the increasingly damaging effects of war. Similarly, the Massada project promised for a moment to let Vichy escape from an unbearable deadlock. People around

Marshal Pétain had clearly come to the conclusion that the deportations were a grave liability. As Lavagne wrote in an 18 January memorandum that Pétain may have seen, Catry and Kadmi Cohen offered "the only truly effectual solution that is both completely humane and Christian."[120] The scheme had a long fantasy life at Vichy because it allowed the regime to reconcile, without painful choices, several utterly unreconcilable goals: to get rid of many Jews, to do so without offending French and foreign opinion, to regain the enthusiasm of the Church, and to change Jewish policy without having to embark on any dangerous confrontation with the Germans. The scheme is a measure of the Pétainist thirst for economical compromise solutions in the midst of total war, a grasping at dreams rather than realities.

The Italian Interlude

According to Bousquet, [the Italian officer] Lospinoso declared: the Germans are very severe in carrying out the measures against the Jews; the French are more severe than the Italians; while the Italians strive for a humane solution to the Jewish problem.
Karl Oberg (July 1943)[121]

The Israelites have emigrated and continue to emigrate en masse to that promised land which the left bank of the Rhône has become.
Alexandre Angéli, regional prefect of
Lyon (May 1943)[122]

When the Germans occupied the southern zone of France in November 1942, their Italian allies occupied eight departments east of the Rhône: Drôme, Isère, Hautes-Alpes, Basses-Alpes, Alpes-Maritimes, Savoie, Haute Savoie, and Var. Nothing was more galling to Vichy than this Italian presence, not because the occupation regime was harsh, but because France in no way felt beaten by Italy. The Italian armies had gained little ground against second-line French divisions in 1940. An Italian occupation of extensive French territory saved the Germans some precious manpower, but for the French it was a gratuitous humiliation. Laval even asked General von Neubronn if German troops could not be stationed among the Italians on the Mediterranean coast, for the sake of public opinion. "The French cannot bear the Italians' presence," observed the prefect of the Savoie, reporting "numerous incidents" between the population and the occupying forces in January

1943.[123] A quarrel soon developed between the two governments, but its basis was entirely unexpected. It concerned the Jews.

Unlike German Nazism, Italian Fascism had never put antisemitism at the center of its program. Until Mussolini decided to throw in his lot with Hitler in 1937, the Italian regime did not persecute Jews. Indeed, it welcomed them into its ranks. Mussolini himself spoke from every possible point of the compass about Jews: he praised them warmly on some occasions, wrote slanderous articles about them on others, and negotiated genially with Zionist leaders. In the fall of 1933, a group of American Jewish publications named Mussolini among twelve Christians who had been "most outstanding in their opposition to anti-Semitism."[124] The Duce was fundamentally indifferent to the matter. He always had important Jewish colleagues. He was prepared to use antisemitism when it seemed useful, and equally happy to support Jews when there was something to be gained.

Mussolini's attitudes reflected Italian reality. There were few Jews in Italy—fewer than fifty thousand in 1938, a highly assimilated minority of whom only a small proportion were foreigners. Antisemitism existed in Italy, but it never approached the intensity or the organization found in Germany or France, for example.[125] Once the Duce's European and imperial ambitions pointed toward a German alliance, however, his policy toward the Jews hardened. In October 1938, Fascist Italy issued its own racial laws and gave further momentum to an official anti-Jewish campaign.

Even after this crucial shift, antisemitism did not strike deep roots in Italy. Despite the backing of party ideologues and part of the bureaucracy, persecution lacked energy. It was weakened by lack of interest, corruption, and even sympathy for the Jews. Many sections of Italian society looked upon racism as a ridiculous notion, cooked up by the Germans in their insufferable campaign of domination. Self-interest also moderated Italian antisemitism. When Vichy proposed to extend aryanization to Tunisia, the Italian Armistice Commission and Foreign Office protested strenuously against the threat to five thousand Italian property-owners in Tunisia and to centuries of Italian development there.[126] If the French anti-Jewish program was less vigorously applied in Tunisia than in Algeria and Morocco, Italian efforts to preserve its national stake there had a lot to do with it. During the summer of 1942, the Italian government obtained its citizens' exemption from the Jewish star in Occupied France; and Italian diplomatic and military representatives posed a real obstacle to the persecution and deportation of Jews in Croatia and Greece, parts of which were under

Italian control. The Italian regime hoped to avoid burning its bridges with the Allies. As the tide of battle began to turn in late 1942, widespread Fascist opposition to the Nazi Final Solution was already apparent.

Italian authorities clashed with Vichy over the Jews almost immediately after their occupation of the eight French departments. When Marcel Ribière, prefect of the Alpes-Maritimes, began to enforce the French December ordinances expelling foreign and stateless Jews from the coast, the Italian authorities quickly blocked the move. Soon after, they forbade him to apply the 11 December 1942 law requiring the stamping of Jews' ID cards and ration books. Calisse, the Italian consul-general in Nice, informed Ribière that Italian officials had sole power to deal with the Jewish question in the Italian zone of occupation. When Ribière suggested that, in that case, the Italians might like to receive all the foreign Jews in Italy, General Carlo Avarna di Gualtieri, the senior representative of the Italian High Command in Vichy, replied that there would be in France what prevailed in Italy, that is, "humane legislation."[127]

Far from welcoming the shield that Italian occupation policy offered to thousands of Jews, French officials grew steadily more irritated at this challenge to their sovereignty. Laval telephoned the Italian embassy in Paris and demanded an explanation.[128] He was willing to concede the Italians' right to intercede on behalf of their own citizens; he even proposed that the Italians repatriate their Jewish citizens, along with foreign Jews if they wished. But he could not admit their pretension to stand between the French government and citizens of third countries on French soil. In discussing the Italian obstructions with Knochen in January, Laval complained that they were putting him in an awkward position in the eyes of French public opinion. According to Knochen, Laval asked the Germans for "appropriate support" *(entsprechende Unterstützung)* in his struggle with the Italians.[129]

Abetz had been urging the German Foreign Ministry for some months to take the matter up with Mussolini. In early 1943, the SS in France sent back to Berlin a steady stream of complaints about Italian noncooperation. Röthke noted on 6 March—along with a long list of "particularly revolting cases" of Italian obstruction—that if the Jewish problem were to be resolved, the Italians would have to abandon their current attitude.[130] One project on which the Foreign Office spent a lot of time in early 1943 was a plan for the repatriation of Jews to noncooperative countries like Italy. The Germans believed that, faced with masses of returning Jews, Italy, Spain, and such nations would quickly fall into line. At the end of February, Ribbentrop agreed to raise all these matters directly with Mussolini. When he saw the Duce in mid-March, he told him, among other things, that Jewish matters in France should be left to the French police who, the Germans were convinced, were undertaking the necessary "cleansing action" on their own. But even after Mussolini had promised the German ambassador, General Hans Georg von Mackensen, "decisive action" in Rome in mid-March, things continued much as before.[131]

Indeed, the conflict had grown much more open when deportations resumed in February 1943. When the prefects attempted to carry out the order of 18 February to arrest and dispatch foreign Jews, the Italians stepped in. In the Savoie, they did not permit the transfer of twenty-five foreign Jews to their first assembly point in a camp at Bressieux. At Annecy, even more dramatically, the Italians established a military zone around the prison demanding that the French release foreign Jews who had been assembled for deportation. When the Italians installed four hundred Jews in resort hotels in Mégève, they refused to hand over twelve of them who had been long sought by the French police. They also blocked the transfer of one hundred foreign Jews rounded up by French police in Grenoble. On 2 March, General Avarna di Gualtieri delivered a note to Secretary of State Admiral Charles Platon: henceforth, not only non-French Jews were under Italian protection but French Jews as well. No Jew in the Italian zone could be coerced or arrested by anyone except Italian authorities, except for violations of the common law.[132] Nor could British subjects and American citizens be moved back from the coast. The February 1943 roundup had been completely frustrated in Italian-occupied France.

In the spring of 1943, Rome appeared to keep its commitment to the Germans for decisive action by sending to France a high-ranking police officer from Bari, Inspector-General Guido Lospinoso, as a kind of Italian *Judenreferent*. A local SEC representative was fooled by Lospinoso's reputation for energy. The SS saw more clearly, however, that the Italians were merely engaging in new forms of obstruction.[133] Oberg reported with exasperation on 1 July that Lospinoso had been promising him a visit since 18 May, but that the man was impossible to pin down. Bousquet finally managed a meeting at the end of June. Lospinoso outlined a plan to house six thousand Jews at Mégève, to which Bousquet objected, since Vichy had planned to lodge children from bombed cities there. The Italian vetoed one of the French police chief's projects to improve armaments for the French police and (according to German reports of the conversation) gave the French a little lecture on the more humane qualities of Italian anti-Jewish policy. Bousquet left the meeting no more able than before to enforce the *Statut des juifs* in the Italian zone.[134]

During the first half of 1943, a stateless or foreign Jew caught in France could improve his chances of survival by reaching a fascist country—Spain, Portugal, or Italy. The Italian zone of France was the only area of fascist administration readily accessible; and as the news spread of Italian occupation policy, thousands of Jews made their way there. Before the war the area contained only about 15,000 to 20,000 Jews. By the end of summer 1943, 30,000 Jews were crowded along thirty kilometers of coast in the Alpes-Maritimes, according to the prefect's information. A report of Röthke for 21 July estimated some 50,000 Jews in the Italian zone. The prefects reported on the "afflux" of Jews, and the prefect of the Alpes-Maritimes observed that "whatever the degree of hostility against the occupying forces by the local population, and their disapproval of the violent methods used by the German authorities against the Jews, a certain amount of antisemitism begins to appear."[135]

According to Knochen, the Jews and the Italians were getting along famously in the Italian zone. Jewish relief agencies intensified their work on behalf of refugees. Some five hundred Jews found shelter in a camp at Saint-Gervais (Haute-Savoie), for example, after having been turned back from Switzerland. Under their leader Joseph Kott, they lived unharassed, a tiny Jewish colony in the very shadow of Vichy, aided by American volunteer refugee services and committed to Zionist agricultural projects.[136]

Nice became a Jewish political and cultural center under the benevolent eye of the Italian army. The Germans learned, to their disgust, that the grateful Jewish community of Nice raised three million francs as a donation to Italian victims of Anglo-American air raids. *Carabinieri* stationed in Nice not only mounted guard in front of the synagogue on the boulevard Dubouchage, a hive of Jewish clandestine activity; they also empowered the Jews to issue their own identity cards. The *carabinieri* commander, Captain Salvi, told the local prefect he would personally order the arrest of any French policeman who interfered. Angelo Donati, an Italian Jew with much influence in Rome, was at the center of Jewish efforts in the Italian zone. He did his best to win his government's support for a policy of protection for Jews, French as well as foreign.[137]

Vichy seems to have decided finally to make use of the Italian policy rather than to rail against it. Unlike many French nationalists and a large part of the French administration, Laval was not fundamentally anti-Italian. He had favored cooperation with the Italian neighbor in French interests since the 1930s. Now, when negotiations with the Germans were proving especially difficult, Italian policy provided him with a rare opportunity to play the two Axis partners off against each other. In his reports of February 1943, Knochen believed that Vichy was hiding behind Italian policy in its own efforts to prevent the deportation of native French Jews from the rest of France.[138]

As the differences between the two occupation powers widened, Laval eagerly played the Italian card. To the Germans he called attention loudly to Italian policy as the excuse for French inability to act more resolutely against the Jews. To his own government, however, Laval does not seem to have pressed the issue seriously once the first shock of Italian intervention had worn off. It was soon apparent that there was little point in doing so; the Italians would not budge. In July the government replaced the ardent Pétainist prefect of the Alpes-Maritimes, Ribière, with Jean Chaigneau, who was sympathetic toward the Jews and determined to help them. Chaigneau assembled local Jewish leaders a few days after taking office and assured them that he would not leave to the Italians the privilege of being the sole defenders of tolerance and humanity. On 23 July he ordered the regularization of residence without penalty for all foreign Jews illegally in the department.[139]

Unfortunately the Italian protection of the Jews in southeastern France was not to last. When Mussolini was overthrown in July 1943, there was little immediate change. Indeed, Lospinoso used the occasion of a new government under Marshal Pietro Badoglio to reinforce his resistance to the Germans' demands. In August, however, the Italian troops began to draw back from most of their occupation zone, gathering the Jews with them to the region of Nice. Angelo Donati attempted to negotiate a large-scale evacuation of Jews to Italy and the liberated zone of North Africa. Everything appeared to be in order when the Italian government agreed to accept thirty thousand Jews. Plans for the evacuation went forward. Suddenly, on 8 September, the Allies prematurely announced the spectacular news of an armistice with Italy. The evacuation plans were not ready, and Donati was caught off guard. Panic reigned in Nice where most of the Jews had been concentrated. Three days later the Germans were there. Chaigneau destroyed the lists of Jews at his prefecture. A few hundred Jews managed to escape to Italy; others were hidden by the local population. Many thousands, however, were trapped in one of the most brutal manhunts in western Europe during the war. In a "veritable climate of terror," the Germans —assisted by PPF volunteers, and accompanied by the "banditry" of a few Frenchmen posing as German police in order to rob rich Jews— carried out "systematic operations against the Jews."[140] Needless to say, the Germans no longer had any scruples about French Jews, naturalized or native-born. Despite the protests of prefects, these, too, were seized and, within days, had left Drancy for Auschwitz. There was no other protection to take the Italians' place.

Denaturalization, August 1943: Laval's Refusal

The German authorities responsible for the deportation of Jews from France were not satisfied as they surveyed the situation in mid-1943. The easily arrested Jews had already been taken from the camps; the rest were becoming harder to find. Many Jews were warned in advance when their names appeared on an arrest list; others slipped into the Italian zone or went underground on their own.

In the department of the Allier, for example, a new census yielded 303 foreign Jews. Orders were issued for the arrest of all of them between eighteen and fifty-five years of age. Only those enrolled in the *groupements de travailleurs étrangers*—that is, those without money and friends and already under state authority—were caught; the rest melted away. Of 21 affected in the *arrondissement* of Vichy, 12 were captured; in Montluçon, only 2 out of 11. Only 18 Jews from the entire department were taken to Gurs.[141] The Germans were clearly running out of Jews to deport.

The French police posed another problem. As the Germans took more direct police action in the southern zone and seized increasing numbers of Jews of formerly protected categories—French citizens including former prisoners of war, distinguished members of the Legion of Honor, even UGIF personnel—the French police felt no less torn than other members of the administration. At the same time, the police were subjected to new burdens in 1943 by the rapid growth of resistance. The adoption of conscription for labor service in Germany, the Service du Travail Obligatoire (STO), in February 1943 was a major turning point. This was almost certainly the single most detested act of the Vichy regime. Compliance varied according to local variations in enforcement and opportunity for escape. In some places there was open defiance. By the summer of 1943, in some rural areas such as the Corrèze, "each designation of a worker for Germany prompted an enlistment in the *maquis*."[142] When the regional prefects gathered in Vichy on 21 September for a meeting with Laval and other ministers, they learned that while 170,000 of the military classes born in 1920–22 had left for Germany, 200,000 were "in default or presumed to be" (not counting another 400,000 who were exempt for one reason or another).[143] The French police were now drawn heavily into what they considered the most disagreeable of their tasks: hunting down those evading the STO. It was with "real repugnance" that the police rounded up their young neighbors for the labor draft, reported the officials who maintained surveillance over the postal and telephone systems in September 1943; there were "numerous" resignations, and other Frenchmen were considering such a step.[144] The prefects' reports now became filled with references to their constituents' resentment of "deportation": the word referred without exception to the French workers destined for German factories.

The work of French policemen was becoming not only disagreeable but dangerous. Sabotage of rails and pylons begins to appear regularly in the prefects' reports, along with the first armed clashes between police and groups of *maquisards* and the first armed attacks upon police stations. The summer of 1943 clearly marked a watershed in the breakdown of public order. At a meeting of intendants of police (the new regional police chiefs) on 29 October 1943, it was reported that thirty-one French police had been killed and thirty-seven injured so far in 1943, mostly since 1 July.[145]

Small wonder that recruitment for the French police began to drop off sharply in the summer of 1943. In the Châlons-sur-Marne region, applications for admission to the police fell from the usual fifty per month to fifteen in May. With fewer applicants, the police had to recruit with less selectivity. In the Bordeaux region, fifteen applicants were accepted out of twenty-two in August 1943, eleven out of fifteen in September; and eight out of eleven in October.[146] A police career had been highly sought after in early 1943 when it offered exemption from the STO; even that inducement did not suffice to attract young Frenchmen later in the year. General Bridoux, minister of defense, grumbled in his diary in July 1943 about the "inertia and complacency" of the French *gendarmerie* and police.[147]

Not coincidentally, it was at this same moment that German evaluations of the French police first became seriously negative. On 19

August, Oberg submitted a long report on the French police. Today, he concluded, the French police could not be counted on "in case of emergency" to intervene in any significant numbers for the defense of German interests. He conceded that the French police provided "indispensable" *(unentbehrliche)* cooperation against the Communists but lacked initiative in the "struggle against Judaism." The French police were trying to strengthen themselves, but he did not trust them. Bousquet, he said, gave "his primary allegiance to France."[148]

The French police still carried out important parts of the deportation enterprise in 1943. They accompanied convoys and escorted trains; they hunted down escapees from the convoys and guarded camps. They treated Jews breaking the numerous regulations as outlaws. But the deportation by the Germans of Jewish French citizens who had been arrested by the French police for common-law violations created serious discontent within the French police, as Bousquet explained to Knochen on 12 February. At the end of March, Bousquet asked that the French not be involved in the deportation of French Jews from Drancy.[149] Surprisingly, the Germans suspended convoys for a time; deportations to the east did not resume until June. In April 1943, Bousquet renewed the accords with Oberg over the autonomy of the French police, under the new conditions of German occupation of the southern zone. The French police promised to defend German security against Jews, Communists, and other enemies; the Germans agreed not to involve the French in the selection of hostages or interfere in purely French police matters. Even so, the French police fell far behind the pace of repression set by the Germans. Out of 44,000 people—Jews and non-Jews—arrested for political activity in France during 1943, the Germans were responsible for 35,000.[150]

It was against this background of rising resistance and declining French police reliability that the Germans launched a new project in the summer of 1943 to increase the flow of Jews to the east. Now they cast their eyes upon a hitherto exempt group of Jews: recently naturalized French citizens. If the Vichy government could be induced to strip these newcomers of their French citizenship, major new roundups would be possible. Himmler himself urged the *Judenreferat* forward in June 1943.[151]

Stripping Jews of their citizenship was not a new idea. It will be remembered that one of the first acts of the Vichy regime was the law of 22 July 1940 which set up a commission to review all French citizens naturalized since 1927 and to propose the revocation of citizenship of all those deemed unworthy. Jews were not mentioned by name in this law, although Jews were numerous—second only to Italians—among those whom it deprived of French citizenship (see page 4). It was still in terms of individual cases that, in his first meeting with the newly appointed commissioner-general for Jewish affairs in April 1941, Abetz urged a denationalization law on Vallat:

> In order that the "old established" ones may also at a later stage be included under the same measures that apply to the foreign and newly naturalized Jews, a law is necessary even at this time authorizing the French commissioner for Jews to declare "old established" Jews who have acted contrary to the social and national interests of the French nation to be "foreign."[152]

When planning began for large-scale deportations from France, the Germans began to think of denationalizing entire categories of Jews *en bloc*. During the planning session in Berlin on 15 June 1942, which led to the beginning of systematic deportation from Western Europe, Dannecker observed that he would get the French government to pass a law, inspired by the second German citizenship ordinance, whereby "all Jews living outside French borders or emigrating subsequently [that is, those deported] will lose their French nationality and their French citizenship rights."[153] The problem was a general one, as client or collaborationist regimes throughout Europe made efforts to protect their nationals and the property or other rights that their passports symbolized. To simplify their task, the German technicians of the Final Solution tried generally to have Jews everywhere made stateless.*[154]

To denationalize the Jews of France, of course, required French help. In a conversation over dinner with Oberg on 2 September 1942, Laval himself had confirmed what seems to have been an agreement already reached to hand over [*uberstellen*] all Jews who had acquired French citizenship since 1933, but had taken no further action. Darquier helped put the matter on the agenda for 1943. He had proposed as early as 1938 placing the entire Jewish population of France in a special noncitizen status; and as soon as he was made commissioner for Jewish affairs, he made this part of his program. In a radio broadcast at the end of February 1943, he declared that the government should strip of citizenship all Jews naturalized since 10 August 1927.[156]

The date was significant, for the law of 10 August 1927 had made it

---

*Even the Vichy government intervened on behalf of French Jews in Salonika; the German government chose not to reply until the Jews in question had already been deported.[155]

considerably easier to become French, notably by reducing the residence requirement from ten to three years.[157] In the debate that followed, 1927 became the goal of the "hard-liners." Bousquet proposed a cut-off of 1 January 1932; and Laval, as we have seen, referred to 1933. At stake were the thousands of Jews naturalized between the two dates. The Germans believed that fifty thousand Jews had been naturalized French between 1927 and 1932—an exaggerated figure, it turned out; unusually large numbers were naturalized in 1932–33.[158] Darquier and the Germans remained adamant on 1927, and the government apparently gave way. On 11 June, Leguay showed Röthke a draft French law denationalizing all Jews who had received French citizenship since 10 August 1927.[159]

Röthke and his colleagues set to work at once to plan an immense police roundup for mid-July. All the newly stateless Jews would be seized at once and deported, the moment the new law went into effect. Knochen asked the RSHA in Berlin for 250 more men for the operation, but when the hard-pressed central office could send him only 4, Röthke observed that French police cooperation would be "essential." The roundups were planned for 15 July and, when the French law had still not been promulgated, rescheduled for 23–24 July. Commissioner François of the Prefecture of Police was alerted and promised to cooperate. The Germans were concerned about leaks from French police, however, and exasperated by François's plan to spend months checking each case against his card file. Yet even without French police help, Röthke reported on 21 July, it ought to be possible to complete the work of deportation by the end of 1943.[160]

In early August the Germans began hearing contradictory stories about whether the law had been signed. Although Laval and Justice Minister Gabolde did sign a draft of the law in June, Laval withdrew his support in early August. In a dramatic confrontation with Knochen on 7 August, he covered his retreat with a cloud of excuses. He had misunderstood the law's purpose, he told the SS commander. He had now learned that the Germans intended to deport the newly denaturalized at once. He would not serve as *rabatteur* and beat the woods for the hunted game. There were also difficulties with the Italians and with the police. Finally, he said, there was the Marshal who did not approve and was especially upset about the denaturalization of women and children.[161] For the first time in the history of the Final Solution in France, Laval had said No.

There followed a flurry of activity as the Germans tried to change the French leaders' minds. Röthke saw Laval on 14 August and reminded him of his past promises. "The Führer's order concerning the 'Final Solution' of the Jewish question in all of Europe was crystal clear."[162] Knochen told Bousquet that the Germans could do the job themselves, as they had a division of *gendarmerie* ready for the purpose.[163] Ambassador de Brinon went to see Pétain, presumably to try to secure a change of heart (as if forgetting that he represented the Vichy government to the Germans, and not vice versa). According to the version of de Brinon's visit with Pétain which Knochen later reported to Kaltenbrunner, the Marshal's objections were no mere invention of Laval. They were genuine. Two days earlier, Monsignor Chapoulie, representing the French episcopacy, had brought him the message that the Pope was "very upset" to learn that the Marshal was about to permit new anti-Jewish measures in France. The Pope was concerned about the Marshal's soul. De Brinon reported that Pétain was "visibly moved" by this visit. Pétain then said that he could not take the responsibility for denaturalizing French citizens in order that the Germans might deport them immediately. He accepted the principle of denaturalization and even agreed to hand over the newly created stateless persons to the Germans, but "he could not accept indiscriminate activity." Among the Jews in question were those "who had served France well." Therefore, "for the sake of his own conscience he wanted to examine each case individually." His duty, he explained further, was to maintain order in France. The proposed measure "would make the job of the government even more difficult." Pétain said he had already given sufficient proof of his willingness to cooperate with the Germans. He said he would work as quickly as possible, and asked them to accept that as satisfactory.[164]

This apparent *volte-face* derived less from solicitude toward Jews than from a changed texture in Vichy's relationship to the Germans. The Nazi Reich no longer appeared invincible after the Allied landing in North Africa. Then disaster followed disaster for the Germans in the spring and summer of 1943: the final collapse at Stalingrad in February, the withdrawal from Tunisia in May, the great Soviet summer advance around Kursk and Orel in July, and the Allied invasion of Sicily in the same month. Knochen attributed Vichy's stiffening on the Jewish question to these events;[165] and the possibilities of some kind of compromise peace or even of some mediating role for France certainly entered into the calculations of both Laval and Pétain. It was in the spring of 1943 that both men began speaking directly to German diplomats about the necessity of keeping doors open to the United States.[166] Laval and Pétain were aware of how deeply the Jewish issue touched opinion abroad, particularly in the United States. They could not afford to appear abject.

There were subtler kinds of reasoning at work as well. Pétain's remark to de Brinon about keeping order in France gives us a clue to them. The costs to Vichy's legitimacy of the mass deportation of French Jews were simply too great. The monthly prefects' reports could not have made very comfortable reading for Laval as minister of the interior in the spring of 1943; they spoke often of the "total disenchantment" of public opinion with the government.* It was no longer possible to pretend that the government enjoyed more than grudging acquiescence. And while many French people still supported restrictions upon Jews and even measures to reduce the number of foreign Jews in France, German arrests of French Jews were generally reported by prefects as a shock to public opinion. The regime was approaching its limits of tolerance when it could no longer protect its own citizens.

Not that popular antisemitism had completely disappeared since its irruption in the southern zone in the summer of 1942. The issue now was jealousy that Jewish youths were exempt from the labor draft for work in German factories, the dreaded STO that cost sleep to every parent and son in France. The old remarks about "lazy individuals" began to crop up again, mixed with resentment of the "privileged condition" of young Jewish men. Their exemption from the labor services aroused such "violent criticism" and the "indignation of those who labor," that André Jean-Faure, regional prefect of Limoges, wished Jews would display "less smug satisfaction with the indirect advantage they have of not being shipped off to Germany."[168] Jean-Faure seemed to forget that Jews were departing for Germany under other auspices, and for other purposes.

At a time when the French were preoccupied by the STO, there was a tendency to view the Jewish issue from that perspective rather than from a perspective informed by the Holocaust. The former point of view led Pierre Laval to hatch a curious plan in the summer of 1943 for a Jewish labor service. Foreign Jews, of course, were already subject to enrollment in the *groupements de travailleurs étrangers,* where they were easily skimmed off to fill deportation convoys. French Jewish youths remained exempt, however. During the summer of 1943, Laval had under consideration a plan for obligatory work for the Germans by French Jewish youths aged twenty to thirty, as an equitable substitute for the STO. They would be "put at the disposition of the occupation

---

*The regional prefects of Montpellier and of Marseille used identical terms.[167]

authorities under the same conditions as other Frenchmen," but they would generally perform their labor in France.[169]* There is no record of this plan going into effect anywhere in France or of its being discussed with the Germans. Their instant refusal was, in any event, a foregone conclusion. The project is a sign, however, of the persistence of French public impressions of Jews as privileged persons rather than as victims, of Vichy's continuing compulsion to do something about the "Jewish problem," and of Laval's eagerness in the summer of 1943 to extricate Vichy's Jewish policy from the grip of the German extermination machine.

It was also in the summer of 1943 that Laval seems to have considered dissolving the CGQJ and dispersing its functions among agencies that were more prestigious, more correct, and—perhaps—better able to maintain an autonomous French policy: the Ministry of Justice for questions of personal status, the Ministry of Finance for aryanization, and the Ministry of the Interior for questions of internal order and police. The Germans were aware of Laval's project; but here too, there is no evidence that he actually discussed it with them.[170]

There are clear signs, then, that Laval wanted to shake Vichy Jewish policy free from the German incubus in the summer of 1943. There are equally clear signs that he drew back from picking a quarrel with the Germans on the Jewish issue. For Laval, the Jews were not worth jeopardizing his effort to persuade the Germans by open-handed cooperation to incorporate France into the New Europe.[171]

Denaturalization was the one issue on which he drew the line. It was a significant refusal; and at the time there was reason to think that by it thousands of French Jews might be saved. On the other hand, its import should not be exaggerated. In the first place, the statistics involved had been inflated by everybody. Estimates of the numbers of Jews naturalized after 1927 varied wildly in the summer of 1943, from a probably incomplete 8,000 reported by the French police to Röthke in July to a certainly excessive 200,000 mentioned by de Brinon. Pétain had promised that the commission on denaturalizations would work on individual cases as rapidly as possible; but in a letter to Laval at the end of August, de Brinon complained that results so far were "utterly insignificant." If things continued in that way, it might not be possible "to secure the favorable settlement with the Germans that we anticipate."[172] Finally, in September 1943, de Brinon received a report from the commission which he immediately forwarded to the SS. Between 1927 and 1940, out of more than 500,000 naturalizations, only 23,648

*Prefect André Jean-Faure had been making similar proposals from Limoges since May.

cases involved Jews. Up to 8 September, the commission had examined 7,055 of these and had maintained the nationality of 1,984. It had reserved the cases of an additional 4,800 (prisoners of war, North Africans, internees). Almost 10,000 cases remained to be examined.[173] The denaturalization haul, then, would amount to less than one tenth of the Jews who still remained in France. There were hardly enough for the Germans to make the effort. In any event, in practical terms, Laval's legal strategy was already obsolete. Röthke reported to his SS colleague in Brussels that, despite the difficulties over denaturalizations, French Jews were being deported anyway. French citizenship, he said, no longer provided protection. The *Judenreferent* urged that French Jews living in other Nazi-held territory be sent to the east without further ado.[174]

Furthermore, Laval did nothing to restrain the momentum of the CGQJ bureaucracy. One of his last appointments, little more than a month before D-day, was Joseph Antignac, the last of the incorruptible "hard-liners" in the organization, whom he named its de facto head, as chief of staff. The CGQJ was to go on its way, with Laval's blessing, to the very end.

Last Days

> During the night of 10 to 11 January [1944] government security forces and the gendarmerie, following German orders and in conformity with government instructions, had to arrest French Israelites, men, women and children. Of a total of 473 Jews on the list, 288 were found and taken to the designated assembly point, the Bordeaux synagogue.
>
> Regional prefect of Bordeaux (January 1944)[175]

The denaturalization dispute had led the *Judenreferent* Röthke to the conclusion that "the French government no longer wants to go along with us on the Jewish question."[176] That judgment was far too sweeping, for the Vichy government, however uncomfortable with the Final Solution, had also chosen not to break with the Germans over it. Nonetheless, the German authorities had already been turning more and more to direct action in the southern zone since their arrival there in November 1942. After the summer of 1943, they went their own way even more resolutely.

Following June 1943 there were no more pauses in the deportation convoys. Thereafter they continued at a regular if reduced pace, usually one or two a month, until the Liberation. To fill these trains, the Germans gradually abandoned all earlier limitations. Former prisoners of war, foreign volunteers for the French armed forces, members of the Legion of Honor, UGIF personnel—all of these categories, which at one time or another the Vichy regime had attempted to hold back, could now be taken away.[177]

As plans unfolded for the deportation of those whom the Vichy government was expected to strip of citizenship, Eichmann sent one of his collaborators to France to speed things up. The man chosen was SS-Hauptsturmführer Alois Brunner, an experienced Final Solution administrator fresh from Salonika where he had helped dispatch Greek and foreign Jews with exemplary brutality and efficiency. Brunner, who outranked the *Judenreferent* Röthke, arrived with a special detachment of twenty-five men, authorized to act independently of the German police chain of command. In effect, he received his orders directly from Berlin.

Brunner's strategy was to ease the French police out of Jewish affairs entirely. With the aid of the collaborationists in Paris, he launched a violent press campaign against Bousquet and Laval and accused them of "protecting" the Jews.[178] He took over the direction of the Drancy camp on 2 July. Vichy thereby lost control of the key point in the administrative network of deportation. Thereafter, the French police and bureaucracy were excluded from any influence on the composition of convoys to the east.

Brunner organized squads that prowled about the country making arrests. His forces included Gestapo, *Feldgendarmerie,* and miscellaneous French forces under German control—SEC, the Doriotists (supporters of the flagging fascist movement of prewar fame), the Francists of Marcel Bucard, and various other auxiliaries—but never the French police. Georges Wellers suggests that this inactivity resulted from Brunner's rivalry with Röthke, the latter alone having the authority to call upon the French police. Vichy now withdrew the cooperation of the French police from operations against Jews who were French citizens. Laval told the assembled regional prefects on 21 September that they should protest the arrests of Jews but not intervene on behalf of foreigners; the French police should not "lend a hand" in the arrests of French Jews. In October, when the *Sicherheitspolizei* in Evreux asked the prefect for help with an arrest operation, he, after referring to Leguay, declined to authorize the arrest by French police of any French-born or recently naturalized Jews. The Germans carried out the arrests themselves, while the French arrested one foreigner.[179]

In the fall, Brunner's squads descended upon the areas formerly occupied by the Italians. Their arrival in the Savoie on 9 August spread a "veritable panic" according to the prefect. In September they were at work in the Alpes-Maritimes in "a real climate of terror." Although the prefect there informed the local *Sicherheitsdienst* director of "the decision taken by the government to protect French Israelites," many of them were arrested. The prefect's protests had no effect.[180] The grim tide of deportation reached department after department as Gestapo detachments were available. In December 1943, they removed foreign Jews undergoing treatment in hospitals in Perpignan and Font-Romeu without notifying the prefect, who was unable even to verify how many had been taken. On 18 February 1944 they carried off sixty-one aged Jews, ranging from sixty to eighty years old, from the Foreigners' Reception Center at Alboussières (Ardèche). The last Jewish families in the Marne were taken away at the end of January. The Oberg-Bousquet agreement was "a dead letter," as observed the prefect of the Lot-et-Garonne.[181]

What was happening to the Jews was still muffled, to some degree, by the simultaneous arrest and deportation in late 1943 and early 1944 of hundreds of prominent French men and women, along with the continued deportation of thousands of young men to work in German factories. Prefects reported public outrage as some local personage such as former mayor Schwab of Epinal or Rabbi Deutsch of Limoges was taken; but when five hundred French Jews were dispatched to Drancy from the Dijon region in February 1944, the regional prefect believed that public emotion was reduced "to a lesser priority" by the many other preoccupations of the time.[182] (Fifteen *Dijonnais* had been sentenced to death for an assassination at the same time.) At Vichy, ministers now said as little as possible about the Jews. Although notes survive of a half-dozen direct conversations in 1943 and early 1944 between Marshal Pétain and German officials ranging from the diplomat Roland Krug von Nidda to the military liaison officer General von Neubronn, the subject of Jews was never raised. Talk was left to a few interested enthusiasts like Darquier and Fernand de Brinon.

Another curious blind spot affected the French railway system, which managed widespread, organized resistance to all kinds of German demands—except deportations to the east. Throughout the war, French railwaymen were asked to operate convoys carrying deportees, prisoners, and conscripted laborers to the German frontier, where German railway crews took charge and French personnel withdrew.[183] In a lengthy study of the French national railways' resistance activity, Paul

Durand describes the energetic protests made by the system's legal division against abuses of the armistice and the Hague Convention; he makes no mention, however, of deportations of Jews.[184] Railwaymen apparently helped about fifty Jewish children escape from one convoy in September 1942, and may also have smuggled some tools into baggage cars to help prisoners to break through the floorboards.[185] Nothing interfered with the transports to Auschwitz, however, even in the summer of 1944 when substantial derailments and sabotage affected other shipments. Not one of the eighty-five convoys of Jewish deportees was derailed or otherwise impeded. Fourteen transports left France in 1944 alone, all but three of which carried a thousand Jews or more. The only incidents noted by SS officers in charge were some individual escapees.[186]

Even in this twilight period of German occupation, French police were still ordered on occasion to obey German commanders in actions against Jews. In Bordeaux, in January 1944, the SS demanded that the local police assist in the mass roundup of Jews, including French citizens, women, and children. Through the regional prefect, the reluctant police authorities appealed to de Brinon, Darnand, and Laval. They were told to carry out the job. "Following government instructions," the regional prefect reported, the police captured 288 out of 473 French Jews on their lists and assembled them in the appointed spot, the Bordeaux synagogue, prior to their deportation. One, the prefect noted, a totally disabled veteran of the 1914–18 war, attempted suicide when arrested, and was removed to a hospital in grave condition. The prefect observed that, as a result of this action, the police "will lose . . . part of the credit it has enjoyed among the people, which is hostile to any action taken against persons who have committed no crime." Throughout the region, he continued, the arrests had provoked "an excitement that is all the more keen since public order and tranquility have not been interrupted and no particular circumstance explains [this operation]."[187] This would seem to have been the last large-scale French police participation in an indiscriminate roundup of Jews under German orders. More than likely it was related to the collapse of the Marshal's last burst of independence when he attempted in November 1943 to make a dramatic radio address announcing the removal of Laval and the recall of the National Assembly in the event of Pétain's disappearance; faced with an adamant German veto, Pétain abandoned his plan and accepted a certain number of extremist collaborators in the cabinet, including Joseph Darnand in the new post of secretary-general for the maintenance of order.

It was the same ministerial reshuffle that carried off Darquier. Vichy, however, did not get rid of its commissioner-general for Jewish affairs; the Germans removed him themselves. They had been disappointed with Darquier from the first months. It was not the corruption of the CGQJ that bothered them. There is no evidence that the embassy or the *Sicherheitsdienst* took offense at improprieties among French officials, although one or the other agency sometimes took steps to stop dishonesty within its own ranks. Darquier's administrative incompetence did not trouble these agencies either, since the most important tasks—the roundup and the deportation of Jews—were in the hands of the French and the German police. But it was apparent to all that Darquier had not been able to impose his will on the French government or his views on the French public. As early as June 1942, an embassy official noted his colleagues' disappointment that Darquier had failed to obtain any French funds to extend the Institute of Study on Jewish Questions into the Unoccupied Zone. By December 1942, Knochen, informed of hostility to Darquier on the part of other ministers at Vichy—such as Minister of Justice Joseph Barthélemy—was understood by embassy observers to be ready to let the ineffectual commissioner disappear *(verschwinden)*.[188*] Dr. Klassen, the head of propaganda services in the German embassy in Paris, wrote Consul-General Schleier that German officials interested in Jewish questions were "unanimous" in their opinion that Darquier was "absolutely useless in everything."[190] For another year, however, no one seems to have wanted to face squarely the problem of finding a new commissioner or openly to admit Darquier's failure. It was not until 20 December 1943 that Darquier's name came down from Paris on a list of officials "whose resignation is required" by the German government, and who were associated oddly with a number of close associates of Marshal Pétain whom the Germans blamed for the Marshal's gesture of independence in November (General Campet, Lucien Romier, Jean Jardel, and others).[191]

It may have been a sign of the CGQJ's increasing marginality that Vichy was allowed to have its own way in the naming of a new commissioner. Jacques de Lesdain, whom Abetz had imposed on *L'Illustration* as political editor, and Louis Thomas, ex-officer and "literary adventurer"[192] who had succeeded in becoming administrator of the aryanized publishing house Calmann-Lévy, were known to enjoy the favor of the German embassy and the *Sicherheitsdienst*. When Darquier's

*We find no evidence to support the assertion that Darquier was arrested by Vichy for improprieties.[189]

"resignation" was announced on 26 February 1944, however, his successor was Charles Mercier du Paty de Clam, a career colonial official who had spent the interwar years working his way slowly up the administrative ladder in Damascus.[193]*

Du Paty de Clam's sole qualification for the office seems to have been his name: he was a descendant of the famous Commandant du Paty de Clam, remembered from the Dreyfus affair as the staff officer who arrested the accused Jewish captain in 1894. Charles Mercier was carrying on in the family tradition. But apart from this sentimental link to the antisemitic past, du Paty brought neither talent nor fervor to the job. According to one German observer, he was more interested in cultural matters than in aryanization; and another summarized his impact as "more of a paralysis than a resumption of activity on the part of the Commissariat-General."[195] Finance Ministry Inspector-General Formery, charged with examining the honesty and competence of the CGQJ in May 1944, found in du Paty "a strangely passive serenity."[196] At his appointment, the violently anti-Jewish *Emancipation national* had remarked sardonically on 11 March that it was a least "a way of recalling to mind the existence of the Commissariat-General for Jewish Affairs." *Au Pilori* soon lamented "his strange and silent self-effacement, so unlike the customary effusive verbosity that usually accompanies the assumption of authority." Du Paty was the only CGQJ leader against whom prosecution was dropped in the postwar purge trials.

By spring 1944, the SS was conducting the deportation practically on its own. Communication between the *Judenreferat* and Vichy virtually ceased. In April, Knochen issued secret orders for an intensification of arrests of Jews in France. Brunner gave his approval. Everyone was now to be taken at once, without regard for nationality or any other consideration. By now the SS felt unable to rely at all on local police for help with mass arrests. The arrest squads were ordered to descend upon labor camps, prisons, and so forth, unannounced, at night; otherwise, "the French would . . . free the Jews" or transfer them elsewhere. To help uncover those in hiding, a system of bonuses offered rewards to individuals who denounced Jews:

> The bonuses should not be too high; nevertheless, they should be high enough to give sufficient encouragement. The amount will be fixed by the [local] commander. The bonus cannot be the same everywhere. It will generally be larger in the cities than in the country.[197]

---

*Laval informed Abetz of the appointment on 28 January, and the Germans scurried about after background information on the new appointee.[194]

The SS could still rely on one source of French assistance, however: the Milice, a paramilitary force created within the veterans' Légion, which acquired more autonomy in its pursuit of the regime's enemies during 1943. Joseph Darnand was its chief. Darnand had received the highest soldier's decoration, the *Médaille militaire,* from the hands of Pétain himself in 1918 for guerrilla exploits behind the lines, and then had vegetated between the wars as a garage owner and as a militant in veterans' organizations in Nice. Vichy's increasing resort to police repression provided the long-sought outlet for Darnand's violence, unscrupulousness, and utter single-mindedness in what he conceived to be obedience to the orders of his chief. Darnand was quick to attack any weakness in repression, whether it came from the police or the head of government. With the Milice, the Germans came closest to what they had always lacked in France, and for what Heydrich had asked during his visit to Paris in May 1942: a parallel police force composed of men chosen for their ideological conviction rather than for professional competence, led by a chief outside the regular police and ready for anything. Darnand's star rose as German strength waned, and when all else had failed to keep the French in line. At the end of 1943, the Germans finally removed Bousquet from office; and in January 1944, Vichy named Darnand to replace him, changing the title of his office appropriately to "secretary-general for the maintenance of order."[198]

The Milice pursued Jews relentlessly, taking up much of this work from the flagging regular police forces. The French *gendarmerie* in the Savoie department, for example, according to a disgruntled SEC agent, ignored the few Jews remaining and did not even bother to keep track of them.[199] Even some German military units were losing their stomach for the business. Röthke warned in May 1944, when informed that German military police had refused on several occasions to act against Jews, that if such behavior continued, the SS would have to reconsider its relationship with the Wehrmacht.[200] No such hesitations affected the Milice. The SS found Darnand's performance exemplary. Indeed, the *miliciens* were the most dangerous of all as far as Jews were concerned. As one historian has pointed out, "while the ordinary police might be friendly or at least neutral, and the Germans were strangers and might be bluffed, *miliciens* were sharp, suspicious characters wholeheartedly devoted to the bad cause and only too fully informed."[201]

Working on their own except for the Milice and those who denounced people to the authorities, the understaffed German SS were unable to reach the numbers that had been deported in 1942 when the full resources of the French police had been at their disposal. About 33,500 Jews were sent to the east in 1943–44—short of the 42,500 deported with greater French help in 1942. But the SS squads at work in 1944 made up for their inadequate numbers with ferocity. Röthke combed the entertainment and nightclub world for Jews. De Brinon's brother-in-law was arrested, despite his certificate stating that he did not belong to the Jewish race. Klaus Barbie, the Gestapo chief in Lyon, led a raid on a Jewish orphanage. The result was 41 children and 10 adults captured, all sent to Drancy.[202]

Such horrors might well have prompted the end of Vichy's own anti-Jewish activity. When du Paty de Clam took indefinite leave in May, however, the Vichy regime was not content to let the CGQJ continue in somnolent passivity. Joseph Antignac, the workhorse of the commissariat, now took charge. He was given the lesser title of "secretary-general," but he exerted the same single-minded energy that had brought him from command of the Limoges region of the Police for Jewish Affairs in 1942 to a position as Darquier's second-in-command in 1943 (see pages 288–89).[203] Where du Paty had been largely indifferent to the commissariat and its goals, Antignac was utterly partisan. "Antisemite first," he told his staff upon taking over the new post; "supporter of the Marshal's policy thereafter"—with a perhaps unintended hint of a new dichotomy. Antignac had assured Röthke a year earlier of his commitment to a view of the Final Solution that went well beyond that of his government: "I remain convinced that total deportation would considerably simplify all these questions, especially the removal of Jews in government positions."[204] To prove his fidelity, Antignac denounced André Baur and Raymond-Raoul Lambert, leaders of the UGIF in the northern and southern zones, respectively, ensuring the prompt deportation and murder in Auschwitz of even the men chosen by the Vichy government to administer the affairs of the Jewish community.[205] This was the man to whom Laval entrusted the machinery of persecution in the last days of Vichy.

It remains to be explained why Vichy gave another turn of the wheel to the faltering CGQJ machinery in the spring of 1944. Our evidence on this point is incomplete, since both Vichy and German records are much more abundant for the first years of the occupation than for the last; current documents may have been destroyed at the last minute in 1944, leaving the older files more intact. The embassy and *Sicherheitsdienst* abandoned their candidate Jacques de Lesdain after Laval observed that his absence in Germany during the 1939–40 campaign would make him ineffective.[206] By this time, the *Judenreferat* and the *Sicherheitspolizei* were going their own way. Nor is there direct evidence of why Laval or his ministers wanted another zealot at the helm of anti-Jewish affairs.

We can draw a kind of indirect evidence, however, from the efforts of the Vichy regime to maintain its authority and to prevent the collapse of any parts of its administration in the spring of 1944. The government's strategy was shaped by its perception of the rising menaces of 1944. An Allied landing on French soil was expected from one day to the next. As seen from Vichy, that event promised not so much to liberate France as to make it a battle zone. Disorder and a challenge to the government's legitimacy were certain; outright civil war was likely. The only chance to preserve civil order, as seen from Vichy, was the firmest possible administrative grip. If the machinery of state remained intact, it might even be possible to transfer authority peaceably from one hand to another. That last desperate hope lay behind several Vichy efforts in the summer of 1944 to arrange an orderly transfer of power.[207] The regime struggled in 1944 to maintain the authority of the state and of all of its agencies.

These concerns seem to have applied to the anti-Jewish sphere as well as to the more traditional government concerns. Laval sent word to this effect to du Paty and then to Antignac.[208] The anti-Jewish machinery ground on, then, partly from bureaucratic momentum, partly from the new impetus that Antignac gave to it. On 1 May 1944 newspapers carried a notice calling attention to a decree of the previous year requiring Jews to pay 360 francs a year as a "solidarity assessment" for the UGIF. It also turned out that local UGIF offices lacked precise information concerning the Jews of their locality, and thus a new census was taken. The CGQJ asked the prefects of the southern zone to provide a "a full list" of all the Jews in each department, arranged by nationality; a reminder followed on 4 July 1944. Thirty-six prefects complied, mostly enclosing 1941 lists with various apologies for the many addresses no longer current. The prefects of the Creuse and the Haute-Loire sent ostensibly up-to-date lists of foreign Jews but omitting French citizens.[209] Also on 4 May, the *Journal officiel* published a law (dated 23 March 1944) raising the deduction, on the blocked accounts of Jewish property, from 10 percent to 20 percent, to fill the coffers of the CGQJ. On 22 May, André Parmentier, the new director-general of the Police under Darnand, ordered prefects in the southern zone to renew Jews' ration cards only at the mayor's office of their commune of residence, "in order to facilitate investigations of Israelites." Letters of denunciation of hidden Jews and "Judaized business" continued to arrive at the CGQJ. On 19 July, the SEC was opening an investigation of a Paris lawyer, at a time when forty-six out of fifty-three of the Jewish lawyers authorized to practice in Paris under the quota had already been interned or deported. Prominent citizens were recommending clients or relatives for positions as *administrateur provisoire* as late as February 1944.[210] The law remained in force. Whatever their repugnance to mass, indiscriminate roundups, many police still regarded it as their duty to arrest individual Jews who in some way violated the *Statuts des juifs.* *

Nor did the Allied landing in Normandy on 6 June 1944 give a signal to close down Vichy's anti-Jewish machinery. Antignac quoted Laval's instructions in an effort to bolster the understandably flagging spirits of his regional directors.[212] After the Liberation, Antignac claimed that Laval also told him to procrastinate and keep out of the Germans' way, "letting me know that it was the end."[213] His statements at the time, however, do not suggest an Antignac resigned to liquidating the anti-Jewish enterprise as quietly and as harmlessly as possible. To Laval he wrote, on 1 June 1944, that he was determined to put the commissariat in order to eliminate dubious elements. "I propose to carry out the necessary improvements in each department, a task that will be very easily accomplished given the confidence that you have so kindly placed in me."[214] To his assembled underlings he gave a speech in early June emphasizing their role in the National Revolution. "Antisemitism first" was still his motto. While he admitted that the situation was grave, and the commissariat "in a critical state," he issued a stirring call for discipline and exactitude. He demanded unconditional obedience: "I will personally ensure that order, confidence, probity, justice, and commitment to the job are the rule around here."[215] To the Ministry of Justice he drafted a long letter on 4 August making a careful defense of new legislation to improve the functioning of aryanization.[216] To his CGQJ directors he wrote on 17 August reminding them of the regional chain of command and urging them to follow the written orders of the regional prefects.[217] In Antignac's world of make-believe, the commissariat had its duty to perform even as the Allied armies were approaching Paris.

As Vichy descended into the conflict it had so feared, government propaganda took an emphatically antisemitic turn. First, there were the radio editorials of Philippe Henriot, the Catholic militant and former deputy from Bordeaux whom Laval accepted as secretary of state for information and propaganda in January 1944, in the government reshuffle following Pétain's abortive moves of the end of 1943. Twice daily thereafter, Henriot embroidered on one theme: the violence and the self-interest of France's pretended "liberators," "our future colonizers" (12 May 1944), who included "all those Jews who surround you" (14 April

---

*A list of nearly seven hundred Jews arrested for violation of the *Statuts* includes eleven arrested in 1944.[211]

1944) such as Mendès-France "in the Finance Ministry [of the provisional government in Algiers] where one would be surprised not to find a Jew" (4 April 1944).[218] Henriot's passion and verve drew listeners far beyond the little circle of those who still believed in what Vichy was trying to do. His evening broadcast on 27 June—in which he boasted of having never defended the Jews—was his last; that night a Resistance group disguised as *miliciens* penetrated to his apartment in the Ministry of Information in Paris and shot him dead. Cardinal Gerlier attended one of the memorial masses in his honor; and Pétain, who had refused to sign his appointment decree, sent a hand-written letter of condolence to Mme. Henriot.[219]

Henriot's successor was none other than Xavier Vallat, who shared the microphone with Paul Marion. The former commissioner-general for Jewish affairs did not refrain from giving an antisemitic edge to the twenty-five radio editorials he delivered during July 1944. Henriot, he said, had been "killed by London, Washington, Moscow, and Jerusalem" (2 July). He lamented "this ideological war desired by Israel" (18 July) and led by Britain, "l'ennemi héréditaire" (20 July). He warned that Allied victory could lead only to what was already visible in North Africa: "the return to power of the Jews and Freemasons . . . who for half a century lived on the backs of the settlers and the natives [until] the Marshal cleared them away" (3 July). He did not hesitate to attack the integrity of Georges Mandel, his old nemesis (20 July), nearly two weeks after Mandel had been shot down by *miliciens*.[220] The anxieties of the summer of 1944 did not diminish anti-Jewish feeling among Vichy leaders but, if anything, sharpened it.

During the last days, as Antignac blamed the CGQJ's troubles on a handful of malcontents, and Xavier Vallat blamed the war on the Jews, the bureaucracy of repression began to melt away. At the end of July, forty gendarmes quit their post at the Sisteron internment center, along with the camp guards. Two thirds of the prisoners escaped.[221] Reports of intrigue and corruption multiplied. The regional delegate of the SEC in Rouen was arrested at the end of May, charged with robbing the apartments of six foreign Jews whom he had discovered in hiding. In early August one of his colleagues wrote to the central office of the CGQJ pleading on his behalf, while praising this official's persistence in reconstituting the Rouen CGQJ office after Allied bombardments in the sequestered Jewish apartment in which he lived.[222] The machinery of the Commissariat-General for Jewish Affairs continued to function and, for at least a few officials, Laval's orders to maintain continuity were obeyed to the very end.

CHAPTER

8

Conclusions: The Holocaust in France

In conclusion, we found no difficulty with the Vichy government in implementing Jewish policy.

Helmut Knochen (1947)[1]

LIKE THE SS, who methodically counted the Jews sent to the east, we can calculate the toll of the Final Solution in France. By the end of 1944, almost 75,000 Jews had been deported from France to killing centers in former Polish territory.* Upon arrival, most were gassed immediately, while the rest were put to work under conditions that meant almost certain death within a few weeks or months. About 2,500, approximately 3 percent, survived.[2] Auschwitz was the destination of about 70,000 of the deportees from France. The rest were sent to other camps—Maidanek, Sobibor, and a few dozen to Buchenwald in August 1944. Close to one third of the total were French citizens. The rest were foreign refugees. Nearly 2,000 were under six years of age, over 6,000 were under thirteen, and 8,700 were sixty years or over.

These statistics emerge from German records—nominative lists of the seventy-nine convoys that left France, and archives of the Auschwitz camp administration—as well as from lists of survivors collected by the French Ministry of Veteran Affairs and similar authorities in other countries. Of course, no slaughter of this magnitude leaves absolutely precise figures, especially a slaughter that was accelerating in the closing months of a lost war; but the totals are accurate within a very small margin of error. The destruction of European Jewry was more meticulously scrutinized by record keepers than have been other massacres in history. The conclusions of the French researchers who have studied

*According to Klarsfeld, at least 815 Jews were arrested in the Nord and the Pas-de-Calais departments and deported from Belgium. Adding these to the total of other deportees, one concludes that a minimum of 75,721 Jews were deported from France.

these lists do not differ substantially. Most recently, in 1978 (see note 2, p. 412), following a thorough evaluation, Serge Klarsfeld has published the names of 75,721 deportees, convoy by convoy. His hundreds of pages remind one of the telephone directory of a medium-sized city, the long columns of names a mute testimony to the scale of the Nazi enterprise. More conservative than some other recent evaluations, and based upon a painstaking critique of the sources, Klarsfeld's assessment seems as close as we are likely to get to a definitive judgment.

The French government, we should add, prefers, in official statements, not to distinguish among the "racial deportees." Responding to a recent question in the Chamber of Deputies about *Jewish* deportees, the Prime Minister cited French documents in referring to 120,000 "racial deportees" of whom only 3,000 returned.[3] The divergence between these statistics and those computed from German lists is probably explained by the French government's use of the term "deportation" to cover involuntary transportation from France by the Germans for a variety of reasons besides the persecution of Jews. French government figures likely also include other groups, such as gypsies, whom the Nazis sent to the east[4] (after being interned, we might add, by the Vichy regime).

However ghastly these totals, they fell short of SS expectations. In mid-1942, Dannecker had looked forward to shipping 100,000 Jews east in the first six months of the program. Röthke, his successor, had projected that 1943 would see the deportation of all the remaining Jews in France, whom he fairly accurately estimated at 270,000.[5] The Germans soon recognized that deportations were falling behind schedule, and officials charged with the Final Solution complained, on various occasions late in the war, about its slow progress in France.

After the Liberation, defenders of Vichy took their cue from the German officials' disappointment. Just as the world learned of the enormity of the Jewish tragedy—two thirds of European Jewry killed, between five million and six million people—Pierre Laval claimed to have limited the damage in France. Xavier Vallat pointed out that, in comparison with other countries, the significant fact in France was that so many Jews had been saved. Vichy, the argument went, had served as a "shield" for thousands of Jews, especially those who were French. Vichy had dirtied its hands, its defenders were sometimes prepared to admit; but the final result was not so terrible as elsewhere, where a far greater proportion of Jews had been murdered.[6*]

*This view has been adopted by a number of historians, including some with no evident predisposition to favor Vichy, such as Gerald Reitlinger: "With the loss of less than

The Germans themselves were not nearly so sure where to place the blame for their mediocre results in France. To be sure, the German police concluded by late 1943 that the French police were no longer reliable for operations against Jews, although the Germans gladly used them whenever possible as late as January 1944. Röthke concluded from the denaturalization quarrel in August 1943 that Vichy was no longer willing to cooperate on anti-Jewish policy. But when Heinrich Himmler himself was asked by his loyal lieutenant Martin Mutschmann, in July 1944, why there were still so many Jews in Normandy to aid the British and Americans, he pointed his finger in a different direction. The total evacuation of Jews from France, Himmler replied, had been "extremely difficult . . . because of the strained relations with the Wehrmacht military authorities there." If French obstruction deserved any part of the blame, Himmler forgot to mention it in July 1944. After the war, under interrogation by French authorities, Helmut Knochen, the head of the German security police in France, asserted that he recalled no serious trouble with the French on the Jewish issue during the occupation.[8]

Whose account are we to believe? In fact, the matter is more complicated than either version would suggest. We must attempt to reconstruct the ways in which Vichy officials perceived the matter of the Jews during the successive phases of the occupation. After the war, comparison with Greece, Holland, or Yugoslavia may have occurred to collaborators as they prepared their defense in 1945 or 1946. During the occupation, however, no one knew the extent of Jewish losses in various European countries. No models of other strategies presented themselves to the Vichy leaders, who knew nothing of what was being done in Denmark or Hungary to impede deportation. Beyond that, we find no evidence that the Vichy leaders even considered such comparisons in 1942 or 1943. They envisaged the matter of policy toward the Jews in terms of French internal policy and of the domestic concerns of the late 1930s and early 1940s. Well into the occupation, and perhaps to the end in some cases, they fitted new information about what was happening to the Jews into conceptions formed when France was hardening its attitude toward refugees in the late 1930s.

The theory of a "shield"—sending some Jews to certain death in order to save a substantial number of other Jews—implies a far clearer consciousness of long-term German intentions than the contemporary

---

25 percent, no Jewish community in Occupied Europe came off so lightly, except in Denmark, and this was due in large measure to the tactics of Laval.[7]

evidence suggests. Like everyone else, Vichy's leaders were slow to fathom the scope of the Final Solution, in the face of mounting evidence, and despite the Nazis' repeated declarations that all the Jews of France would eventually be deported. Although Vichy had the means to understand, its officials for the most part preferred not to delve too far into such matters. Indifference to the fate of Jews was the predominant attitude. To Laval, in particular, the Jews seem generally to have been unimportant, hardly worth the effort that the "shield" strategy implied. Vichy undoubtedly hoped to save some French Jews from whatever was meant by "work" in the east. There is no indication, however, that this aim had a high priority in Vichy's calculations or that it formed part of a well-articulated plan. Laval was content not to press the Germans for any formal agreement limiting deportation to foreign Jews, even after the Germans made it clear to him that, despite some postponement, they would eventually take all the Jews of France. Did Laval know what deportation meant? Did he know what was in store for the Jews whom his police loaded into the cattle cars?

What Did Vichy Know about the Final Solution?

> . . . I see how dumbfounded everyone is when I am asked for news and when I have to reply in agony that Monsieur Roussetzki is deported.
> Everyone knows how terrible that is! And me, I didn't want to believe it, but the facts are there. If he had been treated humanely he would be able to write, to correspond with his family. . . .
> As a Frenchwoman I appeal to your ministry and shout out my indignation. Where is my husband? What has become of my husband?
> A letter to Marshal Pétain (1943)[9]

Immediately after the war, when the death camps had just been revealed in detail to a shocked public, it was more common than it is now to plead ignorance. German officials, almost to a man, said they did not know. Pierre Laval said that he did not know.

> I tried to find out, by questioning them, where the Germans were sending those convoys of Jews, and their reply invariably was: "To Poland, where we want to create a Jewish state." I was well aware that this meant working there in terrible conditions, most often to suffer and to die there.[10]

Xavier Vallat said that he did not know, and cited the horrified amazement of Allied troops who first liberated the death factories in the spring of 1945.[11] Just after the war, Rabbi Jacob Kaplan, summarizing the Jewish ordeal in France for an American audience, implied that there was real uncertainty even among Jewish leaders until close to the Liberation. "There came a moment, *at the beginning of 1944,* when there was no longer any doubt that the Hitlerite program called for the extermination of French Jewry by deportations and massacres" (our italics).[12]

Yet reports of mass killings began to reach the West almost as soon as they began. Unorganized mass killings had begun on the Russian front in fall 1941; systematized early in 1942, they were extended to German-controlled western Europe during July 1942 in the form of massive deportations to the east. As early as March 1942, a long memorandum given to the papal nuncio in Berne, Monsignor Bernardini, by representatives of the Jewish Agency, the World Jewish Congress, and the Swiss Jewish community, referred to the execution of "thousands of Jews in Poland and in parts of Russia occupied by the Germans," along with the more familiar grievances of expulsions, internments, exclusions from jobs and professions, and expropriation of property.[13] It has generally been believed that the first serious warning about an active German program of total extermination, a "final solution" as distinct from episodic killings, was a message sent to London and to Washington by Gerhardt Riegner, representative of the World Jewish Conference in Geneva, on 8 August 1942—less than a month after systematic deportations from western Europe began. Walter Laqueur has recently shown that credible accounts of mass killings, and even of the use of gas, reached the West before August 1942 through a variety of sources: the Polish underground, escapees, witnesses from Italian and other allied armed forces, and even Gestapo agents, some of whom were Jews. "Many more people knew about the extermination than is commonly believed, and many knew *earlier* than generally assumed."[14]

By early fall 1942 these reports were being discussed at the highest levels. It cannot be proven conclusively, without independent verification from the Vatican archives, that SS Colonel Kurt Gerstein's eyewitness account of the use of Zyklon-B gas for mass extermination at Auschwitz actually reached the Vatican through the various churchmen and Swedish diplomats whom he approached as early as August 1942. It is certain that Myron C. Taylor, U. S. ambassador to the Holy See, sent a detailed report on the mass execution of Polish and western Jews in Poland to the papal secretary of state Cardinal Maglione on 26

September 1942 and asked what the Vatican's reactions to these events would be.[15] On the floor of the House of Commons on 17 December 1942, British Foreign Secretary Anthony Eden denounced the massive execution of Jews in the Polish camps. The same day, the Allied governments and the French National Committee released jointly a statement describing in some detail conditions in the "main Nazi abattoir" in Poland and promising retribution for these crimes after the war.[16]

Within France itself, the roundups of Jews and their families in both zones in July–August 1942 were impossible to conceal, despite prefects' efforts at discretion. The prefects of the Unoccupied Zone themselves described in their monthly reports the public's reaction— far more negative than positive—to these shocking scenes. Departure conditions were always better known, of course, than what happened at the destination; but as early as 1 July 1942, the BBC had broadcast accounts in French of the massacre of 700,000 Polish Jews. The fate of the Jews taken from France was discussed without delay in the underground press. The clandestine newspaper *J'Accuse*, dated 20 October 1942, declared that "the Boche torturers are burning and asphyxiating thousands of men, women, and children deported from France." Another Resistance tract of 15 November 1942 reported "the most dreadful rumors" about the fate of the deportees. "According to letters from Poland the trains brought only corpses there. Now we learn that a few convoys of women, old people, the sick and children, in short all who were unfit for work, were asphyxiated by poison gas."[17] The Communist *L'Humanité* clandestinely published in October 1942 the allegation that the Germans had performed experiments with toxic gas on eleven thousand men, women, old people, and children from among the Jews deported from the two zones of France.[18]

Receiving reports was one thing; accepting them as something other than Allied or dissident propaganda was another. Prefects tended to dismiss the more alarming reports as "unlikely," "the most fantastic rumors." Prefect Dauliac of the Haute Savoie grumbled that "the enemies of the regime, exploiting popular sentimentality, did not fail to claim . . . that the 'unfortunate victims' were condemned to certain death." Prefect Gaston Jammet did not think that the upsurge of German arrests he witnessed in August 1942 in the Vendée "would have serious consequences for those concerned."[19] Indeed, there was considerable skepticism on the Allied side as well. A British Foreign Office analyst called Gerhardt Riegner's August 1942 report of a "final solution" policy decision in Germany "a rather wild story"; and the U.S. envoy in Bern commented that "there is what is apparently a wild rumor inspired by Jewish fears that the Nazis will exterminate all at once (possibly with prussic acid) in the autumn about 4 m. Jews whom they have been assembling in Eastern Europe." "For another two or three years [after November 1941]," Walter Laqueur observes, "the general consensus in Whitehall was that the accounts about the mass murder of Jews were exaggerated."[20]

The reluctance of Jews themselves to believe these reports is particularly striking. Not until 23 November 1942, after the arrival in Palestine of a group of women and children from Poland who confirmed the reports about Treblinka and Sobibor, did the Jewish Agency in Palestine feel certain enough to release a major public statement about the extent of the mass murders. Even then it was hard to believe that these stories were not exaggerations or wartime propaganda. Even the inmates of other camps could not believe the rumors about what went on in the killing centers. Léon Blum emerged from Buchenwald (a concentration camp, not a death camp) unaware of the gas chambers.[21] Georges Wellers, a Paris lawyer who had been arrested with the thousand Jewish leaders in December 1941, "had left Drancy [for Auschwitz] on 30 June 1944, without having the slightest idea about the real meaning of the deportation of the Jews." Even though he had access to the other prisoners and had secret correspondence with his wife, he could "affirm categorically that no one had the slightest idea about the systematic murder that in reality awaited the Jews at the other end of their deportation journey."[22]

It is as if this unbearable truth had to be rediscovered and reconfirmed over and over again for those who could not or would not believe it. In the autumn of 1943—more than a year after the Consistoire central had already made an official declaration to Laval about the "exterminations" it believed were taking place in eastern Europe— Jacques Helbronner, the president of the Consistoire, received a detailed report of crematory ovens and systematic extermination which he found "so unbelievable" that he set out to find confirmation from neutral sources.[23] In January 1944, the Abbé Joseph Catry, still eager to persuade the Germans to employ him as a propagandist, implored the *Judenreferent* Röthke to give him the means to disprove the accusations of genocide that he heard around him. "There is a real effort to hide something very grave," he wrote Röthke, "but without success, because the subterfuge is very clumsy."[24] As late as April 1944, two Slovakian Jews who had escaped from Auschwitz created a sensation with their accounts of what they had seen. All along the line, beginning with the *Judenrat* in Bratislava, authorities hesitated to give them full credence; and only in July were the Slovakians' "Notebooks from Auschwitz" published in the *Gazette de Lausanne* and the *Journal de Genève*, and in November 1944 by the United States government.[25]

On reflection, it is naïve to select retroactively—out of the myriad conflicting signals of wartime news, rumor, and propaganda—those reports that conform to the truth finally established upon the opening of the camps in May 1945, and to declare that, once these reports had arrived in the West, everyone of good faith "knew." Most of us, however, "know" only information that accords with prior expectations and patterns of intelligibility. A celebrated example involves the surprise of the Japanese attack on the United States naval base at Pearl Harbor, in the Hawaiian Islands, on 7 December 1941. Having broken Japanese codes, American intelligence analysts possessed enormous quantities of raw data concerning Japanese movements, including indications of a possible strike toward the mid-Pacific. They disregarded these scraps of information, however, in favor of other scraps of information that fitted their expectation of a Japanese advance toward southeast Asia.[26] Identifying important information among a welter of conflicting signals is often possible only after subsequent events have given meaning to one signal rather than another.

The first reports of the death camps competed for attention against many contradictory signals. Even the examples we have quoted conflicted among themselves. Some referred to killings, but local excesses were not necessarily proof of a plan of total extermination. Some signals referred to poison gas, but in terms of "experiments" (as in the *Humanité* article previously quoted) or of "prussic acid," recalling some of the more notoriously discredited propaganda stories of the First World War. Many signals referred to the conditions of departure, which did not necessarily prove anything about the conditions at the point of arrival. A Resistance tract from July 1942, which provided an accurate account of the Vel d'Hiv roundup, then alluded vaguely to the "deportation by groups of one thousand to a prison across the Rhine."[27] In Hungary, the Germans produced a film combining accurate footage of the local fascist Arrow Cross men roughly loading the deportees and faked scenes of solicitous Germans caring for them at the destination.[28] In August 1942, the extremely well-informed Donald Lowrie of the American relief agency YMCA wrote that "no one had any illusions" about the fate of the deportees: "falling into German hands meant either forced labor or slow extermination in the Jewish 'reservation' in Poland." But still there was no certainty. As a humanitarian gesture, the YMCA put a box of books in each railway car leaving southern France for an unknown destination. "As yet no reliable news had been received

[as] to the ultimate destination of these convoys or of what happens there," Lowrie wrote on 7 October.[29] Intimate knowledge of the harsh conditions of the departure carried in itself no certain proof that the Germans had decided to apply a policy of wholesale extermination at the destination.

For one thing, the Nazis did their best to hide, from all but a few administrators and security officials, the murder of millions of Jews. Himmler, acknowledging a long statistical report on the Jewish question sent to him by Kaltenbrunner in April 1943, thanked the chief of the *Sicherheitspolizei* and the *Sicherheitsdienst* for his attention to "camouflage policy" *(Tarnungszwecken)* and for keeping in mind readers of "later times." For instance, "evacuation" *(Evakuierung)*—already a euphemism—appeared in Kaltenbrunner's statistical tables as "migration" *(Abwanderung).*[30] The agencies directly responsible for the extermination preferred to use the term "special treatment" *(Sonderbehandlung),* or "S.B.," to describe their work; at the Nuremberg trials it required repeated questioning to establish that this neutral phrase simply meant killing.*

In France, the German occupation authorities told their subordinates to use guarded language and to hide the real objectives of the deportations. To be sure, sweeping statements can sometimes be found in internal German communications, especially those of Dannecker. In May 1942, for example, the brash and inexperienced *Judenreferent* discussed with General Kohl, head of railway transport in France, the aims of German policy toward Jews, which he described as "the complete annihilation of the enemy" *(restloser Vernichtung des Gegners).*[32] But in that same month the military administration circulated a directive to avoid even the word "deportation," nomenclature held to be too reminiscent of Tsarist expulsions to Siberia. The proper formula now was "sending away for forced labor" *(Verschickung zur Zwangsarbeit),* a phrase that better masked the real significance of the transports.[33] Dannecker himself resorted to euphemisms a few weeks later, advising his staff to use the term "transfer of population" *(Umsiedlung)* which permitted the inclusion of children.[34] Pétain's own office occasionally sounded out the Germans on the fate of noteworthy deportees, operating through the intermediary of the Delegation of Armistice Services (DSA) which reported to Vichy on the coercive measures of the occupation. The Germans refused all interventions on behalf of Jews, however, including even distinguished personalities and war veterans. Reporting for the DSA to the Marshal in November 1943, General Debeney de-

---

*Hans Buchheim has proved the meaning of the term beyond doubt.[31]

clared that "there is a strong impression that no more can be attempted on their behalf."[35]

But we have not adequately explained the reactions of Vichy officialdom to the reports of the Final Solution if we limit ourselves to the contradictory and incomplete nature of those reports, to the incredible nature of their suggestions, or to the Nazis' efforts at secrecy. Many people at Vichy believed the official version because it fit so comfortably within the attitudes formed during the refugee crisis of 1938–41.

The Nazis' cover story had a kind of plausibility, after all, while the truth flew in the face of common sense. Conscripted labor was not uncommon in wartime. The French themselves had used German prisoners of war as labor during and after the First World War, and the Vichy regime, as we have seen, dragooned Spanish, Jewish, and other civilians into *groupements de travailleurs étrangers* after 1940 without any need for German prompting. After the campaign in Russia had bogged down into a war of attrition, the Germans recruited foreign labor, sometimes forcibly, to the point that in the summer of 1942 there were approximately three and one-half million foreigners working in the Reich. The French had intimate experience of the Germans' thirst for foreign labor, as young Frenchmen made up the largest national male contingent after the Service du Travail subjected French youths to a labor draft in February 1943. If young Frenchmen were being "deported" to work in German factories (and we have noted that this was the term universally used to describe the hated STO), what was more natural—and even desirable—than that Jews who had originated in German and German-occupied lands be "deported" for similar purposes? As we have seen, the exemption of young French Jews from labor service was a matter of some jealousy in France in 1943. It was true that some able-bodied Jewish deportees did work for a time in the chemical plant that I. G. Farben had built within the vast Auschwitz complex in order to enjoy the benefits of cheap prison labor. Even the *Manchester Guardian,* whose reporting showed more understanding than most newspapers of what was happening to the Jews, argued on 31 August 1942 that "the deportation of Jews to Poland means that Jewish muscles are needed for the German war effort."[36] Why should the Germans, locked in a life-and-death struggle with the Russians, squander precious resources and manpower on a project devoid of material advantage, and so repugnant that it could not be avowed even within the German governing elite? The "forced labor" alibi had enough verisimilitude to satisfy the indifferent and even some of those concerned.

Moreover, the idea of a Jewish colony where the unwanted refugees could be settled was both familiar and attractive. The French press and public as well as the administration had discussed a number of possible overseas settlements, such as the abortive Madagascar project, before the war and even since the armistice. More to the point, the French government had been actively seeking German cooperation since 1938 in easing the refugee burden, whether by persuading the Germans to cease their expulsions or by some kind of international Jewish settlement project. This is what Foreign Minister Georges Bonnet had talked to Ribbentrop about when the German foreign minister visited Paris in November 1938. After the Germans had dumped over six thousand Jews from Baden and the Palatinate into France in November 1940, the Vichy regime had implored them to take the refugees back. When the German government suddenly announced plans in the summer of 1942 to take them back, it was almost too good to be true. Laval told some American visitors in August 1942 that "the French government was glad that a change in German attitude toward [the foreign Jews] gave France an opportunity to get rid of them." Laval's breathtaking avowal is comprehensible only if we peel away successive layers of experience and knowledge and restore, in a kind of archaeology of consciousness, the commonplace attitudes formed during the refugee crisis of 1938–41.

The Vichy leaders were intellectually and emotionally prepared, therefore, to accept the German explanations as normal—even welcome. Some officials even added glosses of their own. Pierre Huguet, intendant of police in Limoges, issued instructions for the roundups in August 1942 telling Jews that they would be taken to central Europe, to Galicia (in reality, it was Upper Silesia) "where the German authorities intend to set up a great Jewish colony." The operation was to be described as an "ethnic reclassification."[37]

Pierre Laval took pains to validate this reassuring and familiar version of events. At lunch with General Karl Oberg, the Höhere SS- and Polizeiführer in France, on 2 September 1942, Laval reported that several foreign diplomats had questioned him about the transports of Jews leaving the Unoccupied Zone. Laval said he had told them that the convoys were going to southern Poland, but he wanted a conventional response *(Sprachregelung)* to avoid possible conflict with the Germans' version. Oberg's assistant recorded what the French were supposed to say:

> It was agreed that in the future President Laval would reply to such questions by saying that the Jews from the Unoccupied Zone

handed over to the occupation authorities were deported to the Gouvernement General [i.e. Poland] to be put to work.[38]

The French police contributed to these fictions by adopting the Germans' blank formula in response to inquiries: "an unknown destination."[39] At this crucial moment, when the mass deportations had just been extended to the Unoccupied Zone where they had provoked the first important outcry against a Vichy policy, it is not hard to believe that Laval was trying to get his alibi straight.

The very conditions of the departure, obvious to anyone who saw them and fully reported to the authorities in Vichy, ought to have aroused skepticism about the official French and German tales of work colonies for Jews in the east. As long as the deportation convoys were made up of healthy men of working age, even internees like Georges Wellers awaiting their departure from Drancy could cling to the hope that forced labor in the east was "to be sure, a worrisome aggravation, but one that only affected the most hardy of the internees, able-bodied adult men."[40] That illusion was shattered from the time of the third convoy, on 22 June 1942, when women began to be included, sometimes reaching more than half of those on board. Then, from 5 August, the shipments periodically comprised children below fifteen. The papal nuncio in France wrote the Vatican secretary of state on 7 August that people did not believe the official version. The fact that the destination was not Germany but Poland, and the fact that the deportees included the sick and the aged "excludes the design of using them for work." All this, reported Monsignor Valerio Valeri, was producing much uneasiness *(malumore)* in the French population.[41]

Like other observers, the Jewish leaders knew that work colonies were not built by the weak or the unfit. At the end of August 1942, the Consistoire Central des Israélites de France, the traditional governing body of French Judaism, made a desperate appeal to Laval which drew upon the reports already reaching the West:

It has been established and confirmed by the most exact information that hundreds of thousands of Israelites have been murdered in Eastern Europe or have died there after horrible suffering from ill treatment. . . . The government does not want the Jews for labor but for the clear purpose of exterminating them pitilessly and methodically.[42]*

*Even as late as fall 1943, however, the Consistoire was still trying to verify the existence of gas chambers and a plan of total extermination.[43]

Rabbi Kaplan spoke of "exterminations" in a conversation with Cardinal Gerlier on 17 August 1942.[44] The French minister in Bucharest reported to Laval the same day that deportations were taking place there under conditions "few could survive."[45] The Protestant leader Marc Boegner, a number of Catholic prelates, American refugee relief workers, and the U.S. envoy Pinkney Tuck all drew French leaders' attention to the situation of the Jews in France. Pastor Boegner described the character of the deportation itself to Marshal Pétain in a letter on 20 August:

> The "handing over" of these unfortunate foreigners happens in many places under inhumane conditions which have aroused the most hardened consciences and brought tears to the eyes of witnesses. Crammed into freight cars without any concern for hygiene, the foreigners designated for departure were treated like cattle.[46]

Boegner saw Laval on 9 September and repeated what he had heard about killings. Laval, however, stuck to the tale agreed upon with Oberg a week before: the Jews were building an agricultural colony. "I talked to him about murder," Boegner recalled after the war; "he answered me with gardening."[47]

After the summer of 1942, then, the Vichy leaders had a picture of the unfolding catastrophe of the Jews which was no more complete than that of other western governments or of Jewish leaders. There remained uncertainty about the precise conditions that prevailed in the camps of eastern Europe to which the Jews of France were being deported. That uncertainty had not been fully dispelled even in 1943. The Vichy leaders' information was no less complete, however, than that of other governments. If anything, they had more concrete details than had anyone else of the atrocious manner in which the deportees were transported from France. The conditions of the voyage itself meant death for many of the victims. Even the Germans' euphemistic version of deportation meant that many would die. The conditions of the departure in themselves—the subject of the remonstrances by Boegner and others whom we have cited—were reason enough for official French opposition. Instead, the Vichy leaders continued to regard the deportations as merely the next phase of the refugee crisis. If the details were ugly, that was not sufficient reason, in their eyes, to allow this secondary matter to trouble Franco-German relations.

Through 1943, as unbelief slowly was eroding among sections of the French population, Vichy's leaders must have heard more of the occasional rumors that circulated about the murders in the east. But pressure upon Laval abated after the protests about deportations in the summer and autumn of 1942. Ministers now said as little about Jews as possible. More and more, French officials could hide behind German explanations. If private perceptions were any clearer at Vichy, leaders kept the terrible secret to themselves.

A Comparative View

The proportion of Jews killed varied enormously from one part of German-dominated Europe to another, from the nearly complete survival of the Jews of Denmark to the nearly complete disappearance of the Jews of Germany, the Baltic countries, Poland, and Czechoslovakia. It is far from simple, however, to draw conclusions from a comparison of raw statistics. For one runs the risk of comparing the incomparable. No two situations were the same. It is sometimes claimed, for example, that the celebrated rescue of Danish Jewry proves that an alternative policy was available to the Vichy government, that similar resolute action by French authorities could have saved thousands of Jews from the deportation trains. But fewer than 8,000 Jews lived in Denmark when the Nazis decided in September 1943 to deport them, thanks partly to a much more stringent exclusion of Jewish refugees during the 1930s from Denmark than from France. Within easy reach of neutral Sweden, which was ready to accept the Jewish fugitives, the determined Danish rescuers could evacuate Jews by sea almost overnight. By that time, moreover, the dimmed prospects of ultimate German victory encouraged resistance to the Final Solution. It does not belittle the Danish achievement to observe that circumstances were far more favorable in Denmark than in France.

As the Danish case makes clear, sheer numbers could be important. France's Jews were far too numerous to spirit across the Swiss or the Spanish frontiers, or across the Channel to Britain, even assuming those countries would have accepted them. Although the Jews composed considerably less than 1 percent of France's wartime population of 42,-000,000, her Jewish population of about 300,000 was larger than that of any other country of western Europe, occupied by the Germans or not. Our study, indeed, focuses upon the period after which the center of gravity of the European Jewish community shifted to France, which plays today the role toward which she was moving during the 1930s of housing the largest Jewish minority in Europe.

It has been suggested that terrain and dispersal offered important possibilities for Jews to escape, and that, in this respect, France was far more favored than flat, more densely settled countries like Belgium and Holland. In the highly urbanized Netherlands, two thirds of that country's 140,000 Jews were concentrated in Amsterdam, and there were no forested mountains to which they could flee. Dutch Jews, concludes Raul Hilberg, were caught in a "natural trap."[48] In France, by contrast, the scattering of Jews during the débâcle of 1940 helped keep them out of the clutches of German and French police. Vichy further facilitated the dispersal of Jews, in sharp contrast to the ghettoization policies of occupied eastern Europe; but Vichy's was a punitive policy, hardly designed to make life easier for the Jews. Those saved by dispersal owe nothing to the French authorities, who tried to make up for it with their censuses, card files, and specially stamped ID cards. Geography did on occasion aid those in hiding. The few thousand Jews who found themselves in the wild and mountainous Dordogne, for example (including a substantial proportion of the Jewish community of Strasbourg), had a much higher survival rate than those in the rest of the country. Although Jews constituted a high proportion of hostages shot in the Dordogne for various reasons, there were apparently only seventy-nine deportations for "racial" reasons from the entire department.[49]

Generally speaking, however, such factors were not decisive when the cards were stacked against the Jews for other reasons. A remote and inaccessible countryside did not save the Yugoslav Jews, over 80 percent of whom were killed. Small numbers did not protect about one half of the Jewish population of 2,000 in Norway from deportation, despite a thousand-mile frontier with Sweden and the protest resignation of several prominent members of the Norwegian collaborationist Vidkun Quisling's party when the deportations began.

In the last analysis, what governed the scale of the killings was the degree to which the Germans were able to apply their power. The massacre was most complete and extensive in Germany itself, in Poland, and in the territories conquered from Russia. It was after the deposition of Mussolini and the direct occupation of Italy by German forces that the mass deportations of Italian Jews began, in September–October 1943; these eventually took about 16 percent of Italy's 45,000 Jews. Similarly, large numbers of Hungarian Jews were deported to their deaths only beginning in May 1944, after Admiral Miklós Horthy's Hungary first came under direct German military occupation. Both

Rumania and Bulgaria held off German demands to mesh their Jewish policies with that of the Reich, although both nations dealt even more harshly than France with Jews in newly conquered territories. The Nazis could rely on puppet regimes like those in Croatia or Slovakia, and the obstacles they encountered there were largely technical. In Holland, ruled directly by a *Reichskommissar,* the Germans seized control of the civil administration in 1940, providing no leeway for local authorities in Jewish matters. In Denmark, by contrast, the monarchy and the indigenous administration were permitted to function as a result of its concessions to Germany, and preserved a wide discretion in the area of policy toward the Jews.

France fitted none of these patterns, due to the unique terms of the armistice of 1940, by which the French government maintained significant attributes of sovereignty while the victors occupied only a portion of the country. To Dutchmen who fled to France from the Netherlands in 1940, for example, France seemed remarkably free—an impression that encouraged the Zionist underground in Holland to smuggle Jews to French territory.[50] Even in the Occupied Zone, German reliance upon indigenous French administration imposed limitations upon German power greater than those in any other directly occupied country in western or northern Europe.* While France had less autonomy than Germany's allies, such as Hungary or Italy, she enjoyed more autonomy than states administered directly by the Germans, such as Holland, or those with Nazi-imposed local rulers, such as Norway.

Not that the Germans attempted to impose the same policy everywhere, uniform in both space and time. We have shown that in 1940 the German authorities—a few marginal intellectuals like Dr. Friedrich Grimm aside—had no interest in getting unoccupied France to adopt their anti-Jewish policies. On the contrary, the Germans tried in 1940 to use France as a dumping ground for German Jewish refugees; in Nazi eyes, to be allowed to join Germany among the *judenfrei* peoples was too good a' fate for the defeated and racially inferior French. At this early stage, even Hitler's allies were not pressed to imitate the Nuremberg Laws, although it no doubt helped create good will in party circles when Italy, Hungary, Croatia, and Slovakia did so. German pressures were always greater in areas close to real or potential military fronts—along the Channel and North Sea coasts in 1940, on the eastern front

---

*A study by Dr. Werner Best in August–September 1941 showed that 2,898 German civilian personnel were assigned to occupied France, 3,192 to Holland, and 18,724 to Bohemia-Moravia. Citing Freiherr von Stein's maxim "govern little" *(wenig zu regieren),* Best advocated letting occupied countries administer themselves as fully as possible.[51]

after July 1941, and along the Mediterranean coast after November 1942, when the Allies had reached North Africa. The Nazis showed a pathological dread of Jewish concentrations near German armies' operating areas. When extermination fully replaced emigration in German policy, and Germany faced war on multiple fronts, the Nazis tried to impose their aims on a far wider area.

The areas where the Nazis could best apply their will varied considerably with time and the course of the war. If the war had somehow ended suddenly in April 1944, France would have fared much more poorly in the comparisons, and Hungary would be able to claim among the fewest Jewish dead. And had the war in Europe continued for a year or so beyond May 1945, the remaining Jews in all occupied areas would probably have been killed, giving us yet another comparative ranking. The course of the war, and the changing opportunities it gave the RSHA to work its' will under the umbrella of German power, had more to do with the final totals than matters of structure—terrain, dispersal, size of the Jewish population—or local attitudes. The more we contemplate the game of statistical comparisons, the less we feel the raw totals reveal without careful study of local conditions.

Although the Nazis' capacity to work their will was the paramount determinant of the Jews' fate in Europe, it is still important to determine how German force meshed or clashed with indigenous policies concerning Jews. It was extremely rare—the Danish case is the only example—for local forces to thwart a determined German effort. A nearly total absence of Dutch popular support for anti-Jewish measures, and the demonstrations in the Netherlands against them in February 1941[52]—a far bolder act of public resistance to antisemitism than anything known in France—could not save the Jews of Holland. On the other hand, indigenous policies could facilitate the Germans' efforts, or impede them, to some degree. How much did local anti-Jewish activities, such as those of Vichy France, help the RSHA to do its work? How did Vichy compare with other governments in this respect?

Comparison obliges us to look in unaccustomed directions. France was altogether unique among occupied western European nations in having adopted indigenous antisemitic policies. No other occupied country in western Europe took even the most tentative step in this direction on its own; although, to be sure, few of them, including Norway or Denmark, had sufficient autonomy to have done so had they wished. Some of Hitler's allies, however—Hungary and Italy in 1938, and Rumania in 1940, but not Spain or Portugal, which remained neutral—adopted their own antisemitic measures. Pétain thus had more in common, with respect to anti-Jewish measures, with Horthy and Antonescu than with Franco and Salazar.* It is thus to Hungary and Rumania that we must turn for closer comparison.

The three countries were certainly not identical; France was Germany's defeated enemy, while Hungary and Rumania were allies. Part of French territory was subjected to an army of occupation in June 1940, and all of it after November 1942; some German divisions were stationed in Rumania by mutual consent in October 1940; but Hungary received only occasional transient German troops until March 1944. Rumania had a far more virulent antisemitic tradition than had France; and even comparatively tolerant Hungary had turned against its Jewish middle class in 1919–20. These countries came after only Poland and Lithuania in the size and urban-commercial-professional concentration of their Jewish minorities: 5.1 percent of the Hungarian population was Jewish, with 34.4 percent of the doctors and 49.2 percent of the lawyers; 4 percent to 5 percent of the Rumanian population was Jewish, with 14.3 percent of the overall urban population and up to nearly half the town populations in Czernowitz, in Bukovina.[53] The Jewish population of France never exceeded 1 percent between the wars. The authoritarian-nationalist regime of Hungary had already imposed a *numerus clausus* in 1921; and Rumania, though officially proclaiming its Latin kinship with France between the wars, was a country where violence against Jews was winked at, and where the most successful antisemitic party outside Germany and Austria won 15.5 percent of the vote and became the third largest party in the kingdom in December 1937. The France of the Third Republic, by contrast, penalized its antisemitic minority, and so little discrimination was permitted in public life that Jews were not even identified as such in the French vital statistics—an obstacle about which the German police complained after 1940.[54]

Despite these disparities, however, the general lineaments of the three countries' anti-Jewish policies had much in common. Antisemitism was greatly sharpened by defeat in all three—in Hungary in 1919, in France in June 1940, and in Rumania by the loss of two thirds of her territory to Hungary and Russia in summer and fall 1940. In all three countries, leaders lent their considerable authority to native anti-Jewish measures that owed more to religious and cultural protectionism than to Nazi racialism. These leaders believed they were working in the

*Throughout the period of the Final Solution, Rumania was ruled by the military dictatorship of Marshal Ion Antonescu who effectively seized full control in January 1941; Portugal was in the hands of Antonio de Oliveira Salazar, who had ruled since 1928.

national interest, and all hoped that the Germans would be sufficiently impressed with their domestic anti-Jewish measures to leave them to their own devices. All distanced themselves from the German Final Solution when it began in 1942, and made some attempt to protect their own Jewish nationals. The Germans were in a position to blackmail each leader by threatening to replace him with a more radical rival—Doriot (the most powerful contender on the extreme Right in France), the Iron Guard (the Rumanian fascists), the Arrow Cross (their Hungarian equivalent). All three regimes carried out unprecedented spoliations and contributed directly to the deaths of large numbers of Jews. So let our comparison proceed.

The indigenous anti-Jewish legislation of these three countries bore a family resemblance. All shared an economic and cultural protectionism that sought to preserve more places in a shrinking economy for the dominant national group, to expel those minorities deemed unassimilable, and to hasten the assimilation of the rest in the name of cultural homogeneity. Admiral Horthy led the way in Hungary in 1938 with a law limiting Jews to 20 percent of the professions and private businesses and abridging certain property rights; he narrowed these restrictions drastically in 1939 to 6 percent and 12 percent, respectively, and added absolute prohibitions upon state service and influential cultural posts such as publishing and theater directing.[55] In Rumania, continuing the anti-Jewish campaign of his predecessors, General Antonescu enacted a mass of similar legislation during the six months after inheriting in September 1940 the shrunken remnant of the nation from the discredited King Carol.[56] Vichy's legislation was no less harsh, though each regime had its own national priorities. In agrarian Rumania, Jewish landowning was prohibited early (4 October 1940); although Vichy banned absentee Jewish landowning in late 1941. On 8 March 1941, Antonescu excluded Jews from teaching; while Pétain had seen to that in the first *Statut des juifs* on 3 October 1940. During 1941, both Rumania and Hungary imposed harsh labor service on Jews—a plan that Laval only discussed in 1943. Also, in 1941, Hungary copied the German Nuremberg laws forbidding intermarriage—a move that no French official, not even Darquier, dared to make.[57] On the other hand, Vichy's definition of a Jew spread the net wider than the others did—even wider than the Germans' own ordinances in Occupied France and than the laws of the same period in Hungary and Slovakia.[58]* If the Vichy regime had adopted, say, the Hungarian definition of Jewishness (those

*Both Hungary and Slovakia later tightened their definitions beyond a strictly religious criterion.

practicing the Jewish religion and their children, excluding veterans and those converted before 1919), the effect of its *Statuts des juifs* would have been considerably reduced.

All three regimes also made some efforts to protect their own Jewish nationals from the Final Solution, and all three were accused by the Nazis of "a policy of obstruction."[59] Contrary to what prior French tradition would lead us to expect, Marshal Pétain comes out less energetic than Admiral Horthy in these efforts. Apart from one incident in 1941 when Hungary expelled 11,000 to 18,000 foreign refugees into newly occupied Galicia—an episode in the battle over refugees rather than in the Final Solution—Horthy's regime handed over no Jews to the Germans until after German occupation forces arrived on 22 March 1944, nearly two years after Vichy had begun delivering Jews to the Germans from its Unoccupied Zone. Soon after huge mass deportations began in May 1944, Horthy responded to clerical and humanitarian protests and rescinded his agreement in early July. Deportations did not begin again until he had been removed from power, and the Arrow Cross had a free hand under Ferenc Szálasi in October 1944. They doomed about half of Hungary's pre-1940 Jewish population of 400,000 and an overwhelming proportion of the 250,000 Jews in those portions of Transylvania allocated to Hungary by the German-sponsored Vienna Award of 30 August 1940.* That toll was of course heavier than France's 75,000, or one-quarter of its Jews; but it was achieved by a great concentration of German force in 1944. Whether the Germans could or would have employed a comparable force simultaneously in a western European area in 1944 is open to question, and what a similarly vigorous obstruction by Pétain might have achieved in the west can only be imagined.

Antonescu's record in protecting some of Rumanian Jewry from the Final Solution was not so much worse than Pétain's as one would expect, considering the rest of the Rumanian antisemitic record. Rumania stood out as the one European state in addition to Germany that practiced outright extermination on its own, at least in the territories it conquered from the Russians after June 1941. When Rumanian armies cooperated with the Germans in the invasion of the Soviet Union, the Jews of reconquered Bessarabia and Northern Bukovina were herded into camps or ghettos or moved farther east across the Dienster (Transnistria). Almost all 250,000 of them died of forced labor, poor conditions, or simple execution by German or Rumanian *Einsatzkom-*

---

*The statistics in Hilberg remain generally accepted today. See also Nora Levin's and Lucy Dawidowicz's statistical appendices.[60]

mandos.[61] And yet Antonescu blocked the deportation of Jews from the *Regat,* the heartland of the country. Furthermore, he moved against the trend in his relations with the racialist extremists of Rumania, led by the Iron Guard. Although he had assumed power jointly with the Iron Guard in September 1940, he turned against the Guard in January 1941 after it had embarked on a rampage of looting and killing Jews and other "enemies." With German acquiescence, he expelled the Guard from the government and curbed it in a bloody repression. He thereby proved to anyone who wanted to observe that Hitler basically preferred order to ideological fervor in his satellites, and the satellites were less threatened by blackmail from home-grown Nazis than they seem to have feared. When the Final Solution began, Antonescu obstructed deportation from the *Regat,* even though the Iron Guard chief Horia Sima remained in reserve in Berlin. Antonescu made repeated attempts to persuade the Germans to authorize the departure of Jews for Palestine and Syria. The Germans evidently found it too troublesome or expensive to do the work themselves. In the end, most of the 300,000 assimilated Jews in the country's core survived.[62]

Vichy's efforts to afford some protection to native French Jews were thus less vigorous than those of Horthy, and neither more vigorous nor more effective than those of Antonescu insofar as the Rumanian heartland was concerned. The course of the war determined that life chances were better for Jews in France than in either Hungary or Rumania, but it is hard to attribute much credit for that to the Pétain regime itself. The regime began by adopting, on its own initiative, a wide-ranging program of legal disabilities and property spoliations and imposing them on Jews more broadly defined than those of German satellites at the time. It interned thousands of foreign Jews in camps whose conditions, as we have seen, were more primitive than those of the Nazi concentration camps of the 1930s. The first Jewish victims of the Holocaust in France died on *French* soil. Serge Klarsfeld has collected from departmental and prefectoral archives the names of more than two thousand Jews who died in French camps, and the total is probably closer to three thousand.[63]

When the Final Solution began, the Vichy regime volunteered to round up and hand over to the Germans foreign Jews from the Unoccupied Zone of France. This step puts Vichy France among very limited company indeed. Only one other regime in all Europe delivered up numbers of Jews to the Germans from outside the area of direct German military occupation: Bulgaria, which systematically deported the Jews of newly conquered Macedonia and Thrace into German hands, though it refused to deport Jews of the old kingdom's territory.[64]*

These cases remind us how central was the distinction between native and foreign Jews in shaping anti-Jewish policies of the allied or occupied states. Wherever there were large numbers of alien or refugee Jews, allied or occupied governments could be found who were more than willing to get rid of them. This was especially true among peoples who felt insecure or threatened, or who were attempting to reseat their authority and revive their culture in disputed borderlands. We have alluded to the efforts of Rumania to eliminate Jews from the newly reconquered regions of Bessarabia and Northern Bukovina. Non-Magyarized Jews of Galicia and the Serbian city of Novi Sad suffered at the hands of the Hungarians. The Bulgarians willingly delivered up to German deportation the Jews of newly conquered Macedonia and Thrace. Foreign Jews who had found refuge in Holland or Belgium during the 1930s were more vulnerable than native-born Jews, for the former enjoyed less protection from neighbors and public officials—sometimes, indeed, suffering their hostility. Only the Italians and Danes broke this general rule. The Italians defended foreign Jews as well as Italian nationals, not only in their own country but also in France, Tunisia, Croatia, and Greece. These refreshing contrasts have much to do with the tiny, relatively homogeneous, and highly assimilated Jewish communities of Italy and Denmark. There were only about 1,500 Jewish refugees in the latter, and most Danes had probably never heard of them.[66]

Whereas foreign Jews averaged about 25 percent of the total number of Jews in western Europe in general, according to Hilberg,[67] they constituted no less than half of the Jews in France. It is true that far fewer foreign Jews entered France during the 1930s than many observers believed at the time; often the "aliens" had been in France for decades and remained alien simply because the French considered them such. But France received well over 300,000 refugees from central Europe during the 1930s—far more than any other country, including the United States, which let in 136,000.† Moreover, the French government was one of the few anywhere that spent public funds on refugees during the interwar period.[68] The backlash after 1940 was thus all the more severe.

We have discussed the 1930s refugee crisis here at length because

---

*Cf. also Hungary's expulsion of foreign Jewish refugees into Galicia in fall 1941, which should be seen in terms of the struggle over who would accept refugees. It was the Germans who put a stop to this move. Rumanian expulsions of Jews from Transnistria during 1942 may be viewed in the same context.[65]

†Many of the refugees who reached France left the country soon after their arrival.

we felt it essential if one is to understand the general loss of tolerance for foreigners and the more specific antisemitism of the 1940s. No country had a good record with the refugees of the 1930s or with suspicious minorities after the war began. For all its vast open spaces, Canada managed to admit only a handful of Jewish refugees before September 1939.[69] After the Japanese attack upon Pearl Harbor in December 1941 brought the United States into the war, the American authorities rounded up all the Japanese of the Pacific coast states of California, Oregon, and Washington—120,000 of them, some of them settled there for two generations—and put them into camps. Their property was sold for a fraction of its peacetime worth. The Canadian government did the same with its Japanese residents. In September 1939, on the outbreak of the war in Europe, the British government, like the French, interned all holders of German or Austrian passports even though most of those interned were Jewish refugees. Thus, the Vichy regime embarked after 1940 on a path already well trodden by most of the countries of the world when confronted by masses of foreigners under conditions distorted by depression and war. Vichy went farther than most, however, for the refugees were already inside the country, not at the gates. And tragically, their measures dovetailed with the more murderous enterprise of Nazi Germany.

The Vichy leaders wanted to get rid of the Jews of France. Left to themselves—at least up to the time of Darquier—they would not have killed them. They would accept those Jews who were willing to renounce all trace of cultural distinction and to disappear into the dominant nationality, provided they had proven their fitness by many generations of residence and military service, and subject to certain restrictions on careers and professions. Jews who persisted in difference, or rank newcomers, would be sent to some appropriate overseas settlement when the international situation permitted it. The refusal of other countries, such as the United States and Switzerland, to accept large numbers of refugees had already made the re-emigration of foreign Jews from France more difficult before 1940. The spread of war after 1940 made it nearly impossible. And although the Vichy government officially encouraged emigration of Jews, muddle, vindictiveness, and red tape prevented even some who had visas for North or South America from getting out. Emigration—the official goal of both the late Third Republic and the early years of Vichy—was simply not practicable after 1940.

Locked in with its unwanted refugees, the Vichy regime set out to reduce the Jews—all Jews, not merely immigrants or refugees—to a subservient role, to strip them of their property, and to subject them to humiliating restrictions. The nightmare of old assimilated French Jewry had come true: what was perceived as an uncontrollable flood of exotic oriental Jews had compromised the position of them all.

It is striking with what alacrity the Vichy regime, enjoying more popular support at the beginning than had most preceding French governments, deliberately adopted an anti-Jewish policy after the defeat of 1940. We hope there is no longer any possible confusion about the German role in launching that policy. We can find no trace of German attempts to extend their own anti-Jewish policy to the Unoccupied Zone in the summer of 1940; at the beginning, they envisaged France as a dumping ground for their own refugees. Vichy anti-Jewish policy was thus not only autonomous from German policy; it was a rival to it. Vichy struggled with the occupying authority in an attempt to assert its own sovereignty in anti-Jewish matters, and to keep the advantages of property confiscations and refugee control for itself.

Vichy's antisemitism was not merely pre-emptive, however. It was part of a larger national effort to replace with homogeneity the enfeebling disunities of the 1930s. French political cultures from Left to Right —from Jacobinism to integral nationalism—have traditionally perceived cultural pluralism as dangerous. After the defeat of 1940, the things that had divided Frenchmen in the 1930s—class, politics, alien people, and doctrines—seemed almost fatal. Vichy leaders set about to restore the homogeneity that they imagined to have been the traditional state of France (notwithstanding a simultaneous interest in restoring regional cultures, within limits), and to whose loss in the twentieth century they attributed their military defeat. They proposed to submerge class conflict in corporatism; they proposed to replace squabbling politics with obedience and hierarchy. And as for aliens and outsiders, they proposed to put an end to the easy cosmopolitan hospitality of the Third Republic. Jews were not the only outsiders troubled. Gypsies were rounded up and interned, often under harsh conditions.* The Spanish refugees in the southwest of France aroused considerable popular hostility,[71] and a plan was afoot to send as many of them as possible to Mexico. It was not a happy time to be different in France.

Traditional French antisemitism by itself does not explain what happened. Antisemitic outbursts have not been more frequent in the full sweep of French history than in other national histories, nor have

---

*See the reports of Prefect André Jean-Faure on the "nomad" camps of Poitiers, Jargeau (Loiret), and Saliers (Bouches-du-Rhône) and his hopes for the nomads' "stabilization."[70]

the possibilities for Jewish acceptance and success been more limited in France than elsewhere. It is true that antisemitism became much more virulent during the 1930s in France than before. The readiness to blame Jews for the defeat in 1940 clearly had its preparation in widespread readiness in the 1930s to blame Jews for unemployment, for the threat of war, and for the dilution of French culture. Beyond the circle of active antisemites lay a broader circle that felt antipathy for foreigners in general and acquiesced in Vichy's anti-Jewish measures, or at least remained indifferent to them. The refugee problem of the 1930s had spread these antipathies widely in the administration and in the public at large. The backlash against the refugees could spread so far beyond the narrow circle of active antisemites because it drew upon an element of the republican tradition, the doctrine of assimilation.

The French doctrine of assimilation had its positive face. French language and values were deemed universal and open to all who wanted to acquire them. In a tradition leading from the honorary citizens of the 1790s through hospitality to exiles in much of the nineteenth century to warm receptivity to French-speaking African intellectuals such as Leopold Sedor Senghor in the twentieth century, French assimilationism opened the gates to anyone who wanted to be accepted. Michel Debré has written recently that a nation-state with a powerful drive for assimilation, like France, is less susceptible to racism than pluralist federations which allow multiple languages and cultures to persist.[72] In tranquil times, he may well be right. In times of crisis, however, when the national lifeboat seems ready to be swamped by a mass of exotic outsiders, the requirement of cultural assimilation can cut the other way. Difference seemed a threat after 1940; pluralism, a form of weakness. At such times, woe to Jews or gypsies or other peoples refractory to assimilation. Deliberate, obstinate, provocative difference then seems not merely a rejection, but a menace.

The comparative leniency of the Vichy regime toward blacks makes an instructive comparison. Unlike the American melting pot, French assimilationism has tended to test its aspirants by purely intellectual criteria: a willingness to submerge one's cultural identity totally in being French. Assimilated blacks in small numbers have always been more readily accepted in France than in the Anglo-Saxon countries. The Vichy regime even had a black cabinet minister, the Martinique lawyer Henri Lémery, a friend of Marshal Pétain since 1934, who served as minister of colonies until September 1940. There was no longer room, of course, for Senegalese troops in the tiny army permitted France under the armistice.[73] The Vichy regime also enforced German requirements forbidding "colored persons" *(gens de couleur)* from crossing the Demarcation Line into the Occupied Zone, and imposing other limitations upon blacks there, as the black deputy and member of the regime's National Council Gratien Candace complained;[74] but Vichy added no restrictions of its own upon blacks in the Unoccupied Zone, in sharp distinction to its autonomous measures against Jews. Gypsies, those irreducible outsiders, were shut up in camps to be "stabilized." It was the Jews who had always been the traditional targets when difference came to seem threatening in France, and they suffered more than any other identifiable group from the nativist outburst of 1940.

Not that the public clamored for anti-Jewish measures in the summer of 1940. The public was too stunned to do more than look up out of the abyss for leadership. A few convinced antisemites like Raphael Alibert and Xavier Vallat seized that leadership. From positions close to the center of power at Vichy, they gave legitimacy to suspicions that Jews had played a substantial role in the degradation of France, and set up machinery to penalize them. These antisemitic activists were nationalists and hostile to Germany. They disliked Nazism and felt no kinship with the biological racism of the Third Reich. While their overt supporters may never have formed a majority in Vichy France, they were left exceptional freedom by the discredit of the Third Republic values, by the disarray of the first months after defeat, by a general acquiescence in whatever was covered by the authority of Marshal Pétain, and by the widespread dislike and suspicion of foreigners in general and of Jews in particular that had spread during the 1930s.

What added to the persuasiveness of men like Alibert and Vallat was the bargaining advantage that persecution of the Jews seemed likely to afford the hard-pressed Vichy regime. In what proved to be a colossal miscalculation, the Vichy leader assumed that the German authorities would be grateful to the French for pursuing a parallel anti-Jewish policy, and would respond by yielding greater authority to France over this and other spheres of national activity. In reality, the Germans wanted something quite different. At first, they wanted to evacuate large numbers of German Jews to France. Later, they engaged in a subtle form of entrapment. They relieved themselves of much of the trouble of their own racial policy and, by exploiting Vichy's desire to regain control over administration in the Occupied Zone, nudged the French ever deeper into measures against the Jews. Even when these measures aroused private reservations among Vichy ministers and administrators, there was no open dissent from within, no systematic refusal to apply any of the new laws; there were at most a few quiet exceptions in favor of the well-connected. Once the direction of policy had been set by Laval or Darlan, the prestigious mantle of Marshal Pétain and the pulls of administrative unity, duty in times of national peril, and sheer routine turned the machinery of government implacably against the Jews.

The subsequent horrors of the Final Solution have tended to obscure the autonomous French anti-Jewish project of 1940–42. The measures of those first two years had catastrophic effects upon the Jews of France. Snapping the material links that bound Jews to French society, Vichy confiscated their property through aryanization, dismissed them from government service, excluded them from professions and higher education. Thousands of productive French Jews were thus turned into refugees, who swelled the ranks of those already uprooted by other states, and who offered self-fulfilling validation of the popular animus against "parasites." Vichy also snapped the legal links that normally offered protection to citizens and visitors. Officials entrusted with upholding constitutional guarantees deprived a segment of French citizenry of them, owing to circumstances of ancestry rather than for anything individuals had done. The way was open for legal disabilities without limit in the name of administrative convenience or the rulers' taste. Finally, Vichy snapped the links of moral solidarity among peoples. Even though he never pronounced the word "Jew" in a public statement, Marshal Pétain lent his immense prestige implicitly to a systematic propaganda of collective denigration. Two years of government measures that linked national revival to antisemitism dulled the consciences of many French people toward a group officially blamed for everything from high prices to the defeat. The first two years of Vichy made it hard to see Jews as victims rather than as problems.

When the Germans began their systematic deportation and extermination of Jews in 1942, Vichy's rival antisemitism offered them more substantial help than they received anywhere else in western Europe, and more even than they received from such allies as Hungary and Rumania. Having begged the Germans for years to take back their refugees, the Vichy leaders offered to dispatch foreign Jews from unoccupied areas—something that Bulgaria alone, in eastern Europe, did on a similar scale. They had already accumulated large numbers of foreign Jews in internment camps and labor battalions. They had systematically enumerated and identified the Jews of the Unoccupied Zone as well as the Occupied Zone, devoting the best of their new perforated-card statistical technology to the purpose,[75] and setting up elaborate file systems that simplified the task of the SS and the French police who did the work of rounding up Jews for deportation. After December 1942, they marked the ID and ration cards of all Jews—citizens as well as refugees—with a large *Juif* or *Juive,* thus exposing all of them to the increasingly haphazard raids of the SS. The CGQJ, an organ of the French government, performed much of the administrative routine that elsewhere was forced upon the Jewish councils or *Judenräte.* The French police were indispensable. As SS-General Oberg wrote to French Police Chief Bousquet on July 1942, as the two police services solidified their agreement to work together, "I am happy to confirm, moreover, that the French police has up to now performed in a manner worthy of appreciation."[76] The Germans could never have accomplished as much on their own.

Were there reasonable alternatives? Vichy's supporters contend that outright refusal in this matter that engaged the Nazis' emotions so deeply would have precipitated "the worst": the Germans would have turned France over to right-wing fanatics from Paris, so goes this argument, and the Nazis would have become even more directly involved in arrests and deportations. As to the first point, the evidence suggests simply that Vichy miscalculated. Throughout Europe the Germans wisely preferred conservative and nationalist leaders to fascist adventurers. The Nazis knew that the satellite fascists would further drain the Reich's resources by plunging their countries into chaos, civil war, and expansionism. Moderating his own fanaticism with shrewd calculation, Hitler could be sensitive to political limits. In his midnight harangues at the dinner table, he talked of grandiose schemes of ridding the world of Jews; in the sober light of morning he drew back until worsening war situations seemed to demand complete control. The Germans did not expend much effort to bring the Italians into line on the Jewish question, for example, despite the Italians' open sabotage of the Final Solution.[77] In Finland, a much weaker ally, government resistance to deportation policy withstood the menaces of Heinrich Himmler and the presence of a powerful German army. In the end, the Finnish Jews were not deported.[78] Horthy withheld Jews from deportation in Hungary until 1944; and Antonescu, who had successfully turned against the main native pro-Nazi party in 1941, refused the deportation of the Jews from the heartland of Rumania—whatever his barbarities toward the Jews of the reconquered provinces. Stunned by the débâcle, however, Vichy failed to appreciate the limits of German power. With France, the German bluff worked admirably. In the same way, Vichy misjudged the capacity of the Germans to move against Jews on their own. Given the shortages of German manpower in the west, without the exertions of the French police and administration, the Germans would have had to withdraw substantial forces from military uses in order to have sent an equivalent number of Jews to the east by themselves.

A number of modest acts would have obstructed the deportation of Jews in 1942 even without raising any major confrontation with the Germans over police cooperation or otherwise troubling the basic policy of collaboration. The camps could have been emptied before the Germans arrived in November 1942. The emigration of foreign Jews— Vichy's declared policy—could have been eased and simplified, and bureaucratic hostility to individual would-be emigrants at the local level eliminated. Above all, the regime might have refrained from stamping Jews' ID and ration cards with the words *Juif* or *Juive*. A large number of Jewish refugees might have been permitted to retreat to North Africa. This last option was excluded by Vichy's keen ear for European opinion in North Africa; the others were excluded by administrative punctilio. None was imaginable in the climate of anti-Jewish feeling deliberately cultivated by the regime.

Some may wonder how three quarters of the Jews of France survived after all. Some native-born French Jews observed all the laws scrupulously, wearing the star in the Occupied Zone, having their cards stamped, shopping only at the specified times, exercising some modest craft without direct dealings with the public, and not hiring anyone. The files of the Vichy anti-Jewish police, the Sections d'Enquête et Contrôle contain a few such cases too modest for even those zealots.[79] Many other Jews benefited by the assistance or complicity of a friend or neighbor—sometimes out of self-interest, sometimes benevolent— who took over a shop or sheltered young people on a farm (where their labor was desperately needed), received family valuables, or offered simply the gift of silence. Jews of French citizenship sometimes benefited from the Vichy government's preference that foreigners go first, though often the SS took anyone who came to hand. The course of the war saved Jews whose departure Vichy had only postponed. As for foreigners, the chance of finding a helpful friend or neighbor was smaller. The possibilities of escape overseas were mainly reserved for the rich, the famous, or the extremely resourceful—and the lucky ones among these. Even Jews who had volunteered for the French army in 1940, and whom the Vichy leaders felt engaged the regime's prestige, could not be exempted by Vichy's feeble efforts. The most fortunate foreigners escaped from French law by holding a favored passport: British or American, of course, or of a British possession such as Egypt, or of one of the states such as Turkey, Italy, or Hungary that refused to let its citizens be deported. Another way of escaping French law was —ironically enough—to escape to a fascist country: into the Italian zone of occupation as long as the Italians were in charge, or across the Pyrenees to Spain or Portugal. The most vulnerable by far, of course, were those who were most unwelcome in France, the refugees from Germany and eastern Europe for whom no one would speak any more; among that last category, the poorest were most vulnerable of all.

In the summer and autumn of 1942, when the French police and administration lent their hands to the task, some 42,500 Jews were deported from France to their deaths—perhaps one third of them at Vichy's initiative from the Unoccupied Zone. When Vichy began to drag its feet in 1943, the number declined to 22,000 sent east in the year 1943. After the last use of French police in January 1944, and despite feverish last-minute German efforts, the number deported up to August 1944 was 12,500. One can only speculate on how many fewer would have perished if the Nazis had been obliged to identify, arrest, and transport without any French assistance every Jew in France whom they wanted to slaughter.

Principal Occupation Authorities Dealing with Jews 1940–44

Reichsminister
Alfred Rosenberg

Minister of Foreign Affairs
of the Reich
Joachim von Ribbentrop

German Ambassador to Paris
Otto Abetz
[rue de Lille]

Consul-General
Rudolf Schleier

Political Section
Dr. Ernst Achenbach

Jewish Questions
SS-Sturmbannführer
Carl Theo Zeitschel

Reichsführer-SS *Heinrich Himmler*

RSHA: SS-Obergruppenführer
Reinhard Heydrich, 1940–42
SS-Obergruppenführer
Ernst Kaltenbrunner, 1943–44

Gestapo: SS-Gruppenführer
Heinrich Müller

IV B 4: SS-Obersturmbannführer
Adolf Eichmann

Higher SS and Police Leader
(HSSPF), 1942–44
SS-Brigadeführer und Generalmajor der Polizei
Karl-Albrecht Oberg

SS-Obersturmbannführer
Helmut Knochen
[72 avenue Foch]

Judenreferat:
[31 bis avenue Foch]
[11 rue des Saussies]

SS-Obersturmführer *Theodor Dannecker*
1940–42
SS-Obersturmführer *Heinz Röthke*
1942–44

SS-Sturmbannführer
Herbert-Martin Hagen
[Bordeaux]

SS-Sturmbannführer
Kurt Lischka

General *Walther von Brauchitsch*,
Army Commander-in-Chief
(OKH) [at Fontainebleau]

Militärbefehlshaber
in Frankreich
(MBF) [at Hôtel Majestic,
avenue Kléber]

Otto von Stülpnagel
1940–42
Karl Heinrich von Stülpnagel
1942–44

Administrative
Headquarters
(Verwaltungsstab): Administrative Director
SS-Brigadeführer *Werner Best*
1940–42

SS and SD representative
(Befehlshaber der Sipo-SD
or BdS):

Einsatzstab
Rosenberg

Geheime Feldpolizei
(GFP)

Economic Section
Dr. Elmar Michel

Jewish Section
Dr. Blanke

List of Abbreviations

Notes

Index

List of Abbreviations

AA   Auswärtiges Amt (German Foreign Office)
AFSC   American Friends Service Committee (Quakers)
AN   Archives nationales, Paris
APP   Archives de la Préfecture de police, Paris
BA   Bundesarchiv, Koblenz
BDC   Berlin Document Center
BdS   Befehlshaber der Sicherheitsdienstes (chief German security official)
CIAF   Commissione italiano de l'armistizia con la Francia
CDJC   Centre de documentation juive contemporaine, Paris
CGQJ   Commissariat- (or, Commissaire-) général aux questions juives
CHDGM   Comité d'histoire de la deuxième guerre mondiale, Paris
CO   Comité d'organisation
DFCAA   Délégation française auprès de la commission allemande d'armistice (French
        Delegation to the German Armistice Commission)
DGFP   Documents on German Foreign Policy
FRUS   Foreign Relations of the United States
GTE   Groupements de travailleurs étrangers
HICEM   International Jewish refugee relief agency
JO   *Journal officiel de la République française* (or, *de l'Etat français*)
JTA   Jewish Telegraphic Agency
JTS   Jewish Theological Seminary, New York
LBI   Leo Baeck Institute, New York
MBF   Militärbefehlshaber in Frankreich (German military authority in France)
ND   Nuremberg Document
PRO   Public Record Office, London
RHDGM   *Revue d'histoire de la deuxième guerre mondiale*
RSHA   Reichssicherheitshauptamt (German security agency)
SCAP   Service de contrôle des administrateurs provisoires
SD   Sicherheitsdienst (German security agency)
SEC   Sections d'enquête et contrôle (special anti-Jewish police of the CGQJ)
T   Microfilm series, U.S. National Archives, Washington
UGIF   Union générale des Israélites de France
VOBIF   *Verordnungsblatt des Militärbefehlshabers in Frankreich* (official journal of the
        German military authority in France)
WL   Wiener Library, London
YIVO   YIVO Institute for Jewish Research, New York
YMCA   Young Men's Christian Association

Notes

(The numbers in brackets refer to the original, complete citation of a particular reference in each chapter.)

Chapter 1

1. JO (18 October 1940).
2. JO (30 August 1940).
3. JO (25 April 1939).
4. Jacques Polonski, *La Presse, la propagande, et l'opinion publique sous l'occupation* (Paris, 1946), p. 60.
5. JO (23 July 1940).
6. Haute Cour de Justice, Ministère public contre Alibert, 9; *Les Procès de la collaboration* (Paris, 1948), p. 119.
7. JO (18 July 1940).
8. JO (19 August 1940).
9. JO (11 September 1940).
10. JO (18 October 1940).
11. JO (8 October 1940).
12. *Le Monde*, 18 February 1977.
13. Jérôme Carcopino, *Souvenirs de sept ans, 1937–1944* (Paris, 1953), pp. 244–45.
14. Ibid.
15. Haute Cour de Justice, Ministère public contre Alibert, 43.
16. Christopher Browning, *The Final Solution and the German Foreign Office* (New York 1978).
17. U.S. Department of State 851.00/2048; DGFP XI no. 368.
18. Berlin Document Center (Theodor Dannecker, Sippenakte).
19. AA (Inland IIg 189 passim).
20. VOBIF (30 September 1940).
21. Maurice Lagrange, "Le rapatriement des réfugiés après l'exode (juillet-septembre 1940)," RHDGM 27 (July 1977): 48–49.
22. CDJC (CCXLVI–20).
23. VOBIF (21 June 1940).
24. VOBIF (20 October 1940).
25. Faramond to Blanke, 14 November 1941.
26. Joseph Billig, *Le Commissariat général aux questions juives (1941–44)*, 3 vols. (Paris, 1955–60), vol. I, pp. 35–38.
27. Le Directeur du SCAP à Xavier Vallat, 21 August 1941; Joseph Billig, *Le Gouvernement de l'Etat français et la question juive* (Paris, n.d.), p. 11.
28. *Le Procès de Xavier Vallat présenté par ses amis* (Paris, 1948), p. 325.
29. Paul Baudouin, *Neuf Mois au gouvernement: avril–décembre 1940* (Paris, 1948), p. 341.
30. Heydrich memorandum, 5 February 1941; and Heydrich to Luther, 14 February 1941 (AA: Inland II A/B 80–41 Sdh III).

31. Luther to German embassy, Paris, 8 March 1942 (AA: Deutscher Botschaft Paris 1318).

32. Billig, *Commissariat* [26], vol. I, p. 24.

33. Alan Milward, *The New Order and the French Economy* (Oxford, 1970), passim.

34. AA (Inland II A/B 80–41 Sdh III).

35. Bericht über Verschickerung von Juden deutscher Staatsangehörigkeit nach Südfrankreich, 30 October 1940 (AA: Inland IIg 189); Kurt R. Grossmann, *Emigration. Geschichte der Hitler-Flüchtlinge, 1933–45* (Frankfurt-am-Main, 1969), 204; Xavier de Montclos et al. *Eglises et chrétiens dans la IIe guerre mondiale. La région Rhône-Alpes* (Actes du colloque tenu à Grenoble du 7 au 9 Octobre 1976) (Lyon, 1978), p. 210; Zosa Szajkowski, *Analytical Franco-Jewish Gazetteer, 1939–1945* (New York, 1966), pp. 241–43; memorandum of Luther, 31 October 1940, *Trials of War Criminals before the Nuernberg Military Tribunals*, 13 vols. (Washington, D.C., 1951–52), vol. XIII, p. 165.

36. DFCAA (II, 244–45; III, 37, 87–89; IV, 98, 308–9).

37. AA: Deutscher Botschaft Paris 1318; DFCAA III, 88.

38. AA: Deutscher Botschaft Paris 1318; DFCAA IV, 98.

39. Le Sous-préfet de Bayonne au Ministère de l'Intérieur, 7 April 1941 (AN: F1CIII 1180).

40. *Le Statut des juifs en France, en Allemagne, et en Italie* (Express-Documents: Lyon, n.d.), p. 64.

41. Cf. the conversations reported by U.S. Ambassador William C. Bullitt to the Department of State (FRUS 1940 II 462 ff).

42. Hemmen memorandum, 2 August 1940 (T–120/3527H/E021556).

43. Laval-Grimm conversation, 28 August 1940 (T–120/2624H/D525934–947).

44. Billig, *Commissariat* [26], I, p. 31.

45. *Le Figaro,* 6 July 1940.

46. Hencke to Auswärtiges Amt, no. 245, 19 November 1940 (AA: Inland IIg 189). The French text published in DFCAA III 87 is slightly milder.

47. Woermann report, 25 July 1940 (DGFP, series D, X, 292–93).

48. Monique Luirard, "Les Juifs dans la Loire pendant la Seconde Guerre Mondiale," *Cahiers d'histoire* XVI (1971): 193–94.

49. T–120/3697/E036091–2; DFCAA IV 98.

50. Direction général de la Sûreté Nationale, note du 9 March 1941 au sujet de l'institution par décret d'un comité directeur de l'immigration (AN: AGII520 CC104F).

51. *Le Temps,* 24 July 1940.

52. *Le Temps,* 18 October 1940; Jean Thouvenin, *Une Année d'histoire de la France, 1940–41* (Paris, 1941), pp. 256–57; Hubert Thomas-Chevalier, *La Protection légale de la race: essai sur les lois de Nuremberg* (Paris, 1942), pp. 200–201.

53. Le Préfet de l'Oise, 30 October 1940 (An: F1CIII1176); le Préfet du Loiret, 10 November 1940 (AN: FCIII1163); le Préfet de la Sarthe, 5 July 1940 (AN: F1CIII1186).

54. AN (F1CIII1190).

55. Roger Langeron, *Paris 1940* (Paris, 1946), pp. 136, 141, 168–69, 173.

56. Pierre Pierrard, *Juifs et catholiques français: de Drumont à Jules Isaac (1886–1945)* (Paris, 1970), p. 288. British agents reported similarly in September 1940 (PRO: FO 371/24313 [C10842/67/17]).

57. Le Préfet de l'Aube, 28 July 1940 (AN: F1CIII1140); le Préfet de l'Ain, 30 October 1940 (AN: F1CIII1135); le Préfet de la Seine-et-Oise, 5 August 1940 (AN: F1CIII1190).

58. Thouvenin, *Une Année* [52], p. 216.

59. *L'Oeuvre du Maréchal, juillet 1940–juillet 1941* (Vichy, 1941), p. 24.

60. *Le Temps,* 20 September 1940.

61. BA (R 70/Frankreich/32, no. 28). Hagen memorandum, 21 June 1943.

62. André Lavagne to Guionin, 13 October 1941 (AN: AGII 487 CC64bis).

63. Mrs. Pardee to B. Ménétrel, 29 March and 10 April 1941 (AN: AGII 76 SP 3).

64. Baudouin, *Neuf mois* [29], 366.

65. Murphy to Secretary of State, 15 August 1940 (FRUS 1940 II 565).

66. AA (Inland IIg 81).

67. Fred Kupferman, *Pierre Laval* (Paris, 1976), p. 88; cf. Geoffrey Warner, *Pierre Laval and the Eclipse of France* (London, 1968), p. 147.

68. Marc Boegner, "Rapport," in *Les Eglises protestantes pendant la guerre et*

l'occupation. Actes de l'assemblée générale du protestantisme français (Paris, 1946), p. 18.

69. Marquet-Abetz conversation, September 1940 (T–120/364/206021 ff). For a defense of Marquet's posture, see Levi Eligulashvili, "How the Jews of Gruziya in Occupied France Were Saved," *Yad Vashem Studies* VI (1967): 252–53.

70. Maurice Martin du Gard, *Chronique de Vichy* (Paris, 1948), p. 55.

71. Xavier Vallat, *Le Nez de Cléopâtre: souvenirs d'un homme de droite (1919–1944)* (Paris, 1957), pp. 244–45.

72. Le Préfet de l'Oise, 15 November, 15 December 1940 (AN: F¹CIII1176).

73. Le Préfet de l'Indre, 30 January 1941 (AN: F¹CIII1157).

74. *Journal des débats*, 25 October 1940.

Chapter 2

1. *Die Zeit*, 3 November 1978, p. 21; Rita Thalmann and Emmanuel Feinermann, *La Nuit de cristal* (Paris, 1972). For a full account of the murky sequel to the assassination, see Helmut Heiber, "Der Fall Grünspan," *Vierteljahrshefte für Zeitgeschichte* 5 (1957): 134–72.

2. Le Marquis de la Tour du Pin, *Vers un ordre social chrétien* (Paris, 1907), pp. 331, 337, 340.

3. Vendredi saint. Au deuxième nocturne, 5e leçon, *Le Breviaire romain*, 4th ed. (Paris, 1935), pp. 701–2.

4. See Arthur Gilbert, *The Vatican Council and the Jews* (Cleveland and New York, 1968).

5. Zeev Sternhell, *La Droite révolutionnaire, 1885–1914: les origines françaises du fascisme* (Paris, 1978), pp. 23–24.

6. Georges Vacher de Lapouge, *L'Aryen: son rôle social* (Paris, 1899), p. 467.

7. J. Verdès-Leroux, *Scandale financier et antisémitisme catholique: la krach de l'Union générale* (Paris, 1969), p. 207 and passim.

8. P. Sorlin, *"La Croix" et les Juifs (1880–1899): contribution à l'histoire de l'antisemitisme contemporain* (Paris, 1967), p. 219.

9. Dan S. White, *The Splintered Party. National Liberalism in Hessen and the Reich, 1867–1918* (Cambridge, Mass., 1976), pp. 134–147, 171–72.

10. Pierre Pierrard, *Juifs et catholiques français: de Drumont à Jules Isaac (1886–1945)* (Paris, 1970), pp. 235–36.

11. See Norman Cohn, *Warrant for Genocide: The Myth of the Jewish World Conspiracy and the Protocols of Zion* (New York, 1967).

12. Jacques Petit, *Bernanos, Bloy, Claudel, Péguy: quatre écrivains catholiques face à Israël* (Paris, 1972), p. 25.

13. Pierrard, *Juifs et catholiques* [10], p. 298.

14. Report by Xavier Vallat (CDJC: CIX–106).

15. See Marcia Graham Symnott, *The Half-Opened Door: Discrimination and Admissions at Harvard, Yale, and Princeton, 1900–1970* (Westport, Conn., 1979).

16. Geoffrey Alderman, "The Anti-Jewish Riots of August 1911 in South Wales," *The Welsh History Review* VI(2 [December 1972]): 190–200. We thank Dr. Tim Mason for this reference.

17. Stephen Wilson, "The Antisemitic Riots of 1898 in France," *The Historical Journal* XVI 4 [1973]: 789–806.

18. Jules Isaac, *Expériences de ma vie*, vol. I: *Péguy* (Paris, 1959), pp. 20, 43, 64–66.

19. Joseph Bonsirven, *Juifs et chrétiens* (Paris, 1936), p. 7.

20. J.-L. Loubet del Bayle, *Les Non-conformistes des années 30: une tentative de renouvellement de la pensée politique française* (Paris, 1969), p. 11.

21. Georges Dupeux, *La Société française, 1789–1960* (Paris, 1964), p. 231.

22. Jean-Charles Bonnet, *Les Pouvoirs publics français et l'immigration dans l'entre-deux-guerres* (Lyon, 1976), pp. 190–93.

23. Georges Mauco, *Les Etrangers en France: leur rôle dans l'activité économique* (Paris, 1932), p. 134.

24. Bonnet, *Les Pouvoirs* [22], p. 19; Arieh Tartakower and Kurt R. Grossmann, *The Jewish Refugee* (New York, 1944), pp. 132–33.

25. Kurt R. Grossmann, *Emigration. Geschichte der Hitler–Flüchtlinge, 1933–45* (Frankfurt-am-Main, 1969), p. 161. See also Werner Rosenstock, "Exodus, 1933–39: A Survey of Jewish Emigration from Germany," *Leo Baeck Year Book* (1956) I: 373–90; Yehuda Bauer, *My Brother's Keeper: A History of the American Joint Distribution Committee* (Philadelphia, 1974), pp. 138, 237–39.

26. Etat Français, *Annuaire statistique abrégé* (Paris, 1943), vol. I, p. 12.

27. Haim Genizi, "James G. McDonald: High Commissioner for Refugees, 1933–1935," *Wiener Library Bulletin* XXX (43/44, [1977]): 45.

28. Mauco, *Les Etrangers* [23], p. 145.

29. Eugen Weber, *Action Française* (Stanford, 1962), pp. 552, 317.

30. Paula Hyman, *From Dreyfus to Vichy: The Remaking of French Jewry, 1906–1939* (New York, 1979), p. 104.

31. Minutes, 17 December 1933, cited in Hyman, *From Dreyfus* [30], p. 131.

32. Senateur Reynaldi, JO *Documents parlementaires, Sénat,* 8 November 1934, p. 865; cited in Bonnet, *Les Pouvoirs* [22], p. 213.

33. Hyman, *From Dreyfus* [30], p. 107.

34. Centre de Documentation et de Vigilance, *Bulletin,* November 1938, p. 9 (JTS: XII, 26).

35. Ibid., p. 12.

36. Ibid., pp. 7–8.

37. Robert Brasillach, *Notre avant-guerre* (Paris, 1942), p. 189.

38. Jean et Jérôme Tharaud, *Quand Israël n'est plus roi* (Paris, 1933), p. 199.

39. Louis-Ferdinand Céline, *Bagatelles pour un massacre* (Paris, 1937), p. 182.

40. *Action française* (Stanford, Calif., 1962), p. 372, note b.

41. Joseph Bonsirven, "Chronique du judaïsme français: y-a-t-il en France un réveil d'antisémitisme?" *Etudes* CCXXII (1935): 110.

42. Jean Lacouture, *Léon Blum* (Paris, 1977), p. 306.

43. Simone Pétrement, *La Vie de Simone Weil* (Paris, 1973), vol. II, p. 10.

44. *Le Matin,* 3 December 1938.

45. *Le Matin,* 19 November 1938.

46. Pascal Ory, *Les Collaborateurs, 1940–44* (Paris, 1976), p. 32.

47. David Weinberg, *Les Juifs à Paris de 1933 à 1939* (Paris, 1974), pp. 225–26.

48. Centre de Documentation et de Vigilance, *Bulletin,* 6 October 1938, p. 6 (JTS: XII, 26).

49. Quoted in Pierrard, *Juifs et catholiques* [10], p. 260.

50. Centre de Documentation et de Vigilance, *Bulletin,* 6 October 1938, p. 6 (JTS: XII, 26). German consular reports concerning anti-Jewish shop smashings and other demonstrations in Epinal, Lyon, and Dijon in early October 1938 are found in AA (Pol. 36 Frankreich).

51. "Bulletin du jour: le problème juif," *Le Temps,* 17 November 1938.

52. "La Police des étrangers," *Le Temps,* 9 November 1938; "Surveillance et contrôle des étrangers," *Le Temps,* 14 November 1938.

53. Preface to Drieu de la Rochelle's novel *Gilles* (Paris, 1939).

54. Lucien Rebatet, *Les Décombres* (Paris, 1942), p. 127.

55. Louis-Ferdinand Céline, *L'Ecole des cadavres* (Paris, 1938), p. 264.

56. *Les Pavés de Paris,* no. 26, 9 December 1938; *Les Pavés de Paris,* no. 22, 11 November 1938.

57. Marcel Jouhandeau, *Le Péril juif* (Paris, 1939), p. 13.

58. Cf. another call to action in Paul Plancard, *Le Juif démasqué* (Paris, 1937), yet another work published by Henry Coston's Office de Propagande Nationale.

59. *Bulletin municipal officiel de la Ville de Paris,* 7 April 1938.

60. Raymond Millet, "Les Enquêtes du Temps," *Le Temps,* 5 May, 22 May, 24 May 1938, et seq.; also published as *Trois millions d'étrangers en France: les indésirables, les bienvenus* (Paris, 1938).

61. *Le Temps,* 24 May 1938.

62. *Les Pavés de Paris,* no. 21, 4 November 1938.

63. Alfred Kupferman, "Le Bureau Ribbentrop et les campagnes pour le rapproach-ment franco-allemand, 1934–1939," in *Les Relations Franco-Allemandes, 1933–39* (Paris, 1976) pp. 87–98; A. Alperin, "Die antisemitische Propaganda in Frankreich der Milk-ome," in E. Tcherikower, ed., *Yidn in Frankreich* (New York, 1942), II, pp. 264–280 (in Yiddish).

64. Note of July 1939 and 1 August (PP [Seine], 37022–B).

65. Gilles, 1973 ed., Collection "Folio" (Paris). p. 562.

66. World Jewish Congress, "Le Problème juif et l'opinion catholique française," mimeographed, Archives of the World Jewish Congress, Institute of Jewish Affairs, London.

67. Léon Merklen, "Le Problème juif et l'universalité de la Rédemption," *La Croix,* 1 September 1938; Pierrard, *Juifs et catholiques* [10], pp. 266–85; François Delpech, "La persécution des juifs et l'Amitié Chrétienne," in Xavier de Monclos et al., Eglises et chrétiens dans la IIe guerre mondiale: région Rhône-Alpes (Lyon, 1978), p. 143f.

68. *Ce Soir,* 19 February 1939.

69. H. de Kérillis, "L'Antisémitisme, ciment des dictateurs," *L'Epoque,* 12 November 1938; Kérillis, "Une Solution pour les Juifs allemands," *L'Epoque,* 16 November 1938.

70. *Les Pavés de Paris,* 23 September 1938; P.-E. Flandin, "Risques de guerre et chances de Parix, "*Revue politique et parlementaire,* 10 April 1939.

71. See note of 20 November 1940 (WL: PC6 3b 4).

72. L'Epoque, 14 November 1938; Maurice Pujo, *Comment La Rocque a trahi* (Paris, n.d.); *La Rocque et les juifs: un nouveau scandale:* (Paris, n.d.) was published by Henry Coston's agency, one of the busiest antisemitic publishers.

73. Dieter Wolf, *Doriot: du communisme à la collaboration* (Paris, 1969), p. 313.

74. CHDGM: "Questions juives," A.6.I.

75. William D. Irvine, "French Conservatives and the 'New Right' during the 1930s," *French Historical Studies* VIII (1974): 534–62.

76. Centre de Documentation et de Vigilance, *Bulletin,* July 1938, pp. 10–11 (JTS: XII, 26).

77. Ibid., 13 January 1939. Cf., for supporting arguments, *La Liberté,* 7 October 1938; and *Le Petit Journal,* 19 October 1938.

78. "Le Statut des commerçants étrangers," *Le Temps,* 15 April 1939.

79. Centre de Documentation et de Vigilance, *Bulletin,* 3 November 1938.

80. "Le Problème des étrangers," *Le Temps,* 15 April 1939.

81. Mauco, *Les Etrangers* [23], pp. 490, 598. Cf. also Georges Mauco, "Le Général de Gaulle et le Haut Comité de la Population et de la famille," *Espoir: Revue de l'Institut Charles de Gaulle,* no. 21 (December 1977), pp. 20–27.

82. *Le Temps présent,* 9 September 1938.

83. *Le Matin,* 12 November 1938.

84. Pétrement, *Simone Weil* [43], p. 326.

85. Jean Giraudoux, *Pleins Pouvoirs,* 3rd edition (Paris, 1939), pp. 59–76.

86. Bonnet, *Pouvoirs publics* [22], pp. 235–36.

87. Allan Mitchell, "The Xenophobic Style: French Counterespionage and the Emer-gence of the Dreyfus Affair," *Journal of Modern History* 52(September 1980): 414–25.

88. Donald N. Baker, "The Surveillance of Subversion in Interwar France: the Carnet B in the Seine, 1922–40," *French Historical Studies* 10 (1978): 486–516.

89. JO (12 August 1932).

90. Bonnet, *Pouvoirs publics* [22], p. 292.

91. Sir John Hope Simpson, *The Refugee Problem: Report of a Survey* (London, 1939), p. 275.

92. Bonnet, *Pouvoirs publics* [22], part II, passim; Barbara Vormeier, "Quelques aspects de la politique française à l'égard des émigrés allemands, 1933–42," in Hanna Schramm and Barbara Vormeier, *Vivre à Gurs: un camp de concentration français, 1940–44* (Paris, 1949), pp. 213–14.

93. Report of le Préfet de Police (Seine) au Ministre de l'Intérieur, 23 July 1937 (APP [Seine], B/A 1714).

94. Law of 29 May 1938, JO (1–3 May 1938, pp. 4967–68); decree of application, JO (14 May 1938, pp. 5492–94).

95. "La Police des étrangers," *Le Temps*, 5 May 1938; "Questions sociales: le travail des étrangers," *Le Temps*, 20 November 1938; Bonnet, *Pouvoirs publics* [22], p. 350.

96. Arthur Koestler, *Scum of the Earth* (London, 1941), p. 165.

97. JO, Lois et décrets (13 November 1938, p. 12920).

98. J. Lubetzki, *La Condition des Juifs en France sous l'occupation allemande, 1940–44* (Paris, 1945), p. 9.

99. JO, Lois et décrets (13 November 1938, p. 12920).

100. JO (12 April 1935, pp. 4101–16).

101. Bonnet, *Pouvoirs publics* [22], pp. 338–39.

102. Bauer, *My Brother's Keeper* [25], p. 337.

103. *La Nouvelle Revue française*, August 1941.

104. "Le problème des réfugiés," *Le Temps*, 8 July 1938; Shlomo Z. Katz, "Public Opinion in Western Europe and the Evian Conference of July 1938," *Yad Vashem Studies* IX (1973): 105–32; Eliahu Ben Elissar, *La Diplomatie du IIIe Reich et les Juifs (1933–1939)* (Paris, 1969), pp. 240 ff.

105. Reports by George Rublee and Myron Taylor, 23 August, 25 August, and 19 November 1938 (FRUS, 1938, I 769–772, 834).

106. Centre de Documentation et de Vigilance, *Bulletin*, 1938, p. 15 (JTS: XII, 26).

107. Woermann memorandum, 24 October 1938 (DGFP, Series D, V, 902–3); "L'Action antijuive en Allemagne: le sort des réfugiés," *Le Temps*, 20 November 1938; "L'Aide aux réfugiés d'Allemagne et d'Autriche," *Le Temps*, 22 November 1938.

108. Record of Anglo-French conversations, Quai d'Orsay, 24 November 1938 (DBrFP, 3rd Series, III, 294–6).

109. DGFP, Series D, IV, 451–52.

110. Georges Bonnet, *Fin d'une Europe*, vol. II: *De Munich à la Guerre* (Paris, 1967). Roger Errera, "Chroniques de l'indifférence en matière de génocide," *Esprit*, June 1969, pp. 1095–1100, and subsequent exchanges between Bonnet and Errera in *Esprit*, December 1969, pp. 952–58, and February 1970, pp. 445–47.

111. Anthony Adamthwaite, *France and the Coming of the Second World War, 1936–39* (London, 1977), p. 290.

112. Chargé in France (Wilson) to U.S. Secretary of State, 15 December 1938 (FRUS, 1938, I 871–73).

113. Phipps to Halifax, 8 December 1938, DBrFP, 3rd Series, III, 397.

114. Philip Freidman, "The Lublin Reservation and the Madagascar Plan: Two Aspects of Nazi Jewish Policy during the Second World War," in Joshua A. Fishman, ed., *Studies in Modern Jewish Social History* (New York, 1972), pp. 165–67; and the paper on Madagascar in Questions juives, Mesures antisémites (CHDGM).

115. J.B. Trant to Foreign office, 4 April 1946 (PRO: FO 371/57690/1085).

116. Bauer, *My Brother's Keeper* [25], p. 193.

117. Mandel to Bonnet, 25 May 1938 (French Foreign Ministry Archives).

118. Martin Gilbert, *Exile and Return: the Emergence of Jewish Statehood* (London, 1978), p. 188.

119. Kennedy to U.S. Secretary of State, 3 December 1938 (FRUS, 1938, I, 851).

120. Ibid., p. 852.

121. "Audition de M. Georges Bonnet à la Commission des affaires étrangères," *Le Temps*, 16 December 1938.

122. "Le contrôle de l'entrée des étrangers sur notre territoire," *Le Temps*, 20 October 1938.

123. "Discours de M. Albert Sarraut, ministre de l'intérieur," *Le Temps*, 6 February 1939.

124. Quoted in Bonnet, *Pouvoirs publics* [22], p. 358.

125. "Nos hôtes et nous," *Le Temps*, 9 March 1939; "La leçon espagnole," *Le Temps*, 12 March 1939.

126. Louis Stein, *Beyond Death and Exile: The Spanish Republicans in France, 1939–55* (Cambridge, Mass., 1979), p. 85.

127. Schramm and Vormeier, *Vivre à Gurs* [92], p. 260.

128. Bonnet, *Pouvoirs publics* [22], p. 364.

129. "Les Étrangers en France," *Le Temps*, 26 March 1939.

130. JO Débats (Chambre, 8 December 1939, 2120–21).

131. Leo Lania, *The Darkest Hour: Adventures and Escapes,* trans. Ralph Marlowe (Boston, 1941), chap. 3.

132. Maurice Lagrange, "Le Repatriement des réfugiés après l'exode (juillet–septembre 1940)," RHDGM, 27 (July 1977): 39–52; Malcolm J. Proudfoot, *European Refugees, 1939–52: A Study in Forced Population Movements* (London, n.d.); WL: PIII, i (France), no. 635.

133. Heinz Pol, *Suicide of a Democracy* (New York, 1940), pp. 232–33.

134. AA (Inland II A/B 80–41 Sdh III). B. Queller to the German Foreign Office, Berlin, 20 November 1940. The letter was handed to Dr. Kundt who visited the French internment camps to look for political refugees.

135. Joseph Weill, *Contribution à l'étude des camps d'internement dans l'anti-France* (Paris, 1946), p. 154; WL (PIII, i (France), no. 635); Lion Feuchtwanger, *The Devil in France and My Encounter with Him in the Summer of 1940* (New York: 1941), p. 141.

136. Schramm and Vormeier, *Vivre à Gurs* [92], p. 323; René Kapel, "J'étais l'aumônier des camps du sud-ouest de la France (août 1940–décembre 1942)," *Le Monde juif,* no. 87 (July–August 1977); 97–100.

137. Schramm and Vormeier, *Vivre à Gurs* [92], pp. 254–55.

138. HICEM HH 2–FR2–119. The estimation of 70 percent comes from Pierrard, *Juifs et catholiques* [10], p. 316.

139. William A. Nielson, *We Escaped: Twelve Personal Narratives of the Flight to America* (New York, 1941), p. 115.

140. Koestler, *Scum of the Earth* [96]. Koestler had been interned at Le Vernet.

141. See AN: AG^{II}26.

142. Zosa Szajkowski, "The Soldiers France Forgot," *Contemporary Jewish Record,* V (1942): 589–96; and Szajkowski, *Jews and the French Foreign Legion* (New York, 1975); Szajkowski worked for months on the Trans-Sahara Railway. See also Michel Ansky, *Les Juifs d'Algérie: du décret Crémieux à la Libération* (Paris, 1950), pp. 261–62.

143. JO, *Lois et décrets* (1 October 1940).

144. Tartakower and Grossmann, *Jewish Refugee* [24], pp. 145, 181, 208–9.

145. Comité de coordination (Nîmes), minutes of meeting of 15 April 1941 (LBI).

146. Report by Dr. Kundt, 1 November 1940 (AA: Inland II A/B 80–41 Sdh III).

147. DFCAA, I, 84–85, 361–365.

148. For an early French protest, see Ambassadeur de France in Berlin, no. 156, 15 March 1938 (AA: Pol. 36 Frankreich).

149. General Doyen to General Stülpnagel, 18 November 1940 (DFCAA, II, 385).

150. Ibid., 10 February 1941 (DFCAA, IV, 98).

Chapter 3

1. Haute Cour de Justice, Procédure suivie contre Raphael Alibert (AN: W^{III}46).

2. See décrets of 10 December 1941 JO (13 December 1940 and 1 January 1941).

3. For Debré, Halphen, Marc Bloch, and others, see décrets of 5 January 1941.

4. For Rueff, see décret of 22 January 1941 JO (24 January 1941) and for Berr, see décret of 15 April 1941 JO (19 April 1941).

5. "Polizeiverwaltung unter dem MBF" (BA: R70 Frankreich/13, p. 170).

6. Hans Umbreit, *Der Militärbefehlshaber in Frankreich, 1940–44* (Boppard am Rhein, 1968); Lucien Steinberg, *Les Autorités allemandes en France occupée: inventaire commenté de la collection de documents conservés au CDJC* (Paris, 1966), pp. 11–28; Joseph Billig, *Le Commissariat général aux questions juives (1941–44),* 3 vols. (Paris, 1955–60), vol. I, pp. 22–24; Jacques Delarue, *Histoire de la Gestapo* (Paris, 1962), pp. 347–69. See the useful biographical sketches of some important German personalities prepared by Serge Klarsfeld in Joseph Billig, *La Solution finale de la question juive: essai sur les principes dans le IIIe Reich et en France sous l'occupation* (Paris, 1977), pp. 189–201.

7. BDC: SS-Personal-akte, Carl-Theo Zeitschel; Zeitschel to Abetz, 21 August 1941 (CDJC: V–8).

8. Dannecker file (BDC: Sippenakte).

9. Billig, *Commissariat* [6], vol. I, p. 27.

10. BA: R70 Frankreich/23, pp. 36–39.

11. Dannecker's memorandum of 1 July 1941 (ND: RF 1207), in Henri Monneray, ed., *La Persécution des Juifs en France et dans les autres pays de l'Ouest présentée par la France à Nuremberg* (Paris, 1947), p. 85.

12. Dannecker notes, 3 February 1941 and 22 February 1941 (CDJC: XXIV–13 and XXVI–80).

13. Billig, *Commissariat* [6], vol. I, pp. 45–58; Zeitschel, note of 14 February 1941 (CDJC: 7–60).

14. Abetz to Ribbentrop, 6 March 1941 (DGFP, series D, vol. XII, p. 228).

15. Dr. Kurt Ihlefeld, Notiz für Herrn Botschafter, 1 March 1941 (AN: W^{III}212² no. 46[17]).

16. JO (31 March 1941).

17. Note du Contrôleur-général de Faramond, 15 December 1941 (CDJC: CXIV–22).

18. Keitel to General Thomas, 10 January 1941 (OKW/2012:T–77/851/5,596,112f).

19. Jérôme Carcopino, *Souvenirs de sept ans* (Paris, 1953), p. 359; Darlan to Moysset, 15 January 1942 (AN: AG^{II}536 CC130B).

20. AN: AG^{II}82 SP10M.

21. AN: AG^{II}610 CM 26–D. Cf. René Gillouin, *J'étais l'ami du maréchal Pétain* (Paris, 1966), pp. 156–57.

22. Zosa Szajkowski, *Analytical Franco-Jewish Gazetteer, 1939–45* (New York, 1966), pp. 49–50; Philippe Erlanger, *La France sans étoile: souvenirs de l'avant-guerre et du temps de l'occupation* (Paris, 1974), pp. 99–100. Lavagne to Helbronner, 13 November 1941 and 24 November 1943 (CDJC: CCXIII–7 and 9).

23. See Szajkowski, *Gazetteer* [22], p. 69 no. 269; and Serge Klarsfeld, *Le Mémorial de la déportation des Juifs de France* (Paris, 1978).

24. Note by Dr. Bernard Ménétrel, 17 November 1942 (AN: AG^{II}617 MP3); for 1943, see Pétain's meetings with the German diplomat Roland Krug von Nidda, 3 February 1943 (T–120/1832H/418618f) and 22 August 1943 (T–120/3546H/E 022155f).

25. Testimony of Henri du Moulin de Labarthète at the trial of Xavier Vallat, 19 October 1946 (AN: W^{III}213¹[59]).

26. Ménétrel to de Brinon, 3 July 1942 (AN: F^{60} 1485).

27. Jardel to Guérard, 19 July 1943 (AN: AG^{II} 488 CC 66).

28. Pétain to Alibert, 4 February 1942 (AN: AG^{II} 24 SG2); Barthélemy to Pétain, 6 June 1942 (AN: AG^{II} 609 CM 25–A).

29. Pétain to de Brinon, 12 June 1942 (AN: AG^{II}24 SG 1).

30. CDJC: XLIX–42; BA: R 70 Frankreich/27, p. 35.

31. CDJC: LXXI–85a.

32. AA: Inland II A/B 83–26, vol. 4; ibid., vol. 5; Deutscher Botschaft Paris 1318.

33. Barthélemy, Speech of 9 August 1941, Toulouse (CDJC: CCXXXIX–30).

34. Xavier Vallat, preface to Gabriel Malglaive, *Juif ou Français: Aperçus sur la question juive* (Paris, 1942), p. 8.

35. Robert Debré, *L'Honneur de vivre* (Paris, 1974), p. 221.

36. Haute Cour de Justice, Procédure suivie contre Xavier Vallat (AN: W^{III}211¹ no. 5). See also Vallat, *Le Nez de Cléopâtre: souvenirs d'un homme de droite* (1919–1944) (Paris, 1957), p. 232; Vallat, preface to Malglaive, *Juif ou Français* [34], pp. 5–7.

37. *Le Temps*, 7 April 1941, 15 June 1941; *Le Matin*, 5 April 1941; Charles Maurras, *La Seule France: chronique des jours d'épreuve* (Lyon, 1941), p. 194.

38. Coston to Vallat, 23 April 1941 (CDJC: CXCV–75); Pierre Pierrard, *Juifs et Catholiques français: de Drumont à Jules Isaac (1886–1945)* (Paris, 1970), p. 303; Billig, *Commissariat* [6], vol. I, p. 93.

39. *Paris-Soir*, 4 April 1941; *Dépêche marocaine*, 6 April 1941.

40. Vallat press conference, quoted in Michel Ansky, *Les Juifs d'Algérie: du décret Crémieux à la Libération* (Paris, 1950), pp. 149–50.

41. Malglaive, *Juif ou Français* [34], pp. 11–12. "Le problème juif: conférence prononcée par M. Xavier Vallat devant les stagiaires de la 3e session" (AN: W^{III} 211¹ no. 5).

42. AN: W^{III} 211^1 no. 5.

43. Billig, *Commissariat* [6], vol. II, p. 153.

44. Vallat to Best, 23 June 1941 (CDJC: CX–65).

45. AN: W^{III} 211^2 no. 33(2); AJ^{38} 1143 I JA/9–14.

46. Boegner to Vallat, 4 July 1941; Vallat to Boegner, 10 July 1941 (CDJC: CXCV–44).

47. AN: AJ^{38} 1143 I JA/9–14.

48. Vallat, "Le problème juif," (AN: W^{III}211^1 no. 5); Vallat to Préfet de Police (Paris), 30 August 1941 (AN: AJ^{38} 62 M75). Also CDJC: XXXII–39 et seq.

49. Warner Green, "The Fate of Oriental Jews in Vichy France," *Wiener Library Bulletin* XXXII (49/50 [1979]):40–50.

50. Vallat, "Le problème juif" (AN: W^{III}211^1 no. 5); *Le Figaro,* 14 June 1941. For Vallat's opinions on this and other points, see also Henri Baudry and Joannès Ambre, *Condition publique et privée du Juif en France (Statut des Juifs)* (Paris, 1942).

51. BA: R70 Frankreich/31, pp. 55–56, 62.

52. The following three paragraphs are based on AN: AJ^{38} 1143 T JA/9–14.

53. Vallat to Moysset, 7 February 1942 (AN: W^{III}212^1 no. 24[2]).

54. Baudry and Ambre, *Condition publique* [50], p. 49.

55. Best Aktenzeichen, 5 April 1941 (BA: R70 Frankreich/32, pp. 9–13). Also CDJC: LXXV–145.

56. Carl-Theo Zeitschel, "Besprechung mit Kriegsverwaltungschef Ministerial-direktor Dr. Best," 5 April 1941 (BA: R70 Frankreich/23, pp. 3–5). Also CDJC: V–81.

57. Abetz to Ribbentrop, 3 April 1941 (T-120/221/149195–6). Also CDJC: CXXIV–41.

58. JO (14 June 1941).

59. Vallat, "Rapport à M. le maréchal de France, chef de l'état, sur la modification de la loi du 3 octobre 1940 portant statut des juifs," 26 May 1941 (AN: AJ^{38} 1143 I JA/1–4).

60. Ibid.

61. *La Patrie,* no. 1, quoted in J. Lubetzki, *La Condition des Juifs en France sous l'occupation allemande, 1940–44* (Paris, 1945), p. 15.

62. CHDGM: "Statut des Juifs."

63. AN: AJ^{38} 1143 1 JA/1.

64. On the work of the Conseil d'Etat, see H. du Moulin de Labarthète, *Le Temps des illusions: souvenirs (juillet 1940–avril 1942)* (Paris, 1946), p. 268.

65. Loi du 2 June 1941 (JO, 14 June 1941).

66. Lubetzki, *Condition* [61], p. 60. For Jewish reactions, see Vichy police report of 10 July 1941 (CDJC: LXI–38); and Adam Rutkowski, *La lutte des Juifs en France à l'époque de l'Occupation (1940–44)* (Paris, 1975), p. 54.

67. Le Marquis de La Tour du Pin La Charce, *Vers un ordre social chrétien. Jatlons de route* (Paris, 1907), p. 343.

68. Chavin to MM. les préfets, 12 July 1941 (AN: AJ^{38} 1144 2JA/2).

69. JO (26 August 1941).

70. ND: HG–4893, *Trials of War Criminals before the Nürenberg Military Tribunals,* 13 vols. (Washington, D.C., 1951–52), vol. XIII, p. 159.

71. Billig, *Commissariat* [6], vol. III, p. 75. Cf. also German embassy, Paris (Dr. Kuntze) to German Foreign Office, Berlin, 20 July 1942 (AA: Pol. II. Richtlinien. Allgemeines).

72. Billig, *Commissariat* [6], vol. III, p. 119.

73. Vallat, "Le problème juif" (AN: W^{III} 211^1 no. 5).

74. "Polizeiverwaltung unter dem MBF" (BA: R70 Frankreich/13, p. 157).

75. Jacques Delarue, *Trafics et crimes sous l'occupation* (Paris, 1968), p. 70; Jean Cassou, *Le pillage par les Allemands des oeuvres d'art et des bibliotheques appartenant à des Juifs de France* (Paris, 1947), pp. 67–68, 96–97, 206–7, 227.

76. Carcopino, *Souvenirs* [19], pp. 364–67.

77. Cassou, *Pillage* [75], pp. 96–97. See also T-120, serials 3840H and 7236H.

78. Vallat to Moysset, 7 February 1942 (AN: W^{III}211^1 no. 24 [2]).

79. Comptes-rendus of meetings, 7 May and 17 May 1941 (AN: AJ^{38} 116; also CDJC: XXXIX–137).

80. Joseph Barthélemy, "Observations concernant le projet de loi relatif aux entreprises, biens, et valeurs appartenant aux Juifs," 15 June 1941 (AN: AJ^{38} 124 84 JA/1).

81. Vallat to Darlan, 7 July 1941 (CDJC: CVI–23).

82. Vallat to Militärbefehlshaber in Frankreich, 9 October 1941 (AN: W^{III} 213^1 no. 36).

83. Vallat, *Nez de Cléopâtre* [36], p. 225.

84. Lubetzki, *Condition* [61], p. 86.

85. CDJC: CCXXXVIII et seq.; Chavin to Vallat, 20 May 1941 (AN: AJ^{38} 4; AN: W^{III} 212^1 no. 29).

86. Letter of 30 June 1941 (CDJC: CXCV–80).

87. Procédure suivie contre Vallat (AN: W^{III} 213^1 nos. 89, 90, 101, 203–8).

88. Vallat to Bousquet, 30 May 1941 (AN: AJ^{38} 62 M75).

89. Billig, *Commissariat* [6], vol. II, pp. 44–46; (AN: AJ^{38} 19 M2; for one example of a disputed determination of Jewishness, cf. "Note de M. Borione pour M. X. Vallat," July 1941 (AN: AJ^{38} 129).

90. Procédure suivie contre Vallat: commissions rogatoires, Algérie, Maroc (AN: W^{III}212^1 nos. 30, 28).

91. "Vichy extends Anti-Jewish laws to this hemisphere," The *New York Herald Tribune*, 16 November 1941; "Vichy Extends Jewish Ban to Colonies in Western World," *Christian Science Monitor*, 29 November 1941.

92. JTA reports of 13 July 1941 and 31 March 1942.

93. Richard Kuisel, *Ernest Mercier: French Technocrat* (Berkeley and Los Angeles, 1967), p. 145.

94. Vallat, "Rapport à M. le Maréchal de France, chef de l'Etat, sur la modification de la loi du 3 octobre 1940 portant statut des juifs," 26 May 1941 (AN: AJ^{38}1143 1JA).

95. JO (2 December 1941).

96. Loi du 17 November 1941, JO (2 December 1941).

97. AN: AJ^{38} 405, "Artisanat"; W^{III} 213^2 no. 3.

98. R. R. Lambert, "Compte-rendu de mes voyages à Vichy (20 Septembre 1941–9 janvier 1942)," interview with Vallat of 27 September 1941 (YIVO: UG II–1).

99. Vallat to MBF, 6 September 1941 (AN: W^{III}213^1 no. 6); JO (2 December 1941).

100. René Mayer to Vallat, 2 December 1941 (AN: W^{III} 212^2 no. 42 [2]).

101. AN: AG^{II} 487 CC 64 bis.

102. Vallat to MBF, Verwaltungsstab (for Ministerialrat Dr. Storz), 24 September 1941 (AN: W^{III} 213^1 no. 5 [2]).

103. Georges Edinger, "Rapport sur l'U.G.I.F." [1946] (AN: W^{III} 211^1 no. 1); Georges Edinger, "Déclaration au Consistoire," [March 1942?] (AN: W^{III} 212^2 no. 42 [2]). See also Zosa Szajkowski, "The Organization of the 'UGIF' in Nazi-Occupied France," *Jewish Social Studies* 9 (1947): 239–56, and Szajkowski "Glimpses of the History of Jews in Occupied France," *Yad Vashem Studies* II (1958), 133–57; and Billig, *Commissariat* [6], vol. I., pp. 206 ff.

104. Billig, *Commissariat* [6], vol. I, pp. 197–98.

105. AN: AJ^{38} 1155, "UGIF: Caisse des dépôts et consignations." See also Y. Regelsperger to Director-general, Caisse des Dépôts et Consignations, 7 February 1942 (AN: AJ^{38} 329; AJ^{38} 675).

106. JO (18 January 1942).

107. Billig, *Commissariat* [6], vol. III, pp. 224–25; Billig, *Le Gouvernement de l'Etat français et la question juive* (Paris, 1961), p. 12.

108. MBF, Wi I/2, memorandum of 11 November 1941 (AN: W^{III} 213^2 no. 4 [1]).

109. Report of Mr. Lautman (HICEM: HHR FR 2–53).

110. Schellenberg memorandum, 20 May 1941 (AA: Inland IIg 189, "Akten betreffend Juden in Frankreich von 1940 bis 1943)."

111. Compte-rendu des sous-commissions militaires et des affaires politiques, 19 March 1941, La Délégation française auprès de la Commission allemande d'armistice. *Recueil de documents publiés par le gouvernement français*, 5 vols. (Paris, 1947), vol. IV, p. 213; Lubetzki, *Condition* [61], p. 161.

112. Zeitschel to Abetz, 12 August 1941 (CDJC: V–15).

113. Comptes-rendus des conversations de M. Lautman à Foix, Vichy, et Clermont-Ferrand, 29 September–6 October 1941 (HICEM: HH2 FR2 109); letter from Commissaire-adjoint de la Lutte contre le chômage, Vichy, to Directeur of HICEM, 6 March 1942 (HICEM: HH2 FR2 109).

114. "Une déclaration de M. Xavier Vallat sur la question juive," *Le Temps*, 7 April 1941.

115. CDJC, *L'Activité des organisations juives en France sous l'occupation* (Paris, 1947).

116. Administrateur-délégué de l'UGIF to HICEM, 19 March 1942 (HICEM: HH2 FR2–71).

117. HICEM to Louis Oungre, Vichy, 22 August 1940 (HICEM: HH2 FR2–109); Varian Fry, *Surrender on Demand* (New York, 1945), pp. 85, 127–28, 206; Henry L. Feingold, *The Politics of Rescue: the Roosevelt Administration and the Holocaust, 1938–45* (New Brunswick, N.J., 1970), pp. 159–61.

118. Carl Ludwig, *La Politique pratiquée par la Suisse à l'égard des réfugiés au cours des années 1933 à 1955*. Annexe au rapport du Conseil fédéral à L'Assemblée fédérale sur la politique pratiquée par la Suisse à l'égard des réfugiés au cours des années 1933 à nos jours [Berne, 1957], p. 77 and passim; Jean-Baptiste Mauroux, *Du Bonheur d'être suisse sous Hitler* (Geneva, 1968), pp. 161–198.

119. Bernard Wasserstein, *Britain and the Jews of Europe, 1939–45* (Oxford, 1979).

120. "Rapport pour 1941 sur notre activité en faveur des personnes internées" (HICEM: HH2 FR2–33; HICEM to Ministre de l'Intérieur, 28 February 1942). HICEM: HH2 FR2–19; "Rapport de la commission d'émigration," October 1941. LBI–98.

121. "Action de la HICEM en faveur des internés des différents camps," undated (HICEM:HH2 FR2–39); "Relations avec l'administration française au cours des mois d'octobre à décembre 1941" (HICEM: HH2 FR2–11).

122. Szajkowski, *Gazetteer* [22], p. 90.

123. AN: AG^{II}536 CCI 30–B.

124. Best to Knowlton, 31 March 1942 (AN: W^{III}212² no. 48[4]). Also, CDJC: LXXV–148.

125. Billig, *Commissariat* [6], vol. I, p. 53.

126. Vallat to Best, 23 June 1941 (CDJC: CX–65); Vallat to MBF, 9 October 1941 (AN: AJ^{38} 9); AJ^{38} 121.

127. Vallat to MBF, 9 October 1941 (AN: W^{III}213¹ no. 36); MBF, Verwaltungsstab, to Vallat, 25 November 1941 (AN: W^{III} 213² nos. 9–10).

128. CDJC: XXIII–78.

129. Darlan to Moysset, 15 January 1942 (AN: AG^{II} 536 CC130–3).

130. Barthélemy to Vallat, 27 January 1942 (AN: AJ^{38} 118).

131. Dr. Best, note of 20 February 1942 (CDJC: LXXV–148).

132. Vallat to Moysset, 7 February 1942 (AN: W^{III} 212¹ no. 24 [2]).

133. Vallat to Best, 23 December 1941 (AN: AJ^{38} 9); Billig, *Commisariat* [6], vol. I, p. 221.

134. Vallat [to Blanke], 3 December 1941 (AN: AJ^{38} 9).

135. Vallat, "Compte-rendu de ma réunion du 22 janvier au Majestic avec le Ministerialrat Dr. Gelbhaar" (AN: W^{III} 211² no. 33 [3]).

136. Aktennotiz, 17 February 1942 (AN: W^{III} 213¹ no. 6).

137. Best to Knochen, 31 March 1942 (AN: W^{III} 212² no. 48 [4]). Also CDJC: LXXV–148.

138. Billig, *Commissariat* [6], vol. I, p. 184.

139. ND: RF–1210. International Military Tribunal, *Trial of the Major War Criminals*, 42 vols. (Nuremberg, 1947–49), vol. XXXVIII, p. 742.

Chapter 4

1. Jules Jeanneney, *Journal politique: septembre 1939–juillet 1942* (Paris, 1972), p. 282.

2. JO (24 June 1941). Most of the following paragraphs is drawn from CGQJ, Service de législation et de contentieux, "Enseignement" (AN: AJ^{38} 1144 5JA).

3. AN: AJ^{38} 4; Joseph Billig, *Le Commissariat général aux questions juives (1941–44)*, 3 vols. (Paris, 1955–60), vol. III, pp. 45–46.

4. Weygand to Pétain, 15 May 1941 (AN: AJ^{38} 4).

5. CGQJ, Service de législation et de contentieux, "Statut des Juifs" (AN: AJ³⁸ 1143 1JA).

6. CGQJ to Ministre-secrétaire d'état à la guerre, 30 January 1942 (AN: AJ³⁸ 64 M76).

7. Vice-admiral Bourragué to Vallat, 5 November 1941 (AN: AJ³⁸ 64).

8. General de la Porte du Theil to Vallat, 7 February 1942 (AN: AJ³⁸ 64 M7641).

9. CDJC: CCXLVI–11.

10. Vallat to MBF, 27 January 1942 (CDJC:CXCIII–108).

11. AN: AJ³⁸ 64.

12. Gouverneur-général de l'Algérie à Ministre de l'Intérieur, 13 October 1941 (AN: W^III 212¹ no. 30 [18]).

13. AN: AJ³⁸64.

14. Le Préfet des Landes au Délégué-général du gouvernement français dans les territoires occupés, 3 August 1942 (AN: F¹C^III 1160).

15. Law of 19 May 1941, JO (31 May 1941).

16. Law of 6 May 1942, JO (14 May 1942).

17. Billig, *Commissariat* [3], vol. I, p. 146; wage scales appear on p. 147.

18. De Faramond to Vallat, 21 August 1941 (AN: AJ³⁸ 69 M70).

19. Billig, *Commissariat* [3], vol. I, p. 146.

20. "Spoliations," *La Documentation française*, no. 1,107, 12 April 1949, p. 19.

21. Colonel Chomel de Jarnieu "Essai de réorganisation du CGQJ," 30 June 1942 (AN: AJ³⁸ 1); Chomel de Jarnieu, note pour le Commissaire-général, 1 September 1941 (AN: AJ³⁸ 69 M70); Dr. Werner Best, note, 20 February 1942 (CDJC: LXXV–148).

22. "Mémoire sur la situation des agents du CGQJ," 16 March 1944 (CDJC: CVI–128).

23. Ibid.

24. Billig, *Commissariat* [3], vol. III, p. 9.

25. Joseph Barthélemy, note on projet de loi modifying article 2 of law of 29 March 1941 creating the CGQJ (CHDGM: *Statut des juifs*).

26. Report of a meeting of 23 July 1941 to examine the application of the statute of 2 June 1941 to civil servants (CDJC: CXCV–48).

27. Billig, *Commissariat* [3], vol. III, pp. 247–48.

28. Léon Poliakov, *L'Etoile jaune* (Paris, 1949), pp. 56–58.

29. Ibid.

30. Billig, *Commissariat* [3], vol. I, pp. 165–66.

31. Réunion du 17 mai [1941] dans le bureau de M. Bouthillier (AN: W^III 213¹ no. 117 [2]).

32. MBF to Vallat, 16 July 1941; MBF to Bichelonne, 18 July 1941 (AN: W^III 213¹ nos. 34, 33).

33. Dr. Elmar Michel, draft note Wi I/2 4165/41, 19 November 1941 (AN: W^III 213¹ no. 65).

34. Réunion interministérielle du 4 mars 1943 (AN: AJ³⁸ 566).

35. Le Préfet des Alpes-Maritimes à M. le Ministre de l'Intérieur, 4 August 1941, 4 October 1941, and n.d. (early November 1941) (AN: F¹C^III 1137).

36. Le Préfet des Hautes-Pyrénées à M. le Ministre de l'Intérieur, 4 February 1941, 2 March 1941 (AN: F¹C^III1182).

37. Haute Cour de Justice, Ministère public contre Bousquet, fascicule 1, p. 118. For the Nazi state, see Hans Buchheim et al, *Anatomie der SS-Staat* (Olten and Freiburg, 1965).

38. Arrêté ministériel, Ministre de l'Intérieur, 19 October 1941, not published in the JO; the text may be found in Commission Rogatoire-Antignac, no. 78 (CDJC: XCVI). For the resort to special courts in the fall of 1941 and the hostage crisis, see Robert O. Paxton, *Vichy France* (New York, 1972), p. 221; and Hervé Villeré, *Section spéciale* (Paris, 1975).

39. AN: W^III 213¹ no. 53.

40. Dannecker, "Juifs," 22 February 1942 (ND: RF–1210), in Henri Monneray, ed., *La Persécution des Juifs en France et dans les autres pays de l'ouest présentés par la France à Nuremberg* (Paris, 1947), pp. 118–19; Billig *Commissariat* [3], vol. I, pp. 80–81, 203–4, vol. II, pp. 9–15.

41. Report of 18 February 1942, Billig, *Commissariat* [3], vol. II, p. 31.

42. "Instructions sur l'organisation du Service de Police des Questions Juives," 22 October 1941 (CDJC: CXCIV–1).

43. Billig, *Commissariat* [3], vol. II, p. 26.

44. AN: F¹CIII 1183–4.

45. Billig, *Commissariat* [3], vol. II, pp. 31, 39–44.

46. Ibid., vol. I, p. 228.

47. "Die Aufgaben der Verwaltungsaufsicht über die franzosische Polizei," n.d. (probably March 1942) (BA: R70 Frankreich/13).

48. "Préparation psychologique et politique pour la journée du 1er mai," (AN: AG^{II} 27 SG7F); CIAF Notizario no. 11, 16 May 1941 (T–586/441/023520).

49. Archives de chef de l'état, cabinet civil, "Opérations de Police" (AN: AG^{II} 520 CC104C).

50. *Les Institutions de la France Nouvelle,* vol. I, *Droit public* (Paris, n.d., but 1941), vol. I, p. iv.

51. Wladimir Rabi, "Les interventions de la hiérarchie en faveur des juifs: une constatation et une question," in Xavier de Montclos et al., eds., *Eglises et chrétiens dans la IIe guerre mondiale. La Région Rhône-Alpes,* Actes du colloque tenu à Grenoble du 7 au 9 octobre 1976 (Lyon, 1978), p. 198.

52. Roger Bonnard, "La reconstruction de la France," *Revue de droit public* LVII (1941): 145.

53. Roger Bonnard, "A nos lecteurs," *Revue de droit public* LVII (1941): 141–42.

54. Ibid.

55. E.-H. Perreau, "Le nouveau statut des Juifs en France," *La Semaine juridique,* 1941, no. 216, no pagination. Cf. Perreau, "Les mesures complémentaires concernant le statut des Juifs," *La Semaine juridique,* I, Doctrine (1942), p. 244. Pierre Lepaulle, an expert on trusteeship, applied his talents to "L'aryanisation des entreprises," *Gazette du Palais,* 1943 2e semestre, 1–18.

56. Gaston Jèze, "La Definition légale du juif au sens des incapacités légales," *Revue de droit public* (1944): 74–81.

57. H. Balzard et al., *Etudes de droit allemand: mélanges Oflag II B* (Paris, 1943). This curious work is a collection of five studies of contemporary German law written by French prisoners of war who were legal specialists.

58. G. Burdeau, *Cours de droit constitutionnel* (Paris, 1942), pp. 189, 191. Cf. also René Floriot, *Principaux textes des lois, décrets, circulaires, et ordonnances parus entre l'armistice et le 20 novembre, classés d'après leur objet, commentés, et expliqués* (Paris, 1940).

59. Henri Baudry and Joannès Ambre, *La Condition publique et privée du Juif en France (Statut des Juifs)* (Paris, 1942).

60. André Broc, *La Qualité de juif* (Paris, 1943).

61. Dannecker to Vallat, 6 October 1941 (AN: AJ³⁸ 1144 2JA/2). Vallat to Darlan, 28 March 1942 (AJ³⁸ 1143 1JA 9–14).

62. AN: F¹CIII 1142.

63. Lubetzki, *La Condition des Juifs en France sous l'occupation allemande, 1940–44* (Paris, 1945), p. 131.

64. Ibid., p. 38.

65. A list may be found in Vallat's trial (AN: W^{III}213¹ no. 130).

66. Danielle Loschak, *Le Rôle politique du juge administratif français* (Paris, 1972), p. 289.

67. Du Moulin de Labarthète, *Le Temps des illusions* (Paris, 1946), p. 268.

68. Jérôme Carcopino, *Souvenirs de sept ans, 1937–1944* (Paris, 1953), pp. 249, 358–59.

69. Séance of 6 December 1941 (AN: AJ³⁸ 122:33).

70. AN: AJ³⁸ 120.

71. Jèze, "Définition légale" [56], p. 78.

72. CGQJ to director of SEC (Lyon), 25 July 1943 (CDJC: CXCV–201).

73. See "Juifs" in Sirey, *Tables quinquennals,* 1941–45, pp. 279–80; Jèze, "Définition légale" [56], pp. 80–81; Lubetzki, *Condition* [63], p. 115 ff; Loschak, *Rôle politique* [66], p. 289.

74. P. Chauveau, "Juifs," *La Semaine juridique,* II, Jurisprudence (Paris, 1942), no. 1800; Lubetzki, *Condition* [63], pp. 30–1.

75. Joseph Haennig, "Quels moyens de preuve peuvent être fournis par le métis juif pour établir sa non-appartenance à la race juive?" *Gazette du palais,* 1943 (1er semestre): 31–32. Haennig was a member of the bar of the Paris Court of Appeals. Cf. Also Hubert

Thomas-Chevalier, *La Protection légale de la race: essai sur les lois de Nuremberg* (Paris, 1942). Thomas-Chevalier was a lawyer at the court of appeals of Nancy. See also CGQJ note of 10 December 1941 (AN: AJ^{38}19 M2); Maurice Caillez, "Les lois du 2 juin et 17 novembre sur les Juifs," *Gazette du Palais*, 1941 (2e semestre), p. 122.

76. *La Semaine juridique*, 1941, no. 1646.

77. Lubetzki, *Condition* [63], p. 76.

78. AN: AJ^{38} 118.

79. Edmond Bertrand, "Du contrôle judiciaire du déssaisissement de juifs et de la liquidation de leurs biens (étude critique de jurisprudence)", *Juris classeur périodique*, 1943, I, 354.

80. Billig, *Commissariat* [3], vol. III, p. 259.

81. Ibid., pp. 258–59.

82. Maurice Duverger, "La situation des fonctionnaires depuis la révolution de 1940," *La Revue de droit public* LXVII (1941): 227 ff.

83. Ibid.

84. Haute Cour de Justice, Ministère public contre Bousquet, fascicule 1, p. 38.

85. Dr. M. Kahany, report, Geneva, 26 December 1940. PRO: FO 371/28461 (Z821/821/17).

86. Procès-verbal d'interrogatoire, 8 August 1945 (AN: W^{III} 212^1 no. 14 [1]).

87. Donald A. Lowrie, *The Hunted Children* (New York, 1963), pp. 52–53.

88. Pontzen report of 2 March 1941 (HICEM: HH2–FR2–82).

89. Report of Charles Kauffman (WL: PIII, i [France], no. 542).

90. Regional Director, Clermont-Ferrand, to CGQJ, 21 November 1941 (CDJC: CII–74).

91. SEC (Lyon), report of 2 June 1943 (CDJC: LXXIX–86).

92. AN: F^{1}CIII 1188. Le Préfet de la Seine-Inférieure à M. le Ministre de l'Intérieur, 31 October 1942.

93. Monique Luirard, "Les Juifs dans la Loire pendant la Seconde Guerre mondiale," *Cahiers d'histoire* XVI (1971): 193–94.

94. JO (7–8 December 1942, 4026).

95. *Mémento de la législation des questions juives à l'usage des maires et des brigades de gendarmerie* (Vichy, [1943]).

96. JTA report from Toulouse, 7 January 1945.

97. Philip Hallie, *Lest Innocent Blood Be Shed* (New York, 1978).

98. Délégué du conseil auprès la 6ème direction de l'UGIF à M. le Directeur-général de l'UGIF, 25 February 1943 (HICEM: HH2–FR2–73).

99. Jules Jeanneney, *Journal* [1], pp. 278–87 (AN: AJ^{38} 64).

100. Ibid., p. 282.

101. Ibid.

102. JO (18 July 1940).

103. "Note sur le fonctionnement du Service administratif des étrangers de la Préfecture de Police depuis le 14 juin 1940, 1er jour de l'occupation, jusqu'au 1er octobre 1941" (APP: B/A 1714).

104. See Ministère des Affaires étrangères to CGQJ, 16 April 1943 (CDJC: CCXXXVII–54).

105. Carcopino, *Souvenirs* [68], p. 248.

106. Ibid., pp. 247–49.

107. Procès-verbal de la séance du Bureau tenu à Chatel-Guyon le 30 juin 1942," quoted in Jeanneney, *Journal* [1], p. 278, n. 5.

108. Ibid., pp. 277–78.

109. CDJC: CCXXXIX–139.

110. Cf., for example, Knochen to RSHA (Berlin), "Endlösung der Judenfrage in Frankreich," 12 February 1943 (BA: R70 Frankreich/23).

111. Ministre-secrétaire d'Etat à la guerre au général commandant la 15e division militaire, 12 December 1940 (JTS: Box 13, 1).

112. "Vichy Hotels Ban Jews," *New York Herald Tribune*, 29 June 1941.

113. BA: R70 Frankreich/31, 70, contains an example of such a certification.

114. Vallat au président du Groupement National de l'Ameublement, n.d. but spring 1942 (AN: AJ^{38} 405 XXX–78).

115. Vallat speech to students de l'Ecole Nationale des Cadres Civiques, n.d. but March 1942 (AN: W^III 211¹ no. 5).
116. Loi du 22 juillet 1941, JO (26 August 1941).
117. "Spoliations et restitutions," *La Documentation française*, no. 1.107, 12 April 1949, 19.
118. AN: AJ³⁸ 608.
119. Ibid.
120. Ibid.
121. "Spoliations," *La Documentation française*, no. 1.107, 12 April 1949, 20.
122. AN: AJ³⁸ 608.
123. Roger Lehideux, circular to branches of the Union Syndicale des Banquiers de Paris et de la Province, 17 September 1941; ibid., 3 December 1941; Association Professionelle des Banques, réunion du 19 December 1941, Vichy (JTS: Box 14, no. 15).
124. CGQJ to M. l'Amiral de la Flotte, Vice-président du Conseil, Secrétariat-général, 2 March 1942 (AN: W^III 213¹ no. 89). See also Vallat to M. le directeur de la Mutuelle générale Française, n.d. but March 1942 (AN: W^III 213¹ no. 90).
125. CGQJ to Syndicat des Exportateurs Français d'Indochine, 28 February 1942 (AN:W^III 213¹ no. 87).
126. Vallat to Dr. Blanke, 16 December 1941 (AN: W^III 213² no. 17).
127. Vallat to MBF, 9 October 1941 (AN: W^III 213¹ no. 36).
128. Bichelonne to Michel, 7 August 1941 (CDJC: LXXV–48); Billig, *Commissariat* [3], vol. III, pp. 98–99, 114, 180.
129. AN: AJ³⁸ 124:81.
130. Darlan to Vallat, 26 August 1941 (AN: AJ³⁸ 70 M9).
131. Billig, *Commissariat* [3], vol. III, p. 317.
132. Report of 6 June 1941 (CDJC: CCXXXVIII–64).
133. CDJC: XCVI–37, 40.
134. Billig, *Commissariat* [3], vol. III, pp. 267–68.
135. Le rapport Formery, 12–23 May 1944 (AN: W^III 212¹ no. 19 [1–4]).
136. Le rapport Houël, 27 April 1944 (AN: W^III 212¹ no. 19 [8]).
137. Henry W. Ehrmann, *Organized Business in France* (Princeton, N.J., 1957), p. 81.
138. AN: AJ³⁸ 405 XXX–78. Conclusive judgments about the *comités d'organisation* await the doctoral thesis of Henri Rousso. The material in these paragraphs is drawn largely from the Fonds Braun (CDJC: CCCLXXIX–48) and the relevant dossiers of the CGQJ (AN: AJ³⁸ 329, 330, 405, 566, 675).
139. AN: AJ³⁸ 405 XXX–78.
140. Le Délégué-général responsable du Comité Général d'Organisation du Commerce (P. Benaerts) to the Directeur-général du SCAP (M. de Faramond), 24 October 1942 (CDJC: CCCLXXIX–48).
141. Syndicat des Fabricants Français de Lampes Électriques (M. de Saléon-Smith, président) to CGQJ, n.d. (AN: AJ³⁸ 405).
142. Comité des Industries de Bois, Groupement national de l'Ameublement (A. Ducrot, président) to Vallat, 24 January 1942 (AN: AJ³⁸ 405 XXX–74).
143. AN: AJ³⁸ 566.
144. M. Voisin, Président de la Chambre Syndicale de la Nouveauté de Rouen to SCAP, 30 March 1942 (AN: AJ³⁸ 329; AJ³⁸ 405 XXX–81).
145. Henri Rousso, "Les Comités d'organisation: aspects structurels et économiques, 1940–44," (master's thesis, Paris I. 1975–76), p. 132.
146. Le président-délégué-général du Comité d'Organisation des Pelletiers et Fourrures (Roger E. Binet) au Secrétariat d'état à la production industrielle, 14 September 1942 (AN: AJ³⁸ 675).
147. Rousso, "Les Comités" [145], p. 209.
148. CDJC: CCCLXXIX–48.
149. Xavier Vallat, témoignage du 17 janvier 1947 (AN: W^III 213¹ no. 30).
150. Le Préfet des Alpes-Maritimes, Rapport mensuel d'information, 6 March 1941 (AN: F¹CIII 1137).
151. AN: AJ³⁸ 405.
152. Ibid.

153. Le Préfet du Tarn-et-Garonne à M. l'Amiral de la Flotte, Ministre de l'Intérieur, 31 May 1941 (AN: F¹cIII).

154. Cf., for example, memorandum by Direction-général de la Sûreté Nationale, 9 March 1941 (AN: AG II 520 CC104F).

155. Donald N. Baker, "The Surveillance of Subversion in Interwar France: the Carnet B in the Seine, 1922–40," *French Historical Studies* X (1978): 486–516.

156. Zosa Szajkowski, *Analytical Franco-Jewish Gazetteer* (New York, 1966), pp. 90–91.

157. Varian Fry, *Surrender on Demand* (New York, 1945), p. 86.

158. Rapport de la Commission d'Emigration, séance du 31 octobre 1941 (LBI).

159. The following paragraphs are drawn from HICEM archives: HH2–FR2–18 to 96; Fry, *Surrender on Demand* [157]; Lowrie, *Hunted Children*, [87], chap. 9; Joseph Weill, *Contribution à l'histoire des camps d'internement dans l'anti-France* (Paris, 1946), pp. 148–50; Szajkowski, *Gazetteer* [156], pp. 90–94.

160. Rapport de la Commission d'Emigration, séance du 31 octobre 1941 (LBI).

161. Suite des rapports sur l'activité du 2e trimestre 1942 (HICEM: HH2–FR2–18).

162. See Arieh Tartakower and Kurt R. Grossmann, *The Jewish Refugee* (New York, 1944), pp. 201–2.

163. AN: AC^II 75 SP 2.

164. AN: AG^II 520.

165. Xavier Vallat, *Le Nez de Cléopâtre: souvenirs d'un homme de droite (1919–1944)*, (Paris, 1957), p. 269.

166. Gilbert Badia, "Camps répressifs ou camps de concentration?" in Gilbert Badia et al., *Les Barbelés de l'exil: études sur l'émigration allemande et autrichienne (1938–1940)* (Grenoble, 1979), pp. 289–332.

167. "Bericht der Kommission Kundt über die Lager in unbesetzten Frankreich," in Barbara Vormeier, "Beitrag zur französischen Emigrantenpolitik (1933–44), in Hanna Schramm and Barbara Vormeier, *Menschen in Gurs: Erinnerungen an ein Internierungslager (1940–44)* (Worms, 1977), pp. 561–65.

168. Weill, *Camps* [159], pp. 21–22; Szajkowski, *Gazetteer* [156], passim.

169. Weill, *Camps* [159], p. 15.

170. Ibid., p. 16; the North African figure comes from the League of Nations Deputy High Commissioner for Refugees, Dr. Kullman, in 1941 ("Refugee Statistics for France," PRO: FO 371/32681/W 15789/4555/48).

171. Weill, *Camps* [159], p. 22; Dannecker memorandum, 28 February 1941 (ND: NG–4895; AN: AG^II 520).

172. "Refugee Statistics for France," (PRO: FO 371/32681/W 15789/4555/48).

173. Baudry and Ambre, *Condition*, [59], pp. 110–11.

174. Ibid., p. 206.

175. Kurt B. Grossmann, *Emigration. Geschichte der Hitler-Fluchtlinge, 1933–1945* (Frankfur-am-Main, 1969), p. 206.

176. Comité de Coordination pour l'Assistance aux Camps à U.S. Secretary of State, 9 January 1941 (LBI).

177. Hillel Kieval, "Legality and Resistance in Vichy France: the Rescue of Jewish Children," *Proceedings of the American Philosophical Society* 124 (5 [October 1980]), p. 350.

178. Le Préfet de la Seine-Inférieur à M. le délégué du gouvernement dans les territoires occupés, 1 October 1942 (AN: F¹CIII 1188); le Préfet des Alpes-Maritimes à M. le Ministre de l'Intérieur, 1 Novembre 1940 (AN: F¹CIII 1137).

179. CDJC: CXIII–125.

180. Schleier to Foreign Ministry, 24 March 1941 (DGFP, series D, XII, 347).

181. WL: PIII i (France), no. 60.

182. See *Mémento* [95], p. 10, for the terms of instructions sent to local authorities.

183. Le Préfet de la Haute-Savoie à M. l'Amiral de la Flotte, Ministre de l'Intérieur, 11 April 1941 (AN: F¹CIII 1187).

184. Report of André Dupont, 9 August 1941 (AN: AJ³⁸ 4).

185. Ibid.

186. Préfet délégué du Ministre de l'Intérieur dans les Territoires occupés à CGQJ, 6 June 1941 (CDJC: CXI–1).

187. Le Préfet des Alpes-Maritimes à M. le Ministre de l'Intérieur, 6 November 1941, 4 December 1941 (AN: F¹ᶜᴵᴵᴵ 1137).

188. Pucheu's circulars to regional prefects, 3 November 1941 and 26 January 1942 (CDJC: LXV–54, 64).

189. Loi du 27 September 1940, JO (1 October 1940).

190. Szajkowski, *Gazetteer* [156], p. 27; Zosa Szajkowski, *Jews and the French Foreign Legion* (New York, 1975), p. 82.

191. Note pour le CGQJ, n.d., but 1941 (AN: AJ³⁸ 1144).

192. Ministère de l'intérieur, circular no. 76, 2 January 1942. See also circulaire no. 431, 25 November 1941 (AN: AJ³⁸ 1150 71JA/4).

193. Lowrie, *Hunted Children* [87], p. 152.

194. Note pour M. Schah (Marseille), 20 October 1941 (HICEM: HH2–FR2–11); Directeur du HICEM à Commandant Doussau, Inspecteur-général des Formations de Travailleurs Étrangers, 6 February 1942 (HICEM: HH2–FR2–38).

195. *New York Times*, 11 January, 26 January, 23 February, and 29 March 1941; Malcolm J. Proudfoot, *European Refugees, 1939–52: A Study in Forced Population Movement* (London, n.d.), p. 49ff; Tartakower and Grossmann, *Refugees* [162], pp. 168–69; Grossmann, *Emigration* [175], pp. 204–5; Lowrie, *Hunted Children* [87], p. 133.

196. AN: F¹ᶜᴵᴵᴵ 1137.

197. André Lavagne to A. Jean-Faure, 28 February 1942 (AN: AGᴵᴵ 520 CC104E).

198. AN: AGᴵᴵ 27.

199. AA: Inland IIg 189.

200. Le Préfet des Pyrénées-orientales, "Rapport mensuel d'information," 3 January 1942 (AN: F¹ᶜᴵᴵᴵ 1181–2).

201. Arthur Koestler, *Scum of the Earth* (London, 1941), pp. 89–92.

202. A. Plédel to M. Allix, 27 February 1941 (AN: AGᴵᴵ 520).

203. Serge Klarsfeld, *Le Mémorial de la déportation des Juifs de France* (Paris, 1978), no pagination; Tartakower and Grossmann, *Refugees* [162], p. 168; Weill, *Camps* [159], p. 38; H. R. Kedward, *Resistance in Vichy France: A Study of Ideas and Motivations* (Oxford, 1978), p. 116.

204. Honoré Baradat, *Pays Basque et Béarn sous la botte allemande, 1940–44* (Pau, [1968]), p. 45.

Chapter 5

1. Testimony of 19 October 1946, trial of Xavier Vallat (AN: Wᴵᴵᴵ 213¹ no. 59).

2. *Le Procès de Xavier Vallat présenté par ses amis* (Paris, 1948), pp. 59–77.

3. "A la recherche de la 'Gauche': une enquête de l'Institut français d'opinion publique," *Les Temps modernes* (May 1955), pp. 1588–89.

4. Ibid., pp. 1624–25.

5. Léon Poliakov, "An Opinion Poll on Anti-Jewish measures in Vichy France," *Jewish Social Studies* XV (2 [April 1953]): 135–50.

6. "Rapport statistique des renseignements recueillis dans les interceptions postales, télégraphiques, et téléphoniques pendant le mois de décembre 1943" (AN: AGᴵᴵ 461 CCXXXVI–G).

7. Service Civil des Contrôles Techniques, "Synthèse hebdomadaire des interceptions de contrôles télégraphiques, téléphoniques, et postaux," no. 197, 25 August 1942 (AN: AGᴵᴵ 461 CCXXXVI–G).

8. AN: F¹ᶜᴵᴵᴵ 1135–1204.

9. For example, "Les Juifs et le marché noir," *Action française* (Lyon), 16 July 1942.

10. Karl Brandt, *Management of Agriculture and Food in the German-Occupied and Other Areas of Fortress Europe* (Stanford, Calif., 1953); Robert O. Paxton, *Vichy France: Old Guard and New Order, 1940–1944* (New York, 1972), pp. 359–61.

11. Pierre Limagne, *Ephémérides de quatre années tragiques, 1940–44,* 3 vols. (Paris, 1945–47), vol. I, p. 540.

12. AN: AG^{II} 28 SG 9 F. For the black market activities of the German espionage group known as the *Bureau Otto,* see Jacques Delarue, *Trafics et crimes sous l'occupation* (Paris, 1968), pp. 32–35.

13. Le Préfet régional de Limoges, rapport mensuel, 11 July 1942 (F^{1}CIII 1197). Also synthèse des contrôles, 5 August 1942 (AN: AG^{II} 461).

14. Synthèse des contrôles, no. 194, 5 August 1942 (AN: AG^{II} 461 CCXXXIV–G.

15. G. Rougeron, *Départment de l'Allier dans l'Etat français (1940–1944)* ([Moulins], 1969), pp. 257–58.

16. Vallat to Ollivier (Bourbon l'Archambault), 9 June 1941 (AN: AJ^{38} 4).

17. Vallat au Ministre de l'Intérieur, 16 September 1941 (AN: AJ^{38} 4).

18. "Rapport Antignac" (AN: AJ^{38} 253).

19. Community leaders of Mégève to Vallat, 14 February 1942 (CDJC: CXCV–86); Report of Devèze, 9 March 1942 (CDJC: CCXXXIX–59).

20. André Siegfried, "Le problème de l'assimilation des immigrants," *Le Temps,* 6–7 December 1941.

21. Boegner to Gillouin, 23 August 1941 (AN: AG^{II} 610 CM26–D).

22. Comité de Coordination (Paris) to UGIF (UG I–32, 12–13).

23. Pierre Tissier, *The Government of Vichy* (London, 1942), pp. 153, 155–56.

24. Georges Boris, *Servir la république: textes et témoignages* (Paris, 1963), pp. 286, 299.

25. André Gillois, *Histoire secrète des Français à Londres de 1940 à 1944* (Paris, 1973), p. 72; René Cassin, *Les Hommes partis de rien* (Paris, 1975), pp. 136, 151, 403.

26. "Les minorités nationales," *Cahiers (O.C.M.),* June 1942, p. 171. See Arthur Calmette, *L'OCM: organisation civile et militaire: histoire d'un mouvement de résistance de 1940 à 1946* (Paris, 1961), p. 54. The article was left out of a collection of OCM material republished in 1945.

27. "Minorités nationales" [26], pp. 179–87.

28. Cf. René Martial, *Vie et constance des races,* 4th ed. (Paris, 1939); and *Français, qui es tu?* (Paris 1942).

29. Simone Pétrement, *La Vie de Simone Weil* (Paris, 1973), vol. II, pp. 476–77.

30. "Rassemblement," *Le Franc-tireur* (Lyon), December 1941. For a more positive reading of this text, see Dominique Veillon. *Le Franc-tireur: un journal clandestin, un mouvement de résistance, 1940–44* (Paris, 1977).

31. Marie Granet and Henri Michel, *Combat. Histoire d'un mouvement de résistance de juillet 1940 à juillet 1943* (Paris, 1957), p. 121.

32. Maurice Eisenbeth, *Les Juifs d'Afrique du Nord: démographie et onomastique* (Algiers, 1936), pp. 18–22; Moses Jung, "Jews in Northern Africa," *Contemporary Jewish Record* V (1942): 618–25. For an excellent recent discussion of the Jewish situation in Algeria, see Charles-Robert Ageron, *Histoire de l'algérie contemporaine,* vol. II: *De l'insurrection de 1871 au déclenchement de la guerre de libération (1954)* (Paris, 1979).

33. Eisenbeth, *Juifs d'Afrique du Nord* [32], p. 66.

34. *Le Réveil algérien* (Oran), 23 February 1898, quoted in Charles-Robert Ageron, *Les Algériens musulmans et la France (1871–1919)* 2 vols. (Paris, 1968), vol. I, p. 596.

35. Ageron, *Algériens musulmans* [34], vol. I, pp. 586–605; and Ageron, *Histoire de l'Algérie contemporaine (1830–1973),* 5th ed. (Paris, 1974), pp. 55–56; Michel Ansky, *Les Juifs d'Algérie: du décret Crémieux à la libération* (Paris, 1950); Zeev Sternhell, *La Droite révolutionnaire, 1885–1914: les origines françaises du fascisme* (Paris, 1978), pp. 232–34.

36. Ansky, *Juifs d'Algérie* [35], pp. 82–85; Ageron, *Algérie contemporaine* [32], pp. 89–90; "The Jews of Algeria," Institute of Jewish Affairs, *World Jewish Congress Reports,* II (October 1949): 7; World Jewish Congress, *The Abrogation of the Crémieux Decree* (New York, [1943]), pp. 13–14.

37. Ansky, *Juifs d'Algérie* [35], pp. 88–98; Ageron, *Algérie contemporaine* [32], p. 91. For the contrasting situation in Tunisia, see Jacques Sabille, *Les Juifs en Tunisie sous Vichy et l'occupation* (Paris, 1954).

38. *Le Républicain de Constantine,* October 1940, quoted in Ansky *Juifs d'Algérie* [35], p. 93.

39. Darlan to CGQJ, 27 June 1941 (AN: AJ^{38} 5).

40. Ansky, *Juifs d'Algérie* [35], pp. 105, 107–37; Joseph Billig, *Le Commissariat général aux questions juives (1941–44)*, 3 vols. (Paris, 1955–60), vol. III, pp. 40–41.

41. Ansky, *Juifs d'Algérie* [35], p. 96; Yves-Maxime Danan, *La Vie politique à Alger de 1940 à 1944* (Paris, 1963), p. 30.

42. Ibid., p. 46.

43. Ansky, *Juifs d'Algérie* [35], pp. 296–97.

44. Ibid.

45. Ansky, *Juifs d'Algérie* [35], p. 249.

46. "The Government of North Africa: M. Peyrouton's Reply to Criticism," *Manchester Guardian*, 8 February 1943.

47. Ansky, *Juifs d'Algérie* [35], p. 253.

48. Noguès to Darlan, 2 April 1942 (AN: AJ³⁸ 67:92); Roosevelt-Noguès conversation, Casablanca, 17 January 1943 (FRUS, *Conferences at Washington 1941–42 and Casablanca, 1943*, p. 608).

49. Ibid., p. 611.

50. Hagen memorandum, 18 November 1942 (CDJC: XXVI–68b).

51. Roland de Pury, "Engagé dans la lutte," in *Chrétiens sous l'occupation. Sens: Juifs et chrétiens dans le monde d'aujourd'hui*, nos. 9/10 (September–October 1978), p. 31.

52. Pierre Pierrard, *Juifs et catholiques français: de Drumont à Jules Isaac (1886–1945)* (Paris, 1970), p. 298.

53. "Dans un vibrant discours, Mgr. Gerlier engage tous les Français à s'unir autour du Maréchal," *Journal des débats*, 28 December 1940; Roland de Pury, "Engagé" [51], 31. See Claude Langlois, "Le régime de Vichy et le clergé d'après les 'Semaines religieuses' des diocèses de la zone libre," *Revue française de science politique* XXII (1972): 750–74.

54. Renée Bédarida, *Les Armes d'esprit: Témoignage chrétien (1941–44)* (Paris, 1977), p. 14; Jacques Duquesne, "Defensor Judaeorum—the French Episcopate, 1940–44," *Wiener Library Bulletin* XXI (spring 1967): 19.

55. Xavier Vallat, *Le Nez de Cléopâtre: souvenirs d'un homme de droite (1919–44)* (Paris, 1957), pp. 240, 264; *Le Procès de Xavier Vallat* [2], pp. 65, 110–11.

56. Jacques Duquesne, *Les Catholiques français sous l'occupation* (Paris, 1966), p. 252.

57. Langlois, "Le régime de Vichy" [53], p. 757.

58. François Delpech, "La persécution des juifs et l'Amitié chrétienne," in Xavier de Montclos et al., *Eglises et chrétiens dans la IIe guerre mondiale: la région Rhône-Alpes. Actes du Colloque tenu à Grenoble du 7 au 9 Octobre 1976* (Lyon, 1978), p. 158.

59. Ibid., p. 159; Wladimir Rabi, "L'Eglise catholique sous l'occupation," *Le Monde juif* 33 (January–March 1977): 39–40.

60. See, for example, Duquesne, *Catholiques français* [56], p. 255. Cf. interventions of François Delpech and Wladimir Rabi in Montclos, *Eglises et chrétiens* [58], pp. 195–99, 201.

61. 18 July 1941 (AG^II 609 CM25–A).

62. Jean-Marie Mayeur, "Les évêques dans l'avant-guerre," in Montclos, *Eglises et chrétiens* [58]; "Pierre-Marie Gerlier, Cardinal Archbishop of Lyons" (PRO: F0371/31944 [Z8960/81/17]); "Le Cardinal Gerlier associe dans un même hommage le Maréchal Pétain et le Général Franco, *Le Figaro*, 14 June 1941.

63. Delpech, in Montclos, *Eglises et chrétiens* [58], p. 161; Varian Fry, *Surrender on Demand* (New York, 1945), pp. 234–35; Duquesne, *Catholiques français* [56], p. 254; "Rapport sur la situation des centres d'hébergement et des camps en zone non-occupée," 1941 (HICEM: HH2–FR2–38).

64. CDJC: CIX–106.

65. CDJC: CCXXXVIII–61.

66. Among various publications of Bérard's report, see L. Papeleux, "Le Vatican et le problème juif, II, 1941–42," RHDGM 27 (1977): 75–84; *Le Procès de Xavier Vallat* [2], pp. 500–509; Léon Poliakov, "Le Vatican et la question juive," *Le Monde juif*, no. 2 (December 1950): 11–14; Georges Wellers, "Dans le sillage du colloque du CDJC (mars 1979)," *Le Monde juif*, no. 94 (April–June 1979): 40–51.

67. *Actes et documents du Saint-Siège relatifs à la Seconde guerre mondiale*, vol. VIII: *Le Saint-Siège et les victimes de guerre, janvier 1941–décembre 1942* (Vatican City, 1974), pp. 295–97, 333–34.

68. CDJC: CIX–106.
69. Press communiqué of CGQJ, 11 October 1941 (AN: AJ³⁸ 62 M75; CDJC: XLII–110).
70. See Marcel Déat's view that the Church could and should live with racism, "Catholicisme et racisme," *L'Oeuvre*, 27 July 1943.
71. Duquesne, *Catholiques Français* [56], p. 264.
72. Charles Klein, "Le clergé et les chrétiens de France tels que les voyaient certains dirigeants nazis sous l'occupation," in Montclos, *Eglises et chrétiens* [58], p. 9.
73. Letter of 25 August 1942 (CDJC: XXXVIII–60).
74. CDJC: XXXVIII–70.
75. *Un Evêque français sous l'occupation. Extraits des messages de S. Ex. Mgr. Saliège, archevêque de Toulouse* (Paris, 1945), p. 72.
76. Marc Boegner, "Rapport," in *Les Eglises protestantes pendant la guerre et l'occupation. Actes de l'assemblée générale du protestantisme français, 1945* (Paris, 1946), p. 16.
77. Boegner to Gillouin, 23 August 1941 (AN: AG^II 610 CM26–D).
78. A-N. Bertrand, "Rapport," in Violette Mouchon et al., *Quelques Actions des protestants de France en faveur des Juifs persécutés sous l'occupation allemande* (Paris, n.d.), p. 18.
79. Marc Boegner, "Rapport" [76], pp. 4–5.
80. *Eglises protestantes* [76], pp. 22–26.
81. Boegner, "Rapport" in Mouchon, *Quelques Actions* [78], p. 7.
82. Gillouin to Pétain, 29 August and 23 August 1941 (AN: AG^II 610 CM26–D).
83. René Gillouin, *J'etais l'ami du maréchal Pétain* (Paris, 1966). The editors of *Ici Londres. Les Voix de la liberté, 1940–1944* (Paris, 1975) published only one BBC broadcast concerning Jews for the years 1940–41—René Cassin, "Message aux Israélites de France," March 1941, vol. I, p. 217—a text that does not mention foreign Jews.
84. Boegner, *Eglises protestantes* [76], p. 26; Boegner, "Rapport," in Mouchon, *Quelques Actions* [78], pp. 7, 8.
85. Marc Boegner, in Henri Manen, *Le Pasteur A.-N. Bertrand, témoin de l'unité évangélique, 1876–1946* (Nîmes, n.d.), p. 187.
86. Pierre Pierrard, *Juifs et catholiques* [52], p. 316; Saliège, *Un Evêque* [75]; Bedarida, *Témoignage chrétien* [54], pp. 21–23.
87. Lucien Steinberg, *Les Autorités allemandes en France occupée: inventaire commentée de la collection de documents conservés au C.D.J.C.* (Paris, 1966); Charlotte Wardi, *Le Juif dans le roman français, 1933–1948* (Paris, 1972), p. 243.
88. Billig, *Commissariat* [40], vol. II, pp. 114–16.
89. Bédarida, *Témoignage chrétien* [54], passim; Pierrard, *Juifs et catholiques* [52], pp. 312–19; Marialetizia Cravetto, "Il problema ebraico nella resistenza christiana," *Rivista di storia e letteratura religiosa* VI (1970): 3–64.
90. Adam Rutkowski, *La Lutte des Juifs en France à l'époque de l'occupation (1940–1944)* (Paris, 1975), p. 96.
91. See Richard Cobb, "A Personal State of War," *Times Literary Supplement*, 10 March 1978, pp. 270–71.
92. G. Ribière, "Discussion," in Montclos, *Eglises et chrétiens* [58], pp. 205–7.
93. Philip Hallie, *Lest Innocent Blood Be Shed* (New York, 1978).
94. Annie Kriegel, "Résistants communistes et juifs persécutés," *H-Histoire*, no. 3 (November 1979); 93–123.
95. Brazzaville Manifesto, 27 October 1940. Charles De Gaulle, *Oeuvres complètes. Discours et messages. Pendant la guerre: juin 1940–janvier 1946* (Paris, 1970), pp. 38–39.
96. De Gaulle, *Oeuvres*, 10 December 1940, p. 41, and 18 September 1941, p. 105.
97. Maurice Schumann, *La Voix du couvre-feu* (Paris 1964), p. 33.
98. CGQJ au Ministre de l'éducation nationale, 14 March 1942 (CDJC: CIX–125); Report of 25 September 1943 (CDJC: LXXIX–102); Billig, *Commissariat* [40], vol. II, pp. 49, 120–23; vol. III, p. 48.
99. Haguenau to Vallat, 31 July 1941, quoted in David Knout, *Contribution à l'histoire de la résistance juive en France, 1940–44* (Paris, 1947), p. 55.
100. Quoted in Robert E. Herzstein, "Le Nazisme et la France (1939–42): population et racisme," RHDGM, 115 (1979): 14.
101. Knochen to MBF, 28 January 1941 (CDJC: V–64).
102. J. Bellemin to CGQJ (Lyon), 30 July 1942 (AN: AJ³⁸ 4).

103. E.g., Billig, *Commissariat* [40], vol. I, p. 201.
104. Darlan to Délégué-général du gouvernement français dans les territoires oc-cupés, 21 January 1942 (CDJC: V–64).
105. Pierre Mendès-France, *Liberté, liberté chérie* (Paris, 1977), pp. 321–22.
106. CDJC: CCXLVI–15.
107. Report of September 1940 (PRO: FO 371/24313 [C10842/67/17]).
108. Leahy to U.S. Secretary of State, 16 June 1941 (FRUS, 1941, II 508–9).
109. J. Lubetzki, *La Condition des Juifs en France sous l'occupation allemande, 1940–44* (Paris, 1945), pp. 116–19; Rougeron, *Département de l'Allier* [15], pp. 258–59.
110. Joseph Billig, *L'Institut d'étude des questions juives: officine française des autor-ités nazies en France* (Paris, 1974).
111. André Kaspi, " 'Le Juif et la France': une exposition à Paris en 1941," *Le Monde juif,* no. 79 (July–September 1975): 8–20.
112. For the German budget, see AA: Deutscher Botschaft Paris, Paket Nr. 1192, Judenfragen 30b. For other aspects of the exposition, see AA: Inland II A/B 83–26 Frank-reich.
113. Kaspi, " 'Le Juif' [111].
114. Sézille to François, 15 January 1942 (CDJC: XIc–656).
115. H. R. Kedward, *Resistance in Vichy France: A Study of Ideas and Motivations* (Oxford, 1978) p. 168; Bédarida, *Témoignage chrétien* [54], p. 30 no. 1; Claude Bellanger et al., *Histoire générale de la presse française,* vol. IV: *De 1940 à 1944* (Paris, 1969), pp. 78–79; Duquesne, *Catholiques français* [56], p. 255; *Esprit,* 9e année, no. 101 (June 1941); Michel Winock, *Histoire politique de la revue "Esprit," 1930–50* (Paris 1975), p. 228.
116. Malglaive, "Projet de revue mensuelle," undated (CDJC: CXCV–111); Billig, *Com-missariat* [40], vol. II, pp. 268–69.
117. Quoted in Charlotte Wardi, *Le Juif dans le roman français, 1933–48* (Paris, 1972), p. 244.
118. CGQJ au Secrétaire-général à la Jeunesse, 13 May 1942 (AN: AJ38 4); Kedward, *Resistance* [115], p. 170; Hillel Kieval "Legality and Resistance in Vichy France: The Rescue of Jewish Children," *Proceedings of the American Philosophical Society,* vol. 124, no. 5 (October 1980): 342–50, 360–61.
119. Uwe Dietrich Adam, *Judenpolitik im Dritten Reich* (Düsseldorf, 1972), p. 341.
120. JTA report, 23 March 1942 (WL PC6 3b4).
121. Le Préfet du Cher, 3 December 1941 (AN: F1CIII1147).

Chapter 6

1. AN: F60 1485.
2. HICEM: HH2–FR2–71.
3. AN: AJ38 70 M85.
4. BDC: SS-Personalhauptamt, Personal-Akte Werner Best.
5. See Pierre Laroque's broadcast, 23 June 1943, in *Ici Londres, 1940–1944: Les Voix de la liberté,* ed. Jean-Louis Crémieux-Brilhac (Paris, 1975), vol. III, p. 189.
6. Edward L. Homze, *Foreign Labor and Nazi Germany* (Princeton, N.J., 1967), pp. 194, 200; Eberhard Jäckel, *La France dans l'Europe de Hitler* (Paris, 1968), pp. 319–34; Fred Kupferman, "Le Gouvernement Laval et les tentatives de relance de la collabora-tion," *Le Monde juif* 32 (October–December 1976): 133–52.
7. Haute Cour de Justice, Ministère public contre Bousquet, audience du 21 June 1949, fascicule 1, 118ff.
8. ND: PS–710, reprinted in Raul Hilberg, *Documents of Destruction* (Chicago, 1971), p. 88. Cf. Martin Broszat, "Hitler und die Genesis der 'Endlösung': aus Anlass der Thesen von David Irving," *Vierteljahrsheft für Zeitgeschichte* 25 (1977): 739–75.
9. ND: NG–2586, reprinted in Hilberg, *Documents* [8], pp. 89–99; Lucy Dawidowicz,

A Holocaust Reader (New York, 1976), pp. 73–82; and Robert M. W. Kempner, *Eichmann und Komplizen* (Zurich, 1971), pp. 133–47.

10. Abetz to von Ribbentrop, 20 August 1940 (ND: NG–2433).

11. "Zentrales Judenamt in Paris," 21 January 1941 (CDJC: V–59).

12. Best to MBF, 4 April 1941 (BA: R70 Frankreich/32, 9–13; also CDJC: LXXV–145). Henri Monneray, ed., *La Persécution des Juifs en France et dans les autres pays de l'ouest présentése par la France à Nuremberg* (Paris, 1947), pp. 137–38.

13. Joseph Billig, *Le Commissariat-général aux questions juives (1941–44)*, (Paris, 1955–60), vol. I, p. 59.

14. Kurt R. Grossmann, *Emigration. Geschichte der Hitler-Flüchtlinge, 1933–45* (Frankfurt-am-Main, 1969), p. 203.

15. Claude Lévy and Paul Tillard, *La Grande Rafle du Vel d'Hiv (16 juillet 1942)*, (Paris, 1967), p. 249.

16. VOBIF, Nr. 39, 22 August 1941. For French protests of 11 January and 18 April 1942, see CDJC: LXI–63, and AN: AJ³⁸64 M76.

17. Billig, *Commissariat* [13], vol. II, pp. 17–18; "Arrestation des Juifs dans le XIe arrondissement," *Le Matin*, 21 August 1941.

18. "Réunion hebdomadaire du Secrétariat-général à la Délégation française" (AN: AJ³⁸ 67 M75).

19. Schleier to von Weizsäcker (Berlin), 30 October 1941 (ND: NG–5095).

20. Jäckel, *La France* [6], pp. 269–71; Hans Umbreit, *Der Militärbefehlshaber in Frankreich, 1940–44* (Boppard-am-Rhein, 1968), pp. 128–33; Hervé Villeré, *L'Affaire de la Section spéciale* (Paris 1977).

21. Jäckel, *La France* [6], p. 273; Marcelle Adler-Bresse, "La répression de la résistance française par les autorités allemandes d'occupation, 1940–45," unpublished paper, 1963.

22. Umbreit, *Der Militärbefehlshaber* [20], p. 263; Raph Feigelson, *Le Crime du 15 décembre: témoignage* (Paris, 1964), pp. 28–30.

23. "Une note officieuse du gouvernement français," *Le Figaro*, 15 December 1941.

24. *Les procès de la collaboration: Fernand de Brinon, Joseph Darnand, Jean Luchaire: compte-rendu sténographique* (Paris, 1948), pp. 114–18.

25. 10 December 1941. Cf. Jean d'Orsay, "Une mesure bien accueillie," *Le Matin*, 16 December 1941.

26. *Le Temps*, 11 December 1941. J. Lubetzki, *La Condition des Juifs en France sous l'occupation allemande, 1940–44* (Paris, 1945), pp. 187n., 204.

27. Pucheu to regional prefects, 2 January 1942 (CDJC: LXI–61).

28. *Le Temps*, 11 December 1941.

29. Darlan to de Brinon, 11 October 1941 (AN: F⁶⁰1485; also CDJC: CII–11a).

30. CGQJ to Darlan, 20 August 1941, (AN: AJ³⁸ 67 M75); de Brinon to Ministère de défense nationale, 26 March 1942 (AN: F⁶⁰ 1485).

31. Best to Knochen, 2 January 1942 (BA: R70 Frankreich/23, 8–9).

32. ND: RF–1241. Also CDJC: XXVI–19, in Lucien Steinberg, *Les Autorités allemandes en France occupée: inventaire commentée de la collection de documents conservés au CDJC* (Paris, 1966), p. 249.

33. Serge Klarsfeld, *Le Mémorial de la déportation des Juifs de France* (Paris, 1978), no pagination; contains the list of deportees.

34. Jäckel, *La France* [6], pp. 325–26.

35. 12 March 1942 (CDJC: XXVb–10).

36. Schleier to AA, Berlin, 11 September 1942 (AA: Inland IIg 187; also ND: NG–5109).

37. Note of Dannecker for Knochen and Lischka, 13 May 1942 (CDJC: XXVb–29, in Steinberg, *Autorités* [32], p. 111).

38. Abetz to Knochen, 21 May 1942 (CDJC: XLIXa–41).

39. BA: R70 Frankreich/23, p. 13.

40. Dannecker note, 15 June 1942 (ND: RF–1217, in Monneray, *Persécution* [12], pp. 126–27).

41. Zeitschel to BdS, 27 June 1942 (ND: RF–1220, in Monneray, *Persécution* [12], pp. 138–39).

42. Thompson to Secretary of State, 7 August 1942 (FRUS, 1942, I, 464).

43. Fred Kupferman, *Pierre Laval* (Paris, 1976), pp. 6–7, 88.

44. Geoffrey Warner, *Pierre Laval and the Eclipse of France, 1931–45* (London, 1968), p. 147.

45. Philippe Erlanger, *La France sans étoile: souvenirs de l'avant-guerre et du temps de l'occupation* (Paris, 1974), pp. 120–21.

46. Abetz to Berlin, 23 May 1942 (T–120/422/217099ff).

47. Knochen memorandum on the Final Solution, 12 February 1943 (BA: R70 Frankreich/23).

48. Ibid.

49. Zeitschel to Schleier, 28 February 1942 (CDJC: LXXI–84, in Steinberg, *Autorités* [32], pp. 108–9).

50. Pastor Boegner to Pétain, 20 August 1942 (AN: AG^II 495 CC 77–C).

51. Schleier to AA (Berlin), 11 September 1942 (ND: NG–5109).

52. Réunion du conseil des ministres." 26 June 1942 (CHDGM: Gouvernement de Vichy).

53. Ibid., 3 July 1942.

54. Quoted in Jacques Delarue, "La police et l'administration" (CDJC colloque paper, 1979, 15).

55. Dannecker to Knochen, 1 and 6 July 1942, in Joseph Weill, *Contribution à l'histoire des camps d'internement dans l'Anti-France* (Paris, 1946), pp. 193–95.

56. Report of Dannecker, 6 July 1942 (ND: RF–1225, in Monneray, *Persécution* [12], p. 140).

57. Note of Röthke, 13 August 1942 (ND: RF–1234, in Monneray, *Persécution* [12], p. 152).

58. Dannecker to BdS (Brussels), 9 July 1942 (CDJC: XXVb–54), in Steinberg, *Autorités* [32], p. 117.

59. Uwe Dietrich Adam, *Judenpolitik im Dritten Reich* (Dusseldorf, 1972) pp. 334–38.

60. Darlan to de Brinon, 21 January 1942, (CDJC: CCXVI-4), reprinted in Michel Ansky, *Les Juifs d'Algérie: du décret Crémieux à la libération* (Paris, 1950), p. 371.

61. Léon Poliakov, *L'Etoile jaune* (Paris, 1949), pp. 24–27.

62. Steinberg, *Autorités* [32], pp. 57–58; Philip Friedman, "The Jewish Badge and the Yellow Star in the Nazi Era," *Historia Judaica* XVII (1955): 45.

63. Billig, *Commissariat* [13], vol. I, p. 238.

64. Eighth ordinance of 29 May 1942 (VOBIF, 1 June 1942); Poliakov, *Etoile* [61], pp. 41–42.

65. Allaire to CGQJ, 11 June 1942 (CDJC: XLIXa–83).

66. Poliakov, *Etoile* [61], p. 38.

67. Abetz to Berlin, 2 and 7 July 1942 (CDJC: XLIXa–41); AA: Inland IIg 187. Akten betreffend Judenfrage in Frankreich, 1942–44.

68. Pétain to de Brinon, 12 June 1942 (CDJC: XLIXa–90a, and in Poliakov, *Etoile* [61], p. 61).

69. Ménétrel to de Brinon, 3 July 1942 (AN: F^60 1485); Poliakov, *Etoile* [61], p. 62 n.2.

70. Cardinal Suhard's office to de Brinon, 14 October 1942 (AN: F^60 1485).

71. CDJC: XXVa–174.

72. Oberg to Commandant des Sapeurs-pompiers de Paris, 15 June 1942 (CDJC: XLIXa–89), in Steinberg, *Autorités* [32], p. 65.

73. Report of General Reinecke, 10 August 1942 (ND: NOKW–3538).

74. Ninth ordinance of 8 July 1942 (VOBIF, 15 July 1942), and successive notices.

75. "Impudence juive," *Le Matin*, 1 July 1942; "Un Seul Choix pour les juifs: l'étoile jaune ou la prison," *Le Matin*, 3 August 1942; JTA, 3 August 1942; "The Jews of France," *Manchester Guardian*, 23 July 1942; Pierre Limagne, *Ephémérides de quatres années tragiques, 1940–44*, 3 vols. (Paris, 1945–47), vol. I, p. 581. See also the reaction of Dr. Robert Debré, *L'Honneur de vivre: témoignage* (Paris, 1974), p. 231.

76. "Etoiles filantes," *Le Matin*, 6 August 1942; Limagne, *Ephémérides* [75], vol. I, p. 584.

77. AN: F^1CIII 172, 1190, 1197, 1198.

78. JTA, 5 June 1942; Philippe Garnier-Raymond, *Une certaine France: l'antisémitisme, 1940–44* (Paris, 1975), p. 70.

79. Poliakov, *Etoile* [61], pp. 80, 83; Oberg to Schleier, 28 October 1942 (ND: RF–1231, in Monneray, *Persecution* [12], pp. 175–76).

80. Poliakov, *Etoile* [61], pp. 78–86.
81. "Visas for Refugees," *Manchester Guardian,* 4 August 1942; JTA, 7 June, 3 July, and 31 August 1942.
82. Poliakov, *Etoile* [61], pp. 86–89.
83. *Les Eglises protestantes pendant la guerre et l'occupation. Actes de l'assemblée générale du protestantisme français, 1945* (Paris, 1946), pp. 27–28.
84. Maurice Duverger, *L'Autre côté des choses* (Paris, 1977), pp. 86–88.
85. Jean Galtier-Boissière, *Mon journal pendant l'occupation* (Garas, 1944), p. 133.
86. Note of Moritz, 17 June 1942 (CDJC: XLIX–66).
87. MBF to Dr. Bock, 1 June 1942 (ND: RF–1232).
88. Le Préfet de la Vienne, rapport mensuel of 4 July 1942 (AN: F¹CIII 1197).
89. JO (12 December 1942, rectified 27 January 1943).
90. Schleier to Berlin, 11 September 1942 (AA: Inland IIg 187; also ND: NG–5109).
91. Otto Abetz, *Histoire d'une politique franco-allemande, 1930–50: mémoires d'un ambassadeur* (Paris, 1953), p. 308; Raul Hilberg, *The Destruction of the European Jews* (Chicago, 1961), p. 407; Lucien Steinberg, "La collaboration policière, 1940–44," unpublished paper, 1978.
92. Müller (RSHA IV B 4, Berlin) to Oberg and Knochen, 3 July 1943 (BA: R 70 Frankreich/23, 36–37).
93. CDJC: CCCXLV–7.
94. Dannecker, "La Question juive en France et son traitement," 1 July 1941 (ND: RF–1207), in Monneray, *Persécution* [12], pp. 104–5.
95. Dannecker, "Juifs," 22 February 1942 (ND: RF–1210), in Monneray, *Persécution* [12], pp. 117–18; Lévy and Tillard; *Grande Rafle* [15], pp. 243–44, 249–51; Billig, *Commissariat* [13], vol. I, pp. 250, 255, vol. II, pp. 195–96; Jacques Delarue, *Histoire de la Gestapo* (Paris, 1962), p. 373. See the hostile German report on Tulard in 1943 (CDJC: XXVII–29); and the note of Röthke, 10 February 1943 (CDJC: XXVc–204).
96. Billig, *Commissariat* [13], vol. I, p. 36, vol. II, pp. 195–96.
97. Decree of 10 December 1941 (AN: AJ³⁸ 62 M75).
98. Sixième ordonnance, 7 February 1942 (VOBIF 11 February 1942). Cf. Commandant du Grand Paris, Etat-major administratif à Préfet du Police, 16 February 1942 (CDJC: CXCV–21).
99. Oberg to Bousquet, 29 July 1942 (AA: Botschaft Paris *[geheim]* 2468); Warner, *Laval* [44], p. 304.
100. BA: R70 Frankreich/13, "Polizei in Frankreich: allgemeines," pp. 112–13; AA: Botschaft Paris *(geheim)* 2468, "Akten betreffend der Höhere SS- und Polizeiführer im Bereich des Militärbefehlshabers in Frankreich," passim; Tribunal militaire de Paris, Procès Oberg-Knochen (CDJC: LXIV–1); Haute Cour de Justice, Ministère public contre Bousquet.
101. Delarue, *Gestapo* [95], pp. 509–12, gives a charitable interpretation of these accords, from Bousquet's standpoint.
102. Steinberg, "Collaboration policière" [91], p. 28.
103. Billig, *Commissariat* [13], vol. II, pp. 51–63; Darquier to Laval, 31 July 1942 (CDJC: CXIV–25); Bousquet to regional prefects (CDJC: XXXIII–16).
104. Note of Röthke, 19 July 1942 (ND: RF–1226), in Monneray, *Persécution* [12], pp. 131–32.
105. Ibid.
106. Note of Dannecker, 3 August 1942 (CDJC: XXVb–113). Cf. also Michel Mazor "L'influence nazie sur le sort des Juifs dans la zone non-occupée de la France," *Le Monde juif* (April–June 1971), p. 34.
107. Heinrichsohn memorandum, 27 August 1942, in Monneray, *Persécution* [12], p. 154. For the CGQJ's appreciation of the logic of the timetables, cf. CGQJ to Préfet-délégué du Ministère de l'intérieur, 31 July 1942 (CDJC: CII–61).
108. For example, le Préfet des Bouches-du-Rhône, 4 April 1942 (AN: F¹CIII1143); le Préfet de la Haute Garonne, 8 April 1942 (AN: F¹CIII1154).
109. "Action en faveur des internés durant le 1er semestre 1942." HICEM: HH2–FR2–19; HICEM: HH2–FR2–40.
110. Documentation March 1942 (HICEM: HH2–FR2–19).
111. CGQJ (Jarnieu) to Laval, 4 June 1942 (AN: AJ³⁸61 M46); Laval to CGQJ, 5 September 1942 (AN: AJ³⁸ 62 M72).

112. Adam, *Judenpolitik* [59], pp. 306–10; AA: Inland IIg 189, "Verhaftungen ausland-ischen Juden in Frankreich, 1941," 8/1; Best to MBF, 4 April 1941 (CDJC: LXXV–145); Schellenberg to Wilhelmstrasse, 20 May 1941 (ND: NG–3104); Monneray, *Persecution* [12], pp. 165–7.

113. RSHA (Berlin) to SS headquarters in Belgium and France, 23 October 1941 (CDJC: XXVb–7).

114. MBF Circular, 4 February 1942 (CDJC: XXVI–10); ND:RF–1203; AA: Botschaft Paris 1318; Müller to MBF, 19 January 1942 (CDJC: XXVb–5).

115. Continuation of reports on the activity of HICEM in the course of the second semester, 1942 (HICEM: HH2–FR2–18); Commission d'information confessionelle, ac-count of the session of 26 July 1942 (JTS: no. 1 box 13); UGIF to Ministère de l'Intérieur, 27 July 1942 (HICEM: HH2–FR2–110). Cf. also HICEM: HH2–FR2–40.

116. Cado to regional prefects, 4 August 1942 (CDJC: CII–62).

117. UGIF to Secrétaire-général à la Police, 3 August 1942 (HICEM: HH2–FR2–110).

118. "Laval Losing Confidence," *Manchester Guardian*, 30 September 1942.

119. HICEM: HH2–FR2–15 and 72.

120. AFSC Report, "Activities in France, 1940–November 1942," LBI: 741.

121. Dannecker to Knochen, 6 July 1942; photograph in Joseph Weill, *Contribution à l'histoire des camps d'internement dans l'Anti-France* (Paris, 1946), p. 195; also ND: RF–1225, in Monneray, *Persécution* [12], pp. 139–41.

122. Note of Dannecker, 8 July 1942, in Monneray, *Persécution* [12], 142–45; Dan-necker to Oberg, Knochen, and Lischka, 7 July 1942 (CDJC: XXVb–55), in Steinberg, *Autorités* [32], pp. 116–17.

123. François Bondy, "Rapport sur le camp du Vernet (Ariège) et sur les conditions de l'arrestation et de l'internement de nombreux étrangers en France" (Paris, 1940), WL: PIIIh (Camp du Vernet, France), no. 629.

124. Hennequin, "Consignes pour les équipes chargés des arrestations," 12 July 1942, in Monneray, *Persécution* [12], pp. 145–47.

125. Lévy and Tillard, *Grande rafle* [15], pp. 23, 37–38.

126. Ibid., p. 45.

127. "Les réceptions du président Laval," *Le Temps*, 17 July 1942; Pierre Nicolle, *Cinquante mois d'armistice* (Paris, 1947), vol. I, p. 477.

128. "Réunion du conseil des ministres," 18 July 1942 (CHDGM: Gouvernement de Vichy).

129. Report of Röthke, 18 July 1942 (CDJC: XLIX–67).

130. Klarsfeld, *Mémorial* [33].

131. CHDGM: Camps d'internement, Drancy, AII. See also Jacques Darville et Simon Wichené, *Drancy-la-Juive, ou la deuxième inquisition* (Cachan, 1945); Georges Wellers, *De Drancy à Auschwitz* (Paris, 1946); Lévy et Tillard, *Grande rafle* [15], pp. 247–49; Weill, *Camps* [121], pp. 213–26.

132. Le Préfet de la Seine au Ministère de l'intérieur, 21 August 1941 (CDJC: CII–8).

133. Report of 9 December 1941 (CDJC: CII–18).

134. Weill, *Camps* [55], p. 216.

135. Wellers, *Drancy* [131], pp. 91–93.

136. Delarue, "Police" [54]11.

137. Commandant de Drancy to Sous-directeur chargé de la Direction des étrangers et des affairs juives, 26 June 1942, in Klarsfeld, *Mémorial* [33].

138. CHDGM: Camps d'internement, Drancy, A.II.

139. Note (signature illegible), 12 September 1942 (CHDGM: Camps d'internement, Drancy, A. II).

140. Klarsfeld, *Mémorial* [33], n.p.; Wellers, *Drancy* [131], pp. 121–22.

141. Rapport mensuel d'information, 1 September 1942 (AN:F^{1}CIII1186).

142. Rapport mensuel d'information, 3 September 1942 (AN: F^{1}CIII1156).

143. Note of Dannecker, 6 July 1942 (ND: RF–1225), in Monneray, *Persécution* [12], p. 141; note of Zeitschel, 28 February 1941 (CDJC: LXXXI–84).

144. Note of 28 February 1941 (CDJC: V–62), in Michel Mazor, "L'influence mazie sur le sortt des juifs dans la zone non-occupée de la France," *Le monde juif*, April–June 1971, p. 30; Steinberg, *Autorités* [32], p. 102; Notes of Dannecker, 26–29 June 1942 (CDJC: XXVb–41, 43, 44, and XXVI–33)).

145. Report of Dannecker, 20 July 1942, in Monneray, *Persécution* [12], p. 160.

146. Ibid., p. 162.

147. Röthke memorandum, 28 July 1942 (CDJC: XXVb–96); Note of Röthke, 13 August 1942 (ND: RF–1234), in Monneray, *Persécution* [12], p. 152.

148. Dannecker memorandum, 29 July 1942 (CDJC: XXVb–112). Dannecker to Knochen, 3 August 1942 (CDJC: XXVb–113); note of Hagen, 3 August 1942 (CDJC: XXVI–54); both in Steinberg, *Autorités* [32], pp. 123–24.

149. Note for Darquier de Pellepoix, 31 August 1942 (AN: AJ³⁸ M75); Haute Cour de Justice, Ministère public contre Bousquet, audience du 21 June 1949, fascicule 2, 73; Lubetzki, *Condition* [26], p. 231.

150. Note of Heinrichson, 27 August 1942, in Monneray, *Persécution* [12], pp. 153–54.

151. AN: AJ³⁸ 1150 71JA/4.

152. Le préfet de l'Hérault, rapport mensuel d'information, 3 October 1942 (AN: F¹ CIII 1156).

153. Le préfet de la Haute Garonne, rapport mensuel d'information, 5 October 1942 (AN: F¹CIII1154).

154. Donald A. Lowrie, memorandum, 17 September 1942 (PRO: FO371/32056 [Z8804/1716/17]).

155. Lowrie, memorandum, August 1942 (PRO: FO 371/32056 [Z8804/1716/17]).

156. Note of Dannecker, 21 March 1942 (CDJC: XXVb–17), in Steinberg, *Autorités* [32], p. 271; Röthke to Eichmann, 20 July 1942 (CDJC: XXVb–86), in Steinberg, *Autorités* [32], p. 120; and Adam Rutkowski, *La Lutte des Juifs en France à l'époque de l'Occupation (1940–44)* (Paris, 1975), p. 101.

157. *Le Figaro*, 28 August 1942, notes his replacement without explaining it. Cf. CDJC: CCXIV–88; Henri Amoretti, *Lyon capitale, 1940–44* (Paris, 1964), p. 150.

158. Le préfet du Tarn-et-Garonne, 5 October 1942 (AN: F¹CIII1193).

159. Le préfet de la Gironde à de Brinon, 1 October 1942 (AN: F⁶⁰1485); Limagne, *Ephémérides* [75], entry for 11 September 1942, II, 771.

160. Höhere SS- und Polizeiführer im Bereich des MBF, 19 August 1943, (BA: R70 Frankreich/13), "Polizei in Frankreich, allgemeines," 110–14.

161. Le préfet de l'Ardèche, 31 August 1942 (AN: F¹CIII1137); le préfet de la Haute Savoie, 1 September 1942 (AN: F¹CIII1187); le préfet régional de Lyon, September 1942 (AN: F¹CIII1200).

162. Bousquet to Darquier de Pellepoix, 31 August 1942 (CDJC: CV–61); Schleier to Berlin, 11 September 1942 (AA: Inland IIg 187); note of Zeitschel, 16 September 1942 (CDJC: LXXI–106).

163. Note of Röthke, 18 August 1942 (CDJC: XXVb–132); Giessler (SD-Vichy) to Knochen, 29 August 1942 (CDJC: XXVI–58).

164. Lowrie, memorandum, 17 September 1942 (PRO: FO371/32056 [Z8804/1716/17]).

165. Note of Hagen, 3 August 1942 (CDJC: XXVb–112), in Steinberg, *Autorités* [32], p. 124; note of Hagen, 3 September 1942 (CDJC: XLIX–42).

166. Note of Röthke, 1 September 1942 (ND: RF–1228); note of Ahnert, 3 September 1942 (ND: RF–1227), both in Monneray, *Persécution* [12], pp. 157, 192.

167. Note pour le dossier de Zeitschel, 16 September 1942 (CDJC: LXXI–106), in Steinberg, *Autorités* [32], p. 130.

168. Gallien to Laval, 23 July 1942 (CDJC: XXVb–92), in Steinberg, *Autorités* [32], p. 121; note of Hagen, 3 August 1942 (CDJC: XXVI–54), in Steinberg, *Autorités* [32], p. 124.

169. Minutes of Comité de Coordination (Nîmes), 9 September 1942 (LBI: 90); Thompson to U.S. Secretary of State, 7 August 1942 (FRUS, 1942, I 464).

170. Tuck to U.S. Secretary of State, 26 August 1942 (FRUS, 1942, II 710).

171. Knochen to Eichmann, 25 September 1942 (CDJC: XXVb–177); note of Hagen, 3 September 1942 (CDJC: XLIX–42[1]).

172. Report of Donald Lowrie, August 1942 (PRO: 371/32056 [Z8804/1716/17]), and a similar Lowrie report, 10 August 1942, in Zosa Szajkowski, *Analytical Franco-Jewish Gazetteer, 1939–45* (New York; 1966), p. 119; minutes of the Comité de Coordination (Nîmes), 9 September 1942 (LBI: 90); Weill, *Camps* [55], p. 175.

173. Report in the hand of André Lavagne, 24 July 1942 (AN:AG^II 495 CC 77–D).

174. Baur to CGQJ, 28 August 1942 (YIVO: UG, CVIII–10).

175. Report of 29 September 1942 (AN: AG^II 492 CC 72–A).

176. Klarsfeld, *Mémorial* [33], n.p.
177. Note of Dannecker, 15 June 1942 (ND: RF–1217), in Monneray, *Persécution* [12], p. 126.
178. Dannecker to Eichmann, 6 July 1942 (CDJC: XLIX–35).
179. Note of Röthke, 18 July 1942, in Monneray, *Persécution* [12], p. 150.
180. Note of Dannecker, 21 July 1942 (CDJC: XXVI–46), in Steinberg, *Autorités* [32], p. 120, also ND: RF–1233, in Monneray, *Persécution* [12], pp. 197–98.
181. Wellers, *Drancy* [131], pp. 56–57.
182. Notes of Germain Bleckman (CHDGM: Camps d'internement, Drancy, A. 12. I).
183. Report (undated) of Donald Lowrie to Paul Anderson (LBI: 552).
184. Leguay to Darquier de Pellepoix, 3 August 1942 (CDJC: CII–61).
185. Report in the hand of André Lavagne, chief of staff of Marshal Pétain, drawn from information submitted by an official of the Secours National, 24 July 1942 (AN: AG II 495 CC 77–D).
186. Alfred Mallet, *Pierre Laval*, 2 vols. (Paris, 1955), vol. II, p. 261; Warner, *Laval* [44], p. 307.
187. Hillel Kieval, "From Social Work to Resistance: Relief and Rescue of Jewish Children in Vichy France," unpublished B.A. thesis, Harvard University, 1973.
188. UGIF, 6e direction, to Bousquet (HICEM: HH2–FR2–109); Tuck to Hull, 11 September 1942, and Hull to Tuck, 28 September 1942 (FRUS, 1942, II 712–13).
189. Boegner, in *Eglises protestantes* [83], p. 33.
190. Abetz to Berlin, 15 September 1942 (AA: Inland IIg 187: Akten betreffend Judenfrage in Frankreich von 1942 bis 1944); Abetz to Berlin, 12 October and 24 October 1942 (AA: Politische Abteilung Pol II: Politik Frankreich. Akten betreffend Judenfragen: "Politik 36: Judenfragen").
191. Accounts of meeting of 16 October 1942 by Donald Lowrie and Lindsley H. Noble (LBI: 597–98, 601–4).
192. Lindsley H. Noble, "Diary of Emergency Emigration of Jewish Refugee Children," 26 October, 5 November 1942 (LBI: 589, 594–95).
193. Szajkowski, *Gazetteer* [172], p. 74.
194. Cf. Lévy and Tillard, *Grande Rafle* [15], pp. 103–5.
195. Billig, *Commissariat* [13], vol. III, p. 319.
196. Ibid., vol. I, p. 255; vol. III, pp. 316–18.
197. Cf. Haute Garonne (AN: F¹CIII 1154); Lozère (AN: F¹CIII 1164).
198. Warren to U.S. Secretary of State, 28 August 1942 (FRUS, 1942, I 467); Lois Kellog Jessup memorandum, 3 January 1943 (LBI: 853).
199. Krug to Paris, 9 September 1942 (AA: Botschaft Paris 1318).
200. Enquête of SEC, 4 November 1942 (CDJC: LXXXIX–43).
201. Report of 29 September 1942 (AN: AG^II 492 CC 72–A).
202. "Coup de filet dans toute la France," *Le Matin*, 15–16 August 1942.
203. JTA, 14 September 1942.
204. AN: F¹CIII 1187.
205. AN: F¹CIII 1195.
206. AN: AG^II 492 CC 72–A; Jacques Duquesne, *Les Catholiques français sous l'occupation* (Paris, 1966), p. 256.
207. François Delpech, "La persécution des Juifs et l'Amitié chrétienne," in Xavier de Montclos et al., *Eglises et chrétiens dans la IIe guerre mondiale. La région Rhône-Alpes* (Lyon, 1978), p. 168.
208. Duquesne, *Catholiques* [206], p. 257; L. Papeleux, "Le Vatican et le problème juif. II. 1941–42," RHDGM, 27 (July 1977): 78.
209. "Mgr. Théas," *Documentation catholique* (1 May 1977), p. 447; Duquesne, *Catholiques* [206], p. 260.
210. Duquesne, *Catholiques* [206], p. 261.
211. Quoted in Renée Bédarida, *Les Armes de l'esprit: Témoignage chrétien (1941–44)* (Paris, 1977), p. 125.
212. Danielle Delmaire, "Le Cardinal Liénart devant la persécution des Juifs de Lille pendant la Seconde guerre mondiale," CDJC colloque, 1979.
213. Duquesne *Catholiques* [206], p. 262.

214. *La Revue des deux mondes,* 1 January 1941; André Sauvageot, *Marseille dans la tourmente, 1939–44* (Paris, 1949), p. 157, n.2.

215. T–120/4640/B209249.

216. Regnier to de Brinon, 23 July 1942 (AN: F⁶⁰ 1485); Lubetzki, *Condition* [26], p. 120.

217. UGIF to M. le Grand chancelier de la Légion d'honneur, 27 October 1942 (UG: CIX–I, p. 5); Szajkowski, *Gazetteer* [172], p. 118.

218. Edouard Patin to de Brinon, 1 June 1943 (AN: F⁶⁰ 1485).

219. Abetz to Berlin, 2 Sept. 1942 (T–120/434/220345); le préfet du Tarn-et-Garonne, rapport mensuel d'information, 5 September 1942 (AN: F¹CIII 1183–4); Henri Cadier, *Le Calvaire d'Israel et la solidarité chrétienne* (Geneva, 1945), pp. 49; H. O. Kedward, *Resistance in Vichy France: A Study of Ideas and Motivations* (Oxford, 1978) pp. 182–83; Billig, *Commissariat* [13], vol. II, 96–97.

220. Bernard Aulas, *Vie et mort des Lyonnais en guerre, 1939–45* (Roanne, 1974), p. 212, n.11.

221. Le préfet du Tarn-et-Garonne, rapport mensuel d'information, 5 October 1942 (AN: F¹CIII 1154); Duquesne, *Catholiques* [206], p. 257.

222. "Note d'orientation du 4 septembre 1942" (CDJC:CIX–123); Duquesne, *Catholiques* [206], p. 270.

223. Jacques Polonski, *La Presse, la propagande, et l'opinion publique sous l'occupation* (Paris, 1946), pp. 68–69; Limagne, *Ephémérides* [75], vol. II, pp. 737, 753–59.

224. Abetz to Ribbentrop, 28 August 1942 (ND: NG–4578, also CDJC: CXXVIa–12); Papeleux, "Vatican" [208], pp. 79–80.

225. Le Préfet du Tarn-et-Garonne, June 1942 (An: F¹CIII 1193).

226. Abetz to Ribbentrop, 28 August 1942 in (ND: NG–4578, also T–120/434/220–323–4); Valeri to Maglione, 14 August 1942, in *Actes et documents du Saint-Siège relatifs a la Seconde guerre mondiale* (Vatican City, 1970–75), vol. VIII, pp. 620–21.

227. Le préfet du Rhône, rapport mensuel d'information, 5 September 1942 (AN: F¹ CIII 1183–84); Abetz to Ribbentrop, 2 September 1942 (ND: NG–5127); note of Hagen, 4 September 1942 (CDJC: LXV–15).

228. Les préfets de la Corse (AN: F¹CIII 1147), des Bouches-du-Rhône (AN:F¹CIII 1143), and du Tarn-et-Garonne (AN: F¹CIII 1193).

229. Le préfet de l'Isère, rapport mensuel d'information, 4 September 1942 (AN: F¹ CIII 1157–58).

230. Le préfet de la Lozère, 2 September 1942 (AN: F¹CIII 1164); le préfet des Bouches-du-Rhône, 7 October 1942 (AN: F¹CIII 1143). See similar opinion in Haute-Garonne, 5 October 1942 (AN: F¹CIII 1154).

231. *La semaine catholique de Toulouse,* 82ᵉ année, no. 39 (27 September 1942), p. 603.

232. L'église affirme à nouveau son loyalisme envers les pouvoirs publics une conférence du Cardinal Suhard," *Le Moniteur,* 5 October 1942.

233. Report (unsigned), 29 September 1942 (AN: AGᴵᴵ 492 CC72A).

234. Nicolle, *Cinquante mois* [127], vol. II, p. 48; "Second Cardinal to see Laval," *Manchester Guardian,* 29 October 1942.

235. A. Lavagne to R. Brian, 14 December 1942 (AN: AGᴵᴵ 543 CC 141); AGᴵᴵ 495 CC 77–C; law of 24 October 1942, JO 6 January 1943.

236. Note of Hagen, 4 September 1942 (CDJC: LXV–15).

237. Lavagne to Bérard, 4 January 1943, and Valeri to Lavagne, 5 January 1943 (AN: AGᴵᴵ 492 CC 72–A).

238. Bérard to Laval, 18 January 1943 (AN: AGᴵᴵ 492 CC 72–A).

239. Suhard to Pétain, 22 February 1943 (AN: AGᴵᴵ 492 CC 72–A).

240. Chappoulie to Bérard, 15 May 1943 (AN: AGᴵᴵ 492 CC 72–A). Cf. Papeleux, "Vatican" [208], p. 80.

241. For example, le préfet du Tarn, rapport mensuel d'information, 5 October 1942 (AN: F¹CIII 1193).

Chapter 7

1. "Le problème juif," address by M. Xavier Vallat before the students of the third session, Ecole Nationale des Cadres Civiques, [probably March 1942] (AN: W^{III} 211^1 no. 5).
2. *La France enchaînée*, 22 and 29 April 1938. Much of what follows is drawn from the dossier d'instruction of Darquier de Pellepoix (AN: W^{III} 141).
3. Zeitschel note, 4 April 1941 (AN: W^{III} 212^2 no. 46[26]; also BA: R70 Frankreich/23, 3–5.
4. Eugen Weber, *Action française* (Stanford, Calif., 1962), p. 374 n.
5. AA: Pol. II, "Innere Politik: Parlament- und Parteiwesen, Frankreich 5, 1936–40 (T–120/753/269596–604); Report of 1 July 1939 (APP: 37022–B).
6. *Bulletin municipal officiel*, 7 April 1938.
7. Dr. Kurt Ihlefeld, Notiz für Herrn Botschafter, 1 March 1941 (AN: W^{III} 212^2 no. 46[17]; Schleier to Best, 21 March 1942, and Zeitschel to Achenbach, 28 January 1942 (AA: Botschaft Paris 1318, also T–120/4636/E208941–3,E208948); René Gillouin, *J'étais l'ami du maréchal Pétain* (Paris, 1966), p. 159.
8. *Le procès de Xavier Vallat, présenté par ses amis* (Paris, 1948), pp. 144–47; Jacques Isorni, *Philippe Pétain* (Paris, 1973), vol. II, p. 211 n.2; Joseph Billig, *Le Commissariat-général aux questions juives, 1940–44* (Paris, 1955–60), vol. I, p. 130; AN: AG^{II} 536.
9. JO (8 May 1942).
10. CDJC: XLIX–42.
11. "Le problème juif vu par M. Darquier de Pellepoix," *L'Oeuvre*, 12 October 1943.
12. Billig, *Commissariat* [8], vol. I, pp. 127–29.
13. AN: W^{III}213^1 III 30 (1–9).
14. BA: R70 Frankreich/32, pp. 3–8, 17–21.
15. Billig, *Commissariat*, [8], vol. I, pp. 116–20; Gérard, "Irrégularités," 1942 (AN: AJ^{38}4); and Darquier to Gallien, 18 November 1942 (AN: AJ^{38}4).
16. Commission rogatoire: Antignac (CDJC:XCVI); Billig, *Commissariat* [8], vol. I, pp. 120–25.
17. AN: W^{III} 41^I 53, p. 185; AJ^{38}9.
18. CGQJ to Röthke, 29 September and 5 October 1942 (AN: AJ^{38} 67 M9).
19. BdS to Darquier, 9 January 1943, in David Rousset, *Le Pitre ne rit pas* (Paris, 1948), pp. 130–31.
20. For example, Darquier to Achenbach, 19 December 1942 (AN: AJ^{38} 18).
21. Darquier, note de service, 31 January 1944 (AN: AJ^{38} 1, 9).
22. BDC: Sippenakte.
23. "La question juive est facile à résoudre, mais il fault le vouloir!" *Le Matin*, 13–14 March 1943.
24. "Exposé de Darquier de Pellepoix sur l'état de la question juive au moment de sa nomination comme Commissaire-général" (AN: W^{III} 211^{1}no. 10); Transocéan news service, 6 and 23 May 1942; JTA reports of 8, 11, and 12 May 1942, and 13 and 27 March 1943; Billig, *Commissariat* [8], vol. II, p. 297; "La question juive" [23].
25. "La question juive" [23].
26. *Procès de Xavier Vallat* [8], p. 329; Robert Aron, *Histoire de Vichy, 1940–44* (Paris, 1954), p. 528.
27. Note of Hagen, 3 September 1942 (CDJC: XLIX–42).
28. CGQJ to Conseil d'état, 7 May and 9 July 1943. Instruction de Darquier de Pellepoix (AN: W^{III} 141^2 184–86).
29. Darquier to Ministère-Secrétariat d'état à la production industrielle, 21 September 1942 (CJDC: CXIV–96); Billig, *Commissariat* [8], vol. I, p. 262.
30. Secrétaire-général de la Police to CGQJ, 19 May 1942 (AN:AJ^{38}123:66).
31. Direction des étrangers, Préfecture de Police (Paris) to CGQJ, 28 November 1942 (CDJC: CII–75).
32. Le Préfet régional de Limoges, rapport mensuel, April 1943 (AN: F^{1}C^{III}1200).
33. Jacques Delarue, "La Police et l'administration" (CDJC colloque, 1979, 13); W^{III} 141^1 53, pp. 167–87.

34. Laval to Darquier, 30 October 1942 (AN: AJ³⁸67 M9); Pierre Limagne, *Ephémérides de quatre années tragiques,* 3 vols. (Paris, 1945–47), vol. II, p. 1023.
35. AN: AGᴵᴵ 521.
36. Cf. Report, weekly conference of the Ministère de la production industrielle, 4 May 1943 (AN:AJ³⁸ 566).
37. Le Préfet régional de Nancy, rapport mensuel, January 1944 (AN: F¹ᶜᴵᴵᴵ1202).
38. AN: Wᴵᴵᴵ212¹ no. 19.
39. "Note concernant un plan d'ensemble de législation antijuive," [1942] (AN: AJ³⁸ 116).
40. J. Lubetzki, *La Condition des Juifs en France sous l'occupation allemande, 1940–44* (Paris, 1945), p. 101; Billig, *Commissariat* [8], vol. I, pp. 150–52.
41. Billig, *Commissariat* [8], vol. III, pp. 180–85.
42. Ibid., pp. 237–38.
43. Ibid., pp. 287–304.
44. Gérard, "Irrégularités," [1942], and "Note concernant M. Gallien," 23 November 1942 (AN: AJ³⁸ 4).
45. Billig, *Commissariat* [8], vol. I, pp. 313–15.
46. Kommandeur Verwaltungsgruppe 531 to Chambre de Commerce de Troyes, 26 February 1941 (CDJC: CCXLV–15).
47. YIVO: UG, CVIII–20; AN: AJ³⁸ 61 M49, M70; *L'Oeuvre,* 12 October 1943.
48. Billig, *Commissariat* [8], vol. III, pp. 306–9; AN: AJ³⁸ 565; Gérard to Klassen, 18 March 1943 (AA: Botschaft Paris 1190).
49. Billig, *Commissariat* [8], vol. I, 300–301, vol. II, pp. 92–94.
50. Circular of CGQJ, 28 October 1943 (AN: AJ³⁸ 253); Billig, *Commissariat* [8], vol. II, pp. 66–68; Darquier to directors of SEC, [April] 1943 (AN: AJ³⁸2).
51. "Activités de la SEC du 1er au 31 janvier 1943," 7 February 1943; Billig, *Commissariat* [8], vol. I, pp. 302–3.
52. BA: R70 Frankreich/11, pp. 202–38.
53. AN: AJ³⁸ 253,281; Report of Enquête of 6 March 1944 (CDJC: XLII–130); Instruction générale du CGQJ, 11 February 1943 (CDJC: CXCV–188,189); Report of 16 March 1943 (CDJC: LXXIX–71); Billig, *Commissariat* [8], vol. II, pp. 99–127.
54. Billig, *Commissariat* [8], vol. I, pp. 305–6.
55. Ibid., vol. I, p. 115, and vol. II, p. 227; Limagne, *Ephémérides* [34], vol. III, p. 709.
56. RSHA report [probably 1943] (BA: R58/1223); Jean Laloum, *La France antisémite de Darquier de Pellepoix* (Paris, 1979).
57. Jacques Polonski, *La Presse, la propagande, et l'opinion publique sous l'occupation* (Paris, 1946), pp. 138–45; Pascal Ory, "L'Université française face à la persécution antisémite" (CDJC colloque, 1979, pp. 9–11).
58. Darquier de Pellepoix, "Propaganda anti-juive," submitted to Dr. Klassen of the German embassy, 12 December 1942 (AN: AJ³⁸ 18).
59. Note of Hagen, 4 September 1942 (CDJC: LXV–15); CDJC: CXCV–114 et seq.
60. George L. Mosse, *Towards the Final Solution: A History of European Racism* (London, 1978), chapter 4: "From Gobineau to de Lapouge."
61. CDJC: CIX–89, quoted in Billig, *Commissariat* [8], vol. II, pp. 319–20.
62. "L'expulsion totale est le but à atteindre," *Le Matin,* 13–14 March 1943.
63. *Titres et travaux scientifiques de Dr. George Montandon, professor d'ethnologie à l'Ecole d'Anthropologie* (unpublished, 1941. BN: 4°LN²⁷69894); George Montandon, *L'Ethnie française* (Paris, 1935), Lauréat de l'Institut (Académie des Science morales et politiques) pp. 139–43; Pascal Ory, *Les Collaborateurs, 1940–45* (Paris, 1976), pp. 154–55.
64. CGQJ to UGIF (Paris), 23 February 1944, YIVO: UG, CVIII–1, 13; Billig, *Commissariat* [8], vol. II, pp. 242–44.
65. Billig, *Commissariat* [8], vol. II, pp. 244–48.
66. Note de service, 9 September 1942 (AN: AJ³⁸71).
67. Memorandum concerning Festnahme-Aktion von Juden, 7 July 1943 (BA: R70 Frankreich/23).
68. Eberhard Jäckel, *La France dans l'Europe de Hitler* (Paris, 1968), pp. 335–61; Robert O. Paxton, *Vichy France: Old Guard and New Order, 1940–1944* (New York, 1972), pp. 280–88.

69. Dalüge to Wolff, 28 February 1943 (ND: NO–2861), cited in Raul Hilberg, *Destruction of the European Jews* (Chicago, 1961), p. 413.

70. Monique Luirard, "Les Juifs dans la Loire pendant la Seconde Guerre Mondiale," *Cahiers d'histoire* XVI (1971): 206.

71. Knochen to OKW, KdS(France), RSHA, and HSSPF, 11 November 1942 (CDJC: VII–9, 12) in Lucien Steinberg, *Les Autorités Allemandes en France occupée: inventaire commentée de documents conservés au CDJC* (Paris, 1966), p. 244.

72. Arieh Tartakower and Kurt R. Grossmann, *The Jewish Refugee* (New York, 1944), p. 153.

73. Report of 12 December 1942 (PRO: FO 3194 [Z10348/81/17].

74. Bousquet to prefects of southern zone, 12 December 1942 (AN: AJ³⁸ 281).

75. Le Préfet du Tarn-et-Garonne au Ministère de l'intérieur, 4 February 1943 (AN: F¹CIII₁₁₉₃).

76. Reichsführer SS-Persönlicher Stab (T–175/103/625028); also ND: PS–1994, CDJC: CCLXI–6.

77. Knochen to Müller, 12 February 1943 (BA: R70 Frankreich/23, pp. 26–30); also CDJC: I–38.

78. Schleier to SD (Berlin), 22 January 1943 (CDJC: XXVa–254a); Röthke to Oberbefehlshaber West, 3 February 1943 (CDJC: XXVa–260).

79. JO (18 April 1943); Lubetzki, *Condition* [40], pp. 115, 215–16; Zosa Szajkowski, *Analytical Franco-Jewish Gazetteer, 1939–1945* (New York, 1966), p. 83.

80. Le Préfet de la Creuse au Ministère de l'intérieur, 31 January 1943 (AN: F¹CIII₁₁₅₀); le Préfet de l'Ariège au Ministère de l'intérieur, 31 January 1943 (AN: F¹CIII₁₁₃₈).

81. Knochen to Eichmann, 31 December 1942 (ND: RF–1229, CDJC: XXVI–69); Steinberg, *Autorités* [71], pp. 193–94; Knochen to SD Kommandos, 26 January 1943 (BA: R70 Frankreich/23, p. 25).

82. Lubetzki, *Condition* [40], p. 111; Limagne, *Ephémérides* [34], vol. II, pp. 937,971.

83. AA: Pol. Abt. Pol. II, Politik FR.: Betreffend Judenfragen, Po 36; also T–120/3466/E017871.

84. Knochen to Müller, 12 February 1943 (BA: R70 Frankreich/23, pp. 26–30); also CDJC: I–38.

85. Notes of Röthke, 16 and 19 February 1943 (CDJC: XXVC–207 and LXV–13).

86. Le Préfet régional de Limoges au Ministère de l'Intérieur, rapport de février 1943 (AN: F¹CIII₁₂₀₀).

87. See rapports des préfets de la Creuse, la Haute Loire, la Lozère, la Rhône, la Saône-et-Loire, and la Savoie for February 1943 (AN: F¹CIII₁₁₅₀, 1162, 1165, 1183–86). The order to regional prefects was Ministère de l'Intérieur circular no. 56 of 18 February 1943.

88. Note of Röthke, 6 March 1943 (CDJC: XXVc–214).

89. Le Préfet régional de Lyon, January 1943 (AN: F¹CIII 1200).

90. Reichsführer SS-Persönlicher Stab, T–175/65/580606.

91. Le Préfet régional de Marseille, February 1943 (AN: F¹CIII₁₂₀₀).

92. Jardin to Guérard, 19 May 1943, Rapport sur les évenements à Marseille du 28 au mai 1943, and letter of Jacques Helbronner to Marshal Pétain (AN: W^III 141²180).

93. Rapport du Préfet régional de Clermont-Ferrand, 5 May 1943 (AN: F¹CIII₁₁₉₉).

94. Malcolm J. Proudfoot, *European Refugees, 1939–52: A Study in Forced Population Movement* (London, n.d.), p. 56.

95. Radio Lyon, broadcast of 5 October 1942 (WL: PC 6 3B4).

96. *L'Activité des organisations juives en France sous l'Occupation* (Paris, 1947), p. 95; Haim Avni, *Sefarad veha Yehudim bi Yemai ha Shoah veha Emansipatzyah* (in Hebrew) (Tel Aviv, 1975), p. 115.

97. Monique Lewi, *Histoire d'une communauté juive: Roanne: étude historique et sociologique d'un judaisme* (Roanne, 1976), p. 54.

98. Luirard, "Juifs dans la Loire" [70], p. 186.

99. Szajkowski, *Gazetteer* [79], pp. 73–75, 234–35, 256 and passim.

100. Nicolas Bondy, "The Affair of the Finaly Children," *Commentary*, 15, no. 6 (June 1953): 547–58; Moïse Keller, *L'Affaire Finaly* (Paris, 1960).

101. Le Préfet du Tarn-et-Garonne au Ministère de l'Intérieur, 1 August 1943 (AN: F¹CIII₁₁₉₄).

102. *Activité des organisations* [96], p. 96.

103. JO (18 April 1943); le Préfet de la Haute Garonne au Ministère de l'Intérieur, 5 April 1943 (AN: F¹CIII1154); le Préfet des Pyrénées-Orientales au Ministère de l'Intérieur, 29 April 1943 (AN: F¹CIII1181–2).

104. Kurt R. Grossmann, *Geschichte der Hitler-Flüchtlinge, 1933–45* (Frankfurt-am-Main, 1969), p. 211; Tartakower and Grossmann, *Jewish Refugee* [72], p. 200.

105. Lucien Steinberg, "La collaboration policière, 1940–44," (11 May 1978), unpublished paper (CHDGM); Oberg's text of the accords is in BA: 70 Frankreich/13, pp. 112–13.

106. Note of André Lavagne, 6 February 1943 (AN: AG^II 495).

107. Note of Catry, 18 January 1943 (AN: AG^II495).

108. Kadmi Cohen to Pétain, 28 June 1943 (AN: AG^II495).

109. Note of Catry, 18 January 1943 (AN: AG^II495).

110. Kadmi Cohen, letter to Dr. Klassen, 6 January 1943, covering letter by Joseph Catry, 18 January 1943 (AA: Inland IIg 187, also T–120/2257H/478637–40).

111. Kadmi Cohen to Pétain, 28 June 1943 (AN: AG^II495).

112. André Lavagne to Kadmi Cohen, 18 January 1943 (AN: AG^II495).

113. Joseph Catry, covering letter of 18 January 1943, footnote 105.

114. SD (Paris) to SD (Frankfurt), 4 November 1943, ND: NG–1729:2 (CDJC: CXVIII–19).

115. Catry to Erwin Reifenrath (Weltdienst), 10 June 1943, and to Röthke, 22 January 1944; note of Roland Krug von Nidda, 1 April 1943—all in T–120/2257H/478623–36.

116. Legationsrat von Thadden, note of 15 October 1943 (AA: Inland IIg 187; also T–120/2275H/478611–14).

117. German Embassy, Paris, to von Thadden (Berlin), T–120/2257H/478619–20.

118. Serge Klarsfeld, *Le Mémorial de la déportation des Juifs de France* (Paris, 1978).

119. Pétain to Pope Pius XII (draft), 5 August 1942 (AN: AG^II495 CC77).

120. André Lavagne, "Note sur le mouvement Massada," 18 January 1943 (AN: AG^II 495).

121. Oberg to Himmler and Kaltenbrunner, 1 July 1943 (BA: R70 Frankreich/23, also CDJC:XXVII–22).

122. Le Préfet régional de Lyon au Ministère de l'Intérieur, 9 May 1943 (AN: F¹CIII 1200).

123. Report of General von Neubronn, 15 November 1942, OKW/133: Wehrmachtführungsstab: Sonderakte, Vorgänge Frankreich (T–77/770/5502117); le Préfet de la Savoie au Ministère de l'Intérieur, 5 January 1943 (AN: F¹CIII1186).

124. John P. Diggins, *Mussolini and Fascism: The View from America* (New York, 1972), p. 202.

125. Meir Michaelis, *Mussolini and the Jews: German-Italian Relations and the Jewish Question in Italy, 1922–45* (Oxford, 1978), p. 187; Michel Mazor, "Les Juifs dans la clandestinité sous l'occupation italienne en France," *Le Monde juif,* July–September 1970, pp. 21–31; Renzo De Felice, *Gli Ebrei Italiani sotto il fascismo* (Torino, 1961), p. 13.

126. Luther to Paris, 7 September 1942 (AA: Inland IIg.187); CDJC: XLVIII, passim; Michaelis, *Mussolini and the Jews* [125], p. 305.

127. Rapport du Préfet des Alpes-Maritimes no. 145, 14 January 1943 (CDJC: XXVa–324/325).

128. Léon Poliakov and Jacques Sabille, *Jews under the Italian Occupation* (Paris, 1955), pp. 25–26.

129. Knochen to Müller, 13 January 1943 (CDJC: L–35), also in Poliakov and Sabille, *Jews under Italian Occupation* [128], pp. 49–50.

130. AA: Inland IIg187; Steinberg, *Autorités* [71], pp. 198–204; note of Röthke, 6 March 1943 (ND: RF–1230), in Henri Monneray, *La Persécution des Juifs en France et dans les autres pays de l'ouest présentée par la France à Nuremberg* (Paris, 1947), p. 195.

131. Eichmann to Knochen, 26 February 1943, in Poliakov and Sabille, *Jews under Italian Occupation* [128], p. 67; Christopher Browning, *The Final Solution and the German Foreign Office* (New York, 1978), pp. 168–69; Mackensen to Foreign Office (Berlin), 18 March 1943 (CDJC: CXXIII–91).

132. Note of Lischka, 22 February 1943 (CDJC: XXVa–274a); Barbie to Röthke, 15 May 1943 (CDJC: XXVa–331); ND: NG–5087; Browning, *Final Solution* [131], pp. 167–68; le Préfet de la Haute Savoie, 4 March 1943 (AN: F¹CIII1187); le Préfet de la Savoie, 27

February 1943 (AN: F¹CIII1186); Gualtieri to Bourragué, 29 March 1943, in Poliakov and Sabille, *Jews under Italian Occupation* [128], p. 87.
133. Note of Müller (Marseille), 10 July 1943, SEC report of 2 August 1943, in Poliakov and Sabille, *Jews under Italian Occupation* [128], pp. 101–3, 107–11.
134. Le Préfet régional de Lyon au Ministère de l'Intérieur, 9 May 1943 (AN: F¹CIII 1200).
135. Zanvel Diamant, "Jewish Refugees on the French Riviera," *YIVO Annual of Jewish Social Sciences,* VIII (1953), pp. 264–80; Lewi, *Roanne* [97]; Szajkowski, *Gazetteer* [79], p. 260; le Préfet des Alpes-Maritimes, 8 September 1943 (AN: F¹CIII1137); le Préfet de la Savoie, February–August 1943 (AN: F¹CIII1186).
136. Lewi, *Roanne* [97], p. 53.
137. Diamant, "Jewish Refugees" [135]; Donati report, June–July 1945, in Adam Rutkowski, *La Lutte des Juifs en France à l'époque de l'Occupation (1940–44)* (Paris, 1975), pp. 319–20.
138. Knochen to Müller, 12 and 22 February 1943 (CDJC: I–38 and XXVI–71), in Steinberg, *Autorités* [71], p. 202, and Poliakov and Sabille, *Jews under Italian Occupation* [128] pp. 62–63.
139. Diamant, "Jewish Refugees" [135]; CDJC: XXVa–247; Poliakov and Sabille, *Jews under Italian Occupation* [128], pp. 30–31.
140. Le Préfet des Alpes Maritimes, September–October 1943 (AN: F¹CIII1137); le Préfet de la Savoie, 27 October 1943 (AN: F¹CIII1186).
141. G. Rougeron, *Le Département de l'Allier sous l'Etat français (1940–44),* ([Moulins], 1969), p. 262.
142. Le Préfet régional de Limoges, rapport mensuel, August 1943 (AN: F¹CIII1200).
143. Réunion des préfets régionaux, 21 September 1943 (AN: AGII460 9/S.A.).
144. Monthly synthèsis of telephone, telegraph, and postal surveillance, no. 52, 10 August–10 September 1943 (AN: AGII461 CCXXXVI).
145. AN: AGII460 CC 35 K.
146. Le Préfet régional de Châlons-sur-Marne, 4 May 1943; le Préfet régional de Bordeaux, rapport mensuel, September 1943 (AN: F¹CIII1199).
147. Le journal du général Bridoux, 23 July 1943.
148. BA:R70 Frankreich/13, pp. 110–31; see also notes of Röthke, 31 July and 14 August 1943 (CDJC: XXVII–31,36), and Steinberg, "Collaboration policière" [105], p. 33.
149. Knochen to Müller, 12 February 1943 (CDJC: XXVI–71); note of Hagen, 25 March 1943 (CDJC: XXVc–232).
150. Steinberg, "Collaboration policière" [105]. Hans Umbreit, *Der Militärbefehlshaber in Frankreich, 1940–44* (Boppard am Rhein, 1968), p. 143; Jacques Delarue, *Histoire de la Gestapo* (Paris, 1962), pp. 532–33.
151. Hagen to Röthke, 16 June 1943 (CDJC: XXVII–17), cited in Joseph Billig, *La Solution finale de la question juive: essai sur ses principes dans le IIIe Reich et en France sous l'Occupation* (Paris, 1977), p. 181.
152. Abetz to German Foreign Ministry, 3 April 1941 (DGFP, series D, vol. 12, 438).
153. Note of Dannecker, 15 June 1942 (ND: RF–1217), in Monneray, *Persécution* [130], p. 127.
154. The German Foreign Office was brought into the picture by the efforts of some governments to protect their Jewish nationals. See Browning, *Final Solution* [131], passim.
155. AA: Inland II A/B 83–26, vol. 5; Deutscher Botschaft Paris 1318.
156. JTA report, 27 February 1943.
157. Jean-Charles Bonnet, *Les Pouvoirs publics français et l'immigration dans l'entre-deux-guerres* (Lyon, 1976), p. 159.
158. Knochen to Oberg, 21 May 1943 (CDJC: XXVI–74), in Steinberg, *Autorités* [71], p. 144; Bonnet, *Pouvoirs publics* [157], p. 162.
159. Röthke to Knochen, 11 June 1943 (CDJC: XXVII–13), in Steinberg, *Autorités* [71], p. 145.
160. Memorandum concerning Festnahme-Aktion von Juden, 7 July 1943 (BA: R70 Frankreich/23); BA: 70 Frankreich/23, pp. 42–43; Steinberg, *Autorités* [71], pp. 148–49.
161. Notes of Hagen, 6 and 11 August, and of Röthke, 14 August 1943 (CDJC: XXVII–33, 35, 36), in Steinberg, *Autorités* [71], pp. 150–51.

162. CDJC:XXVII–36, in ibid., p. 151.

163. Note of Hagen, 25 August 1943 (CDJC: XXVII–39).

164. Knochen to Kaltenbrunner, 25 August 1943 (CDJC: XXVII–40), in Billig, *Commissariat* [8], vol. I, pp. 271–72; Pétain to de Brinon, 24 August 1943, (AG^{II} 24 SG2).

165. Note of Hagen, 25 August 1943, in Steinberg, *Autorités* [71], 152. Dr. Klassen to Schleier, 6 April 1943 (AN: W^{III} 141^{3}X no. 4).

166. Geoffrey Warner, *Pierre Laval and the Eclipse of France, 1931–45* (London, 1968), 359–60, 365–66, 391, 419.

167. 3 December 1942 (AN: F^{1}C^{III}1201) and 9 September 1943 (AN: F^{1}C^{III}1200), respectively.

168. Le Préfet des Alpes-Maritimes, 12 July and 8 September 1943 (AN: F^{1}C^{III}1137); le Préfet de la Haute-Vienne, 3 February 1943 (AN: F^{1}C^{III}1197); le Préfet régional de Limoges, rapport mensuel, May 1943 (AN: F^{1}C^{III}1200).

169. Réunions des préfets, 24 June, 18 August, and 21 September 1943, (AG^{II}460 CC35–G).

170. Vallat testimony, 6 November 1945 (AN: W^{III}212^1 no. 22).

171. Warner, *Laval* [166], pp. 366, 419.

172. Röthke to Lischka, 31 July 1943 (CDJC:XXVII–31), in Steinberg, *Autorités* [71], p. 149; de Brinon to Hagen, CDJC: XXVII–44; de Brinon to Laval, 26 August 1943, in *Les Procès de la collaboration: Fernand de Brinon, Joseph Darnand, Jean Luchaire: compte-rendu sténographique* (Paris, 1948), p. 119.

173. De Brinon to Knochen, 8 September 1943 (CDJC: XXVII–47).

174. Röthke to Ehlers, 15 July 1943 (CDJC: XXVII–31), in Steinberg, *Autorités* [71], p. 149.

175. Le Préfet régional de Bordeaux, rapport mensuel, January 1944 (AN: F^{1}C^{III}1199).

176. Report of Röthke, 14 August 1943 (CDJC: XXVII–36), in Steinberg, *Autorités* [71], p. 151.

177. UGIF to service 37, 10 January 1943 (YIVO: UG, XVI–16, p. 7); Darquier to prefects, 18 December 1942 (AN: AJ^{38}61 M 45); CGQJ to UGIF (Marseille), 16 January 1943 (YIVO: UG, CVIII–19, p. 1); "Statut du personnel," UGIF, 24 March 1943 (HICEM: HH2–FR2–65).

178. Delarue, *Gestapo* [150], p. 389; André Brissaud, *La Dernière Année de Vichy (1943–44)* (Paris, 1965), pp. 42–43.

179. Georges Wellers, *De Drancy à Auschwitz* (Paris, 1946), pp. 108–9; réunion des préfets régionaux, 21 September 1943 (AN: AG^{II}460 CC35–G; le Préfet de l'Eure au Ministère de l'Intérieur, 3 November 1943 (AN: F^{1}C^{III}1152; le Préfet régional de Rouen, rapport mensuel, October 1943 (AN: F^{1}C^{III}1204).

180. Le Préfet de la Savoie, rapport sur la période 1 June–30 August 1943 (AN: F^{1}C^{III} 1186); le Prefet des Alpes-Maritimes, rapport bimensuel, September–October 1943 (AN: F^{1}C^{III}1137).

181. Le Préfet des Pyrénées-Orientales au Ministère de l'Intérieur, 31 December 1943 (AN: F^{1}C^{III}1181–2); le Préfet régional de Lyon au Ministère de l'Intérieur, 15 March 1944 (AN: F^{1}C^{III}1200); le Préfet de la Marne au Ministère de l'Intérieur, 29 February 1944 (AN: F^{1}C^{III}1166); le Préfet du Lot-et-Garonne au Ministère de l'Intérieur, 1 December 1943 (AN: F^{1}C^{III}1164).

182. Le Préfet régional de Dijon, report of February 1944 (AN: F^{1}C^{III}1199).

183. Olga Wormser-Migot, *Le Système concentrationnaire* (Paris, 1968) pp. 222–23.

184. Paul Durand, *La S.C.N.F. pendant la guerre: résistance à l'occupant* (Paris, 1968), pp. 210–15.

185. Wormser-Migot, *Système* [183], p. 223.

186. Klarsfeld, *Mémorial* [118]; Steinberg, *Autorités* [71], pp. 161–63.

187. Le Préfet régional de Bordeaux à Laval, Brinon, and Darnand, 11 January 1944 (AN: F^{60}1485); le Préfet régional de Bordeaux, rapport mensuel, January 1944 (AN: F^{1}C^{III} 1199).

188. Legationsrat Buscher, Aufzeichnung, 25 June 1942 (AA: Deutscher Botschaft Paris 1125a); Aufzeichnung für Herrn Gesandter Rahn, 18 December [1942] (AA: Deutscher Botschaft Paris 1318).

189. See also Laloum, *Darquier de Pellepoix*, p. 25.

190. Klassen to Schleier, 5 April 1943 (AN: W^{III} 141^{3}X, no. 4).

191. German Embassy, Paris, telegram for Ambassador Rintelen, 20 December 1943 (AN: W^{III}213^2 no. 253 [1]).

192. Ory, *Les Collaborateurs* [63], p. 154.

193. JO (27 February 1944).

194. T–120/5549H/E387672.

195. AA: Botschaft Paris, Paket 143/43, Pol. 3 Nr. 5; Billig, *Commissariat* [8], vol. I, pp. 125–26.

196. AN: W^{III}212^1 no. 19(3).

197. 14 April 1944 (ND: NO–1411). Cf. Adam Rutkowski, "Directives allemandes concernent les arrestations et les depoΓtations des Juifs de France en avril-août 1944," *Le Monde juif*, no. 82 (April-June 1976): 53–65.

198. Bertram Gordon, "Un soldat du fascisme: l'évolution politique de Joseph Darnand," RHDGM, no. 108 (October 1977): 43–70.

199. SEC report, 3 January 1944 (AN: AJ^{38}281).

200. Note of Röthke, 17 May 1944 (CDJC: XLVI–chemise M), in Steinberg, *Autorités* [71], p. 161.

201. M.R.D. Foot, *SOE in France: An Account of the Work of the British Special Operations Executive in France, 1940–44* (London, 1966), p. 120; for the Milice in general, see Jacques Delperrie de Bayac, *Histoire de la milice, 1918–45* (Paris, 1969).

202. Note of Röthke, 21 March 1944 (CDJC: XLVI–chemise I–J); dossier Guy Frank, 21 March 1944 (CDJC: XLVI–chemise F); Barbie to GdS, 6 April 1944 (CDJC: VII–10), all in Steinberg, *Autorités* [71], pp. 158–60; "Programme . . . ou pas," *Au Pilori*, 20 April 1944.

203. "Rapport Antignac [undated]" (AN: AJ^{38} 253); Billig, Commissariat [8], vol. I, pp. 120–26.

204. Antignac to BdS, 15 March 1943 (CDJC: XXXIII–17b).

205. Léon Poliakov, "Le Commissariat-général aux questions juives devant la cour de justice," *Le Monde juif* (August–September 1949), p. 4.

206. Abetz telegram to Berlin 17 January 1944, AN: W^{III} 141^{3}X no. 7.

207. Robert O. Paxton, "Le régime de Vichy en 1944," in Comité d'histoire de la 2e guerre mondiale, *La Libération de la France: actes du colloque international tenu à Paris du 28 au 31 octobre 1974* (Paris, 1976), pp. 323–42.

208. Instruction of du Paty de Clam, 29 April 1944 (AN: AJ^{38}281); Antignac to regional director of CGQJ (Lyon), 23 June 1944 (AN: AJ^{38}69 M 70).

209. "Recensement des Juifs–Z.S. (1944)" (AN: AJ^{38}147).

210. Parmentier to prefects, 22 May 1944 (AN: AJ^{38}147; AJ^{38}565); Pierre Taittinger to CGQJ, 3 February 1944 (AJ^{38}330).

211. AN: W^{III} 213^1 no. 130.

212. Antignac to regional director of CGQJ (Lyon), 23 June 1944 (AN: AJ^{38}69 M 70).

213. Quoted in Billig, *Commissariat* [8], vol. III, p. 304.

214. Antignac to Laval, 1 June 1944 (AN:AJ^{38}4).

215. Billig, *Commissariat* [8], vol. I, pp. 124–25.

216. Antignac to Garde des Sceaux, 4 August 1944 (AN: AJ^{38} 67 M9).

217. Note of Antignac, 17 August 1944 (CDJC: CXCV–215).

218. AN: AG^{II}81 S.P.9A, "Emissions Philippe Henriot"; Philippe Amaury, *Les Deux Premières Expériences d'un 'ministère de l'information' en France* (Paris, 1969), pp. 272–79; Amaury omits all aspects of anti-Jewish propaganda.

219. Pétain's handwritten note to Mme Henriot (AN: AG^{II} 24 SG 1 A no. 467).

220. AN: W^{III}211^2 Dossier C, "Editoriaux prononcés à la radio."

221. Le Préfet des Basses-Alpes au Ministère de l'Intérieur, 31 July 1944 (AN: F^{1}C^{III} 1136.)

222. Le Préfet régional de Rouen to CGQJ, 27 May 1944 (AN: AJ^{38}4); Billig, *Commissariat* [8], vol. III, 305.

Chapter 8

1. Knochen to commissaire de police Marc Berge, 4 January 1947, AN: W^{III} 141²193.

2. Serge Klarsfeld, *Le Mémorial de la déportation des Juifs de France* (Paris, 1978); Martin Broszat, "Selektion der Juden in Auschwitz," *Gutachten des Instituts für Zeitgeschichte* (Munich, 1958), pp. 231–33; Adam Rutkowski, "Les déportations des Juifs de France vers Auschwitz-Birkenau et Sobibor," *Le Monde juif* (January–June 1970), pp. 35–75; Lucien Steinberg, "Statistiques de la déportation des Juifs de France d'après les dossiers de la Gestapo à Paris," *Le Monde juif* (January–March 1966), pp. 26–30; Steinberg, *Les Autorités allemandes en France occupée: inventaire commentée de documents conservés au CDJC* (Paris, 1966), pp. 167–73.

3. JO, Assemblée nationale, February 1979, p. 857.

4. Eberhard Jäckel, *La France dans l'Europe de Hitler* (Paris 1968), p. 433.

5. Report of Röthke, 21 July 1943 (CDJC I–54), in Steinberg, *Autorités* [2], p. 149.

6. *Laval parle: notes et mémoires rédigés à Fresnes, d'août à octobre 1945* (Paris, 1948), pp. 105–6; *Le Procès de Xavier Vallat présenté par ses amis* (Paris, 1948), pp. 117–18.

7. Gerald Reitlinger, *The Final Solution: The Attempt to Exterminate the Jews of Europe, 1939–45* (New York, 1961), p. 328.

8. Himmler to Mutschmann, 21 July 1944, Persönlicher Stab, Reichsführer-SS (T–175/155/685770–3); Knochen testimony, 4 January 1947 (AN: W^{III} 141² 193).

9. Mme. Roussetzki to Pétain, 1943 (AN: AJ³⁸ 70 M85).

10. *Laval parle* [6], p. 102.

11. Xavier Vallat, *Le Nez de Cléopâtre: souvenirs d'un homme de droite* (Paris, 1957), pp. 271–72.

12. Jacob Kaplan, "French Jewry under the Occupation," *American Jewish Yearbook* 47 (1945–46): 108.

13. Saul Friedländer, *Pie XII et le IIIe Reich* (Paris, 1964), pp. 104–9; Walter Laqueur, *The Terrible Secret: An Investigation into the Suppression of Information About Hitler's Final Solution* (London, 1980).

14. Friedländer, *Pie XII* [13], p. 115; Walter Laqueur, "The First News of the Holocaust," The Leo Baeck Memorial Lecture No. 23 (New York, 1979), p. 29. See also Laqueur, "Jewish Denial and the Holocaust," *Commentary* (December 1979), pp. 44–55.

15. FRUS, 1942, III, 775ff.

16. Friedländer, *Pie XII* [13], pp. 121–22; John P. Fox, "The Jewish Factor in British War Crimes Policy in 1942," *English Historical Review* XCII (January 1977): 82–106.

17. Adam Rutkowski, *La Lutte des Juifs en France à l'époque de l'occupation (1940–44)* (Paris, 1975), pp. 115, 121.

18. Georges Wellers, *L'Etoile jaune à l'heure de Vichy: de Drancy à Auschwitz* (Paris, 1973), p. 229.

19. Le Préfet du Gard, 1 October 1942 (AN: F¹CIII1153; le Préfet régional de Marseille, 7 September 1942 (AN: F¹CIII1200); le Préfet de la Haute Savoie, 1 September 1942 (AN: F¹CIII1187); le Préfet de la Vendée, 3 September 1942 (AN: F¹CIII1196).

20. Laqueur, "First News" [14], p. 30.

21. Jean Lacouture, *Léon Blum* (Paris, 1977), p. 504.

22. Wellers, *L'Etoile jaune* [18], pp. 4–5.

23. Ibid., p. 231.

24. Catry to Röethke, 22 January 1944 (T–120/2257H/478626).

25. John S. Conway, "Frühe Augenzeugenberichte aus Auschwitz: Glaubwürdigkeit und Wirkungsgeschichte," *Vierteljahrshefte für Zeitgeschichte* 27 (1947): 260–83; Wellers, *L'Etoile jaune* [18], p. 230. See the excellent analysis of this process in Fred Weinstein, *The Dynamics of Nazism: Leadership, Ideology, and the Holocaust* (New York, 1980), chap. 1.

26. Roberta Wohlstetter, *Pearl Harbor: Warning and Decision* (Stanford, Calif., 1962).

27. Rutkowski, *Lutte* [17], p. 103.

28. C. A. Macartney, *October 15: A History of Modern Hungary* (Edinburgh, 1957), vol. II, p. 286, n. 3.

29. Report of Donald Lowrie, August 1942 and 7 October 1942 (PRO: FO 371/32056 [Z8804/1716/17]).

30. Himmler to Kaltenbrunner, 9 April 1943, Persönilicher Stab, Reichsführer-SS (T–175/003/625028).

31. Hans Buchheim, "Der Ausdruck 'Sonderbehandlung,' " *Gutachten des Instituts für Zeitgeschichte* (Munich, 1958), pp. 62–63,

32. Dannecker to Knochen and Lischka, 13 May 1942 (CDJC: XXVb–29).

33. 13 May 1942 (ND: RF–1215), in Henri Monneray, *La Persécution des Juifs en France et dans les autres pays de l'ouest, présentée par la France à Nuremberg* (Paris, 1947), pp. 121–22.

34. Note of Dannecker, 15 June 1942, in Steinberg, *Autorités* [2], pp. 111–12.

35. General Debeney, "Etude sur la question des arrestations en France," 12 November 1943 (AN: AG^{II} 530 CC 119).

36. Laqueur, "First News" [14], p. 27.

37. David Knout, *Contribution à l'histoire de la résistance juive en France, 1940–44* (Paris, 1947), pp. 62–63.

38. Note of Hagen, 3 September 1942 (CDJC: XLIX–42), also in Steinberg, *Autorités* [2], p. 128.

39. Steinberg, *Autorités* [2], p. 135.

40. Georges Wellers, introduction to Rutkowski, *Lutte* [17], pp. 16, 21–22.

41. Valeri to Cardinal Maglione, 7 August 1942, in *Le Saint-Siège et les victimes de la guerre, janvier 1941–décembre 1942* (Vatican City, 1974), p. 614.

42. Quoted in Joseph Billig, *La Solution finale de la question juive: essai sur ses principes dans le IIIe Reich en France sous l'occupation* (Paris, 1977), pp. 176–77.

43. Wellers, *L'Etoile jaune* [18], p. 231.

44. Xavier de Montclos, ed., *Eglises et chrétiens dans la IIe guerre mondiale. La région Rhône-Alpes. Actes du colloque tenu à. Grenoble du 7 au 9 octobre 1976* (Lyon, 1978), pp. 167–68.

45. CDJC: LXXXVIII–27.

46. Boegner to Pétain, 20 August 1942, in Pierre Bolle, "Les Protestants et leurs églises devant la persécution des Juifs en France" (CDJC colloque, 1979, pp. 23–24).

47. *Les Eglises protestantes pendant la guerre et l'occupation. Actes de l'assemblée générale du protestantisme français, 1945* (Paris, 1946), pp. 32–33.

48. Raul Hilberg, *The Destruction of the European Jews* (Chicago, 1961), p. 365.

49. M. G. Morquin, *La Dordogne sous l'occupation allemande*, vol. I., *Déportations, fusillades* (Périgueux, [1961]), p. 15.

50. Haim Avni, "The Zionist Underground in Holland and France and the Escape to Spain," in Yisrael Gutman and Efraim Zuroff, eds., *Rescue Attempts during the Holocaust: Proceedings of the Second Yad Vashem International Historical Conference, Jerusalem, April 8–11, 1974* (Jerusalem, 1977), p. 562.

51. T–501/101/1367.

52. Jacob Presser, *The Destruction of the Dutch Jews* (New York, 1969), pp. 56–57; B. A. Sijes, *De Februari-Staking* ('s-Gravenhage, 1954).We thank Jacob Willem Smit for help on this point.

53. Mario D. Fenyo, *Hitler, Horthy, and Hungary* (New Haven, 1972), pp. 68n–69n; Joseph Rothschild, *East Central Europe Between the Wars* (Seattle, 1974), p. 289.

54. "Die Polizeiverwaltung unter dem MBF," BA: R70 Frankreich/13, pp. 167–68.

55. Macartney, *October 15* [28], vol. I, pp. 218–29, 324–25, 330.

56. Martin Broszat, "Das Dritte Reich und die Rumänische Judenpolitik," *Gutachten des Instituts für Zeitgeschichte* (Munich, 1958), p. 135.

57. Randolph L. Braham, *The Hungarian Labor Service System, 1939–45* (New York, 1977); Macartney, *October 15* [28], vol. II, p. 15.

58. J. Lubetzki, *La Condition des Juifs en France sous l'occupation allemande, 1940–44* (1945), 29; Hilberg, *Destruction* [48], pp. 459–60, 512–13; Macartney, *October 15* [28], vol. I, pp. 218–19, 324–25.

59. Broszat, "Dritte Reich" [56], p. 139.

60. Nora Levin, *The Holocaust: The Destruction of European Jewry, 1939–45* (New York, 1973), pp. 715–18; and Lucy Dawidowicz, *The War Against the Jews* (New York, 1975), pp. 483–544.

61. The documentary evidence is published in Matatias Carp, *Cartea Neagra,* 4 vols. (Bucharest, 1947). See also Broszat, "Dritte Reich" [56], pp. 102–83. We thank Peter Black for help on this point.

62. Broszat, "Dritte Reich," [56], pp. 167, 176; Andreas Hillgruber; *Hitler, König Carol und Marschall Antonescu: Die Deutsch-Rumänischen Beziehungen, 1938–1944,* 2nd ed. (Wiesbaden, 1965), pp. 236–46.

63. Serge Klarsfeld, *Mémorial* [2].

64. Frederick B. Chary, *The Bulgarian Jews and the Final Solution, 1940–44* (Pittsburgh, 1972), chap. 4: "Deportation from the New Territories."

65. Macartney, *October 15* [28], vol. II, pp. 37–38; Hilberg, *Destruction* [48], 496–97.

66. Leni Yahil, *The Rescue of Danish Jewry: Test of a Democracy* (Philadelphia, 1969), pp. 19–20; Yahil, "Methods of Persecution: A Comparison of the 'Final Solution' in Holland and Denmark," *Scripta Hierosolymita* 23 (1972): 279–300.

67. Hilberg, *Destruction* [48], p. 364.

68. Malcolm J. Proudfoot, *European Refugees, 1939–52: A Study in Forged Population Movement* (London, n.d.), pp. 27–30.

69. Irving Abella and Harold Troper, " 'The Line Must Be Drawn Somewhere': Canada and Jewish Refugees, 1933–9," *Canadian Historical Review* LX (1979): 180–209.

70. AN: AG^{II}27.

71. Le Préfet régional de Bordeaux au Ministère de l'Intérieur, July 1943 (AN: F^{1C}III 1199).

72. Michel Debré, "De nouveau, le racisme . . . ," *Le Figaro,* 11 December 1978; cf. reply by Bernard de Fallois, "Contre le racisme," *Le Monde,* 19 January 1979.

73. Robert O. Paxton, *Parades and Politics at Vichy* (Princeton, 1966), p. 45.

74. Gratien Candace to Pétain, 2 September 1942 and October 1942 (AN: AG^{II}543).

75. Le contrôleur-général René Carmille to CGQJ, "Exploitation mécanographique du recensement juif," 2 June 1942 (AN: AJ^{38} 147).

76. Oberg to Bousquet, 29 July 1942 (AA: Botschaft Paris (g) 2468, "Akten betreffend der Höhere SS- und Polizeiführer im Bereich des Militärbefehlshabers in Frankreich").

77. Meir Michaelis, *Mussolini and the Jews: German-Italian Relations and the Jewish Question in Italy, 1922–45* (Oxford, 1978), p. 179.

78. Felix Kersten, *The Kersten Memoirs, 1940–45* (London, 1956), pp. 141–45.

79. See the SEC report on a watchmaker in Limoges, June 1943 (AN: AJ^{38} 565).

Index

Abbeville, destruction of, 14–15
Abetz, Otto, *xiv*, 6, 9, 19, 222, 223, 228*n*, 273*n*, 333, 334*n*; aryanization and, 101; clerical protests of deportations and, 274, 275; Darlan and, 84; denaturalization suggested by, 324; deportations approved by, 227; on expulsion of Jews from Occupied Zone, 10; and founding of CGQJ, 82, 83; on French police, 243; on Italian obstruction, 317; Laval supported by, 18, 81, 230, 231; on political importance of antisemitism, 78; on Star of David, 237, 240; Vallat and, 89, 97
Abomination américaine, L' (Cohen), 311
Abrial, Jean, 194
Abyssinia, Jews in, 93
Académie Française, 5
Academy of Medicine, 285
Academy of Paris, 5, 151
Action Catholique, 200
Action Française, 19, 46, 47, 53, 182, 199; in Algeria, 193; avoidance of war with Germany urged by, 40, 41; criticized by Rebatet, 42; Darquier in, 284; early history of, 31, 32; on *Kristallnacht*, 48; Pius XII and, 51; Vallat and, 88, 89, 91
Adam, Uwe Dietrich, 213*n*
Adamthwaite, Anthony, 60*n*
Administrateurs provisoires, 8, 20, 132, 133, 152–59; cooperation with SEC of, 297; definition of, 8, 152; nominated by Darquier, 295; syndicates of, 296
Administration des Domaines, 156
Agriculture Ministry, 125
Air Force, *Statut des juifs* and, 126
Aix, arrests of Jews in, 308
Alboussières, arrests of Jews in, 331
Algeria, 4, 49, 123, 142, 316; Allied invasion of, 302; aryanization in, 105, 106; dismissal of Jewish civil servants in, 127; internment of Jews in, 166; Jesuit views on, 198; popular antisemitism in, 191–97; provi-

sional government of, 339; youth camps in, 127
Algiers, University of, 124–25, 127
Alibert, Raphaël, *xiv*, 19, 81, 368; Pétain and, 86; *Statut des juifs* of, 5, 19, 75, 92, 98
Alliance Israëlite Universel, 108
Allies: invasion of France by, 337; Italian armistice with, 320; liberation of death camps by, 347; Normandy landing of, 338; in North Africa, 195, 267, 287, 302, 304, 326, 359; response of, to reports of Final Solution, 348–49; *see also* Britain; United States
Allix, M., 165*n*
Alsace-Lorraine: antisemitic incidents in, 40; expulsion of French citizens from, 11, 70; expulsion of Jews from, 7, 10, 93; German propaganda in, 45
Ambre, Joannès, 96, 167
American Friends Service Committee, 167, 171, 265–66
Amicale des Volontaires Etrangers, 68
Amitié Chrétienne, 207
Amsterdam, Jews in, 357
Anarchists, arrests of, 225
Angéli, Alexandre, 315
Annecy, Italian protection of Jews in, 318
Anthropo-Sociology Institute, 190*n*, 298, 300
Antignac, Joseph, 188, 289, 295, 297; as head of CGQJ, 329, 336–39
Anti-Communist Police, 224
Anti-Jewish League, 40, 192
Anti-Jewish Union, 285
Antisemitism, 15–16, 179–97; in Algeria, 191–97; climax of, 181–86; distribution of, 186–91
Antisémitisme d'état, 138, 144; Darquier and, 286–87; definition of, 89; and deportation of children, 263; public support for, 182; of Vallat, 89, 93, 104, 111

Deportations *(continued)*
policy replaced by, 247–48; failure to ac-
knowledge meaning of, 346; first an-
nouncement of, 226; French railwaymen
and, 331–32; German policy of, 118–19,
123, 145; from Hungary, 361–62; institution of mass arrests for, 249–52; Italian
opposition to, 318–20; litigation during,
142–43; logistical preparations for, 227–
28; from North Africa, 196; from Norway,
357; obscuring of objectives of, 351; public disapproval of, 270–79, 326, 348, 356;
public opinion on, 181–82, 186–88, 191;
railway schedules for, 245–47; in retalia-
tion for assassinations, 225–27; role of
French police in, 241–45, 249; role of *Milice* in, 335–36; segregation prior to, 238;
sheltering of Jews during, 148; statistical
information on, 343; temporary suspen-
sion of, 323; after total occupation, 304–
10; from Unoccupied Zone, 255–62;
Vichy's request for, 232
Depression of 1930s, *xiii*, 34–35, 49; in
North Africa, 192
Deutsch, Rabbi, 331
Diamond merchants, 160
Didkowski (prefect), 276
Dijon: antisemitic incidents in, 40; arrests
of Jews in, 258
Dijon Law Faculty, 140
Direction Générale de L'Enregistrement
des Domaines et du Timbre, 102
Ditte, Jacques, 151
Djelfa concentration camp, 166
Dominican Republic, 268
Dommange, René, 285–86
Donati, Angelo, 319–20
Doriot, Jacques, 144, 229, 230, 285, 361; Al-
gerian following of, 193; French police
aided by followers of, 251; Mussolini's
support of, 47
Dorten, Adam, 69
Doubrovsky, Serge, *xiv*
Dousseau, Commandant, 170
Doyen, General Paul, 11, 13
Drancy internment camp, 86, 166, 223, 227,
251–55, 308; Brunner's takeover of, 330;
children at, 264–65, 336; deportations
from, 249, 252–55, 294, 306–7, 314, 321,
323, 349; French Jews at, 331; Jews from
Unoccupied Zone sent to, 257–59; non-
Jewish protesters at, 239; physical exami-
nations to establish Jewishness at, 301;
Wellers at, 354
Dreyfus affair, 26, 30–33, 47, 49, 334
Drieu La Rochelle, Pierre, 46, 58
Droit de vivre, Le (Lecache), 288
Drumont, Edouard, 30, 31, 45, 46, 192
Druon, Maurice, 4–5

DSA, *see* Delegation of Armistice Services
Dumoulin, Georges, 137
Dupy, J. M. Etienne, 199
Durand, Paul, 331–32
Duverger, Maurice, 144–45, 239

East Prussia: facilities for mass executions
in, 221; SS in, 218
Eclaireur de Nice (newspaper), 299
Ecole d'Anthropologie, 300
Ecole Nationale des Cadres Civiques, 88,
90, 93, 102
Eden, Anthony, 348
Edict of Nantes, 205
Edinger, Georges, 110
Editions de la Porte Latine, 313
Education, Ministry of, 124, 125
Eichmann, Adolph, 218, 233, 234, 244, 306,
330; and deportation of children, 263,
268; deportation quotas established by,
227–28; Final Solution and, 220, 221;
Hagen and, 79; and imposition of Star of
David, 235; insistence on maintaining
deportation schedules of, 246; terror
campaign against Austrian Jews
launched by, 58
EIF, *see* Israelite Boy Scouts of France
Einsatzgruppen, 220–22
Einsatzstab Rosenberg, 8, 79–80,
102–3
Eisenbeth, Maurice, 192
Einstein, Albert, 37
Electric light-bulb manufacturers, 159
Emancipation nationale (periodical), 334
Emigdirect, 113
Emigration, 112–15, 161–64; bureaucratic
obstructions to, 162–64; of children, 266;
Darquier and, 292; deportation policy re-
placing, 247–48, 359; Nazi policy on,
220–21; practical problems in, 365
Endlösung, *see* Final Solution
England, *see* Britain
Enlightenment, the, 27
Enterprises, trusteeship over, *see* Aryani-
zation
Epoque, L' (periodical), 47
Ere nouvelle, L' (periodical), 37
Erlanger, Philippe, 230*n*
Esprit (periodical), 212
Ethnie française, L' (Montandon), 300
Evian-les-Bains, conference on refugees in,
58
Evreux, arrests of Jews in, 330
Express, L' (newspaper), *xv*

Faisceau movement, 88
Falkenhausen, General Ludwig von,
236
Family Affairs, Secretariat for, 134